# BRIEF CONTENTS

## Unit 3 Pronouns



## Unit 4 Modifiers



## Unit 5 Punctuation



## Unit 6 Mechanics



## Unit 7 Effective Sentences



## Unit 8 Choosing the Right Word

# CONTENTS

# PART II WRITING EFFECTIVE ESSAYS 111

# PREFACE

## PREFACE TO THE INSTRUCTOR

Experience tells us that students have the best chance of succeeding in college if they learn how to respond productively to the varying academic demands made on them throughout the curriculum. One extremely important part of this process is being able to analyze ideas and think critically about issues in many different subject areas. *Mosaics: Focusing on Essays* is the third in a series of three books that teach the basic skills essential to all good academic writing. This series illustrates how the companion skills of reading and writing are parts of a larger, interrelated process that moves back and forth through the tasks of prereading and reading, prewriting and writing, and revising and editing. In other words, the *Mosaics* series shows how these skills are integrated at every stage of the writing process.

## THE *MOSAICS* SERIES

This second edition of the *Mosaics* series consists of three books, each with a different emphasis: *Focusing on Sentences in Context*, *Focusing on Paragraphs in Context*, and *Focusing on Essays*. The first book highlights sentence structure, the second book paragraph development, and the third the composition of essays. Each book introduces the writing process as a unified whole and asks students to begin writing in the very first chapter. Each volume also moves from personal to more academic writing. The books differ in the length and level of their reading selections, the complexity of their writing assignments, the degree of difficulty of their revising and editing strategies, and the length and level of their student writing samples.

This entire three-book series is based on the following fundamental assumptions:

- Students build confidence in their ability to read and write by reading and writing.

- Students learn best from discovery and experimentation rather than from instruction and abstract discussions.
- Students need to discover their personal writing process.
- Students learn both individually and collaboratively.
- Students profit from studying both professional and student writing.
- Students benefit most from assignments that actually integrate thinking, reading, and writing.
- Students learn how to revise by following clear guidelines.
- Students learn grammar and usage rules by editing their own writing.
- Students must be able to transfer their writing skills to all their college courses.
- Students must think critically and analytically to succeed in college.

## HOW THIS BOOK WORKS

*Mosaics: Focusing on Essays* teaches students how to write effective essays. For flexibility and easy reference, this book is divided into five parts:

Part I: The Writing Process
Part II: Writing Effective Essays
Part III: The Research Paper: Sources in Context
Part IV: From Reading to Writing
Part V: The Handbook

**Part I: The Writing Process** All eight chapters in Part I demonstrate the cyclical nature of the writing process. They begin with the logistics of getting ready to write and then move systematically through the interlocking stages of the process by following a student essay from prewriting to revising and editing. Part I ends with a quiz that students can take to identify their "Editing Quotient"—their strengths and weaknesses in grammar and mechanics.

**Part II: Writing Effective Essays** Part II, the heart of the instruction in this text, teaches students how to write essays by introducing the rhetorical modes as patterns of development. It moves from personal writing to more academic types of writing: describing, narrating, illustrating, analyzing a process, comparing and contrasting, dividing and classifying, defining, analyzing causes and effects, and arguing. Within each chapter, students write their own essays, read professional essays, study the essays of other students, and finally revise and edit the essay they wrote earlier in the chapter. By following specific guidelines, students learn how to produce a successful essay using each rhetorical mode.

**Part III: The Research Paper: Sources in Context** The next section of this text helps students move from writing effective essays to writing a research paper. It systematically illustrates the details of writing a term paper. Then it explains the research paper through student examples. Part III ends with a series of writing assignments and workshops designed to encourage your students to write, revise, and edit a research paper and then reflect on their own writing process.

**Part IV: From Reading to Writing** Part IV of this text is a collection of readings arranged by rhetorical mode. Multiple rhetorical strategies are at work in most of these essays, but each is classified according to its primary rhetorical purpose. As a result, you can refer your students to particular essays in this part that demonstrate a rhetorical mode you are studying in Part II. In this way, students can actually see the features of each rhetorical mode at work in different pieces of writing. Each professional essay is preceded by prereading activities that will help your students focus on the topic at hand and then is followed by 10 questions that move students from literal to analytical thinking skills as they consider the essay's content, purpose, audience, and paragraph structure.

**Part V: The Handbook** Part V is a complete handbook, including exercises, that covers eight main categories: Sentences, Verbs, Pronouns, Modifiers, Punctuation, Mechanics, Effective Sentences, and Choosing the Right Word. These categories are coordinated with the Editing Checklist that appears periodically throughout this text. Each chapter starts with five self-test questions so that students can determine their strengths and weaknesses in a specific area. The chapters provide at least three types of practice after each grammar concept, moving the students systematically from identifying exercises to writing their own sentences. Each unit ends with a practical "Editing Workshop" that asks students to use the skills they just learned to edit another student's writing and then their own writing.

## APPENDIXES

The appendixes will help your students keep track of their progress in the various skills they are learning throughout this text. References to these appendixes are interspersed throughout the book so that students know when to use them as they study the concepts in each chapter:

Appendix 1: Critical Thinking Log
Appendix 2: Revising and Editing Peer Evaluation Forms

Appendix 3: Revising and Editing Peer Evaluation Forms for a Research Paper
Appendix 4: Test Yourself Answers
Appendix 5: Editing Quotient Error Chart
Appendix 6: Error Log
Appendix 7: Spelling Log

## OVERALL GOAL

Ultimately, each book in the *Mosaics* series portrays writing as a way of thinking and processing information. One by one, these books encourage students to discover how the "mosaics" of their own writing process work together to form a coherent whole. By demonstrating the interrelationship among thinking, reading, and writing on progressively more difficult levels, these books promise to help prepare your students for success in college throughout the curriculum.

## UNIQUE FEATURES

Several unique and exciting features separate this book from other basic writing texts:

- It moves students systematically from personal to academic writing.
- It uses both student writing and professional writing as models.
- It demonstrates all aspects of the writing process through student writing.
- It integrates reading and writing throughout the text.
- It teaches revising and editing through student writing.
- It features culturally diverse reading selections that are of high interest to students.
- It teaches rhetorical modes as patterns of thought.
- It helps students discover their own writing process.
- It includes a complete handbook with exercises.
- It offers worksheets for students to chart their progress in reading and writing.

## INSTRUCTOR'S TEACHING PACKAGE

*Annotated Instructor's Edition*—ISBN 0-13-094212-X. For the first time, *Mosaics* has an *Annotated Instructor's Edition*. Written by Kim Flachmann and Cheryl Smith, the *AIE* contains in-text answers and marginal annotations to help instructors prepare thoroughly for class. The *AIE* gives both experienced and new instructors tips on how to get the most out of the text, providing teaching tips, summaries of the readings, readability levels for the essays, additional writing activities, ideas for incorporating the Internet into class, and much more. This supplement is free to adopters.

*Instructor's Resource Manual*—ISBN 0-13-094693-1. Also written by Kim Flachmann and Cheryl Smith, the *Instructor's Resource Manual* contains sample syllabi, additional teaching strategies (both general and specific), sample quizzes, journal assignments, additional writing assignments, rubrics for marking essays, and much more. It is available in print or electronic format and is free to adopters.

*Instructor's Resource CD.* This CD contains video clips of the author discussing how to use the *Mosaics* series effectively in class. Designed with the new instructor in mind and organized around specific parts of each text in the series, this CD will provide instructors with concrete teaching strategies taken from Kim Flachmann's own classroom. It is free to adopters. Contact your local Prentice Hall representative for a copy.

## STUDENT'S LEARNING PACKAGE

*Writing Pro* An Internet-based assessment tool like no other in the developmental English market, *Writing Pro* provides students with summary instruction and practice on each element of writing as presented in the *Mosaics* series. *Writing Pro* includes over 200 learning modules covering the writing process, paragraph and essay development, and grammar. For each module, students have access to the following online features:

*Watch Screens* that provide an audio and animated summary of the content;

*Recall Questions* that test their comprehension of the content;

*Apply Questions* that test their ability to apply the concepts to existing writing;

*Write Questions* that prompt students to generate their own prose using the concepts.

This technology solution frees up class time by allowing students to work individually on their areas of weakness. The software measures and tracks students' progress through the course with an easy-to-use management system. *Writing Pro* is available at a discount when packaged with the text. Contact your local Prentice Hall representative for more information and a demonstration.

*Companion Web Site:* www.prenhall.com/flachmann. The Companion Web Site allows students to gain a richer perspective and a deeper understanding of the concepts and issues discussed in *Mosaics: Focusing on Essays*. This site is free to all students. Features of this site include the following:

- Chapter learning objectives that help students organize key concepts;
- On-line quizzes, which include instant scoring and coaching;
- Essay questions that test students' critical thinking skills;
- Built-in routing that gives students the ability to forward essay responses and graded quizzes to their instructors.

*The New American Webster Handy College Dictionary, Third Edition*—ISBN 0-13-032870-7. With over 1.5 million Signet copies in print and over 115,000 definitions, this dictionary is available *free* to your students when packaged with the text.

*English on the Internet 2001: Evaluating Online Resources*—ISBN 13-019484-0. This completely revised guide helps students develop the critical thinking skills needed to evaluate on-line sources critically. This supplement is available *free* when packaged with the text.

*The Prentice Hall ESL Workbook*—ISBN 0-13-092323-0. This 138-page workbook is designed for use with a developmental English textbook to improve English grammar skills. Divided into seven major units, this workbook provides thorough explanations and exercises in the most challenging grammar topics for non-native speakers of English. With over 80 exercise sets, this guide provides ample instruction and practice with nouns, articles, verbs, modifiers, pronouns, prepositions, and sentence structure. The *PH ESL Workbook* also contains an annotated listing of key ESL Internet sites for further study and practice, an answer key to all the exercises so that students may study at their own pace, and a glossary for students to look up difficult words and phrases. Contact your local Prentice Hall representative for a copy.

*The Prentice Hall Grammar Workbook*—ISBN 0-13-042188-X. This 21-chapter workbook is a comprehensive source of instruction for students who need additional grammar, punctuation, and mechanics instruction. Covering such topics as subject-verb agreement, conjunctions, modifiers, capital letters, and vocabulary, each chapter provides ample explanations, examples, and exercises. The exercises contain enough variety to ensure students' mastery of each concept. This supplement is available to students packaged by itself or with the text at a discount.

*The Prentice Hall TASP Writing Study Guide*—ISBN 0-13-041585-5. Designed for students studying for the Texas Academic Skills Program test, this guide prepares students for the TASP by familiarizing them with the elements of the test and giving them strategies for success. The authors, both from Prairie View A&M,

provide practice exercises for each element of the writing and multiple-choice portions of exam, and the guide ends with a full-length practice test with answer key so that students can evaluate their own progress. Contact your local Prentice Hall representative for a copy.

Ask your local Prentice Hall representative for information about ever-growing list of supplements for both instructors and students.

## ACKNOWLEDGMENTS

I want to acknowledge the support, encouragement, and sound advice of several people who have helped me through the development of the *Mosaics* series. First, Prentice Hall has provided guidance and inspiration for this project through the wisdom of Craig Campanella, acquisitions editor; the insights and vision of Harriett Prentiss, development editor; the diligence and clairvoyance of Maureen Richardson, project manager; the foresight and prudence of Leah Jewell, editor-in-chief; the creative inspiration of Rachel Falk, marketing manager; the brilliant observations of Charlyce Jones-Owen, editorial director for humanities; the hard work and patience of Celeste Parker-Bates, permissions editor; the guidance and fortitude of Bruce Emmer, copy-editor; and the common sense and organization of Joan Polk, administrative assistant for developmental English. Also, this book would not be a reality without the insightful persistence of Phil Miller, publisher for modern languages.

I want to give very special thanks to Cheryl Smith, my consultant and adviser for the duration of this project and author of the margin annotations and the *Mosaics Instructor's Resource Manual.* I am also grateful to Valerie Turner, Rebecca Hewett, and Kelly Osdick for their discipline and hard work and to Monique Idoux, Matt Woodman, Carlos Castillo, Thomas Board, Victoria Bockman, and Li'i Pearl for their dedication and expertise. I also want to thank Rebecca Juarez, Heather Morgan, Richard Marquez, Lynette Betty, Marilyn Cummings, Jessica Sanchez, Jolene Christie, Katie Greer, Beth Olson, and Kathy Angelini for their assistance and support.

In addition, I am especially grateful to the following reviewers who have guided me through the development and revision of this book: Lisa Berman, Miami-Dade Community College; Patrick Haas, Glendale Community College; Jeanne Campanelli, American River College; Dianne Gregory, Cape Cod Community College; Clara Wilson-Cook, Southern University at New Orleans; Thomas Beery, Lima Technical College; Jean Petrolle, Columbia College; David Cratty, Cuyahoga Community College; Allison Travis, Butte State College; Suellen Meyer,

Meramec Community College; Jill Lahnstein, Cape Fear Community College; Stanley Coberly, West Virginia State University at Parkersville; Jamie Moore, Scottsdale Community College; Nancy Hellner, Mesa Community College; Ruth Hatcher, Washtenaw Community College; Thurmond Whatley, Aiken Technical College; W. David Hall, Columbus State Community College; and Marilyn Coffee, Fort Hays State University.

I also want to express my gratitude to my students, from whom I have learned so much about the writing process, about teaching, and about life itself. I am especially grateful to Cheryl Smith's classes, who tested the book and gave me good ideas for revising in spring 1999, fall 2000, and winter 2001, and to Rebecca Hewett's classes for doing the same in spring 1999. Thanks especially to the students who contributed paragraphs and essays to this series: Josh Ellis, Jolene Christie, Mary Minor, Michael Tiede, and numerous others.

Finally, I owe a tremendous personal debt to the people who have lived with this project for the last two years; they are my closest companions and my best advisers: Michael, Christopher, and Laura Flachmann. To Michael, I owe additional thanks for the valuable support and feedback he has given me through the entire process of creating and revising this series.

Kim Flachmann

# THE WRITING PROCESS

*Writing, like life itself, is a voyage of discovery.*

—Henry Miller

In Part I, you will be working with the entire writing process. The goal of this part is to help you develop your self-confidence as a writer. It will give you the tools you need to construct your personal writing process. Then, as you move through these eight chapters, you will discover how to adjust the writing process to suit your own needs and preferences. As you become more aware of the choices you have to make, you will also develop a better understanding of your strengths and weaknesses as a writer. With practice, your personalized writing process will soon be a routine part of your academic life and will help you confirm your place in the community of writers.

# Writing in College

Words help us solve problems, discover new ideas, feel better, make people laugh, and understand the world around us. Writing is simply one way of using words. It lets us connect with our immediate environment. Eric Zorn, a reporter for the *Chicago Tribune*, tries to explain more precisely the power of writing in our everyday lives:

> We write to enlarge and preserve that which we know, that which we have felt. We write because organizing our jumbled impressions into sentences is sometimes the only way to figure out what we think. We write because words—inadequate as they always are—are the best and most lasting way to connect with ourselves and with others.

## WHY LEARN HOW TO WRITE WELL?

The better you write, the more completely you can connect with your environment and the more control you have over your daily life. Writing well lets you communicate exactly what you mean and actually helps you get what you want out of life. So writing well can give you power—in all aspects of your life.

### Writing as Discovery

Often you will not really know the points you want to make until you start writing. When you write, a very interesting process takes place: the physical act of writing helps your mind sort through lots of ideas and helps you decide exactly what you want to say. Sometimes new ideas will come out of something you have written. Or you might understand an idea better once you start writing about it.

The simple act of writing leads to understanding. Also, the more you write, the more ideas you generate. This is why your instructor might suggest that you write if you are stuck on a topic or don't know what to say next.

Writing helps you discover and express the good ideas that are already in your mind.

## Writing as Critical Thinking

Writing can also help you think critically. Critical thinking is the highest form of mental activity that human beings engage in, and it is a major source of success in college and in life.

Thinking critically involves grappling with the ideas, issues, and problems that surround you in your immediate environment and in the larger world. It means constantly questioning and analyzing the world. Since critical thinking is complex, it requires a great deal of concentration and practice. Once you have a sense of how your mind works at this level, you will be able to think critically whenever you want.

With some guidance, learning how to write according to different rhetorical modes or strategies (like describing, narrating, or dividing and classifying) can give you the mental workout you need to think critically in much the same way that physical exercise warms you up for various sports. As you move through the chapters in Part II, you will be asked to isolate each rhetorical mode—just as you isolate your abs, thighs, and biceps in a weight-lifting workout. Each rhetorical mode offers a slightly different way of seeing the world, processing information, and solving problems. So each rhetorical mode is really a different way of thinking and making sense of the world.

## Writing as Necessity

Most important of all, writing is necessary for surviving both in college and on the job. You will have to write more in today's electronic age than any previous generation has. Some of your writing will be reports or projects that extend over a long period of time. Other writing tasks will have to be completed immediately, like responses to e-mail messages. Whatever the terms, writing will be a significant part of your life throughout college and beyond.

One way to set yourself apart from others is to be a good writer. The better your writing skills, the better grades you will make in college and the further you will get in a career. Everything you learn about writing in this text applies to writing in all your courses. On the job, these strategies will also be helpful, especially when you have to write that difficult letter asking for a raise or a promotion or when you are asked to summarize your accomplishments on the job so far. The same writing guidelines apply to all writing tasks.

## Practice 1

1. Why should you learn to write?

______________________________________________

______________________________________________

2. Why should you learn to write well?

______________________________________________

______________________________________________

3. In what ways is writing a process of discovery?

______________________________________________

______________________________________________

4. How can writing help you think critically?

______________________________________________

______________________________________________

5. Why is writing necessary in today's world?

______________________________________________

______________________________________________

## THINKING OF YOURSELF AS A WRITER

Using words on paper or on the computer screen makes a person a writer. Whether you write a note on the refrigerator, e-mail a friend, write a paper for economics class, or draft a report for your boss, you are part of a community of writers. In fact, you *are* a writer.

Any piece of writing more formal than a note on the refrigerator, however, is usually the result of a sequence of activities that may seem on the surface to have nothing directly to do with the act of writing itself. This sequence of activities is called the *writing process*, and learning to use this process is what this book is all about.

Even though each writer is different, some general principles apply to everyone—students and professional writers alike. Before you actually begin to write, a wise move is to get your surroundings ready. That involves setting aside a time and place to write, gathering supplies, and establishing a routine.

1. ***Set aside a special time to write, and plan to do nothing else during that time.*** The bird's cage can wait to be cleaned until tomorrow, the furniture doesn't have to be dusted today, the garage can be hosed down some other time, and the dirt on your kitchen floor won't turn to concrete overnight. When you first get a writing assignment, a little procrastination can be good. Procrastinating lets your mind plan your approach to the writing task. The trick is to know when to quit procrastinating and get down to work.
2. ***Find a comfortable place with few distractions.*** Joyce Carol Oates, a famous contemporary writer, claims that writing is a very private act that requires lots of patience, time, and space. First, you need to set up a place to write that suits your specific needs as a writer. It should be a place where you are not distracted or interrupted. Some people work best in a straight-back chair sitting at a table or desk, while others get their best ideas sitting cross-legged in bed. The exact place doesn't matter, as long as you can write there.

   Even if you are fortunate enough to have a private study area, you may find that you still want to make some adjustments. You may decide to unplug your phone during your writing time. Or you may discover that an all-night R&B radio station helps you shut out all kinds of noises but doesn't distract you the way talk shows and rock stations do. One student may do her best writing after a soaking in a hot tub; another might play jazz when he is getting down to work; and still another may have a Pepsi on one side of his table and a Snicker's bar on the other as he writes. Whatever your choices, you need to set up a comfortable working environment.
3. ***Gather your supplies before you begin to write.*** Don't risk losing your great ideas by not being able to find a pen and paper or a formatted disk. Some writers use a yellow tablet and a mechanical pencil to get started on a writing task; others go straight to their computers. One of the main advantages of working on a computer is that once you type your ideas onto a computer, changing them or moving them around is easy.

As a result, you are more likely to revise when you work on a computer, and you will therefore turn in a better paper. Whatever equipment you choose, make sure it is ready for the time you have set aside to write.

4. ***Establish a personal writing ritual.*** As a member of the community of writers, acknowledging your own writing habits and rituals is a major part of discovering your writing process. These rituals begin the minute you are given a writing assignment. What activities help you get ready to write? Some people exercise, others catch up on e-mail, and still others clean their rooms before they write. Most people do these activities without even realizing why. But they are preparing their minds for writing. So in the course of confirming yourself as a writer, take a moment now to record some of your own preferences and rituals for when you write.

**Practice 2** Explain the ritual you instinctively follow as you prepare to write. How do you prepare your mind for writing? Where do you write? At what time of day do you produce your best work? Do you like noise? Quiet? What other details describe your writing environment? What equipment do you use to write?

## KEEPING A JOURNAL

The word *journal* refers to a daily log of your writing. It is a place where you can record ideas, snatches of conversation, dreams, descriptions of people, pictures of places, and thoughts about objects—whatever catches your attention.

If you use a notebook for your journal, choose one that you really like. You might even keep your journal on your computer. However, unless you have a laptop computer, you won't have your electronic journal with you all the time. The choice is yours (unless your instructor has specific requirements). Just remember that a journal should be a notebook you enjoy writing in and carrying with you.

As you move from college to the professional world, you will find a personal journal a particularly valuable tool because—in the case of writing as in many other activities—the more you write, the more you will improve your writing. In addition, your journal can become an excellent bank of thoughts and topics for you. If used thoughtfully, it can become an incredible resource—a place to both generate and retrieve your ideas. Writing in your journal can help you discover your thoughts and feelings about specific issues as well as let you think through important choices you have to make. So writing can help you solve problems and work your way through various college projects.

A good way to establish the habit of journal writing is to use your journal for answering the questions that accompany the instruction in Parts II and III and the readings in Part IV of this text. You can also use your journal to jot down ideas and plans for essays as they occur to you. In addition, you might want to complete your prewriting activities in your journal. Keeping track of a journal is much easier than finding your notes on assorted scraps of paper.

Keeping a section of your journal private is also a good idea. Sometimes, when you think on paper or let your imagination run free, you don't want to share the results with anyone. Yet those notes can be very important in finding a subject to write about or in developing a topic.

The content of your journal entries depends to a great extent on your instructor's directions. But some basic advice applies to all entries, whether on paper or on a computer.

1. Date your entries, and note the time; you may find it useful to see when your best ideas occur.
2. Record anything that comes to your mind, and follow your thoughts wherever they take you (unless your instructor gives you different directions).
3. Glue or tape anything into your journal that stimulates your thinking or writing—cartoons, magazine ads, poems, pictures, advice columns.
4. Think of your journal as someone to talk to—a friend who will keep your cherished ideas safe and sound and won't talk back or argue with you.

**Practice 3** Begin your own journal.

1. Buy a notebook that you like, and write in it.
2. Make at least two journal entries on your computer.
3. Which type of journal do you prefer—notebook or disk? Write an entry explaining your preference.

## WRITING WITH A COMPUTER

Many people—in school and at work—find that they write most efficiently directly on a computer. This strategy saves them time and energy and helps them meet deadlines. First of all, writing directly on the computer lets you change words and sentences as you go along. It also saves you time since you don't have to write out a draft by hand and then type it up later. When you complete a first draft on the computer, you can move your ideas around without having to rewrite the whole paper. Finally, you can correct your grammar and spelling errors right on the final draft.

To compose on your computer, follow some simple rules so you don't lose your work or make word processing more complex than it is. Here are five guidelines for writing on the computer:

1. Give your document a name before you start writing.
2. Save your work often (or set the computer to save at short intervals). This will help you avoid losing your writing in a power failure or other accident.
3. Save your work in two different places—on your hard drive and on a disk. Then if one becomes damaged, you always have the other.
4. Print out your work frequently so that you can refer to printed copies as well as electronic copies.
5. Name and number each draft so that you can go back to earlier drafts if you want. For example, you might name and number an assignment this way: Description Essay D1, Description Essay D2, and so forth (D = draft).

## Practice 4

1. What are the advantages of writing directly on a computer?

______________________________

______________________________

______________________________

______________________________

______________________________

2. What five guidelines should you remember if you write on a computer?

 1. ______________________________

 2. ______________________________

 3. ______________________________

4. ______________________________

5. ______________________________

## THE WRITING PROCESS

The writing process begins the minute you get a writing assignment. It involves all the activities you do, from choosing a topic to turning in a final draft, including trips to the library, phone calls, and late-night snacks. The main parts of the process are outlined here.

### Prewriting

"Prewriting" refers to activities that help you explore a general subject, generate ideas about it, select a specific topic, establish a purpose, and learn as much as possible about your readers. Chapter 2 will teach you different strategies for accomplishing these goals before you actually begin to write a draft of your essay. Your mission at this stage is to stimulate your thinking before and during the act of writing. Whenever you generate new material throughout the writing process, you are prewriting.

### Writing

You can start writing after you have some ideas to work with. Writing includes developing some of your ideas further, organizing your thoughts with your purpose in mind, and writing a first draft. To begin writing, you should go back to your notes, journal entries, and other prewriting activities and then mold these ideas into a logical, coherent essay. As you write, you should concentrate on what you are saying and how your ideas fit together. Don't let grammar and spelling distract you from your task at this point. You can correct your grammar and mechanical errors later.

### Revising

Most people do not want to take the time to revise their writing. But revising always pays off, because it will make your writing stronger and better. Revising involves rethinking your content and organization so that your words say exactly what you mean. (Editing, the last step, focuses on your grammar, punctuation, mechanics, and spelling.) Your main goal in revising is to make sure that the purpose of your essay is clear to your audience and that your main ideas are supported with adequate details and examples. In addition, you should check that your paper is organized logically.

## Editing

Editing is the final stage of the writing process. After you revise, read your writing slowly and carefully to find errors in grammar, punctuation, mechanics, and spelling. Such errors can distract your reader from the message you are trying to convey or can even cause communication to break down altogether. Editing gives you the chance to clean up your draft so that your writing is clear, precise, and effective.

Once you start writing, these "stages" of writing do not necessarily occur in any specific order. You may change a word (revise) in the very first sentence that you write, then think of another detail that you want to add to your opening sentence (prewrite), and next cross out and rewrite a misspelled word (edit)—all in the first two minutes of your writing task. Although you may never approach any two writing projects in the same way, the chapters in Part I will help you establish a framework for your personal writing process and start to feel comfortable as a writer working within that framework.

### Practice 5

1. When does the writing process start for a writing assignment?

   ______________________________

2. Explain "prewriting" in your own words.

   ______________________________

   ______________________________

3. Describe your writing environment.

   ______________________________

4. What does "writing" consist of?

   ______________________________

   ______________________________

5. What is the difference between revising and editing?

______________________________________________

______________________________________________

______________________________________________

## VISUALIZING THE WRITING PROCESS

Even though we talk about the stages of writing, writing is actually a cyclical process, which means that at any point you may loop in and out of other stages. As you work with the writing process in this textbook, the following graphic design might help you understand how various stages of the process can overlap.

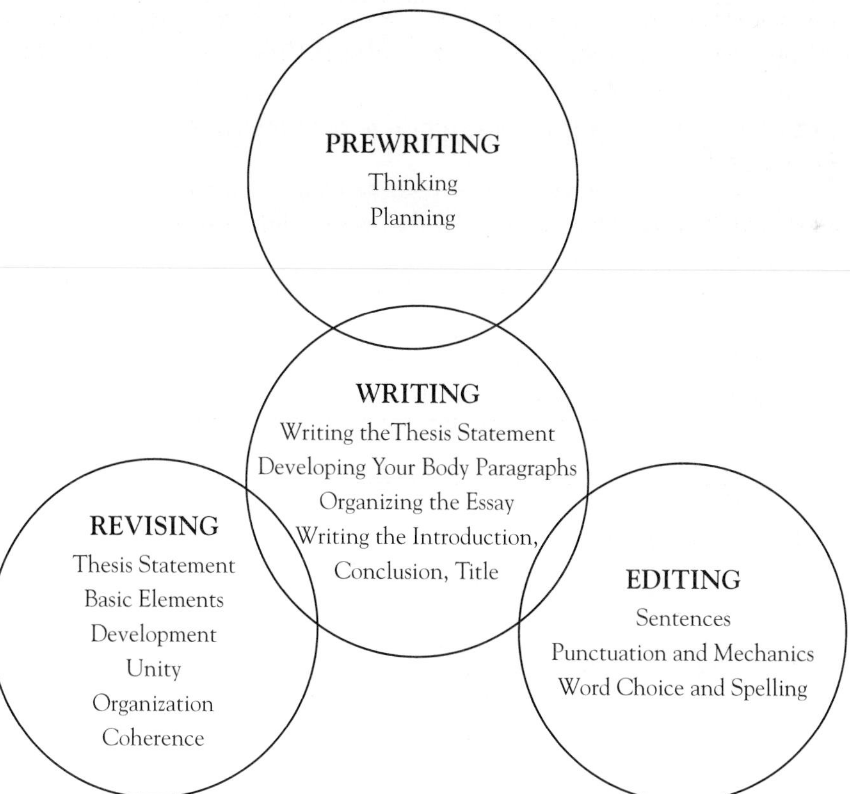

### Practice 6

1. List the two elements of prewriting.

_______________________________________________

2. List the four elements of writing.

_______________________________________________

_______________________________________________

3. List the six elements of revising.

_______________________________________________

4. List the three elements of editing.

_______________________________________________

## WRITING IN TANDEM WITH A STUDENT

In the rest of Part I, you will be writing in tandem with (along with) another student who has already completed the assignments you will be doing. In other words, this student writer will be demonstrating what you have to do for each essay. This approach will make the requirements for each writing task easy to follow, but you might find that you want to borrow the student's ideas. When this happens, force yourself to discover the original ideas in your mind as you do each assignment.

### Practice 7

1. What does writing in tandem mean in this text?

_______________________________________________

2. How can this approach help you?

_______________________________________________

3. What problem can it cause?

______________________________________________

4. How can you best deal with this problem?

______________________________________________

## WRITING ASSIGNMENT

This first writing assignment is much like the writing tasks you will be asked to do throughout this book. You'll be working on this assignment yourself over the next seven chapters as you apply what you are learning about the writing process. At the same time, we will follow the work of student Beth Olson so you can see how she approaches and completes the same assignment. By the end of Chapter 8, you will have a feel for the entire writing process, which is essential to strengthening your identity as a writer.

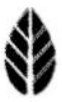

***Write Your Own Essay***

We all learn about life in a variety of ways. These lessons help us become who we are. What have you learned over the years? How did you learn these lessons? What experiences have made you the person you are today? Based on a combination of your observations, reading, and personal experience, write an essay explaining how you learn best.

# Prewriting

Activities that take place before you actually start writing your paper fall into the general category of *prewriting*. This is a time when you should be generating as many new ideas on a topic as you can, using the right side of your brain over the left. This is the part of your brain that thinks up new ideas and sees relationships among old ideas. More specifically, prewriting consists of activities that help you do the following tasks:

- Explore a subject
- Generate ideas about the subject
- Settle on a specific topic
- Establish a purpose
- Analyze your audience

Let's begin by looking at activities that many writers use to stimulate their minds as they approach a writing task. You will get a chance to try each one. Consider recording your responses to the following exercises and questions in your journal so that you can refer to them throughout the course.

## THINKING

Thinking is always the place to start any writing project. Thinking means exploring your topic and letting your mind run freely over the ideas you generate. We'll explore six activities that students often use to stimulate their best thoughts: reading, freewriting, brainstorming, clustering, questioning, and discussing. You will see how Beth Olson uses each strategy and then have a chance to try out the strategy yourself.

### Reading

Sometimes a good way to start your writing process is to surf the Net or read an article on your topic. Taking notes on your reading will give you material to work with as you begin to write. In fact, you may find yourself wandering off into your own thoughts on the subject, which you should also get down in writing.

**Beth's Reading** Beth read the following paragraph from an essay titled "Survive the Savage Sea" by Dougal Robertson. It stimulated her thoughts about learning in general because she believes that the most important part of learning is taking risks. She jots several notes to herself in the margins as she reads.

> That Sunday morning stands out clearly in my memory, however, as one of the nice days. I had put the kettle on the hot plate of the solid fuel cooker and while waiting for it to boil switched on the radio to listen to news, which contained a commentary on the Round the World yacht race. I had carried the mugs of tea upstairs on a tray, calling out to Anne, our sixteen-year-old daughter, to come through to our room where nine-year-old twins Neil and Sandy rocked with laughter as they lay in bed with their mother watching our son Douglas perform one of his special slapstick comedy acts. As Douglas rolled his eyes and cavorted around the bedroom in stiff-legged imitation of a disabled robot, Neil's face reddened as he laughed all the breath from his lungs, and even the more serious-minded Sandy chuckled in ecstasy as he watched his fifteen-year-old brother's antics.

*My family would <u>never</u> have a Sunday like this.*

> Neil and Sandy had become silent while Anne and Douglas questioned and Lyn talked of our sailing adventures in Hong Kong before we had started farming, but suddenly Neil shouted, "Daddy's a sailor. Why can't we go round the world?" Lyn burst out laughing, and "What a lovely idea!" she exclaimed. "Let's buy a boat and go round the world." I realized that Neil, who thought Manchester was one of the four brown corners of the earth, had no conception of the meaning of his remark, and that his mother was entering into the spirit of the game, but suddenly, to me, it was no game. Why not? I looked at Anne and Douglas, both handsome children but the horizons of their minds stunted by the limitations of their environment. In two years they would both have reached school leaving age and neither had shown any leaning toward academic aptitude, and the twins, already backward compared with their contemporaries in town, were

*I wish my dad were a sailor.*

*Sounds like quite a learning experience!*

unlikely to blossom into sudden educational prodigies. In two years' time they would finish their primary schooling and then. . . . Why not indeed?

Two years later, after selling our entire holdings in stock and land, we had acquired enough money to embark on the initial stage of our planned circumnavigation of the world.

*I can't believe they sold every-thing.*

*I can't imagine spending so much time with my family.*

Later, Beth made this entry in her journal.

> The more I think about Robertson's essay, the more I think about how much I could learn from a trip like this. How great it would be to pick up and leave for a while! I could get some perspective on the world. I can't imagine not having any responsibilities except for those on a boat. My head might actually be clear. I would like to travel around the States for about a year or so, but in an RV or something. I've only been to Texas, Illinois, and New York, but I'd love to see the rest of the country. I can't imagine leaving my family or school, though. I think it would be a waste of time for me right now to just leave. I guess I can plan for that after I retire. That is, if I can get through school.

**Your Reading** Read "I Just Wanna Be Average," an essay by Mike Rose (p. 419) on learning, and take notes in the margins as you read. Then, in your journal, write down any thoughts this essay stimulates.

## Freewriting

The strategy of freewriting involves writing about anything that comes to your mind. You should write without stopping for five to ten minutes, because the act of writing alone will make you think of other ideas. Do not worry about grammar, punctuation, mechanics or spelling. If you get stuck, repeat an idea or start rhyming words. Just keep writing.

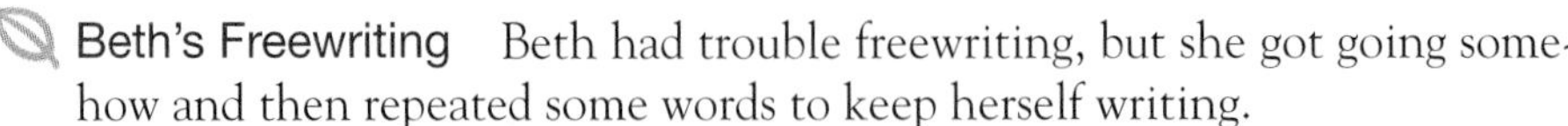

**Beth's Freewriting** Beth had trouble freewriting, but she got going somehow and then repeated some words to keep herself writing.

> My English teacher wants us to freewrite about whatever comes to our minds, but I can't think of anything to say. It's hard for me to just start writing. I still can't think of

anything to say. And it's hard for me to just write. I don't even know what to write about. Everyone in here is writing furiously in their notebooks; I wonder what they're writing about. How many are writing about their girlfriends? their families? their dreams? I wonder what their dreams are. No one could ever guess that one of my dreams is to someday be my own boss in a company that will make enough money for my family to live comfortably. I suppose that's everyone's dream, really, but I don't think many people would think I had enough guts to go out on my own. But I will someday, and it's going to be a great life.

*Focused freewriting* is the same procedure focused on a specific topic—either one your instructor gives you or one you choose. Apply your guidelines for freewriting to a specific topic. More specifically, just write freely about a designated topic so that you find words for your thoughts and impressions.

**Beth's Focused Freewriting** Beth produced the following focused freewriting in her journal. She is trying to get her mind ready to write her essay about learning.

People can learn about life from just about everything they do. It seems that every action can result in some sort of lesson. It's like all those fairy tales that have morals at the end of the story. If we keep our eyes open, everything we do can have a moral at the end. We can learn about how to study when we join a study group. We can decide how to treat our boyfriends or girlfriends when we watch our friends. And we can even learn from what's on the tube, I also like asking questions and talking to people about problems I'm having. I often get answers that way. Everywhere we look there's something to learn.

**Your Freewriting** Try a focused freewriting assignment by writing in your journal about ways that you learn so you can prepare for the essay you are going to write.

## Brainstorming

Like freewriting, brainstorming is based on free association. When you are brainstorming, you let one thought naturally lead to another, generally in the form of a list. You can brainstorm by yourself, with a friend, or with a group. Regardless of the method, list whatever comes into your mind on a topic—ideas, thoughts, examples, facts. As with freewriting, don't worry about grammar, punctuation, mechanics, or spelling.

 **Beth's Brainstorming** Here is Beth's brainstorming on learning about life:

everyone learns about life through everyday lessons

- from our parents
- from our brothers and sisters
- from our friends
- by watching our friends make mistakes
- by listening to others
- by listening to the radio
- by watching TV
- by asking questions
- by listening to music
- by taking risks
- by succeeding and failing
- by reading books or newspapers
- by studying or going to school
- by observing

 **Your Brainstorming** Brainstorm in your journal about how you think you learn.

## Clustering

Clustering, like brainstorming, is based on free association, but it also shows how your thoughts are related. To cluster, take a sheet of blank paper, write a key word or phrase in the center of the page, and draw a circle around it. Next, write down and circle any related ideas that come to mind. As you add ideas, draw lines to the thoughts they came from. After two or three minutes, you'll have a map of your ideas that can guide you toward a good essay.

**Beth's Cluster** Here is Beth's cluster on learning about life.

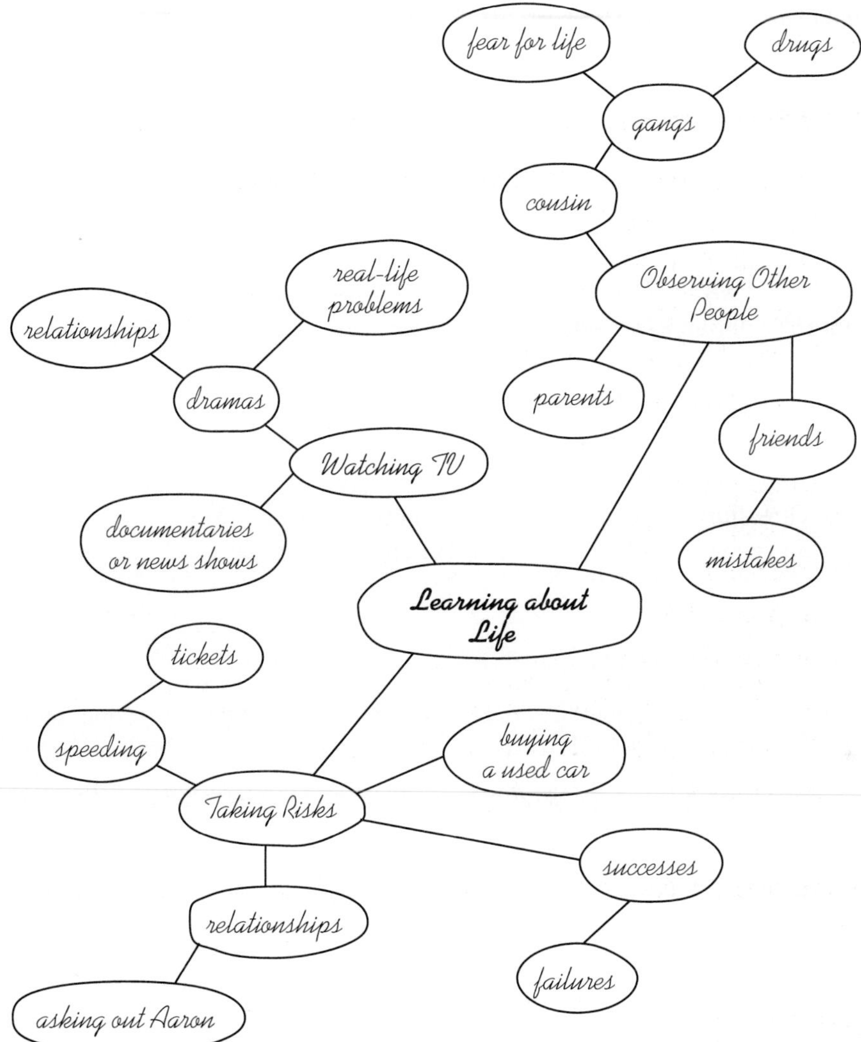


**Your Cluster** Write "Learning About Life" in the middle of a piece of paper, circle it, and create a cluster of your own associations with this concept.

## Questioning

Journalists use the questions known as the "five *W*s and one *H*"—Who? What? When? Where? Why? and How?—to check that they've covered all the important information in a news story. Other writers use these questions to generate ideas on a writing topic. Ask yourself each question as it relates to a particular topic. Then answer the questions one by one.

 **Beth's Questions** Here is how Beth used questioning to generate ideas on her topic, learning about life:

**Who?** everyone I know learns about life

**What?** learning about life

**When?** all day, every day
People learn every day even though they don't know it

**Where?** depends on what's being learned

**Why?** to better themselves in life, for fun, for a variety of reasons

**How?** by paying attention and taking action
I guess we can even learn without realizing it

 **Your Questions** In your journal, answer these six questions about learning for your essay: Who? What? When? Where? Why? How?

## Discussing

Discussing involves talking your ideas out with friends, relatives, classmates, tutors, or anyone who will listen. Often someone else will have a completely new perspective on your topic that will help you come up with even more ideas. Be sure to record your notes from these conversations so that you don't lose the ideas.

 **Beth's Discussion** Here are Beth's notes from a conversation she had with her running partner about how we learn about life.

> When I spoke with my friend Alison, I realized we all learn about life in just about everything we do. I guess it's really how much we want to pay attention. Alison reminded me about how much I learned from my cousin when she was involved in gangs. And we talked about how I asked Aaron, my boyfriend, out when I thought he was out of my league. We talked about all the ways we learn in life, but realized we learn by watching what other people do and how they act, by taking risks throughout our lives, and by watching different television shows. We figured these were the best ways to learn about life--for us.

**Your Discussion** Discuss learning about life with someone, and record notes from your conversation in your journal.

**Practice 1A** Now that you have been introduced to several prewriting strategies, which is your favorite? Why do you like it best?

**Practice 1B** Using two prewriting strategies on one assignment is often a good idea. What is your second favorite prewriting strategy? Why do you like this strategy?

## PLANNING

In this course, you'll be writing essays. Although essays may differ a great deal in design, organization, and content, they share certain identifying features that distinguish them from other types of writing. At the simplest level, how an essay looks on the page tells its audience "Here's an essay!" An essay usually has a title that names its broad subject. Many longer, more complex essays also have subtitles. When writers move from one topic to another, they indicate this shift by indenting a new paragraph. Most essays have a thesis that is either stated or implied in the introduction, several body paragraphs explaining or supporting that thesis, and a conclusion.

In content, essays are nonfiction, as opposed to short stories, poetry, or drama; that is, they deal with real-life subjects rather than made-up ones. Most essays concentrate on one specific subject and focus on a single purpose. For an essay to be successful, most writers choose methods of development that both suit their purpose and appeal to the audience they hope to inform or persuade. A successful essay gets the reaction from the readers that its author hopes for—whether this response is to appreciate a special scene, identify with someone's grief, or leap into action over a controversial issue.

If you haven't already discovered it, you will learn in this book that writing an essay takes planning. If you make some decisions about your topic, audience, and purpose before you actually write, the job of writing will be much smoother and less stressful.

- *What is your subject (person, event, object, idea, etc.)?* An essay focuses on a single subject, along with related thoughts and details. In approaching an essay assignment, then, deciding what you are going to write about is very important. Sometimes your topic is given to you, as when your sociology instructor assigns a paper on abused children. But other times, you choose your own subject. In such cases, choosing a subject that interests you is best. You will have more to say, and you will enjoy writing much more if you know something about your topic.

- *What is your purpose?* Your purpose is your reason for writing an essay. Your purpose could be to explore your feelings on a topic (*to do personal writing*), to tell a friend about something funny that happened to you (*to entertain*), to explain something or share information (*to inform*), or to convince others of your position on a controversial issue (*to persuade*). Whatever your purpose, deciding on it in advance makes writing the rest of your paragraph easier.
- *Who is your audience?* Your audience consists of the people for whom your message is intended. The more you know about your audience, the more likely you will accomplish your purpose. The audience for your writing in college is usually your instructor, who represents what is called a "general audience"—people with an average amount of knowledge on most subjects. A general audience is a good group to aim for in all your writing unless you are given other directions.

**Practice 2** Identify the subject, purpose, and audience of each of the following paragraphs.

1. Schools have been dealing with the issue of bilingual education for many years. The big debate is whether or not students should be allowed to study in their native language in order to learn English. Many people believe that students should be forced to learn in English, even if they don't know the language. Other people believe that this method of teaching will cause students not to learn, but they know bilingual education programs aren't teaching the students. Obviously, a compromise must be reached in order to help the students.

**Subject:** ______________________________

**Purpose:** ______________________________

**Audience:** ______________________________

2. The world of computers has reached a point where people can conduct all of their business transactions from the comfort of their homes. Internet companies have made it possible for people to shop and do all of their business on-line. While most people using these services enjoy the convenience of being able to have a business meeting in their bathrobes, the idea of never having to leave the house worries other computer users.

People will be able to do everything from home and won't have to interact with other people face to face. Eventually, the art of human interaction will be lost.

**Subject:** ______________________________

**Purpose:** ______________________________

**Audience:** ______________________________

3. Playing sports came naturally to me and also taught me a valuable lesson. I began playing soccer and T-ball when I was 5 years old and continued playing all different types of sports through high school. I had times when I would get tired of constantly having to be at practice for one sport or another. Having a social life became very difficult because I was always busy with sports or trying to stay caught up in my classes. Through the years of playing sports, I realized I had learned something that none of the teachers in my classes could ever teach me. I had learned how to deal with people. Competing against people taught me how to play with a team and how to keep calm when something wasn't going my way.

**Subject:** ______________________________

**Purpose:** ______________________________

**Audience:** ______________________________

4. Reading a good book can be a fine substitute for a vacation. Every once in a while, people get the feeling that they need to get away from their normal routine and take a vacation. Unfortunately, dropping everything and leaving on vacation is not always possible. In this case, reading a book about somewhere far away can make people believe that they have really left their normal surroundings. People can become so involved in a book that they are completely oblivious to the world around them. Sometimes reading a book is just what people need to get away.

**Subject:** ______________________________

**Purpose:** ______________________________

**Audience:** ______________________________

5. Last summer, my family and I went on a two-day rafting trip. The morning our trip began, we loaded all of the camping gear and food into the gear trailer and were on our way. The first day the rapids were class 2 and 3, which means that they were moderate rapids and perfect for beginners. Everyone had fun playing in the rapids, swimming, and jumping off of the rocks on the side of the river. That night in camp, the entire group was tired from such a full day on the river, so everyone was ready to go to bed early. The rapids the second day were class 4 because they had large holes and waves and were considered intermediate. I have to admit that the second day was more exciting than the first day. At the end of the trip, everyone was ready to get a good night's sleep but eager to come back and do it all again.

**Subject:** ______________________________

**Purpose:** ______________________________

**Audience:** ______________________________

Beth's Plans Beth made the following decisions before beginning to write on learning about life:

**Subject:** learning about life
**Purpose:** informative--to really talk about the different ways to learn
**Audience:** general--anyone from the general population

Your Plans Identify the subject, purpose, and audience of the essay you will write on learning about life.

**Subject:** ______________________________

**Purpose:** ______________________________

**Audience:** ______________________________

# Writing a Thesis Statement

By now, you have a subject (learning about life) and have used several prewriting techniques with this subject, which means you have generated a number of thoughts that you can use in your essay. You have also decided on a purpose and audience. In this chapter, you will learn how to write a thesis statement, which you will develop into an essay in the next three chapters. Again, you will be writing alongside Beth Olson as she works through her writing process.

Your writing assignments in college are most often broad subjects. To compose a good essay, you need to narrow a broad subject to an idea that you can discuss in a limited number of pages. Your thesis statement is what puts limits on your essay. A **thesis statement** is the controlling idea of an essay. It is the main point that all other sentences relate to. Like a high-powered telescope, your thesis statement zooms in on the specific topic that you will discuss in the body of your essay. The decisions you made in Chapter 2 about subject, purpose, and audience lead you to your thesis statement.

A thesis statement is usually in the first paragraph of an essay. It works best as the last sentence of the opening paragraph. Ending the introduction with the thesis statement lets the writer use the beginning of the paragraph to hook the reader's interest or give background information.

A thesis statement has two parts—a topic and an opinion you hold on that topic.

| Subject | Limited Subject + | Opinion | = | Thesis Statement |
|---|---|---|---|---|
| Sports | Playing a team sport | has lots of benefits | | Playing a team sport teaches a person self-discipline, cooperation, and leadership. |

| | | | |
|---|---|---|---|
| Anger | Road rage | is very dangerous | Road rage is dangerous because it puts the driver, the victim, and the surrounding cars at risk. |
| Writing | College writing | is similar to writing in the business world | College writing is similar to writing in the business world in three important ways: Both types of writing must be logical, well-developed, and clear. |

**Practice 1** Fill in the blanks.

1. A thesis statement is ______________________________

   ______________________________

2. A thesis statement has two parts, a ______________ and an

   ______________________________

3. Where should you put your thesis? ______________________________

   ______________________________

**Practice 2** Limit the following subjects that aren't already limited, add an opinion, and make them into thesis statements.

| Subject | Limited Subject | + Opinion | = Thesis Statement |
|---|---|---|---|
| 1. Friendship | ________ | ________ | ________ |
| 2. Work | Bosses | ________ | ________ |
| 3. Winning | ________ | ________ | ________ |
| 4. Love | Dating | ________ | ________ |
| 5. Winter | ________ | ________ | ________ |

When you write a thesis statement, keep the following guidelines in mind:

1. ***Your subject should not be too broad or too narrow.*** A subject or topic that is too broad needs a book to develop it. One that is too narrow leaves you nothing to say. A manageable subject is one that you can write about in about three body paragraphs. You may find it necessary to limit your subject several times before you arrive at one that will work.

   | | |
   |---|---|
   | **Subject:** | Television |
   | **Too broad:** | Prime-time TV |
   | **Still too broad:** | New TV shows of the 2000 season |
   | **Good:** | *Who Wants to Be a Millionaire* |
   | **Too narrow:** | My favorite competitor |

2. ***State your opinion clearly.*** When you give your opinion on the topic, choose your words carefully. Be direct and take a stand. Opinions like "is interesting," "are not good," "is a problem," or "can teach us a lot" are vague and boring. In fact, if you are specific enough about the opinion you hold, you will be very close to your thesis statement.

   | | |
   |---|---|
   | **Vague Opinion:** | *Who Wants to Be a Millionaire* is fun to watch. |
   | **Specific Opinion:** | *Who Wants to Be a Millionaire* teaches us to be greedy. |

3. ***Do not simply announce your topic.*** Make an interesting statement about your topic.

   | | |
   |---|---|
   | **Announcement:** | My paper is going to be about *Who Wants to Be a Millionaire*. |
   | | *Who Wants to Be a Millionaire* is the topic of this essay. |
   | **Statement:** | *Who Wants to Be a Millionaire* is a TV show that teaches us to be greedy. |

4. ***Try your thesis statement (TS) as a question.*** This does not mean that you should actually express your thesis statement as a question in your essay. Rather, you should try thinking of your thesis statement as a question that you will answer in the rest of your essay. You might want to write out your "TS Question" and keep it in front of you as you draft your paper. It will help you keep your focus.

**Thesis Statement:** The television program *Who Wants to Be a Millionaire* teaches us to be greedy.

**TS Question:** How does *Who Wants to Be a Millionaire* teach us to be greedy?

**Practice 3** Which of the following are good thesis statements? Mark B for too broad, N for too narrow, MO for missing opinion, and C for complete. Test each thesis statement by turning it into a question.

1. _____ Schools have good education programs.

2. _____ In America today, we face the problem of keeping our air clean.

3. _____ Vehicles powered by natural gas will cut down on the pollution expelled by automobiles.

4. _____ When using a computer, the user should know many things.

5. _____ Human cloning is being studied to determine the scientific and moral consequences of the process.

6. _____ Children in America are becoming desensitized to violence because of TV.

7. _____ Many people do not eat meat because they cannot stand the thought of eating something that was once alive.

8. _____ A lot of people avoid math because they have difficulty with analytical problem solving.

9. _____ Our campus drama department will be performing *Noises Off* this spring.

10. _____ Since the early 1980s, people have been on various health-craze diets and exercise programs.

**Practice 4** Complete the following thesis statements.

1. Marriage today ______________________________________________.

2. ______________________________ is my favorite class because

______________________________________________________.

3. Sleeping ______________________________________________.

4. TV award shows __________________________________________.

5. ______________________________ is a role model for college students today.

**Beth's Thesis Statement** Beth writes a thesis statement by stating her opinion about her subject.

| Limited Subject | Opinion |
| --- | --- |
| Learning about life | is easy for me. |

**Your Thesis Statement** Write a thesis statement here that can serve as the controlling idea for your essay.

| Limited Subject | Opinion |
| --- | --- |
| ______________________ | ______________________ |

**Thesis Statement**

______________________________________________________

# Developing Body Paragraphs

Now that you have written a thesis statement that comes at the end of your introduction, you are ready to write the body paragraphs of your essay. The body paragraphs explain and support the thesis statement.

## SUPPORT FOR YOUR THESIS STATEMENT

What ideas will support the statement you make in your thesis? This is the question you need to answer at this point. The supporting ideas are what make up the body of your essay. Each body paragraph covers one major idea in the discussion of your thesis. The body paragraphs consist of a topic sentence and concrete details that support that topic sentence.

**Practice 1A** For each of the following lists, cross out any ideas that do not support the thesis statement.

1. Children are desensitized to violence by television, video games, and comic books.

   Children aren't even affected by violent acts they see on TV.
   Children do not care when the heroes beat up the villains in comic books.
   Many video games cost too much.
   Children often want to be just like the sports figures they watch on TV.
   Most children learn very early in life to shoot figures in video games.

2. Political campaigns often bring out the worst in candidates.

   Most people are either Republican or Democrat.
   Candidates try to find secrets from their opponents' past.

Candidates use the media to help ruin other candidates' reputations.

Presidential campaigns occur every four years.

Some candidates even resort to name-calling and twisting their opponents' words.

3. To qualify for the FBI, applicants must meet certain requirements.

   People interested in joining the FBI must have a college degree.

   FBI applicants must be in great physical shape and have excellent eyesight.

   *The X-Files* has caused a great interest in the FBI.

   FBI agents work within the United States, while CIA agents work outside the United States.

   FBI applicants must be willing to go through rigorous training and to move anywhere in the United States.

4. Starting your own business takes a lot of planning and work.

   Prospective business owners must create a business plan in order to borrow money from a bank.

   Owning your own business is rewarding.

   People should research the current trends in the market for the type of business they plan to open.

   Sometimes business owners can get their families to work for free.

   People should determine how much money they will spend and how much money they will make so they can project possible earnings.

5. To maintain a long-distance relationship, both people must be willing to sacrifice.

   Separations often happen when couples go to different universities.

   Both parties must be sensitive to the other's needs—even at a distance.

   People have to communicate often with each other, even if it's hard to find the time.

   Both people must put extra effort into the relationship to make it work.

   My parents had a long-distance relationship.

**Practice 1B** For each of the following thesis statements, list three supporting ideas.

1. People should always look for three things when searching for a job.

   ________________________________________

2. Moving away from home for the first time can be hard.

3. Animals can help people live longer.

4. Vacations can often be more strenuous than restful.

5. Studying the right way can make a difference in a test grade.

Essays are of different lengths and often have a varying number of ideas that support their thesis statements. The thesis statement generally determines the length of an essay and the amount of support necessary to make your point. Some statements require very little proof and might need only one body paragraph; others might require much more support and might need four or more body paragraphs for a complete explanation. An essay that falls somewhere in the middle has an introduction, three body paragraphs, and a conclusion. That is what Beth has decided on—three topics, calling for one body paragraph each.

**Beth's Supporting Ideas** Beth decided on three supporting ideas for her essay, which call for three body paragraphs.

**Thesis Statement:** Learning about life is easy for me.
**Supporting Idea 1:** Other people
**Supporting Idea 2:** Risks
**Supporting Idea 3:** TV

**Your Supporting Ideas** Now list the support you might use for your thesis statement.

**Your Thesis Statement:** ______________________________

**Supporting Idea 1:** ______________________________

**Supporting Idea 2:** ______________________________

**Supporting Idea 3:** ______________________________

## OUTLINING

At this stage of the writing process, many people benefit from putting their main ideas in the form of a rough or working outline. A rough outline can help you plan your essay and let you see the relationship of your ideas to one another. In this way, you can easily identify ideas that don't support your thesis and locate places where you need more information. A rough outline can evolve and become more detailed as your paper develops.

**Beth's Rough Outline** Here is a rough outline of Beth's ideas so far.

**Thesis Statement:** Learning about life is easy for me.

A. Observing other people is natural for me.
B. Taking risks is important.
C. Watching TV teaches us values.

**Your Rough Outline** Now put your ideas so far in outline form.

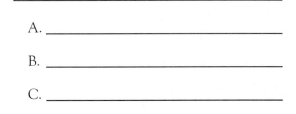

**Thesis Statement:** ________________________________

A. ________________________________

B. ________________________________

C. ________________________________

## TOPIC SENTENCES

Writing is made up of several steps that lead you to your first draft. So far, you have been given a subject (learning about life) and worked through a number of prewriting techniques. You have also generated ideas that you can use in your essay and decided on a purpose and audience. Now you will learn how to write topic sentences for your body paragraphs. Then you will add some specific, concrete details to your notes from prewriting activities and choose a method of organization for each paragraph. At that point, you will be ready to write your essay. This portion of the chapter will help you start your first draft, which you will then revise and edit in Chapters 7 and 8. Again, you will be writing alongside Beth as she works through the writing process with you.

First, you need to state each of your supporting ideas in the form of a topic sentence that will be developed into a body paragraph. The decisions you made in Chapter 2 about subject, purpose, and audience will lead you to your topic sentences. Look back at your prewriting notes and think about which topics will best support your thesis statement. These will be the topics of your body paragraphs. These paragraphs will each include a topic sentence.

The *topic sentence* of a paragraph is its controlling idea. A typical paragraph consists of a topic sentence and details that expand on that topic sentence. A topic sentence performs two important tasks in its paragraph: (1) It supports the essay's thesis statement, and (2) it tells what the paragraph will be about. It functions best as the first or last sentence in its paragraph. Beginning or ending a paragraph with the topic sentence gives direction to the paragraph and provides a kind of road map for the reader.

Like a thesis statement, a topic sentence has two parts—a topic and a statement about that topic. The topic should be limited enough that it can be developed in a paragraph. It should also be focused and not vague or scattered.

| Topic | Limited Topic | Statement |
|---|---|---|
| Reading | Frequent reading | improves thinking skills. |
| Lotteries | Winning the lottery | will change a person's life forever. |
| Children | Having children | is a huge responsibility. |
| Hate | Hate crimes | are one of life's worst horrors. |

**Practice 2A** Limit the following topics. Then develop them into statements that could be topic sentences.

| Topic | Limited Topic | Statement |
|---|---|---|
| 1. Mondays | ____________________ | ____________________ |
| 2. Hobbies | ____________________ | ____________________ |
| 3. Theme parks | ____________________ | ____________________ |
| 4. Writing | ____________________ | ____________________ |
| 5. Summer | ____________________ | ____________________ |

**Practice 2B** Complete the following topic sentences. Make sure they are general enough to be developed into a paragraph but not too broad.

1. Work-related injuries ________________________________________.
2. ________________________________ is my favorite television show.
3. Sex education ________________________________________.
4. Stray dogs and cats ________________________________________.
5. ____________________________ must be looked at on my college campus.

**Practice 2C** Write topic sentences for the following paragraphs.

1. ______________________________

She watches the old ones like *Perry Mason* and can't get enough of the newer ones like *Law and Order*. But my mom really prefers the not-old and not-new mystery shows like *Matlock* and *Murder She Wrote*. My mom will watch any of these shows for hours. My dad has a joke that she's watching all these TV shows so she can learn how to get rid of him and get away with it. I think she's just gathering information to write a book similar to these shows she loves to watch.

2. ______________________________

First, you must follow the directions to install it onto your computer. Then you must read the directions to learn what you should do first with the program. It's best to read all the directions first, but most times people just go straight to the program and try to navigate their way through it. Once you get a handle on how to work the program, it's best just to play around and only use the book for when you have questions. Mastering computers can be hard, but once you've done it, you can be sure you'll never forget how to use them.

3. ______________________________

Because she wanted to save money for other parts of her wedding, the consultant was the first expense she cut. Everything went fine until the day of the wedding. My sister didn't get the flowers she ordered, but the ones that were delivered were OK. The cake arrived four hours late, and the receptio hall wouldn't let us attach anything to the walls. And the wedding train just before my sister walked into the church was completely disorganized. Luckily, no one but my sister and our family knew of the mishaps, but a wedding consultant would have been worth every penny on the actual day of the wedding.

**Practice 3A** Supply three topic sentences for each thesis statement.

1. Many people enjoy resting on Sundays.

   ________________________________________

   ________________________________________

   ________________________________________

2. Teachers should encourage all students to learn.

   ________________________________________

   ________________________________________

   ________________________________________

3. Computers will enable people to function more efficiently at work, at home, and at play.

   ________________________________________

   ________________________________________

   ________________________________________

4. Planning is the key to a successful vacation.

   ________________________________________

   ________________________________________

   ________________________________________

5. The abilities to think critically, to act quickly, and to communicate clearly are essential in the business world.

______________________________

______________________________

______________________________

**Practice 3B** Fill in the following rough outlines.

1. Subject: College life

   Limited Subject: ______________________________

   Thesis Statement: ______________________________

   Topic Sentence: ______________________________

   Topic Sentence: ______________________________

   Topic Sentence: ______________________________

2. Subject: Animal rights

   Limited Subject: ______________________________

   Thesis Statement: ______________________________

   Topic Sentence: ______________________________

   Topic Sentence: ______________________________

   Topic Sentence: ______________________________

3. Subject: Intercollegiate sports

   Limited Subject: ______________________________

   Thesis Statement: ______________________________

   Topic Sentence: ______________________________

Topic Sentence: ______________________________

Topic Sentence: ______________________________

4. Subject: Summer jobs

Limited Subject: ______________________________

Thesis Statement: ______________________________

Topic Sentence: ______________________________

Topic Sentence: ______________________________

Topic Sentence: ______________________________

5. Subject: The Internet

Limited Subject: ______________________________

Thesis Statement: ______________________________

Topic Sentence: ______________________________

Topic Sentence: ______________________________

Topic Sentence: ______________________________

**Beth's Topic Sentences** Beth writes three topic sentences that she thinks will support her thesis statement.

| | |
|---|---|
| **Thesis:** | Learning about life is easy for me. |
| **Topic Sentence:** | I have always been aware that I learn a lot through secondhand experiences. |
| **Topic Sentence:** | I have also learned a lot about life by taking risks and making my own mistakes. |
| **Topic Sentence:** | TV is also a source of learning for me. |

**Your Topic Sentences** Develop each of the ideas you listed on page 33 into a topic sentence that is directly related to your thesis statement. List your thesis first.

**Thesis:** ______________________________

**Topic Sentence:** ______________________________

**Topic Sentence:** ______________________________

**Topic Sentence:** ______________________________

## SPECIFIC DETAILS

Now you are ready to generate the specific details that will make up the bulk of your body paragraphs. Later in this text, you will learn about different methods of developing your ideas, such as describing, comparing and contrasting, and analyzing causes and effects. For now, we are simply going to practice generating concrete supporting details and examples that are directly related to a specific topic. Concrete words refer to anything you can see, hear, touch, smell, or taste, like *trees*, *boats*, *water*, *friends*, *fire alarm*, and *fresh bread*. They make writing come alive because they help the reader picture what the writer is talking about.

**Practice 4A** Put a check by the details and examples listed that support each topic sentence.

1. Many people are addicted to soap operas.

   ______ viewers get caught up in the story

   ______ people care about the characters

   ______ soap operas are often a springboard for actors wanting more work

   ______ people want certain situations to happen in certain ways

   ______ mindless but entertaining TV

   ______ can watch every once in a while to catch up

   ______ CBS has had the number one soap opera for years

2. My parents have reversed the stereotypical roles in their marriage.

_____ my dad decorates the house

_____ my mom and dad both work

_____ my sister wants to be just like our mom

_____ my mom mows and takes care of the lawn

_____ my mom builds furniture for our house

_____ my dad cleans the inside of the house

_____ I hope to marry someone like my mom

3. The members of every generation think they'll understand their kids' music—until they actually hear it.

_____ parents don't understand today's rock music

_____ parents who listened to rock-and-roll don't understand heavy metal

_____ parents become wary of bands like Kid Rock and Marilyn Manson

_____ no parents understand new wave or punk music

_____ Dick Clark has helped all kinds of music get established

_____ parents have a hard time letting their kids listen to rap music

_____ Elvis helped put rock-and-roll on the map

4. Students change their majors often throughout their academic careers.

_____ general education courses make students learn about a variety of subjects

_____ in college students discover interests in subjects they hadn't considered

_____ professors bring new subjects to life for many students

_____ math is difficult for many students

______ other students often influence the decisions about majors

______ the reality of the job market creates changes in majors

______ academic performance sometimes makes students look for alternative interests

5. The best way to lose weight is through a good diet and exercise.

______ snacking all day long can cause a person to eat more than usual

______ people should avoid eating late at night before they go to bed

______ skipping meals is counterproductive for people on diets

______ people should do cardiovascular exercise at least three times per week

______ running is great exercise

______ people should eat three sensible meals per day

______ ESPN has many exercise shows

**Practice 4B** For each of the following topic sentences, list five details or examples to develop them.

1. Everywhere I go, I seem to see someone that I know.

______________________________________________

______________________________________________

______________________________________________

______________________________________________

______________________________________________

2. When I was in high school, I enjoyed many different extracurricular activities.

______________________________________________

______________________________________________

3. People are beginning to use their personal computers for many different business transactions.

4. Friends and family are a very important part of life.

5. People must be careful when they are swimming.

**Beth's Development** To come up with concrete details and examples that would support her topic sentence, Beth uses the brainstorming and focused freewriting techniques she learned in Chapter 2. This is what she wrote.

I have always been aware that I learn a lot through secondhand experiences.

- watching my friends make mistakes with their boyfriends
- watching my parents make their rules
- seeing my cousin ruin her life
- watching my brother mess up
- watching people around me get involved with drugs
- learning about other people's mistakes from my friends

I have also learned a lot about life by taking risks and making my own mistakes.

- procrastinating in school
- buying a used car
- quitting my new job
- asking Aaron out for the first time
- driving way too fast
- trying new foods
- changing majors
- moving in with roommates I don't know

TV is also a source of learning for me.

- watching the news
- watching the magazine channels
- learning about history or nature
- learning about everyday problems from shows like Dawson's Creek
- learning to cook from the best chefs
- watching documentaries

Here is Beth's new freewriting:

I know I learn a lot by watching people, taking risks, and watching TV. I'm sure I learn in other ways, but these are the ways that seem to give me the most knowledge about life in general.

Watching other people really helps me learn about life because I see the mistakes of others. I've learned a lot about boyfriends through the mistakes my friends have made. And I've learned how to be treated by a boyfriend by watching how my brother treats his girlfriend. They're going to be married next year. But I think I have learned the biggest lesson by watching my cousin throw away her life by staying involved in gangs.

Taking risks also teaches me lessons about life. I can learn from any risk--whether it is big or small. I'll never forget the risk I took when I chose to room with a person I had never met. This was a good decision in the long run, but it sure took us a while to get used to living with each other. And I will always be glad I took the risk to ask Aaron out. We've been together for almost two years, and it's wonderful. What a great risk to take!

And even though I would never admit it to my friends, I learn a lot from TV. I love Dawson's Creek, and I have learned how not to treat people by watching this show. I also love ER. I think it's neat how those actors show real-life situations. I'm actually thinking of becoming a nurse because of all the real-life-looking stuff on that show. It's taught me a lot about a hospital. I think TV is a great way to learn about anything in life that people want to know.

I will always learn about life from these sources. I guess I will always learn about life as long as I keep my eyes open, but these ways seem the most important to me right now.

 Your Development Choose at least one of the prewriting strategies that you learned in Chapter 2, and use it to generate more specific details and examples for each of your topic sentences.

# Organizing Your Essay

You are moving along quite well in the writing process. You have determined your subject, purpose, and audience, and you have written your thesis statement. You have also written topic sentences for your body paragraphs and thought of details, examples, and facts to develop those topic sentences. Now you are ready to organize your ideas. What should come first? What next?

To organize the ideas in your essay, you need to consider the purpose of your essay and the way each body paragraph serves that purpose. Then you should arrange your body paragraphs in a logical manner to achieve that purpose. If your essay's main purpose is informative—to describe the layout of a building, for example—you would probably arrange the details spatially. That is, you might begin with the entrance and move to the other parts of the building as if you were strolling through it. If, however, you want to persuade a reader to buy one type of car over another, you might arrange the essay so that it moves from one extreme to another—for example, from the least important feature of the car to the most important. Once you decide on the order of your paragraphs, you need to organize the details in each paragraph.

Most paragraphs and essays are organized in one of five ways:

1. From general to particular
2. From particular to general
3. Chronologically (by time)
4. Spatially (by physical order)
5. From one extreme to another

Let's look at these methods of organization one by one.

## GENERAL TO PARTICULAR

The most common method of organizing an essay or paragraph is from general to particular. This method begins with a general topic and becomes more specific as it progresses. A paragraph organized from general to particular might look like this:

Topic Sentence
 Detail
 Detail
 Detail
 Detail

Here is an example of a paragraph organized from general to particular:

> When I began attending college, I was very nervous because I was afraid I would not do very well in my classes. My first year, I took general education classes that reviewed a lot of the material I learned in high school. There was a lot of studying involved in these classes, but I was able to pass all of them. Soon I decided that my major would be business, so I began taking classes that dealt with business. All of the business classes were harder than the classes I had taken in general education. Just when I thought I would not pass a class, I would do well on a test, which would raise my confidence level again. I worked very hard in every class I had to take and was able to pass every one. Tomorrow I am graduating with my bachelor's degree in business.

This paragraph moves from the general idea of going to college to the specific notion of taking classes, graduating, and receiving a degree. Notice that it includes such transitions as *when*, *but*, *soon*, and *which*. They show the relationship among the writer's ideas.

The skeleton of a general-to-particular essay looks like this, although the number of paragraphs and details will vary:

Introduction
Topic sentence stating the most general point
 Detail
 Detail
 Detail
Topic sentence stating a more specific supporting point
 Detail
 Detail
 Detail

Topic sentence stating the most specific supporting point
Detail
Detail
Detail
Conclusion

An example of an essay organized from general to particular is "A Family Dilemma: To Scout or Not to Scout" on page 472. The essay begins by introducing the nephew of the author and the Supreme Court's ruling that the Boy Scouts can legally fire gay men from their organization. The author then explains how these two general topics are affecting his present life, moving to topics that become more and more specific as the essay progresses. You might want to read this selection to see how this method of organization works in a full essay.

**Practice 1A** Turn to the essay "El Hoyo" on page 398, and find two paragraphs organized from general to specific.

**Practice 1B** Write a topic sentence for the following group of sentences. Then organize the sentences into a paragraph using general-to-particular order. Add words, phrases, or sentences as necessary to smooth out the paragraph.

**Topic Sentence:** ________________________________

During these events, not only do you get to watch the athletes play their games, but you get to see former athletes announcing the play-by-play action.

Anytime you turn on the TV, there are at least 14 sporting events happening at one time.

You can see anything from basketball to golf to racing to fishing.

Let's face it; the likelihood of seeing a sports figure on the TV is great.

And just when you think you've seen enough of the players, you are flooded with commercials that have athletes selling various products.

## PARTICULAR TO GENERAL

When you reverse the first method of organization, you arrange your material from particular to general. In this case, more specific ideas start the essay or paragraph and lead up to a general statement. This type of organization is particularly effective if you suspect that your reader might not agree with the final point you are going to make. With this method, you can lead your reader to your opinion slowly and carefully.

A paragraph organized from particular to general looks like this:

Detail
Detail
Detail
Detail
Topic Sentence

Here is a paragraph of particular-to-general organization.

> The water is so crystal-clear that I can see every pebble settled on the bottom. A small sandy beach reaches the water's edge and makes a perfect spot to spend the afternoon. Across the water I can see the mountainside covered in the greenest trees imaginable. A log cabin also sits among the trees halfway up the mountain, so peaceful and secluded. The puffy white clouds make the sky appear to be a brighter blue, and the birds seem to enjoy floating on the soft breeze. I could sit all day next to the lake in the valley and just stare at my surroundings.

This paragraph starts with specific details about the area around the lake and ends with a topic sentence. Such transitions as *and*, *across the water*, and *also* move readers through the paragraph.

This is how a particular-to-general essay looks, though the number of details will vary:

Introduction
Topic sentence stating the most specific point
Detail
Detail
Detail
Topic sentence stating a less specific point
Detail
Detail
Detail
Topic sentence stating the most general point
Detail

Detail
Detail
Conclusion

The essay titled "Healing Myself with the Power of Work" on page 467 is a good example of organization from particular to general. It moves from examples out of the writer's life to his thesis at the end—that work is his therapy. If you read this selection, you will see firsthand how this method of organization works in a complete essay.

**Practice 2A** Turn to essay "What Are Friends For?" on page 458, and find two paragraphs that demonstrate particular-to-general organization.

**Practice 2B** Write a topic sentence for the following group of sentences. Then organize the sentences into a paragraph using particular-to-general order. Add words, phrases, or sentences as necessary to smooth out the paragraph.

**Topic Sentence:** ______________________________

My mom hopes I'll order something more grown-up, but I never will.
My family knew I loved pizza and always let me order one once a week.
I have always loved pepperoni, even on sandwiches and in soups.
I used to love pizza night when I lived at home.
And pizza is just the best food ever created in the world.
Now when I go home, we just go to an Italian restaurant where I can order pizza.

## CHRONOLOGICAL ORDER

When you organize ideas chronologically, you are organizing them according to the passage of time—in other words, in the order in which they occurred. Most of the time, when you tell a story or explain how to do something, you use chronological order: First this happened, and then that. Or first you do this, next you do that, and so on.

A paragraph organized chronologically looks like this:

Topic Sentence
First

Then
Next
Finally

Here is an example of a paragraph organized chronologically:

> Preparing to go snowboarding for the first time can be a lot of fun. First of all, you must get into full gear upon arriving at the mountain. Then you ride a ski lift to the top of the mountain. Once at the top, it is time to buckle the boots into the bindings on the board. The bindings must be tight, but not so tight that they are uncomfortable. Next, it is time to begin the descent down the mountain. On the way down the mountain, you should pay attention to how the board moves when pressure is applied to the toes and heels of the feet. Finally, you find out where to lean in order to turn right and left so you can fly down the mountain. Once you have learned the basics, you will have fun perfecting your new hobby.

This paragraph is chronological because it explains snowboarding according to a time sequence and uses transitions such as *first of all*, *then*, *next*, and *finally*.

Here is what an essay organized chronologically looks like:

Introduction
What happened first
  Detail
  Detail
  Detail
What happened next
  Detail
  Detail
  Detail
What happened after that
  Detail
  Detail
  Detail
Conclusion

A good example of this method of organization is the essay titled "Black Music in Our Hands" on page 452. It begins with the author explaining the three types of music she sang in the early 1960s. She then explains according to a time sequence all the circumstances that caused her to look at music differently. Reading through it will help you understand this method of organization.

**Practice 3A** Turn to the essay "Writer's Retreat" on page 412, and find two paragraphs that are organized chronologically.

**Practice 3B** Write a topic sentence for the following group of sentences. Then organize the sentences into a paragraph using chronological order. Add words, phrases, or sentences as necessary to smooth out the paragraph.

**Topic Sentence:** ______________________________

Spread the jelly on top of the peanut butter.
Unscrew the lids from a jar of peanut butter and a jar of jelly.
Using the knife again, remove a small amount of jelly from the jar.
Place two slices of bread on a plate.
Using the knife, remove a small amount of peanut butter from the jar.
Place the second slice of bread on top of the slice with the peanut butter and jelly on it.
First, remove a butter knife from the drawer.
Spread the peanut butter with the knife on one slice of bread.

## SPATIAL ORDER

Another method of arranging details is by their relationship to each other in space. You might describe the layout of your campus from its front entrance to its back exit or the arrangement of a beautiful garden from one end to the other. Explaining a home page from top to bottom and a screened-in porch from inside to outside are also examples of spatial order. Beginning at one point and moving detail by detail around a specific area is the simplest way of organizing by space.

A paragraph organized spatially might look like this:

Topic Sentence
  Here
  There

Next
Across
Beyond

Here is an example of a paragraph organized spatially:

> It was the first football game of the season and her first football game ever as a cheerleader. Standing in front of the huge crowd made the butterflies in her stomach begin to flutter again. In the front row sat a group of her friends cheering her on. Two rows behind them sat her psychology professor. Next to him sat a few of her new sorority sisters. As the cheerleader looked across the aisle, she noticed a group of rowdy students screaming and cheering for their team. Beyond the crowd, the tall announcer's booth where all of the press people and the athletic director sat seemed to glare down at her. Any minute the music would begin to blare from that very booth, and she would begin her first half-time dance routine.

This paragraph is arranged spatially because it moves physically around the football stadium, using such words as *in front of*, *behind*, *next to*, and *beyond* as transitions.

Here is what an essay organized spatially looks like:

Introduction
Here
  Detail
  Detail
  Detail
There
  Detail
  Detail
  Detail
Next
  Detail
  Detail
  Detail
Across
  Detail
  Detail
  Detail

Beyond
  Detail
  Detail
  Detail
Conclusion

An example of this method of organization is the essay titled "Dwelling" on page 402. It moves in spatial order around the vicinity of the author's home. Reading through it will help you understand this method of organization.

**Practice 4A** Turn to the essay "Sanctuary of School" on page 409, and find two paragraphs that use spatial organization.

**Practice 4B** Write a topic sentence for the following group of sentences. Then write a paragraph putting the sentences in spatial order. Add words, phrases, or sentences as necessary to smooth out the paragraph.

**Topic Sentence:** ______________________________

The hotel's check-in desk is located on the left side of the lobby.

Two little boys are sitting quietly on the couches next to the check-in counter waiting for their parents to finish checking in.

In the center of the lobby are four massive couches arranged in a conversational setting.

Directly across from the check-in desk is the activities counter where people can plan their stay.

Walking through the front door, a guest's attention is immediately drawn to the ceiling.

Painted as a sky, the ceiling gives guests the feeling that they have never left the outdoors.

Framing the front door are two huge water dolphins perched in the center of two water fountains.

## ONE EXTREME TO ANOTHER

Sometimes the best way to organize a paragraph is from one extreme to another: from most expensive to least expensive, from most humorous to least humorous, from most frustrating to least frustrating, and so on. (Of course, you can also move from least to most.) Use whatever extremes make sense for your topic. You might explain how to choose a pet by elaborating on the most important qualities and then considering the least important. For example, an apartment dweller's most important consideration would be the size of the pet and its need for exercise. Least important would be a dog's watchdog qualities. To accomplish another purpose, you might reverse this order and begin with the least important quality; this method is good in persuasive writing, because you end with your most important idea.

This method of organization has one distinct advantage over the other four approaches: It is the most flexible. When no other method of organization works, you can always arrange details from one extreme to another.

Here is an outline of a paragraph organized from one extreme to another:

Topic Sentence
- Most
- Next most
- Somewhat
- Least

Here is an example of a paragraph that moves from one extreme to another:

> Ever since I was old enough to join Little League teams, I have played a variety of sports. I would have to say that my favorite sport has always been football. Absolutely nothing can top the feeling of running for a touchdown and passing the last person on defense. My next favorite sport would have to be baseball. I used to love to pitch to catchers when we would work as though we were one athlete. My next favorite sport is basketball. As a teenager, I played guard in basketball, but eventually I got bored with the position. My least favorite sport is soccer. No matter how much I trained and ran before soccer season, I always got exhausted during the games—all we did was run up and down the field. Now that I'm in college, I'm grateful for the intramural teams that let me keep playing the sports that I love.

This paragraph moves from most to least preferred sport and is marked by such words as *favorite*, *next favorite*, and *least favorite*.

Here is what an essay organized according to extremes looks like:

Introduction

Most
- Detail
- Detail
- Detail

Next most
Detail
Detail
Detail
Somewhat
Detail
Detail
Detail
Least
Detail
Detail
Detail
Conclusion

"What Are Friends For?" on page 458 is a good example of this method of organization. It begins with a discussion of "relative friends" and moves to an explanation of "new friends." The author organizes her essay from least meaningful to most meaningful friends. Reading through it will help you understand this strategy.

**Practice 5A** Turn to the essay "Happiness Is Catching" on page 475, and find two paragraphs that are organized from one extreme to another.

**Practice 5B** Write a topic sentence for the following group of sentences. Then write a paragraph arranging the sentences from one extreme to another. Add words, phrases, and sentences as necessary to smooth out the paragraph. Also, label your system of classification (from

most ____________________ to least ____________________ or from least

__________________ to most __________________).

**Topic Sentence:** ______________________________________________

First, they have a hard time asking people for money.
Consequently, they allow debtors extra time to pay the bill.

But after a few months, the new employee has heard all the sob stories and is immune to their power.
That just makes it harder to get the money.
This is probably because they believe the sob stories they hear that probably aren't true.
Unfortunately, once the date has been extended, we all have to agree to it.

**Practice 6A** List the best method of development for paragraphs on the following topics.

1. How to make homemade salsa.
2. I think I am going to rearrange my dorm room to get more space.
3. What I will have for dinner tonight.
4. Today, people question the ethics of capital punishment.
5. I lift weights for an hour and run five miles every day.

**Practice 6B** Write a topic sentence that introduces the following details in a paragraph. Then arrange the details in logical order, and write a paragraph.

**Topic Sentence:** ______________________________

exercising three times a week
the advantages of aerobic exercise
exercising with a friend
the difficulty of starting an exercise routine

**Beth's Organization** Beth decided to organize her essay from one extreme to another—from the least important ways of learning for her to the most important. She first wants to introduce the idea of watching others, which comes so naturally for her. Next she will discuss taking risks and finally learning from television because she spends a lot of time watching TV. She thinks this order might work, so she lists as many concrete details as she can under each main idea.

Here is Beth's working outline at this point.

| | |
|---|---|
| **Thesis:** | Learning about life is easy for me. |
| **Observing Other People (*important*):** | watching other people making mistakes in their lives |
| **Specific Details:** | watching my cousin in gangs<br>living in fear<br>not in a gang because of her |
| **Taking Risks (*more important*):** | taking risks in order to learn from them |
| **Specific Details:** | making mistakes<br>asking my boyfriend out<br>learning whether good or bad |
| **Watching TV (*most important*):** | watching TV to learn about everyday stuff |
| **Specific Details:** | TV silly but helpful<br>TV can teach a wide range of topics<br>TV represents real-life experiences |
| **Concluding Thoughts:** | people can learn from everything they do |
| **Specific Details:** | watching other people<br>taking risks<br>watching TV |

Does the method of organization that Beth has chosen suit her topic? Would any other method of organization work as well?

 Your Organization What method of organization will work best for your ideas about learning? Why do you think this method will be best?

# Writing the Introduction, Conclusion, and Title

By now, you have written your thesis statement and topic sentences for your body paragraphs. You've thought of supporting details, facts, examples, and the most effective way of organizing your thoughts. At the end of this chapter, you will write a complete first draft of your essay. First, though, let's look at three important parts of your essay: the introduction, the conclusion, and the title.

You might have written some of these parts already. Some people write their introduction with their thesis; some write the introduction last. Some have an idea of how they want to conclude from the time they begin their papers; others write the conclusion last. Some struggle with a title; others write their titles as they generate their drafts. The order in which you write these three parts of an essay depends on your own personal writing process. All that matters is that your papers have a title, an introduction, several body paragraphs, and a conclusion that work together.

## INTRODUCTION

The introduction to your essay—your first paragraph—should both introduce your subject and stimulate your audience's interest. The introduction of an essay captures the readers' interest, gives necessary background information, and presents your thesis statement. This paragraph essentially tells readers what the essay is going to cover without going into detail or discussing specifics.

Writers generally use the introduction to lead up to their thesis statement. As a result, the sentences at the beginning of the introductory paragraph need to grab your readers' interest. Some effective ways of catching your audience's attention and giving necessary background information are to (1) furnish a vivid description, (2) tell a brief story, (3) give a revealing fact, statistic, or definition, (4) make an interesting comparison, (5) present a dramatic example, and (6) use an exciting quotation.

Also be sure that your introduction gives your readers any information that they may need to follow your train of thought. One way to check that your readers have all the necessary background is to apply the five *W*s and one *H*: who, what, when, where, why, and how. Any of this information that is important to your readers' understanding of your thesis statement should go in the introduction. You might also ask a friend to read your first draft and tell you if any background information is missing.

**Beth's Introduction and Thesis** Beth wrote a first draft of her introduction just to get started. She knew she would have to work with it later, but at least she was able to get some of her ideas down on paper.

> We all learn about life in different ways. Some people learn by watching, while others learn by doing. Some people learn by reading, and others learn by listening. My mom has always said that people can learn from any experience. But everyone learns in some way or another. Learning about life is easy for me.

**Your Introduction** Use the guidelines suggested here to capture your readers' interest and, if necessary, give them background information. Write two different introductions for your essay. End each with your thesis statement.

## CONCLUSION

The concluding paragraph is the final paragraph in an essay. It draws your essay to a close, giving readers a sense of completion. That is, readers feel that all the loose ends are wrapped up and the point of the essay is clear. As with introductions, there are many good techniques for writing a conclusion. You might (1) summarize the main ideas, (2) highlight the most important issue, (3) ask a question that gets readers to think about something in particular, (4) predict the future, (5) offer a solution to a problem, or (6) call readers to action. In some cases, you might want to use several of these strategies.

You should avoid two common problems in writing a conclusion. First, do not begin your conclusion with the words "in conclusion," "in summary," or "as you can see." Your conclusion should *show*—not *tell*—that you are at the end of your essay. Second, do not introduce a new idea. The main ideas of your essay should be in your body paragraphs. The conclusion is where you *finish* your essay, leaving your readers with a sense of closure or completeness.

**Beth's Conclusion** Here is a rough outline of what Beth wants to include in her conclusion. These are the notes that she came up with at this point.

People learn about life from just about anything.

- made me the person I am
- observing other people
- taking some risks myself
- watching TV

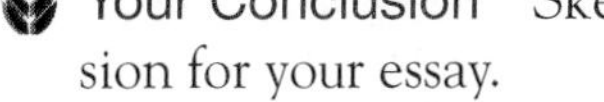

**Your Conclusion** Sketch an outline or write a draft of a possible conclusion for your essay.

## TITLE

A title is a phrase, usually no more than a few words. A title gives a hint about the subject, purpose, or focus of what is to follow. For example, the main title chosen for this book, *Mosaics*, reflects a particular view of the writing process—as many bright pieces logically connected to complete a picture. In other words, that title expresses in capsule form this textbook's purpose, which is to guide writers through the process of fitting the separate pieces of their ideas into a single meaningful whole for their audiences. The title of this chapter, however, is a straightforward naming of its contents: "Writing the Introduction, Conclusion, and Title."

Besides suggesting an essay's purpose, a good title catches an audience's attention or "hooks" readers so that they want to read more. Look at some of the essay titles in the readings in Part IV. For example, "Happiness Is Catching: Why Emotions Are Contagious" attracts the readers' attention because they will probably want to find out exactly how happiness is catching. "What Are Friends For?" is a title that will draw in anyone. And "I Just Wanna Be Average" is intriguing because the title is not a typical goal for most people. Do not underline or use quotation marks around your essay title. Do not put a period at the end of your title, and be sure to capitalize it correctly. The first word and last word in a title are always capitalized. Capitalize all other words except articles (*a*, *an*, *the*) and short prepositions (such as *in*, *by*, *on*, or *from*; see page 515 for a more complete list of prepositions).

**Beth's Title** Beth has several possible titles for her essay. She doesn't really know which one to use.

Learning About Life
The Way We Learn
Everyone Can Learn

**Your Title** Write three titles for your essay: (1) one that gives a hint of your subject, (2) one that gives a hint of your purpose, and (3) one that gives a hint of your focus. Make each title as catchy as you can.

**Beth's First Draft** In Chapters 1 through 5, and again in this chapter, you have watched Beth thinking about, planning, developing, and organizing her essay. It is time now to get a complete first draft down on paper. Here is Beth's first draft.

The Way We Learn

We all learn about life in different ways. Some people learn by watching, while others learn by doing. Some people learn by reading, and others learn by listening. My mom has always said that people can learn from any experience. But everyone learns in some way or another. Learning about life is easy for me.

I have always been aware that I learn a lot through secondhand experiences. When my cousin became heavily involved with gangs, I watched my cousin live her life in constant fear. By watching my cousin, I made a conscious decision to be nothing like my cousin. I was never drawn into a life of gangs because I saw what it did to my cousin.

I have also learned a lot about life by taking risks and making my own mistakes. Some risks I have taken were really difficult. One time I took a risk to ask out my best friend's roommate. Every risk I have taken has taught me something--whether good or bad.

TV is also a source of learning for me. Even though people make fun of TV and its silly shows. I still think it's a good way to learn about life. TV shows can teach people about life, as long as people are smart enough to understand that TV shows aren't real. The situations on TV represent real-life experiences.

People can learn about life from just about anything they do. What has made me the person I am today is observing other people, taking some risks myself, and watching TV.

**Your First Draft** Now write a complete first draft of your essay on taking risks.

# Revising

No matter how hard you wish, writing does not end with your first draft. The fun of revising and editing still lies ahead of you. *Revising* means "seeing again," and that is exactly what you should try to do when you revise to improve your writing—see it again from as many different angles as possible.

More specifically, revising your writing means changing it so that it says exactly what you mean in the most effective way. Revision involves both *content* (what you are trying to say) and *form* (how you deliver your message). Having a friend or tutor read your paper before you revise is a good idea so that you can see if you are communicating clearly.

Revising content means working with your words until they express your ideas as accurately and completely as possible. Revising form consists of working with the organization of your writing. When you revise, you should look closely at the six basic categories listed in the following checklist.

## Revising Checklist

**THESIS STATEMENT**

✔ Does the thesis statement contain the essay's controlling idea and appear as the last sentence of the introduction?

**BASIC ELEMENTS**

✔ Does the title draw in the readers?

✔ Does the introduction capture the readers' attention and build up to the thesis statement effectively?

✔ Does each body paragraph deal with a single topic?

✔ Does the conclusion bring the essay to a close in an interesting way?

**DEVELOPMENT**

✔ Do the body paragraphs adequately support the thesis statement?

✔ Does each body paragraph have a focused topic sentence?

✔ Does each body paragraph contain *specific* details that support the topic sentence?

✔ Does each body paragraph include *enough* details to explain the topic sentence fully?

UNITY

✔ Do the essay's topic sentences relate directly to the thesis statement?

✔ Do the details in each body paragraph support its topic sentence?

ORGANIZATION

✔ Is the essay organized logically?

✔ Is each body paragraph organized logically?

COHERENCE

✔ Are transitions used effectively so that paragraphs move smoothly and logically from one to the next?

✔ Do the sentences move smoothly and logically from one to the next?

Let's look at these revision strategies one by one.

## Thesis Statement

✔ Does the thesis statement contain the essay's controlling idea and appear as the last sentence of the introduction?

As you learned in Chapter 3, every successful essay has a thesis statement that states the essay's controlling idea. This sentence gives direction to the rest of the essay. It consists of a limited subject and the writer's position on that subject. Although a thesis statement can appear anywhere in an essay, it is usually the last sentence in the introduction.

Here are two examples:

| **Limited Subject** + | **Opinion** = | **Thesis Statement** |
|---|---|---|
| 1. Children today | grow up too fast | Children today grow up too fast. |
| 2. Children today | grow up too fast | Children today grow up too fast because of television, advertising, and working parents. |

As in the second example, the thesis statement should introduce all the topics in its essay. The first example includes the limited subject and the writer's position on that subject but needs to also introduce its topics.

**Practice 1A** Review the guidelines for developing a thesis statement in Chapter 3. Then write a thesis statement for each group of topic sentences listed here.

1. Thesis Statement: ____________________________________________

   ________________________________________________________________

   Everyone needs a friend who likes to do the same things.
   Everyone needs someone to share the good news.
   Equally important, everyone needs a good listener during bad times.

2. Thesis Statement: ____________________________________________

   ________________________________________________________________

   Watching a movie on the big screen of a theater makes the story and characters bigger and more interesting than life.
   The sound system in a movie theater makes me feel that I'm right there, in the action.
   The concession stand has all sorts of candy and goodies, and I don't have to clean up my own mess afterward.

3. Thesis Statement: ____________________________________________

   Driving behind slow drivers can cause other drivers to experience road rage.
   Likewise, having people driving too closely behind others can cause people to get angry.
   People who weave in and out of traffic at extreme speeds make many people furious.

4. Thesis Statement: ____________________________________________

   Asking someone out on a first date can take a lot of courage.
   Suggesting places to go or things to do is harder than it sounds.
   It seems that there's always one very embarrassing moment on a first date that would never happen on a later date.

5. Thesis Statement: ______________________________

Signing up for a skydiving class is exciting, and all your friends think you're really cool.
Boarding the plane for your first jump is a strong dose of reality, but still nothing like getting up the nerve to actually jump.
Free-falling and landing safely provide a rush that skydivers never forget.

**Practice 1B** Write thesis statements for the following introductions.

1. ______________________________

No matter how much I tell myself I am going to get up in the morning and go, I cannot seem to do it. Every night before I go to bed, I lay out my sweats and shoes and set my alarm. In the morning when the alarm rings, I push the snooze button and promise myself that I will get up in 10 minutes. This routine goes on for the next hour until I have to get up in order to make it to work on time. Once again, I have failed to get up and go to the gym, and I have deprived myself of one more hour of sleep.

2. ______________________________

The most important detail is to determine the number of rooms in the house. A family must consider the needs of the people living in the house and the plans in the near future. Of course, don't forget the backyard. Does the family need a fenced yard for animals or an area for the kids to play? And the family must pay attention to how well the house has been kept up. All of these items are very important details to pay attention to when looking for a new home.

3. ______________________________

Every morning, at precisely 8:00, the couple eats breakfast at the corner café. Afterward, they go to the market for fresh fruit or vegetables and run any errands. If there is no shopping to be done, the couple goes home and does housework or yard work. Every afternoon at 1:00, they sit down to lunch and watch a little television. In the late afternoon, they go for a walk around the lake for a bit of exercise before preparing their dinner. After dinner, they watch the news and play a hand of cards. Soon the sun dips behind the mountain, and the couple retires for the night.

Beth's Revision When Beth looks back at her thesis statement, she realizes it does not completely introduce what she talks about in her essay. Her thesis only tells readers that learning about life is easy for her, not that she has three important ways that she learns about life.

**Thesis Statement:** Learning about life is easy for me.

She decides to expand her thesis statement so that it more accurately introduces the topics that will follow in her essay:

**Revised Thesis Statement:** Learning about life ~~is easy for me~~ **happens for me by observing other people, by taking risks, and by watching TV**.

She feels that this thesis statement introduces the notion of learning and the different ways that she learned.

Your Revision With these guidelines in mind, revise your thesis statement.

**Your Revised Thesis Statement:** ______________________________

______________________________________________________________

## Basic Elements

- ✔ Does the title draw in the readers?
- ✔ Does the introduction capture the readers' attention and build up to the thesis statement effectively?
- ✔ Does each body paragraph deal with a single topic?
- ✔ Does the conclusion bring the essay to a close in an interesting way?

These revision items ask you to check that all the basic elements of the essay are present and are doing the jobs they are supposed to do. If all the essay's parts are in place, you can spend more time polishing what you have to say.

This is the time you should review these basic elements and look at them again now that you have written a complete draft of your essay. What changes do you want to make in your title? In your introduction? In your conclusion? Is your thesis statement at the end of your introduction? Do you need to split any body paragraphs?

**Practice 2A** Write an alternate title for "Venus Envy" (page 448).

**Practice 2B** Write an alternate introduction for "Don't Be Cruel" (page 429).

**Practice 2C** Write an additional body paragraph for "Sanctuary of School" (page 409).

**Practice 2D** Write an alternate conclusion for "How to Find True Love: Or, Rather, How It Finds You" (page 463).

**Beth's Revision** Beth sets out to answer each of these questions one by one. Here are her responses.

✔ Does the title draw in the readers?
No. It's kind of boring.

✔ Does the introduction capture the readers' attention and build up to the thesis statement effectively?
Not really--it's too short; I could use one of the ideas introduced in Chapter 6 to make it more interesting.

✔ Does each body paragraph deal with a single topic?
Yes. So I don't have to break any of them into two or more paragraphs.

✔ Does the conclusion bring the essay to a close in an interesting way?
Sort of. I guess I should look at it again and try to apply some of the material in Chapter 6 to my conclusion.

You saw Beth's first draft at the end of Chapter 6. Here is draft 2 of her introduction, conclusion, and title with her changes highlighted.

**Introduction**

We all learn about life in different ways. Some people learn by watching, while others learn by doing. Some people learn by reading, and others learn by listening. My mom has always said that people can learn from any experience. But everyone learns in some way or another. **To prove her point, when I experienced disappointment as I was growing up, my mom would always ask, "What did you learn from this experience?" It used to really irritate me. But now that I think about it, I realize she was right.** Learning about life happens for me by observing other people, by taking risks, and by watching TV.

**Conclusion**

People can learn about life from just about anything they do. What has made me the person I am today is observing other people, taking some risks myself, and watching TV. **I'm not finished learning yet. Are you?**

**Title**

~~The Way We Learn~~

**The Learning Curve**

Your Revision Apply these questions one by one to your essay.

- ☐ Does the title draw in the readers?
- ☐ Does the introduction capture the readers' attention and build up to the thesis statement effectively?
- ☐ Does each body paragraph deal with a single topic?
- ☐ Does the conclusion bring the essay to a close in an interesting way?

## Development

- ✔ Do the body paragraphs adequately support the thesis statement?
- ✔ Does each body paragraph have a focused topic sentence?

- ✔ Does each body paragraph contain *specific* details that support the topic sentence?
- ✔ Does each body paragraph include *enough* details to explain the topic sentence fully?

When you develop an essay, you build the body paragraphs. Body paragraphs provide supporting evidence for the thesis statement. They are made up of a clearly focused topic sentence and details that support the topic sentence. Supporting details should be as *specific* as possible, and you need to provide *enough* details to support the point you are making in each paragraph.

### Specific Details

An important part of developing a good essay is being able to recognize ideas that are more general (for example, *entertainment* and *exercise*) and more specific (the opening scene in *The Green Mile*). Two other essential terms to know in choosing details are *abstract* and *concrete*. As you learned in Chapter 3, concrete words refer to items you can see, hear, touch, smell, or taste—as opposed to abstract words, which refer to ideas and concepts, such as *entertainment*, *frustration*, and *peacefulness*. Look at the following examples, and notice how each line becomes more detailed.

entertainment (general, abstract)
movies
suspense films
Stephen King films
*The Green Mile*
opening scene in *The Green Mile* (specific, concrete)

exercise (general, abstract)
sports
team sports
football
college football
college football championship
Rose Bowl
2002 Rose Bowl in Pasadena (specific, concrete)

Don't confuse levels of detail with examples. Compare the previous ladder with this one:

sports

team sports

football

college football

UCLA Bruins
Wisconsin Wolverines
University of Texas Longhorns
Florida State Gators

In this ladder, the four college teams are at the same level of detail. One is not more specific than another. So these last four items are just a list of examples.

As a rule, your thesis statement should be the most general statement in your essay. Your topic sentences are more specific than your thesis, and the details in your body paragraphs are the most specific items in the essay. So an outline of these elements looks like this:

Thesis statement (general)

Topic sentence

Detail (specific and concrete)
Detail (specific and concrete)
Detail (specific and concrete)

Here is one of Beth's body paragraphs with more specific details in bold type in her revision.

**First Draft**

I have also learned a lot about life by taking risks and making my own mistakes. Some risks I have taken were really difficult. One time I took a risk to ask out my best friend's roommate. Every risk I have taken has taught me something--whether good or bad.

**Revised with Specific Details**

I have also learned a lot about life by taking risks and making my own mistakes. Some risks I have taken were really difficult. One time I took a risk to ask out my best friend's roommate. **I was attracted to his smile from the minute I met him.** Every risk I have taken has taught me something--whether good or bad.

**Practice 3A** Underline the most specific word or phrase in each group.

1. books, library, shelves, page 42, stairs
2. computer, technology, software, on-off switch, on-line help
3. backyard, swimming pool, Coppertone lotion, pool party
4. drinks, thirst, soda, root beer, root beer in a frosty mug
5. pink candles on a birthday cake, dessert dinner, sweets, chocolate candy

**Practice 3B** Fill in each blank with a new level of concrete detail as indicated by the indentions.

1. ____________________

    state lottery

        ____________________

            ____________________

2. ____________________

    brother

        ____________________

            ____________________

3. boat

    ____________________

        ____________________

            ____________________

4. ____________________

____________________

____________________

blue shirt with stripes

5. ____________________

____________________

Thursday's newspaper

## Enough Details

Not only should your details be specific and concrete, but you should furnish enough details to support your topic sentence. No matter how good one detail is, it is not adequate to develop a topic sentence. Without enough details, facts, or reasons, a paragraph can be too short and weak to support a thesis statement. So Beth needs to add more details to her paragraph.

Here is Beth's body paragraph on learning with more details.

**Revised with More Details**

I have also learned a lot about life by taking risks and making my own mistakes. Some risks I have taken were really difficult, **but the risks were important steps in my life.** One time I took a risk to ask out my best friend's roommate. I was attracted to his smile from the minute I met him**, but I thought he was too good-looking for me. I finally asked him out, we have been dating ever since. Our first date was at an amusement park. He bought me cotton candy. Other risks like driving too fast to be cool were just plain stupid.** Every risk I have taken has taught me something--whether good or bad.

**Practice 4A** List three details that could support each of the following topic sentences.

1. My favorite pastime is swimming.

____________________________________________

2. Eating a balanced diet is an important part of feeling good.

3. A simple gift is often the best.

4. Working for people you like is easy.

5. Spending time outside can change a person's mood.

**Practice 4B** Develop the following topic sentences with enough specific details.

1. Before taking a test, take a moment to relax.
2. Always discuss major decisions with someone you trust.
3. When interviewing for a job, dress appropriately.

4. My roommate is a real neatness freak.
5. When reading a book, think about what you are reading.

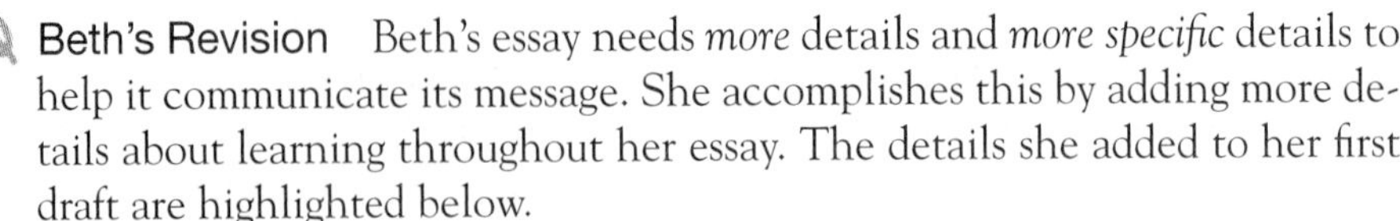

Beth's Revision Beth's essay needs *more* details and *more specific* details to help it communicate its message. She accomplishes this by adding more details about learning throughout her essay. The details she added to her first draft are highlighted below.

The Learning Curve

We all learn about life in different ways. Some people learn by watching, while others learn by doing. Some people learn by reading, and others learn by listening. My mom has always said that people can learn from any experience. But everyone learns in some way or another. To prove her point, when I experienced disappointment as I was growing up, my mom would always ask, "What did you learn from this experience?" It used to really irritate me. But now that I think about it, I realize she was right. **Now that I think about it, the way we learn is a major part of who we are.** Learning about life happens for me by observing other people, by taking risks, and by watching TV.

I have always been aware that I learn a lot through secondhand experiences. When my cousin became heavily involved with gangs, I watched my cousin live her life in constant fear. **She was worried she would end up in jail, lose her boyfriend, and maybe even lose her life.** By watching my cousin, I made a conscious decision to be nothing like my cousin. I was never drawn into a life of gangs because I saw what it did to my cousin.

I have also learned a lot about life by taking risks and making my own mistakes. Some risks I have taken were really difficult**, but the risks were important steps in my life.** One time I took a risk to ask out my best friend's roommate. **I was attracted to his smile from the minute I met him, but I thought he was too good-looking for me. I finally asked him out, we have been dating ever since. Our first date was at an amusement park. He bought me cotton candy. Other risks like driving too fast to be cool were just plain stupid.** Every risk I have taken has taught me something--whether good or bad.

TV is also a source of learning for me. Even though people make fun of TV and its silly shows. I still think it's a good way to learn about life. **Shows like Dawson's Creek and Boston Public may overdo the drama, but I still learn about people from the way the characters interact with each other. I especially love ER.** TV shows can teach people about life, as long as people are smart enough to understand that TV shows aren't real. The situations on TV represent real-life experiences.

People can learn about life from just about anything they do. What has made me the person I am today is observing other people, taking some risks myself, and watching TV. I'm not finished learning yet. Are you?

 Your Revision Add more details to your essay, making your explanations and descriptions as specific as possible.

## Unity

- ✔ Do the essay's topic sentences relate directly to the thesis statement?
- ✔ Do the details in each body paragraph support its topic sentence?

An essay is unified when its topic sentences are all related to the thesis statement and when each body paragraph discusses only one idea. Irrelevant paragraphs in essays are those that don't support their essay's thesis statement. They should be deleted or revised to fit into the essay's plan.

A paragraph's main idea is introduced in its topic sentence. All other sentences in a paragraph should expand on this idea and relate to it in some way. Information that is not about the topic sentence is irrelevant and does not belong in the paragraph.

 Practice 5A Cross out the topic sentences that don't support each thesis statement.

1. Holidays are fun times in my family.

   My favorite holiday is Thanksgiving.
   July 4th always scares my dogs.

Chanukah is a time of great celebration in my house.
My boyfriend doesn't understand my family.

2. I love working with children.

   Children's games still make me laugh.
   I hate foods that are good for me.
   I want a good paying job.
   I have always liked babysitting.
   I have applied to work at the Children's Center on our campus.

3. Exercise is essential for good shape.

   Exercise keeps our hearts in good shape.
   Exercise is fun.
   Exercise is difficult when you are on a tight schedule.
   Exercise is necessary for weight control.
   Exercise is good for us emotionally.

4. I have learned over the years how to control my anger.

   One way is to count to 10 before I do anything.
   I get angry easily.
   Another solution is to take a deep breath before I act.
   The solution I use most often is to take a walk.

5. I really like to cook, but I never have the time.

   I am most creative at breakfast.
   My favorite dish to make is beef stroganoff.
   My class schedule keeps me busy right through dinner.
   My philosophy class is my toughest class.
   I don't like spicy foods.

**Practice 5B** Cross out the three irrelevant sentences in the following paragraph.

I have a very bad habit of waiting until the night before an exam to begin studying, so it is very important for me to have a well-planned and productive cramming session. One time during my junior year of high school, I failed a test. I begin by putting on comfortable clothes so that when I begin to squirm and twist to try and get comfortable, I am able to move around. Next, I get a large glass of milk and several cookies to snack on. Peanut butter cookies have always been my favorite. Once I have my snack, I spread all my books and study materials out on the living room floor. I have a hardwood floor. Finally, I am ready to begin studying for the next few hours.

**Practice 5C** Cross out the three irrelevant sentences in the following paragraph.

Most people wonder what it would be like to win the lottery and be able to spend money as they please. The odds are that even the people who buy a lottery ticket every day will never win the lottery. Winning the lottery would change most people's lives drastically. Many people say that they would begin by paying all their debts. There are people in the world who buy so many items on credit that they are constantly trying to get out of debt. Other people say that they would buy a new house or a new car to spoil themselves a little bit. Some people simply say that they would invest the money, and use it when they retire so that they can live comfortably. Many elderly people are unable to continue the lifestyles they are accustomed to after retirement.

**Beth's Revision** When Beth reads her paper for unity, she sees that three sentences are off topic. So she deletes them.

**In Paragraph 3:** ~~Our first date was at an amusement park. He bought me cotton candy.~~

**In Paragraph 4:** ~~I especially love ER.~~

**Your Revision** Read your essay carefully, and cross out any irrelevant sentences or paragraphs.

## Organization

- ✔ Is the essay organized logically?
- ✔ Is each body paragraph organized logically?

In Chapter 3, you learned five ways to organize your paragraphs and essays:

1. From general to particular
2. From particular to general
3. Chronologically (by time)
4. Spatially (by physical arrangement)
5. From one extreme to another

The organization that you choose for your essay depends chiefly on your topic and overall purpose. What are you trying to accomplish? In what order should you present your evidence? Is point A the most important? Maybe it should be the last paragraph so you can build up to it.

After you put your paragraphs in order, you are ready to look at the organization of each individual paragraph. It's very likely that your essay will be organized one way (say, from least important to most important) and each of your body paragraphs will have its own method of organization. As you revise, you should check to see that your essay is organized as effectively as possible for what you are trying to accomplish and that your body paragraphs are each arranged logically as well.

**Practice 6A** Reorganize the following topics so that they are in a logical order. Then label your method of organization.

1. east at the mall to the stop light
   west at the grocery store to the flower shop
   north at the flower shop until you get to Amy's
   south at the stop light until you hit the grocery store

**Method of Organization:** ____________________

2. sitcoms
   dramas
   documentaries
   musicals
   awards shows

**Method of Organization:** ____________________

3. community servants
   police badges
   police officers
   police office staff
   police uniforms

**Method of Organization:** ______________________________

**Practice 6B** Reorganize the following sentences so that they are in a logical order. Then identify your method of organization.

Next, I decide what I will have for dinner and begin to cook.
Then I change into comfortable clothes.
Before I completely wind down, I lay out my clothes for the next day and set my alarm clock.
This is always a good time to look at the mail or return phone calls.
While I am cooking, I listen to music or turn on the evening news.
First, I begin to relax by taking a shower.
When I return home in the evenings, I always follow the same routine.
After I eat, I do the dishes and sit down in the living room.
Then I watch television or read a book until I am ready to go to bed.

**Method of Organization:** ______________________________

**Practice 6C** Reorganize the following sentences so that they are in a logical order. Then identify your method of organization.

Sweatshirts belong next to long-sleeved shirts, so they come next.
When I walk in the closet door, all of my T-shirts are hanging directly to my left in the closet.
My shoes follow the same pattern on the floor as the clothes hanging up do.
Next to the T-shirts are my long-sleeved shirts.
Starting the summer clothes are the tank-tops, followed by summer dresses.

Everything in my closet must be in order, or I will never be able to find anything.

All of my sweaters can be found stacked neatly on the shelf just above my long-sleeved sweatshirts.

Jackets, of course, go along with sweatshirts, so they are hanging next to the sweatshirts.

I have winter shoes immediately as I walk in the door, with sandals for summer toward the back of the closet.

After the jackets come the summer clothes.

**Method of Organization:** ______________________________

Beth's Revision In Chapter 3, Beth decided that the best way to organize her essay was from one extreme to another (from least to most important). But now she needs to make sure that this is the most effective order for her ideas and that every paragraph is in the right place.

This is the order of the main ideas in her first draft:

| | |
|---|---|
| **Least important:** | Observing people |
| **Next most important:** | Taking risks |
| **Most important:** | Watching TV |

After thinking about this order, Beth realizes that she learns more from taking risks than from watching TV. So she decides to reverse these two topics. She also remembers that she has to revise her thesis statement and her concluding sentence to reflect this new order.

| | |
|---|---|
| **Revised Thesis Statement:** | Learning about life happens for me by observing other people, **by watching TV,** and **by taking risks.** |
| **Revised Concluding Sentence:** | What has made me the person I am today is observing other people, **watching TV,** and **taking some risks myself.** |

Also in Chapter 3, Beth organized her three body paragraphs from general to particular. At this point, she checks to see if this is the most effective order for these ideas. She thinks that this order is a good choice for her body paragraphs.

 Your Revision Double-check the method of organization you chose in Chapter 3 for your essay. Do you still think this is the most effective order for what you are trying to say? Then check each body paragraph to see that the details are arranged logically.

## Coherence

- ✔ Are transitions used effectively so that the paragraphs move smoothly and logically from one to the next?
- ✔ Do the sentences move smoothly and logically from one to the next?

A well-written paragraph is coherent—that is, its parts *cohere*, or stick together. It is smooth, not choppy, and readers move logically from one thought to the next, seeing a clear relationship among the ideas. Here are four different strategies that writers use to help their readers follow their train of thought from one paragraph to the next and within paragraphs: *transitions*, *repeated words*, *synonyms*, and *pronouns*.

### Transitions

*Transitional words and phrases* provide bridges or links between paragraphs and ideas. They show your readers how your paragraphs or thoughts are related or when you are moving to a new point. Good use of transitions makes your writing smooth rather than choppy.

**Choppy:** TV shows can teach people about life, as long as people are smart enough to understand that TV shows aren't real. The situations on TV represent real-life experiences.

**Smooth:** TV shows can teach people about life, as long as people are smart enough to understand that TV shows aren't real. **However,** the situations on TV represent real-life experiences.

Transitions have very specific meanings, so you should take care to use the most logical one.

**Confusing:** TV shows can teach people about life, as long as people are smart enough to understand that TV shows aren't real. **Consequently,** the situations on TV represent real-life experiences.

Here is a list of some common transitional words and phrases that will make your writing more coherent. They are classified by meaning.

**Some Common Transitions**

| | |
|---|---|
| **Addition:** | *moreover, further, furthermore, besides, and, and then, likewise, also, nor, too, again, in addition, next, first, second, third, finally, last* |
| **Comparison:** | *similarly, likewise, in like manner* |
| **Contrast:** | *but, yet, and yet, however, still, nevertheless, on the other hand, on the contrary, after all, in contrast, at the same time, otherwise* |
| **Emphasis:** | *in fact, indeed, to tell the truth, in any event, after all, actually, of course* |
| **Example:** | *for example, for instance, in this case* |
| **Place:** | *here, there, beyond, nearby, opposite, adjacent to, near* |
| **Purpose:** | *to this end, for this purpose, with this objective* |
| **Result:** | *hence, therefore, accordingly, consequently, thus, as a result, then, so* |
| **Summary:** | *to conclude, to sum up, to summarize, in brief, on the whole, in sum, in short, as i have said, in other words, that is* |
| **Time:** | *meanwhile, at length, immediately, soon, after a few days, now, in the meantime, afterward, later, then, sometimes, (at) other times, still* |

See pages 517–518 in the Handbook (Part V) for more information on transitions.

Practice 7A Fill in the blanks in the following paragraph with logical transitions.

Today, an unlimited amount of information is available through the Internet. ____________, some of this information may not be suitable for younger audiences. Many concerned parents asked for a way to block Internet sites that they did not want their children to view. _____________, a system was developed by which a parent uses a password to choose which Internet sites the household computer will and won't access. _____________, children who do not know the password cannot access the blocked Internet sites. _____________, parents have control over the technology in their homes and feel their children are safe when they use the Internet.

**Practice 7B** Rewrite the following paragraph, adding at least three transitions to make it more coherent.

In high school, I thought I had everything figured out. I never considered what I would do after graduation. I never made any plans. When I graduated, I was completely lost. I went to see a guidance counselor at the local college. I decided to go to college. I am in college and have made many plans for the future.

### Repeated Words

*Repeating key words* also helps bind the ideas of an essay together and guide readers through the details. A key word is usually the topic of the essay or paragraph. At the same time, too much repetition becomes boring.

**Effective Repetition:** **TV shows** can teach people about life, as long as people are smart enough to understand that **TV shows** aren't real.

**Practice 8A** Underline five effective repeated words in the following paragraph.

All my life, I have gone to my grandmother's house near a lake out in farm country during the summer. This year, I'm taking my best friend at college with me. What I like most about summers at the lake is that the weather is so warm, so I can swim all day long. I swim near the bridge and see the small fish swimming around the columns. Sometimes I even swim over to the docks where all of the people are loading and unloading their boats. I used to try to swim faster and faster to beat my own record. Now I just go to relax, forget about school, and think about the future.

**Practice 8B** Underline at least five effective repeated words in the following paragraph.

For many people, reading the daily newspaper is their main source of information about the world. The front page usually gives the national news or an international political event that affects the United States. Major world events, such as an earthquake, always make front-page news. On the last page of the first section is the op-ed (opposite editorial) page, where editors and readers give their opinions on current news. The editorial and op-ed pages are among the few places in the newspaper where the writing is not objective, along with book and movie reviews and columnists like Molly Ivins or Dear Abby. Most newspapers have separate sections for sports, business, entertainment, classified ads, and comics. All in all, a half hour spent with the newspaper over morning coffee keeps a person up-to-date on world affairs and local people, places, and events.

### Synonyms

*Synonyms* are another way to link your ideas and help you avoid needless repetition. Synonyms are words that have identical or similar meanings—*movie/film*, *feeling/emotion*, *fantastic/unbelievable*. They add variety and interest to your writing. A thesaurus, or book of synonyms, can help you choose synonyms for specific words. Be aware, however, that all the words in a thesaurus listing are not interchangeable. *Retreat* is listed as a synonym for *escape*, but the two words suggest two very different ways of leaving a place.

**Boring Repetition:** But **now that I think about it,** I realize she was right. **Now that I think about it,** the way we learn is a major part of who we are.

**Revision:** But **now that I think about it,** I realize she was right. **In fact,** the way we learn is a major part of who we are.

In the following example from Beth's essay, Beth uses *programs* in place of one of her references to *shows*.

**Original Reference:** **Shows** like Dawson's Creek and Boston Public may overdo the drama, but I still learn about people from the way the characters interact with each other.

**Synonym:** **Programs** like Dawson's Creek and Boston Public may overdo the drama, but I still learn about people from the way the characters interact with each other.

**Practice 9A** Underline at least four synonyms for *friend* in the following paragraph.

My younger brother and his friends were always starting clubs when I was young. The clubhouse and the club name were very important. The pals usually decided on a name first. I think my favorite name that they had was "The Three Amigos," even though it was not very original. Every once in a while, an acquaintance of the boys would be allowed to join the club, and the name would have to be changed. Since the boys always thought that they were so sophisticated, they had a sign on the door that read "Associates Only—No Girls Allowed." The boys are all grown now, but I still smile every time I think about all of the meetings of "The Three Amigos" that I sat outside and listened to.

**Practice 9B** Replace two uses of the word *actor* with two different synonyms in the following paragraph.

Being an actor seems like a glamorous career choice, but becoming famous is not easy. Many actors start out waiting on tables in restaurants, hoping to be discovered by agents dining there. Other actors go from bit part to bit part in movies and never really earn enough for a living. In the unlikely event that an actor makes it big, he or she suddenly loses all privacy. Still, there are advantages to fame, and most actors adjust quite well to the lifestyle.

### Pronouns

Finally, you can link your sentences with *pronouns*. Pronouns not only help you avoid needless repetition but also keep your writing moving at a fairly fast pace. Personal pronouns (*I*, *you*, *he*, *she*, *it*, *we*, *they*) and indefinite pronouns (*any*, *some*, *other*, *one*) are the ones most commonly used as replacements.

Beth uses a pronoun to get rid of a repetition of the words *my cousin*.

**Repetition:** When my cousin became heavily involved with gangs, I watched my cousin live her life in constant fear.

**Revision:** When my cousin became heavily involved with gangs, I watched ~~my cousin~~ **her** live her life in constant fear.

For more information on pronouns, see pages 508–510 in the Handbook (Part V).

**Practice 10A** Underline 10 personal and indefinite pronouns in the following paragraph.

The people down the street have a very large family, which means that there is always something going on in their house. Sometimes when I am at their house, I cannot keep up with everything that is happening. For example, when Sandy answers the phone, she yells that it's for Ryan. Of course, Ryan has to know who it is, and the yelling continues back and forth until Ryan decides to finally pick up the phone. Sometimes when the family are really busy, they all make dinner for themselves. Everyone is in the kitchen at one time trying to find something to eat while trying not to step on one another. I'm not sure I could live at the Mitchells' house, but I definitely like visiting.

**Practice 10B** Add five pronouns where appropriate in the following paragraph.

A few days ago, Brian, Carol, Katie, and I went out to dinner. Brian, Carol, Katie, and I went to a new Italian restaurant on First Street. As soon as Brian, Carol, Katie, and I walked in the door, Brian, Carol, Katie, and I could smell the garlic, basil, and oregano in the rich tomato sauces of pizza, lasagna, and, of course, spaghetti and meatballs. Brian, Carol, Katie, and I couldn't stand it, so Brian, Carol, Katie, and I ordered immediately. The food was even better than it smelled. Before the dinner was over, Brian, Carol, Katie, and I set a date to return.

**Beth's Revision** When Beth checks her essay for coherence, she thinks her writing could be smoother if she used some of these techniques. So she makes the following revisions that help bind her sentences together and show the relationship between her ideas.

Here is Beth's essay with transitions, repeated words, synonyms, and pronouns highlighted.

The Learning Curve

We all learn about life in different ways. Some people
learn by watching, while others learn by doing. Some
people learn by reading, and others learn by listening.
My mom has always said that people can learn from any
experience. But everyone learns in some way or another.
To prove her point, when I experienced disappointment
as I was growing up, my mom would always ask, "What
did you learn from this experience?" It used to really irritate me. But now that I think about it, I realize she was
*Transition* right. **In fact,** the way we learn is a major part of who we
are. Learning about life happens for me by observing
other people, by watching TV, and by taking risks.

I have always been aware that I learn a lot through
secondhand experiences. When my cousin became heav-
ily involved with gangs, I watched ~~**my cousin**~~ **her** live her *Pronoun*
life in constant fear. She was worried she would end up
in jail, lose her boyfriend, and maybe even lose her life.
By watching my cousin, I made a conscious decision to
*Pronoun* be nothing like ~~**my cousin**~~ **her. Therefore,** I was never *Transition*
drawn into a life of gangs because I saw what it did to my
cousin.

TV is also a source of learning for me. Even though
people make fun of TV and its silly shows. I still think
it's a good way to learn about life. ~~**Shows**~~ **Programs** *Synonym*
like Dawson's Creek and Boston Public may overdo the
drama, but I still learn about people from the way the
characters interact with each other. **TV shows** can teach *Repetition*
people about life, as long as people are smart enough to
*Repetition* understand that **TV shows** aren't real. **However,** the sit- *Transition*
uations on TV represent real-life experiences.

I have also learned a lot about life by taking risks and
making my own mistakes. Some risks I have taken were

really difficult, but **~~the risks~~ they** were important steps *Pronoun*
*Transition* in my life. **For instance,** one time I took a **~~risk~~ chance** to *Synonym*
ask out my best friend's roommate. I was attracted to his smile from the minute I met him, but I thought he was too good-looking for me. I finally asked him out, we have
*Repetition* been dating ever since. Other **risks** like driving too fast to be cool were just plain stupid. Every **risk** I have taken *Repetition*
has taught me something--whether good or bad.

People can learn about life from just about anything they do. What has made me the person I am today is observing other people, watching TV, and taking some
*Transition* risks myself. **Of course,** I'm not finished learning yet. Are you?

**Transitions** In addition to *however*, Beth added four more transitions to her essay. What are they?

______________________________________________

List the meaning of all five transitions in Beth's essay:

1. Transition: ________________ Meaning: ________________
2. Transition: ________________ Meaning: ________________
3. Transition: ________________ Meaning: ________________
4. Transition: ________________ Meaning: ________________
5. Transition: ________________ Meaning: ________________

**Repeated Words** When Beth checked her essay for repeated key words, she saw that she referred directly to *risk* twice. She decided this was an effective repetition and chose to keep it in her essay.

**Synonyms** When Beth looked at her essay again, she found another opportunity to use a synonym to link her ideas more clearly. Besides the addition of *program* for *show*, what other synonym does Beth use in her revision?

______________________ for ______________________

Pronouns Finally, in addition to substituting *her* for *my cousin*, Beth found two more places to use pronouns to bind her essay together. Where are these places in her essay?

____________________ for ____________________

____________________ for ____________________

 Your Revision Now it's time to make your essay more coherent.

Transitions Check the transitions in your essay. Do you use enough transitions so that your essay moves smoothly and logically from one paragraph to the next and from one sentence to the next? Do you use your transitions correctly?

Repeated Words Look at your essay to see when you might want to repeat a key word. Then revise your essay accordingly.

Synonyms Now look for places in your essay where you might add synonyms to link your sentences. Use a thesaurus in book form or on your computer if you need help.

Pronouns Now check your essay for opportunities to use pronouns. Add appropriate pronouns.

Beth's Revised Essay After revising her thesis statement, her development of ideas, and the unity, organization, and coherence of her writing, Beth produced the following revised essay. All of her revisions are in bold type.

~~The Way We Learn~~

**The Learning Curve**

We all learn about life in different ways. Some people learn by watching, while others learn by doing. Some people learn by reading, and others learn by listening. My mom has always said that people can learn from any experience. But everyone learns in some way or another. **To prove her point, when I experienced disappointment as I was growing up, my mom would always ask, "What did you learn from this experience?" It used to really irritate me. But now that I think about it, I realize she**

**was right. In fact, the way we learn is a major part of who we are.** Learning about life ~~**is easy for me**~~. **happens for me by observing other people, by watching TV, and by taking risks.**

I have always been aware that I learn a lot through secondhand experiences. When my cousin became heavily involved with gangs, I watched ~~**my cousin**~~ **her** live her life in constant fear. **She was worried she would end up in jail, lose her boyfriend, and maybe even lose her life.** By watching my cousin, I made a conscious decision to be nothing like ~~**my cousin**~~ **her. Therefore,** I was never drawn into a life of gangs because I saw what it did to my cousin.

TV is also a source of learning for me. Even though people make fun of TV and its silly shows. I still think it's a good way to learn about life. ~~**Shows**~~ **Programs like Dawson's Creek and Boston Public may overdo the drama, but I still learn about people from the way the characters interact with each other.** ~~**I especially love ER.**~~ **TV shows** can teach people about life, as long as people are smart enough to understand that **TV shows** aren't real. **However,** the situations on TV represent real-life experiences.

I have also learned a lot about life by taking risks and making my own mistakes. Some risks I have taken were really difficult, **but** ~~**the risks**~~ **they were important steps in my life. For instance,** one time I took a ~~**risk**~~ **chance** to ask out my best friend's roommate. **I was attracted to his smile from the minute I met him, but I thought he was too good-looking for me. I finally asked him out, we have been dating ever since.** ~~**Our first date was at an amusement park. He bought me cotton candy.**~~ **Other risks like driving too fast to be cool were just plain stupid.** Every **risk** I have taken has taught me something--whether good or bad.

People can learn about life from just about anything they do. What has made me the person I am today is observing other people, watching TV, and taking some risks myself. **Of course, I'm not finished learning yet. Are you?**

Your Revised Essay Now that you have applied all the revision strategies to your own writing, rewrite your revised essay.

# Editing

After you have revised your writing, you are ready to edit it. Editing involves finding grammar, punctuation, mechanics, and spelling errors and correcting them. Correct writing helps you communicate just as clearly as well-chosen words. Nothing distracts readers from what you are saying more than editing errors.

As the checklist here shows, we have divided the editing strategies into three categories: sentences, punctuation and mechanics, and word choice and spelling. This checklist doesn't cover all the grammar and usage problems you may find in your writing, but it focuses on the main errors college students make.

## Editing Checklist

**SENTENCES**

- ✔ Does each sentence have a main subject and verb?
- ✔ Do all subjects and verbs agree?
- ✔ Do all pronouns agree with their nouns?
- ✔ Are modifiers as close as possible to the words they modify?

**PUNCTUATION AND MECHANICS**

- ✔ Are sentences punctuated correctly?
- ✔ Are words capitalized properly?

**WORD CHOICE AND SPELLING**

- ✔ Are words used correctly?
- ✔ Are words spelled correctly?

## YOUR EQ (OR EDITING QUOTIENT)

A good way to approach editing is by finding your EQ (Editing Quotient). Knowing your EQ will help you look for specific errors in your writing and make your editing more efficient.

**Practice 1 EQ Test** In each of the following paragraphs, underline the errors you find, and label them a, b, c, and so on. Then list them on the lines below the paragraph. The number of lines corresponds to the number of errors in each paragraph.

The possible errors are listed here:

| | | |
|---|---|---|
| apostrophe | end punctuation | run-on |
| capitalization | fragment | spelling |
| comma | modifier error | subject-verb agreement |
| confused word | pronoun | verb form |
| dangling modifier | pronoun agreement | |

1. Many people seem to have a telephone permanently attached to one ear people have several phone lines going into their homes. And cell phones hanging off of their belts. People are talking on their cell phones in restaurants, in cars, and even in public bathrooms. When they go home, they go on-line to check e-mail. While the second line is ringing off the hook. Why would someone want to be available every second of the day? This rushed society will eventually have to slow down, people can't live at this pace for long.

   a. ______________________________

   b. ______________________________

   c. ______________________________

   d. ______________________________

2. Recently, a major computer software company was accused of being a monopoly. That is, it seemed to be trying to control the whole software industry. The company, reality software, sells many different types of software at a reasonable price. Which results in the company selling more products than its competitors. Reality Software also signed contracts with Computer Manufacturers that allow the manufacturers to install

Reality programs on computers before they are sold. The courts, which guard against monopolies, say this is unfair to consumers, they should be able to choose their software. It is also unfair to other software companies. Because they are not given a fair chance to sell their products.

(a.) ______

(b.) ______

(c.) ______

(d.) ______

(e.) ______

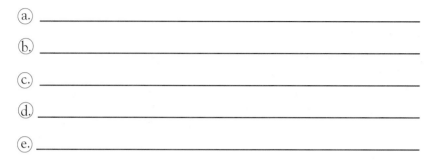

3. Public speaking is a valuable tool no matter what career path a person take. At some point in every career, if a person is going to advance, they will have to speak to a group. In fact, the higher up the career ladder a person climb, the more public speaking will be required. It is good preparation, therefore, to take a public speaking course in college, a public speaking course not only teaches the skills involved in making a presentation but also builds a person's confidence.

(a.) ______

(b.) ______

(c.) ______

(d.) ______

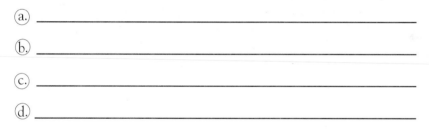

4. If you think a surprise birthday party takes a lot of time and work, try planning a wedding. Until a person plans his or her own wedding, they can't fully understand all the details that must be considered. Too my way of thinking, long engagements aren't to find out how compatible the couple is. There to allow enough time to find a place to hold the reception. On the date you want. Plus a good caterer and music. Even the smallest detail must be considered, such as whether guests should throw rice birdseed or confetti at the happy couple after the ceremony.

(a.) ______

(b.) ______

(c.) ______________________________

(d.) ______________________________

(e.) ______________________________

(f.) ______________________________

(g.) ______________________________

5. A famous author once said that his messy handwriting, almost kept him from becoming a writer. Struggling to be legible, the pages were impossible to read. No matter how hard he tried, after only a few words his handwriting would become rushed and scribbled. He would write wonderful novels that only he could read, for his twenty-third birthday, his wife bought him a typewriter. He then began to write books. That people all over the world have read. If he were alive today, he could write with a computer.

(a.) ______________________________

(b.) ______________________________

(c.) ______________________________

(d.) ______________________________

6. Everyone has heard the term "best freind." But what is a best friend? Some people beleive that their oldest friend is they're best friend. Yet a best friend can be someone you meet in college or even someone who is family. Such as a brother or sister. No matter who qualifies as a best friend, two facts is true: A best freind is someone special and the person you trust the most. People may wonder how they could get along without their best friend? Most people couldn't.

(a.) ______________________________

(b.) ______________________________

(c.) ______________________________

(d.) ______________________________

(e.) ______________________________

(f.) ____________________

(g.) ____________________

7. If I had my way, I would require every college student to take a course in geography. It is embarassing how little the average American knows about his own country, to say nothing of other countries. For instance, do you know the capital of virginia? Could you name all the Great Lakes? On which continent is greece? If you can answer these questions you are one of very few people. People think geography is boring but it isn't. Its fascinating to learn about the world we live in.

(a.) ____________________

(b.) ____________________

(c.) ____________________

(d.) ____________________

(e.) ____________________

(f.) ____________________

(g.) ____________________

8. I believe that fast-food restaurants should change there names to "fast food sometimes, but at least faster than a sit-down restaurant." When I go through the drive-up window at a fast-food restaraunt, it is because I am in a hurry and want to get something to eat quickly, however, sometimes it would be quicker for me to go home and cook a three-course meal. I do not understand what could take so long. I pull up to the intercom, order my food, procede to the window, and wait. If fast food always lived up to its name I would be able to get food fast.

(a.) ____________________

(b.) ____________________

(c.) ____________________

(d.) ____________________

(e.) ____________________

9. Doing the family laundry used to be a chore for me but now I am a pro. First, I sort the clothes according to colors or whites. Before I learned this basic rule, my poor brother had to wear pink underwear from time to time. Next, I put the clothes in the washing machine, and add detergent. If I'm doing whites I also add bleach. I close the lid, turn the dial to hot wash and cold rinse, and push the "start" button. I allow the washing machine to do it's work while I read a magazine. When it's time to put the clothes in the dryer, I pay attention to the drying instructions on the tags. Once I neglected this step, and my favorite pants shrinked. When the dryer has done its work, remove the clothes immediately so they do not become rinkled.

   (a.) ______________________________

   (b.) ______________________________

   (c.) ______________________________

   (d.) ______________________________

   (e.) ______________________________

   (f.) ______________________________

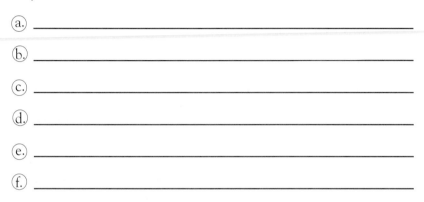

10. It's fun to watch a person with their animals. For instance, each morning, the lady down the street takes her dog for a walk. The dog is a tiny rat terrier, it is really cute. The lady puts a little leash on the dog. To keep him from running away. Even though the dogs legs are short, he can run real fast. The dog seems so happy during his walks. He jumps and yips. The lady and her dog are a good pair, they enjoy walking with each other and keeping each other company.

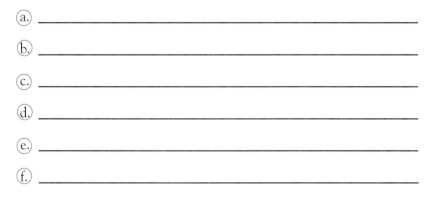

   (a.) ______________________________

   (b.) ______________________________

   (c.) ______________________________

   (d.) ______________________________

   (e.) ______________________________

   (f.) ______________________________

**Practice 2 EQ Answers** Score your answers in Practice 1 using the following answer key.

1. ⓐMany people seem to have a telephone permanently attached to their ear people have several phone lines going into their homes. ⓑAnd cell phones hanging off of their belts. People are talking on their cell phones in restaurants, in cars, and even in public bathrooms. When they go home, they go on-line to check e-mail. ⓒWhile the second line is ringing off the hook. Why would someone want to be available every second of the day? ⓓThis rushed society will eventually have to slow down, people can't live at this pace for long.

   ⓐ run-on

   ⓑ fragment

   ⓒ fragment

   ⓓ run-on

2. Recently, a major computer software company was accused of being a monopoly. That is, it seemed to be trying to control the whole software industry. The company, ⓐreality software, sells many different types of software at a reasonable price. ⓑWhich results in the company selling more products than its competitors. Reality Software also signed contracts with ⓒComputer Manufacturers that allow the manufacturers to install Reality programs on computers before they are sold. ⓓThe courts, which guard against monopolies, say this is unfair to consumers, they should be able to choose their software. It is also unfair to other software companies. ⓔBecause they are not given a fair chance to sell their products.

   ⓐ capitalization

   ⓑ fragment

   ⓒ capitalization

   ⓓ run-on

   ⓔ fragment

3. Public speaking is a valuable tool no matter what career path a ⓐperson take. At some point in every career, if a person is going to advance,

(b) they will have to speak to a group. In fact, the higher up the career ladder a (c) person climb, the more public speaking will be required. (d) It is good preparation, therefore, to take a public speaking course in college, a public speaking course not only teaches the skills involved in making a presentation but also builds a person's confidence.

(a.) subject-verb agreement

(b.) pronoun agreement

(c.) subject-verb agreement

(d.) run-on

4. If you think a surprise birthday party takes a lot of time and work, try planning a wedding. Until a person plans his or her own wedding, (a) they can't fully understand all the details that must be considered. (b) Too my way of thinking, long engagements aren't to find out how compatible the couple is. (c) There to allow enough time to find a place to hold the reception. (d) On the date you want. (e) Plus a good caterer and music. Even the smallest detail must be considered, such as whether guests should throw rice (f) birdseed (g) or confetti at the happy couple after the ceremony.

(a.) pronoun agreement

(b.) confused word

(c.) confused word

(d.) fragment

(e.) fragment

(f.) comma

(g.) comma

5. A famous author once said that his messy handwriting, (a) almost kept him from becoming a writer. (b) Struggling to be legible, the pages were impossible to read. No matter how hard he tried, after only a few words his handwriting would become rushed and scribbled. (c) He would write

wonderful novels that only he could read, for his twenty-third birthday his wife bought him a typewriter. He then began to write books. ⓓThat people all over the world have read. If he were alive today, he could write with a computer.

ⓐ comma

ⓑ dangling modifier

ⓒ run-on

ⓓ fragment

6. Everyone has heard the term "best ⓐfreind." But what is a best friend? Some people ⓑbeleive that their oldest friend is ⓒthey're best friend. Yet a best friend can be someone you meet in college or even someone who is family. ⓓSuch as a brother or sister. No matter who qualifies as a best friend, two ⓔfacts is true: A best ⓕfreind is someone special and the person you trust the most. People may wonder how they could get along without their best friend?ⓖ Most people couldn't.

ⓐ spelling

ⓑ spelling

ⓒ confused word

ⓓ fragment

ⓔ subject-verb agreement

ⓕ spelling

ⓖ end punctuation

7. If I had my way, I would require every college student to take a course in geography. It is ⓐembarassing how little the average American knows about ⓑhis own country, to say nothing of other countries. For instance, do you know the capital of ⓒvirginia? Can you name all the Great Lakes? On which continent is ⓓgreece? If you can answer these questionsⓔ you are one of very few people. People think geography is boringⓕ but it isn't. ⓖIts fascinating to learn about the world we live in.

ⓐ spelling

ⓑ pronoun

ⓒ capitalization

ⓓ capitalization

ⓔ comma

ⓕ comma

ⓖ confused word

8. I believe that fast-food restaurants should change ⓐthere names to "fast food sometimes, but at least faster than a sit-down restaurant." ⓑWhen I go through the drive-up window at a fast-food ⓒrestaraunt, it is because I am in a hurry and want to get something to eat quickly, however, sometimes it would be quicker for me to go home and cook a three-course meal. I do not understand what could take so long. I pull up to the intercom, order my food, ⓓprocede to the window, and wait. If fast food always lived up to its nameⓔ I would be able to get food fast.

ⓐ confused word

ⓑ run-on

ⓒ spelling

ⓓ spelling

ⓔ comma

9. Doing the family laundry used to be a chore for meⓐ but now I am a pro. First, I sort the clothes according to colors or whites. Before I learned this basic rule, my poor brother had to wear pink underwear from time to time. Next, I put the clothes in the washing machine,ⓑ and add detergent. If I'm doing whitesⓒ I also add bleach. I close the lid, turn the dial to hot wash and cold rinse, and push the "start" button. I allow the washing machine to do ⓓit's work while I read a magazine. When it's time to put the clothes in the dryer, I pay attention to the drying instructions on the tags. Once I neglected this step, and my favorite pants ⓔshrinked. When the dryer has done its work, remove the clothes immediately so they do not become ⓕrinkled.

(a.) comma

(b.) comma

(c.) comma

(d.) confused word

(e.) verb form

(f.) spelling

10. It's fun to watch a person with (a) their animals. For instance, each morning, the lady down the street takes her dog for a walk. (b) The dog is a tiny rat terrier, it is really cute. The lady puts a little leash on the dog. (c) To keep him from running away. Even though the (d) dogs legs are short, he can run (e) real fast. The dog seems so happy during his walks. He jumps and yips. (f) The lady and her dog are a good pair, they enjoy walking with each other and keeping each other company.

(a.) pronoun agreement

(b.) run-on

(c.) fragment

(d.) apostrophe

(e.) modifier error

(f.) run-on

**Practice 3 Finding Your EQ** Turn to Appendix 5, and chart the errors you didn't identify in Practice 1. Then place your errors on the second EQ chart, and see what pattern they form.

## HOW TO EDIT

Editing is a two-part job: First, you must locate the errors. Then you must know how to correct them.

## Finding Your Errors

A major part of editing is proofreading. Proofreading is reading to catch grammar, punctuation, mechanics, and spelling errors. If you do not proofread carefully, you will not catch your errors and make the final changes that will improve your writing.

There are some specific techniques for finding errors. One good method is to read your essay backward, sentence by sentence, starting with the last sentence. Taking sentences out of context lets you concentrate on individual sentences and not get caught up in reading for meaning.

Many students like to keep error logs like the one for grammar, punctuation, and mechanics in Appendix 6 and the one for spelling in Appendix 7. By the second or third paper you write, the logs will show the types of errors you make most frequently. Then you can proofread your paper for one type of error at a time. For example, if you often write run-on sentences, you should read your paper once just to catch run-ons. Then read it again to find a second type of error, and so on. The error logs can help you reduce the number of errors in your writing. By recording the correction for each error you find, you will eventually learn the corrections.

You can also use the "grammar check" feature on your computer, which will point out possible grammar errors and suggest ways to reword sentences. This is not foolproof, however; you need to decide if you want to accept or reject the grammar suggestions the computer makes.

Asking a tutor or a friend to read your writing is also a good idea. A fresh pair of eyes may see errors you have missed. When others read your writing, they might want to use the editing symbols on the inside back cover to highlight your errors for you. You can then use the page references on the chart to guide you to the part of this textbook that explains how to correct those errors.

## Correcting Your Errors

Whenever you find errors, you need to correct them. To guide you through this phase of the writing process, Part V of this text provides a complete handbook. The cross-references in the EQ Score Yourself section are to this handbook. You may also want to refer to the list on the inside back cover if your instructor uses editing symbols when reading your essays.

As you proofread, record your errors in the Error Log in Appendix 6 and the Spelling Log in Appendix 7. If you do this regularly as you write, these logs will eventually help you control the most common errors in your writing.

Finally, use the Editing Checklist at the beginning of this chapter. Apply each question in the checklist to your essay. If you are not sure whether you have made an error or not, look up the problem in Part V. Work with your writing until you can answer yes to every question on the checklist.

**Practice 4 Using the Handbook** Using the Handbook in Part V, list the page references for the 14 different types of errors you worked with in Practice 1. This will help you learn to use the Handbook as a reference guide.

| | |
|---|---|
| apostrophe | page ______________ |
| capitalization | page ______________ |
| comma | page ______________ |
| confused word | page ______________ |
| dangling modifier | page ______________ |
| end punctuation | page ______________ |
| fragment | page ______________ |
| modifier error | page ______________ |
| pronoun | page ______________ |
| pronoun agreement | page ______________ |
| run-on | page ______________ |
| spelling | page ______________ |
| subject-verb agreement | page ______________ |
| verb form | page ______________ |

**Practice 5 Using the Error Log and Spelling Log** Turn to Appendixes 6 and 7, and start an Error Log and a Spelling Log of your own with the errors you didn't identify in Practice 1. For each error, write out the mistake and the rule from the Handbook. Then make the correction. See Appendix 6 for an example.

**Practice 6 Using the Editing Checklist** Using the Editing Checklist at the beginning of this chapter, edit two of the paragraphs from Practice 1. Rewrite the entire paragraphs.

**Beth's Editing** When Beth proofreads her paper for grammar, punctuation, mechanics, and spelling, she finds two errors that she looks up in Part V and corrects. The first error is a run-on sentence:

> **Run-on:** I finally asked him out, we have been dating ever since.

Beth realizes that this sentence has too many subjects and verbs without any linking words or end punctuation between them. She looks up "run-on" on page 552 of Part V and corrects the error by putting a comma and a coordinating conjunction (*and*) between the two sentences.

> **Correction:** I finally asked him out, **and** we have been dating ever since.

Beth also finds a sentence that doesn't sound complete—it is not a sentence but a fragment:

> **Fragment:** Even though people make fun of TV and its silly shows.

When she looks up the problem in Part V (page 538), she learns that a fragment is easily corrected by connecting it to another sentence.

> **Correction:** Even though people make fun of TV and its silly shows/**,** I still think it's a good way to learn about life.

**Beth's Edited Draft** Both of these errors are corrected here in Beth's edited draft.

The Learning Curve

We all learn about life in different ways. Some people learn by watching, while others learn by doing. Some people learn by reading, and others learn by listening. My mom has always said that people can learn from any experience. But everyone learns in some way or another. To prove her point, when I experienced disappointment as I was growing up, my mom would always ask, "What did you learn from this experience?" It used to really irritate me. But now that I think about it, I realize she was right. In fact, the way we learn is a major part of who we are. Learning about life happens for me by observing other people, by watching TV, and by taking risks.

I have always been aware that I learn a lot through secondhand experiences. When my cousin became heavily involved with gangs, I watched her live her life in constant fear. She was worried she would end up in jail, lose her boyfriend, and maybe even lose her life. By watching my cousin, I made a conscious decision to be nothing like her. Therefore, I was never drawn into a life of gangs because I saw what it did to my cousin.

TV is also a source of learning for me. Even though people make fun of TV and its silly shows/**,** I still think it's a good way to learn about life. Programs like Dawson's Creek and Boston Public may overdo the drama, but I still learn about people from the way the characters interact with each other. TV shows can teach people about life, as long as people are smart enough to understand that TV shows aren't real. However, the situations on TV represent real-life experiences.

I have also learned a lot about life by taking risks and making my own mistakes. Some risks I have taken were really difficult, but they were important steps in my life. For instance, one time I took a chance to ask out my best friend's roommate. I was attracted to his smile from the minute I met him, but I thought he was too good-looking for me. I finally asked him out, **and** we have been dating ever since. Other risks like driving too fast to be cool were just plain stupid. Every risk I have taken has taught me something--whether good or bad.

People can learn about life from just about anything they do. What has made me the person I am today is observing other people, watching TV, and taking some risks myself. Of course, I'm not finished learning yet. Are you?

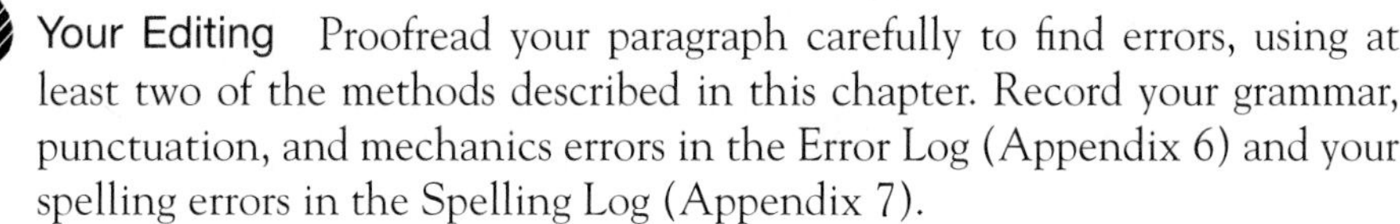

**Your Editing** Proofread your paragraph carefully to find errors, using at least two of the methods described in this chapter. Record your grammar, punctuation, and mechanics errors in the Error Log (Appendix 6) and your spelling errors in the Spelling Log (Appendix 7).

**Your Edited Draft** Now write out a corrected draft of your essay.

## Review of the Writing Process

**Clues for Review**

- The **writing process** is a series of tasks that involve prewriting, writing, revising, and editing. At any time, one activity may loop in and out of the other.
- **Prewriting** consists of thinking about and planning your essay.

  *Thinking:* Reading, freewriting, brainstorming, clustering, questioning, discussing

  *Planning:* Deciding on a subject, purpose, and audience
- **Writing** includes writing a thesis statement, developing your ideas, organizing your essay, and writing a first draft.

  *Writing a thesis statement:* Stating a limited subject and an opinion about that subject

  *Developing:* Explaining your ideas and adding specific details, examples, facts, and reasons

  *Organizing:* Arranging ideas from general to particular, particular to general, chronologically, spatially, or from one extreme to another

  *Drafting:* Writing a first draft, then revising to write a second draft, a third draft, and so on, until you have written your final draft
- **Revising** means "seeing again" and improving all aspects of an essay's organization and development.

  Thesis statement

  Basic elements

  Development

  Unity

  Organization

  Coherence
- **Editing** involves proofreading and correcting your grammar, punctuation, mechanics, and spelling errors.

### Review Practice 1

1. What are the four main parts of the writing process?

   ______________________________

2. What is your favorite prewriting activity? Why is it your favorite?

______________________________________________

3. What personal rituals do you go through when you write?

______________________________________________

______________________________________________

4. Where do you usually do your academic writing? Do you write your first draft on a computer? What time of day do you do your best writing?

______________________________________________

______________________________________________

5. What is a thesis statement?

______________________________________________

6. What is the difference between topic sentences and details?

______________________________________________

______________________________________________

7. What are the five main methods of organization?

______________________________________________

______________________________________________

8. Do you usually ask a tutor or friend to look at your draft before you revise it?

______________________________________________

9. What is the difference between revising and editing?

______________________________________________

______________________________________________

10. Draw a picture or graphic version of your own writing process. What happens first, second, third, and so on from the time you get a writing assignment? Don't use any words in your picture.

**Review Practice 2** Write a thesis statement for five of the following topics. Then develop one thesis statement into a first draft of an essay.

1. My best friend
2. Politics
3. My best adventure
4. Animals
5. In the middle of the night
6. My family
7. My future career
8. The best car
9. Parents should never
10. Sports

**Review Practice 3** Revise the essay you wrote for Review Practice 2, using the checklist on page 64–65.

**Review Practice 4** Edit the essay you wrote for Review Practice 2, using the checklist on page 93.

# WRITING EFFECTIVE ESSAYS

*We do not write in order to be understood; we write in order to understand.*

—CECIL DAY LEWIS

In Part I of *Mosaics,* you learned about the different stages of the writing process—prewriting, writing, revising, and editing—and the form of an essay. You know that essays typically have an introduction with a thesis statement, several body paragraphs, and a conclusion. Part II of *Mosaics* focuses on ways to develop and organize an essay's body paragraphs. You will learn strategies for thinking on paper that will help you discover your best thoughts on a particular topic. Then you will find out your options for organizing those ideas.

The nine basic writing strategies—also called rhetorical modes—are introduced in this part. Each chapter gives specific guidelines for using a strategy and then applies those guidelines to an essay. Next, the chapter takes you through the phases of revising and editing a student essay and then your own essay, showing you systematically how to improve your writing.

# Describing

*When you show, you get out of the readers' way and let them come right at the experience itself.*

—DONALD MURRAY

Description is an essential part of your life every day. Your friends might want to know what kind of car you just bought; your parents may ask what your new friend is like; your boss might need a description of the project you just finished. You constantly need to describe people, places, objects, and activities for different audiences if you want to communicate clearly and effectively.

In addition, you frequently use description when writing. Actually, description is a major part of our writing in our personal lives, in college, and at work. Think about the following situations:

You describe your new leather jacket in an e-mail message to a friend.

You describe the damage to your car in an insurance report.

A student describes a cell and its parts on a biology exam.

A nurse describes the appearance of a wound in a patient report.

A landscape contractor describes a design for a rock garden.

**Description** creates a picture in words to help a reader visualize something a writer has seen, heard, or done. It helps the reader understand or share a sensory experience through "showing" rather than "telling." Description is one of our primary forms of self-expression.

At times, description is used as an end in itself. That is, you write a description for the sole purpose of telling what something looks, sounds, feels, tastes, or smells like. For instance, you might use pure description to tell a friend about your new apartment. More often, though, description is used to help accomplish another purpose—to explain a problem, to analyze the causes and effects of an event, or to persuade your readers to change their thinking or take some specific action.

Writing about the dust storms of the 1930s, Margaret Bourke-White describes their various trails of destruction. In what ways has nature played a role in your life? What is this role? Is it a positive or negative one?

**Margaret Bourke-White**

## DUST CHANGES AMERICA

Vitamin K they call it—the dust which sifts under the door sills, and stings in the eyes, and seasons every spoonful of food. The dust storms have distinct personalities, rising in formation like rolling clouds, creeping up silently like formless fog, approaching violently like a tornado. Where has it come from? It provides topics of endless speculation. Red, it is the topsoil from Oklahoma; brown, it is the fertile earth of western Kansas; the good grazing land of Texas and New Mexico sweeps by as a murky yellow haze. Or, tracing it locally, "My uncle will be along pretty soon," they say; "I just saw his farm go by." 1

The town dwellers stack their linen in trunks, stuff wet cloths along the window sills, estimate the tons of sand in the darkened air above them, paste cloth masks on their faces with adhesive tape, and try to joke about Vitamin K. But on the farms and ranches there is an attitude of despair. 2

By coincidence I was in the same parts of the country where last year I photographed the drought. As short a time as eight months ago there was an attitude of false optimism. "Things will get better," the farmers would say. "We're not as hard hit as other states. The government will help out. This can't go on." But this year there is an atmosphere of utter hopelessness. Nothing to do. No use digging out your chicken coops and pigpens after the last "duster" because the next one will be coming along soon. No use trying to keep the house clean. No use fighting off that foreclosure any longer. No use even hoping to give your cattle anything to chew on when their food crops have literally blown out of the ground. 3

It was my job to avoid dust storms, since I was commissioned by an airplane company to take photographs of its course from the air, but frequently the dust storms caught up with us, and as we were grounded anyway, I started to photograph them. Thus I saw five dust-storm states from the air and from the ground. 4

In the last several years there have been droughts and sand storms and dusters, but they have been localized, and always one state could borrow from another. But this year the scourge assumes tremendous proportions. Dust storms 5 are bringing distress and death to 300,000 square miles; they are blowing over all of Kansas, all of Nebraska and Wyoming, strips of the Dakotas, about half of Colorado, sections of Iowa and Missouri, the greater part of Oklahoma, and the northern panhandle of Texas, extending into the eastern parts of New Mexico.

6 Last year I saw farmers harvesting the Russian thistle. Never before had they thought of feeding thistles to cattle. But this prickly fodder became precious for food. This year even the Russian thistles are dying out and the still humbler soap weed becomes as vital to the farmer as the fields of golden grain he tended in the past. Last year's thistle-fed cattle dwindled to skin and bone. This year's herds on their diet of soap weed develop roughened hides, ugly growths around the mouth, and lusterless eyes.

7 Years of the farmers' and ranchers' lives have gone into the building up of their herds. Their herds were like their families to them. When AAA officials spotted cows and steers for shooting during the cattle-killing days of last summer, the farmers felt as though their own children were facing the bullets. Kansas, a Republican state, has no love for the AAA. This year winds whistled over land made barren by the drought and the crop-conservation program. When Wallace removed the ban on the planting of spring wheat he was greeted by cheers. But the wheat has been blown completely out of the ground. Nothing is left but soap weed, or the expensive cotton-seed cake, and after that—bankruptcy.

8 The storm comes in a terrifying way. Yellow clouds roll. The wind blows such a gale that it is all my helper can do to hold my camera to the ground. The sand whips into my lens. I repeatedly wipe it away trying to snatch an exposure before it becomes completely coated again. The light becomes yellower, the wind colder. Soon there is no photographic light, and we hurry for shelter to the nearest farmhouse.

9 Three men and a woman are seated around a dust-caked lamp, on their faces grotesque masks of wet cloth. The children have been put to bed with towels tucked over their heads. My host greets us: "It takes grit to live in this country." They are telling stories: A bachelor harnessed the sandblast which ripped through the keyhole by holding his pots and pans in it until they were spick and span. A pilot flying over Amarillo got caught in a sand storm. His motor clogged; he took to his parachute. It took him six hours to shovel his way back to earth. And when a man from the next county was struck by a drop of water, he fainted, and it took two buckets of sand to revive him.

10 The migrations of the farmer have begun. In many of the worst-hit counties 80 percent of the families are on relief. In the open farm country one crop failure follows another. After perhaps three successive crop failures the farmer can't stand it any longer. He moves in with relatives and hopes for a job in Arizona or Illinois or some neighboring state where he knows he is not needed. Perhaps he gets a job as a cotton picker, and off he goes with his family, to be turned adrift again after a brief working period.

We passed them on the road, all their household goods piled on wagons, one lucky family on a truck. Lucky, because they had been able to keep their truck when the mortgage was foreclosed. All they owned in the world was packed on it; the children sat on a pile of bureaus topped with mattresses, and the sides of the truck were strapped up with bed springs. The entire family looked like a Ku Klux Klan meeting, their faces done up in masks to protect them from the whirling sand. 11

Near Hays, Kansas, a little boy started home from school and never arrived there. The neighbors looked for him till ten at night, and all next day a band of two hundred people searched. At twilight they found him, only a quarter of a mile from home, his body nearly covered with silt. He had strangled to death. The man who got lost in his own ten-acre truck garden and wandered around choking and stifling for eight hours before he found his house considered himself lucky to escape with his life. The police and sheriffs are kept constantly busy with calls from anxious parents whose children are lost, and the toll is mounting of people who become marooned and die in the storms. 12

But the real tragedy is the plight of the cattle. In a rising sand storm cattle quickly become blinded. They run around in circles until they fall and breathe so much dust that they die. Autopsies show their lungs caked with dust and mud. Farmers dread the birth of calves during a storm. The newborn animals will die within twenty-four hours. 13

And this same dust that coats the lungs and threatens death to cattle and men alike, that ruins the stock of the storekeeper lying unsold on his shelves, that creeps into the gear shifts of automobiles, that sifts through the refrigerator into the butter, that makes housekeeping, and gradually life itself, unbearable, this swirling drifting dust is changing the agricultural map of the United States. It piles ever higher on the floors and beds of a steadily increasing number of deserted farmhouses. A half-buried plowshare, a wheat binder ruffled over with sand, the skeleton of a horse near a dirt-filled water hole are stark evidence of the meager life, the wasted savings, the years of toil that the farmer is leaving behind him. 14

*Preparing to Write Your Own Description*

What are some memorable experiences you have had with nature (for example, a snowstorm, a sunny day, a drought, a tornado, a thunderstorm)? Why do you remember these experiences? Do any of them form a single impression when you think about them? Use one or more of the prewriting techniques that you learned in Chapter 2 to generate your thoughts about these memories.

## HOW TO WRITE A DESCRIPTION ESSAY

Describing is a very natural process that is based on good observing. But some people describe things more vividly than others. When they describe an experience, you feel as though you were there too. We can all improve our skill at describing by following a few simple guidelines:

1. ***Decide on a dominant impression—the feeling or mood you want to communicate.*** How do you want your readers to feel after reading your description? Good about the characters in the scene? Angry at the situation? Satisfied with the outcome? Choosing a dominant impression gives your description focus and unity. You can't possibly write down everything you observe about a person, place, incident, or object. The result would be a long, confusing—and probably boring—list. But if you first decide on a dominant impression for your description, you can then choose the details that will best convey that impression.

   The dominant impression Bourke-White conveys is a feeling of frustration and despair at the thought of the destruction that nature can bring. This dominant impression gives her essay focus and helps her choose the details that will best communicate this feeling.

2. ***Decide how much of your description should be objective (factual) and how much should be subjective (personal reactions).*** An objective description is like a dictionary definition—accurate and without emotion. Scientific and technical writing are objective. If, for example, you are describing a piece of equipment used in a chemistry experiment or the packaging needed to ship a computer, you would be objective. Subjective description, in contrast, tries to produce a specific emotional response in the reader. It focuses on feelings rather than facts and tries to activate as many senses as possible. An advertisement describing a Caribbean cruise would be very subjective, as would a restaurant or movie review. Most descriptive writing has a combination of objective and subjective elements. The degree to which you emphasize one over the other depends on your purpose and your audience.

   Bourke-White's essay demonstrates a good balance of objective and subjective writing. She presents the facts about the dust storms and the ways the midwesterners deal with the dust—putting linen in trunks, stuffing wet cloths in window sills, using masks on their faces, and so on. Then she mixes these facts with subjective stories about families who are suffering, children who never make it home from school, and cattle who are like family to their owners. This combination of objective and subjective elements makes the essay realistic and powerful at the same time.

3. ***Draw on your five senses to write a good description.*** Although observing is at the heart of good description, limiting yourself to what you see is a mistake. Good description relies on all five senses: sight, hearing, touch, smell, and taste. If you use all your senses to relay your description, your readers will be able to see, hear, touch, smell, and taste what you are describing as if they were there with you participating in the same experience.

   Look again at Bourke-White's description. She draws on sight throughout the essay but especially in paragraph 8 when she describes her attempts at taking pictures. She refers to our sense of touch when she talks about the dust stinging the eyes (paragraph 1) and cloth masks on people's faces (paragraph 2). She relies on taste when she mentions the dust seasoning the food (paragraph 1) and the cattle eating thistles (paragraph 6). Her description of the wind whistling over the barren land (paragraph 7) appeals to our sense of hearing. Her entire essay is vivid because of all the specific sensory details she furnishes.

4. ***When you describe, try to show*** **rather than** ***tell*** **your readers what you want them to know.** Your ultimate goal in writing a descriptive essay is to give your readers an experience as close to yours as possible. Therefore, do not simply tell your readers what you saw or experienced; *show* them. Use your writing skills to re-create the event so that your readers can see, hear, feel, smell, taste, and understand as if they were there. For example, you can tell someone you bought a "terrific new car." But if you say you bought a "beautiful, new blue Mustang with a gray interior, custom wheels, and an awesome stereo," you're *showing* your readers why you are so excited about your purchase.

   If Bourke-White had simply stated her dominant impression (that dust storms bring frustration and despair to the Midwest) with no examples or details to support her statement, she would only be *telling* her readers how she felt. Instead, she *shows* them. Her sensory details demonstrate her main point.

5. ***Organize your description so that your readers can easily follow it.*** Most descriptions are organized from general to particular (from main idea to details), from particular to general (from details to main idea), or spatially (from top to bottom or left to right). Because the organization of your essay often depends on your point of view, you should choose a specific perspective from which to write your description. If

your description jumps around your house, referring to a picture on the wall in your bedroom, then to the refrigerator in the kitchen, and next to the quilt on your bed, your readers are likely to become confused and disoriented. They will not be able to follow you. If, however, you move from room to room in a logical way, your audience will be able to stay with you. In fact, your vision will become their vision.

Bourke-White organizes her essay from one extreme to another—in this case, from least to most tragic. She starts by describing the inconveniences of the dust storms on a personal level—the dirty houses, the piles of dust in the fields, the health problems. Then she moves on to the more serious issues of death on 300,000 square miles of land. The essay ends with references to farms collapsing financially, children dying from the dust, and whole families being displaced. The author leaves us at the end of her essay with a sense of loss and hopelessness that reflects the feelings of the farmers in the Midwest during a drought.

***Writing Your Own Description Essay***

What direct encounters have you had with nature? What are some of the details of these encounters? Was your general impression good or bad? Write an essay describing one of these encounters. Describe your experience through the senses, following the guidelines for writing a description essay. Remember to show rather than tell your readers about your memory. Begin by reviewing your prewriting notes. Then choose your dominant impression, and put it into a thesis statement.

## DESCRIPTION AT WORK

In an essay about a fond memory, a student named Abby Reed reminisces about her grandfather. As you read it, ask yourself what dominant impression Abby is trying to communicate to her readers.

### Grandma's House

1 My grandma lives in the country, near a large, blue lake and a small, green forest. I look forward to visiting her house. I think of my grandpa when I'm there.

2 Whenever I walk into my grandma's house, I always go directly to my grandpa's favorite room--the den. I am immediately reminded of my

grandpa in this room. My grandma has a soft, brown sofa and a brown leather loveseat in this small, dark room, but all I see is the old, worn chair that was my grandpa's. The chair was recovered in an itchy tweed fabric. I used to pretend to be asleep in his chair so my grandpa would gently lift me from the coarse fabric and place me on his lap. I would lie there even though I wasn't sleeping and enjoy the warmth of his body. I remember the times I sat on his sturdy lap in that chair while he read *One Fish, Two Fish, Red Fish, Blue Fish* or *The Cat in the Hat* in his deep voice.

Now when I sit in his chair, I look on the mantle and see an old Air 3
Force picture of my grandpa and three of his Air Force buddies. They are all dressed in informal flight clothes and are standing in front of a World War II airplane. Next to this picture is a single portrait of my grandpa. When he was 70. This picture represents the way I still see him in my mind. His gray hair is thin, his face has light brown sun spots on it that show his years of working outdoors. His gentle, light blue eyes sparkle in a way that usually meant he was up to something mischievous. But most of all. I love looking at his smile. The right side of his mouth always turned slightly downward, but it is a smile that I would give anything to see in person just one more time.

I also love to play with the pipe stand that sits on the table next to my 4
grandpa's chair. I love the worn feeling of the pipe. It once was rough with ridges but is now smooth from use. When I quietly pick up his pipe and smell the sweet tobacco that was once housed in its shell, I think of all the times I knew my grandpa were near me because of this same aroma.

I have wonderful memories of my grandpa. When I go to my grandma's 5
house, I can sit in my grandpa's old chair in my grandpa's favorite room and reminisce about all the times I felt safe when my grandpa was near. I will always treasure this one tiny room, with its smells from the past and its picture of my grandpa smiling.

1. This essay creates a certain mood. What is the dominant impression that Abby creates?

   ____________________________________________

2. Is this description primarily subjective or objective? Explain your answer.

   ____________________________________________

   ____________________________________________

   ____________________________________________

3. In this particular essay, the student writer describes her subjects mainly through the sense of sight, with a few references to hearing, touch, and smell. Find at least one example of each of these senses in this essay?

   Seeing: ______________________________

   Hearing: ______________________________

   Touching: ______________________________

   Smelling: ______________________________

4. Abby works hard in this essay to *show* rather than *tell* us what she sees in the house. What three details go beyond telling to *show* us what she observes?

   ______________________________

   ______________________________

   ______________________________

5. How does Abby organize her essay? List the topics of each of her body paragraphs, and then identify her method of organization.

   ______________________________

   ______________________________

   ______________________________

   Method of organization: ______________________________

## REVISING AND EDITING A STUDENT ESSAY

This essay is Abby's first draft, which now needs to be revised and edited. First, apply the Revising Checklist on page 121 to Abby's draft so that you are working with her content. When you are satisfied that her ideas are fully developed and well organized, use the Editing Checklist on page 125 to correct her grammar and mechanics errors. Answer the questions after each checklist. Then write your suggested changes directly on Abby's draft.

## Revising Checklist

**Thesis Statement**

- ✔ Does the thesis statement contain the essay's controlling idea and appear as the last sentence of the introduction?

**Basic Elements**

- ✔ Does the title draw in the readers?
- ✔ Does the introduction capture the readers' attention and build up to the thesis statement effectively?
- ✔ Does each body paragraph deal with a single topic?
- ✔ Does the conclusion bring the essay to a close in an interesting way?

**Development**

- ✔ Do the body paragraphs adequately support the thesis statement?
- ✔ Does each body paragraph have a focused topic sentence?
- ✔ Does each body paragraph contain *specific* details that support the topic sentence?
- ✔ Does each body paragraph include *enough* details to explain the topic sentence fully?

**Unity**

- ✔ Do the essay's topic sentences relate directly to the thesis statement?
- ✔ Do the details in each body paragraph support its topic sentence?

**Organization**

- ✔ Is the essay organized logically?
- ✔ Is each body paragraph organized logically?

**Coherence**

- ✔ Are transitions used effectively so that paragraphs move smoothly and logically from one to the next?
- ✔ Do the sentences move smoothly and logically from one to the next?

## Thesis Statement

- ✔ Does the thesis statement contain the essay's controlling idea and appear as the last sentence of the introduction?

1. Put brackets around the last sentence in Abby's introduction. Does it contain her dominant impression? ____________________
2. Rewrite Abby's thesis statement if necessary so that it states her dominant impression and introduces her topics.

____________________________________________

____________________________________________

## Basic Elements

- ✔ Does the title draw in the readers?
- ✔ Does the introduction capture the readers' attention and build up to the thesis statement effectively?
- ✔ Does each body paragraph deal with a single topic?
- ✔ Does the conclusion bring the essay to a close in an interesting way?

1. Give Abby's essay an alternate title. ____________________

____________________________________________

2. Rewrite Abby's introduction so that it captures the readers' attention and builds up to the thesis statement at the end of the paragraph.

____________________________________________

____________________________________________

____________________________________________

____________________________________________

3. Does each of Abby's body paragraphs deal with only one topic? _______

4. Rewrite Abby's conclusion using at least one suggestion from Part I.

________________________________________

________________________________________

________________________________________

________________________________________

## Development

- ✔ Do the body paragraphs adequately support the thesis statement?
- ✔ Does each body paragraph have a focused topic sentence?
- ✔ Does each body paragraph contain *specific* details that support the topic sentence?
- ✔ Does each body paragraph include *enough* details to explain the topic sentence fully?

1. Write out Abby's thesis statement (revised, if necessary), and list her three topic sentences below it.

Thesis statement: ________________________________

________________________________

Topic 1: ________________________________

________________________________

Topic 2: ________________________________

________________________________

Topic 3: ________________________________

________________________________

2. Do Abby's topics adequately support her thesis statement? ___________

3. Does each body paragraph have a focused topic sentence? ___________

4. Does the essay draw on all five senses? ___________

5. Add at least one detail to Abby's essay that refers to a new sense. Label the detail you are adding.

   Sense: ___________ Detail: ___________

6. In what way does Abby's essay *show* rather than *tell* her readers about her memories of her grandfather?

   ___________

   ___________

## Unity

- ✔ Do the essay's topic sentences relate directly to the thesis statement?
- ✔ Do the details in each body paragraph support its topic sentence?

1. Read each of Abby's topic sentences with her thesis statement (revised, if necessary) in mind. Do they go together? ___________
2. Revise them if necessary so they are directly related.
3. Drop or rewrite any of the sentences in her body paragraphs that are not directly related to their topic sentences.

## Organization

- ✔ Is the essay organized logically?
- ✔ Is each body paragraph organized logically?

1. Read Abby's essay again to see if all the paragraphs are arranged logically.
2. Move any paragraphs that are out of order.

3. Look closely at Abby's body paragraphs to see if all her sentences are arranged logically within paragraphs.
4. Move any sentences that are out of order.

## Coherence

- ✔ Are transitions used effectively so that paragraphs move smoothly and logically from one to the next?
- ✔ Do the sentences move smoothly and logically from one to the next?

1. Circle five transitions Abby uses. For a list of transitions, see page 84.
2. Explain how two of these make Abby's essay easier to read.

_______________________________________________

_______________________________________________

Now rewrite Abby's essay with your revisions.

## Editing Checklist

**SENTENCES**

- ✔ Does each sentence have a main subject and verb?
- ✔ Do all subjects and verbs agree?
- ✔ Do all pronouns agree with their nouns?
- ✔ Are modifiers as close as possible to the words they modify?

**PUNCTUATION AND MECHANICS**

- ✔ Are sentences punctuated correctly?
- ✔ Are words capitalized properly?

**WORD CHOICE AND SPELLING**

- ✔ Are words used correctly?
- ✔ Are words spelled correctly?

## Sentences

> ✔ Does each sentence have a main subject and verb?
> For help with subjects and verbs, see Chapter 34.

1. Underline the subjects once and verbs twice in paragraphs 3 and 4 of your revision of Abby's essay. Remember that sentences can have more than one subject-verb set.
2. Does each of the sentences have at least one subject and verb that can stand alone? ______________
3. Did you find and correct Abby's two fragments? If not, find and correct them now. For help with fragments, see Chapter 35.
4. Did you find and correct Abby's run-on sentence? If not, find and correct it now. For help with run-ons, see Chapter 36.

> ✔ Do all subjects and verbs agree?
> For help with subject-verb agreement, see Chapter 39.

1. Read aloud the subjects and verbs you underlined in your revision of Abby's essay.
2. Did you find and correct the subject and verb that do not agree?

> ✔ Do all pronouns agree with their nouns?
> For help with pronoun agreement, see Chapter 43.

1. Find any pronouns in your revision of Abby's essay that do not agree with their nouns.
2. Correct any pronouns that do not agree with their nouns.

> ✔ Are modifiers as close as possible to the words they modify?
> For help with modifier errors, see Chapter 46.

1. Find any modifiers in your revision of Abby's essay that are not as close as possible to the words they modify.
2. Rewrite sentences if necessary so that modifiers are as close as possible to the words they modify.

## Punctuation and Mechanics

✔ Are sentences punctuated correctly?
For help with punctuation, see Chapters 47–51.

1. Read your revision of Abby's essay for any errors in punctuation.
2. Find the two fragments and the run-on sentence you revised, and make sure they are punctuated correctly.

✔ Are words capitalized properly?
For help with capitalization, see Chapter 52.

1. Read your revision of Abby's essay for any errors in capitalization.
2. Be sure to check Abby's capitalization in the fragments and run-on you revised.

## Word Choice and Spelling

✔ Are words used correctly?
For help with confused words, see Chapter 58.

1. Find any words used incorrectly in your revision of Abby's essay.
2. Correct any errors you find.

✔ Are all words spelled correctly?
For help with spelling, see Chapter 59.

1. Use spell-check and a dictionary to check the spelling in your revision of Abby's essay.
2. Correct any misspelled words.

Now rewrite Abby's essay again with your editing corrections.

## REVISING AND EDITING YOUR OWN ESSAY

Returning to the description you wrote earlier in this chapter, revise and edit your own writing. The checklists here will help you apply what you have learned to your essay.

### Revising

#### Thesis Statement

☐ Does the thesis statement contain the essay's controlling idea and appear as the last sentence of the introduction?

1. What dominant impression are you trying to communicate in your essay?

   ______________________________

2. Put brackets around the last sentence in your introduction. Does it contain your dominant impression? ______________________________
3. Rewrite your thesis statement if necessary so that it states your dominant impression and introduces your topics.

#### Basic Elements

☐ Does the title draw in the readers?

☐ Does the introduction capture the readers' attention and build up to the thesis statement effectively?

- ☐ Does each body paragraph deal with a single topic?
- ☐ Does the conclusion bring the essay to a close in an interesting way?

1. Give your essay a title if it doesn't have one. ______________________
2. Does your introduction capture your readers' attention and build up to your thesis statement at the end of the paragraph? ______________
3. Does each of your body paragraphs deal with only one topic? ________
4. Does your conclusion follow some of the suggestions offered in Part I?

   ______________________________________________

## Development

- ☐ Do the body paragraphs adequately support the thesis statement?
- ☐ Does each body paragraph have a focused topic sentence?
- ☐ Does each body paragraph contain *specific* details that support the topic sentence?
- ☐ Does each body paragraph include *enough* details to explain the topic sentence fully?

1. Write out your thesis statement (revised, if necessary), and list your topic sentences below it.

   Thesis statement: ______________________________

   Topic 1: ______________________________

   Topic 2: ______________________________

   Topic 3: ______________________________

2. Do your topics adequately support your thesis statement? __________

3. Does each body paragraph have a focused topic sentence? ____________

4. Does your essay draw on all five senses? ____________________

5. Record three details from your essay that draw on three different senses. Label each example with the sense it refers to.

| Sense | Detail |
|---|---|
| ____________ | ____________________________ |
| ____________ | ____________________________ |
| ____________ | ____________________________ |

6. Add at least one new detail to your essay.
7. Does your essay *show* rather than *tell* readers what they need to know? Give three examples.

____________________________________________

____________________________________________

____________________________________________

## Unity

- ☐ Do the essay's topic sentences relate directly to the thesis statement?
- ☐ Do the details in each body paragraph support its topic sentence?

1. Read each of your topic sentences with your thesis statement in mind. Do they go together? ____________
2. Revise them if necessary so they are directly related.
3. Drop or rewrite any of the sentences in your body paragraphs that are not directly related to their topic sentences.

## Organization

- ☐ Is the essay organized logically?
- ☐ Is each body paragraph organized logically?

1. Read your essay again to see if all the paragraphs are arranged logically.
2. Refer to your answers to the development questions. Then identify your method of organization: ______________
3. Is the order you chose for your paragraphs the most effective approach to your topic? ______________
4. Move any paragraphs that are out of order.
5. Look closely at your body paragraphs to see if all the sentences are arranged logically within paragraphs.
6. Move any sentences that are out of order.

## Coherence

- ☐ Are transitions used effectively so that paragraphs move smoothly and logically from one to the next?
- ☐ Do the sentences move smoothly and logically from one to the next?

1. Circle five transitions you use. For a list of transitions, see page 84.
2. Explain how two of these make your essay easier to read.

____________________________________________

____________________________________________

Now rewrite your essay with your revisions.

# Editing

## Sentences

☐ Does each sentence have a main subject and verb?
For help with subjects and verbs, see Chapter 34.

1. Underline the subjects once and verbs twice in a paragraph of your revised essay. Remember that sentences can have more than one subject-verb set.
2. Does each of your sentences have at least one subject and verb that can stand alone? ______________
3. Correct any fragments you have written. For help with fragments, see Chapter 35.
4. Correct any run-on sentences you have written. For help with run-ons, see Chapter 36.

☐ Do all subjects and verbs agree?
For help with subject-verb agreement, see Chapter 39.

1. Read aloud the subjects and verbs you underlined in your revised essay.
2. Correct any subjects and verbs that do not agree.

☐ Do all pronouns agree with their nouns?
For help with pronoun agreement, see Chapter 43.

1. Find any pronouns in your revised essay that do not agree with their nouns.
2. Correct any pronouns that do not agree with their nouns.

☐ Are modifiers as close as possible to the words they modify?
For help with modifier errors, see Chapter 46.

1. Find any modifiers in your revised essay that are not as close as possible to the words they modify.
2. Rewrite sentences if necessary so that your modifiers are as close as possible to the words they modify.

## Punctuation and Mechanics

☐ Are sentences punctuated correctly?

For help with punctuation, see Chapters 47–51.

1. Read your revised essay for any errors in punctuation.
2. Make sure any fragments and run-ons you revised are punctuated correctly.

☐ Are words capitalized properly?

For help with capitalization, see Chapter 52.

1. Read your revised essay for any errors in capitalization.
2. Be sure to check your capitalization in any fragments or run-ons you revised.

## Word Choice and Spelling

☐ Are words used correctly?

For help with confused words, see Chapter 58.

1. Find any words used incorrectly in your revised essay.
2. Correct any errors you find.

☐ Are all words spelled correctly?

For help with spelling, see Chapter 59.

1. Use spell-check and a dictionary to check your spelling.
2. Correct any misspelled words.

Now rewrite your essay again with your editing corrections.

## READING SUGGESTIONS

In Chapter 25, you will find two essays that demonstrate good descriptive writing: "El Hoyo" by Mario Suarez describes a small town near Tucson and its citizens, and "Dwellings" by Linda Hogan focuses on the habitats of different animals. You might want to read these selections before writing another description essay. As you read, notice how the writers pull you into each experience through sensory details.

## IDEAS FOR WRITING

**Guidelines for Writing a Description Essay**

1. Decide on a dominant impression—the feeling or mood you want to communicate.
2. Decide how much of your description should be objective (factual) and how much should be subjective (personal reactions).
3. Draw on your five senses to write a good description.
4. When you describe, try to *show* rather than *tell* your readers what you want them to know.
5. Organize your description so that your readers can easily follow it.

1. Place yourself in the scene on the next page, and describe it in as much detail as possible. Imagine that you can see, hear, touch, smell, and taste everything in this picture. What are your sensations? How do you feel? Before you begin to write, decide on the dominant impression you want to convey. Then choose your details carefully.
2. Describe for your classmates a class environment that is ideal for you. What kind of classroom atmosphere makes you thrive? What should the people in your class understand about you as a student? What kind of instructor brings out the best in you? Why?

3. A national travel magazine is asking for honest descriptions (positive or negative) of places people have visited. They are offering $100 to the writers of the essays chosen for publication. You may decide to write about a place with a marvelous beach or about an absolutely awful place. In either case, remember to begin with the dominant impression you want to create.
4. Create your own description assignment (with the help of your instructor), and write a response to it.

## Revising Workshop

**Small Group Activity (5–10 minutes per writer)** In groups of three or four, each person should read his or her description essay to the other members of the group. Those listening should record their reactions on a copy of the Peer Evaluation Form in Appendix 2A. After your group goes through this process, give your evaluation forms to the appropriate writers so that each writer has two or three peer comment sheets for revising.

**Paired Activity (5 minutes per writer)** Using the completed Peer Evaluation Forms, work in pairs to decide what you should revise in your essay. If time allows, rewrite some of your sentences, and have your partner look at them.

**Individual Activity** Rewrite your paper, using the revising feedback you received from other students.

## Editing Workshop

**Paired Activity (5–10 minutes per writer)** Swap papers with a classmate, and use the editing portion of your Peer Evaluation Form to identify as many grammar, punctuation, mechanics, and spelling errors as you can. If time allows, correct some of your errors, and have your partner look at them. Record your grammar, punctuation, and mechanics errors in the Error Log (Appendix 6) and your spelling errors in the Spelling Log (Appendix 7).

**Individual Activity** Rewrite your paper again, using the editing feedback you received from other students.

## Reflecting on Your Writing

When you have completed your own essay, answer these six questions.

1. What was most difficult about this assignment?
2. What was easiest?
3. What did you learn about description by completing this assignment?
4. What do you think are the strengths of your description? Place a squiggly line by the parts of your essay that you feel are very good.
5. What are the weaknesses, if any, of your paper? Place an X by the parts of your essay you would like help with. Write any questions you have in the margin.
6. What did you learn from this assignment about your own writing process—about preparing to write, about writing the first draft, about revising, and about editing?

CHAPTER 10

# Narrating

*I try to remember times in my life, incidents in which there was the dominating theme of cruelty or kindness or generosity or envy or happiness or glee. Then I select one.*

—Maya Angelou

Because we are constantly telling other people about various events in our lives, we all know how to use narration. Think of how many times a day you tell someone about an event that happened to you: your accident on the way to school; the conversation you had at the bus stop yesterday; your strange experience at the restaurant last night. Narrating is an essential part of all of our lives. In fact, stories teach us how to live our lives.

Narration also plays an important role in our writing. Think about how many times we tell a story when we write—in our personal lives, in classes, and at work. Consider these situations:

You tell a friend in an e-mail about how you met the person you're now dating.

On a history exam, a student summarizes the chain of events that led to the United States' entry into World War II.

A student summarizes a short story in an English class.

An emergency medical technician gives an account of her 911 calls for the day.

A supervisor writes a report explaining an employee's accident on the job.

**Narration,** or storytelling, is an interesting way of getting someone's attention by sharing thoughts or experiences. Like description, narration is sometimes used as an end in itself (for example, when you tell a friend a joke or the plot of a movie). But very often it's used in conjunction with explaining or persuading. You might start a term paper analyzing drug abuse, for example, with a brief story of one addict's life, or a lawyer might seek a not-guilty verdict by telling the jury about the hardships his or her client suffered as a child.

Jane Maher, who teaches college in New York City, wrote the following autobiographical essay to help her come to terms with the loss of her father. Can you think of an event that taught you something important about life? What was the event? What did you learn?

**Jane Maher**

## GIRL

1 I don't remember exactly when I began to be offended when my father called me, or other girls or women, "girl." I guess he always did it; at least I don't remember him ever not doing it. He'd often use it as a term of affection: "How's my girl today?" But just as often, he'd use it carelessly or callously, the way some men use the expression "sweetie." "Listen girl," my father would say, "I make the rules around here."

2 Women, girls, were perceived by my father as less than men: less important, less intelligent, less capable, less in need of education or direction. In fact, for a long period of my life, I was so indoctrinated by my father's views, and by society's confirmation of those views, that I agreed with him.

3 But as I grew older, the term "girl" began to hurt me and make me angry. As my father became aware of my strong and growing aversion to the word, he'd use it even more often. "What's the matter," he'd ask. "you don't like it anymore when your old man calls you girl? You're my daughter, I'll call you whatever I want." Or he'd ask my mother, pretending I wasn't in the room, "What kind of daughter did you raise that she wants to become a man? Is she ashamed to be a girl?" The word took on stronger and stronger connotations for me as I began to realize how permanently, and adversely, my father's attitudes had affected my life. I had been sent to an all-girls commercial high school. "Listen girl," my father declared, "as long as you know typing and stenography, you'll never starve." College was not mentioned very much in our house—I was one of three daughters. If one of us had a date, my father would tell my mother to remind us "what can happen to a girl if she's not careful." When I got married, I heard my father joking with my uncle: "One down, two to go." We were objects to be dispensed with, burdens of no conceivable use to him.

4 This does not mean that he did not love us or care for us; for my entire childhood he worked two jobs so that he could afford to send us away to the country

every summer. But it was the terms upon which he loved and cared for us which were so distressing to me. Nor did I always get angry when he used the term. When my first daughter was born, he arrived at the hospital carrying a silver dollar he had saved in his collection for many years as a gift for her. "Now I've got four of you girls instead of three," he said, knowing that I knew at this special time he was only teasing and did not intend to hurt me.

I saw less and less of my father after I moved to Connecticut in 1980. He and my mother kept their house in Brooklyn but spent most of the winter months in Florida. Sometimes when I called on the phone, I could tell how happy he was to hear my voice. "Hey, girl, is that husband of yours taking as good care of you as I did?" But other times, over Thanksgiving dinner or while opening Christmas presents, he'd use the term as he had when I was young. "Girl, get me a little more coffee will you?" Or when I enrolled my daughter in an expensive private school: "Why spend money you don't have to, girl? She's just going to get married the way you did." I'd keep my countenance at those times; I had grown wise to my father—I wouldn't give him the satisfaction of showing my anger. That's not to say he didn't keep trying: "So now you like it when your old man calls you girl, huh? You're finally getting wise to the fact that men aren't so bad to have around when you need something." 5

And I suspected that secretly he was proud of me. Soon after I got married, I returned to college, part time, in the evening, and graduated magna cum laude. By then, both of my daughters were in school, so I earned my master's degree from Columbia University, again part time. It was my father who picked up my daughters from the school bus stop on the day I took my comprehensive exam. When I began to teach part time at a local community college, my father asked my mother, again pretending I wasn't in the room, "if there was a girl around here who thought her father was going to start calling her Professor." 6

My father had always had a heart condition, exacerbated by twenty-two years as a New York City fireman, two packs of cigarettes a day, and my mother's delicious Italian cooking. When he suddenly became seriously ill, my mother got him home from Florida and into a hospital in Brooklyn in less than 24 hours. But it still wasn't soon enough. My father died before they could perform a triple bypass, and before I got to say goodbye to him. 7

I had left Connecticut at nine in the morning, intending to wait out the surgery with my mother and to be with my father when he awoke. Instead, when I arrived at the hospital, one of my sisters and my mother were in a small, curtained-off section of the intensive care unit being told by a busy, preoccupied young resident that my father had experienced very little discomfort before he died. It sounded too pat, too familiar, too convenient to me. I was overcome with the fear that my father had been alone that entire morning, that no one in that overcrowded municipal hospital had even known that he was dead until they arrived to prepare him for surgery. 8

9 They left us alone to say goodbye to him, but I was so concerned over my mother's anguish that I didn't take the time I should have to kiss him or even to touch his forehead. A nurse came in and suggested, gently, that it was time to leave. She was right of course; another moment and my mother would have collapsed.

10 I thanked the nurse and asked her, nonchalantly, if she knew exactly when my father had died, secretly convinced that she didn't have an answer, that he had been alone all morning. "I didn't see him this morning," she replied, "but I'll get the nurse who did."

11 A young, pretty nurse appeared several minutes later. "My shift is over," she said, "but I was waiting around to see the family."

12 "Was he in pain?" my mother asked.

13 "No, not at all. He even teased me a bit. I remember his exact words. "Go take care of the patients who need you girl," he said, "I'm perfectly fine."

14 I wasn't exactly fine, but I have never felt more comforted in my life than when I heard that word.

*Preparing to Write Your Own Narration Essay*

We have all learned important lessons from various events in our lives. Over time, we find that some lessons are more worthwhile than others. What events in your life have taught you important lessons? Use one or more of the prewriting techniques you learned in Chapter 2 to gather your thoughts on these events. What lessons did you learn?

## HOW TO WRITE A NARRATION ESSAY

Narrating involves telling a story about an experience—one of yours or someone else's. When you write a narrative essay, you focus on a particular event and make a specific point about it. You should provide enough detail so that readers can understand as completely as possible what going through your experience was like. Here are some guidelines to help you make your narrative interesting.

1. ***Make sure your essay has a point.*** The most important feature of a narrative essay is that it makes a point. Simply recording your story step by step is a boring exercise for both writer and reader. Writing an account of your walk to class in the morning is not interesting. The

walk becomes interesting when something important or significant happens on the way. An event is significant if it helps both writer and reader understand something about themselves, about other people, or about the world we live in. If you can complete one of the following sentences, you will produce a focused narrative:

This essay shows that . . .

This essay teaches us that . . .

In Jane Maher's essay, the narrator focuses on the pain she felt, growing up, when her father referred to her as a "girl." She thought the term was degrading until she understood, after he died, that it was really a term of endearment. Maher is able to communicate the process of growing up through her experience with this one word. Her essay teaches us that the relationship between words and emotions is complex.

2. ***Use the five Ws and one H to construct your story.*** The five *Ws* and one *H* are the six questions—*Who? What? When? Where? Why?* and *How?*—that journalists use to make sure they cover all the basic information when they write a news story. These questions can help you come up with details and ideas for a well-developed narrative essay. You should make sure that your essay answers each of these questions in detail.

   When you look at Maher's narrative again, you can see that she covered the answers to all these questions:

   *Who* was involved? Maher, her father, her mother, and the nurses

   *What* was the central problem? Maher was offended by her father's use of the word "girl."

   *When* did this story take place? As Maher was growing up

   *Where* were they? At home

   *Why* was Maher offended? Because she thought the word "girl" was degrading to her as a person and to other females

   *How* did the author learn from this event? She finally understood that her father's use of "girl" wasn't as offensive as she thought it was.

   Since Maher covers all these basic details, the reader can appreciate her full story and understand its significance.

3. ***Develop your narrative with vivid details.*** Your readers will be able to imagine the events in your narrative essay if you provide them with specific details. In fact, the more specific your details, the more vivid your essay will become. These details should develop the ideas you generated with the six journalistic questions. At the same time, you should omit any irrelevant details that don't support your thesis statement.

Look again at Maher's essay. In this narrative, the author provides many vivid details about the narrator: She is a girl whose father thinks girls are less important than boys; he calls her "girl"; this term starts to bother the narrator as she is growing up; she gets married and moves to Connecticut; she has two daughters; she gets her master's degree at Columbia University and starts teaching at a local community college; and her father dies of a heart attack. The amount of detail and its specificity help readers participate in this narrative.

4. ***Build excitement in your narrative with careful pacing.*** To be most effective, narration should prolong the exciting parts of a story and shorten the routine facts that simply move the reader from one episode to another. If you were robbed on your way to work, for example, a good narrative describing the incident would concentrate on the traumatic event itself rather than on such boring details as what you had for breakfast or what clothes you were wearing. One writer might say, "I was robbed this morning." A better writer would draw out the exciting parts: "As I was walking to work around 7:30 this morning, a huge, angry-looking man ran up to me, thrust a gun into my belly, and demanded my money, my new wristwatch, my credit cards, and my pants—leaving me broke and embarrassed." The details themselves tell the story.

   Maher reveals the details in her story through some of her father's quotations that bothered her: "Listen girl, I make the rules around here"; "Listen girl, as long as you know typing and stenography, you'll never starve." She feels frustrated and belittled by her father, even as an adult: "Hey, girl, is that husband of yours taking as good care of you as I did?" Finally, she works through the hurtfulness when her father dies. At this point, Maher draws out the search for the nurse who could tell her if her father died alone. The pacing of her story holds our interest throughout the essay.

5. ***Organize your narration so that your readers can easily follow it.*** Most narrative essays follow a series of actions through time, so they are organized chronologically, or according to a time sequence. Once you choose the details you will use, you should arrange them so that your story has a clear beginning, middle, and end. If you add clear, logical transitions, such as "then," "next," "at this point," and "suddenly," you will guide your readers smoothly through your essay from one event to the next.

   Jane Maher organizes her narrative chronologically. It moves through time from her childhood to going to high school to getting married and having a baby as her father raises her, retires, and grows old. In other words, the two main characters—Maher and her father—move through normal life events. Because it follows a logical time sequence and does not jump around, Maher's narrative is easy to follow. She guides her readers through her essay with such transitions as "in fact," "as I grew older," "when," "sometimes," and "soon."

**Writing Your Own Narration Essay**

Choose one of the events from your prewriting notes that taught you an important lesson in life, and write a narration essay explaining this incident and the lesson you learned. Follow the guidelines in this chapter to develop your essay.

## NARRATION AT WORK

In an essay about a terrifying incident in his life, student writer Tommy Poulos tells a story that taught him an important lesson in life. Here is his first draft. As you read this paragraph, try to figure out what Tommy's main point is.

**"My Brother"**

My family and I lead a fairly quiet life. My parents go to work, and my brother and I go to school. We never make headlines with sports events or science fairs. We essentially live a normal American life out of the spotlight. It was quite a shock, then, when a lot of attention was focused on our family. 1

My brother, Wayne, was driving on a highway that is nicknamed "The Death Loop." It got its name because it's a two-lane highway that loops around the city, and many people have died because of drivers who take too many chances and cause head-on collisions. One afternoon, Wayne saw a woman's car wrecked into a guardrail with her passenger side of the car completely smashed in. The driver's side was mangled, and my brother could tell the woman inside was in trouble. Wayne didn't think twice about running up to help them. She was badly injured, but my brother knew not to move her! 2

The woman had not been wearing her seat belt. Her car was too old to have an airbag. She had obviously hit her head because she had blood gushing from a gaping wound in her forehead. She was conscious, so my brother sat with her, trying to keep her calm and awake. He kept asking her questions like if she had any children? Two other cars stopped, and 3 my brother remembers telling one man to call 911. Wayne stayed with the woman until the paramedics arrived.

4 Wayne left the scene after giving a statement to the police. Later, he heard from the local newspapers and news stations that his heroic actions had saved the woman. In these stories, the woman's husband said he believed his wife was still alive because she had a guardian angel keeping her awake. Even the paramedics said Wayne probably kept her alive. By keeping her awake. In public, Wayne acts very humble, but in private, he is loving the attention.

5 Now my brother is the local hero. Our house used to be quiet, but since Wayne's act of heroism, it's become Grand Central Station. Everyone wants to talk to Wayne. I'm happy for him. But most of all, I'm glad Wayne realizes the importance of seat belts. He used to be macho and say seat belts were too uncomfortable to wear. Now he won't leave the driveway until everyone has buckled their seat belts. Perhaps the woman will save Wayne's life as well.

1. All the details in Tommy's essay lead to one main point. What is that point? ______________________________

2. Tommy covers all the journalistic questions in his essay. Record at least one detail he uses for each question:

   Who? ______________________________

   What? ______________________________

   When? ______________________________

   Where? ______________________________

   Why? ______________________________

   How? ______________________________

3. In your opinion, which two details of Tommy's are most vivid? What makes them so vivid?

   ______________________________

   ______________________________

4. How does Tommy pace his essay to build excitement?

_______________________________________________

_______________________________________________

_______________________________________________

5. How does Tommy organize his essay? List the topic of each of his body paragraphs; then identify his method of organization.

_______________________________________________

_______________________________________________

_______________________________________________

Method of organization: _______________________

## REVISING AND EDITING A STUDENT ESSAY

This essay is Tommy's first draft, which now needs to be revised and edited. First, apply the Revising Checklist below to Tommy's draft so that you are working with his content. When you are satisfied that his ideas are fully developed and well organized, use the Editing Checklist on pages 149–150 to correct his grammar and mechanics errors. Answer the questions after each checklist. Then write your suggested changes directly on Tommy's draft.

### Revising Checklist

**Thesis Statement**

✔ Does the thesis statement contain the essay's controlling idea and appear as the last sentence of the introduction?

**Basic Elements**

✔ Does the title draw in the readers?

✔ Does the introduction capture the readers' attention and build up to the thesis statement effectively?

✔ Does each body paragraph deal with a single topic?

✔ Does the conclusion bring the essay to a close in an interesting way?

**DEVELOPMENT**

✔ Do the body paragraphs adequately support the thesis statement?

✔ Does each body paragraph have a focused topic sentence?

✔ Does each body paragraph contain *specific* details that support the topic sentence?

✔ Does each body paragraph include *enough* details to explain the topic sentence fully?

**UNITY**

✔ Do the essay's topic sentences relate directly to the thesis statement?

✔ Do the details in each body paragraph support its topic sentence?

**ORGANIZATION**

✔ Is the essay organized logically?

✔ Is each body paragraph organized logically?

**COHERENCE**

✔ Are transitions used effectively so that paragraphs move smoothly and logically from one to the next?

✔ Do the sentences move smoothly and logically from one to the next?

## Thesis Statement

✔ Does the thesis statement contain the essay's controlling idea and appear as the last sentence of the introduction?

1. Put brackets around the last sentence in Tommy's introduction. Does it contain his main point? ______________
2. Rewrite Tommy's thesis statement if necessary so that it states his main point and introduces his topics.

______________________________________________

______________________________________________

## Basic Elements

- ✔ Does the title draw in the readers?
- ✔ Does the introduction capture the readers' attention and build up to the thesis statement effectively?
- ✔ Does each body paragraph deal with a single topic?
- ✔ Does the conclusion bring the essay to a close in an interesting way?

1. Give Tommy's essay an alternate title. Also drop the quotation marks, since original titles should not be in quotation marks. ______________

2. Rewrite Tommy's introduction so that it captures the readers' attention and builds up to the thesis statement at the end of the paragraph.

   ______________________________________________

   ______________________________________________

   ______________________________________________

3. Does each of Tommy's body paragraphs deal with only one topic? _______

4. Rewrite Tommy's conclusion using at least one suggestion from Part I.

   ______________________________________________

   ______________________________________________

   ______________________________________________

## Development

- ✔ Do the body paragraphs adequately support the thesis statement?
- ✔ Does each body paragraph have a focused topic sentence?
- ✔ Does each body paragraph contain *specific* details that support the topic sentence?
- ✔ Does each body paragraph include *enough* details to explain the topic sentence fully?

1. Write out Tommy's thesis statement (revised, if necessary), and list his three topic sentences below it.

   Thesis statement: ______________________________

   ______________________________

   Topic 1: ______________________________

   ______________________________

   Topic 2: ______________________________

   ______________________________

   Topic 3: ______________________________

   ______________________________

2. Do Tommy's topics adequately support his thesis statement? __________
3. Does each body paragraph have a focused topic sentence? __________
4. Add more specific information to two of Tommy's supporting details.
5. Add two new details to Tommy's essay that support his main idea.

## Unity

> ✔ Do the essay's topic sentences relate directly to the thesis statement?
> ✔ Do the details in each body paragraph support its topic sentence?

1. Read each of Tommy's topic sentences with his thesis statement (revised, if necessary) in mind. Do they go together?

   ______________________________

2. Revise them if necessary so they are directly related.
3. Drop or rewrite any of the sentences in his body paragraphs that are not directly related to their topic sentences.

## Organization

- ✔ Is the essay organized logically?
- ✔ Is each body paragraph organized logically?

1. Read Tommy's essay again to see if all the paragraphs are arranged chronologically.
2. Move any paragraphs that are out of order.
3. Look closely at Tommy's body paragraphs to see if all his sentences are arranged logically within paragraphs.
4. Move any sentences that are out of order.

## Coherence

- ✔ Are transitions used effectively so that paragraphs move smoothly and logically from one to the next?
- ✔ Do the sentences move smoothly and logically from one to the next?

1. Circle five words or phrases Tommy repeats.
2. Explain how two of these make Tommy's essay easier to read.

______________________________________________

______________________________________________

Now rewrite Tommy's essay with your revisions.

## Editing Checklist

**Sentences**

- ✔ Does each sentence have a main subject and verb?
- ✔ Do all subjects and verbs agree?
- ✔ Do all pronouns agree with their nouns?
- ✔ Are modifiers as close as possible to the words they modify?

PUNCTUATION AND MECHANICS

✔ Are sentences punctuated correctly?

✔ Are words capitalized properly?

WORD CHOICE AND SPELLING

✔ Are words used correctly?

✔ Are words spelled correctly?

## Sentences

✔ Does each sentence have a main subject and verb?

For help with subjects and verbs, see Chapter 34.

1. Underline the subjects once and verbs twice in paragraph 4 of your revision of Tommy's essay. Remember that sentences can have more than one subject-verb set.
2. Does each of the sentences have at least one subject and verb that can stand alone? ____________
3. Did you find and correct Tommy's fragment? If not, find and correct it now. For help, see Chapter 35.

✔ Do all subjects and verbs agree?

For help with subject-verb agreement, see Chapter 39.

1. Read aloud the subjects and verbs you underlined in your revision of Tommy's essay.
2. Correct any subjects and verbs that do not agree with each other.

✔ Do all pronouns agree with their nouns?

For help with pronoun agreement, see Chapter 43.

1. Find any pronouns in your revision of Tommy's essay that do not agree with their nouns.

2. Did you find and correct the two pronouns that do not agree with their nouns? If not, find and correct them now.

> ✔ Are modifiers as close as possible to the words they modify?
> For help with modifier errors, see Chapter 46.

1. Find any modifiers in your revision of Tommy's essay that are not as close as possible to the words they modify.
2. Rewrite sentences if necessary so that modifiers are as close as possible to the words they modify.

## Punctuation and Mechanics

> ✔ Are sentences punctuated correctly?
> For help with punctuation, see Chapters 47–51.

1. Read your revision of Tommy's essay for any errors in punctuation.
2. Find the fragment you revised, and make sure it is punctuated correctly.
3. Did you find and correct Tommy's two other punctuation errors?

> ✔ Are words capitalized properly?
> For help with capitalization, see Chapter 52.

1. Read your revision of Tommy's essay for any errors in capitalization.
2. Be sure to check Tommy's capitalization in the fragment you revised.

## Word Choice and Spelling

> ✔ Are words used correctly?
> For help with confused words, see Chapter 58.

1. Find any words used incorrectly in your revision of Tommy's essay.
2. Correct any errors you find.

✔ Are all words spelled correctly?
For help with spelling, see Chapter 59.

1. Use spell-check and a dictionary to check the spelling in your revision of Tommy's essay.
2. Correct any misspelled words.

Now rewrite Tommy's essay again with your editing corrections.

## REVISING AND EDITING YOUR OWN ESSAY

Returning to the narration you wrote earlier in this chapter, revise and edit your own writing. The checklists here will help you apply what you have learned to your essay.

### Revising

#### Thesis Statement

☐ Does the thesis statement contain the essay's controlling idea and appear as the last sentence of the introduction?

1. What is the main point of your essay?

_______________________________________________

2. Put brackets around the last sentence in your introduction. Does it contain your main point? ______________________________

3. Rewrite your thesis statement if necessary so that it states your main point and introduces your topics.

## Basic Elements

- ☐ Does the title draw in the readers?
- ☐ Does the introduction capture the readers' attention and build up to the thesis statement effectively?
- ☐ Does each body paragraph deal with a single topic?
- ☐ Does the conclusion bring the essay to a close in an interesting way?

1. Give your essay a title if it doesn't have one. ____________________
2. Does your introduction capture your readers' attention and build up to your thesis statement at the end of the paragraph? ________________
3. Does each of your body paragraphs deal with only one topic? __________
4. Does your conclusion follow some of the suggestions offered in Part I?

   ______________________________________________________

## Development

- ☐ Do the body paragraphs adequately support the thesis statement?
- ☐ Does each body paragraph have a focused topic sentence?
- ☐ Does each body paragraph contain *specific* details that support the topic sentence?
- ☐ Does each body paragraph include *enough* details to explain the topic sentence fully?

1. Write out your thesis statement (revised, if necessary), and list your topic sentences below it.

Thesis statement: ______________________________

______________________________

Topic 1: ______________________________

______________________________

Topic 2: ______________________________

______________________________

Topic 3: ______________________________

______________________________

2. Do your topics adequately support your thesis statement? __________
3. Does each body paragraph have a focused topic sentence? __________
4. Record at least one detail you use in response to each journalistic question.

   Who? ______________________________

   What? ______________________________

   When? ______________________________

   Where? ______________________________

   Why? ______________________________

   How? ______________________________

5. Add at least two new details to your essay that support your main idea.

## Unity

- ☐ Do the essay's topic sentences relate directly to the thesis statement?
- ☐ Do the details in each body paragraph support its topic sentence?

1. Read each of your topic sentences with your thesis statement in mind. Do they go together?
2. Revise them if necessary so they are directly related.
3. Drop or rewrite any of the sentences in your body paragraphs that are not directly related to their topic sentences.

## Organization

- ☐ Is the essay organized logically?
- ☐ Is each body paragraph organized logically?

1. Read your essay again to see if all the paragraphs are arranged logically.
2. Refer to your answers to the development questions. Then identify your method of organization: ______________________________
3. Is the order you chose for your paragraphs the most effective approach to your topic? ____________
4. Move any paragraphs that are out of order.
5. Look closely at your body paragraphs to see if all the sentences are arranged logically within paragraphs.
6. Move any sentences that are out of order.

## Coherence

- ☐ Are transitions used effectively so that paragraphs move smoothly and logically from one to the next?
- ☐ Do the sentences move smoothly and logically from one to the next?

1. Circle five words or phrases you repeat.
2. Explain how two of these make your essay easier to read.

______________________________________________________________

______________________________________________________________

Now rewrite your essay with your revisions.

##  Editing

## Sentences

- ☐ Does each sentence have a main subject and verb?
  For help with subjects and verbs, see Chapter 34.

1. Underline the subjects once and verbs twice in a paragraph of your revised essay. Remember that sentences can have more than one subject-verb set.
2. Does each of your sentences have at least one subject and verb that can stand alone? ______________
3. Correct any fragments you have written. For help with fragments, see Chapter 35.
4. Correct any run-on sentences you have written. For help with run-ons, see Chapter 36.

- ☐ Do all subjects and verbs agree?
  For help with subject-verb agreement, see Chapter 39.

1. Read aloud the subjects and verbs you underlined in your revised essay.
2. Correct any subjects and verbs that do not agree.

- ☐ Do all pronouns agree with their nouns?
  For help with pronoun agreement, see Chapter 43.

1. Find any pronouns in your revised essay that do not agree with their nouns.
2. Correct any pronouns that do not agree with their nouns.

- ☐ Are modifiers as close as possible to the words they modify?
  For help with modifier errors, see Chapter 46.

1. Find any modifiers in your revised essay that are not as close as possible to the words they modify.
2. Rewrite sentences if necessary so that your modifiers are as close as possible to the words they modify.

## Punctuation and Mechanics

☐ Are sentences punctuated correctly?
For help with punctuation, see Chapters 47–51.

1. Read your revised essay for any errors in punctuation.
2. Make sure any fragments and run-ons you revised are punctuated correctly.

☐ Are words capitalized properly?
For help with capitalization, see Chapter 52.

1. Read your revised essay for any errors in capitalization.
2. Be sure to check your capitalization in any fragments or run-ons you revised.

## Word Choice and Spelling

☐ Are words used correctly?
For help with confused words, see Chapter 58.

1. Find any words used incorrectly in your revised essay.
2. Correct any errors you find.

☐ Are all words spelled correctly?
For help with spelling, see Chapter 59.

1. Use spell-check and a dictionary to check your spelling.
2. Correct any misspelled words.

Now rewrite your essay again with your editing corrections.

## READING SUGGESTIONS

In Chapter 26, you will find two essays that illustrate good narrative writing: "The Sanctuary of School," in which Linda Barry tells a story about using her school as an escape from her home life, and "Writer's Retreat" by Stan Higgins, which talks about his life as a writer in prison. You might want to read these selections before writing another narration essay. As you read, notice how the writers cover the journalistic questions and use vivid descriptive details to pull you into their narratives, making the main point of the essays all the more meaningful.

## IDEAS FOR WRITING

**Guidelines for Writing a Narration Essay**

1. Make sure your essay has a point.
2. Use the five *W*s and one *H* to construct your story.
3. Develop your narrative with vivid details.
4. Build excitement in your narrative with careful pacing.
5. Organize your narration so that your readers can easily follow it.

1. Place yourself in the scene on the previous page, and write a narrative about what is happening. How did you get here? Why are you here? Where are you going from here? Be sure to decide on a main point before you begin to write.
2. Your old high school has asked you, as a graduate, to submit an essay to the newsletter, recalling a job or volunteer experience that you enjoyed. The editors want to inform current high school students about options for volunteer and paid work. Your purpose is to tell your story in enough interesting detail so that you convince the current high school students that the job you had is worth looking into.
3. Your college class is putting together a collection of essays that explain how classmates decided to go to their current college. What happened first? When did you decide? What helped you decide? What activities or people influenced your decision the most? Tell your story in vivid detail.
4. Create your own narration assignment (with the help of your instructor), and write a response to it.

## Revising Workshop

**Small Group Activity (5–10 minutes per writer)** In groups of three or four, each person should read his or her narration essay to the other members of the group. Those listening should record their reactions on a copy of the Peer Evaluation Form in Appendix 2B. After your group goes through this process, give your evaluation forms to the appropriate writers so that each writer has two peer comment sheets for revising.

**Paired Activity (5 minutes per writer)** Using the completed Peer Evaluation Forms, work in pairs to decide what you should revise in your essay. If time allows, rewrite some of your sentences, and have your partner look at them.

**Individual Activity** Rewrite your paper, using the revising feedback you received from other students.

## Editing Workshop

**Paired Activity (5–10 minutes per writer)** Swap papers with a classmate, and use the editing portion of your Peer Evaluation Form to identify as many grammar, punctuation, mechanics, and spelling errors as you can. If time allows, correct some of your errors, and have your partner look at them. Record your grammar, punctuation, and mechanics errors in the Error Log (Appendix 6) and your spelling errors in the Spelling Log (Appendix 7).

Individual Activity Rewrite your paper again, using the editing feedback you received from other students.

## Reflecting on Your Writing

When you have completed your own essay, answer these six questions.

1. What was most difficult about this assignment?
2. What was easiest?
3. What did you learn about narration by completing this assignment?
4. What do you think are the strengths of your narration? Place a squiggly line by the parts of your essay that you feel are very good.
5. What are the weaknesses, if any, of your paper? Place an X by the parts of your essay you would like help with. Write any questions you have in the margin.
6. What did you learn from this assignment about your own writing process—about preparing to write, about writing the first draft, about revising, and about editing?

# Illustrating

*When I began to write, I found it was the best way to make sense out of my life.*

—JOHN CHEEVER

Giving examples to make a point is a natural part of communication. For example, if you are trying to demonstrate how much time you waste, you can cite the fact that you talk on the phone about two hours every day. Or to tell your friends how much fun you are having, you might say, "College is great because no one tells me what to do or when to go to bed. I am completely on my own." The message is in the examples you choose.

We also use examples every day to make various points in our writing. Think about the following situations that take place in our personal lives, at school, and at work.

In a letter to your parents, you tell them how hard you are studying in college by giving them examples of your weekend study schedule.

A student gives examples of gestures, facial expressions, and posture in a paper on nonverbal communication for a psychology course.

A student answers a sociology exam question by giving examples to show how children are integrated into society.

A human resource director of a large company writes a memo on sexual harassment in the workplace, including examples of inappropriate behavior.

The owner of a catering business writes a brochure listing examples of dinners available in different price ranges.

An example is an **illustration** of the point you want to make. Well-chosen examples then are the building blocks of an illustration essay. You draw examples from your experience, your observations, and your reading.

They help you show rather than tell what you mean, usually by supplying concrete details (what you see, hear, touch, smell, or taste) to support abstract ideas (such as faith, hope, understanding, and love), by providing specifics ("I like chocolate") to explain generalizations ("I like sweets"), and by giving definite references ("Turn left at the second stoplight") to clarify vague statements ("Turn left in a few blocks").

Not only do examples help you make your point, but they also add interest to your writing. Would you rather read an essay stating that being a server in a restaurant is a lot harder than it looks? Or would you be more interested in reading an essay describing what it is like having to serve too many tables, carrying heavy trays, taking the wrong order to a table, and dealing with rude customers? The first statement *tells*, but vivid examples *show* your readers the point you want to make.

In her essay "Hold the Mayonnaise," Julia Alvarez uses examples to explain the difficulties involved in blending two cultures—American and Latino—in a stepfamily. Have you ever visited a foreign country? What was it like to be in a different culture? Have you ever been part of a group that blended two or more cultures? What did you learn?

**Julia Alvarez**

## HOLD THE MAYONNAISE

1 "If I die first and Papi ever gets remarried," Mami used to tease when we were kids, "don't you accept a new woman in my house. Make her life impossible, you hear?" My sisters and I nodded obediently and a filial shudder would go through us. We were Catholics, so of course, the only kind of remarriage we could imagine had to involve our mother's death.

2 We were also Dominicans, recently arrived in Jamaica, Queens, in the early '60s, before waves of other Latin Americans began arriving. So, when we imagined who exactly my father might possibly ever think of remarrying, only American women came to mind. It would be bad enough having a *madrastra,* but a "stepmother. . . ."

3 All I could think of was that she would make me eat mayonnaise, a food which I identified with the United States and which I detested. Mami understood, of course, that I wasn't used to that kind of food. Even a madrastra, accustomed to our rice and beans and tostones and pollo frito, would understand. But an American stepmother would think it was normal to put mayonnaise on

food, and if she were at all strict and a little mean, which all stepmothers, of course, were, she would make me eat potato salad and such. I had plenty of my own reasons to make a potential stepmother's life impossible. When I nodded obediently with my sisters, I was imagining not just something foreign in our house, but in our refrigerator.

So it's strange now, almost 35 years later, to find myself a Latina stepmother 4
of my husband's two tall, strapping, blond, mayonnaise-eating daughters. To be honest, neither of them is a real aficionado of the condiment, but it's a fair thing to add to a bowl of tuna fish or diced potatoes. Their American food, I think of it, and when they head to their mother's or off to school, I push the jar back in the refrigerator behind their chocolate pudding and several open cans of Diet Coke.

What I can't push as successfully out of sight are my own immigrant child- 5
hood fears of having a *gringa* stepmother with foreign tastes in our house. Except now, I am the foreign stepmother in a gringa household. I've wondered what my husband's two daughters think of this stranger in their family. It must be doubly strange for them that I am from another culture.

Of course, there are mitigating circumstances—my husband's two daugh- 6
ters were teen-agers when we married, older, more mature, able to understand differences. They had also traveled when they were children with their father, an eye doctor, who worked on short-term international projects with various eye foundations. But still, it's one thing to visit a foreign country, another altogether to find it brought home—a real bear plopped down in a Goldilocks house.

Sometimes, a whole extended family of bears. My warm, loud Latino family 7
came up for the wedding: my *tía* from Santo Domingo; three dramatic, enthusiastic sisters and their families; my papi, with a thick accent I could tell the girls found it hard to understand; and my mami, who had her eye trained on my soon-to-be stepdaughters for any sign that they were about to make my life impossible. "How are they behaving themselves?" she asked me, as if they were 7 and 3, not 19 and 16. "They're wonderful girls," I replied, already feeling protective of them.

I looked around for the girls in the meadow in front of the house we were 8
building, where we were holding the outdoor wedding ceremony and party. The oldest hung out with a group of her own friends. The younger one whizzed in briefly for the ceremony, then left again before the congratulations started up. There was not much mixing with me and mine. What was there for them to celebrate on a day so full of confusion and effort?

On my side, being the newcomer in someone else's territory is a role I'm 9
used to. I can tap into that struggling English speaker, that skinny, dark-haired, olive-skinned girl in a sixth grade of mostly blond and blue-eyed giants. Those

tall, freckled boys would push me around in the playground. "Go back to where you came from!" "*No comprendo!*" I'd reply, though of course there was no misunderstanding the fierce looks on their faces.

10 Even now, my first response to a scowl is that old pulling away. (My husband calls it "checking out.") I remember times early on in the marriage when the girls would be with us, and I'd get out of school and drive around doing errands, killing time, until my husband, their father, would be leaving work. I am not proud of my fears, but I understand—as the lingo goes—where they come from.

11 And I understand, more than I'd like to sometimes, my stepdaughters' pain. But with me, they need never fear that I'll usurp a mother's place. No one has ever come up and held their faces and then addressed me, "They look just like you." If anything, strangers to the remarriage are probably playing Mr. Potato Head in their minds, trying to figure out how my foreign features and my husband's fair Nebraskan features got put together into these two tall, blond girls. "My husband's daughters," I kept introducing them.

12 Once, when one of them visited my class and I introduced her as such, two students asked me why. "I'd be so hurt if my stepmom introduced me that way," the young man said. That night I told my stepdaughter what my students had said. She scowled at me and agreed. "It's so weird how you call me Papa's daughter. Like you don't want to be related to me or something."

13 "I didn't want to presume," I explained. "So it's O.K. if I call you my stepdaughter?"

14 "That's what I am," she said. Relieved, I took it for a teensy inch of acceptance. The takings are small in this stepworld, I've discovered. Sort of like being a minority. It feels as if all the goodies have gone somewhere else.

15 Day to day, I guess I follow my papi's advice. When we first came, he would talk to his children about how to make it in our new country. "Just do your work and put in your heart, and they will accept you!" In this age of remaining true to your roots, of keeping your Spanish, of fighting from inside your culture, that assimilationist approach is highly suspect. My Latino students—who don't want to be called Hispanics anymore—would ditch me as faculty adviser if I came up with that play-nice message.

16 But in a stepfamily where everyone is starting a new life together, it isn't bad advice. Like a potluck supper, an American concept my mami never took to. ("Why invite people to your house and then ask them to bring the food?") You put what you've got together with what everyone else brought and see what comes out of the pot. The luck part is if everyone brings something you like. No potato salad, no deviled eggs, no little party sandwiches with you know what in them.

***Preparing to Write Your Own Illustration Essay***

When did you last try something new in your life? Was it difficult? Did you plan this new experience, or did it just happen? Do you like new experiences, or do you prefer keeping your life routine? Use one or more of the prewriting strategies you learned in Chapter 2 to recall several times you tried something new, planned or not. Then think about the positive and negative aspects of trying new experiences. What value do they have in your life? What are the disadvantages of trying new experiences?

## HOW TO WRITE AN ILLUSTRATION ESSAY

In the art world, a good illustrator is someone who makes an image or an idea come alive with the perfect drawing. The same principle applies in writing: Someone who uses illustrations, or examples, effectively makes an essay or other piece of writing come alive. Moreover, in college, most essay exam questions are based on illustration—finding the best examples to support your main point. Here are some guidelines to help you use examples effectively.

1. ***State your main point in the last sentence of your introduction.*** Write a thesis statement that clearly and plainly states the main idea of your essay, and place it at the end of your introduction. This is the controlling idea of your essay and should consist of a limited subject and your opinion about that subject. You will explain this main point through the examples you furnish in the following body paragraphs.

   In the sample essay, Alvarez uses many examples to show the difficulties of bringing two cultures together in a stepfamily. Alvarez's introduction is two paragraphs long. She expresses her main point in the last sentence of the second paragraph: "It would be bad enough having a *madrastra,* but a 'stepmother.'" She introduces this idea as the focus of her essay and then explains it with examples. Through her examples, the author is talking about her new family as much as her fears as a child.

2. ***Choose examples that are relevant to your point.*** In an illustration essay, examples serve as the writer's explanation. Well-chosen examples are an essay's building blocks. They help you prove your point and must directly support the point you are trying to make. Examples that

are not relevant are distracting, causing readers to lose their train of thought. Your readers will appreciate the point you are making not because you tell them what to think but because you show them with relevant examples what you are trying to say. Keep in mind, too, that the more specific your examples are, the more likely your readers are to agree with your point.

Finding relevant examples is a fairly easy task. The best examples often come from your own experience and observation. You can also draw examples from your reading—books, newspapers, magazines. In addition, as technology advances, more and more information is available on-line, making the Internet a good place to find examples for an illustration essay.

In Alvarez's essay, all of her examples focus on how difficult the role of stepmother is. Since Alvarez's point has to do with merging two cultures in a stepfamily, her examples refer to either her Dominican experience or her stepdaughters' American experience. Alvarez uses her dislike of mayonnaise to help her illustrate some of the differences people have to deal with when they combine cultures. These focused examples make her essay coherent and unified.

3. ***Choose examples that your readers can identify with.*** To do this, you need to know as much as possible about your audience. Once you know who your readers are, you can tailor your examples to them. In this way, your readers are most likely to follow your line of reasoning. Suppose, for instance, that you want your parents to finance an off-campus apartment for you. You are not likely to make your point by citing examples of European universities that do not provide any student housing because this is not an example that American parents can identify with.

   Alvarez's essay was first published in the *New York Times*, so she chose examples that a diverse group of educated people would relate to. She knew that many of these readers would also be parents, so they would understand the issue of merging families and cultures. In that way, she could keep the attention of her readers for her entire essay and get them to sympathize with her particular point of view.

4. ***Use a sufficient number of examples to make your point.*** Nobody has a set formula for determining the perfect number of examples, because that depends on the point you are trying to make. Sometimes several short examples will make your point best. Or perhaps three or four fairly detailed examples—each in its own body paragraph—work best. At other times the most effective way to develop an essay is with a single extended example. Usually, however, three or four examples are sufficient. If you are in doubt whether to add another example or more vivid

details, you should probably do so. Most students err on the side of using too few examples or not adding enough detail to their examples.

Alvarez opens her essay with a fairly extended example (three paragraphs) to show her dislike of mayonnaise and stepmothers. Later, in paragraph 7, she provides four short examples—all in one sentence—of how her stepdaughters might find her Dominican family difficult to be around. In paragraphs 9 and 11 through 14, Alvarez develops her examples in single paragraphs. She also tries to put herself in her stepdaughters' place. Overall, she gives enough examples from many perspectives so that we understand the complexity and importance of the point she is making. These different types of examples give her essay variety and make it interesting.

5. ***Organize your examples to make your point in the clearest, strongest way.*** When you have gathered enough relevant examples, you are ready to organize them into an essay. Most illustration essays are organized from general to particular—from a general statement (the thesis) to specific examples that support the general statement—or chronologically—according to a time sequence.

   The examples themselves must also be organized within their paragraphs in some logical way—chronologically, spatially, or by extremes. Which example should come first? Second? Last? The simple act of arranging examples can help you and your reader make sense of an experience or idea. Use basic logic to try different patterns.

   Alvarez opens her essay with a childhood memory (fearing a stepmother), moves to present time (she's now a stepmother), and then looks back at episodes in her life and her stepdaughters' lives that show how blending two cultures can be difficult. For every point she makes, she provides an example. Overall, her organization is chronological, though someone else might have arranged these examples a different way.

**Writing Your Own Illustration Essay**

Based on the prewriting that you did earlier, write an essay about three new experiences you have had. Which were planned? Which were unplanned? Did they affect you in positive ways? In negative ways? Or were the outcomes mixed? What did you learn from these experiences? Draft a thesis statement. Then write a first draft of your essay, including an introduction and a conclusion. Use examples in your body paragraphs to support your thesis statement.

## ILLUSTRATION AT WORK

In the following essay, student writer Taleah Trainor uses examples to explain her relationship with Murphy's Law. As you read this essay, try to find Taleah's main point.

### Murphy's Law

1 Murphy's Law: If something can go wrong, it will. I have always been familiar with the concept of this law, but never from actual experience. It was not until the summer before my first year in college that different events taught me about Murphy's Law.

2 The first event was when my father informed me that on our family trip to Washington D.C. we would be using my car. Since I had made previous plans I was not bubbling with enthusiasm. I had 14, "fun-filled" days in D.C. And to top it all off, on the way home from D.C., my car decided to have a breakdown between two Louisiana towns. Louisiana has a really long stretch of highway that driver's hate. People feel like they're on it forever. Luckily, my father had AAA, our delay was short.

3 This particular instance had familiarized me with Murphy's Law, and for the remainder of the summer, I began to notice it every time I turned around. At first it was little things like catching the flu just hours before a date. After a while, it turned into bigger hassles, like getting flat tires on the way to job interviews. I prayed my luck would take a turn for the better rather then the worse.

4 Murphy showed up again on August 29, when I left my hometown to travel to my new school. Having to entrust my 397-mile journey to an old AAA map, I pictured getting sidetracked onto an out-of-the-way farm road leading me to an uncharted town. But I did not get lost until arriving at the infamous "traffic circle" in my new hometown. Realizing my highway map was of know use in town, I frantically looked around and happened to catch a glimpse of the "I ♥ Bulldogs" bumper sticker plastered on the car in front of me. I said to myself, "Now how many cars could have <u>that</u> sticker?" I convinced myself that I was in luck and that the car in front of me was headed toward campus. I decided to follow it. After arriving in a gruesome alley, which accurately resembled the pictures I had seen of a Third World country, I came to the conclusion the car was not headed toward campus but probably to the local chicken fights. Pulling in to the nearest Texaco station, directions were given to me. Three service stations later, their I was, at my new dorm on campus. Once again, I knew that Murphy's Law had decided to play with me.

I realized Murphy's Law was becoming a permanent part of my life. 5
If something in my life could possibly go wrong, Murphy would be there to make sure of it. I had finally come to the conclusion that Murphy, and I would be friends for life--unless, of course, something went wrong.

1. What main idea do you think Taleah is trying to communicate in this essay? ______________________

   Does her thesis communicate this main idea? ______________________

2. How is each of Taleah's examples related to her main point? List three examples she furnishes, and explain how they are related to her thesis statement. ______________________

   ______________________

   ______________________

3. Knowing that this essay was written for her college writing class, do you think Taleah's audience could identify with these examples? Explain your answer. ______________________

   ______________________

4. Does Taleah include enough examples to make her point? Explain your answer. ______________________

   ______________________

   ______________________

5. How are the examples in Taleah's essay arranged? List some of her examples in the order they appear; then identify her method of organization.

   ______________________ ______________________

   ______________________ ______________________

______________________ ______________________

Method of organization: ______________________

## REVISING AND EDITING A STUDENT ESSAY

This essay is Taleah's first draft, which now needs to be revised and edited. First, apply the Revising Checklist below to Taleah's draft so that you are working with her content. When you are satisfied that her ideas are fully developed and well organized, use the Editing Checklist on page 174 to correct her grammar and mechanics errors. Answer the questions after each checklist. Then write your suggested changes directly on Taleah's draft.

### Revising Checklist

**THESIS STATEMENT**

✔ Does the thesis statement contain the essay's controlling idea and appear as the last sentence of the introduction?

**BASIC ELEMENTS**

✔ Does the title draw in the readers?

✔ Does the introduction capture the readers' attention and build up to the thesis statement effectively?

✔ Does each body paragraph deal with a single topic?

✔ Does the conclusion bring the essay to a close in an interesting way?

**DEVELOPMENT**

✔ Do the body paragraphs adequately support the thesis statement?

✔ Does each body paragraph have a focused topic sentence?

✔ Does each body paragraph contain *specific* details that support the topic sentence?

✔ Does each body paragraph include *enough* details to explain the topic sentence fully?

**UNITY**

✔ Do the essay's topic sentences relate directly to the thesis statement?

✔ Do the details in each body paragraph support its topic sentence?

ORGANIZATION

✔ Is the essay organized logically?

✔ Is each body paragraph organized logically?

COHERENCE

✔ Are transitions used effectively so that paragraphs move smoothly and logically from one to the next?

✔ Do the sentences move smoothly and logically from one to the next?

## Thesis Statement

✔ Does the thesis statement contain the essay's controlling idea and appear as the last sentence of the introduction?

1. Put brackets around the last sentence in Taleah's introduction. Does it introduce her main point?

______________________________________________

2. Rewrite Taleah's thesis statement if necessary so that it states her main point and introduces her topics.

______________________________________________

______________________________________________

## Basic Elements

✔ Does the title draw in the readers?

✔ Does the introduction capture the readers' attention and build up to the thesis statement effectively?

✔ Does each body paragraph deal with a single topic?

✔ Does the conclusion bring the essay to a close in an interesting way?

1. Give Taleah's essay an alternate title. ______________________________

2. Rewrite Taleah's introduction so that it captures the readers' attention and builds up to the thesis statement at the end of the paragraph.

______________________________

______________________________

______________________________

3. Does each of Taleah's body paragraphs deal with only one topic? ______

4. Rewrite Taleah's conclusion using at least one suggestion from Part I.

______________________________

______________________________

______________________________

## Development

- ✔ Do the body paragraphs adequately support the thesis statement?
- ✔ Does each body paragraph have a focused topic sentence?
- ✔ Does each body paragraph contain *specific* details that support the topic sentence?
- ✔ Does each body paragraph include *enough* details to explain the topic sentence fully?

1. Write out Taleah's thesis statement (revised, if necessary), and list her three topic sentences below it.

   Thesis statement: ______________________________

   ______________________________

   Topic 1: ______________________________

   ______________________________

Topic 2: ____________________________________________

____________________________________________

Topic 3: ____________________________________________

____________________________________________

2. Do Taleah's topics adequately support her thesis statement? __________
3. Does each body paragraph have a focused topic sentence? __________
4. Are Taleah's examples specific?
   Add another more specific detail to one of the examples in her essay.
5. Does she offer enough examples to make her point?
   Add at least one new example to strengthen Taleah's essay.

## Unity

- ✔ Do the essay's topic sentences relate directly to the thesis statement?
- ✔ Do the details in each body paragraph support its topic sentence?

1. Read each of Taleah's topic sentences with her thesis statement (revised, if necessary) in mind. Do they go together? __________________
2. Revise them if necessary so they are directly related.
3. Drop or rewrite the two sentences in paragraph 2 that are not directly related to their topic sentence.

## Organization

- ✔ Is the essay organized logically?
- ✔ Is each body paragraph organized logically?

1. Read Taleah's essay again to see if all the paragraphs are arranged logically.
2. Move any paragraphs that are out of order.

3. Look closely at Taleah's body paragraphs to see if all her sentences are arranged logically within paragraphs.
4. Move any sentences that are out of order.

## Coherence

- ✔ Are transitions used effectively so that paragraphs move smoothly and logically from one to the next?
- ✔ Do the sentences move smoothly and logically from one to the next?

1. Circle five transitions, repetitions, synonyms, or pronouns Taleah uses.
2. Explain how two of these make Taleah's essay easier to read.

________________________________________________

________________________________________________

Now rewrite Taleah's essay with your revisions.

##  Editing Checklist

**Sentences**

- ✔ Does each sentence have a main subject and verb?
- ✔ Do all subjects and verbs agree?
- ✔ Do all pronouns agree with their nouns?
- ✔ Are modifiers as close as possible to the words they modify?

**Punctuation and Mechanics**

- ✔ Are sentences punctuated correctly?
- ✔ Are words capitalized properly?

**Word Choice and Spelling**

- ✔ Are words used correctly?
- ✔ Are words spelled correctly?

## Sentences

✔ Does each sentence have a main subject and verb?
For help with subjects and verbs, see Chapter 34.

1. Underline the subjects once and verbs twice in paragraph 2 of your revision of Taleah's essay. Remember that sentences can have more than one subject-verb set.
2. Does each of Taleah's sentences have at least one subject and verb that can stand alone? ______________
3. Did you find and correct Taleah's run-on sentence? If not, find and correct it now. For help with run-ons, see Chapter 36.

✔ Do all subjects and verbs agree?
For help with subject-verb agreement, see Chapter 39.

1. Read aloud the subjects and verbs you underlined in your revision of Taleah's essay.
2. Correct any subjects and verbs that do not agree.

✔ Do all pronouns agree with their nouns?
For help with pronoun agreement, see Chapter 43.

1. Find any pronouns in your revision of Taleah's essay that do not agree with their nouns.
2. Correct any pronouns that do not agree with their nouns.

✔ Are modifiers as close as possible to the words they modify?
For help with modifier errors, see Chapter 46.

1. Find any modifiers in your revision of Taleah's essay that are not as close as possible to the words they modify.
2. Did you find and correct her dangling modifier? If not, find and correct it now.

## Punctuation and Mechanics

> ✔ Are sentences punctuated correctly?
> For help with punctuation, see Chapters 47–51.

1. Read your revision of Taleah's essay for any errors in punctuation.
2. Find the run-on sentence you revised, and make sure it is punctuated correctly.
3. Did you find and correct Taleah's two comma errors?

> ✔ Are words capitalized properly?
> For help with capitalization, see Chapter 52.

1. Read your revision of Taleah's essay for any errors in capitalization.
2. Be sure to check Taleah's capitalization in the run-on you revised.

## Word Choice and Spelling

> ✔ Are words used correctly?
> For help with confused words, see Chapter 58.

1. Find any words used incorrectly in your revision of Taleah's essay.
2. Did you find and correct the three confused words in Taleah's essay. If not, find and correct them now.

> ✔ Are all words spelled correctly?
> For help with spelling, see Chapter 59.

1. Use spell-check and a dictionary to check the spelling in your revision of Taleah's essay.
2. Correct any misspelled words.

Now rewrite Taleah's essay again with your editing corrections.

## REVISING AND EDITING YOUR OWN ESSAY

Returning to the illustration you wrote earlier in this chapter, revise and edit your own writing. The checklists here will help you apply what you have learned to your essay.

### Revising

#### Thesis Statement

- ☐ Does the thesis statement contain the essay's controlling idea and appear as the last sentence of the introduction?

1. What is the main point you are trying to convey in your essay? ______________________________

2. Put brackets around the last sentence in your introduction. Does it convey your main point? ____________
3. Rewrite your thesis statement if necessary so that it states your main point and introduces your topics.

#### Basic Elements

- ☐ Does the title draw in the readers?
- ☐ Does the introduction capture the readers' attention and build up to the thesis statement effectively?
- ☐ Does each body paragraph deal with a single topic?
- ☐ Does the conclusion bring the essay to a close in an interesting way?

1. Give your essay a title if it doesn't have one. ______________________

2. Does your introduction capture your readers' attention and build up to your thesis statement at the end of the paragraph? ________________

3. Does each of your body paragraphs deal with only one topic? __________

4. Does your conclusion follow some of the suggestions offered in Part I?

______________________________________________

## Development

- ☐ Do the body paragraphs adequately support the thesis statement?
- ☐ Does each body paragraph have a focused topic sentence?
- ☐ Does each body paragraph contain *specific* details that support the topic sentence?
- ☐ Does each body paragraph include *enough* details to explain the topic sentence fully?

1. Write out your thesis statement (revised, if necessary), and list your topic sentences below it.

   Thesis statement: ______________________________________

   ______________________________________

   Topic 1: ______________________________________

   Topic 2: ______________________________________

   Topic 3: ______________________________________

2. Do your topics adequately support your thesis statement? ____________

3. Does each body paragraph have a focused topic sentence? ____________

4. Are your examples specific? Add another more specific detail to an example in your essay.

5. Do you give enough examples to make your point? Add at least one new example to your essay.

6. Can your readers identify with your examples? ____________________

## Unity

- ☐ Do the essay's topic sentences relate directly to the thesis statement?
- ☐ Do the details in each body paragraph support its topic sentence?

1. Read each of your topic sentences with your thesis statement in mind. Do they go together? ____________________
2. Revise them if necessary so they are directly related.
3. Drop or rewrite any of the sentences in your body paragraphs that are not directly related to their topic sentences.

## Organization

- ☐ Is the essay organized logically?
- ☐ Is each body paragraph organized logically?

1. Read your essay again to see if all the paragraphs are arranged logically.
2. Refer to your answers to the development questions. Then identify your method of organization: ____________________
3. Is the order you chose for your paragraphs the most effective approach to your topic? ____________________
4. Move any paragraphs that are out of order.
5. Look closely at your body paragraphs to see if all the sentences are arranged logically within paragraphs.
6. Move any sentences that are out of order.

## Coherence

- ☐ Are transitions used effectively so that paragraphs move smoothly and logically from one to the next?
- ☐ Do the sentences move smoothly and logically from one to the next?

1. Circle five transitions, repetitions, synonyms, or pronouns you use.
2. Explain how two of these make your essay easier to read.

______________________________________________

______________________________________________

Now rewrite your essay with your revisions.

# Editing

## Sentences

- ☐ Does each sentence have a main subject and verb?
  For help with subjects and verbs, see Chapter 34.

1. Underline the subjects once and verbs twice in a paragraph of your revised essay. Remember that sentences can have more than one subject-verb set.
2. Does each of your sentences have at least one subject and verb that can stand alone? ______________
3. Correct any fragments you have written. For help with fragments, see Chapter 35.
4. Correct any run-on sentences you have written. For help with run-ons, see Chapter 36.

- ☐ Do all subjects and verbs agree?
  For help with subject-verb agreement, see Chapter 39.

1. Read aloud the subjects and verbs you underlined in your revised essay.
2. Correct any subjects and verbs that do not agree.

☐ Do all pronouns agree with their nouns?
For help with pronoun agreement, see Chapter 43.

1. Find any pronouns in your revised essay that do not agree with their nouns.
2. Correct any pronouns that do not agree with their nouns.

☐ Are modifiers as close as possible to the words they modify?
For help with modifier errors, see Chapter 46.

1. Find any modifiers in your revised essay that are not as close as possible to the words they modify.
2. Rewrite sentences if necessary so that your modifiers are as close as possible to the words they modify.

## Punctuation and Mechanics

☐ Are sentences punctuated correctly?
For help with punctuation, see Chapters 47–51.

1. Read your revised essay for any errors in punctuation.
2. Make sure any fragments and run-ons you revised are punctuated correctly.

☐ Are words capitalized properly?
For help with capitalization, see Chapter 52.

1. Read your revised essay for any errors in capitalization.
2. Be sure to check your capitalization in any fragments or run-ons you revised.

## Word Choice and Spelling

☐ Are words used correctly?
For help with confused words, see Chapter 58.

1. Find any words used incorrectly in your revised essay.
2. Correct any errors you find.

☐ Are all words spelled correctly?
For help with spelling, see Chapter 59.

1. Use spell-check and a dictionary to check your spelling.
2. Correct any misspelled words.

Now rewrite your essay again with your editing corrections.

## READING SUGGESTIONS

In Chapter 27, you will find two essays that use examples to make their point: "I Just Wanna Be Average" by Mike Rose gives examples from his life to show the importance to him of being average, and "Getting to Know About You and Me" by Chana Schoenberger uses examples to talk about personal biases. You might want to read these selections before writing another illustration essay. As you read, notice how the writers use examples to support and advance their ideas.

## IDEAS FOR WRITING

**Guidelines for Writing an Illustration Essay**

1. State your main point in the last sentence of your introduction.
2. Choose examples that are relevant to your point.
3. Choose examples that your readers can identify with.
4. Use a sufficient number of examples to make your point.
5. Organize your examples to make your point in the clearest, strongest way.

1. Identify some common themes in this collage. Then come up with a thesis statement that explains the message of the collage. Write an essay that is developed with relevant examples from the picture and from your own experience to support your thesis statement.
2. Share with your classmates your opinion on a national issue, such as capital punishment, abortion, or gun laws. Use examples in your body paragraphs to support your main point.
3. Why do you think Americans are interested in exercise and weight loss? What actions illustrate this attitude? Use examples or illustrations to explain your observations on the current interest in health and weight among Americans.
4. Create your own illustration assignment (with the help of your instructor), and write a response to it.

## Revising Workshop

**Small Group Activity (5–10 minutes per writer)** In groups of three or four, each person should read his or her illustration essay to the other members of the group. Those listening should record their reactions on a copy of the Peer Evaluation Form in Appendix 2C. After your group goes through this process, give your evaluation forms to the appropriate writers so that each writer has two or three peer comment sheets for revising.

**Paired Activity (5 minutes per writer)** Using the completed Peer Evaluation Forms, work in pairs to decide what you should revise in your essay. If time allows, rewrite some of your sentences, and have your partner look at them.

**Individual Activity** Rewrite your paper, using the revising feedback you received from other students.

## Editing Workshop

**Paired Activity (5–10 minutes per writer)** Swap papers with a classmate, and use the editing portion of your Peer Evaluation Form to identify as many grammar, punctuation, mechanics, and spelling errors as you can. If time allows, correct some of your errors, and have your partner look at them. Record your grammar, punctuation, and mechanics errors in the Error Log (Appendix 6) and your spelling errors in the Spelling Log (Appendix 7).

**Individual Activity** Rewrite your paper again, using the editing feedback you received from other students.

## Reflecting on Your Writing

When you have completed your own essay, answer these six questions.

1. What was most difficult about this assignment?
2. What was easiest?
3. What did you learn about using illustrations by completing this assignment?
4. What do you think are the strengths of your illustration? Place a squiggly line by the parts of your essay that you feel are very good.
5. What are the weaknesses, if any, of your paper? Place an X by the parts of your essay you would like help with. Write any questions you have in the margin.
6. What did you learn from this assignment about your own writing process—about preparing to write, about writing the first draft, about revising, and about editing?

# Analyzing a Process

*I see but one rule: to be clear.*

—STENDHAL

Process analysis satisfies our natural desire for basic information—how to be more assertive, how the stock market works, how to eat more healthfully, or how to help your child do a better job in school.

Process analysis writing, more than other types of writing, helps you understand the world around you and improve yourself—in your personal life, in college, and in the workplace. Consider the following situations:

People who are coming to visit you from out of town e-mail you for directions to your house.

A student needs to write a paper on how to improve employee morale for a course in business management.

A student needs to explain how to be a good listener for the midterm exam in speech communication.

The owner of an apartment building posts a notice in the laundry room explaining how to operate the new washers and dryers.

The manager of a shoe store has to write a memo reminding employees about the correct procedure for taking returns.

**Process analysis** is a form of explaining. Process analysis essays fall into one of two main types—giving directions or giving information. The first type, giving directions, tells *how to do something,* such as how to write a research paper or change the oil in your car. The second type, giving information, analyzes *how something works,* such as satellite TV or a bread machine, or *how something happened,* such as how the Soviet Union broke into separate nations. In each case, the explanation starts at the beginning and moves step by step, usually in chronological order, to the end result. Process analysis can be about something mental (how to solve a math problem) or something physical (how to pitch a tent).

In "Dare to Change Your Job and Your Life in 7 Steps," Carole Kanchler explains how to take the right risks in order to change jobs and improve your life. In other words, the essay demonstrates the first type of process analysis: how to do something. Kanchler tells you what to do first, then second, and so on until reaching the desired outcome—success in a job you like. Have you ever held a job that you intensely disliked? Were you able to quit? Why or why not? Do you know what career you want to follow? What steps are you taking to prepare for it?

**Carole Kanchler**

## DARE TO CHANGE YOUR JOB AND YOUR LIFE IN 7 STEPS

1 Small, dark-haired, attractive and warm, Melissa belies her 44 years. In a sharp gray suit and becoming blouse, she projects a professional yet approachable image. She is now director of training and development for a large retail outlet—and loves it.

2 "I feel good about myself," she says, "and at the end of the day, I have lots of energy left over." Melissa feels content because she believes she is doing something worthwhile. Her new position gives her life meaning and purpose. But getting there wasn't easy.

3 First a flight attendant, then a high school English teacher, then a manager in a retail store, Melissa stumbled about from what was for her one dead-end job to another. How did she finally find a meaningful, fulfilling, well-paid career? And how did she do what so many of us fail to do—dare to change?

4 A career change can take months or even years of soul-searching—10 months in Melissa's case. You need to know the steps, how to master the troublesome feelings that accompany change, where the possible dangers lie, and how to maximize your gains while minimizing your losses. While creating a life worth living isn't easy, Melissa and millions of others have shown that anything is possible.

5 In interviews and surveys with more than 30,000 people over the past 25 years, I have identified seven steps that are key to a successful career and life shift.

## 1. Become AWARE of Negative Feelings

Your body and mind may be sending you messages about your job satisfaction. The messages may be physical—lingering colds, flu or headaches—or verbal—"23 minutes till lunch!" or "One more day till Friday!" 6

Perhaps you've been working for several years in your job and it appears to be going well. You've had steady promotions, praise from superiors and admiration from colleagues. Then one day you get a queasy feeling that something is lacking. But what? You run the film of your life in reverse but you can't figure it out. These feelings may persist for months or even years, depending on your ability to tolerate them, but, sooner or later, you have to admit you have a problem. 7

## 2. DEFINE the Problem

A good written definition of your problem can help to put you on the road toward change. 8

First, ask yourself, "What's making me feel this way? What is it about my situation that is unpleasant? Does this job help me reach my goals?" If not, why? 9

Next, describe any barriers that may be blocking you from making a move—perhaps fear of change; fear of losing a secure income, pension or other benefits; fear that the change will interfere with your relationships; or fear that you'll lose power or status. 10

Fear is the result of conditioning, and because it is learned, it can be unlearned. Reprogram your old attitudes and beliefs with new ones by learning and practicing specific ways to overcome the fears blocking your path toward change. Think of FEAR as an acronym for "False Expectations Appear Real." Don't spend time worrying about what *might* happen. Focus on the now. 11

## 3. Listen to AMBIVALENCE

Milton, a rehabilitation counselor, was approached by a prospective partner to start an executive recruitment agency. For weeks before making the move, he went straight to bed immediately after dinner and pulled the sheets up over his head. He tried to make light of this behavior, but he had undertaken many risks before and had never felt this way about them. 12

His underlying fears were prophetic. He later discovered that the hard-sell, aggressive style required for executive recruiting was not for him. The difference in basic values between Milton and his partner proved such a handicap that, within five months, the two parted ways. 13

The decision to change can provoke mixed feelings. A certain amount of ambivalence is natural. Inner emotional preparation—weighing losses as well as gains, fears as well as hopes—is a necessary prerequisite for successful risk taking. 14

15 But if the prospect of undertaking a change is so great that your stomach is churning, you can't sleep, you have constant headaches or you feel you're developing an ulcer, your body, in its wisdom, is telling you to forgo the risk.

### 4. PREPARE for Risk

16 The key to avoiding potential potholes is to set tentative career goals before you explore new roads. Goals force you to focus on what you really want. Years from now, as you review your life, what would you regret not having done?

17 Fantasize about the ultimate goal, your shining star. If you could do anything in the world, what would it be? Write all of your ideas or fantasies in a notebook. Include everything you want to do, be and have. The sky is the limit. Once you know what you want, you'll be more willing to take the risks necessary to achieve it.

18 Choosing a satisfying career and lifestyle also requires a basic understanding of yourself. A variety of exercises can help. To identify your strengths, for example, list some of the successes you've had—say, substituting for your son's soccer coach. Next to each success, identify what gave you the positive feelings. Did you contribute to the team's first win of the season?

19 Also list the skills and abilities you used to bring about that success. Were you well organized and adept at working with parents? Finally, decide how your interests, needs, accomplishments and other personal strengths add up. What pattern do they form?

20 Self-exploration is just part of the process. You also need to take a careful look at your current situation, as well as the available alternatives. Some popular reference tools, available at your local library, can help. Check out the *Occupational Handbook,* the *Dictionary of Occupational Titles* and the *Encyclopedia of Careers and Work Issues.* The Internet also offers excellent sites for exploring general occupational fields, job descriptions and educational opportunities.

### 5. NARROW Your Options

21 Successful career management hinges on finding a position that's compatible with your personal qualities and goals. Do you have the necessary intelligence and skills to do the work? Can you afford the training required for the job? Might your shortcomings—health, vision, size or strength, for example—pose a problem?

22 To help narrow your options, draw a series of vertical and horizontal lines so that your paper is divided into squares. Across the top of the page, list the most important elements of your ideal job: income, responsibility, public image, creativity, challenge and so on (one in each square). Down the left side of the page, list each occupational option you're considering.

Next, for each alternative, place a −1 in the appropriate box if that job option doesn't satisfy the criterion listed at the top of the page. If the criterion is met, but not as much as you'd like, record a 0. If the criterion is well met, record a +1. Add the points for each job option and place them in a column labeled "total" at the far right. The job with the highest score meets the greatest number of criteria that you have deemed important. 23

## 6. Take ACTION

Once you've determined your occupational goal, take steps to realize it. You'll need a well-planned campaign to market yourself for the job, establish your own business or return to school. 24

Stay focused on your goals and believe you will achieve them. View failures along the way as learning experiences—detours that might offer an unexpected dividend. 25

## 7. EVALUATE the Decision

When you have worked hard at making a decision, take the time not just to enjoy the outcome, but to evaluate it. Ask yourself: 26

- Do I feel good about the move?
- What other gains did I derive from the move? What did I lose?
- What factors contributed to the success of my move?
- If could do it all over again, what would I do differently?
- Who was most helpful in the process? Who let me down?

Evaluation is a continuous process. Assess your needs, goals, and job satisfaction periodically to determine if your developing personality fits your position and lifestyle. Don't wait for a crisis to clear your vision. 27

There really is no substitute for risk as a way to grow. Knowing you have honestly faced the painful struggle and accepted the trade-offs, and yet proceeded in spite of them, is extremely gratifying. 28

Melissa learned that the tremendous investment of energy a successful job search demands is exactly what enables people to look back and say, "Win, lose or draw, I gave it my everything." Being able to say with satisfaction that you risked for a dream may be the biggest prize of all. 29

To remain fulfilled, however, you'll need to risk again and again until you've created a life in which you feel comfortable being yourself, without apology or pretense—a life in which you can continue to have choices. 30

*Preparing to Write Your Own Process Analysis*

Think of some advice that you would like to give to a friend or classmate—for example, how to survive your first year of college, how to find the partner of your dreams, how to buy a used car, or how to find good day care for your child. Use one or more of the prewriting strategies you learned in Chapter 2 to generate ideas about advice you have for others.

## HOW TO WRITE A PROCESS ANALYSIS ESSAY

Both types of a process analysis call for careful step-by-step thinking, but especially the first—how to do something. If you leave out even one detail, you may confuse your reader or even endanger someone's life. If, for example, you forget to tell a patient who is coming to a doctor's office for some tests that she shouldn't eat after midnight and she has breakfast, the test results will not be accurate, and a serious medical condition might go unnoticed.

Good process analysis of the second type—how something works or how something happened—can help your reader see a product or an event in a totally new light. Someone looking at a product that is already assembled or at a completed event has no way of knowing how it got to the final stage without an explanation. Good process analysis gives the reader a new way of "seeing" something. The following guidelines will help you write clear and complete process analysis essays.

1. ***State in the thesis statement what the reader should be able to do or understand by the end of the essay.*** Stating the end result at the beginning, in the thesis statement, gives your readers a road map for what follows. The thesis statement in a process essay should also state the number of steps or stages in the process. For example, someone giving directions might start by saying, "It's easy to get to the library from here with just four turns." Even if a process involves many separate steps, you should divide the list into a few manageable groups: "Most experts agree that there are four stages in overcoming an addiction." Stating the end result and the number of steps or stages in the thesis statement helps the reader follow your explanation. These statements set up the tasks.

   Carole Kanchler's thesis statement, which appears in paragraph 5, at the end of her introduction, tells her readers exactly what they will be able to do by the end of her article: make "a successful career and life shift." She also tells them how many steps are involved—seven. In this way, she gives a very clear road map for reading her essay.

2. ***Know your audience.*** In a process analysis essay, more than in others, the success of your essay depends on how well you know your audience. Knowing your audience helps you decide how much detail to include, how many examples to add, and which terms to define. Also keep in mind that your readers won't be able to ask you questions, so if they can't follow your explanation, they will become confused and frustrated. Whoever your audience is, explaining clearly is essential.

   Kanchler's essay was first published in *Psychology Today*, which is read mostly by educated adults. The author's audience seems to be working adults of any age who are unhappy in their jobs. Kanchler addresses them in a very businesslike way; she doesn't talk down. Knowing that being unhappy in a job is very depressing, she strives for an upbeat "you can do it" tone.

3. ***Explain the process clearly in the body of your essay.*** By the end of a how-to essay, the reader should be able to perform the activity. By the end of a how-something-works essay, the reader should understand what is going on behind the scenes, and by the end of a how-something-happened essay, the reader should understand more about a specific event.

   In writing the body paragraphs of a process essay, pay special attention to transitions. Use transitions such as *first, next, then, after that*, and *finally* to guide your readers through the process, from beginning to end.

   Since Kanchler's process has seven parts, she numbers each step. This is a good idea if a process is complicated. If you are writing about a process with only three or four steps, you can use transitions to indicate to your readers where you are in the process.

4. ***Organize your material logically.*** Most process analysis essays are organized chronologically or according to a time sequence. The explanation starts at one point and progresses through time to the final point. If a process is complicated, figure out the most logical organization for the process you are explaining. For instance, playing the guitar involves pressing the strings with the fingers of one hand and strumming with the other hand. You might therefore explain each part of the process separately and then explain how the hands work together to make music.

Kanchler's essay is organized chronologically. She moves from recognizing the problem to taking action and then to evaluating the action. To help readers follow along smoothly, she numbers the steps and uses transitions such as *first*, *next*, and *then*.

5. ***End your essay by considering the process as a whole.*** Don't just stop after you have explained the last step of a process. Instead, in the conclusion, look at the process as a whole. There are many ways to do this. You might state why knowing about this process is important: Knowing how to perform CPR (cardiopulmonary respiration) can save a life; knowing how your car runs might save you money in repair bills. Or you might review your introduction, summarize the steps of the process, call for action, or end with a fitting quotation. Whatever your method, leave your reader feeling that your essay has reached a natural close.

   Kanchler concludes by returning to her introduction. She brings back Melissa, the person from the opening example, to emphasize the rewards of taking risks. She ends her essay by saying that a satisfying life requires taking risks again and again.

### *Writing Your Own Process Analysis Essay*

Look at the prewriting you did earlier on the topic of giving advice to a friend or classmate. If your directions involve many steps, divide them into three groups. Come up with a thesis statement that states the end result of the process and tells how many steps or stages are involved. Then write the first draft of your essay by following the guidelines for writing a process analysis essay. Make sure you have an introduction and a conclusion.

## PROCESS ANALYSIS AT WORK

A student writer named Emily Bliss wrote the following essay about procrastination. See if you can follow her steps.

**You Too Can Procrastinate**

1 My name is Emily, and I am a procrastinator. But I have discovered over the years that procrastination is not all bad. Especially when I have to write. At my college, the English instructors requires rough drafts. I have somehow mastered the art of procrastinating but still meeting

deadlines with my papers. So I have perfected a successful plan for procrastinating that I now want to share with the world.

You will know the dreaded day you have to write has arrived when you wake up with a start. This day is different from the rest. You actually have to do something about your paper today. But whatever you do, resist the temptation to sit down and write early in the day by following two more steps. First (step 2), to avoid sitting down to write, you can clean, take a bike ride, do the laundry, rearrange the furniture, dust the light bulbs, and so on. But don't write. Then (step 3), when you finally think you are ready to start writing, call a friend. Talk about anything but your paper for about 15 or 20 minutes. This final delay is what creates the tension that a real procrastinator needs to do his or her best work. 2

First, you will naturally think about the assignment from the moment you get it whether you want to or not. If you have two weeks or two months, you will spend most quiet moments haunted by your paper topic. No matter what you do, your paper topic will be bouncing around in your head giving you headaches, making you worry, wanting attention. But that's OK. Don't give in and write. Ignore it until the day before it is due. 3

At this point, your fourth step is to prepare your immediate environment for work. You need to get ready for serious business. Sharpen your pencils, and lay them in a row. Get out the white paper if you can't think on yellow, or get out the yellow paper if you ca'nt think on white. Go to the kitchen for snacks. Whether or not you actually drink or eat these item's is irrelevant—as long as they are by your side. You can't be distracted if you don't have them next to you. My stomach growls really loudly when I'm hungry. Some sort of bread usually takes away the hunger pangs. Step 5 is to sit back in your chair and stare at the computer while you think long and hard about your paper. Sixth, brainstorm, list, or cluster your ideas on the colored paper of your choice. Seventh, put all your procrastination strategies aside. It's finally time to write. 4

If you follow these seven simple steps, you too can become a master procrastinator. You can perform your very own procrastinating ritual and still get your first draft in on time. If you go through the same ritual every time you write. You can perfect it and get your own system for writing essays down to a science. The trick is just to make sure you start writing before you has to join Procrastinators Anonymous. 5

1. What should the reader be able to do by the end of this essay?

______________________________________________

2. Who do you think Emily's audience is? Does she meet their needs?

_______________

_______________

3. Do you understand how to procrastinate and still meet your deadlines? If so, list the seven steps of this process.

Step 1: _______________

Step 2: _______________

Step 3: _______________

Step 4: _______________

Step 5: _______________

Step 6: _______________

Step 7: _______________

If you do not understand, what else do you need to know?

_______________

4. Are the details in the essay organized logically? Is this order effective for what the author is trying to say? Why or why not?

_______________

_______________

5. Does the essay conclude by considering the process as a whole? Explain your answer.

_______________

_______________

_______________

## REVISING AND EDITING A STUDENT ESSAY

This essay is Emily's first draft, which now needs to be revised and edited. First, apply the Revising Checklist below to Emily's draft so that you are working with her content. When you are satisfied that her ideas are fully developed and well organized, use the Editing Checklist on page 199 to correct her grammar and mechanics errors. Answer the questions after each checklist. Then write your suggested changes directly on Emily's draft.

### Revising Checklist

**THESIS STATEMENT**

✔ Does the thesis statement contain the essay's controlling idea and appear as the last sentence of the introduction?

**BASIC ELEMENTS**

✔ Does the title draw in the readers?

✔ Does the introduction capture the readers' attention and build up to the thesis statement effectively?

✔ Does each body paragraph deal with a single topic?

✔ Does the conclusion bring the essay to a close in an interesting way?

**DEVELOPMENT**

✔ Do the body paragraphs adequately support the thesis statement?

✔ Does each body paragraph have a focused topic sentence?

✔ Does each body paragraph contain *specific* details that support the topic sentence?

✔ Does each body paragraph include *enough* details to explain the topic sentence fully?

**UNITY**

✔ Do the essay's topic sentences relate directly to the thesis statement?

✔ Do the details in each body paragraph support its topic sentence?

**ORGANIZATION**

✔ Is the essay organized logically?

✔ Is each body paragraph organized logically?

COHERENCE

- ✔ Are transitions used effectively so that paragraphs move smoothly and logically from one to the next?
- ✔ Do the sentences move smoothly and logically from one to the next?

## Thesis Statement

- ✔ Does the thesis statement contain the essay's controlling idea and appear as the last sentence of the introduction?

1. Put brackets around the last sentence in Emily's introduction. Does it state her purpose? ______________________________

2. Rewrite Emily's thesis statement if necessary so that it states her purpose and introduces her topics.

______________________________

______________________________

## Basic Elements

- ✔ Does the title draw in the readers?
- ✔ Does the introduction capture the readers' attention and build up to the thesis statement effectively?
- ✔ Does each body paragraph deal with a single topic?
- ✔ Does the conclusion bring the essay to a close in an interesting way?

1. Give Emily's essay an alternate title. ______________________________

2. Rewrite Emily's introduction so that it captures the readers' attention and builds up to the thesis statement at the end of the introduction.

______________________________

______________________________

______________________________________________

______________________________________________

3. Does each of Emily's body paragraphs deal with only one topic? _______

4. Rewrite Emily's conclusion using at least one suggestion from Part I.

______________________________________________

______________________________________________

______________________________________________

______________________________________________

## Development

- ✔ Do the body paragraphs adequately support the thesis statement?
- ✔ Does each body paragraph have a focused topic sentence?
- ✔ Does each body paragraph contain *specific* details that support the topic sentence?
- ✔ Does each body paragraph include *enough* details to explain the topic sentence fully?

1. Write out Emily's thesis statement (revised, if necessary), and list her three topic sentences below it.

   Thesis statement: ______________________________________________

   ______________________________________________

   Topic 1: ______________________________________________

   ______________________________________________

   Topic 2: ______________________________________________

   ______________________________________________

Topic 3: ______________________________________________

______________________________________________

2. Do Emily's topics adequately support her thesis statement? __________

3. Do Emily's details in the essay explain the process step by step? ________

4. Where do you need more information?

______________________________________________

5. Add at least two new details to make the steps clearer. ______________

## Unity

> ✔ Do the essay's topic sentences relate directly to the thesis statement?
> ✔ Do the details in each body paragraph support its topic sentence?

1. Read each of Emily's topic sentences with her thesis statement (revised, if necessary) in mind. Do they go together? ______________
2. Revise them if necessary so they are directly related.
3. Drop or rewrite the two sentences in paragraph 4 that are not directly related to their topic sentence.

## Organization

> ✔ Is the essay organized logically?
> ✔ Is each essay paragraph organized logically?

1. Read Emily's essay again to see if all the paragraphs are arranged logically. Look at your list of steps in response to question 3 after Emily's essay.
2. Reverse the two paragraphs that are out of order.
3. Look closely at Emily's body paragraphs to see if all her sentences are arranged logically within paragraphs.
4. Move any sentences that are out of order.

## Coherence

✔ Are transitions used effectively so that paragraphs move smoothly and logically from one to the next?

✔ Do the sentences move smoothly and logically from one to the next?

1. Circle five transitions Emily uses. For a list of transitions, see page 00.
2. Explain how two of these make Emily's essay easier to read.

_______________________________________________

_______________________________________________

Now rewrite Emily's essay with your revisions.

## Editing Checklist

**Sentences**

✔ Does each sentence have a main subject and verb?

✔ Do all subjects and verbs agree?

✔ Do all pronouns agree with their nouns?

✔ Are modifiers as close as possible to the words they modify?

**Punctuation and Mechanics**

✔ Are sentences punctuated correctly?

✔ Are words capitalized properly?

**Word Choice and Spelling**

✔ Are words used correctly?

✔ Are words spelled correctly?

## Sentences

✔ Does each sentence have a main subject and verb?

For help with subjects and verbs, see Chapter 34.

1. Underline the subjects once and verbs twice in paragraphs 1 and 5 of your revision of Emily's essay. Remember that sentences can have more than one subject-verb set.
2. Does each of the sentences have at least one subject and verb that can stand alone? ______________
3. Did you find and correct Emily's two fragments? If not, find and correct them now. For help with fragments, see Chapter 35.

✔ Do all subjects and verbs agree?

For help with subject-verb agreement, see Chapter 39.

1. Read aloud the subjects and verbs you underlined in your revision of Emily's essay.
2. Did you find and correct the two subjects and verbs that do not agree? If not, find and correct them now.

✔ Do all pronouns agree with their nouns?

For help with pronoun agreement, see Chapter 43.

1. Find any pronouns in your revision of Emily's essay that do not agree with their nouns.
2. Correct any pronouns that do not agree with their nouns.

✔ Are modifiers as close as possible to the words they modify?

For help with modifier errors, see Chapter 46.

1. Find any modifiers in your revision of Emily's essay that are not as close as possible to the words they modify.
2. Rewrite sentences if necessary so that modifiers are as close as possible to the words they modify.

## Punctuation and Mechanics

✔ Are sentences punctuated correctly?
For help with punctuation, see Chapters 47–51.

1. Read your revision of Emily's essay for any errors in punctuation.
2. Find the two fragments you revised, and make sure they are punctuated correctly.
3. Did you find and correct Emily's two apostrophe errors? If not, find and correct them now.

✔ Are words capitalized properly?
For help with capitalization, see Chapter 52.

1. Read your revision of Emily's essay for any errors in capitalization.
2. Be sure to check Emily's capitalization in the fragments you revised.

## Word Choice and Spelling

✔ Are words used correctly?
For help with confused words, see Chapter 58.

1. Find any words used incorrectly in your revision of Emily's essay.
2. Correct any errors you find.

✔ Are all words spelled correctly?
For help with spelling, see Chapter 59.

1. Use spell-check or a dictionary to check the spelling in your revision of Emily's essay.
2. Correct any misspelled words.

Now rewrite Emily's essay again with your editing corrections.

# REVISING AND EDITING YOUR OWN ESSAY

Returning to the process analysis you wrote earlier in this chapter, revise and edit your own writing. The checklists here will help you apply what you have learned to your essay.

## Revising

### Thesis Statement

- ☐ Does the thesis statement contain the essay's controlling idea and appear as the last sentence of the introduction?

1. What is your purpose in the essay?

   ______________________________

2. Put brackets around the last sentence in your introduction. Does it state your purpose? ______________________________

3. Revise your thesis statement if necessary so that it states your purpose and introduces your topics.

### Basic Elements

- ☐ Does the title draw in the readers?
- ☐ Does the introduction capture the readers' attention and build up to the thesis statement effectively?
- ☐ Does each body paragraph deal with a single topic?
- ☐ Does the conclusion bring the essay to a close in an interesting way?

1. Give your essay a title if it doesn't have one. ______________________

2. Does your introduction capture your readers' attention and build up to your thesis statement at the end of the paragraph?

3. Does each of your paragraphs deal with only one topic? ____________

4. Does your conclusion follow some of the suggestions offered in Part I?

____________________________________________

## Development

- ☐ Do the body paragraphs adequately support the thesis statement?
- ☐ Does each body paragraph have a focused topic sentence?
- ☐ Does each body paragraph contain *specific* details that support the topic sentence?
- ☐ Does each body paragraph include *enough* details to explain the topic sentence fully?

1. Write out your thesis statement (revised, if necessary), and list your topic sentences below it.

   Thesis statement: ____________________________________

   Topic 1: ____________________________________

   ____________________________________

   Topic 2: ____________________________________

   ____________________________________

   Topic 3: ____________________________________

   ____________________________________

2. Do your topics adequately support your thesis statement? ____________

3. Does each body paragraph have a focused topic sentence? ____________

4. Do the details in your essay explain the process step by step? __________

5. Where do you need more information?

   ____________________________________________

6. Add at least two new details to make the steps clearer.

## Unity

- ☐ Do the essay's topic sentences relate directly to the thesis statement?
- ☐ Do the details in each body paragraph support its topic sentence?

1. Read each of your topic sentences with your thesis statement in mind. Do they go together?
2. Revise them if necessary so they are directly related.
3. Drop or rewrite any of the sentences in your body paragraphs that are not directly related to their topic sentences.

## Organization

- ☐ Is the essay organized logically?
- ☐ Is each body paragraph organized logically?

1. List the steps in your essay to make sure your process analysis is in chronological order.
2. Move any steps or paragraphs that are out of order.
3. What word clues help your readers move logically through your paragraph?

   ______________________________

4. Look closely at your body paragraphs to see if all the sentences are arranged logically within paragraphs.
5. Move any sentences that are out of order.

## Coherence

- ☐ Are transitions used effectively so that paragraphs move smoothly and logically from one to the next?
- ☐ Do the sentences move smoothly and logically from one to the next?

1. Circle five transitions you use. For a list of transitions, see page 84.
2. Explain how two of these make your essay easier to read.

_______________________________________________

_______________________________________________

Now rewrite your essay with your revisions.

## Editing

### Sentences

☐ Does each sentence have a main subject and verb?
For help with subjects and verbs, see Chapter 34.

1. Underline your subjects once and verbs twice in a paragraph of your revised essay. Remember that sentences can have more than one subject-verb set.
2. Does each of your sentences have at least one subject and verb that can stand alone? ______________
3. Correct any fragments you have written. For help with fragments, see Chapter 35.
4. Correct any run-on sentences you have written. For help with run-ons, see Chapter 36.

☐ Do all subjects and verbs agree?
For help with subject-verb agreement, see Chapter 39.

1. Read aloud the subjects and verbs you underlined in your revised essay.
2. Correct any subjects and verbs that do not agree.

☐ Do all pronouns agree with their nouns?
For help with pronoun agreement, see Chapter 43.

1. Find any pronouns in your revised essay that do not agree with their nouns.
2. Correct any pronouns that do not agree with their nouns.

☐ Are modifiers as close as possible to the words they modify?
For help with modifier errors, see Chapter 46.

1. Find any modifiers in your revised essay that are not as close as possible to the words they modify.
2. Rewrite sentences if necessary so that your modifiers are as close as possible to the words they modify.

## Punctuation and Mechanics

☐ Are sentences punctuated correctly?
For help with punctuation, see Chapters 47–51.

1. Read your revised essay for any errors in punctuation.
2. Make sure any fragments and run-ons you revised are punctuated correctly.

☐ Are words capitalized properly?
For help with capitalization, see Chapter 52.

1. Read your revised essay for any errors in capitalization.
2. Be sure to check your capitalization in any fragments or run-ons you revised.

## Word Choice and Spelling

☐ Are words used correctly?
For help with confused words, see Chapter 58.

1. Find any words used incorrectly in your revised essay.
2. Correct any errors you find.

☐ Are all words spelled correctly?

For help with spelling, see Chapter 59.

1. Use spell-check or a dictionary to check your spelling.
2. Correct any misspelled words.

Now rewrite your essay again with your editing corrections.

## READING SUGGESTIONS

In Chapter 28, you will find two essays that illustrate good process analysis writing: "Don't Be Cruel" by Roger Flax explains how to criticize people without humiliating them, and "Access Activism" by Geeta Dardick explains the origins of the Americans with Disabilities Act (ADA). You might want to read these selections before writing another process analysis essay. As you read, notice how the writers explain every step of the process carefully and completely.

## IDEAS FOR WRITING

**Guidelines for Writing a Process Analysis Essay**

1. State in the thesis statement what the reader should be able to do or understand by the end of the essay.
2. Know your audience.
3. Explain the process clearly in the body of your essay.
4. Organize your material logically.
5. End your essay by considering the process as a whole.

1. Place yourself in a scene similar to the one on the next page, and write a process analysis essay explaining something that you find as interesting as this person finds this activity. Be sure to cover all steps or stages of the process you are discussing.
2. Choose an appliance or a piece of equipment that you understand well, and write a process analysis essay explaining how it works. Don't identify

the item in your essay. Then see if the class members can guess what device you are talking about.

3. Research the history of your college or university, and write an essay explaining its background to prospective students. Be sure to give a focus to your study and decide on a purpose before you begin writing.
4. Write your own process analysis assignment (with the help of your instructor), and write a response to it.

## Revising Workshop

**Small Group Activity (5–10 minutes per writer)** In groups of three or four, each person should read his or her process analysis essay to the other members of the group. Those listening should record their reactions on a copy of the Peer Evaluation Form in Appendix 2D. After your group goes through this process, give your evaluation forms to the appropriate writers so that each writer has two or three peer comment sheets for revising.

**Paired Activity (5 minutes per writer)** Using the completed Peer Evaluation Forms, work in pairs to decide what you should revise in your essay. If time allows, rewrite some of your sentences, and have your partner look at them.

**Individual Activity** Rewrite your paper, using the revising feedback you received from other students.

## Editing Workshop

**Paired Activity (5–10 minutes per writer)** Swap papers with a classmate, and use the editing portion of your Peer Evaluation Form to identify as many grammar, punctuation, mechanics, and spelling errors as you can. If time allows, correct some of your errors, and have your partner look at them. Record your grammar, punctuation, and mechanics errors in the Error Log (Appendix 6) and your spelling errors in the Spelling Log (Appendix 7).

**Individual Activity** Rewrite your paper again, using the editing feedback you received from other students.

## Reflecting on Your Writing

When you have completed your own essay, answer these six questions.

1. What was most difficult about this assignment?
2. What was easiest?
3. What did you learn about process analysis by completing this assignment?
4. What do you think are the strengths of your process analysis? Place a squiggly line by the parts of your essay that you feel are very good.
5. What are the weaknesses, if any, of your paper? Place an X by the parts of your essay you would like help with. Write any questions you have in the margin.
6. What did you learn from this assignment about your own writing process—about preparing to write, about writing the first draft, about revising, and about editing?

# Chapter 13: Comparing and Contrasting

*The difference between the right word and the almost-right word is really a large matter—'tis the difference between the lightning-bug and the lightning.*

—Mark Twain

Comparison and contrast are at the heart of our democratic society. Our competitive natures encourage us to compare our lives to those of others so we can try to better ourselves. Even if we simply attempt to improve on our "personal best," comparison and contrast keep us striving for more. In school, we learn about different writers, different cultures, different musical instruments, and different political platforms by comparing them to one another. And every day we make decisions based on comparisons of one sort or another—which clothes we should wear, which person we should date, which apartment we should rent, which job we should take. Comparisons help us establish a frame of reference and figure out where we fit into the larger world around us.

On another level, comparison and contrast are also part of our writing. They play an important role in our personal lives, in our college courses, and in the workplace. Think about these situations:

Someone looking for a new car does comparison shopping on the Internet.

A student doing a report in a nursing course compares and contrasts traditional and alternative approaches to medical care.

A student compares and contrasts two Native American cultures for an exam in anthropology.

An insurance agent prepares a report for a client that compares and contrasts several different insurance policies.

A travel agent compares and contrasts two travel packages for a client.

**Comparison and contrast** help us understand one subject by putting it next to another. When we *compare*, we look for similarities, and when we *contrast*, we look for differences. Nearly always, however, comparison and contrast are part of the same process. For this reason, we often use the word *compare* to refer to both techniques.

In the essay "Thrills and Chills," Eric Minton compares and contrasts roller coasters and haunted houses to show how amusement parks play on our deepest fears. Do you like being scared? Do you like roller coasters and haunted houses? Are they a means of escape for you?

**Eric Minton**

## THRILLS AND CHILLS

In Orlando, Florida, David Clevinger stands in a back corridor of *Terror on Church Street* and listens expectantly as customers make their way through the haunted house's passages. Suddenly screams erupt, sending Clevinger, the attraction's artistic director and operations manager, into gales of glee. "I love that sound," he chortles. So does Dave Focke. Watching shrieking riders hurtle through the drops of *The Beast,* the massive wooden coaster at Paramount's Kings Island near Cincinnati, Ohio, Focke beams with pride. "Guests come off breathless, hearts pounding, scared out of their wits," exults Focke, the park's vice president of construction and maintenance. "And wanting to get in line to go again!" 1

Call them shockmeisters, terror tacticians, spookologists and boo-ologists. The small band of designers who create the roller coasters and haunted houses that are amusement parks' premier attractions are master manipulators of our deepest fears. They get us to walk through pitch black hallways and step into cutaway coaster cars that dangle our arms and legs. They exploit our most closely held vulnerabilities—and make us like it. 2

For designers, primarily engineers for coasters and theatrical artists for haunted houses, turning fear into fun depends on illusion. No matter how precarious a roller coaster or alarming a haunted house may appear, it must be totally safe. "We always try to make them look and feel more dangerous than they 3 really are," says Michael Boodley, president of Great Coasters International, Inc., of Santa Cruz, California.

4 Though the experience offered by roller coasters and haunted houses diverges dramatically—it's the difference between pushing a wagon over a steep hill versus telling campfire ghost stories—the attractions are constructed of common elements. Both draw on all our senses, both rely on surprise for their shocks and both quote heavily from the movies (coasters replicate action-adventure perils, à la *Indiana Jones* and *Star Wars,* and haunted houses feature quasi-Frankensteins and *Friday the 13th* Jasons).

5 But the biggest common denominator is that the two feed on the same basic fear: loss of control. Once a coaster takes off, passengers can do nothing but sit, or on some rides stand, and scream. "The closest thing to compare it to is driving with an idiot," observes Boodley. Lynton Harris, director of *Madison Scare Garden,* an annual fright fest in New York City, also uses an auto analogy for haunted houses. "It's a hundred degrees outside, and you'd expect to get in a car and have air conditioning, and all of a sudden the heater gets turned on," he says. "Then the doors lock. Cocky as you are, you realize you're not in charge."

6 With roller coasters, the psychological games start before customers even get into the train. Boodley purposely makes his wooden coasters as diabolical looking as possible. "It's kind of like a black widow spider web," he explains. "It's a very, very pretty thing, but when the black widow gets you . . ." Queueing customers at *Outer Limits: Flights of Fear,* one of 12 coasters at Kings Island, are treated to dim lights, alien noises and a video of a space station in the grip of a mysterious force. "Even after having ridden that ride probably close to a hundred times, I sit there anticipating the start, and my palms still sweat," says *Outer Limits* designer Jim Seay, president of Premier Rides of Millersville, Maryland.

7 Whether the traditional chain-driven wooden or steel clackers or the newer linear induction motor (LIM) rides that harness electromagnetic force to blast off trains, all roller coasters play on two related—and universal—terrors: fear of heights and fear of falling. "The loops and elements, they come and go, but the coaster always has to have the big drop," says Focke of Kings Island.

8 Traditional coasters provide an excruciatingly slow buildup to the plunge. "There's a lot of self-abuse on that chain lift," says Boodley. "Your own mind puts you in a state of paralysis." (Wooden coasters also creak, rumble and clickity-clack naturally as they flex, but riders get a queasy feeling that the structure is about to collapse. "That's probably one of the funniest things we as designers get to appreciate," says Boodley.) LIMs, on the other hand, rocket you into terror with trains that go from 0 to 60 mph in under four seconds. The big drops are actually shorter on LIMs, but the sense of speed sets hearts pounding.

9 Most coasters travel below 70 miles an hour, slower than many people drive, but designers heighten the sense of speed and danger with close flybys of

terrain, buildings, people, even other trains. At Busch Gardens Tampa Bay, *Montu* dives riders into five trenches, one of which emerges through the patio of an ersatz Egyptian temple. "Not knowing exactly where the bottom is or where you come out is important," says Mark Rose, the park's vice president of design and engineering. "If you could see the whole thing, then you could kind of play it out in your mind." Some coasters, like *Outer Limits* and Disney World's *Space Mountain,* intensify the fear and suspense by keeping passengers in the dark for the entire ride.

Upping the vulnerability quotient even further is a recent innovation: inverted coasters which suspend riders below the track and carve away as much of the train as possible. "There is less fiberglass, less coach around you, so your feet are just hanging out there," notes Rose. During one stretch of track on *Montu,* passengers' soles skim just 24 inches above the ground. Riders also get dangled over a pit of live Nile crocodiles. 10

A coaster's effects, though, are not all illusory. Passengers pull close to 4 positive G's on some plummets. They turn upside down on loops and rotate head over heels through corkscrews. They literally feel the wind in their hair and, on a LIM coaster launch, the air in their eyes. Human bodies don't commonly experience such acrobatic maneuvers, and that in itself is psychologically disorienting. "Anytime you put riders in a situation they're not used to, there's an element of the unknown," declares Boodley. "And for 80% of people, fear is the unknown." 11

The biggest unknown of all is death, and creators of haunted houses are masters at exploiting our fear of dying, especially in a gruesome manner. To unnerve guests, designers depend on two elements. The first is setting a spooky mood with sights, sounds, smells and "feels"—"all the things that make you uneasy," says Drew Edward Hunter, co-chairman of the International Association of Haunted Attractions and design director of haunted attractions at Sally Corporation of Jacksonville, Florida. "Then you have the second part, the attack, the out-and-out scare. I don't think you can have one without the other." 12

For the "creep-out" effect, haunts are always dark; skeletons, skulls, fog, ticking clocks and screaming ghouls abound. "On my sets, I try to capture a claustrophobic feeling," says *Terror on Church Street's* Clevinger. "I bring my ceilings low, the walls close." To further emphasize the sense of enclosure, he hangs tree branches, Spanish moss, rags and spider webs. 13

Just the suggestion of something loathsome will give customers the screaming meemies. "Do the sounds of insects, and people scratch their heads all the way through," says John Denley, president and owner of Boneyard Productions of Salem, Massachusetts. Run a soundtrack that whispers of rats, turn on ankle-aimed air hoses and professional football players tap dance. A strong whiff of formaldehyde and you have the scent of death, "no matter what country you're in," says Clevinger. 14

15 The second part of the equation is the scare, which, say spookologists, is really a "startle." "All scares are primarily based on two things," instructs Edward Marks, president of Jets Productions of Chatsworth, California. "One, it's there and does something you don't expect it to do, or two, it's not there and it appears."

16 In *Terror on Church Street,* customers come upon Hannibal Lecter, the cannibal psychiatrist of *Silence of the Lambs*. He yells and lunges against his cell's bars, drawing yelps from viewers. The cries quickly subside into nervous tittering. As guests make their way around the bars, Lecter follows along inside. Then, just when viewers feel safest, Lecter opens the cage door and steps out. "The guys who were taunting him usually scream the loudest," observes Clevinger.

17 In the second type of gag, designers have people or objects suddenly emerge from in front, beside, above or below patrons. A surefire gag—and the simplest of all—is dropping a spider on a person's head. "We call that a $2 scare," says Harris of *Madison Scare Garden.* "It's the best value-for-money scare we've ever used."

18 Another never-fail gotcha goes by the generic term "UV Dot Man." Guests enter a dark room with ultraviolet dots on the wall (variations would be skeletons or geometric patterns). A black-masked actor wearing a black bodysuit, likewise bearing UV dots, stands against the wall and jumps out. "You are actually looking at him before he leaps out at you," Marks says. "It works every time, and it's so simple." (Another certain scare that designers hate, but feel compelled to use, is the hockey-masked goon waving a whirring chainsaw. Customers complain if a haunted house doesn't have one.)

19 For designers, combining the two types of gags may be the most satisfying scare of all. In his favorite trick, Denley once draped sheets over padding, topped them with masked and wigged heads, and attached the forms to the caging on oscillating fans. He plugged the fans into a power strip but left the cords clearly visible. These "monsters" started moving in unison when people entered the room. After the initial surprise, guests noticed the power strip and began mocking the amateurish setup. Suddenly, the middle white-sheeted monster—actually a man with one of the plugged-in extension cords tied to his leg—leaped out.

20 "It was hilarious," recalls a chuckling Denley, who is also known as Professor Nightmare. "We had a woman hyperventilate. We had people wet themselves. They thought they knew the gag—and, bam! we hit them with something totally different."Guests losing control of their bladders is considered a badge of honor among haunt producers. "We call it yellow control," Clevinger says. Getting an entire group to cower on the ground is another measure of success.

21 While the live actors who sometimes assume roles in haunted production are forbidden to touch patrons, they are encouraged to invade their personal space. "Everybody's got this wonderful circle around them," says Denley, who likes to have actors suddenly appear as close to a person as possible, then disappear. "We want to leave you thinking, 'What was that?'"

Designers also like to pick their victims. "We call it 'slicing the group,'" says Marks at Jets Productions. "We actually can single out a person from 20 people. A guy and girl clinging together—I can slice them apart with the right scare." A trained actor watches their body language, whether they tighten up, stare him down, or avert their eyes. 22

Male customers are a favorite target. "We try to take the guys who are hecklers and make examples of them," observes Denley. "If you nail them, the rest of the group will follow." Men also pose a special challenge. "Guys are harder to read than women," Denley explains. "They don't do body language as much. Women are more animated, more intent on being scared. Guys play it cool." Designers usually get them with strikes from above or below, but they're careful. Men sometimes lash out with their fists. 23

"The scariest things come from your mind," sums up Edward Hunter. "With the right setup, the right imagination, the right story, your mind creates things we couldn't possibly show you." "No matter how good the makeup or the costume, nothing is more effective than your imagination," echoes Denley. One proof: guests at *Terror on Church Street* scream loud and long when, at a particular point, they catch a glimpse of lurking monsters. The fiends: themselves, reflected in strategically placed mirrors. 24

***Preparing to Write Your Own Comparison/Contrast Essay***

Think of several ways you escape and relax. What do you like about these methods of relaxation? Use one or more of the prewriting strategies you learned in Chapter 2 to generate ideas about these forms of relaxation. Why do they work for you?

## HOW TO WRITE A COMPARISON/CONTRAST ESSAY

To write a comparison/contrast essay, you should consider two items that have something in common, such as cats and dogs (both are family pets) or cars and motorcycles (both are means of transportation). A discussion of cats and motorcycles, for example, would not be very interesting or useful because the two do not have common features. This is the basic rule underlying the following guidelines for writing a good comparison/contrast essay.

1. ***Decide what point you want to make with your comparison, and state it in your thesis statement.*** A comparison/contrast essay is usually written for one of two purposes: to examine the subjects separately or to show the superiority of one over the other. This purpose should be made clear in your thesis statement.

   In the sample essay, Minton's main idea is that the experience of roller coasters and of haunted houses plays in a similar manner on people's deepest fears. Minton makes the purpose of his essay clear in his thesis statement at the end of paragraph 2: "They exploit our most closely held vulnerabilities—and make us like it." This thesis promises to examine its subjects separately. If, however, this essay was going to show the superiority of one of its subjects over the other, its thesis statement might read something like this: "Although roller coasters and haunted houses both draw on our deepest fears, roller coasters are far more popular." In either case, readers would be interested in reading further to find out why they are attracted to roller coasters and haunted houses.

2. ***Choose items to compare and contrast that will make your point most effectively.*** Usually, the subjects you plan to compare and contrast have many similarities and differences. Your task, then, is to look over the ideas you generated in prewriting and choose the best points for making your comparison clearly and strongly.

   In his essay, Minton compares his subjects—roller coasters and haunted houses—on four points:

   Point 1: They draw on all five senses.
   Point 2: They rely on surprise.
   Point 3: They refer to movies.
   Point 4: They feed on loss of control.

3. ***Use as many specific details and examples as possible to expand your comparison.*** The most common way of developing a comparison/contrast essay is to use description and example. Generate as many details and examples as you can for each of your subjects. Try to think of both obvious and not-so-obvious points of comparison.

   In "Thrills and Chills," Minton relies heavily on description and examples. First, he describes both of these attractions with equal attention to detail throughout the essay. You can look at almost any body paragraph (paragraphs 6 to 23) in Minton's essay and find an example with vivid description. When he finally gets down to the common elements that make both of these subjects appeal to people who like to be scared, Minton makes his details more and more specific. Here is an example of his varying level of detail:

haunted houses
    fear of death
        spooky mood
        low ceilings
        close walls
        sound of insects
        smell of formaldehyde
    the attack
        unexpected action
        jumping from cage
        unexpected appearance
        spider
        "UV Dot Man"

These specific examples draw the readers into the essay.

4. ***Develop your comparison in a balanced way.*** Having selected the points on which you will compare your two subjects, you are ready to develop the comparison in your body paragraphs. You should make sure, however, that your treatment of each subject is balanced. That means, first, you cover the same topics for each subject. In other words, you should give equal coverage to both subjects, no matter what your conclusion is. In addition, you should spend the same amount of time on each point. If you describe one of your subjects in detail, you should also describe the other. In like manner, you should provide a similar number of examples for both subjects. In this way, your readers will feel that you have been fair to both subjects and that you are not presenting a biased discussion that favors one subject over the other.

   Minton covers all four of his points for both of his subjects and spends approximately the same amount of time developing both subjects. In discussing the ways that roller coasters make us feel out of control, for example, he names specific roller coasters and describes the way they build fear and suspense. Then he names specific haunted house attractions and describes how they "creep out" and scare people.

5. ***Organize your essay subject by subject or point by point—or combine the two approaches.*** When you are ready to write, you have three choices for organizing a comparison-and-contrast essay: (1) subject by subject (AAA, BBB), (2) point by point (AB, AB, AB), or (3) a combination of the two.

   In the subject arrangement, you say everything you have to say about the first subject, A, before you move on to talk about the second subject, B. In a point-by-point arrangement, both subjects are compared on point 1; then both are compared on point 2; and so on through all the points.

   To choose which method of organization would be most effective, just use your common sense. If the subjects themselves are the most interesting part of your essay, use the subject pattern. But if you want single characteristics to stand out, use the point-by-point pattern.

   Minton's essay is organized point by point. He spends most of his time on point 4 for both subjects. Here is what Minton's organization looks like:

   Point 1: They draw on all five senses.
   - A. Roller coasters
   - B. Haunted houses

   Point 2: They rely on surprise.
   - A. Roller coasters
   - B. Haunted houses

   Point 3: They refer to movies.
   - A. Roller coasters
   - B. Haunted houses

   Point 4: They feed on loss of control.
   - A. Roller coasters
     - i. Fear of heights
     - ii. Fear of falling
   - B. Haunted houses
     - i. Spooky mood
     - ii. The scare

*Writing Your Own Comparison/Contrast Essay*

Write an essay comparing and contrasting two methods of escape, based on the ideas you generated in your prewriting activities. How are they alike? How are they different? Decide what point you want to make before you start writing. Then spend some time choosing and organizing your topics and deciding on your method of organization (subject by subject, point by point, or a combination of the two). Form a clear thesis statement, and follow the guidelines for writing a comparison/contrast essay.

## COMPARISON AND CONTRAST AT WORK

Let's look at a student's management of a comparison/contrast essay. This next essay, called "The Truth About Cats and Dogs," was written by a student named Maria Castillo. See if you can identify her main point as you read her essay.

### The Truth About Cats and Dogs

The majority of people in the world will say that dogs are man's best friends and that cats were put on this earth to aggravate dogs. Some people are closet cat lovers, meaning he or she is afraid to tell family and friends that they actually like cats. Others will proudly state, "I hate cats, except for yours." People who resist cats do so because they believe they are; aloof, self-centered, and dull. People prefer dogs because they are friendly, protective, and playful. However, cats exhibit these same qualities and deserve the same respect as dogs. 1

Dogs have always been considered to be friendly, but cats can also fit this description. Dogs stay by their owners' sides and live to make their masters happy. They are the first to greet their family at the front door, they want nothing more than to be praised by their owners. Yet cats are much the same way. They, too, will be at the front door when their family gets home and are always excited to see them. They usually sit near their owners just to be by their sides. And despite what some people believe, a cat does come when they're called. Birds do not sit with their owners unless they are trained. Cats are very friendly to their owners. 2

As much as dogs love to play, so do cats. Most dogs love to play with chew toys, searching for the hidden-squeaker treasure. They often parade around with their "kill" until their masters notice their triumph. 3

Some owners will awaken to find that their dogs have strewn all their toys all over the house. Dogs love the toys they know are theirs. However, so do cats. Cats will make a toy out of anything that will slide across a tile floor, whether it's a hair tie, a milk jug ring, a toy mouse, or a paper clip. They can amuse themselves for hours. If the toy-of-the-day gets trapped under the refrigerator, cats will whine and wait for their owner to get the toy. Cats just love to play.

4 Even though dogs are great defenders, cats have been known to protect the family as well. Dogs bark or growl whenever they want to alert their owners to possible danger. They stand at the door and wait for their owners to check for danger. If they see their owner being attacked, they will attack the enemy. Most people think cats would just stand by and watch, but this simply isn't true. Cats also alert their owners of danger by growling or standing to stiff attention. They, too, stand near the door waiting for their owner to react. Cats have been known to bite people who harm their loved ones. Cats can be excellent watch animals.

5 Dogs and cats are a lot alike. People say cats are very different from dogs, but this is not the case. The truth is, most people love to hate cats. It's now an old American pastime. But it's time for all cat lovers to unite and prove that it can be a cat-eat-cat world too.

1. What is Maria's main point in this essay?

_______________________________________________

2. What exactly is Maria comparing or contrasting in this essay? List her points under the subjects below.

| **Dogs** | **Cats** |
|---|---|
| ______________________ | ______________________ |
| ______________________ | ______________________ |
| ______________________ | ______________________ |
| ______________________ | |

3. Does Maria use as many specific details and examples as possible? List three of her specific references.

_______________________________________________

______________________________________________

______________________________________________

4. Does Maria develop her comparison in a balanced way? Explain your answer. ______________________________________________

______________________________________________

5. How does Maria organize her essay: subject by subject, point by point, or a combination of the two?

______________________________________________

## REVISING AND EDITING A STUDENT ESSAY

This essay is Maria's first draft, which now needs to be revised and edited. First, apply the Revising Checklist below to Maria's draft so that you are working with her content. When you are satisfied that her ideas are fully developed and well organized, use the Editing Checklist on pages 225–226 to correct her grammatical and mechanical errors. Answer the questions after each checklist. Then write your suggested changes directly on Maria's draft.

### Revising Checklist

**Thesis Statement**

✔ Does the thesis statement contain the essay's controlling idea and appear as the last sentence of the introduction?

**Basic Elements**

✔ Does the title draw in the readers?

✔ Does the introduction capture the readers' attention and build up to the thesis statement effectively?

✔ Does each body paragraph deal with a single topic?

✔ Does the conclusion bring the essay to a close in an interesting way?

**DEVELOPMENT**

- ✔ Do the body paragraphs adequately support the thesis statement?
- ✔ Does each body paragraph have a focused topic sentence?
- ✔ Does each body paragraph contain *specific* details that support the topic sentence?
- ✔ Does each body paragraph include *enough* details to explain the topic sentence fully?

**UNITY**

- ✔ Do the essay's topic sentences relate directly to the thesis statement?
- ✔ Do the details in each body paragraph support its topic sentence?

**ORGANIZATION**

- ✔ Is the essay organized logically?
- ✔ Is each body paragraph organized logically?

**COHERENCE**

- ✔ Are transitions used effectively so that paragraphs move smoothly and logically from one to the next?
- ✔ Do the sentences move smoothly and logically from one to the next?

## Thesis Statement

- ✔ Does the thesis statement contain the essay's controlling idea and appear as the last sentence of the introduction?

1. Put brackets around the last sentence in Maria's introduction. Does it contain her main point? ______________

2. Rewrite Maria's thesis statement if necessary so that it states her main point and introduces her topics.

____________________________________________________________

____________________________________________________________

## Basic Elements

- ✔ Does the title draw in the readers?
- ✔ Does the introduction capture the readers' attention and build up to the thesis statement effectively?
- ✔ Does each body paragraph deal with a single topic?
- ✔ Does the conclusion bring the essay to a close in an interesting way?

1. Give Maria's essay an alternate title. ______________________________
2. Rewrite Maria's introduction so that it captures readers' attention and builds up to the thesis statement at the end of the paragraph. ________

   ______________________________________________

   ______________________________________________

   ______________________________________________
3. Does each of Maria's body paragraphs deal with only one topic? _____
4. Rewrite Maria's conclusion using at least one suggestion from Part I.

   ______________________________________________

   ______________________________________________

   ______________________________________________

## Development

- ✔ Do the body paragraphs adequately support the thesis statement?
- ✔ Does each body paragraph have a focused topic sentence?
- ✔ Does each body paragraph contain *specific* details that support the topic sentence?
- ✔ Does each body paragraph include *enough* details to explain the topic sentence fully?

1. Write out Maria's thesis statement (revised, if necessary), and list her three topic sentences below it.

   Thesis statement: ______________________________

   ______________________________

   ______________________________

   Topic 1: ______________________________

   ______________________________

   Topic 2: ______________________________

   Topic 3: ______________________________

   ______________________________

2. Do Maria's topic sentences adequately support her thesis statement?

   ______________

3. Does each body paragraph have a focused topic sentence? ___________
4. Do Maria's details adequately characterize both cats and dogs? __________
5. Where do you need more information? __________________________
6. Make two of Maria's details more specific.
7. Add at least two new details to make her comparison clearer.

## Unity

> ✔ Do the essay's topic sentences relate directly to the thesis statement?
> ✔ Do the details in each body paragraph support its topic sentence?

1. Read each of Maria's topic sentences with her thesis statement (revised, if necessary) in mind. Do they go together? __________________________
2. Revise them if necessary so they are directly related.

3. Drop or rewrite the sentence in paragraph 2 that is not directly related to its topic sentence.

## Organization

> ✔ Is the essay organized logically?
> ✔ Is each body paragraph organized logically?

1. Read Maria's essay again to see if all the paragraphs are arranged logically.
2. Reverse the two paragraphs that are out of order.
3. Look closely at Maria's body paragraphs to see if all her sentences are arranged logically within paragraphs.
4. Move any sentences that are out of order.

## Coherence

> ✔ Are transitions used effectively so that paragraphs move smoothly and logically from one to the next?
> ✔ Do the sentences move smoothly and logically from one to the next?

1. Add two transitions to Maria's essay.
2. Circle five synonyms that Maria uses.
3. Explain how two of these make Maria's essay easier to read.

______________________________________________

______________________________________________

Now rewrite Maria's essay with your revisions.

## Editing Checklist

> **SENTENCES**
> ✔ Does each sentence have a main subject and verb?
> ✔ Do all subjects and verbs agree?

✔ Do all pronouns agree with their nouns?
✔ Are modifiers as close as possible to the words they modify?

PUNCTUATION AND MECHANICS
✔ Are sentences punctuated correctly?
✔ Are words capitalized properly?

WORD CHOICE AND SPELLING
✔ Are words used correctly?
✔ Are words spelled correctly?

## Sentences

✔ Does each sentence have a main subject and verb?
For help with subjects and verbs, see Chapter 34.

1. Underline Maria's subjects once and verbs twice in paragraph 2 of your revision of Maria's essay. Remember that sentences can have more than one subject-verb set.
2. Does each of Maria's sentences have at least one subject and verb that can stand alone? ______________
3. Did you find and correct Maria's run-on sentence? If not, find and correct it now. For help, see Chapter 36.

✔ Do all subjects and verbs agree?
For help with subject-verb agreement, see Chapter 39.

1. Read aloud the subjects and verbs you underlined in your revision of Maria's essay.
2. Correct any subjects and verbs that do not agree.

✔ Do all pronouns agree with their nouns?
For help with pronoun agreement, see Chapter 43.

1. Find any pronouns in your revision of Maria's essay that do not agree with their nouns.
2. Did you find and correct the two pronouns that do not agree with their nouns?

> ✔ Are modifiers as close as possible to the words they modify?
> For help with modifier errors, see Chapter 46.

1. Find any modifiers in your revision of Maria's essay that are not as close as possible to the words they modify.
2. Rewrite sentences if necessary so modifiers are as close as possible to the words they modify.

## Punctuation and Mechanics

> ✔ Are sentences punctuated correctly?
> For help with punctuation, see Chapters 47–51.

1. Read your revision of Maria's essay for any errors in punctuation.
2. Find the run-on you revised, and make sure it is punctuated correctly.
3. Did you find and correct Maria's semicolon error? If not, find and correct it now.

> ✔ Are words capitalized properly?
> For help with capitalization, see Chapter 52.

1. Read your revision of Maria's essay for any errors in capitalization.
2. Be sure to check Maria's capitalization in the run-on you revised.

## Word Choice and Spelling

> ✔ Are words used correctly?
> For help with confused words, see Chapter 58.

1. Find any words used incorrectly in your revision of Maria's essay.
2. Correct any errors you find.

✔ Are all words spelled correctly?
For help with spelling, see Chapter 59.

1. Use spell-check and a dictionary to check the spelling in your revision of Maria's essay.
2. Correct any misspelled words.

Now rewrite Maria's essay again with your editing corrections.

## REVISING AND EDITING YOUR OWN ESSAY

Returning to the comparison/contrast you wrote earlier in this chapter, revise and edit your own writing. The checklists here will help you apply what you have learned to your essay.

### Revising

#### Thesis Statement

☐ Does the thesis statement contain the essay's controlling idea and appear as the last sentence of the introduction?

1. What main point are you trying to make in your essay?

   ______________________________

2. Put brackets around the last sentence in your introduction. Does it contain your main point? ______________

3. Rewrite your thesis statement if necessary so that it states your main point and introduces your topics.

## Basic Elements

- ☐ Does the title draw in the readers?
- ☐ Does the introduction capture the readers' attention and build up to the thesis statement effectively?
- ☐ Does each body paragraph deal with a single topic?
- ☐ Does the conclusion bring the essay to a close in an interesting way?

1. Give your essay a title if it doesn't have one. ______________
2. Does your introduction capture your readers' attention and build up to your thesis statement at the end of the paragraph? ______________
3. Does each of your body paragraphs deal with only one topic? ______________
4. Does your conclusion follow some of the suggestions offered in Part I? ______________

## Development

- ☐ Do the body paragraphs adequately support the thesis statement?
- ☐ Does each body paragraph have a focused topic sentence?
- ☐ Does each body paragraph contain *specific* details that support the topic sentence?
- ☐ Does each body paragraph include *enough* details to explain the topic sentence fully?

1. Write out your thesis statement (revised, if necessary), and list your topic sentences below it.

   Thesis statement: ______________

   Topic 1: ______________

Topic 2: ______________________________

Topic 3: ______________________________

2. Do your topics adequately support your thesis statement? __________
3. Does each body paragraph have a focused topic sentence? __________
4. Do you cover the same characteristics of both topics? __________
5. Where do your readers need more information? __________
6. Make two of your details more specific.
7. Add at least two new details to make your comparison clearer.

## Unity

- ☐ Do the essay's topic sentences relate directly to the thesis statement?
- ☐ Do the details in each body paragraph support its topic sentence?

1. Read each of your topic sentences with your thesis statement in mind. Do they go together? __________
2. Revise them if necessary so they are directly related.
3. Drop or rewrite any of the sentences in your body paragraphs that are not directly related to their topic sentences.

## Organization

- ☐ Is the essay organized logically?
- ☐ Is each body paragraph organized logically?

1. Read your essay again to see if all the paragraphs are arranged logically.
2. How is your essay organized: subject by subject, point by point, or a combination of the two? __________

3. Is the order you chose for your paragraphs the most effective approach to your subject? ____________
4. Move any paragraphs that are out of order.
5. Look closely at your body paragraphs to see if all the sentences are arranged logically within paragraphs.
6. Move any sentences that are out of order.

## Coherence

- ☐ Are transitions used effectively so that paragraphs move smoothly and logically from one to the next?
- ☐ Do the sentences move smoothly and logically from one to the next?

1. Add two transitions to your essay.
2. Circle five synonyms you use.
3. Explain how two of these make your essay easier to read.

______________________________________________

______________________________________________

Now rewrite your essay with your revisions.

# Editing

## Sentences

- ☐ Does each sentence have a main subject and verb?
  For help with subjects and verbs, see Chapter 34.

1. Underline the subjects once and verbs twice in a paragraph of your revised essay. Remember that sentences can have more than one subject-verb set.

2. Does each of your sentences have at least one subject and verb that can stand alone? ______________
3. Correct any fragments you have written. For help, see Chapter 35.
4. Correct any run-on sentences you have written. For help, see Chapter 36.

☐ Do all subjects and verbs agree?
For help with subject-verb agreement, see Chapter 39.

1. Read aloud the subjects and verbs you underlined in your revised essay.
2. Correct any subjects and verbs that do not agree.

☐ Do all pronouns agree with their nouns?
For help with pronoun agreement, see Chapter 43.

1. Find any pronouns in your revised essay that do not agree with their nouns.
2. Correct any pronouns that do not agree with their nouns.

☐ Are modifiers as close as possible to the words they modify?
For help with modifier errors, see Chapter 46.

1. Find any modifiers in your revised essay that are not as close as possible to the words they modify.
2. Rewrite sentences if necessary so that your modifiers are as close as possible to the words they modify.

## Punctuation and Mechanics

☐ Are sentences punctuated correctly?
For help with punctuation, see Chapters 47–51.

1. Read your revised essay for any errors in punctuation.
2. Make sure any fragments and run-ons you revised are punctuated correctly.

☐ Are words capitalized properly?
For help with capitalization, see Chapter 52.

1. Read your revised essay for any errors in capitalization.
2. Be sure to check your capitalization in any fragments or run-ons you revised.

## Word Choice and Spelling

☐ Are words used correctly?
For help with confused words, see Chapter 58.

1. Find any words used incorrectly in your revised essay.
2. Correct any errors you find.

☐ Are all words spelled correctly?
For help with spelling, see Chapter 59.

1. Use spell-check and a dictionary to check your spelling.
2. Correct any misspelled words.

Now rewrite your essay again with your editing corrections.

## READING SUGGESTIONS

In Chapter 29, you will find two essays that illustrate good comparison/contrast writing: "The American Family" by Stephanie Coontz compares the institution of the family over the years, and "Venus Envy" by Patricia McLaughlin compares and contrasts the images of men and women in contemporary society. You might want to read these selections before writing another comparison/contrast essay. As you read, notice how the writers make their points through well-thought-out, detailed comparisons and contrasts.

## IDEAS FOR WRITING

**Guidelines for Writing a Comparison/Contrast Essay**

1. Decide what point you want to make with your comparison, and state it in your thesis statement.
2. Choose items to compare and contrast that will make your point most effectively.
3. Use as many specific details and examples as possible to expand your comparison.
4. Develop your comparison in a balanced way.
5. Organize your essay subject by subject or point by point—or combine the two approaches.

1. Compare and contrast the two buildings. What details in both buildings are different? What is the same? What is the overall message you get

from these two buildings? Look at both the obvious and the not-so-obvious.

2. Choose a job being advertised in your local newspaper's classified section, and write a cover letter to the employer comparing yourself to your probable competition. What are your best qualifications compared to others who might be applying for this job? What are your weaknesses in comparison to them? Why would you be the best candidate for the job?
3. Discuss the similarities and differences between two cities that you know well. How are they the same? How are they different? What do you think accounts for these similarities and differences? When you write your essay, consider whether a subject-by-subject or a point-by-point organization would be more effective.
4. Create your own comparison/contrast assignment (with the help of your instructor), and write a response to it.

## Revising Workshop

**Small Group Activity (5–10 minutes per writer)** In groups of three or four, each person should read his or her comparison/contrast essay to the other members of the group. Those listening should record their reactions on a copy of the Peer Evaluation Form in Appendix 2E. After your group goes through this process, give your evaluation forms to the appropriate writers so that each writer has two or three peer comment sheets for revising.

**Paired Activity (5 minutes per writer)** Using the completed Peer Evaluation Forms, work in pairs to decide what you should revise in your essay. If time allows, rewrite some of your sentences, and have your partner look at them.

**Individual Activity** Rewrite your paper, using the revising feedback you received from other students.

## Editing Workshop

**Paired Activity (5–10 minutes per writer)** Swap papers with a classmate, and use the editing portion of your Peer Evaluation Form to identify as many grammar, punctuation, mechanics, and spelling errors as you can. If time allows, correct some of your errors, and have your partner look at them. Record your grammar, punctuation, and mechanics errors in the Error Log (Appendix 6) and your spelling errors in the Spelling Log (Appendix 7).

**Individual Activity** Rewrite your paper again, using the editing feedback you received from other students.

## Reflecting on Your Writing

When you have completed your own essay, answer these six questions.

1. What was most difficult about this assignment?
2. What was easiest?
3. What did you learn about using comparison/contrast by completing this assignment?
4. What do you think are the strengths of your comparison/contrast essay? Place a squiggly line by the parts of your essay that you feel are very good.
5. What are the weaknesses, if any, of your paper? Place an X by the parts of your essay you would like help with. Write any questions you have in the margin.
6. What did you learn from this assignment about your own writing process—about preparing to write, about writing the first draft, about revising, and about editing?

# Dividing and Classifying

*There is an art of reading, as well as an art of thinking and an art of writing.*

—ISAAC D'ISRAELI

Division and classification ensure that we have a certain amount of order in our lives. In fact, we constantly use these two processes to navigate through our daily lives. Thanks to classification, you know where to find the milk in the grocery store and the chapter on World War II in your history textbook. Also, when you choose a major and a career, you use division and classification to make your choice. Division and classification are such a natural part of everyday life that we often don't even know we are using them.

In addition, we regularly use division and classification when we write. Actually, division and classification are a vital part of our written communication every day—in our personal lives, in college courses, and in the workplace. Think about these situations:

You divide your expenses into categories to create a budget.

A student describes three types of bacteria on a biology exam.

A student writes a report on types of hazardous materials for a science course.

A personal banker prepares a flyer about the types of savings accounts that are available.

The manager of a music store suggests to the home office a new system for arranging CDs.

Like comparison and contrast, division and classification are really two parts of the same process. **Division** is sorting—dividing something into its basic parts, such as a home into rooms. Division moves from a single, large category (home) to many smaller subcategories (kitchen, bath, living room, and so forth). **Classification,** grouping items together, moves in the opposite direction, from many subgroups to a single, large category. For example, all the pieces of furniture in a home can be classified as living room furniture or bedroom furniture. Division and classification help us organize information so that we can make sense of our complex world. Both dividing large categories into smaller ones (division) and grouping many items into larger categories (classification) help us put lots of information into useful groups.

Here is a sample division/classification essay by Fran Lebowitz called "The Sound of Music: Enough Already." It classifies the types of music Lebowitz dislikes the most. What are some of your dislikes? Are these also your biggest pet peeves? Why do you dislike these things or behaviors?

**Fran Lebowitz**

## THE SOUND OF MUSIC: ENOUGH ALREADY

1 First off, I want to say that as far as I am concerned, in instances where I have not personally and deliberately sought it out, the only difference between music and Muzak is the spelling. Pablo Casals practicing across the hall with the door open—being trapped in an elevator, the ceiling of which is broadcasting "Parsley, Sage, Rosemary, and Thyme"—it's all the same to me. Harsh words? Perhaps. But then again these are not gentle times we live in. And they are being made no more gentle by this incessant melody that was once real life.

2 There was a time when music knew its place. No longer. Possibly this is not music's fault. It may be that music fell in with a bad crowd and lost its sense of common decency. I am willing to consider this. I am willing even to try and help. I would like to do my bit to set music straight in order that it might shape up and leave the mainstream of society. The first thing that music must understand is that there are two kinds of music—good music and bad music. Good music is music that I want to hear. Bad music is music that I don't want to hear.

3 So that music might more clearly see the error of its ways I offer the following. If you are music and you recognize yourself on this list, you are bad music.

### 1. Music in Other People's Clock Radios

4 There are times when I find myself spending the night in the home of another. Frequently the other is in a more reasonable line of work than I and must arise at a specific hour. Ofttimes the other, unbeknownst to me, manipulates an appliance in such a way that I am awakened by Stevie Wonder. On such occasions I

announce that if I wished to be awakened by Stevie Wonder I would sleep with Stevie Wonder. I do not, however, wish to be awakened by Stevie Wonder and that is why God invented alarm clocks. Sometimes the other realizes that I am right. Sometimes the other does not. And that is why God invented *many* others.

## 2. Music Residing in the Hold Buttons of Other People's Business Telephones

I do not under any circumstances enjoy hold buttons. But I am a woman of reason. I can accept reality. I can face the facts. What I cannot face is the music. Just as there are two kinds of music—good and bad—so there are two kinds of hold buttons—good and bad. Good hold buttons are hold buttons that hold one silently. Bad hold buttons are hold buttons that hold one musically. When I hold I want to hold silently. That is the way it was meant to be, for that is what God was talking about when he said, "Forever hold your peace." He would have added, "and quiet," but he thought you were smarter. 5

## 3. Music in the Streets

The past few years have seen a steady increase in the number of people playing music in the streets. The past few years have also seen a steady increase in the number of malignant diseases. Are these two facts related? One wonders. But even if they are not—and, as I have pointed out, one cannot be sure—music in the streets has definitely taken its toll. For it is at the very least disorienting. When one is walking down Fifth Avenue, one does not expect to hear a string quartet playing a Strauss waltz. What one expects to hear while walking down Fifth Avenue is traffic. When one does indeed hear a string quartet playing a Strauss waltz while one is walking down Fifth Avenue, one is apt to become confused and imagine that one is not walking down Fifth Avenue at all but rather that one has somehow wound up in Old Vienna. Should one imagine that one is in Old Vienna one is likely to become upset when one realizes that in Old Vienna there is no sale at Charles Jourdan. And that is why when I walk down Fifth Avenue I want to hear traffic. 6

## 4. Music in the Movies

I'm not talking about musicals. Musicals are movies that warn you by saying, "Lots of music here. Take it or leave it." I'm talking about regular movies that extend no such courtesy but allow unsuspecting people to come to see them and then assault them with a barrage of unasked-for tunes. There are two major offenders in this category: black movies and movies set in the fifties. Both types of movies are afflicted with the same misconception. They don't know that movies are supposed to be movies. They think that movies are supposed to be records with pictures. They have failed to understand that if God had wanted records to have pictures, he would not have invented television. 7

### 5. Music in Public Places Such as Restaurants, Supermarkets, Hotel Lobbies, Airports, Etc.

8 When I am in any of the above-mentioned places I am not there to hear music. I am there for whatever reason is appropriate to the respective place. I am no more interested in hearing "Mack the Knife" while waiting for the shuttle to Boston than someone sitting ringside at the Sands Hotel is interested in being forced to choose between sixteen varieties of cottage cheese. If God had meant for everything to happen at once, he would not have invented desk calendars.

### Epilogue

9 Some people talk to themselves. Some people sing to themselves. Is one group better than the other? Did not God create all people equal? Yes, God created all people equal. Only to some he gave the ability to make up their own words.

***Preparing to Write Your Own Division/Classification Essay***

Everyone has pet peeves. What are yours? How did you develop these pet peeves? Do your pet peeves form any particular patterns? Use one or more of the prewriting strategies that you learned in Chapter 2 to explore this topic.

## HOW TO WRITE A DIVISION/CLASSIFICATION ESSAY

To write a division/classification essay, keep in mind that the same items can be divided and classified in many different ways. Your friends probably don't all organize their closets the way you do, and no two kitchens are organized exactly alike. The United States can be divided many different ways—into 50 states, four regions (Northeast, Midwest, South, and Pacific), and six time zones (Eastern, Central, Mountain, Pacific, Alaska, and Hawaii). Similarly, in writing you can divide and classify a topic in different ways. Whatever your method of dividing or classifying, use the following guidelines to help you write an effective division/classification essay.

1. ***Decide on your purpose for writing, and make it part of your thesis statement.*** Dividing and classifying in themselves are not particularly interesting. But they are very useful techniques if you are trying to

make a specific point. That point, or purpose, should be in your thesis statement. Look at these two examples:

**A.** There are three types of dangerous drivers on the road today.
**B.** Being aware of three types of dangerous drivers on the road today could save your life.

Both thesis statements name a category—dangerous drivers—but only thesis statement B gives the reader a good reason to keep reading: Knowing the three types could save your life.

In our sample essay, Lebowitz uses division and classification to make fun of the types of music she dislikes. She divides all music into good music and bad music. Then she breaks bad music into five categories. She captures the humor of her essay in her thesis at the end of paragraph 3: "If you are music and you recognize yourself on this list, you are bad music."

2. ***Divide your topic into categories that don't overlap.*** Since most subjects can be classified in different ways, your next task in writing a division/classification essay is to decide on what basis you will divide your subject into categories. First, gather information to come up with a list of all the possible topics. Second, decide on what basis you will put these topics into categories. Next, make sure some of your topics don't fall into two categories. Your categories should be separate enough that your topics fall into one category only. Also, don't add a category at the last minute to accommodate a topic. Keep adjusting your categories until they work with your thesis.

   In the sample essay, the author uses a combination of division and classification to make her point. First, she divides all music into good and bad. Then she classifies bad music into five categories: (1) music in other people's clock radios, (2) music in the hold buttons of other people's business telephones, (3) music in the streets, (4) music in the movies, and (5) music in public places such as restaurants, supermarkets, hotel lobbies, and airports. She might have tried to classify bad music in other ways, such as public and private; indoor, outdoor, and a combination of the two; or personal, business-related, and involving other people. But none of these options would be effective. The first two groupings are too general to supply the detailed information that Lebowitz's categories give us. The third set of categories would force the author to classify many topics, like music in the movies and music in public places, in two categories, which would be confusing. Lebowitz's more specific categories are all about the same size and are very effective in sending her humorous message.

3. ***Clearly explain each category.*** With division, you are trying to show what differences break the items into separate groups or types. With classification, you let the similarities in the items help you set up categories that make sense. In either case, you need to explain each category fully and provide enough details to help your readers see your subject in a new way. To do this, use vivid description and carefully chosen examples. Comparison and contrast (Chapter 13) is also a useful technique because when you classify items, you are looking at how they are alike (comparison) and how they are different (contrast).

   Lebowitz uses comparison and contrast to place her ideas into categories. Then she describes each category and provides detailed examples, such as Stevie Wonder, a Strauss waltz, and "Mack the Knife," to fill out her descriptions. As a result, she explains each of her categories fully and clearly.

4. ***Organize your categories logically.*** Your method of organization should make sense and be easy for readers to follow. Most often, this means organizing from one extreme to another. For example, you might organize your types from most obvious to least obvious. Or you might move from least important to most important, from least humorous to most humorous, from largest to smallest—or the other way around. In every case, though, try to end with the category that is most memorable.

   Fran Lebowitz's essay is arranged from one extreme to another—from personal to public. The categories move from clock radios to business phones to music in the streets to music in movies to music in public places. Each category gets farther from the personal realm, which helps Lebowitz prove that bad music is everywhere.

5. ***Use transitions to move your readers through your essay.*** Transitions will help your readers move from one category to another and follow your train of thought. They will also keep your essay from sounding choppy or boring.

   Since Lebowitz gives her categories headings, she doesn't need to use transitions to move from one category to another. But she does use transitions within her paragraphs. Here are some effective transitions from Lebowitz's essay: "first off" (paragraph 1), "there was a time when" (paragraph 2), "frequently" (paragraph 4), "on such occasions" (paragraph 4), "but" (paragraph 5), and "when" (paragraphs 6 and 8). These words and phrases serve as traffic signals that guide Lebowitz's readers through her essay.

*Writing Your Own Division/Classification Essay*

Write an essay explaining your various pet peeves. How did these pet peeves start? Why do you have them? Begin by reviewing your prewriting notes. Next, divide your subject into distinct categories, and write a clear thesis statement. Then develop your essay with specific examples that explain each category.

## DIVISION AND CLASSIFICATION AT WORK

Sergio Mendola, a student writer, uses division and classification in an essay about neighbors. Called "Won't You Be My Neighbor?" it divides and classifies neighbors into specific categories to prove a point. See if you can identify his main point as you read his essay.

**Won't You Be My Neighbor?**

Neighborhoods can be strange places. Every one is different, but they are all made up of the same ingredient--neighbors. In today's world, though, most people don't know there neighbors. It's not like the '50s. When people knew what their neighbors were doing. But in every neighborhood today, you can find at least one Mystery Neighbor, one Perfect Cleaver Family, and one Good Neighbor Family. 1

The first type of neighbor everyone has is the Perfect Cleaver Family. This family has the perfect parents and the perfect children. They are the June and Wally Cleavers of today. They have 2.5 perfect children. Although these children get in their share of minor trouble, the children never repeat the same mistake after the parents express their disappointment. And then, to avoid future disappointments, the children always keep their parents' values in mind before making decisions. Eddie Haskell left a lot to be desired. I don't know what his values are. The Cleaver-type children later become heart surgeons or police chiefs in order to help the world around them. These neighbors are the role models for everyone else. 2

Then there is the Mystery Neighbor. The Mystery Neighbor remains aloof, and the only way the other neighbors know someone lives at the Mystery House is because the newspaper disappears sometime during the day and the lawn somehow gets mowed every week. Every once in a while, a car will sit in the driveway, but no one knows for sure if the car belongs to the people who own the house. Neighborhood children make up stories about the Mystery Neighbor, which are based on nothing and 3 compete with the best urban legends. The Mystery Neighbor is usually a workaholic or a traveling sales person, but this doesn't stop the neighbors from wondering.

4 The best type of neighbor in any neighborhood is the Good Neighbor Family. Made up of very reliable people. This family is always reaching out to other neighbors. Whenever something goes wrong, someone from the Good Neighbor Family is the first person at the doorstep too lend a helping hand. These neighbors will water the plants and feed the animals for people on vacation who always want to help others. They create the kinds of friendships that continue even when one family moves away. Sometimes the parents might try to "fix up" their boy and girl children so that the families relationship can be legally cemented for life. The Good Neighbor Family is one that everyone hopes to encounter at least once in a lifetime.

5 This mixture of neighbors makes up a very good neighborhood. It creates a neighborhood that functions smoothly and thoughtfully. And even though people don't no their neighbors like they used to 50 years ago, they will probably find at least three different types of neighbors if they look hard enough: the Perfect Cleaver Family, the Mystery Neighbor, and the Good Neighbor Family. It would be sad to be missing any one of them.

1. This essay doesn't simply classify neighbors for their own sake. It has a broader message. What is Sergio's general purpose in this essay?

_______________________________________________

_______________________________________________

2. Does Sergio divide his subject into categories that don't overlap?

_______________________________________________

3. Does Sergio clearly explain each of his categories? Explain your answer.

_______________________________________________

_______________________________________________

4. How does Sergio organize his categories? Is this the most logical order for this purpose? Explain your answer.

_______________________________________________

_______________________________________________

5. What transitions does Sergio use to move his essay along smoothly?

______________________________________________

______________________________________________

______________________________________________

## REVISING AND EDITING A STUDENT ESSAY

This essay is Sergio's first draft, which now needs to be revised and edited. First, apply the Revising Checklist below to Sergio's draft so that you are working with his content. When you are satisfied that his ideas are fully developed and well organized, use the Editing Checklist on page 249 to correct his grammar and mechanics errors. Answer the questions after each checklist. Then write your suggested changes directly on Sergio's draft.

### Revising Checklist

THESIS STATEMENT

✔ Does the thesis statement contain the essay's controlling idea and appear as the last sentence of the introduction?

BASIC ELEMENTS

✔ Does the title draw in the readers?

✔ Does the introduction capture the readers' attention and build up to the thesis statement effectively?

✔ Does each body paragraph deal with a single topic?

✔ Does the conclusion bring the essay to a close in an interesting way?

DEVELOPMENT

✔ Do the body paragraphs adequately support the thesis statement?

✔ Does each body paragraph have a focused topic sentence?

✔ Does each body paragraph contain *specific* details that support the topic sentence?

✔ Does each body paragraph include *enough* details to explain the topic sentence fully?

UNITY

✔ Do the essay's topic sentences relate directly to the thesis statement?

✔ Do the details in each body paragraph support its topic sentence?

ORGANIZATION

✔ Is the essay organized logically?

✔ Is each body paragraph organized logically?

COHERENCE

✔ Are transitions used effectively so that paragraphs move smoothly and logically from one to the next?

✔ Do the sentences move smoothly and logically from one to the next?

## Thesis Statement

✔ Does the thesis statement contain the essay's controlling idea and appear as the last sentence of the introduction?

1. Put brackets around the last sentence in Sergio's introduction. Does it introduce his purpose? ______________

2. Rewrite Sergio's thesis statement if necessary so that it states his purpose and introduces his topics.

______________________________________________

## Basic Elements

✔ Does the title draw in the readers?

✔ Does the introduction capture the readers' attention and build up to the thesis statement effectively?

✔ Does each body paragraph deal with a single topic?

✔ Does the conclusion bring the essay to a close in an interesting way?

1. Give Sergio's essay an alternate title. ______________________________

2. Rewrite Sergio's introduction so that it captures the readers' attention and builds up to the thesis statement at the end of the paragraph. ______

______________________________________________________________

______________________________________________________________

______________________________________________________________

3. Does each of Sergio's body paragraphs deal with only one topic? ______

4. Rewrite Sergio's conclusion using at least one suggestion from Part I.

______________________________________________________________

______________________________________________________________

______________________________________________________________

## Development

- ✔ Do the body paragraphs adequately support the thesis statement?
- ✔ Does each body paragraph have a focused topic sentence?
- ✔ Does each body paragraph contain *specific* details that support the topic sentence?
- ✔ Does each body paragraph include *enough* details to explain the topic sentence fully?

1. Write out Sergio's thesis statement (revised, if necessary), and list his three topic sentences below it.

   Thesis statement: ______________________________________________

   ______________________________________________

   Topic 1: ______________________________________________

   Topic 2: ______________________________________________

   Topic 3: ______________________________________________

2. Do Sergio's topics adequately support his thesis statement? __________

3. Does each body paragraph have a focused topic sentence? __________

4. Do Sergio's details adequately explain his categories? __________

__________

5. Where do you need more information? __________

6. Make two of Sergio's details more specific. __________

7. Add two new details to make his essay clearer. __________

## Unity

- ✔ Do the essay's topic sentences relate directly to the thesis statement?
- ✔ Do the details in each body paragraph support its topic sentence?

1. Read each of Sergio's topic sentences with his thesis statement (revised, if necessary) in mind. Do they go together?
2. Revise them if necessary so they are directly related.
3. Drop or rewrite the two sentences in paragraph 2 that are not directly related to their topic sentences.

## Organization

- ✔ Is the essay organized logically?
- ✔ Is each body paragraph organized logically?

1. Read Sergio's essay again to see if all the paragraphs are arranged logically.
2. Reverse the two paragraphs that are out of order.
3. Look closely at Sergio's body paragraphs to see if all his sentences are arranged logically within paragraphs.
4. Move any sentences that are out of order.

## Coherence

- ✔ Are transitions used effectively so that paragraphs move smoothly and logically from one to the next?
- ✔ Do the sentences move smoothly and logically from one to the next?

1. Add two transitions to Sergio's essay.
2. Circle five transitions, repetitions, synonyms, or pronouns Sergio uses.
3. Explain how two of these make Sergio's essay easier to read.

______________________________________________

______________________________________________

Now rewrite Sergio's essay with your revisions.

## Editing Checklist

SENTENCES
- ✔ Does each sentence have a main subject and verb?
- ✔ Do all subjects and verbs agree?
- ✔ Do all pronouns agree with their nouns?
- ✔ Are modifiers as close as possible to the words they modify?

PUNCTUATION AND MECHANICS
- ✔ Are sentences punctuated correctly?
- ✔ Are words capitalized properly?

WORD CHOICE AND SPELLING
- ✔ Are words used correctly?
- ✔ Are words spelled correctly?

## Sentences

- ✔ Does each sentence have a main subject and verb?

For help with subjects and verbs, see Chapter 34.

1. Underline the subjects once and verbs twice in paragraphs 1 and 4 of your revision of Sergio's essay. Remember that sentences can have more than one subject-verb set.
2. Does each of the sentences have at least one subject and verb that can stand alone? ______________
3. Did you find and correct Sergio's two fragments? If not, find and correct them now. For help with fragments, see Chapter 35.

✔ Do all subjects and verbs agree?
For help with subject-verb agreement, see Chapter 39.

1. Read aloud the subjects and verbs you underlined in your revision of Sergio's essay.
2. Correct any subjects and verbs that do not agree.

✔ Do all pronouns agree with their nouns?
For help with pronoun agreement, see Chapter 43.

1. Find any pronouns in your revision of Sergio's essay that do not agree with their nouns.
2. Correct any pronouns that do not agree with their nouns.

✔ Are modifiers as close as possible to the words they modify?
For help with modifier errors, see Chapter 46.

1. Find any modifiers in your revision of Sergio's essay that are not as close as possible to the words they modify.
2. Did you find and correct Sergio's modifier error? If not, find and correct it now.

## Punctuation and Mechanics

> ✔ Are sentences punctuated correctly?
> For help with punctuation, see Chapters 47–51.

1. Read your revision of Sergio's essay for any errors in punctuation.
2. Find the two fragments you revised, and make sure they are punctuated correctly.
3. Did you find and correct the missing apostrophe in Sergio's essay?

> ✔ Are words capitalized properly?
> For help with capitalization, see Chapter 52.

1. Read your revision of Sergio's essay for any errors in capitalization.
2. Be sure to check Sergio's capitalization in the fragments you revised.

## Word Choice and Spelling

> ✔ Are words used correctly?
> For help with confused words, see Chapter 58.

1. Find any words used incorrectly in your revision of Sergio's essay.
2. Did you find and correct his three confused words? If not, find and correct them now.

> ✔ Are all words spelled correctly?
> For help with spelling, see Chapter 59.

1. Use spell-check and a dictionary to check the spelling in your revision of Sergio's essay.
2. Correct any misspelled words.

Now rewrite Sergio's essay again with your editing corrections.

# REVISING AND EDITING YOUR OWN ESSAY

Returning to the division/classification essay you wrote earlier in this chapter, revise and edit your own writing. The checklists here will help you apply what you have learned to your essay.

## Revising

### Thesis Statement

- ☐ Does the thesis statement contain the essay's controlling idea and appear as the last sentence of the introduction?

1. What is the purpose or general message you want to send to your readers?

   ______________________________

2. Put brackets around the last sentence in your introduction. Does it explain your purpose? ______________
3. Rewrite your thesis statement if necessary so that it states your purpose and introduces your topics.

### Basic Elements

- ☐ Does the title draw in the readers?
- ☐ Does the introduction capture the readers' attention and build up to the thesis statement effectively?
- ☐ Does each body paragraph deal with a single topic?
- ☐ Does the conclusion bring the essay to a close in an interesting way?

1. Give your essay a title if it doesn't have one. ______________________

2. Does your introduction capture your readers' attention and build up to your thesis statement at the end of the paragraph? ________________

3. Does each of your body paragraphs deal with only one topic? ________

4. Does your conclusion follow some of the suggestions offered in Part I?

____________

## Development

- ☐ Do the body paragraphs adequately support the thesis statement?
- ☐ Does each body paragraph have a focused topic sentence?
- ☐ Does each body paragraph contain *specific* details that support the topic sentence?
- ☐ Does each body paragraph include *enough* details to explain the topic sentence fully?

1. Write out your thesis statement (revised, if necessary), and list your topic sentences below it.

   Thesis statement: ________________________________

   Topic 1: ________________________________

   Topic 2: ________________________________

   Topic 3: ________________________________

2. Do your topics adequately support your thesis statement? ____________

3. Does each body paragraph have a focused topic sentence? __________

4. Do your details adequately explain your categories? ________________

5. Where do you need more information? ______________________

6. Make two of your details more specific.

7. Add at least two new details to make your essay clearer.

## Unity

- ☐ Do the essay's topic sentences relate directly to the thesis statement?
- ☐ Do the details in each body paragraph support its topic sentence?

1. Read each of your topic sentences with your thesis statement in mind. Do they go together? ______________
2. Revise them if necessary so they are directly related.
3. Drop or rewrite any of the sentences in your body paragraphs that are not directly related to their topic sentences.

## Organization

- ☐ Is the essay organized logically?
- ☐ Is each body paragraph organized logically?

1. Read your essay again to see if all the paragraphs are arranged logically.
2. Refer to your answers to the development questions. Then identify your method of organization: ________________________________________
3. Is the order you chose for your paragraphs the most effective approach to your topic?
4. Move any paragraphs that are out of order.
5. Look closely at your body paragraphs to see if all the sentences are arranged logically within paragraphs.
6. Move any sentences that are out of order.

## Coherence

- ☐ Are transitions used effectively so that paragraphs move smoothly and logically from one to the next?
- ☐ Do the sentences move smoothly and logically from one to the next?

1. Add two transitions to your essay.
2. Circle five transitions, repetitions, synonyms, or pronouns you use.
3. Explain how two of them make your paragraphs easier to read.

______________________________________________

______________________________________________

Now rewrite your essay with your revisions.

## Editing

### Sentences

☐ Does each sentence have a main subject and verb?
For help with subjects and verbs, see Chapter 34.

1. Underline the subjects once and verbs twice in a paragraph of your revised essay. Remember that sentences can have more than one subject-verb set.
2. Does each of your sentences have at least one subject and verb that can stand alone? ______________
3. Correct any fragments you have written. For help with fragments, see Chapter 35.
4. Correct any run-on sentences you have written. For help with run-ons, see Chapter 36.

☐ Do all subjects and verbs agree?
For help with subject-verb agreement, see Chapter 39.

1. Read aloud the subjects and verbs you underlined in your revised essay.
2. Correct any subjects and verbs that do not agree.

☐ Do all pronouns agree with their nouns?
For help with pronoun agreement, see Chapter 43.

1. Find any pronouns in your revised essay that do not agree with their nouns.
2. Correct any pronouns that do not agree with their nouns.

☐ Are modifiers as close as possible to the words they modify?
For help with modifier errors, see Chapter 46.

1. Find any modifiers in your revised essay that are not as close as possible to the words they modify.
2. Rewrite sentences if necessary so your modifiers are as close as possible to the words they modify.

## Punctuation and Mechanics

☐ Are sentences punctuated correctly?
For help with punctuation, see Chapters 47–51.

1. Read your revised essay for any errors in punctuation.
2. Make sure any fragments and run-ons you revised are punctuated correctly.

☐ Are words capitalized properly?
For help with capitalization, see Chapter 52.

1. Read your revised essay for any errors in capitalization.
2. Be sure to check your capitalization in any fragments or run-ons you revised.

## Word Choice and Spelling

☐ Are words used correctly?
For help with confused words, see Chapter 58.

1. Find any words used incorrectly in your revised essay.
2. Correct any errors you find.

☐ Are all words spelled correctly?
For help with spelling, see Chapter 59.

1. Use spell-check and a dictionary to check your spelling.
2. Correct any misspelled words.

Now rewrite your essay again with your editing corrections.

## READING SUGGESTIONS

In Chapter 30, you will find two essays that illustrate good division and classification writing: "Black Music in Our Hands" by Bernice Reagon categorizes different kinds of music she has encountered, while "What Are Friends For?" by Marion Winik discusses different types of friends. You might want to read these selections before writing another division and classification essay. As you read, notice how the authors' categories support the points they are making.

## IDEAS FOR WRITING

**Guidelines for Writing a Division/Classification Essay**

1. Decide on your purpose for writing, and make it part of your thesis statement.
2. Divide your topic into categories that don't overlap.
3. Clearly explain each category.
4. Organize your categories logically.
5. Use transitions to move your readers through your essay.

1. Looking at the picture on the next page, think of the types of activities college students do in their spare time. Classify these activities into a few categories, and explain their advantages and disadvantages.

2. What are some rituals that you follow in your own life? Do these rituals serve a purpose in your life? Use division and classification to explain three rituals that you follow.
3. We all dream about trips we'd like to take. Sometimes we get to take one of these trips. Others have to remain dreams. What are your ideal trips? Discuss the types of trips you would like to take. What categories do they fall into? Why do you dream about these types of travel?
4. Create your own division/classification assignment (with the help of your instructor), and write a response to it.

## Revising Workshop

**Small Group Activity (5–10 minutes per writer)** In groups of three or four, each person should read his or her division/classification essay to the other members of the group. Those listening should record their reactions on a copy of the Peer Evaluation Form in Appendix 2F. After your group goes through this process, give your evaluation forms to the appropriate writers so that each writer has two or three peer comment sheets for revising.

**Paired Activity (5 minutes per writer)** Using the completed Peer Evaluation Forms, work in pairs to decide what you should revise in your essay. If time allows, rewrite some of your sentences, and have your partner look at them.

**Individual Activity** Rewrite your paper, using the revising feedback you received from other students.

## Editing Workshop

**Paired Activity (5–10 minutes per writer)** Swap papers with a classmate, and use the editing portion of your Peer Evaluation Form to identify as many grammar, punctuation, mechanics, and spelling errors as you can. If time allows, correct some of your errors, and have your partner look at them. Record your grammar, punctuation, and mechanics errors in the Error Log (Appendix 6) and your spelling errors in the Spelling Log (Appendix 7).

**Individual Activity** Rewrite your paper again, using the editing feedback you received from other students.

## Reflecting on Your Writing

When you have completed your own essay, answer these six questions.

1. What was most difficult about this assignment?
2. What was easiest?
3. What did you learn about dividing and classifying by completing this assignment?
4. What do you think are the strengths of your division/classification essay? Place a squiggly line by the parts of your essay that you feel are very good.
5. What are the weaknesses, if any, of your paper? Place an X by the parts of your essay you would like help with. Write any questions you have in the margin.
6. What did you learn from this assignment about your own writing process—about preparing to write, about writing the first draft, about revising, and about editing?

# Defining

*Writers, most of all, need to define their tasks . . . their themes, their objectives.*

—Henry Seidal Canby

All communication depends on our understanding of a common set of definitions. If we did not work from a set of shared definitions, we would not be able to carry on coherent conversations, write clear letters, or understand any form of media.

It's no surprise, then, that we regularly use definitions in writing as well—in our personal lives, in college courses, and in the workplace. Consider these situations:

You e-mail a friend to tell him or her about the equipment at the fitness center you just joined.

A student has to define *melody, harmony,* and *rhythm* on a music appreciation quiz.

A student begins a report for a criminal justice course with a definition of *criminal law* and *civil law.*

A financial planner prepares a summary sheet defining the basic financial terms a client should know.

The manager of a sporting goods shop writes a classified ad for an opening on the staff.

**Definition** is the process of explaining what a word, an object, or an idea is. A good definition focuses on what is special about a word or an idea and what sets it apart from similar words or concepts. Definitions help us understand basic concrete terms (*cell phone, large fries, midterm exams*), discuss events in our lives (*baseball game, graduation, dentist appointment*), and grasp complex ideas (*friendship, courage, success*). Definitions are the building blocks that help us make certain both writer and reader (or speaker and listener) are working from the same basic understanding of terms and ideas.

Definitions vary greatly. They can be as short as one word (a "hog" is a motorcycle) or as long as an essay or even a book. Words or ideas that require such extended definitions are usually abstract, complex, and controversial. Think, for example, how difficult it might be to define an abstract idea like *equality* compared to concrete words such as *dog* or *cat*.

In the following essay, Lars Eighner writes an extended definition of the fine art of "Dumpster diving," or living out of Dumpsters, the big containers designed to be raised and emptied into a garbage truck. Have you ever witnessed someone Dumpster diving? Have you yourself ever found something in the trash that you took home? How would you feel if you lost your home and with it your sense of security?

**Lars Eighner**

## DUMPSTER DIVING

I began Dumpster diving about a year before I became homeless. I prefer the term *scavenging.* I have heard people, evidently meaning to be polite, use the word *foraging,* but I prefer to reserve that word for gathering nuts and berries and such, which I also do, according to the season and opportunity. 1

I like the frankness of the word *scavenging.* I live from the refuse of others. I am a scavenger. I think it a sound and honorable niche, although if I could I would naturally prefer to live the comfortable consumer life, perhaps—and only perhaps—as a slightly less wasteful consumer owing to what I have learned as a scavenger. 2

Except for jeans, all my clothes come from Dumpsters. Boom boxes, candles, bedding, toilet paper, medicine, books, a typewriter, a virgin male love doll, coins sometimes amounting to many dollars: All came from Dumpsters. And, yes, I eat from Dumpsters, too. 3

There is a predictable series of stages that a person goes through in learning to scavenge. At first the new scavenger is filled with disgust and self-loathing. He is ashamed of being seen. 4

This stage passes with experience. The scavenger finds a pair of running shoes that fit and look and smell brand-new. He finds a pocket calculator in perfect working order. He finds pristine ice cream, still frozen, more than he can eat or keep. He begins to understand: People do throw away perfectly good stuff, a lot of perfectly good stuff. 5

6 At this stage he may become lost and never recover. All the Dumpster divers I have known come to the point of trying to acquire everything they touch. Why not take it, they reason, it is all free. This is, of course, hopeless, and most divers come to realize that they must restrict themselves to items of relatively immediate utility.

7 The finding of objects is becoming something of an urban art. Even respectable, employed people will sometimes find something tempting sticking out of a Dumpster or standing beside one. Quite a number of people, not all of them of the bohemian type, are willing to brag that they found this or that piece in the trash.

8 But eating from Dumpsters is the thing that separates the dilettanti from the professionals. Eating safely involves three principles: using the senses and common sense to evaluate the condition of the found materials; knowing the Dumpsters of a given area and checking them regularly; and seeking always to answer the question Why was this discarded?

9 Yet perfectly good food can be found in Dumpsters. Canned goods, for example, turn up fairly often in the Dumpsters I frequent. I also have few qualms about dry foods such as crackers, cookies, cereal, chips, and pasta if they are free of visible contaminants and still dry and crisp. Raw fruits and vegetables with intact skins seem perfectly safe to me, excluding, of course, the obviously rotten. Many are discarded for minor imperfections that can be pared away.

10 A typical discard is a half jar of peanut butter—though non-organic peanut butter does not require refrigeration and is unlikely to spoil in any reasonable time. One of my favorite finds is yogurt—often discarded, still sealed, when the expiration date has passed—because it will keep for several days, even in warm weather.

11 No matter how careful I am I still get dysentery at least once a month, oftener in warm weather. I do not want to paint too romantic a picture. Dumpster diving has serious drawbacks as a way of life.

12 I find from the experience of scavenging two rather deep lessons. The first is to take what I can use and let the rest go. I have come to think that there is no value in the abstract. A thing I cannot use or make useful, perhaps by trading, has no value, however fine or rare it may be.

13 The second lesson is the transience of material being. I do not suppose that ideas are immortal, but certainly they are longer-lived than material objects.

14 The things I find in Dumpsters, the love letters and rag dolls of so many lives, remind me of this lesson. Now I hardly pick up a thing without envisioning the time I will cast it away. This, I think, is a healthy state of mind. Almost everything I have now has already been cast out at least once, proving that what I own is valueless to someone.

15 I find that my desire to grab for the gaudy bauble has been largely sated. I think this is an attitude I share with the very wealthy—we both know there is plenty more where whatever we have came from. Between us are the rat-race

millions who have confounded their selves with the objects they grasp and who nightly scavenge the cable channels for they know not what.

I am sorry for them. 16

*Preparing to Write Your Own Definition Essay*

What do you think of when you hear the word *security*? What associations do you make with this word? What examples does it bring to mind? Use one or more of the prewriting strategies you learned in Chapter 2 to generate ideas for writing an extended definition of *security*.

## HOW TO WRITE A DEFINITION ESSAY

Clear definitions give writer and reader a mutual starting point on the road to successful communication. Sometimes a short summary and an example are all the definition that's needed. But in the case of abstract and complex words or ideas, a writer may use several approaches to a definition. Use the following guidelines to help you write an extended definition essay.

1. ***Choose your word or idea carefully, and give a working definition of it in your thesis statement.*** First, you need to choose a word or idea that can be defined and explained from several angles, or you will end up with a short, lifeless essay. At the same time, you need to give your readers a working definition right at the start. Put that brief, basic definition in your thesis statement so that readers have a mental hook on which to hang the definitions and explanations in the rest of your essay. Also include the purpose of your essay in your thesis statement.

   At the start of his essay, Eighner defines *Dumpster diving* as "scavenging," explaining, "I live from the refuse of others." This simple, direct definition—given at the beginning—guides readers through the rest of the essay.

2. ***Decide how you want to define your term: by synonym, by negation, or by category.*** These are the three common ways to develop a definition.

   When you define using a *synonym*, you furnish readers with a similar word or a short explanation with synonyms. Eighner uses a synonym right at the beginning of his essay. "Dumpster diving" is an informal term that is used by city people to refer to taking garbage out of trash bins. Apartment houses and office buildings often use Dumpsters to hold garbage until it is taken to the dump. Because *Dumpster* is not a term that everyone knows and because the meaning of the expression "Dumpster diving" is not immediately obvious, Eighner provides the synonym "scavenging," which most people understand.

When you define a word by *negation*, you say what it is *not*. That is, you define a term by contrasting it with something else. Eighner uses definition by negation twice in his essay. First, he states that "scavenging" is not "foraging," meaning that it is not gathering nuts and berries. He also says that life as a scavenger is not a comfortable consumer life. The rest of his essay explains his life as a scavenger.

Defining a term by *category* is a more formal type of definition, as in a dictionary. Defining by category has two parts: the class or general category that the word belongs to and the way the word is different from other words in that group. For example, *heart* might be defined as "the organ that pumps blood through the body." The general category is *organ*, and it is different from other organs (brain, lungs, stomach, liver, and so on) because *it pumps blood*. Eighner doesn't use this type of definition directly. He does, however, suggest that scavenging falls into the category of lifestyle in paragraph 2 when he compares his life as a scavenger to the life of a consumer.

3. ***Develop your definition with examples.*** Nearly every definition can be improved by adding examples. Well-chosen examples show your definition in action. Definitions can be *objective*—strictly factual, as in a dictionary definition—or *subjective*—combined with personal opinions. A definition essay is usually more subjective than objective because you are providing your personal opinions about a word or concept. You are explaining to your readers your own meaning, which is what makes your essay interesting. If your readers wanted an objective definition, they could go to a dictionary.

   Eighner uses examples throughout his essay to expand on his definition. Paragraph 3 consists entirely of examples of things he has found in Dumpsters. Later he gives examples of the kinds of food he finds, including canned goods, cookies and crackers, raw fruits and vegetables, peanut butter, and yogurt. These examples help Eighner strike a balance in his definition between objective (factual) and subjective (personal) references. From these and Eighner's other examples, we get a very clear idea of how a person could live by Dumpster diving.

4. ***Use other rhetorical strategies, such as description, comparison, or process analysis, to support your definition.*** When you write a definition essay, you want to look at your word or idea in many

different ways. The other techniques you have learned for developing body paragraphs can help you expand your definition even further. Perhaps a description, a short narrative, or a comparison will make your definition come alive.

In addition to examples, Eighner uses process analysis, classification, and cause and effect to expand his definition. He uses process analysis to explain the four stages that new Dumpster divers go through—how something happens. His three rules for eating safely are also process analysis—how to do something. He draws on classification to name the types of foods he finds and then gives examples of each category. At the end of his essay, he uses cause and effect when he explains that Dumpster diving (the cause) has taught him two lessons (the effects): that only items you can use are valuable and that material objects don't last.

5. ***Organize your essay in a logical way.*** Because a definition essay can be developed through several strategies and techniques, there is no set pattern of organization. So you need to figure out the most logical way to explain your word or idea. You might move from particular to general or from general to particular. Or you might arrange your ideas from one extreme to the other, such as from most important to least important, least dramatic to most dramatic, or most familiar to least familiar. In some cases, you might organize your definition chronologically or spatially. Or you might organize part of your essay one way and the rest another way. What's important is that you move in some logical way from one point to another so that your readers can follow your train of thought.

   Eighner organizes his essay chronologically. He says he started Dumpster diving about a year before he became homeless. Now he is homeless and lives by Dumpster diving. He defines the term in two ways (synonym and negation) and gives examples of what he finds. Then he switches to a general-to-particular organization in paragraphs 7 to 11, explaining how someone learns to dive and then how to actually dive for food in particular. The last five paragraphs conclude the essay.

### *Writing Your Own Definition Essay*

If you have a roof over your head, food to eat, and money in your pocket, you have a sense of security. Write an essay defining "security." Begin by reviewing your prewriting notes. Then decide how you are going to approach your subject. Next, write your essay, starting with a clear thesis statement.

## DEFINITION AT WORK

In the following essay, titled "True Friends," a student named Francine Feinstein defines *friendship*. See if you can identify her main point as you read her essay.

### True Friends

1 Many people throw the term "friend" around loosely. They think they have friends at work, friends at school, and friends from the Internet. But is all these people really friends? The word "friend" seems to be used today to refer to anyone from long-term to short-term relationships. However, a true friend is someone who will always be there in times of need, who will always be the best company, and who will always listen and give advice.

2 Without any questions asked, a good friend will always be there in times of need. No matter how bad a problem is, a true friend will be the person who sits up nights and take days off work just to sit with a friend. If someone is in trouble with a difficult paper a friend will help brainstorm to figure out the problem. If someone is sick, a friend will be the first one at the door with chicken soup and will baby-sit the kids until the sick person feel better. I hate the feeling of being sick. If someone is stranded across town with a broken-down car, a friend will drop everything to make a rescue and drive the person wherever he or she needs to go. Not everyone has a friend like this a true friend will always be the first one there, no matter what.

3 Most of all, a true friend is also someone who will listen and give reliable advice. Some people will listen to problems and then give the advice that they think will work best for them, but that advice isn't necessarily best for their friend. Other people will listen but then interject personal stories that relate to the problem but don't solve it. But a true friend listens to a problem and gives suggestions to help a friend figure out the best solution for himself or herself. In other words, a true friend knows how to listen and help a person solve problems.

4 In addition, a friend is someone who is always great company, because friends have so much in common with each other. Imagine working out together, grabbing a sandwich, and then spending the evening just talking--about life, about good times, about bad times, about classes at school. Right now my classes are really hard. At the end of the day, friends might rent their favorite DVD and make some fresh popcorn. Sometimes they even seem to be on the same biological clock, getting tired and waking up at the same time. Friends can always be themselves around each other.

The word "friend" may be misused in the English language, but at least we can agree on what true friends are. True friends are hard to find. But once you find them, they will always be there, listen to you and be the best people to spend time with. No wonder true friends are so rare! 5

1. What is this essay defining?

   ______________________________

2. Does this author define mainly by synonym, by negation, or by category in her essay? Explain your answer.

   ______________________________

   ______________________________

3. List three specific examples that Francine uses to develop her definition.

   ______________________________

   Are her examples more objective or subjective? ______________

4. What other techniques does Francine use to develop her definition?

   ______________________________

   ______________________________

5. How does Francine organize the examples in her essay? ______________

   ______________________________

   Explain your answer.

   ______________________________

   ______________________________

   ______________________________

## REVISING AND EDITING A STUDENT ESSAY

This essay is Francine's first draft, which now needs to be revised and edited. First, apply the Revising Checklist on page 268 to Francine's draft so that you are working with her content. When you are satisfied that her ideas are fully developed and well organized, use the Editing Checklist on page 272 to correct her grammar and mechanics errors. Answer the questions after each checklist. Then write your suggested changes directly on Francine's draft.

## Revising Checklist

**THESIS STATEMENT**

✔ Does the thesis statement contain the essay's controlling idea and appear as the last sentence of the introduction?

**BASIC ELEMENTS**

✔ Does the title draw in the readers?

✔ Does the introduction capture the readers' attention and build up to the thesis statement effectively?

✔ Does each body paragraph deal with a single topic?

✔ Does the conclusion bring the essay to a close in an interesting way?

**DEVELOPMENT**

✔ Do the body paragraphs adequately support the thesis statement?

✔ Does each body paragraph have a focused topic sentence?

✔ Does each body paragraph contain *specific* details that support the topic sentence?

✔ Does each body paragraph include *enough* details to explain the topic sentence fully?

**UNITY**

✔ Do the essay's topic sentences relate directly to the thesis statement?

✔ Do the details in each body paragraph support its topic sentence?

**ORGANIZATION**

✔ Is the essay organized logically?

✔ Is each body paragraph organized logically?

**COHERENCE**

✔ Are transitions used effectively so that paragraphs move smoothly and logically from one to the next?

✔ Do the sentences move smoothly and logically from one to the next?

## Thesis Statement

> ✔ Does the thesis statement contain the essay's controlling idea and appear as the last sentence of the introduction?

1. Put brackets around the last sentence in Francine's introduction. Does it state her purpose? ____________

2. Rewrite Francine's thesis statement if necessary so that it states her purpose and introduces her topics. ______________________________

______________________________________________________

## Basic Elements

> ✔ Does the title draw in the readers?
> ✔ Does the introduction capture the readers' attention and build up to the thesis statement effectively?
> ✔ Does each body paragraph deal with a single topic?
> ✔ Does the conclusion bring the essay to a close in an interesting way?

1. Give the writer's essay an alternate title. ______________________

2. Rewrite Francine's introduction so that it captures the readers' attention and builds up to the thesis statement at the end of the paragraph.

______________________________________________________

______________________________________________________

______________________________________________________

______________________________________________________

3. Does each of Francine's body paragraphs deal with only one topic? ____________

4. Rewrite Francine's conclusion using at least one suggestion from Part I.

________________________________________

________________________________________

________________________________________

________________________________________

## Development

- ✔ Do the body paragraphs adequately support the thesis statement?
- ✔ Does each body paragraph have a focused topic sentence?
- ✔ Does each body paragraph contain *specific* details that support the topic sentence?
- ✔ Does each body paragraph include *enough* details to explain the topic sentence fully?

1. Write out Francine's thesis statement (revised, if necessary), and list her three topic sentences below it.

   Thesis statement: ________________________________________

   ________________________________________

   ________________________________________

   Topic 1: ________________________________________

   ________________________________________

   Topic 2: ________________________________________

   ________________________________________

   Topic 3: ________________________________________

   ________________________________________

2. Do Francine's topic sentences adequately support her thesis statement?

___________

3. Does each body paragraph have a focused topic sentence? ___________

4. Do the examples in the essay help define "friend"? ___________

___________

5. Where do you need more information? ___________

6. Make two of Francine's details more specific. ___________

7. Add at least two new details to make her essay clearer. ___________

## Unity

- ✔ Do the essay's topic sentences relate directly to the thesis statement?
- ✔ Do the details in each body paragraph support its topic sentence?

1. Read each of Francine's topic sentences with her thesis statement in mind. Do they go together? ___________
2. Revise them if necessary so they are directly related.
3. Drop or rewrite the sentences in paragraph 2 and in paragraph 4 that are not directly related to their topic sentence.

## Organization

- ✔ Is the essay organized logically?
- ✔ Is each body paragraph organized logically?

1. Read Francine's essay again to see if all the paragraphs are arranged logically.

2. Reverse the two paragraphs that are out of order.
3. Look closely at Francine's body paragraphs to see if all her sentences are arranged logically within paragraphs.
4. Move any sentences that are out of order.

## Coherence

✔ Are transitions used effectively so that paragraphs move smoothly and logically from one to the next?

✔ Do the sentences move smoothly and logically from one to the next?

1. Add two transitions to Francine's essay.
2. Circle five transitions Francine uses. For a list of transitions, see page 84.
3. Explain how two of these make Francine's essay easier to read.

______________________________________________

______________________________________________

Now rewrite Francine's essay with your revisions.

## Editing Checklist

SENTENCES

✔ Does each sentence have a main subject and verb?

✔ Do all subjects and verbs agree?

✔ Do all pronouns agree with their nouns?

✔ Are modifiers as close as possible to the words they modify?

PUNCTUATION AND MECHANICS

✔ Are sentences punctuated correctly?

✔ Are words capitalized properly?

WORD CHOICE AND SPELLING

✔ Are words used correctly?

✔ Are words spelled correctly?

## Sentences

> ✔ Does each sentence have a main subject and verb?
> For help with subjects and verbs, see Chapter 34.

1. Underline the subjects once and verbs twice in paragraphs 1 and 2 of your revision of Francine's essay. Remember that sentences can have more than one subject-verb set.
2. Does each of the sentences have at least one subject and verb that can stand alone? ______________
3. Did you find and correct Francine's run-on sentence? If not, find and correct it now. For help with run-ons, see Chapter 36.

> ✔ Do all subjects and verbs agree?
> For help with subject-verb agreement, see Chapter 39.

1. Read aloud the subjects and verbs you underlined in your revision of Francine's essay.
2. Did you find and correct the three subjects and verbs that do not agree?

> ✔ Do all pronouns agree with their nouns?
> For help with pronoun agreement, see Chapter 43.

1. Find any pronouns in your revision of Francine's essay that do not agree with their nouns.
2. Correct any pronouns that do not agree with their nouns.

> ✔ Are modifiers as close as possible to the words they modify?
> For help with modifier errors, see Chapter 46.

1. Find any modifiers in your revision of Francine's essay that are not as close as possible to the words they modify.
2. Rewrite sentences if necessary so that modifiers are as close as possible to the words they modify.

## Punctuation and Mechanics

> ✔ Are sentences punctuated correctly?
> For help with punctuation, see Chapters 47–51.

1. Read your revision of Francine's essay for any errors in punctuation.
2. Find the run-on sentence you revised, and make sure it is punctuated correctly.
3. Did you find and correct the two comma errors in Francine's essay?

> ✔ Are words capitalized properly?
> For help with capitalization, see Chapter 52.

1. Read your revision of Francine's essay for any errors in capitalization.
2. Be sure to check Francine's capitalization in the run-on you revised.

## Word Choice and Spelling

> ✔ Are words used correctly?
> For help with confused words, see Chapter 58.

1. Find any words used incorrectly in your revision of Francine's essay.
2. Correct any errors you find.

> ✔ Are all words spelled correctly?
> For help with spelling, see Chapter 59.

1. Use spell-check and a dictionary to check the spelling in your revision of Francine's essay.
2. Correct any misspelled words.

Now rewrite Francine's essay again with your editing corrections.

## REVISING AND EDITING YOUR OWN ESSAY

Returning to the definition essay you wrote earlier in this chapter, revise and edit your own writing. The checklists here will help you apply what you have learned to your essay.

### Revising

#### Thesis Statement

☐ Does the thesis statement contain the essay's controlling idea and appear as the last sentence of the introduction?

1. What are you defining? ______________________________
2. What is the purpose of your definition essay? ______________________________
3. Put brackets around the last sentence in your introduction. Does it state your purpose? ______________
4. Rewrite your thesis statement if necessary so that it states your purpose and introduces your topics. ______________________________

______________________________

## Basic Elements

- ☐ Does the title draw in the readers?
- ☐ Does the introduction capture the readers' attention and build up to the thesis statement effectively?
- ☐ Does each body paragraph deal with a single topic?
- ☐ Does the conclusion bring the essay to a close in an interesting way?

1. Give your essay a title if it doesn't have one. ______________________
2. Does your introduction capture your readers' attention and build up to your thesis statement at the end of the paragraph? ______________________
3. Does each of your body paragraphs deal with only one topic? __________
4. Does your conclusion follow some of the suggestions offered in Part I? ______________

## Development

- ☐ Do the body paragraphs adequately support the thesis statement?
- ☐ Does each body paragraph have a focused topic sentence?
- ☐ Does each body paragraph contain *specific* details that support the topic sentence?
- ☐ Does each body paragraph include *enough* details to explain the topic sentence fully?

1. Write out your thesis statement (revised, if necessary), and list your topic sentences below it.

   Thesis statement: ______________________________________

   Topic 1: ______________________________________

   Topic 2: ______________________________________

Topic 3: ______________________________

2. Do your topics adequately support your thesis statement? __________
3. Does each body paragraph have a focused topic sentence? __________
4. Do the examples in the essay help develop your definition? __________
5. Where do you need more information? ______________________
6. Make two of your details more specific.
7. Add at least two new details to make your definition clearer.

## Unity

- ☐ Do the essay's topic sentences relate directly to the thesis statement?
- ☐ Do the details in each body paragraph support its topic sentence?

1. Read each of your topic sentences with your thesis statement in mind. Do they go together? __________
2. Revise them if necessary so they are directly related.
3. Drop or rewrite any of the sentences in your body paragraphs that are not directly related to their topic sentences.

## Organization

- ☐ Is the essay organized logically?
- ☐ Is each body paragraph organized logically?

1. Read your essay again to see if all the paragraphs are arranged logically.
2. Refer to your answers to the development questions. Then identify your method of organization: ______________________
3. Is the order you chose for your paragraphs the most effective approach to your topic? ______________________

4. Move any paragraphs that are out of order.
5. Look closely at your body paragraphs to see if all the sentences are arranged logically within paragraphs.
6. Move any sentences that are out of order.

## Coherence

- ☐ Are transitions used effectively so that paragraphs move smoothly and logically from one to the next?
- ☐ Do the sentences move smoothly and logically from one to the next?

1. Add two transitions to your essay.
2. Circle five transitions you use.
3. Explain how two of them make your essay easier to read.

________________________________________

________________________________________

Now rewrite your essay with your revisions.

# Editing

## Sentences

- ☐ Does each sentence have a main subject and verb?
  For help with subjects and verbs, see Chapter 34.

1. Underline the subjects once and verbs twice in a paragraph of your revised essay. Remember that sentences can have more than one subject-verb set.
2. Does each of your sentences have at least one subject and verb that can stand alone? _______________

3. Correct any fragments you have written. For help with fragments, see Chapter 35.
4. Correct any run-on sentences you have written. For help with run-ons, see Chapter 36.

☐ Do all subjects and verbs agree?
For help with subject-verb agreement, see Chapter 39.

1. Read aloud the subjects and verbs you underlined in your revised essay.
2. Correct any subjects and verbs that do not agree.

☐ Do all pronouns agree with their nouns?
For help with pronoun agreement, see Chapter 43.

1. Find any pronouns in your revised essay that do not agree with their nouns.
2. Correct any pronouns that do not agree with their nouns.

☐ Are modifiers as close as possible to the words they modify?
For help with modifier errors, see Chapter 46.

1. Find any modifiers in your revised essay that are not as close as possible to the words they modify.
2. Rewrite sentences if necessary so that your modifiers are as close as possible to the words they modify.

## Punctuation and Mechanics

☐ Are sentences punctuated correctly?
For help with punctuation, see Chapters 47–51.

1. Read your revised essay for any errors in punctuation.
2. Make sure any fragments and run-ons you revised are punctuated correctly.

☐ Are words capitalized properly?
For help with capitalization, see Chapter 52.

1. Read your revised essay for any errors in capitalization.
2. Be sure to check your capitalization in any fragments or run-ons you revised.

## Word Choice and Spelling

☐ Are words used correctly?
For help with confused words, see Chapter 58.

1. Find any words used incorrectly in your revised essay.
2. Correct any errors you find.

☐ Are all words spelled correctly?
For help with spelling, see Chapter 59.

1. Use spell-check and a dictionary to check your spelling.
2. Correct any misspelled words.

Now rewrite your essay again with your editing corrections.

## READING SUGGESTIONS

In Chapter 31, you will find two good definition essays: "How to Find True Love: Or, Rather, How It Finds You" by Lois Smith Brady defines how true love actually finds the lovers, and "Healing Myself with the Power of Work" by Michael Norlen reveals through definition how work helps the author overcome depression. You might want to read these selections before writing another definition essay. As you read, notice how the writers make their points through well-chosen examples and details.

# IDEAS FOR WRITING

**Guidelines for Writing a Definition Essay**

1. Choose your word or idea carefully, and give a working definition of it in your thesis statement.
2. Decide how you want to define your term: by synonym, by negation, or by category.
3. Develop your definition with examples.
4. Use other rhetorical strategies, such as description, comparison, or process analysis, to support your definition.
5. Organize your essay in a logical way.

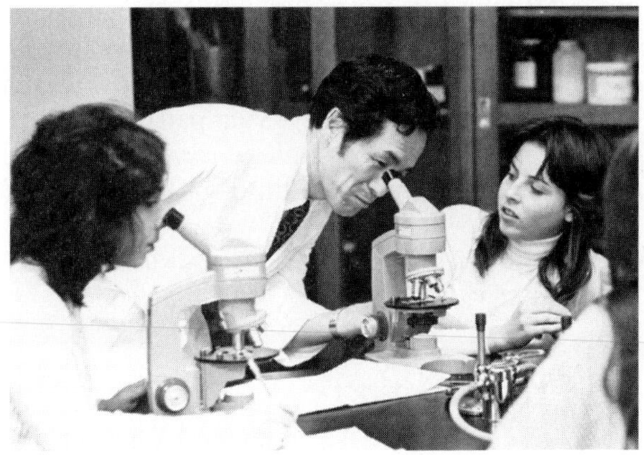

1. What does education mean to you? Define "education" from your point of view.
2. The concept of "family" has undergone a number of changes over the past few years. How would you define this term in our current society?
3. Define one of the following abstract terms: *fear*, *love*, *inferiority*, *wonder*, *pride*, *self-control*, *discipline*, *anger*, *freedom*, *violence*, *assertiveness*, *courtesy*, *kindness*.
4. Create your own definition assignment (with the help of your instructor), and write a response to it.

## Revising Workshop

**Small Group Activity (5–10 minutes per writer)** In groups of three or four, each person should read his or her definition essay to the other members of the group. The listeners should record their reactions on a copy of the Peer Evaluation Form in Appendix 2G. After your group goes through this process, give your evaluation forms to the appropriate writers so that each writer has two or three peer comment sheets for revising.

**Paired Activity (5 minutes per writer)** Using the completed Peer Evaluation Forms, work in pairs to decide what you should revise in your essay. If time allows, rewrite some of your sentences, and have your partner look at them.

**Individual Activity** Rewrite your paper, using the revising feedback you received from other students.

## Editing Workshop

**Paired Activity (5–10 minutes per writer)** Swap papers with a classmate, and use the editing portion of your Peer Evaluation Form to identify as many grammar, punctuation, mechanics, and spelling errors as you can. If time allows, correct some of your errors, and have your partner look at them. Record your grammar, punctuation, and mechanics errors in the Error Log (Appendix 6) and your spelling errors in the Spelling Log (Appendix 7).

**Individual Activity** Rewrite your paper again, using the editing feedback you received from other students.

## Reflecting on Your Writing

When you have completed your own essay, answer these six questions.

1. What was most difficult about this assignment?
2. What was easiest?
3. What did you learn about using definition by completing this assignment?
4. What do you think are the strengths of your definition essay? Place a squiggly line by the parts of your essay that you feel are very good.
5. What are the weaknesses, if any, of your paper? Place an X by the parts of your essay you would like help with. Write any questions you have in the margin.
6. What did you learn from this assignment about your own writing process—about preparing to write, about writing the first draft, about revising, and about editing?

# Analyzing Causes and Effects

*The act of writing is one of the most powerful problem-solving tools humans have at their disposal.*

—Toby Fulwiler

We are born with a natural curiosity. Wanting to know why things happen is one of our earliest, most basic instincts: Daddy, why is the sky blue? Closely related to this desire to understand *why* is our interest in *what* will happen as a result of some particular action: If I stay outside much longer, will I get a bad sunburn? But thinking about causes and effects is not only part of human nature but also an advanced mental process and the basis for most decisions we make. When faced with a decision, we naturally consider it from different perspectives. If we choose option A, what will happen? What if we choose B—or C? In other words, we look at the possible results—the effects—of the choices and then make up our minds.

Analyzing causes and effects is also an essential part of our writing lives. We use cause-and-effect writing in our personal lives, in college, and in the marketplace. Think about these situations:

A volunteer for a mayor's campaign designs a poster telling how a vote for this candidate will benefit the city.

A student discusses the causes of schizophrenia in a paper for a psychology course.

A student explains the effects of the Civil Rights Act of 1964 on a history exam.

A sales representative writes a report to her manager explaining why she didn't meet her sales projections.

The owner of a florist shop writes a letter of complaint to one of the suppliers about the negative effect of late deliveries on sales.

**Analyzing causes and effects** requires the ability to look for connections between two or more items or events and to analyze the reasons for those connections. As the name implies, this writing strategy is composed of two parts: cause and effect. To understand **causes,** we look in the past for reasons why something happened. To discover **effects,** we look to the future for possible results of an action. In other words, we break a situation into parts so we can look at the relationships between these parts and then reach conclusions that are logical and useful.

In "Why Do Schools Flunk Biology?" Lynnell Hancock makes the point that education in the United States is stuck in the nineteenth century. She deals with both the causes and the effects of students' ability to learn. What do you think of our educational system on the high school level? What do you think of your local high schools?

**Lynnell Hancock**

## WHY DO SCHOOLS FLUNK BIOLOGY?

1 Biology is a staple at most American high schools. Yet when it comes to the biology of the students themselves—how their brains develop and retain knowledge—school officials would rather not pay attention to the lessons. Can first graders handle French? What time should school start? Should music be cut? Biologists have some important evidence to offer. Not only are they ignored, but their findings are often turned upside down.

2 Force of habit rules the hallways and classrooms. Neither brain science nor education research has been able to free the majority of America's schools from their 19th-century roots. If more administrators were tuned in to brain research, scientists argue, not only would schedules change, but subjects such as foreign language and geometry would be offered to much younger children. Music and gym would be daily requirements. Lectures, work sheets and rote memorization would be replaced by hands-on materials, drama and project work. And teachers would pay greater attention to children's emotional connections to subjects. "We do more education research than anyone else in the world," says Frank Vellutino, a professor of educational psychology at State University of New York at Albany, "and we ignore more as well."

Plato once said that music "is a more potent instrument than any other for education." Now scientists know why. Music, they believe, trains the brain for higher forms of thinking. Researchers at the University of California, Irvine, studied the power of music by observing two groups of preschoolers. One group took piano lessons and sang daily in chorus. The other did not. After eight months the musical 3-year-olds were expert puzzlemasters, scoring 80 percent higher than their playmates did in spatial intelligence—the ability to visualize the world accurately. 3

This skill later translates into complex math and engineering skills. "Early music training can enhance a child's ability to reason," says Irvine physicist Gordon Shaw. Yet music education is often the first "frill" to be cut when school budgets shrink. Schools on average have only one music teacher for every 500 children, according to the National Commission on Music Education. 4

Then there's gym—another expendable hour by most school standards. Only 36 percent of schoolchildren today are required to participate in daily physical education. Yet researchers now know that exercise is good not only for the heart. It also juices up the brain, feeding it nutrients in the form of glucose and increasing nerve connections—all of which make it easier for kids of all ages to learn. Neuroscientist William Greenough confirmed this by watching rats at his University of Illinois at Urbana-Champaign lab. One group did nothing. A second exercised on an automatic treadmill. A third was set loose in a Barnum & Bailey obstacle course requiring the rats to perform acrobatic feats. These "supersmart" rats grew "an enormous amount of gray matter" compared with their sedentary partners, says Greenough. Of course, children don't ordinarily run such gantlets: still, Greenough believes, the results are significant. Numerous studies, he says, show that children who exercise regularly do better in school. 5

The implication for schools goes beyond simple exercise. Children also need to be more physically active in the classroom, not sitting quietly in their seats memorizing subtraction tables. Knowledge is retained longer if children connect not only aurally but emotionally and physically to the material, says University of Oregon education professor Robert Sylwester in *A Celebration of Neurons*. 6

Good teachers know that lecturing on the American Revolution is far less effective than acting out a battle. Angles and dimensions are better understood if children chuck their work sheets and build a complex model to scale. The smell of the glue enters memory through one sensory system, the touch of the wood blocks another, the sight of the finished model still another. The brain then creates a multidimensional mental model of the experience—one easier to retrieve. "Explaining a smell," says Sylwester, "is not as good as actually smelling it." 7

Scientists argue that children are capable of far more at younger ages than schools generally realize. People obviously continue learning their whole lives, 8 but the optimum "windows of opportunity for learning" last until about the age of 10 or 12, says Harry Chugani of Wayne State University's Children's Hospital of Michigan. Chugani determined this by measuring the brain's consumption of its chief energy source, glucose. (The more glucose it uses, the more active the brain.) Children's brains, he observes, gobble up glucose at twice the adult rate from the age of 4 to puberty. So young brains are as primed as they'll ever be to process new information. Complex subjects such as trigonometry or foreign language shouldn't wait for puberty to be introduced. In fact, Chugani says, it's far easier for an elementary-school child to hear and process a second language—and even speak it without an accent. Yet most U.S. districts wait until junior high to introduce Spanish or French—after the "windows" are closed.

9 Reform could begin at the beginning. Many sleep researchers now believe that most teens' biological clocks are set later than those of their fellow humans. But high school starts at 7:30 a.m., usually to accommodate bus schedules. The result can be wasted class time for whole groups of kids. Making matters worse, many kids have trouble readjusting their natural sleep rhythm. Dr. Richard Allen of Johns Hopkins University found that teens went to sleep at the same time whether they had to be at school by 7:30 a.m. or 9:30 a.m. The later-to-rise teens not only get more sleep, he says; they also get better grades. The obvious solution would be to start school later when kids hit puberty. But at school, there's what's obvious, and then there's tradition.

10 Why is this body of research rarely used in most American classrooms? Not many administrators or school-board members know it exists, says Linda Darling-Hammond, professor of education at Columbia University's Teachers College. In most states, neither teachers nor administrators are required to know much about how children learn in order to be certified. What's worse, she says, decisions to cut music or gym are often made by noneducators, whose concerns are more often monetary than educational. "Our school system was invented in the late 1800s, and little has changed," she says. "Can you imagine if the medical profession ran this way?"

---

***Preparing to Write Your Own Cause/Effect Essay***

What can be improved in our educational system on the high school level? What do you want to change? What would be the possible results of these changes? What do you want to keep the same? Use one or more of the prewriting techniques that you learned in Chapter 2 to generate ideas on this subject.

## HOW TO WRITE A CAUSE/EFFECT ESSAY

When you write a cause/effect essay, your purpose is to give your readers some insight into the causes and effects of an event or a situation. Cause/effect writing is based on your ability to analyze. Good cause/effect essays follow a few simple guidelines.

1. ***Write a thesis statement that tells what you are analyzing.*** Cause/effect thinking requires that you look for connections between two or more situations. That is, you want to discover what caused an incident or what its results might be. Then you can focus on the causes (what made something else happen) or the effects (the results), or some combination of the two.

   In her essay, Hancock puts her thesis statement at the end of her first paragraph: "Not only are they [the biology lessons] ignored, but their findings are often turned upside down." She goes on to say that if school administrators paid attention to research (the cause), we would see many changes (the effects), which she names. The rest of the essay examines each effect in detail.

2. ***Choose facts, details, and reasons to support your thesis statement.*** Cause/effect essays are usually written to prove a specific point. As a result, your body paragraphs should consist mainly of facts, details, and reasons—not opinions. Your reader should be able to check what you are saying, and any opinions that you include should be based on clear evidence.

   Since Hancock sets out to prove that American education ignores research, she must name specific research studies that help her prove her point. She breaks her subject into five areas: music, gym, teaching methods, curriculum (subjects studied), and school hours. She then cites evidence in each area. For example, in the area of music, she describes research at the University of California, Irvine; for gym, she discusses rat studies from the University of Illinois; for curriculum, she describes research done at Wayne State University's Children's Hospital.

   Hancock also quotes many experts, such as Frank Vellutino, a professor of educational psychology at State University of New York at Albany (paragraph 2), and gives statistics from the National Commission on Music Education (paragraph 4). A reader could check every one of Hancock's research studies, quotations, statistics, and observations (such as when most high schools begin classes in the morning). By providing facts and reasons rather than opinions in her body paragraphs, Hancock proves her point—that American education is behind the times.

3. ***Do not mistake coincidence for cause or effect.*** If you get up every morning at 5:30, just before the sun rises, you cannot conclude that the sun rises *because* you get up. The relationship between these two events is coincidence. Confusing coincidence with cause and effect is faulty reasoning—reasoning that is not logical. To avoid this kind of faulty reasoning, you can look deeper into the issues connected with your subject. The more you search for real causes and effects, the less likely you will be thrown off by coincidence.

   Hancock does not seem to mistake coincidence for cause or effect in any part of her essay. If, however, she had said that ignoring research on how teens learn has resulted in fewer students studying foreign languages today compared to 40 years ago, her reasoning would be faulty. She has no evidence to prove that the research about how students learn and the decline in students taking foreign languages in high school are related. It's only a coincidence that the research has been ignored and that fewer students study foreign languages today.

4. ***Search for the real causes and effects connected with your subject.*** Just as you wouldn't stop reading halfway through a good murder mystery, you shouldn't stop too early in your analysis of causes and effects. Keep digging. The first reasons or results that you uncover are often not the *real* reasons or results. Suppose that a character in a mystery dies by slipping in the shower. You should try to find out what caused the fall. A good detective who keeps digging might find that someone administered a drug overdose, which caused her to fall in the shower. In other words, you are looking for the most basic cause or effect.

   Hancock shows us through the large amount of evidence she presents that she has searched hard to discover the real causes and effects of education's lagging behind the times. She names two causes—administrators ignore research and noneducators make decisions about education—and gives the effects of ignoring research in five areas of education.

5. ***Organize your essay so that your readers can easily follow your analysis.*** Though it may be difficult to think through the causes and effects of a situation, organizing this type of essay is usually straightforward. Your thesis statement tells what you are going to analyze. Then your body paragraphs discuss the main causes or main effects in the order they occurred, from one extreme to another, from general to

particular, or from particular to general. You might, for example, use chronological order to show how one effect led to another and then to a third. Or you might move from the most important cause or effect to the least important. Your goal in a cause/effect essay is to get your readers to agree with you and see a certain issue or situation the way you do. To accomplish this purpose, your readers need to be able to follow what you are saying.

Hancock discusses five effects of ignoring research on how students learn, moving from particular to general. First, she deals with the two subjects that school boards cut for budget reasons, music and gym. From these specific classes she moves to more general concerns—teaching methods and curriculum. Finally, she discusses high school hours, the most general topic of all. In other words, she organizes her essay from specific to general, moving from specific classes to the general logistics of the school day.

***Writing Your Own Cause/Effect Essay***

Write an essay analyzing one of the changes you think is necessary in our high school educational system. What caused the current problem as you see it? Why is this change necessary? What will be the results of this change? Review your prewriting notes first. Then draft a thesis statement and write your analysis, following the guidelines for writing a cause/effect essay.

## CAUSE AND EFFECT AT WORK

Jefferson Wright, the student writer of the following essay, titled "The Budget Crisis," explores the problems of budget cuts at his college. Can you find the points in his essay when he deals with causes? When does he focus on effects?

### The Budget Crisis

The local college has a budget crisis. Now, when a staff person quits their job or retires, no one is hired to replace that person. This wouldn't be of great concern to most students, except now the lack of money is starting to affect the campus grounds. The college no longer has the money to replace some of the maintenance and facilities crew, which means the campus grounds, classrooms, and offices are no longer well maintained. 1

2 A campus that used to be beautiful has turned into a wasteland because of the neglect in keeping up its grounds. The small maintenance crew simply cannot handle the workload necessary to maintain the campus. The flower beds in front of the buildings have not been weeded, so now it has more weeds than flowers. Trash that is thrown around the campus has not been picked up. Around every doorway are cigarette butts ground into the concrete. People shouldn't smoke anyway. It's not a great habit. There are old newspapers and candy wrappers caught on grass that has not been mowed in over two weeks, making the grounds look like the aftermath of a concert. Trash cans are overflowing with garbage and have colonies of flies circling them. The outside of the campus just looks unkempt and uncared for.

3 However, the campus grounds are not all that is ugly. The classroom buildings are also neglected. Everything inside is as messy as outside. The floors that used to shine are now covered with a sticky gray film. There are spills on the floors by all the soft drink machines. The bulletin boards are never cleaned off, so people just put new flyers over three or four layers of old flyers. On warm days, a strange smell overwhelms the classrooms, which the students have named "the biohazard." Restrooms are in desperate need of attention. And would probably fail any government check. The campus is really disgusting.

4 But the students aren't the only people suffering; the teachers are feeling the effects also. Their offices have ants crawling from various crevices in the walls. The dust in their offices is two inches thick. Spiders have woven cobwebs high in the windows and corners of the offices. Making both teachers and students wonder exactly where the insects hide during the day. Many light bulbs are broken near the offices, and the fluorescent bulbs flicker as if it is dancing to an unheard rhythm. The offices are as bad as the rest of the campus.

5 The condition of the campus can hardly be blamed on the maintenance crew. They are constantly working and trying to keep up with the workload. The problem lies in the fact that by the time they finish one job, two or more weeks pass by before they can get back to that job. There just isn't enough money to hire the necessary personnel to cover the demands of the job. The college should put money into hiring more maintenance personnel before students transfer to other colleges because of the condition of this one. Why can't the college just spend the necessary money to make the campus beautiful again.

1. What is Jefferson analyzing in this essay?

_______________________________________________

2. Do Jefferson's facts, details, and reasons support his thesis statement? Explain your answer.

_______________________________________________

_______________________________________________

3. Does Jefferson confuse any coincidences with causes and effects? Explain your answer.

_______________________________________________

4. Do you feel that Jefferson gets to the real problems connected with his college's budget crisis? Explain your answer.

_______________________________________________

_______________________________________________

5. How does Jefferson organize the topics in his essay?

_______________________________________________

## REVISING AND EDITING A STUDENT ESSAY

This essay is Jefferson's first draft, which now needs to be revised and edited. First, apply the Revising Checklist below to Jefferson's draft so that you are working with his content. When you are satisfied that his ideas are fully developed and well organized, use the Editing Checklist on page 296 to correct his grammar and mechanics errors. Answer the questions after each checklist. Then write your suggested changes directly on Jefferson's draft.

### Revising Checklist

**THESIS STATEMENT**

✔ Does the thesis statement contain the essay's controlling idea and appear as the last sentence of the introduction?

**Basic Elements**

✔ Does the title draw in the readers?

✔ Does the introduction capture the readers' attention and build up to the thesis statement effectively?

✔ Does each body paragraph deal with a single topic?

✔ Does the conclusion bring the essay to a close in an interesting way?

**Development**

✔ Do the body paragraphs adequately support the thesis statement?

✔ Does each body paragraph have a focused topic sentence?

✔ Does each body paragraph contain *specific* details that support the topic sentence?

✔ Does each body paragraph include *enough* details to explain the topic sentence fully?

**Unity**

✔ Do the essay's topic sentences relate directly to the thesis statement?

✔ Do the details in each body paragraph support its topic sentence?

**Organization**

✔ Is the essay organized logically?

✔ Is each body paragraph organized logically?

**Coherence**

✔ Are transitions used effectively so that paragraphs move smoothly and logically from one to the next?

✔ Do the sentences move smoothly and logically from one to the next?

## Thesis Statement

✔ Does the thesis statement contain the essay's controlling idea and appear as the last sentence of the introduction?

1. Put brackets around the last sentence in Jefferson's introduction. What does it say he is analyzing?

_______________________________________________

2. Rewrite Jefferson's thesis statement if necessary so that it states his purpose and introduces all his topics.

## Basic Elements

- ✔ Does the title draw in the readers?
- ✔ Does the introduction capture the readers' attention and build up to the thesis statement effectively?
- ✔ Does each body paragraph deal with a single topic?
- ✔ Does the conclusion bring the essay to a close in an interesting way?

1. Give Jefferson's essay an alternate title. ______________________________

2. Rewrite Jefferson's introduction so that it captures the readers' attention and builds up to the thesis statement at the end of the paragraph.

______________________________________________________________

______________________________________________________________

______________________________________________________________

______________________________________________________________

3. Does each of Jefferson's body paragraphs deal with only one topic?

______________

4. Rewrite Jefferson's conclusion using at least one suggestion from Part I.

______________________________________________________________

______________________________________________________________

______________________________________________________________

______________________________________________________________

## Development

✔ Do the body paragraphs adequately support the thesis statement?
✔ Does each body paragraph have a focused topic sentence?
✔ Does each body paragraph contain *specific* details that support the topic sentence?
✔ Does each body paragraph include *enough* details to explain the topic sentence fully?

1. Write out Jefferson's thesis statement (revised, if necessary), and list his topic sentences below it.

   Thesis statement: ______________________________

   ______________________________

   ______________________________

   Topic 1: ______________________________

   ______________________________

   Topic 2: ______________________________

   ______________________________

   Topic 3: ______________________________

   ______________________________

2. Do the topics adequately develop the essay's thesis statement? __________
3. Does each body paragraph have a focused topic sentence? __________
4. Does Jefferson get to the *real* causes and effects in his essay __________

   ______________________________

5. Where do you need more information?

   ______________________________

6. Make two of Francine's details more specific.

7. Add at least two new details to make his essay clearer.

## Unity

- ✔ Do the essay's topic sentences relate directly to the thesis statement?
- ✔ Do the details in each body paragraph support its topic sentence?

1. Read each of Jefferson's topic sentences with his thesis statement. Do they go together? ____________________
2. Revise them if necessary so they are directly related.
3. Drop or rewrite the two sentences in paragraph 2 that are not directly related to their topic sentence. ____________________

## Organization

- ✔ Is the essay organized logically?
- ✔ Is each body paragraph organized logically?

1. Read Jefferson's essay again to see if all the paragraphs are arranged logically.
2. Move any paragraphs that are out of order.
3. Do you think his method of organization is the most effective one for his purpose? Explain your answer.

____________________

____________________

4. Look closely at Jefferson's body paragraphs to see if all his sentences are arranged logically within paragraphs.
5. Move the sentence in paragraph 2 that is out of order.

## Coherence

- ✔ Are transitions used effectively so that paragraphs move smoothly and logically from one to the next?
- ✔ Do the sentences move smoothly and logically from one to the next?

1. Add two transitions to Jefferson's essay.
2. Circle five pronouns Jefferson uses. For a list of pronouns, see page 509.
3. Explain how two of these make Jefferson's essay easier to read.

_______________________________________________

_______________________________________________

Now rewrite Jefferson's essay with your revisions.

## Editing Checklist

**SENTENCES**
- ✔ Does each sentence have a main subject and verb?
- ✔ Do all subjects and verbs agree?
- ✔ Do all pronouns agree with their nouns?
- ✔ Are modifiers as close as possible to the words they modify?

**PUNCTUATION AND MECHANICS**
- ✔ Are sentences punctuated correctly?
- ✔ Are words capitalized properly?

**WORD CHOICE AND SPELLING**
- ✔ Are words used correctly?
- ✔ Are words spelled correctly?

## Sentences

- ✔ Does each sentence have a main subject and verb?
  For help with subjects and verbs, see Chapter 34.

1. Underline the subjects once and verbs twice in paragraphs 3 and 4 of your revision of Jefferson's essay. Remember that sentences can have more than one subject-verb set.
2. Does each of the sentences have at least one subject and verb that can stand alone? ______________
3. Did you find and correct Jefferson's two fragments? If not, find and correct them now. For help with fragments, see Chapter 35.

✔ Do all subjects and verbs agree?
For help with subject-verb agreement, see Chapter 39.

1. Read aloud the subjects and verbs you underlined in your revision of Jefferson's essay.
2. Correct any subjects and verbs that do not agree.

✔ Do all pronouns agree with their nouns?
For help with pronoun agreement, see Chapter 43.

1. Find any pronouns in your revision of Jefferson's essay that do not agree with their nouns.
2. Did you find and correct the three pronoun agreement errors in Jefferson's essay? If not, find and correct them now.

✔ Are modifiers as close as possible to the words they modify?
For help with modifier errors, see Chapter 46.

1. Find any modifiers in your revision of Jefferson's essay that are not as close as possible to the words they modify.
2. Rewrite sentences if necessary so that modifiers are as close as possible to the words they modify.

## Punctuation and Mechanics

✔ Are sentences punctuated correctly?
For help with punctuation, see Chapters 47–51.

1. Read your revision of Jefferson's essay for any errors in punctuation.
2. Find the two fragments you revised, and make sure they are punctuated correctly.
3. Did you find and correct Jefferson's two errors in end punctuation? If not, find and correct them now.

✔ Are words capitalized properly?
For help with capitalization, see Chapter 52.

1. Read your revision of Jefferson's essay for any errors in capitalization.
2. Be sure to check Jefferson's capitalization in the fragments you revised.

## Word Choice and Spelling

✔ Are words used correctly?
For help with confused words, see Chapter 58.

1. Find any words used incorrectly in your revision of Jefferson's essay.
2. Correct any errors you find.

✔ Are all words spelled correctly?
For help with spelling, see Chapter 59.

1. Use spell-check and a dictionary to check the spelling in your revision of Jefferson's essay.
2. Correct any misspelled words.

Now rewrite Jefferson's essay again with your editing corrections.

# REVISING AND EDITING YOUR OWN ESSAY

Returning to the cause/effect essay you wrote earlier in this chapter, revise and edit your own writing. The checklists here will help you apply what you have learned to your essay.

## Revising

### Thesis Statement

- ☐ Does the thesis statement contain the essay's controlling idea and appear as the last sentence of the introduction?

1. What are you analyzing? ______________________________
2. Put brackets around the last sentence in your introduction. What do you say you are analyzing in this sentence? ______________________
3. Rewrite your thesis statement if necessary so that it states your purpose and introduces your topics.

### Basic Elements

- ☐ Does the title draw in the readers?
- ☐ Does the introduction capture the readers' attention and build up to the thesis statement effectively?
- ☐ Does each body paragraph deal with a single topic?
- ☐ Does the conclusion bring the essay to a close in an interesting way?

1. Give your essay a title if it doesn't have one. ____________________
2. Does your introduction capture your readers' attention and build up to your thesis statement as the end of the paragraph? ______________

3. Does each of your body paragraphs deal with only one topic? __________

4. Does your conclusion follow some of the suggestions offered in Part I? ____

## Development

- ☐ Do the body paragraphs adequately support the thesis statement?
- ☐ Does each body paragraph have a focused topic sentence?
- ☐ Does each body paragraph contain *specific* details that support the topic sentence?
- ☐ Does each body paragraph include *enough* details to explain the topic sentence fully?

1. Write out your thesis statement (revised, if necessary), and list your topic sentences below it.

   Thesis statement: ______________________________

   Topic 1: ______________________________

   Topic 2: ______________________________

   Topic 3: ______________________________

2. Do your topics adequately support your thesis statement? __________

3. Does each body paragraph have a focused topic sentence? __________

4. Do you get to the *real* causes and effects in your essay? __________

5. Where do you need more information? ______________________

6. Make two of your details more specific.

7. Add at least two new details to make your cause/effect clearer.

## Unity

- ☐ Do the essay's topic sentences relate directly to the thesis statement?
- ☐ Do the details in each body paragraph support its topic sentence?

1. Read each of your topic sentences with your thesis statement in mind. Do they go together? ____________
2. Revise them if necessary so they are directly related.
3. Drop or rewrite any of the sentences in your body paragraphs that are not directly related to their topic sentences.

## Organization

- ☐ Is the essay organized logically?
- ☐ Is each body paragraph organized logically?

1. Read your essay again to see if all the paragraphs are arranged logically.
2. Refer to your answers to the development questions. Then identify your method of organization: ______________________________
3. Move any paragraphs that are out of order.
4. Look closely at your body paragraphs to see if all the sentences are arranged logically within paragraphs.
5. Move any sentences that are out of order.

## Coherence

- ☐ Are transitions used effectively so that paragraphs move smoothly and logically from one to the next?
- ☐ Do the sentences move smoothly and logically from one to the next?

1. Add two transitions to your essay.
2. Circle five pronouns you use. For a list of pronouns, see page 509.
3. Explain how two of these make your essay easier to read.

______________________________________________

______________________________________________

Now rewrite your essay with your revisions.

# Editing

## Sentences

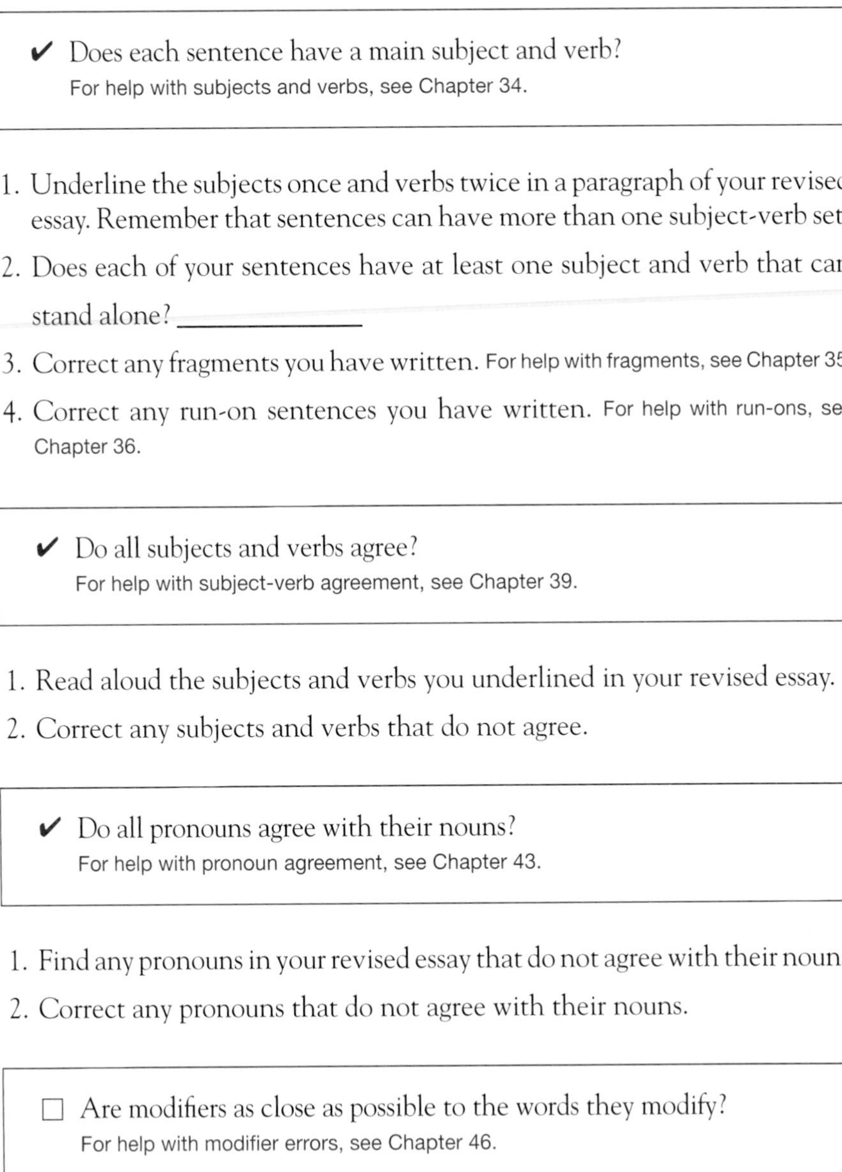

✔ Does each sentence have a main subject and verb?
For help with subjects and verbs, see Chapter 34.

1. Underline the subjects once and verbs twice in a paragraph of your revised essay. Remember that sentences can have more than one subject-verb set.
2. Does each of your sentences have at least one subject and verb that can stand alone? ____________
3. Correct any fragments you have written. For help with fragments, see Chapter 35.
4. Correct any run-on sentences you have written. For help with run-ons, see Chapter 36.

✔ Do all subjects and verbs agree?
For help with subject-verb agreement, see Chapter 39.

1. Read aloud the subjects and verbs you underlined in your revised essay.
2. Correct any subjects and verbs that do not agree.

✔ Do all pronouns agree with their nouns?
For help with pronoun agreement, see Chapter 43.

1. Find any pronouns in your revised essay that do not agree with their nouns.
2. Correct any pronouns that do not agree with their nouns.

☐ Are modifiers as close as possible to the words they modify?
For help with modifier errors, see Chapter 46.

1. Find any modifiers in your revised essay that are not as close as possible to the words they modify.

2. Rewrite sentences if necessary so that your modifiers are as close as possible to the words they modify.

## Punctuation and Mechanics

☐ Are sentences punctuated correctly?
For help with punctuation, see Chapters 47–51.

1. Read your revised essay for any errors in punctuation.
2. Make sure any fragments and run-ons you revised are punctuated correctly.

☐ Are words capitalized properly?
For help with capitalization, see Chapter 52.

1. Read your revised essay for any errors in capitalization.
2. Be sure to check your capitalization in any fragments or run-ons you revised.

## Word Choice and Spelling

☐ Are words used correctly?
For help with confused words, see Chapter 58.

1. Find any words used incorrectly in your revised essay.
2. Correct any errors you find.

☐ Are all words spelled correctly?
For help with spelling, see Chapter 59.

1. Use spell-check and a dictionary to check your spelling.
2. Correct any misspelled words.

Now rewrite your essay again with your editing corrections.

## READING SUGGESTIONS

In Chapter 32, you will find two essays that follow the guidelines you have studied in this chapter. "A Family Dilemma: To Scout or Not to Scout?" by Michael Alvear discusses the dilemma that the ruling about gay scout leaders put on one family, and "Happiness Is Catching: Why Emotions Are Contagious" by Stacey Colino analyzes the role of moods in our daily lives. You might want to read these selections before writing another cause/effect essay. As you read, notice how the writers make their points through well-thought-out, detailed reasoning.

## IDEAS FOR WRITING

**Guidelines for Writing a Cause/Effect Essay**

1. Write a thesis statement that tells what you are analyzing.
2. Choose facts, details, and reasons to support your thesis statement.
3. Do not mistake coincidence for cause or effect.
4. Search for the real causes and effects connected with your subject.
5. Organize your essay so that your readers can easily follow your analysis.

1. Explain how this scene got started. What caused this reaction? Why did it happen? What were the results of the actions pictured here? Write an essay focusing on either the causes or the effects of this scene.

2. We all deal with change differently, but it is generally difficult to accept change in life. Think of a significant change in your life, and write about its causes and effects. What was the incident? What were the circumstances connected with the incident?
3. Write an essay that analyzes a current social problem—homelessness, drugs, environmental concerns—including the reasons for its existence.
4. Create your own cause/effect assignment (with the help of your instructor), and write a response to it.

## Revising Workshop

Small Group Activity (5–10 minutes per writer) In groups of three or four, each person should read his or her cause/effect essay to the other members of the group. Those listening should record their reactions on a copy of the Peer Evaluation Form in Appendix 2H. After your group goes through this process, give your evaluation forms to the appropriate writers so that each writer has two or three peer comment sheets for revising.

Paired Activity (5 minutes per writer) Using the completed Peer Evaluation Forms, work in pairs to decide what you should revise in your essay. If time allows, rewrite some of your sentences, and have your partner look at them.

Individual Activity Rewrite your paper, using the revising feedback you received from other students.

## Editing Workshop

Paired Activity (5–10 minutes per writer) Swap papers with a classmate, and use the editing portion of your Peer Evaluation Form to identify as many grammar, punctuation, mechanics, and spelling errors as you can. If time allows, correct some of your errors, and have your partner look at them. Record your grammar, punctuation, and mechanics errors in the Error Log (Appendix 6) and your spelling errors in the Spelling Log (Appendix 7).

Individual Activity Rewrite your paper again, using the editing feedback you received from other students.

## Reflecting on Your Writing

When you have completed your own essay, answer these six questions.

1. What was most difficult about this assignment?
2. What was easiest?

3. What did you learn about using cause and effect by completing this assignment?
4. What do you think are the strengths of your cause/effect essay? Place a squiggly line by the parts of your essay that you feel are very good.
5. What are the weaknesses, if any, of your paper? Place an X by the parts of your essay you would like help with. Write any questions you have in the margin.
6. What did you learn from this assignment about your own writing process—about preparing to write, about writing the first draft, about revising, and about editing?

CHAPTER 17

# Arguing

*Those who do not know their opponent's arguments do not completely understand their own.*

—DAVID BENDER

Argument may be our most important form of communication because it helps us get what we want in life. The main reason people argue is to persuade someone of something. When you want to get a certain job, sell your car, or borrow some money, you need to present your request clearly and convincingly. On the flip side, others try to persuade you to do things all the time: Politicians make speeches trying to persuade you to vote for them; your friends try to persuade you to go to a movie when you know you should study for an exam; TV commercials, magazine ads, and billboards everywhere try to persuade you to buy this cereal or that car.

As you might suspect, your ability to argue in writing is also important in life. In fact, writing arguments is fundamental to your success on a personal level, in college courses, and in the workplace. Consider these situations:

The chairperson for your college reunion sends a letter with clear reasons why everyone should attend this year.

A student writes an essay in a freshman composition course arguing for or against the death penalty.

A student writes a paper in a sociology course arguing that laws against hate crimes need to be stronger.

A sales representative writes a letter arguing that customers should order supplies from him rather than from his competitor.

A restaurant owner writes an advertisement to persuade people to eat at her restaurant.

The purpose of **arguing** is to persuade someone to take a certain action or to think or feel a specific way. You can use either logical arguments (based on facts and reasoning) or emotional arguments (based on vivid description and details) to achieve your purpose.

Some of the most important laws affecting people's lives in the United States are the result of arguments made to the Supreme Court. Lawyers argue such issues as gun control, abortion, immigrants' rights, and drunk driving. If, for instance, lawmakers are trying to get stricter jail sentences for drunk driving, they might rely heavily on facts and statistics (logical evidence). But then they might add an emotional element by describing the mangled bike, the bloodstained clothes, and the pain in the faces of the parents of a 12-year-old girl killed by a drunk driver as the girl rode her bike home from school. Such an appeal to feelings would create a much stronger argument than statistics alone.

The better you become at arguing—in both thinking and writing—the more you will get what you want out of life (and out of college). Arguing effectively means getting the pay raises you hope for, the refund you deserve, and the grades you've worked hard for. Argumentation is a powerful tool.

The following argument, "Racial Profiling Is Unjust" by Bob Herbert, tries to persuade its readers that law-enforcement agents should not take action based on race alone. It uses a combination of logic and emotion to achieve its purpose. Have you ever been stopped by the police because of your appearance? If you have, what was your reaction? If you haven't, what do you think your reaction would be?

**Bob Herbert**

# RACIAL PROFILING IS UNJUST

1 An anti-loitering law that allowed the Chicago police to arrest more than 42,000 people from 1992 to 1995 was declared unconstitutional in June of 1999 by the Supreme Court.

2 [Supreme Court justice] Antonin Scalia howled in dissent, which should tell you something. The law was an abomination, just like the practice in New York of stopping and frisking black and Hispanic people by the tens of thousands for no good reason. And just like the practice of pulling over and harassing perfectly innocent black and Hispanic motorists on streets and highways in many parts of the country.

## The Faces of Ethnic Profiling

3 Ethnic profiling by law-enforcement authorities in the United States comes in many forms, and all of them are disgusting.

In the summer of 1998, sadistic members of the State Police in Oklahoma spent more than two hours humiliating Rossano Gerald, a 37-year-old Army sergeant, and his 12-year-old son, Greg. 4

Sergeant Gerald was pulled over and interrogated. He was ordered out of his car and handcuffed. The troopers asked if he had any guns. They asked permission to search the car and when he refused they searched it anyway. They separated Greg from his father and locked him in a police vehicle. They interrogated him. They brought drug-sniffing dogs to the scene. They dismantled parts of the car. When they finally tired of the madness, they told Sergeant Gerald he was free to go. No arrest was made. Greg, of course, was petrified. When the ordeal ended he wept uncontrollably. 5

Why did this happen? Greg and Sergeant Gerald were guilty of America's original sin. They were born black. 6

## Profiling Targets the Innocent

In New York, profiling was not only perpetuated but elevated to astonishing new heights during the regime of [New York City mayor] Rudolph Giuliani. Here, the targets are mostly pedestrians, not motorists. Young black and Hispanic males (and in some cases females) are stopped, frisked and harassed in breathtaking numbers. 7

By the Police Department's own count, more than 45,000 people were stopped and frisked by members of the Street Crimes Unit in 1997 and 1998. But the total number of arrests made by the unit over those two years was less than 10,000. And it is widely believed that the number of people stopped during that period was far higher than the 45,000 reported by the cops. The true number likely was in the hundreds of thousands. 8

Ira Glasser, executive director of the American Civil Liberties Union [ACLU], noted that two things characterize the New York City stops: "Virtually everybody is innocent, and virtually everybody is not white." 9

Mayor Giuliani, like most public officials, will not acknowledge that his police officers are targeting people by race. "The stops are driven by the descriptions of the person who committed the crime," Mr. Giuliani said. 10

Spare me. The vast majority of these stops are in no way connected to the commission of a specific crime, and the mayor knows it. They are arbitrary and unconscionable intrusions on the rights of New Yorkers who are supposed to be protected, not humiliated, by the police. 11

## Profiling Is Extensive

Most Americans have no idea of the extent of the race-based profiling that is carried out by law-enforcement officials, and the demoralizing effect it has on its victims. The ACLU, in a report called "Driving While Black: Racial Profiling on Our Nation's Highways," said: "No [people] of color [are] safe from this treatment 12 anywhere, regardless of their obedience to the law, their age, the type of car they drive, or their station in life."

13 The Chicago law that resulted in more than 42,000 arrests over three years was aimed at curbing gang activity. It was clearly unconstitutional. It made it a crime for anyone in the presence of suspected gang members to "remain in any one place with no apparent purpose" after being told by the police to move on.

14 Why should one's purpose for being in a public place have to be apparent? As a reporter for *The New York Times,* I might be in the presence of a suspected gang member. What business is that of the police? And how could that possibly be a legitimate basis for an arrest?

15 The suit challenging the law was brought by the Chicago office of the ACLU. A spokesman for the group noted that the "vast majority" of the people arrested under the law were African-American or Hispanic.

16 What a surprise.

*Preparing to Write Your Own Argument Essay*

Choose a controversial issue on your campus or in the news that is important to you, and use one or more of the prewriting techniques that you learned in Chapter 2 to generate ideas on the issue. Consult your campus or local newspaper for ideas if you want. What is the exact issue? Why is it important? Why do people care about it? How do you think the issue should be resolved?

## HOW TO WRITE AN ARGUMENT ESSAY

When you write an argument essay, choose a subject that matters to you. If you have strong feelings, you will find it much easier to gather evidence and convince your readers of your point of view. Keep in mind, however, that your readers might feel just as strongly about the opposite side of the issue. The following guidelines will help you write a good argument essay.

1. ***State your opinion on your topic in your thesis statement.*** To write a thesis statement for an argument essay, you must take a stand for or against an action or an idea. In other words, your thesis statement should be debatable—a statement that can be argued or challenged and will not be met with agreement by everyone who reads it. Your thesis statement should introduce your subject and state your opinion about that subject.

Bob Herbert's thesis is in his third paragraph: "Ethnic profiling by law-enforcement authorities in the United States comes in many forms, and all of them are disgusting." This is a debatable thesis. But similar statements on the topic of ethnic profiling would not be good thesis statements.

**Not debatable:** Ethnic profiling by law-enforcement authorities in the United States often involves African Americans and Hispanics.

**Not debatable:** Some law-enforcement agencies have strict rules regarding ethnic profiling.

Herbert sets up his essay with some facts about anti-loitering laws and a reference to the practice in New York of stopping and frisking blacks and Hispanics. This background information leads up to his thesis statement.

2. ***Find out as much as you can about your audience before you write.*** Knowing your readers' background and feelings on your topic will help you choose the best supporting evidence and examples. Suppose that you want to convince people in two different age groups to quit smoking. You might tell the group of teenagers that cigarettes make their breath rancid, their teeth yellow, and their clothes smell bad. But with a group of adults, you might discuss the horrifying statistics on lung and heart disease associated with long-term smoking.

   Herbert's essay was first published in the *New York Times*, which addresses a fairly educated audience. The original readers probably thought a lot like he does on this issue. So he chooses his support as if he is talking to people who agree with him.

3. ***Choose evidence that supports your thesis statement.*** Evidence is probably the most important factor in writing an argument essay. Without solid evidence, your essay is nothing more than opinion; with it, your essay can be powerful and persuasive. If you supply convincing evidence, your readers will not only understand your position but perhaps agree with it.

   Evidence can consist of facts, statistics, statements from authorities, and examples or personal stories. Examples and personal stories can be based on your own observations, experiences, and reading, but your opinions are not evidence. You can also develop your ideas with the writing strategies you've learned in Chapters 9 through 16. Comparison/contrast, definition, and cause/effect may be particularly useful in building an argument. Use any combination of evidence and writing strategies that will help you support your thesis statement.

In his essay, Herbert uses several different types of evidence. Here are some examples:

**Facts**

An anti-loitering law was declared unconstitutional in June 1999 (paragraph 1)

Sergeant Rossano Gerald was stopped by the Oklahoma police in the summer of 1998 (paragraph 4)

**Statistics**

Chicago police arrested over 42,000 people from 1992 to 1995 for loitering (paragraph 1)

In New York, more than 45,000 people were stopped and frisked by the Street Crimes Unit in 1997 and 1998 (paragraph 8)

Only 10,000 arrests were made in New York in 1997 and 1998 (paragraph 8)

**Statements from Authorities**

Quote by Ira Glasser, ACLU director (paragraph 9)

Quote by Mayor Giuliani (paragraph 10)

ACLU report (paragraph 12)

**Examples and Personal Stories**

Story about Sergeant Gerald and his son (paragraphs 4–6)

4. ***Anticipate opposing points of view.*** In addition to stating and supporting your position, anticipating and responding to opposing views is important. Presenting only your side of the argument leaves half the story untold—the opposition's half. If you admit that there are opposing arguments and answer them, you will move your reader more in your direction.

   In paragraph 10, Herbert acknowledges a statement made by Mayor Giuliani as his opposition. Giuliani flatly denies the claims against his police force. "The stops are driven by the descriptions of the person who committed the crime." Acknowledging this statement raises Herbert's credibility and then lets him counter Giuliani's claim, which he does in the next paragraph.

5. ***Find some common ground.*** Pointing out common ground between you and your opponent is also an effective strategy. *Common ground* refers to points of agreement between two opposing positions. For example, one person might be in favor of gun control and another strongly opposed. But they might find common ground—agreement—in the need to keep guns out of teenagers' hands. Locating some common ground is possible in almost every situation. When you state in your essay that you agree with your opponent on certain points, your reader sees you as a fair person.

   Herbert assumes that most of his readers know that ethnic profiling by law-enforcement agencies is going on around the country. His job, then, is to prove the extent and unfairness of it.

6. ***Maintain a reasonable tone.*** Just as you probably wouldn't win an argument by shouting or making nasty or sarcastic comments, don't expect your reader to respond well to such tactics. Keep the "voice" of your essay calm and sensible. Your readers will be much more open to what you have to say if they think you are a reasonable person.

   Herbert maintains a reasonable tone throughout his essay. Even when he quotes some unbelievable statistics, as in paragraphs 1 and 8, he keeps his voice under control and therefore earns the respect of his readers.

7. ***Organize your essay so that it presents your position as effectively as possible.*** By the end of your essay, you want your audience to agree with you. So you want to organize your essay in such a way that your readers can easily follow it. The number of your paragraphs may vary, depending on the nature of your assignment, but the following outline shows the order in which the features of an argument essay are most effective:

   **Outline**

   Introduction
   - Background information
   - Introduction of subject
   - Statement of your opinion

   Body Paragraphs
   - Common ground
   - Lots of evidence (logical and emotional)
   - Opposing point of view
   - Response to opposing point of view

Conclusion
- Restatement of your position
- Call for action or agreement

The arrangement of your evidence in an argument essay depends to a great extent on your readers' opinions. Most arguments will be organized from general to particular, from particular to general, or from one extreme to another. When you know that your readers already agree with you, arranging your details from general to particular or from most to least important is usually most effective. With this order, you are building on your readers' agreement and loyalty as you explain your thinking on the subject.

If you suspect that your audience does not agree with you, reverse the organization of your evidence and arrange it from particular to general or from least to most important. In this way, you can take your readers step by step through your reasoning in an attempt to get them to agree with you.

Bob Herbert's essay follows the general outline just presented. Here is a skeleton outline of his essay.

| | |
|---|---|
| Introduction | |
| Background statistics and facts about anti-loitering laws and stopping and frisking | |
| Body Paragraphs | |
| The Faces of Ethnic Profiling | |
| Subject introduced: | racial profiling |
| Statement of opinion: | racial profiling is disgusting |
| Evidence—example: | Sergeant Gerald's story |
| Profiling Targets the Innocent | |
| Evidence—fact: | blacks and Hispanics stopped in New York |
| Evidence—statistics: | more than 45,000 people stopped, less than 10,000 arrested |
| Evidence—statements from authorities: | Ira Glasser, ACLU director |
| Opposing point of view: | Mayor Giuliani |
| Response to opposition: | Herbert's opinion |
| Conclusion: | Profiling Is Extensive |
| Restatement of problem: | extent of race-based profiling |

| | |
|---|---|
| Evidence—statements from authorities: | quotation from ACLU report |
| Evidence—statistics: | over 42,000 arrests in Chicago in three years |
| Herbert's opinion | |
| Evidence—fact: | ACLU lawsuit |
| Herbert's final comment | |

*Writing Your Own Argument Essay*

Write an essay that presents your opinion on the controversial issue you considered in your prewriting. Begin with a debatable thesis statement. Then follow the guidelines for writing an argument essay. As you write your essay, be sure you support your opinions with reasons. If a newspaper article inspired this assignment, attach it to your paper before you turn it in.

## ARGUMENTATION AT WORK

Melinda Jackson, the student writer of the following essay, titled "A Call for Policies on Drinking," argues that drinking on college campuses is a serious problem. See if you can identify her main point and supporting evidence as you read her essay.

### A Call for Policies on Drinking

College and drinking, drinking and college--most students believe the two go hand in hand. If asked, they would say that drinking in college is just a part of life, and it is not a major concern. However, when we examine drinking in college more closely, we see it is a serious problem that people on all levels are not facing. Drinking on college campuses is a bigger problem than parents and administrators realize, and something needs to be done about it--now. 1

No one would ever realistically believe that college students will never drink. In fact, most students, parents, and administrators are in favor of students taking a break and having fun. Studying during every available minute, parents and administrators realize the strain students are under. And they know that students will probably drink. What they don't understand is the trap students can fall into. 2

3 Jerry, a college student, explained how he got involved with alcohol and how it soon took over his life. Jerry went to a different fraternity party every weekend night, where his main goal was to get as drunk as possible. What he didn't know was that he was confrontational when he drank and that people didn't want to be around him. He didn't know his limit, so he often exceeded it. He usually passed out on someone's couch after drinking. In the morning he would wake up and find the next party. Jerry is just one of many students on every U.S. college campus.

4 Whereas most people think drinking occurs just during parties, it actually occurs for many students on a daily basis. Students like Jerry begin by drinking on weekends then they all too easily start drinking every day. They begin to need alcohol in order to feel normal. Once they fall into this pattern, several other serious problems can occur. Not only are they missing classes and falling behind in their coarses, but they are also endangering their lives. Drinking becomes the most important aspect in their lives. But it's not just the drinker who's life is effected. Drinkers disrupt their roommates, who are either distracted from their studying or awakened from their sleep. When the roommate complains about being disturbed. The drinker gets angry. And so the pattern repeats itself again and again.

5 According to our dean of students, students who drink often take risks that endanger their lives and the lives of others. The most obvious risk involves a drinker who gets behind the wheel of a car. Drinkers also tend to get into more fights, because they mistakenly believe they are invincible. In this case, they risk harming the people they fight with and themselves, because they are in no condition to defend themselves. Everyone on the road is a potential victim of the drinker. Drinkers are also likely to have unprotected sex. This could lead to unwanted pregnancies, sexually transmitted diseases, or even AIDS. With the widespread drinking that occurs on college campuses, these consequences are very likely to occur to a student who drinks.

6 Drinking is a major problem on college campuses, but like every other controversial issue, some people say it has been given too much publicity by overzealous worriers. They believe that the college knows light drinking occurs and that the administration has control of the students who drink. They believe that kids will be kids, students will drink no matter what. These people say that letting students have fun is what's important. But to adopt this attitude is possibly placing someone's life in danger. If even one person is in danger from a drunken student. Then the college must take action.

7 Drinking in college is definitely going to happen, but there are measures that can be taken to prevent serious harm to students who do

decide to drink. Campuses could have alcohol awareness programs and give students easy access to condoms. Campuses could set up a response team that would pick up any student who was incapable of driving. They could require all sororities and fraternities to confiscate keys before anyone is given a drink to ensure that a person who has been drinking won't drive. They can offer literature on organizations that can help students who become addicted to alcohol. Its time for students, parents, and administrators to see the problem before them and take steps to fix it before it's too late.

1A. What is Melinda's thesis statement?

______________________________________________

______________________________________________

1B. Does it state her opinion clearly? Explain your answer.

______________________________________________

______________________________________________

1C. Is it debatable? (Does it have more than one side?)

______________________________________________

2. Who do you think Melinda is addressing in this essay? How did you come to this conclusion?

______________________________________________

3. What evidence does the author use to support her thesis statement? Find an example of each type of evidence in her essay.

Facts: ______________________________________

Statistics: __________________________________

Statements from authorities: ____________________

Examples and personal stories: __________________

4. Does Melinda anticipate an opposing point of view? Explain your answer.

   ______________________________________________

5. Did Melinda find some common ground with her readers? Explain your answer. ______________________________________________

   ______________________________________________

6. Does Melinda maintain a reasonable tone? Explain your answer. ______

   ______________________________________________

7. How does Melinda organize the topics in her essay: general to particular, particular to general, or from one extreme to another?

   Method of organization: ______________________________

## REVISING AND EDITING A STUDENT ESSAY

This essay is Melinda's first draft, which now needs to be revised and edited. First, apply the Revising Checklist below to Melinda's draft so that you are working with her content. When you are satisfied that her ideas are fully developed and well organized, use the Editing Checklist on pages 323–324 to correct her grammar and mechanics errors. Answer the questions after each checklist. Then write your suggested changes directly on Melinda's draft.

### Revising Checklist

**THESIS STATEMENT**

✔ Does the thesis statement contain the essay's controlling idea and appear as the last sentence of the introduction?

**BASIC ELEMENTS**

✔ Does the title draw in the readers?

✔ Does the introduction capture the readers' attention and build up to the thesis statement effectively?

- ✔ Does each body paragraph deal with a single topic?
- ✔ Does the conclusion bring the essay to a close in an interesting way?

DEVELOPMENT

- ✔ Do the body paragraphs adequately support the thesis statement?
- ✔ Does each body paragraph have a focused topic sentence?
- ✔ Does each body paragraph contain *specific* details that support the topic sentence?
- ✔ Does each body paragraph include *enough* details to explain the topic sentence fully?

UNITY

- ✔ Do the essay's topic sentences relate directly to the thesis statement?
- ✔ Do the details in each body paragraph support its topic sentence?

ORGANIZATION

- ✔ Is the essay organized logically?
- ✔ Is each body paragraph organized logically?

COHERENCE

- ✔ Are transitions used effectively so that paragraphs move smoothly and logically from one to the next?
- ✔ Do the sentences move smoothly and logically from one to the next?

## Thesis Statement

- ✔ Does the thesis statement contain the essay's controlling idea and appear as the last sentence of the introduction?

1. Put brackets around the last sentence in Melinda's introduction. Does it contain her opinion? ______________ Is it debatable? ______________
2. Rewrite Melinda's thesis statement if necessary so that it states her opinion and introduces her topics.

## Basic Elements

- ✔ Does the title draw in the readers?
- ✔ Does the introduction capture the readers' attention and build up to the thesis statement effectively?
- ✔ Does each body paragraph deal with a single topic?
- ✔ Does the conclusion bring the essay to a close in an interesting way?

1. Give Melinda's essay an alternate title. ______________________

2. Rewrite Melinda's introduction so that it captures the readers' attention and builds up to the thesis statement at the end of the paragraph.

______________________________________________

______________________________________________

______________________________________________

______________________________________________

3. Does each of Melinda's body paragraphs deal with only one topic?

__________

4. Rewrite Melinda's conclusion using at least one suggestion from Part I.

______________________________________________

______________________________________________

______________________________________________

______________________________________________

## Development

- ✔ Do the body paragraphs adequately support the thesis statement?
- ✔ Does each body paragraph have a focused topic sentence?

- ✔ Does each body paragraph contain *specific* details that support the topic sentence?
- ✔ Does each body paragraph include *enough* details to explain the topic sentence fully?

1. Write out Melinda's thesis statement (revised, if necessary), and list her topic sentences below it.

   Thesis statement: ______________________________

   ______________________________

   ______________________________

   Topic 1: ______________________________

   ______________________________

   Topic 2: ______________________________

   ______________________________

   Topic 3: ______________________________

   ______________________________

   Topic 4: ______________________________

   ______________________________

   Topic 5: ______________________________

   ______________________________

   ______________________________

2. Do Melinda's topics adequately support her thesis statement? __________

3. Does each body paragraph have a focused topic sentence? __________

4. Does her evidence support her topic sentences? __________

5. What type of evidence does Melinda provide in each body paragraph?

   Paragraph 2: ______________________________

   Paragraph 3: ______________________________

   Paragraph 4: ______________________________

   Paragraph 5: ______________________________

   Paragraph 6: ______________________________

   What type of evidence does she use the most? ______________

6. Is this a good choice for what she is trying to argue? ______________

   ______________________________________________

7. Where do you need more information?

   ______________________________________________

## Unity

> ✔ Do the essay's topic sentences relate directly to the thesis statement?
> ✔ Do the details in each body paragraph support its topic sentence?

1. Read each of Melinda's topic sentences with her thesis statement in mind. Do they go together? ______________
2. Revise them if necessary so they are directly related.
3. Drop or rewrite any sentences in her body paragraphs that are not directly related to their topic sentences.

## Organization

> ✔ Is the essay organized logically?
> ✔ Is each body paragraph organized logically?

1. Outline Melinda's essay to see if all her ideas are arranged logically.
2. Do you think her method of organization is the most effective one for her purpose? Explain your answer. ______________________________

_____________________________________________

3. Move any paragraphs that are out of order.
4. Look closely at Melinda's body paragraphs to see if all her sentences are arranged logically within paragraphs.
5. Move any sentences that are out of order.

## Coherence

- ✔ Are transitions used effectively so that paragraphs move smoothly and logically from one to the next?
- ✔ Do the sentences move smoothly and logically from one to the next?

1. Add two transitions to Melinda's essay.
2. Circle five transitions, repetitions, synonyms, or pronouns Melinda uses.
3. Explain how two of these make Melinda's essay easier to read.

_____________________________________________

_____________________________________________

Now rewrite Melinda's essay with your revisions.

## Editing Checklist

**Sentences**

- ✔ Does each sentence have a main subject and verb?
- ✔ Do all subjects and verbs agree?
- ✔ Do all pronouns agree with their nouns?
- ✔ Are modifiers as close as possible to the words they modify?

**Punctuation and Mechanics**

✔ Are sentences punctuated correctly?

✔ Are words capitalized properly?

**Word Choice and Spelling**

✔ Are words used correctly?

✔ Are words spelled correctly?

## Sentences

✔ Does each sentence have a main subject and verb?

For help with subjects and verbs, see Chapter 34.

1. Underline the subjects once and verbs twice in paragraphs 4 and 6 of your revision of Melinda's essay. Remember that sentences can have more than one subject-verb set.
2. Does each of Melinda's sentences have at least one subject and verb that can stand alone? ______________
3. Did you find and correct Melinda's two fragments and two run-on sentences? If not, find and correct them now. For help with fragments and run-ons, see Chapters 35 and 36.

✔ Do all subjects and verbs agree?

For help with subject-verb agreement, see Chapter 39.

1. Read aloud the subjects and verbs you underlined in your revision of Melinda's essay.
2. Correct any subjects and verbs that do not agree.

✔ Do all pronouns agree with their nouns?

For help with pronoun agreement, see Chapter 43.

1. Find any pronouns in your revision of Melinda's essay that do not agree with their nouns.
2. Correct any pronouns that do not agree with their nouns.

✔ Are modifiers as close as possible to the words they modify?
For help with modifier errors, see Chapter 46.

1. Find any modifiers in your revision of Melinda's essay that are not as close as possible to the words they modify.
2. Did you find and correct Melinda's two modifier errors? If not, find and correct them now.

## Punctuation and Mechanics

✔ Are sentences punctuated correctly?
For help with punctuation, see Chapters 47–51.

1. Read your revision of Melinda's essay for any errors in punctuation.
2. Find the two fragments and two run-ons you revised, and make sure they are punctuated correctly.

✔ Are words capitalized properly?
For help with capitalization, see Chapter 52.

1. Read your revision of Melinda's essay for any errors in capitalization.
2. Be sure to check Melinda's capitalization in the fragments and run-ons you revised.

## Word Choice and Spelling

✔ Are words used correctly?
For help with confused words, see Chapter 58.

1. Find any words used incorrectly in your revision of Melinda's essay.
2. Did you find and correct the four words Melinda uses incorrectly? If not, find and correct them now.

> ✔ Are all words spelled correctly?
> For help with spelling, see Chapter 59.

1. Use spell-check and a dictionary to check the spelling in your revision of Melinda's essay.
2. Correct any misspelled words.

Now rewrite Melinda's essay again with your editing corrections.

## REVISING AND EDITING YOUR OWN ESSAY

Returning to the argument essay you wrote earlier in this chapter, revise and edit your own writing. The checklists here will help you apply what you have learned to your essay.

### Revising

#### Thesis Statement

> ☐ Does the thesis statement contain the essay's controlling idea and appear as the last sentence of the introduction?

1. What is the subject of your essay? ______________________
2. Put brackets around the last sentence in your introduction. Does it contain your opinion? ______________ Is it debatable? ______________

3. Rewrite your thesis statement if necessary so that it states your opinion and introduces your topics. ______________________________

______________________________________________

## Basic Elements

- ☐ Does the title draw in the readers?
- ☐ Does the introduction capture the readers' attention and build up to the thesis statement effectively?
- ☐ Does each body paragraph deal with a single topic?
- ☐ Does the conclusion bring the essay to a close in an interesting way?

1. Give your essay a title if it doesn't have one. ____________________
2. Does your introduction capture your readers' attention and build up to your thesis statement at the end of the paragraph? ________________
3. Does each of your body paragraphs deal with only one topic? ________
4. Does your conclusion follow some of the suggestions offered in Part I? ____________

## Development

- ☐ Do the body paragraphs adequately support the thesis statement?
- ☐ Does each body paragraph have a focused topic sentence?
- ☐ Does each body paragraph contain *specific* details that support the topic sentence?
- ☐ Does each body paragraph include *enough* details to explain the topic sentence fully?

1. Write out your thesis statement (revised, if necessary), and list your topic sentences below it.

Thesis statement: ______________________________

Topic 1: ______________________________

Topic 2: ______________________________

Topic 3: ______________________________

Topic 4: ______________________________

Topic 5: ______________________________

2. Do your topics adequately support your thesis statement? ____________

3. Does each body paragraph have a focused topic sentence? ____________

4. Does your evidence support your topic sentences? List and label at least one type of evidence you use for each of your topics.

   Topic 1: Evidence: ______________________________

   Type: ______________________________

   Topic 2: Evidence: ______________________________

   Type: ______________________________

   Topic 3: Evidence: ______________________________

   Type: ______________________________

   Topic 4: Evidence: ______________________________

   Type: ______________________________

   Topic 5: Evidence: ______________________________

   Type: ______________________________

   What type of evidence do you use the most? ____________

   Is this a good choice for what you are trying to argue? ____________

5. Where do you need more information? ____________

## Unity

- ☐ Do the essay's topic sentences relate directly to the thesis statement?
- ☐ Do the details in each body paragraph support its topic sentence?

1. Read each of your topic sentences with your thesis statement in mind. Do they go together? ____________
2. Revise them if necessary so they are directly related.
3. Drop or rewrite any of the sentences in your body paragraphs that are not directly related to their topic sentences.

## Organization

- ☐ Is the essay organized logically?
- ☐ Is each body paragraph organized logically?

1. Outline your essay to see if all the paragraphs are arranged logically.
2. Do you think your method of organization is the most effective one for your purpose? Explain your answer.

   ______________________________________________

   ______________________________________________
3. Move any paragraphs that are out of order.
4. Look closely at your body paragraphs to see if all the sentences are arranged logically within paragraphs.
5. Move any sentences or ideas that are out of order.

## Coherence

- ☐ Are transitions used effectively so that paragraphs move smoothly and logically from one to the next?
- ☐ Do the sentences move smoothly and logically from one to the next?

1. Add two transitions to your essay.
2. Circle five transitions, repetitions, synonyms, or pronouns you use.
3. Explain how two of these make your essay easier to read.

______________________________________________

______________________________________________

Now rewrite your essay with your revisions.

# Editing

## Sentences

☐ Does each sentence have a main subject and verb?
For help with subjects and verbs, see Chapter 34.

1. Underline the subjects once and verbs twice in a paragraph of your revised essay. Remember that sentences can have more than one subject-verb set.
2. Does each of your sentences have at least one subject and verb that can stand alone? ______________
3. Correct any fragments you have written. For help with fragments, see Chapter 35.
4. Correct any run-on sentences you have written. For help with run-ons, see Chapter 36.

☐ Do all subjects and verbs agree?
For help with subject-verb agreement, see Chapter 39.

1. Read aloud the subjects and verbs you underlined in your revised essay.
2. Correct any subjects and verbs that do not agree.

☐ Do all pronouns agree with their nouns?
For help with pronoun agreement, see Chapter 43.

1. Find any pronouns in your revised essay that do not agree with their nouns.
2. Correct any pronouns that do not agree with their nouns.

☐ Are modifiers as close as possible to the words they modify?
For help with modifier errors, see Chapter 46.

1. Find any modifiers in your revised essay that are not as close as possible to the words they modify.
2. Rewrite sentences if necessary so that your modifiers are as close as possible to the words they modify.

## Punctuation and Mechanics

☐ Are sentences punctuated correctly?
For help with punctuation, see Chapters 47–51.

1. Read your revised essay for any errors in punctuation.
2. Make sure any fragments and run-ons you revised are punctuated correctly.

☐ Are words capitalized properly?
For help with capitalization, see Chapter 52.

1. Read your revised essay for any errors in capitalization.
2. Be sure to check your capitalization in any fragments or run-ons you revised.

## Word Choice and Spelling

☐ Are words used correctly?
For help with confused words, see Chapter 58.

1. Find any words used incorrectly in your revised essay.
2. Correct any errors you find.

☐ Are all words spelled correctly?
For help with spelling, see Chapter 59.

1. Use spell-check and a dictionary to check your spelling.
2. Correct any misspelled words.

Now rewrite your essay again with your editing corrections.

## READING SUGGESTIONS

In Chapter 33, you will find three examples of good argument essays: "The Neglected Heart" by Thomas Lickona, which analyzes the reasons teenagers are often not emotionally ready for sex, and two essays on loitering and gang violence—"Anti-Loitering Laws Can Reduce Gang Violence" by Richard Willard and "Anti-Loitering Laws Are Ineffective and Biased" by David Cole. You might want to read these selections before writing another argument essay. As you read, notice how the writers make their points through well-thought-out, detailed reasoning.

## IDEAS FOR WRITING

**Guidelines for Writing an Argument Essay**

1. State your opinion on your topic in your thesis statement.
2. Find out as much as you can about your audience before you write.
3. Choose evidence that supports your thesis statement.
4. Anticipate opposing points of view.
5. Find some common ground.
6. Maintain a reasonable tone.
7. Organize your essay so that it presents your position as effectively as possible.

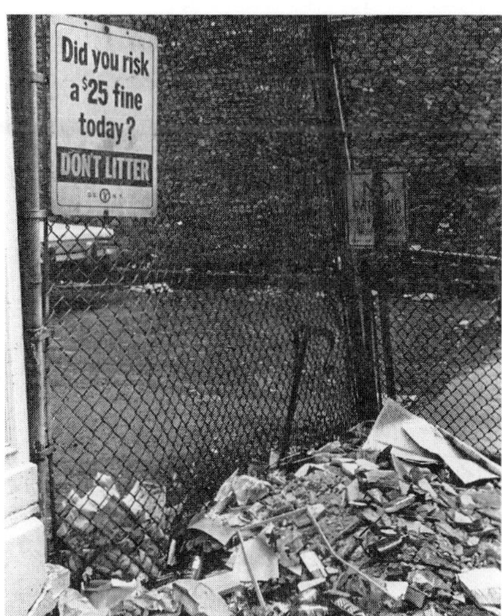


1. Explain what the photographer had in mind in creating this statement about littering. How does it appeal to its viewers? Write an essay explaining what the ad communicates.
2. Argue for or against a controversial political issue. Take a firm stand, and develop an essay supporting your position. You might want to look at the headlines in the newspaper to get some ideas for this assignment.
3. Write a letter to a potential employer for the job of your dreams, arguing that you are the best candidate for the job. Try to convince the employer not only that you are the perfect person for the job but also that you can take the position into new directions. Follow the format for a well-developed argument essay.
4. Create your own argument essay assignment (with the help of your instructor), and write a response to it.

## Revising Workshop

**Small Group Activity (5–10 minutes per writer)** In groups of three or four, each person should read his or her argument essay to the other members of the group. Those listening should record their reactions on a copy of the Peer Evaluation Form in Appendix 2I. After your group goes through this process, give your evaluation forms to the appropriate writers so that each writer has two or three peer comment sheets for revising.

**Paired Activity (5 minutes per writer)** Using the completed Peer Evaluation Forms, work in pairs to decide what you should revise in your essay. If time allows, rewrite some of your sentences, and have your partner look at them.

Individual Activity Rewrite your paper, using the revising feedback you received from other students.

## Editing Workshop

Paired Activity (5–10 minutes per writer) Swap papers with a classmate, and use the editing portion of your Peer Evaluation Form to identify as many grammar, punctuation, mechanics, and spelling errors as you can. If time allows, correct some of your errors, and have your partner look at them. Record your grammar, punctuation, and mechanics errors in the Error Log (Appendix 6) and your spelling errors in the Spelling Log (Appendix 7).

Individual Activity Rewrite your paper again, using the editing feedback you received from other students.

## Reflecting on Your Writing

When you have completed your own essay, answer these six questions.

1. What was most difficult about this assignment?
2. What was easiest?
3. What did you learn about arguing by completing this assignment?
4. What do you think are the strengths of your argument? Place a squiggly line by the parts of your essay that you feel are very good.
5. What are the weaknesses, if any, of your paper? Place an X by the parts of your essay you would like help with. Write any questions you have in the margin.
6. What did you learn from this assignment about your own writing process—about preparing to write, about writing the first draft, about revising, and about editing?

# THE RESEARCH PAPER: SOURCES IN CONTEXT

*In order to understand complex issues and situations and events, we need to analyze them from multiple perspectives; every position or every viewpoint ought to have reasons to support it; and the quality of the conclusion is dependent on the quality of the reasoning that went before it.*

—John Chaffee

Part III discusses the college research paper, from assignment to final draft. It explains not only what a research paper is but also how to write one, step by step. It provides you with a student model of a research paper and then guides you through the process of writing a research paper on a topic of your own.

# CHAPTER 18 Recognizing a Research Paper

The content of a research paper is based mainly on facts and statistics. The main difference between a research paper and other essays is that writers use sources other than themselves to make their points in a research paper. In other words, writers consult books, periodicals, and the Internet to find facts, statistics, and other supporting material or evidence.

In a research paper, the title gives the reader a clue to the subject of the essay. The introduction gives some background for understanding the topic and states the purpose of the paper in a thesis statement. Body paragraphs provide evidence to back up the thesis statement. And the conclusion wraps up the essay by restating the thesis statement and bringing the paper to an end.

Just as you develop the body of most essays with evidence that is common knowledge or personal experience, you develop the research paper with trustworthy evidence from outside sources. To begin choosing appropriate sources, you must have a firm grasp of your thesis statement. Then various information from your sources will back up your thesis statement.

The following essay by Mary Minor, a student, is a good example of a research paper. She solidly proves her thesis statement using articles from many different sources as evidence in her supporting paragraphs. As you read the first paragraph of the essay, take note of her thesis statement. Then, in each supporting paragraph that follows the introductory paragraph, notice how the author develops her essay and supports her thesis statement with material from outside sources.

*Catchy title*

**Children as Robots**

1 When children are infants, there are certain "norms" they are measured by to see if they are progressing through developmental stages at the rate of other infants their age. The "norms" are

never clear-cut and leave room for individual differences. When a child hits the age of two or enters day care, "norms" become all-important. More than in any other time in history, the 1990s brought about a change in "norms" that leaves parents confused. The "terrible twos" and "trying threes" no longer seem to be the best descriptions of toddlerhood. Today children who are "too" terrible at the age of two or "too" trying at the age of three are diagnosed with either "Attention Deficit Disorder (ADD) or its more severe variation, Attention Deficit Hyperactivity Disorder (ADHD). Both neurological conditions seem to be the childhood plague of the '90s" (Higdon 84). Children are often misdiagnosed with ADD or ADHD and suffer unnecessarily when medicated for a disorder they may not have.

*Interesting comparison*

*Direct quotation*

*In-text citation (MLA)*

*Thesis statement*

Because medical professionals cannot agree on "whether this is one disease with subcategories or two entirely different diseases" (Brink 80), the terms ADD and ADHD are often used interchangeably. Both terms, however, refer to "a short attention span" (Schmitt), with or without hyperactivity. The Diagnostic and Statistical Manual of Mental Disorders (DSM-IV) (American Psychiatric Association, 1994) defines ADHD as a "persistent pattern of inattention and/or hyperactivity-impulsivity that is more frequent and severe than typically observed in individuals at a comparable level of development" (Kendall 839). 2

The disease ADD has become "one of the most commonly diagnosed" (LeFever, Dawnson, and Morrow 1359) childhood diseases in the United States today, afflicting "approximately 4 to 7 percent" (Durall 38) of American children. Given the fact that children are identified as having this disease based on what a person may consider "normal" behavior, it is unfortunate for the children being diagnosed that nobody can agree on what "normal" means. The National Institute of Mental Health (NIMH) claims that "differences do not a 3

*Statistic*

disorder make. The differences could simply be part of human variation. . . . We don't know if perhaps we shouldn't treat ADD as the far end of normal behavior, just like height, weight, or muscle mass" (Koch 918).

*Quotation used to define problem*

4 Many children today who do not fit the "norm" of adult expectations may be diagnosed as having ADD. Labeling a child's behavior based on a set of "norms" is ludicrous since these qualities cannot accurately be measured, let alone defined. According to Thomas Armstrong, author of The Myth of the ADD Child, "Once the influential American Psychiatric Association (APA) declared ADD a disorder in 1980, the DSM defined it more and more broadly. . . . Increasing numbers of children are caught in the ever-widening definition net and are then labeled ADD" (914).

*Author and book introduced before quotation*

*Only page number needed since author already introduced*

5 Although we have a definition for this disorder, nobody really knows for sure what the disorder is. According to psychologist Stephen P. Hinshaw, "There's clearly not a single cause of all cases of well-diagnosed ADHD" (qtd. in Bower 343). Other professionals agree that accurate diagnosis "remains elusive and controversial" (Koch 907). If our leading professionals in the field don't know what a "well-diagnosed" case is, how can we be sure that they even know what any case of ADHD is?

*Transition from definition to further problems*

*Question used as transition*

6 Because there are no reliable tests for ADD, nobody is really able to tell if a child has the disorder. "Given the explosion in ADHD diagnoses . . . , the disorder is surprisingly ill defined. . . . There is no blood test, no PET scan, no physical exam that can determine who has it and who does not" (Gibbs 90). Professionals in the field argue over what the disease is, what causes it, how it should be treated, or whether it is a disease at all (Bower 343).

*Citation after paraphrase*

*Transition sentence to new topic*

7 There are as many definitions of ADD as there are experts doing the defining. Unfortunately, the ones losing this war are the children, and this is due to one fact: Ritalin, the most widely used

method of treatment for this disorder, works so well that additional medical tests are not done. According to Dr. Sydney Walker, neither doctors nor insurance companies want to take the time or spend the money to track down the "real" cause of the problem. Instead, they mask the symptoms with Ritalin (Barkley and Walker 921).

*Transition sentence to next paragraph about Ritalin*

While Ritalin seems to work for many children, 8
nobody knows why or how it works, not to mention what the long-term effects of the drug might be (Gibbs 89). We have no absolute information about ADD, only a set of symptoms, which include excessive talking, fidgeting, and similar behaviors. In other words, parents face deciding whether or not to put their child on strong drugs when nobody has yet proved that a disorder exists.

Unfortunately, teachers are often the first to be 9
involved in diagnosing a child, and "sometimes the school systems insist on a brain-disorder label" (Brink 81). One parent describes his experience and feelings about the matter in a U.S. News and World Report article:

> First it was the teacher. Then the school counselor. Then the heavies in the school, the principal, start to show up. You go to meetings, and everybody thinks your child has a problem. . . . Doctors and therapists each had a different diagnosis--ADHD, anxiety disorder, obsessive-compulsive disorder, depression--and each diagnosis called for a different drug. . . . Social conformity and mental health are becoming the same terms. . . . The person with a different perspective is seen as a candidate for medication. (Brink 81)

*Block indention for long quotations*

Parents are often pressured to place their children on drugs with the hope that they will achieve "academic and social success" (Brink 76). However, this pressure may be unwarranted. "There is no solid evidence that stimulant medicine [such as Ritalin] has any impact on scholastic achievement. . . . Teachers and parents tend to approve of the drug because it makes unruly kids more manageable and more social" (Sheppard 46).

*Questions used as transitions*

10 What does this say about American perceptions of children today? Are we so impatient with unruly behavior that we willingly drug our children? Every resource should be exhausted before any of us allows the label of an unknown disease to be placed on our children. Some children are so hard to control that mind-altering drugs such as Ritalin appear to be a blessing, but drugs, if used at all, should be used only for a short period of time--until the "real" cause of the problem behavior is found. Pediatrician Lawrence Diller states his opinion on the subject well when he says, "I just don't believe a pill is the moral equivalent of good parenting and good schooling. . . . I prescribe it because . . . my job is to relieve suffering, and Ritalin, in the short term, will ease suffering" (qtd. in Brink 81).

*Credible opinion used to support argument*

*Opposite argument addressed*

11 Despite major controversy in the medical field, there has been no proof that drugs are being overprescribed for American children. Some experts even feel that children may be undertreated (Koch 912). No studies have been found that would prove one claim over the other, which again means that each child is treated according to the most popular opinion. As a result, "Students who were younger than their classmates were 21 times more likely to be medicated" for ADD or ADHD (920).

*Opposite argument refuted with quotation*

12 Although drugs can be beneficial in some instances, long-term usage is potentially dangerous because these drugs are presently "classified as 'having a high potential for abuse with severe liability for physical and/or psychic dependence'" (Morrow, Morrow, and Haislip 1121). Also, "a very small percentage of children treated at high doses have hallucinogenic responses" (Gibbs 90). To give a prescription for drugs to a child without comprehensive medical testing is, as Walker states, "inexcusable" (Barkley and Walker 921).

Many children exhibit the symptoms of ADHD due to family problems or other environmental factors. Diet may also play a major role in this scenario. The removal of certain foods, especially those containing "allergenic food additives and dyes" (Koch 916), may very well eliminate the symptoms. When doctors quote the Hippocratic Oath, they say these words: "I will apply dietetic measures for the benefit of the sick according to my ability and judgment; I will keep them from harm and injustice" ("Hippocratic Oath"). Sworn to dietetically treat their patients, doctors should remember this oath before prescribing drugs for a disease that nobody can prove exists. 13

*Facts used to show other possible reasons for hyperactivity in children*

*Conclusion*

Nobody can deny that this "disease" is anything more than a belief system in an ever-increasing "conformist" society. Every effort should be made to find the cause of the "real" medical problems underlying ADD and ADHD before we even think about giving our children drugs. A doctor who doesn't order medical tests for a child with symptoms of ADD is negligent, to say the least, and the failure of a doctor to discuss alternatives to drug therapy with parents when diagnosing ADD is more than "inexcusable"; it's unforgivable. More parents would seek alternative treatments if they knew that their child was diagnosed on the basis of nothing more than a list of symptoms with no proof that there is a disorder. After all, most parents do not want their child placed on long-term stimulant drugs. It's time to say good-bye to "conformist" American classrooms and diagnoses. People don't fit "norms"; they fit personalities. 14

*Reference to thesis statement*

*Call to action*

*Concluding statement*

## Works Cited

*Alphabetical order*

American Psychiatric Association. <u>The Diagnostic and Statistical Manual of Mental Disorders</u>. 4th ed. Washington: APA, 1994.

*Book*

Armstrong, Thomas. The Myth of the ADD Child: 50 Ways to Improve Your Child's Behavior and Attention Span Without Drugs, Labels, or Coercion. New York: Dutton, 1995.

*Double spaced with no extra spaces between entries*

Barkley, Russell, and Sydney Walker III. "At Issue: Are Attention Deficit Disorder (ADD) and Attention Deficit Hyperactivity Disorder (ADHD) Legitimate Medical Diagnoses?" CQ Researcher 9 (1999): 921.

Bower, Bruce. "Kid's Attention Disorder Attracts Concern." Science News 154 (1998): 343.

*All lines after the first indented*

Brink, Susan. "Doing Ritalin Right." U.S. News and World Report 23 Nov. 1998: 76–81.

Durall, John. "Toward an Understanding of ADHD: A Developmental Delay in Self-Control." Camping Magazine Jan. 1999: 38–41.

*General-circulation magazine*

Gibbs, Nancy. "The Age of Ritalin." Time 30 Nov. 1998: 86–96.

Higdon, Hal. "Getting Their Attention." Runner's World July 1999: 84–87.

"Hippocratic Oath." World Book Encyclopedia. Vol. 9. 1999 ed.

*Encyclopedia*

Kendall, Judy. "Outlasting Disruption: The Process of Reinvestment in Families with ADHD Children." Qualitative Health Research 8 (1998): 839–857.

*Journal article*

Koch, Kathy. "Rethinking Ritalin." CQ Researcher 9 (1999): 907–914+.

LeFever, Gretchen B., Keila V. Dawson, and Ardythe L. Morrow. "The Extent of Drug Therapy for Attention Deficit-Hyperactivity Disorder Among Children in Public Schools." American Journal of Public Health 89 (1999): 1359–1364.

Morrow, Robert C., Ardythe L. Morrow, and Gene Haislip. "Methylphenidate in the United States, 1990–1995." American Journal of Public Health 88 (1998): 1121.

Schmitt, B. D. "Attention Deficit Disorder (Short Attention Span)." Clinical Reference Systems 1 July 1999 <http://www.epnet.com/ehost/login.html>. 17 Feb. 2000.

*Online source*

Sheppard, Robert. "Growing Up Hyperactive." Maclean's 7 Sept. 1998: 45–46.

Before continuing, choose one of the following topics for your own work in the rest of Part III:

| | | |
|---|---|---|
| Police brutality | Censorship | Cloning |
| Alzheimer's disease | Government spending | Date rape |
| Herbal medicine | Steroids | Child abuse |
| Assisted suicide | Pollution | Alcohol and crime |
| Nursing homes | Drug treatment programs | Bilingual education |

# Avoiding Plagiarism

*Plagiarism* is using someone else's words or ideas as if they were your own. It is a serious offense in college and in life after college, because it is dishonest. By not citing your sources properly, your readers will think certain words and ideas are yours when they came from someone else. When you steal material in this way in college, you can get dismissed from school. When you commit the same offense in the professional world, you can end up in court. So make sure you understand what plagiarism is as you move through this chapter.

## COMMON KNOWLEDGE

If you are referring to such information as historical events, dates of presidents' terms, and known facts such as the effects of ultraviolet rays or smoking, you do not have to cite a source. This material is called *common knowledge* because it can be found in a number of different sources. You can use this information freely because you are not dealing with anyone's original words or ideas.

## ORIGINAL IDEAS

If, however, you want to use someone's words or ideas, you must give that person credit by recording where you found this information. This process is called citing or documenting your sources, and it involves noting in your paper where you found the idea. Since research papers are developed around sources that support your position, citations are an essential ingredient in any research paper.

As you can see in Mary Minor's paper in Chapter 18, every source is acknowledged at least twice in her research paper: (1) in the paper right after a quotation or idea and then (2) at the end of the paper as part of a list of sources used in the paper. At the note-taking stage, you simply have to make sure that you have all the information on your sources that you need so you can acknowledge them in your paper.

## MATERIAL FROM OUTSIDE SOURCES

The best way to avoid plagiarism is at the note-taking stage, when you are actually reading the original sources. One way to learn how to cite sources is to see the different ways you might use information from an original passage. The following paragraph is from "A Family Dilemma: To Scout or Not to Scout" by Michael Alvear. It was published in *Newsweek* magazine on November 6, 2000, on pages 12–13. The quoted passage is from page 12.

### Original Source

> When my sister first called to tell me she was thinking of putting Ricky in the Cub Scouts (a program run by Boy Scouts of America), I could hear the torment in her voice. Ricky is a bright, athletic boy who suffers from a shyness so paralyzing he doesn't have any friends. The other day my sister asked who he had played with at recess. "Nobody," he mumbled, looking at the floor. "I just scratched the mosquito bites on my leg till it was time to go back to class."

### Direct Quotation

If you use a direct quotation from another source, you must put the exact material you want to use in quotation marks:

> Michael Alvear, in his essay "A Family Dilemma: To Scout or Not to Scout," states, "Ricky is a bright, athletic boy who suffers from a shyness so paralyzing he doesn't have any friends" (12).

### Direct Quotation with Some Words Omitted

If you want to leave something out of the quotation, use three dots (with spaces before and after each dot). Omitting words is known as *ellipsis*.

> Michael Alvear, in his essay "A Family Dilemma: To Scout or Not to Scout," states, "Ricky is a bright, athletic boy who . . . doesn't have any friends" (12).

## Paraphrase

When you paraphrase, you are restating all the main ideas in your own words. *Paraphrase* literally means "similar phrasing," so it is usually about the same length as the original. Even though this information is in your own words, you still need to let your readers know where you found it. A paraphrase of our original source might look like this:

> Michael Alvear, in his essay "A Family Dilemma: To Scout or Not to Scout," states that he could hear his sister's worry when he talked to her. She was thinking of putting her very shy son in the Cub Scouts. Even though his nephew, Ricky, was both athletic and intelligent, his shyness prevented him from making any friends (12).

## Summary

When you summarize, you state the author's main idea in your own words. A summary is much briefer than the original or a paraphrase. You still need to cite in your paper where you found the information. Here is a summary of the original source:

> Michael Alvear, in his essay "A Family Dilemma: To Scout or Not to Scout," says his nephew, Ricky, was too shy to have any friends, so Alvear's sister was thinking of signing Ricky up for the Cub Scouts (12).

## TAKING NOTES ON SOURCES

When you take notes, notecards are an excellent tool because you can move them around as your paper takes shape. Put only one idea on a notecard. To avoid plagiarism when taking notes and when writing your paper, write down all the information you need to cite a source both in your paper and on the Works Cited page. For a book, you need the following information:

- Book title
- Author or authors
- City where published
- Publisher
- Year of publication

For an article, you must include the following:

- Title of the article
- Author or authors
- Title of the magazine or journal
- Date of the issue (for a magazine)
- Year and volume number (for a journal)
- Pages on which the article appeared

In both cases, you should also always record the number of the page where you found the information. That way you can find it again or cite it in your paper. If you put all this information on one card, you can use just the author's last name on all other cards from that source. The format in which this information should be presented may depend on the field of study. A good handbook will help you with the formats of the various documentation styles; these include Modern Language Association (MLA) style for the humanities, American Psychological Association (APA) style for the social sciences, and Council of Biology Editors (CBE) style for mathematics and science.

In this book, we are using the Modern Language Association style of citation. The Alvear essay in the MLA format would look like this:

> Alvear, Michael. "A Family Dilemma: To Scout or Not to Scout." Newsweek 6 Nov. 2000: 12–13.

**Practice 1** Identify the following information as either common knowledge (CK) or original (O).

1. _____ In a typical day, for human beings to drink the equivalent of what the glassy-winged sharpshooter insect drinks, humans would have to drink 4,000 gallons of liquid, half the amount in a standard swimming pool.

2. _____ William Shakespeare was born and died on the same day, April 23, 52 years apart.

3. _____ Abraham Lincoln was shot in Ford's Theater by John Wilkes Booth.

4. _____ A human being cannot survive beyond three days without water.

5. _____ The Paleozoic era produced the first shellfish and corals in the Cambrian period, the first fishes in the Ordovician period, and the first land plants in the Silurian period.

6. _____ Tom Hanks has won two Oscars, one for his role in *Philadelphia* and one for the title role in *Forrest Gump*.

7. _____ Aerobic respiration consists of oxygen plus organic matter that produces carbon dioxide, water, and energy.

8. _____ The success of *Survivor* caused many other reality shows to be produced.

9. _____ The longest palindromic word in the English language is *saippuakivikauppias*.

10. _____ AIDS is a disease that can be caught through unprotected sex.

**Practice 2** Quote from, paraphrase, and summarize the following original sources. Document the source correctly in each case by looking up the MLA documentation style in a handbook.

1. The following paragraph is from "Venus Envy" by Patricia McLaughlin. It was originally published in *Philadelphia Inquirer Magazine* on November 5, 1995, on page 27.

> You think of anorexia and bulimia as disorders that strike teenage girls, but men get them, too—not many, but "a bit more" than used to, according to Pertschuk, a psychiatrist who sees patients (including men) with eating disorders. Because eating disorders virtually always start with a "normal" desire to lose weight and look slimmer, the increase among men suggests that men are worrying about their looks more than they used to.

**Quotation:** ______________________________

______________________________

______________________________

**Paraphrase:** ______________________________

______________________________

______________________________

**Summary:** ______________________________

______________________________

______________________________

**Works Cited Citation:** ______________________________

______________________________

2. The following paragraph is from "Writer's Retreat" by Stan Higgins. It was originally published in *The Writer* in November 1991, on pages 21–23. The quoted paragraph appeared on page 21.

> During the day I wash dishes, clean tables, and mop floors. They call it Vocational Training. And today, as every day at three P.M., I return to my cozy, bathroom-size suite and drag out my tiny portable. We've all night, just the two of us, my blue typewriter that has been my steady cell-mate for six years, through seven facilities across two states, and I. Today's goal is three pages. I blow dust from the cover and clean the keys. The Muse calls. *Tack-tack. Tack. Tack-tack-tack.* My typewriter sings its staccato song as I search for a fertile word or idea, some harmonious junction of thought and paper. Locked in solitary combat with my machine, nothing exists outside my cell, or so I pretend. I type a line. My door opens. Two blue-uniformed guards stand there grinning. "Guess what?" one says. "Your number came up."

**Quotation:** ______________________________

______________________________

______________________________

**Paraphrase:** ______________________________

______________________________

______________________________

**Summary:** ______________________________

______________________________

______________________________

**Works Cited Citation:** ______________________________

______________________________

3. The following paragraph is from "Don't Be Cruel" by Roger Flax. It was originally published in *TWA Ambassador* in March 1992, on pages 49–51. The quoted paragraph appeared on page 49.

> Picture this scenario: Seymour Axshun (we'll call him), a terrific manager who has been a loyal employee for several years, messes up on an assignment. He misses a deadline on a proposal, and that three-day delay costs the company $9,100. Seymour's boss, Sy Kottick, has a near coronary over the incident, lashes out at Seymour, and criticizes him mercilessly. In front of four of Seymour's co-workers, Kottick shouts, "Axshun, how many times do I have to tell you to be more efficient with your planning? You blew it, and your mistake will cost us almost $10,000. I don't know what it takes to drill into your head that you must meet deadlines. It's disgusting, and I'm fed up. If you treated the money as if it were your own, you wouldn't be so careless."

**Quotation:** ______________________________

______________________________

______________________________

**Paraphrase:** ______________________________

______________________________

______________________________

**Summary:** ______________________________

______________________________

______________________________

**Works Cited Citation:** ______________________________

______________________________

4. The following paragraph is from "Healing Myself with the Power of Work" by Michael Norlen. It was originally published in *Newsweek*, on October 25, 1999, on page 12.

> It all changed 12 months ago. For the second time in six years, I abandoned my solo law practice. I stopped returning phone calls, forgot to pay bills, and ignored court dates. I began to sleep 16 hours a day. By July of last year I stopped coming into the office, leaving it to fill up with unopened mail and indignant phone messages. By August I was behind on my office rent, and by October my landlord asked me to leave. I ate, but nothing tasted good. I slept, but woke up tired. I felt like a stranger around my wife and two daughters. Thought of suicide shadowed me. And in the midst of all this, I knew. *It* had returned.

**Quotation:** ______________________________

______________________________

______________________________

**Paraphrase:** ______________________________

______________________________

______________________________

**Summary:** ______________________________

______________________________

______________________________

**Works Cited Citation:** ______________________________

______________________________

5. The following paragraph is from the essay "What Are Friends For?" by Marion Winik. It was originally published on pages 85–89 in a book titled *Telling: Confessions, Concessions, and Other Flashes of Light*, which was published by Villard Books in New York City in 1994. The quoted paragraph appeared on page 89.

> At the other end of the spectrum are Hero Friends. These people are better than the rest of us; that's all there is to it. Their career is something you wanted to be when you grew up—painter, forest ranger, tireless doer of good. They have beautiful homes filled with special handmade things presented to them by villagers in the remote areas they have visited in their extensive travels. Yet they are modest. They never gossip. They are always helping others, especially those who have suffered a death in the family or an illness. You would think people like this would just make you sick, but somehow they don't.

**Quotation:** ______________________________

______________________________

______________________________

**Paraphrase:** ______________________________

______________________________

______________________________

**Summary:** ______________________________

______________________________

______________________________

**Works Cited Citation:** ______________________________

______________________________

______________________________

# Finding Sources

No matter what you are studying in college, you should know how to find research materials using the library through a computer. You can access an enormous amount of information that will help you generate paper topics, teach you new information, challenge your thinking, support your strong opinions, and make you smile. In today's electronic world, learning how to use the resources available through the library's services is a basic survival skill.

## CONSULTING ONLINE DATABASES, FULL-TEXT INDEXES, AND ELECTRONIC JOURNAL COLLECTIONS

The best places to begin searching for research materials are online databases, full-text indexes, and electronic journal collections. You should have access to these services from home through your library's home page or from a computer in your library. We will discuss each one separately.

### Online Databases

Online databases can direct you to an incredible number of books and journals on a wide range of subjects. The following are some online indexes found in SilverPlatter's WebSPIRS database, which is an information retrieval system that contains indexes on many different subjects and is used by many libraries.

| Index | Primary Use |
|---|---|
| Biological and Agriculture Index | Science |
| ERIC | Education |
| GeoRef | Geology |
| MLA | Literature, language, and linguistics |

| | |
|---|---|
| Philosopher's Index | Philosophy |
| Sociological Abstracts | Sociology |

## Full-Text Indexes

The following are indexes that take you directly to complete journal articles on-line. In other words, you can print the journal articles you find right from your computer.

| Index | Primary Use |
|---|---|
| ABI Inform | News and business |
| Dow Jones | News and business |
| EBSCOhost* | Many subject areas |
| HRAF | Ethnographies |
| Lexis-Nexis | News, business, and law |
| WilsonWeb* | Popular magazines and newspapers, social science, humanities, business, general science, and education journals |

*Not all articles will be available in full-text.

## Electronic Journal Collections

Electronic journal collections are similar to on-line databases in that you can print complete journal articles directly from your computer. The following collections might help you find information about the topic you have chosen.

| Collection | Primary Use |
|---|---|
| Academic Press's IDEAL | Articles published by academic publishers |
| American Chemical Society's Web Editions | American Chemical Society's 26 scientific journals |
| American Mathematical Society Journals | American Mathematical Society's proceedings and transactions |

| | |
|---|---|
| JSTOR | Back issues of core journals in the humanities, social sciences, and sciences |
| Project Muse | Humanities, social sciences, and math |

Once you access an on-line database, index, or collection, you can easily find articles and books on your topic. You can do on-line searches by author, title, or subject; since you will most likely be looking for articles on a topic, you will use the subject function most often. When you are searching for a title by subject, you should be aware of "Boolean connectors," which are shortcuts to help you narrow the search field.

## Using Boolean Connectors

The Boolean connectors for requesting a search are *AND*, *OR*, and *NOT*. By using these words, you can limit the search and find information directly related to your topic. If you type "AND" between your key words (for example, *TV AND violence*), you are asking the computer to combine the key words for the search. If you put "OR" between the key words (*TV OR video games*), you are separating the words and asking the computer to find articles and books with either one of them. If you add "NOT" (*TV NOT video games*), you limit the search by excluding certain terms from the search.

## Accessing Sources

Once you type your topic into the search function of a database, index, or journal collection, the computer will display the number of articles and books it has found in a "results list." Following are some examples of articles found on the topic of *violence AND television* in an on-line database, a full-text index, and an electronic journal collection.

**From an Online Database**

Record 40 of 313 in *Sociological Abstracts* [in WebSPIRS] 1986-2001/06

TI: The National Television Violence Studies

AU: Chaffee, -Steven

IN: Stanford U, CA 94305

SO: Journal of Communications; 1997, 47, 4, autumn, 170-173.

DT: aja Abstract-of-Journal-Article

AB: A review essay on books by four university research teams - U California (Santa Barbara), U North Carolina (Chapel Hill), U Texas (Austin), & U Wisconsin (Madison) - (1) National **Television Violence** Study, Vol. 1 (Thousand Oaks, CA: Sage, 1997); & National **Television Violence** Study, Vol. 1. & Vol. 2 (Thousand Oaks, CA: Sage, 1997 & 1998, respectively). These works report on recent university studies of TV **violence** in diverse sectors of the US. The Executive Summary provides an overview of the project & policy recommendations & is appropriate for parents & teachers. The two main volumes present the coding system for **violence,** the effects of ratings & antiviolence advertising, & content analysis based on earlier literature. It is concluded that this team effort offers much useful information for the study of TV **violence,** & presents the studies in such a way that they can be easily replicated. 3 References. M. Cella

DEM: *__Television__ (D859500); *Mass-Media-**Violence** (D497700); *Communication-Research (D151900); *Programming-Braodcast (D668400)

AN: 9904482

### From a Full-Text Index

Entry 1 of 194 (from the Social Science Index in WilsonWeb)

Programming Behavior; Augmented title: restricting violent **television** programming during hours when children may be watching; Psychology Today v 34 no 1 Jan/Feb 2001. p. 10

### From an Electronic Journal Collection

2. Warning: The Surgeon General Has Determined That TV Violence Is Moderately Dangerous to Your Child's Mental Health
   Leo Bogart
   *Public Opinion Quarterly*, Vol. 36, No. 4. (Winter, 1972-1973), pp. 491-521.
   [Citation/Abstract] [View Article] [Page of First Match] [Print] [Download]

Notice that the screens you are taken to, like those in the examples, contain all of the information you will need for citing those works in the text and at the end of your paper. So make sure you keep lists like this when you print them so that you can cite your sources correctly.

**Practice 1** For each of the following topics, find a book from an on-line database, an article from a full-text journal, and an article from an electronic journal source. Record the title and the database, index, or source where you found it.

**Example:** Topic: Violence and TV
Database: Sociological Abstracts—in WebSPIRS
Title: *The National Television Violence Studies*
Index: Social Science Index in WilsonWeb
Title: *Programming Behavior*
Electronic Journal: JSTOR
Title: *Warning: The Surgeon General Has Determined That TV Violence Is Moderately Dangerous to Your Child's Mental Health*

1. Topic: Drug testing in college sports

   Database: ________________________________

   Title: ________________________________

   Index: ________________________________

   Title: ________________________________

   Electronic Journal: ________________________________

   Title: ________________________________

2. Topic: Affirmative action and the workforce

   Database: ________________________________

   Title: ________________________________

   Index: ________________________________

   Title: ________________________________

   Electronic Journal: ________________________________

   Title: ________________________________

3. Topic: Prison pampering

   Database: ______________________________

   Title: ______________________________

   Index: ______________________________

   Title: ______________________________

   Electronic Journal: ______________________________

   Title: ______________________________

4. Topic: Women in combat

   Database: ______________________________

   Title: ______________________________

   Index: ______________________________

   Title: ______________________________

   Electronic Journal: ______________________________

   Title: ______________________________

5. Topic: Using animals for testing

   Database: ______________________________

   Title: ______________________________

   Index: ______________________________

   Title: ______________________________

   Electronic Journal: ______________________________

   Title: ______________________________

## SEARCHING FOR WEB SITES

To find a Web site related to your topic, you should go to the Internet through whatever browser you have (Netscape Communicator or Navigator, Microsoft Internet Explorer, etc.). Your browser probably has a search engine of its own, which will let you search the Internet. Or you might want to use a search engine that automatically refers you to sites related to your topic: Both www.dogpile.com and www.google.com are examples of search engines that can save you a lot of time. For example, www.google.com searches nearly 1.5 million Web sites in mere seconds and is an excellent source for research.

Once you access a search engine, type in your topic as if you were searching a database. Most search engines will then begin helping you narrow your search, and most will provide a list of other possible topics. Here are some examples for the topic of *violence and television.*

| **Topic** | **Other Possible Topics** |
|---|---|
| Violence and television | TV violence |
| | On TV violence |
| | Television violence |
| | TV violence children |
| | Violence on television |
| | Causes of TV violence |
| | Media violence |

When the search is complete, your search engine will list the different Web sites in the order it thinks they will be most helpful to you. It will also briefly describe each Web site. After the description, you will most often find the Web site address. The following are the first three "hits" or Web sites from www.dogpile.com for the topic *violence and television.*

1. National Coalition on TV Violence

Learn about the effects of TV violence and facts about the V-Chip, and get ideas to help kids avoid violent entertainment.

www.nctvv.org

2. American Psych. Association - Violence on Television

Association investigates the effect of television violence on children and discusses ways parents can intervene to minimize its impact.

www.apa.org

3. <u>APA HelpCenter: Warning Signs of Teen Violence</u>

The American Psychological Association and MTV team up to get important information to the nation's youth about warning signs of violent behavior, including violence in schools. The Warning Signs site provides a violence prevention guide and resource.

helping.apa.org

**Practice 2** For each of the following topics, find a different Web page through a different search engines and list the Web page title, the explanation, and the Web address.

**Example:** Topic: Violence and television

Search engine: GoTo.com through dogpile.com

Web page title: Center for Educational Priorities: Two Studies

Explanation: Read brief overview of the 1996 National Violence Study and the 1995 UCLA Television Violence Monitoring Report

Web address: www.cep.org

1. Topic: Bilingual education in California

   Search engine: ______________________________

   Web page title: ______________________________

   Explanation: ______________________________

   ______________________________

   Web address: ______________________________

2. Topic: Benefits of the U.S. space program

   Search engine: ______________________________

   Web page title: ______________________________

   Explanation: ______________________________

   ______________________________

   Web address: ______________________________

3. Topic: Legalizing marijuana

   Search engine: ______________________________

   Web page title: ______________________________

   Explanation: ______________________________

   ______________________________

   Web address: ______________________________

4. Topic: Homeopathic medicine

   Search engine: ______________________________

   Web page title: ______________________________

   Explanation: ______________________________

   ______________________________

   Web address: ______________________________

5. Topic: Women's soccer

   Search engine: ______________________________

   Web page title: ______________________________

   Explanation: ______________________________

   ______________________________

   Web address: ______________________________

## USING THE LIBRARY

Once you have compiled a list of books and journals from databases and indexes or from Web sites, you should use your library to check out books or copy journal articles that were not available online.

First, you need to access your library's on-line catalog to see if your library has the book. (If your library does not have computers, use the traditional card catalog.) Ask a librarian how to access your particular catalog through your school. You might also ask if this information is available to you online. You can search for authors and subjects through your library's catalog in much the same way that you would search online databases or program search engines. But since you have already done the preliminary research, all you have to do is search for the books and journals you need. So find the "title" section of the catalog, and type in the title of the book or journal you need in this section. If you need help finding books and journals in your college library, ask a librarian.

If you are searching for a chapter or an essay contained in a book, be sure to type in the main book title. For example, if you searched for "I Just Wanna Be Average" (by Mike Rose), your library computer will tell you that the library does not carry this book. You must type the title of the book it came from, *Lives on the Boundary*, to find the essay. Once you have located the titles of your books or journals in the library's catalog, you should write down the call numbers so you can find the sources in your library. Then it's just a matter of finding the book itself in the stacks of your library.

**Practice 3** Find five books from your research, and using the "title" portion of your library's catalog, locate the call numbers.

**Example:** Title: *Youth Culture: Identity in a Postmodern World*
Call number: HV 1431 Y684 1998

1. Title: ______________________________

   Call number: ______________________________

2. Title: ______________________________

   Call number: ______________________________

3. Title: ______________________________

   Call number: ______________________________

4. Title: ______________________________

   Call number: ______________________________

5. Title: ______________________________

   Call number: ______________________________

# How to Write a Research Paper

A *research paper* is really just an essay with supporting material that comes from outside sources. This type of writing assignment has all the elements of a typical essay. The following chart compares an essay and a research paper.

| Essay | | Research Paper |
|---|---|---|
| Introductory paragraph with thesis statement | ⟷ | Introductory paragraph with thesis statement |
| Body paragraphs with evidence | ⟷ | Body paragraphs with documented evidence to support thesis statement |
| Concluding paragraph | ⟷ | Concluding paragraph |

Keep this outline in mind as you read how to construct a good research paper. Laying out some clear guidelines is the best place to start.

1. ***Choose a subject.*** You might be choosing a subject from infinite possibilities or working with an assigned topic. Whatever the case, you must ask one very important question before you begin planning your paper: Will you be able to find enough information to back up your thesis statement? To make sure you are able to find enough material to use as good evidence in the body paragraphs of your research paper, you must do a good job of choosing a subject, narrowing that subject, and then writing a very clear thesis statement. You will prove this thesis statement with the information you find when you research your topic. If you were writing a research paper on pursuing

a degree in college, for example, your initial prewriting for the thesis statement might look like this:

**General Subject:** College and university degrees
**More Specific:** Bachelor's degree
**More Specific:** Bachelor's degree in English

This limited subject would be perfect for a research paper. You could search for books, catalogs, and periodicals on what it takes to earn a bachelor's degree in English from various colleges and universities. While you are looking, you could be thinking about how to narrow your subject even further.

Mary Minor (in Chapter 18) might have started with a general topic like "childhood disorders," limited it to "childhood behavioral disorders," and finally settled on "ADD and ADHD as childhood behavioral disorders."

**Practice 1** Choose a topic from the list on page 343. Why did you choose this topic?

**Practice 2** Limit this topic so that you can write a paper about five pages long.

2. ***Write a good, clear thesis statement about your subject.*** Just as a thesis statement is the controlling idea of an essay, a thesis statement also provides the controlling idea for your research. This statement will guide the writing of your entire paper. Your assignments throughout college will usually be broad topics. To compose a good research paper, you need to narrow a broad topic to an idea that you can prove within a limited number of pages. A working thesis statement will provide the direction for your research, and the evidence you collect in your research is what proves the thesis statement.

Since the thesis statement presents your controlling idea for the entire paper, one good way to begin your first draft is to write a sentence that clearly states your topic and your position on that topic. Even though your thesis statement may change several times before your essay is finished, making this statement and taking a position is a necessary first step. It will help you move from the broad subject of your assignment to your own perspective on the topic. This will also help you focus your research and save you time in your search for good resources to back up your thesis statement.

Just as in an essay, your research paper's thesis statement is a contract between you and your readers. The thesis statement tells your readers what the main idea of your essay will be and controls the paragraphs in the body of your essay. If you don't deliver what your thesis statement promises, your readers will be disappointed. The thesis statement is usually the last sentence in the introduction. It outlines your purpose and position on the essay's general topic and gives the reader an idea of the type of resources that you will use to develop your essay.

Mary Minor's controlling idea or thesis statement appears at the end of her first paragraph:

> Children are often misdiagnosed with ADD or ADHD and suffer unnecessarily when medicated for a disorder they may not have.

Her entire essay is about children who are too readily diagnosed with ADD or ADHD simply because they do not fall into society's "norm" for children's behavior. The paragraphs following this thesis statement supply evidence that proves that her claim is true.

**Practice 3** List your thoughts and opinions on the topic you chose in Practice 1.

**Practice 4** Put your topic and your position on that topic into a working thesis statement.

3. ***Find sources that are relevant, reliable, and recent to support your thesis statement.*** The thesis statement of a research paper is really only the beginning. To convince your readers that what you say in your essay is worth reading, you must support your thesis statement with evidence. The evidence of a research paper lies in the sources that you use to back up your thesis statement. The sources must be relevant, reliable, and recent. This "three *R*'s" approach to supporting evidence in a research paper will help you write a solid essay with convincing evidence.

Mary Minor's thesis statement suggests that young children are being too readily diagnosed with ADD and ADHD. To convince her readers that her thesis statement is correct, she uses a book, scientific journals, an encyclopedia, on-line journal articles, and general circulation magazines as sources of evidence. Here is a breakdown of how she used her sources.

- **Book:** *The Myth of the ADD Child*

  This source provides well-researched information from an expert's point of view. Mary uses this source early in her paper to help define the scope of her study.
- **Scientific journals:** *CQ Researcher, Science News, Qualitative Health Research, American Journal of Public Health*

  These sources supply the reader with specific evidence put forth by experts in the field of ADD and ADHD research and diagnosis. Mary uses this information to prove that her thesis statement is true.
- **Encyclopedia:** *World Book Encyclopedia*

  Mary uses this source to provide the reader with an understandable definition of the "Hippocratic Oath." This definition plays an important role in Mary's stance on her topic.
- **On-line journal articles:** *Clinical Reference Systems*

  The article from this source was printed from WilsonWeb. The information in this article defines hyperactivity in children for the general reader.
- **General-circulation magazines:** *U.S. News and World Report, Camping Magazine, Time, Runner's World, Maclean's*

  These sources supply information readily available at a newsstand, yet highly informative and applicable to Mary's topic. Information from articles in these magazines speaks to the average citizen. Even though these magazines are not scientific journals, the evidence in them is powerful because it was intended to make specialized information understandable to the general reader.

Mary Minor uses sources in her research paper that do a thorough job of supporting her thesis statement. You should do the same when you are planning and writing your research paper, and also like Mary, you should attempt to use a variety of sources that are relevant, reliable, and recent.

**Practice 5** Review Chapter 20 so that you understand the options available to you for your research.

**Practice 6** Find five sources that give you information about the limited topic that you chose. Make sure they are relevant, reliable, and recent.

4. ***Take notes to avoid plagiarism.*** Now is the time to read your sources and take careful notes, putting the writer's words in quotation marks and recording the page numbers of all information you take down. If

you don't take notes carefully, you will never be able to trace information that you want to use in your paper to its original source. Also, trying to put someone's ideas into your own words is a very good skill that will help you as you write.

Taking notes on notecards also gets you away from your original sources and allows you to move your cards around and put ideas into different paragraphs. When you rearrange cards, you can work with them until you think the order will support what you are trying to prove.

Mary Minor now has to read and take notes on all the sources she found. She first makes a set of bibliography cards with a notecard for every source she has found. For the books, she puts book title, author, city where published, publisher, and year of publication on each card; for the articles, she records author, title of the article, title of the magazine or journal, date of the issue or volume and issue numbers, and page numbers on each card. Then she begins to read her sources. She writes only one idea or quotation on a notecard, and she labels each card so that she knows the book and page it came from. She also makes sure, as she takes notes, to put information in her own words or else record the author's exact words between quotation marks. Finally, she remembers to record on each notecard the author's name and the page number on which she found the information. As she reads, she sees some patterns that she can use in her paper.

**Practice 7** Review Chapter 19 to make sure you understand what plagiarism is and how to avoid it.

**Practice 8** Read and take notes on these sources using notecards. Make sure each of your cards has a source and page number on it.

5. ***Make a working outline of your paper.*** To do this, you just need to start rearranging the notecards you have made. Start by putting all your notecards into small stacks of related ideas. Which ideas will work well together? Which should you put in the introduction? Which do you want to save for your conclusion? When you get all your notecards in stacks, label each group of cards according to its topic. These labels will then become the topics of your paper. You are now ready to start your working outline.

A good way to begin a working outline is to write your tentative thesis statement at the top of a page and then list the topics you have developed under that thesis. These topics should be arranged in some logical order that the reader can easily follow and that will help you prove your point. Each topic should also directly support your thesis statement. Leave room in your outline to add subtopics and details throughout the paper. This outline then becomes a guide for your writing. It will change and grow with every paragraph that you add to your paper.

Mary started developing her paper by putting related notecards into stacks. Next, she labeled her stacks of notecards and started organizing these topics in different ways until they started making sense to her. Her list of topics, with her thesis statement at the top, became the bulk of her working outline. She eventually turned these topics into topic sentences for her body paragraphs. The stack of cards for each topic became the content of her body paragraphs.

**Practice 9** Divide your notecards into topics that logically support your thesis statement. Then label each stack of cards.

**Practice 10** Start a working outline of your paper by listing your thesis statement and your supporting topics.

6. ***Construct an introduction that leads up to your thesis statement.*** The introduction to a research paper is your chance to make a great first impression. Just like a firm handshake and a warm smile in a job interview, an essay's introduction should capture your readers' interest, set the tone for your essay, and state your specific purpose. Introductions often have a funnel effect. They typically begin with general information and then narrow the focus to your position on a particular issue. Regardless of your method, your introduction should "hook" your readers by grabbing their attention and letting them know what you seek to prove in your research paper.

To lead up to the thesis statement, your introductory paragraph must stimulate readers' interest. Some effective ways of catching your audience's attention and giving necessary background information are (1) to use a quotation, (2) to tell a story that relates to your topic, (3) to provide a revealing fact, statistic, or definition, (4) to offer an interesting comparison, or (5) to ask an intriguing question. Be sure your introduction gives readers all the information they may need to follow your train of thought through the rest of your paper.

Mary's introduction starts out with a hypothetical situation that parents face as their children may or may not develop "normally." The second paragraph begins by focusing on the later development of children and adds some dates, statistics, and brief definitions of ADD and ADHD by citing a source. The last sentence of the first paragraph contains the thesis statement of the essay and ends the introduction.

**Practice 11** Make a rough outline of your ideas for a possible introduction to your research paper.

**Practice 12** Write a rough draft of your introduction, ending with your thesis statement.

7. ***Develop as many supporting paragraphs or body paragraphs as you think are necessary to explain your thesis statement.*** Following the introductory paragraph, a research paper includes several body paragraphs that support and explain the essay's thesis statement. Each body paragraph covers a topic that is directly related to the thesis statement.

Supporting paragraphs, or body paragraphs, usually include a topic sentence, which is a general statement of the paragraph's contents, and examples or details that support the topic sentence. (See Chapters 4 and 5 for methods to use when you develop and organize paragraphs.)

To write your supporting paragraphs, you should first organize your notecards within each of your stacks. Next, add these details to your working outline. Then write your supporting paragraphs by following your working outline and your notecards. Make adjustments in your outline as you write so that you can keep track of your ideas and make sure you are developing them in a logical order. The body of the paper and your outline should change and develop together with each sentence that you write.

After you write your body paragraphs, you should look at your thesis statement again to make sure it introduces what you say in the rest of your paper. Your thesis statement should refer to all of your topics, even if only indirectly, in the order you discuss them. It should also prepare your readers for the conclusions you are going to come to.

Mary's research paper contains 12 body paragraphs, each making a separate point that is directly related to her thesis:

| Paragraph | Point |
|---|---|
| 2 | ADD and ADHD can be defined as "a short attention span." |
| 3 | ADD is one of the most commonly diagnosed childhood diseases. |
| 4 | Diagnosing children who do not fit a "norm" is ludicrous. |

5 There is no accurate definition or diagnosis of ADD or ADHD.

6 No physical exam can determine if a child has ADD or ADHD.

7 There are as many definitions of ADD as there are experts doing the defining.

8 We are treating symptoms with these disorders.

9 Teachers, parents, and students get caught up in the diagnosis.

10 Are drugs (Ritalin) the answer?

11 It seems younger children are more often diagnosed and medicated.

12 Drugs can cause side effects and even be abused.

13 Diet may be a factor in the behavior of children.

Like the foundation of a solid building, these paragraphs provide support for the position Mary takes in her thesis statement. The stronger the supporting paragraphs are, the stronger the research paper will be.

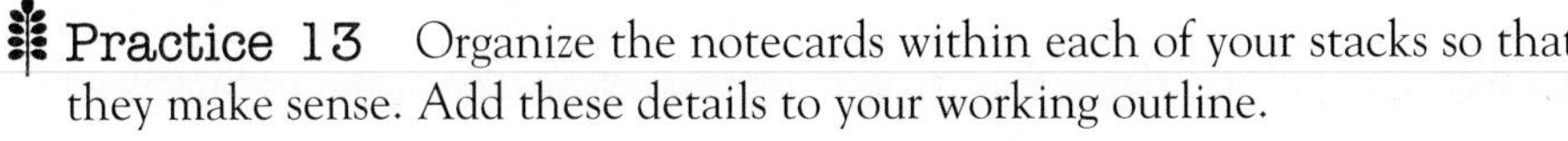

**Practice 13** Organize the notecards within each of your stacks so that they make sense. Add these details to your working outline.

**Practice 14** Write a rough draft of your body paragraphs. Remember that you will be revising and editing this draft a little later, so just concentrate on getting your ideas written up in an organized way. Revise your thesis statement, if necessary, to introduce all your body paragraphs.

8. ***Write a concluding paragraph.*** The concluding paragraph is the final paragraph of an essay. In its most basic form, it should summarize the main points of the essay and remind readers of the thesis statement.

The best conclusions expand on these two basic requirements and bring the essay to a close with one of these creative strategies: (1) Ask a question that provokes thought on the part of the reader, (2) predict the future, (3) offer a solution to a problem, or (4) call the reader to action. Each of these options sends a specific message and creates a slightly different effect at the end of the paper. The most important responsibility of the last paragraph is to bring the essay to an effective close. It is the last information that readers see before they form their own opinions or take action.

Mary's conclusion offers a solution to the problem raised in the second sentence of the paragraph:

> Every effort should be made to find the cause of the "real" medical problems underlying ADD and ADHD before we even think about giving our children drugs.

She then calls the reader to action:

> It's time to say good-bye to "conformist" American classrooms and diagnoses.

She ends by reflecting on her thesis in one last, short line:

> People don't fit "norms"; they fit personalities.

Her concluding paragraph refocuses the reader's attention on the problem, offers a solution to the problem, and then calls the reader to action.

**Practice 15** Make a rough outline of your ideas for a possible conclusion to your research paper. Choose a strategy that you want to use to bring your paper to a conclusion.

**Practice 16** Write a rough draft of your conclusion, reminding your readers of your thesis statement.

9. ***Think of a catchy title.*** Your title is what readers see first in your research paper. A title is a phrase, usually no more than a few words, placed at the beginning of your essay that suggests or sums up the subject, purpose, or focus of the essay. Some titles are very imaginative, drawing on different sources for their meaning. Others are straightforward, like the title of this chapter—"How to Write a Research Paper." These are just two of the many different approaches you can take to creating a title.

Besides suggesting an essay's purpose, a good title catches an audience's attention. For instance, Mary Minor's title, "Children as Robots," will catch most readers' attention because referring to children as "robots" is intriguing, and readers will want to find out just how and why this might occur. That's exactly what a title should do—make your readers want to read your paper.

**Practice 17** Jot down some catchy titles for your research paper.

**Practice 18** Choose a title for your paper.

10. ***Check your sources and documentation format throughout the paper and at the end.*** Finding and using good, solid sources for evidence in a research paper is important, and equally important is the citation of those sources. If you use a source and do not cite it correctly or forget to cite it altogether, you are guilty of plagiarism, which can lead to a failing grade on the paper. So you need to learn when to cite a source (see Chapter 19), what documentation style to use (MLA, APA, or other appropriate format), and how to cite sources. You should check with your instructor to find out which format you should use for a research paper you are writing in any course.

Mary uses the MLA format on this paper, which she wrote for an English class. Usually, English instructors ask their students to use the MLA format for their papers. Many textbooks demonstrate the various forms of documentation. You should find one of these books and keep it handy when you write research papers. Mary includes a variety of sources in her paper; we can use these to illustrate how sources should be documented.

Citations are of two types: (a) The *in-text citation* indicates the source of a quotation or idea right after it appears in the essay or research paper; (b) then, at the end, a list of all the sources used in the paper must appear on the *Works Cited page*. Listed here are some sample Works Cited entries, with the corresponding in-text citations in parentheses.

**Book**—name of author, title of book, city of publication, publisher, date of publication

**Works Cited:** Armstrong, Thomas. The Myth of the ADD Child: 50 Ways to Improve Your Child's Behavior and Attention Span Without Drugs, Labels, or Coercion. New York: Dutton, 1995.

**In-Text Citation:** (Armstrong 42)

**Journal**—name of author, title of article, name of journal, volume number, year, page number

**Works Cited:** Bower, Bruce. "Kid's Attention Disorder Attracts Concern." Science News 154 (1998): 343.

**In-Text Citation:** (Bower 343)

**Encyclopedia**—name of author, title of article, name of encyclopedia, volume number, year

**Works Cited:** "Hippocratic Oath." World Book Encyclopedia. Vol. 9. 1999 ed.

**In-Text Citation:** ("Hippocratic Oath")

*Note:* If an article is unsigned, begin with the title of the article.

**On-line Database**—name of author, title of article, date of publication, name of database, URL in angle brackets, date you accessed the material

**Works Cited:** Schmitt, B. D. "Attention Deficit Disorder (Short Attention Span)." Clinical Reference Systems. 1 July 1999 <http://www.epnet.com/ehost/login. html>. 17 Feb. 2000.

**In-Text Citation:** (Schmitt)

*Note:* If some components are missing, include whatever is available.

**General-Circulation Magazine**—name of author, title of article, name of magazine, date of publication, page numbers

**Works Cited:** Sheppard, Robert. "Growing Up Hyperactive." Maclean's 7 Sept. 1998: 45–46.

**In-Text Citation:** (Sheppard 45)

*Note:* If an article is unsigned, begin with the title of the article.

The examples from Mary's essay are just a few of the various types of sources that you will probably use in your research papers. Every source is cited in a slightly different way. Not even the best writers know the correct MLA format for every source they use. Therefore, you should have a good reference manual handy to check the format for every source in your paper. When you have determined that the source you have found is relevant, reliable, and recent (the three *R*'s), your last step is to consult an MLA manual to make sure you cite the source correctly.

**Practice 19** Make sure that all material from another source in your research paper has an in-text citation. Then create a Works Cited page, following an approved documentation format.

**Practice 20** Check the format of your in-text citations and your Works Cited page by consulting a current handbook.

CHAPTER 22

# Revising and Editing a Student Research Paper

Here is the first draft of an essay written by Michael Tiede, a student. It demonstrates the guidelines for writing a successful research paper that you have learned in Chapters 18 through 21.

**Nuclear Insurance**

Nuclear weapons have been tested for decades. This testing has pro- 1
duced a lot of controversy in the United States. The United States has not decided whether a complete nuclear test ban would benefit the nation's security. One argument states that testing must take place to maintain the threat that our military is powerful. The opposing argument simply says that ending nuclear testing and the use of nuclear weapons will make the world a safer place to live. The idea of no nuclear force and no nuclear testing brings thoughts of world peace and happiness. However, the same idea brings thoughts of insecurity. Without nuclear weapons, the nation will not be able to prevent attacks from other countries. Nuclear testing must take place.

Two classifications of nuclear testing exist. The first classification is 2
known as atmospheric tests. This includes all atmospheric, surface, space, and underwater testing. The other classification is underground testing (Robbins, Makaijani, and Yih 2–3). Many tests are conducted on old battleships and submarines, while other tests are conducted on buildings and other military artillery. These tests will assist in improving nuclear technology and in answering questions about how much power is actually needed to create the desired level of destruction (Trinity and Beyond).

Nuclear testing is the only way to improve the safety of these 3
weapons. Tests have to be run so that the military will know how to properly insert what is known as an "environmental sensing device." This

device will prevent enemies from knowing where a specific target is if a missile falls into their hands. Another safety measure being tested is the "permissive action links." The permissive action links is an "electro-mechanical lock on the weapon's arming system." Which can become operational only with the correct authorization code. This is used to make sure the arming system is used only by authorized personnel. A third safety device that requires extensive testing is the use of insertable nuclear parts. With this technology, the fissile material (the matter that splits to make the nuclear explosion) would be inserted into the weapon when it is delivered to the target (Fetter 38–39). All of these safety issues are important, nuclear testing is important to maintain this safety. Testing for safety also helps the military dicover new insights into nuclear weapons.

4 Learning about new delivery systems would be another result of testing. New technology can deliver nuclear weapons to their target more effectively and more accurately. Refining old methods of delivery will increase the survival of aircraft and other delivery veicles. Cruise missile technology will enable an aircraft to have the capability to drop a nuclear weapon and guide it to a specific location many miles away. With the advances in stealth technology, nuclear missile delivery is safe and accurate and is difficult to counterattack (Fetter 40).

5 Our faith in nuclear weapons and their reliability depends on testing. By enforcing a test ban, confidence in the available nuclear weapons would significantly decrease. The designers and people responsible for nuclear weapons need to be confident that their product is reliable. For these weapons to be reliable, the percentage of weapons that perform properly needs to be high. The only way to ensure a high percentage is to conduct many tests. Experts must have high confidence in the reliable performance of their nuclear weapons if these weapons will help prevent war (Fetter 69–70). A test ban could backfire and eliminate the United States' ability to fight wars.

6 Under a test ban, preventing a war would be difficult. Furthermore, it would also be difficult to detect and monitor testing by other countries. Monitoring systems are between 10 and 20 years from being operational (Snowe B7). Nuclear testing is necessary to test monitoring systems because researchers need nuclear material to test the monitoring systems. Without affective monitoring systems, other countries can conduct nuclear tests without consequences because no one can monitor their activities. A test ban could bring conflict for the countries who still test, and this premise is the opposite idea of what the ban is about. A test ban has the potential for allowing enemy countries to become nuclear power forces, and no one would know of this power.

Nuclear testing is essential for many reasons. It is needed to "increase the safety and security of nuclear warheads" (Fetter 34) and "to remain at the forefront of knowledge about nuclear weapons, their effects, potential developments, and new applications" (Van Cleave and Cohen 54). Nuclear testing is necessary "to develop custom-designed nuclear warheads for new delivery systems" (Fetter 34), "to understand the effects of nuclear detonations on our own systems, and to help maintain confidence in the reliability and effectiveness of our deployed and stockpiled weapons" (Van Cleave and Cohen 54). Essentially, to ban nuclear testing would be more harmful than helpful. Many reasons explain why a complete test ban is not in the United States' best interest. For the military to be able to continue defending the nation, nuclear testing must take place. Having nuclear weapons deters future attacks. The more technology and effort given to nuclear development, the more effective nuclear deterrence will be. 7

**Works Cited**

Fetter, Steve. Toward a Comprehensive Test Ban. Cambridge: Ballinger, 1988.

Robbins, Anthony, Arjun Makaijani, and Katherine Yih. Radioactive Heaven and Earth. London: Zed, 1991.

Snowe, Olympia. "Much Too Soon to Pass a Test Ban Treaty." Seattle Times 21 Oct. 1999: B7.

Trinity and Beyond: The Atomic Bomb Movie. Dir. Peter Kuran. Prod. Peter Kuran and Alan Munro. Visual Concept Entertainment, 1997.

Van Cleave, William R., and S. T. Cohen. Nuclear Weapons, Policies, and the Test Ban Issue. New York: Praeger, 1987.

Michael's first draft now needs to be revised and edited. The following checklists will help you revise and edit Michael's writing. First, apply the Revising Checklist below to Michael's draft, working with his content. When you are satisfied that his ideas are fully developed and well organized, use the Editing Checklist on page 382 to correct his grammatical and mechanical errors. Answer the questions after each checklist. Then rewrite the essay with your suggested changes.

## Revising Checklist

**THESIS STATEMENT**

✔ Does the thesis statement contain the essay's controlling idea and appear as the last sentence of the introduction?

Basic Elements

- ✔ Does the title draw in the readers?
- ✔ Does the introduction capture the readers' attention and build up to the thesis statement effectively?
- ✔ Does each body paragraph deal with a single topic?
- ✔ Does the conclusion bring the essay to a close in an interesting way?

Development

- ✔ Do the body paragraphs adequately support the thesis statement?
- ✔ Does each body paragraph have a focused topic sentence?
- ✔ Does each body paragraph contain *specific* details that support the topic sentence?
- ✔ Does each body paragraph include *enough* details to explain the topic sentence fully?
- ✔ Are the sources relevant, reliable, and recent?
- ✔ Are references given for original sources to avoid plagiarism?
- ✔ Is the documentation format correct—in the paper and at the end?

Unity

- ✔ Do the essay's topic sentences relate directly to the thesis statement?
- ✔ Do the details in each body paragraph support its topic sentence?

Organization

- ✔ Is the essay organized logically?
- ✔ Is each body paragraph organized logically?

Coherence

- ✔ Are transitions used effectively so that paragraphs move smoothly and logically from one to the next?
- ✔ Do the sentences move smoothly and logically from one to the next?

## Thesis Statement

- ✔ Does the thesis statement contain the essay's controlling idea and appear as the last sentence of the introduction?

1. What is Michael's main idea in this research paper?

_______________________________________________

2. Put brackets around Michael's thesis statement. Does it introduce his main point? ____________

3. Rewrite it to introduce all the topics in his essay.

_______________________________________________

_______________________________________________

## Basic Elements

- ✔ Does the title draw in the readers?
- ✔ Does the introduction capture the readers' attention and build up to the thesis statement effectively?
- ✔ Does each body paragraph deal with a single topic?
- ✔ Does the conclusion bring the essay to a close in an interesting way?

1. Give Michael's essay an alternate title.

_______________________________________________

2. Rewrite Michael's introduction so that it captures readers' attention and builds up to the thesis statement at the end of the paragraph.

_______________________________________________

_______________________________________________

_______________________________________________

_______________________________________________

3. Does each of Michael's body paragraphs deal with only one topic? _______

4. Rewrite Michael's conclusion.

## Development

- ✔ Do the body paragraphs adequately support the thesis statement?
- ✔ Does each body paragraph have a focused topic sentence?
- ✔ Does each body paragraph contain *specific* details that support the topic sentence?
- ✔ Does each body paragraph include *enough* details to explain the topic sentence fully?
- ✔ Are the sources relevant, reliable, and recent?
- ✔ Are references given for original sources to avoid plagiarism?
- ✔ Is the documentation format correct—in the paper and at the end?

1. Do Michael's topic sentences support his thesis statement? Write out your revision of Michael's thesis statement, and list his six topic sentences.

   **Thesis:** ______________________________

   ______________________________

   **Topics:** ______________________________

   ______________________________

   ______________________________

   ______________________________

   ______________________________

   ______________________________

2. Does your revised thesis statement accurately introduce Michael's topic sentences? ______________________________
3. Are Michael's examples specific? ____________ Add an even more specific detail to one of his paragraphs.
4. Does he offer enough examples or details in each paragraph? __________

5. Are Michael's sources relevant, reliable, and recent? ____________

6. Does he give references for all original sources in his paper? Find the one sentence in paragraph 3 that is plagiarized and needs the reference "(Fetter 38)."

7. Is the documentation format correct in his paper? ____________

8. Is the format on his Works Cited page correct? ____________

## Unity

- ✔ Do the essay's topic sentences relate directly to the thesis statement?
- ✔ Do the details in each body paragraph support its topic sentence?

1. Read each of Michael's topic sentences with his thesis statement in mind.

   Do they go together? ____________

2. Revise any topic sentences that are not directly related to his thesis.

3. Read each of Michael's paragraphs with its topic sentence in mind. Drop or rewrite any sentences that are not directly related to the paragraph's topic sentences.

## Organization

- ✔ Is the essay organized logically?
- ✔ Is each body paragraph organized logically?

1. Review your list of Michael's topics in item 1 under "Development," and decide if his body paragraphs are organized logically.
2. What is his method of organization?
3. Read Michael's research paper again to see if all his sentences are arranged logically.
4. Move any sentences that are out of order.

## Coherence

- ✔ Are transitions used effectively so that paragraphs move smoothly and logically from one to the next?
- ✔ Do the sentences move smoothly and logically from one to the next?

1. Circle five transitions that Michael uses.
2. Explain how three of these transitions make Michael's research paper easier to read.

Now rewrite Michael's essay with your revisions.

## Editing Checklist

SENTENCES

- ✔ Does each sentence have a main subject and verb?
- ✔ Do all subjects and verbs agree?
- ✔ Do all pronouns agree with their nouns?
- ✔ Are modifiers as close as possible to the words they modify?

PUNCTUATION AND MECHANICS

- ✔ Are sentences punctuated correctly?
- ✔ Are words capitalized properly?

WORD CHOICE AND SPELLING

- ✔ Are words used correctly?
- ✔ Are words spelled correctly?

## Sentences

- ✔ Does each sentence have a main subject and verb?

For help with subjects and verbs, see Chapter 34.

1. Underline the subjects once and verbs twice in paragraph 3 of Michael's essay. Remember that sentences can have more than one subject-verb set.
2. Does each sentence have at least one subject and verb that can stand alone? ______________
3. Did you find and correct Michael's fragment in paragraph 3? If not, find and correct it now. (For help with fragments, see Chapter 35.)
4. Did you find and correct Michael's run-on sentence in paragraph 3? If not, find and correct it now. (For help with run-ons, see Chapter 36.)

✔ Do all subjects and verbs agree?
For help with subject-verb agreement, see Chapter 39.

1. Read aloud the subjects and verbs in paragraph 5 of Michael's revised essay.
2. Correct any subjects and verbs that do not agree.
3. Now read aloud the subjects and verbs in the rest of his revised essay.
4. Correct any subjects and verbs that do not agree.

✔ Do all pronouns agree with their nouns?
For help with pronoun agreement, see Chapter 43.

1. Find any pronouns in your revision of Michael's essay that do not agree with their nouns.
2. Correct any pronouns that do not agree with their nouns.

✔ Are modifiers as close as possible to the words they modify?
For help with modifier errors, see Chapter 46.

1. Find any modifiers in your revision of Michael's essay that are not as close as possible to the words they modify.
2. Rewrite sentences if necessary so that modifiers are as close as possible to the words they modify.

## Punctuation and Mechanics

✔ Are sentences punctuated correctly?
For help with punctuation, see Chapters 47–51.

1. Read your revision of Michael's essay for any errors in punctuation.
2. Make sure any fragments and run-ons you revised are punctuated correctly.

✔ Are words capitalized properly?
For help with capitalization, see Chapter 52.

1. Read your revisions of Michael's essay for any errors in capitalization.
2. Be sure to check the capitalization in fragments and run-ons you revised.

## Word Choice and Spelling

✔ Are words used correctly?
For help with confused words, see Chapter 58.

1. Find any words used incorrectly in your revision of Michael's essay.
2. Did you find and correct the confused word?

✔ Are words spelled correctly?
For help with spelling, see Chapter 59.

1. Use spell-check and a dictionary to check the spelling in your revision of Michael's essay.
2. Did you find and correct his misspelled word?

Now rewrite Michael's research paper again with your editing corrections.

# Revising and Editing Your Own Research Paper

Now revise and edit the essay that you wrote in Chapter 21. The checklists here will help you apply what you have learned in Chapter 22 to your own writing.

## Revising Checklist

**Thesis Statement**

- ☐ Does the thesis statement contain the essay's controlling idea and appear as the last sentence of the introduction?

**Basic Elements**

- ☐ Does the title draw in the readers?
- ☐ Does the introduction capture the readers' attention and build up to the thesis statement effectively?
- ☐ Does each body paragraph deal with a single topic?
- ☐ Does the conclusion bring the essay to a close in an interesting way?

**Development**

- ☐ Do the body paragraphs adequately support the thesis statement?
- ☐ Does each body paragraph have a focused topic sentence?
- ☐ Does each body paragraph contain *specific* details that support the topic sentence?
- ☐ Does each body paragraph include *enough* details to explain the topic sentence fully?
- ☐ Are the sources relevant, reliable, and recent?
- ☐ Are references given for original sources to avoid plagiarism?
- ☐ Is the documentation format correct—in the paper and at the end?

UNITY

☐ Do the essay's topic sentences relate directly to the thesis statement?

☐ Do the details in each body paragraph support its topic sentence?

ORGANIZATION

☐ Is the essay organized logically?

☐ Is each body paragraph organized logically?

COHERENCE

☐ Are transitions used effectively so that paragraphs move smoothly and logically from one to the next?

☐ Do the sentences move smoothly and logically from one to the next?

## Thesis Statement

☐ Does the thesis statement contain the essay's controlling idea and appear as the last sentence of the introduction?

1. What is the main idea of your research paper? ____________________

____________________________________________

2. Put brackets around your thesis statement. Does it introduce your main idea? ____________

3. How can you change it to introduce all the topics in your paper?

## Basic Elements

☐ Does the title draw in the readers?

☐ Does the introduction capture the readers' attention and build up to the thesis statement effectively?

☐ Does each body paragraph deal with a single topic?

☐ Does the conclusion bring the essay to a close in an interesting way?

1. Give your essay an alternate title.

_______________________________________________

2. Does your introduction capture the readers' attention and build up to the thesis statement at the end of the paragraph?

_______________________________________________

3. Does each of your body paragraphs deal with only one topic?

_______________________________________________

4. Does your conclusion bring the essay to a close in an interesting way?

_______________________________________________

## Development

- ☐ Do the body paragraphs adequately support the thesis statement?
- ☐ Does each body paragraph have a focused topic sentence?
- ☐ Does each body paragraph contain *specific* details that support its topic sentence?
- ☐ Does each body paragraph include *enough* details to explain its topic sentence fully?
- ☐ Are the sources relevant, reliable, and recent?
- ☐ Are references given for original sources to avoid plagiarism?
- ☐ Is the documentation format correct—in the paper and at the end?

1. Do your topics support your thesis statement? List your revised thesis statement and your topics.

**Thesis:** _______________________________________________

**Topics:** _______________________________________________

_______________________________________________

_______________________________________________

2. Are your examples specific? Add another more specific detail to one of your paragraphs.
3. Do you furnish enough examples or details in each paragraph? Add at least one new example or detail to one of your paragraphs.
4. Check your sources to make sure they are relevant, reliable, and recent. Find new sources if necessary.
5. Do you give references for all original sources in your paper to avoid plagiarism?
6. Is the documentation format correct in your paper?
7. Is the format on your Works Cited page correct?

## Unity

- ☐ Do the essay's topic sentences relate directly to the thesis statement?
- ☐ Do the details in each body paragraph support its topic sentence?

1. Read each of your topic sentences with your thesis statement in mind. Do they go together?
2. Revise them so that they are directly related.
3. Read each of your paragraphs with its topic sentence in mind.
4. Drop or rewrite any sentences in your body paragraphs not directly related to their topic sentences.

## Organization

- ☐ Is the essay organized logically?
- ☐ Is each body paragraph organized logically?

1. Review the list of your topics in item 1 under "Development," and decide if your body paragraphs are organized logically.
2. What is your method of organization:

_______________________________________________

3. Do you think your method of organization is the most effective one for your purpose? Explain your answer.

_______________________________________________

_______________________________________________

4. Read your essay again to see if all your sentences are arranged logically.
5. Move any sentences that are out of order.

## Coherence

- ☐ Are transitions used effectively so that paragraphs move smoothly and logically from one to the next?
- ☐ Do the sentences move smoothly and logically from one to the next?

1. Circle five transitions, repetitions, synonyms, or pronouns you use. (For a list of transitions, see page 84.)
2. Explain how two of these make your essay easier to read.

_______________________________________________

_______________________________________________

Now rewrite your essay with your revisions.

## Editing Checklist

**SENTENCES**

- ☐ Does each sentence have a main subject and verb?
- ☐ Do all subjects and verbs agree?
- ☐ Do all pronouns agree with their nouns?
- ☐ Are modifiers as close as possible to the words they modify?

**Punctuation and Mechanics**

- ☐ Are sentences punctuated correctly?
- ☐ Are words capitalized properly?

**Word Choice and Spelling**

- ☐ Are words used correctly?
- ☐ Are words spelled correctly?

## Sentences

☐ Does each sentence have a main subject and verb?

For help with subjects and verbs, see Chapter 34.

1. In a paragraph of your choice, underline your subjects once and verbs twice. Remember that sentences can have more than one subject-verb set.
2. Does each sentence have at least one subject and verb that can stand alone?

   ______________

3. Correct any fragments you have written. (For help with fragments, see Chapter 35.)
4. Correct any run-on sentences you have written. (For help with run-ons, see Chapter 36.)

☐ Do all subjects and verbs agree?

For help with subject-verb agreement, see Chapter 39.

1. Read aloud the subjects and verbs you underlined in your revised essay.
2. Correct any subjects and verbs that do not agree.

☐ Do all pronouns agree with their nouns?

For help with pronoun agreement, see Chapter 43.

1. Find any pronouns in your revised essay that do not agree with their nouns.
2. Correct any pronouns that do not agree with their nouns.

- [ ] Are modifiers as close as possible to the words they modify?
For help with modifier errors, see Chapter 46.

1. Find any modifiers in your revised essay that are not as close as possible to the words they modify.
2. Rewrite sentences if necessary so that your modifiers are as close as possible to the words they modify.

## Punctuation and Mechanics

- [ ] Are sentences punctuated correctly?
For help with punctuation, see Chapters 47–51.

1. Read your revised essay for any errors in punctuation.
2. Make sure any fragments and run-ons you revised are punctuated correctly.

- [ ] Are words capitalized properly?
For help with capitalization, see Chapter 52.

1. Read your revised essay for any errors in capitalization.
2. Be sure to check your capitalization if you revised any fragments or run-ons.

## Word Choice and Spelling

- [ ] Are words used correctly?
For help with confused words, see Chapter 58.

1. Find any words used incorrectly in your revised essay.
2. Correct any errors you find.

☐ Are words spelled correctly?

For help with spelling, see Chapter 59.

1. Use spell-check and a dictionary to check your spelling.
2. Correct any misspelled words.

Now rewrite your essay again with your editing corrections.

# Ideas for Writing

**Guidelines for Writing a Research Paper**

1. Choose a subject.
2. Write a good, clear thesis statement about your subject.
3. Find sources that are relevant, reliable, and recent to support your thesis statement.
4. Take notes to avoid plagiarism.
5. Make a working outline of your paper.
6. Construct an introduction that leads up to your thesis statement.
7. Develop as many supporting paragraphs or body paragraphs as you think are necessary to explain your thesis statement.
8. Write a concluding paragraph.
9. Think of a catchy title.
10. Check your sources and documentation format throughout the paper and at the end.

1. Research the changes in the antidrug ads over the past five years. How have they changed? Are they more or less effective now? Write an essay explaining these changes.
2. Research a controversial political issue of your choice. Then take a firm stand on the issue, and develop an essay supporting your position. You might want to look at headlines in the newspaper to get some ideas for this assignment.
3. Research a special trip that you want to take or a special activity that you want to participate in. Get all the facts, including costs, time, and supplies needed. Then write a letter to your parents or guardians asking them to pay for or support this activity in some way. Try to convince them to see the event from your perspective.
4. Create your own research assignment (with the help of your instructor), and write a response to it.

## Revising Workshop

**Small Group Activity (10 minutes per writer)** In groups of three or four, each person should read his or her research paper to the other members of the group. The listeners should record their reactions on a copy of the Peer Evaluation Form in Appendix 3A. After your group goes through this process, give your evaluation forms to the appropriate writers so that each writer has two or three peer comment sheets for revising.

**Paired Activity (5 minutes per writer)** Using the completed Peer Evaluation Forms, work in pairs to decide what you should revise in your essay. If time allows, rewrite some of your sentences, and have your partner check them.

**Individual Activity** Rewrite your paper, using the revising feedback you received from other students.

## Editing Workshop

**Paired Activity (10 minutes per writer)** Swap papers with a classmate, and use the editing portion of your Peer Evaluation Forms to identify as many grammar, punctuation, mechanics, and spelling errors as you can. Mark the errors on the student paper with the correction symbols on the inside back cover. If time allows, correct some of your errors, and have your partner check them.

**Individual Activity** Rewrite your paper again, using the editing feedback you received from other students. Record your grammar errors in the

Error Log (Appendix 6) and your spelling errors in the Spelling Log (Appendix 7).

## Reflecting on Your Writing

When you have completed your own essay, answer these six questions:

1. What was most difficult about this assignment?
2. What was easiest?
3. What did you learn about research papers by completing this assignment?
4. What do you think are the strengths of your research paper? Place a squiggly line in the margin by the parts of your essay that you feel are very good.
5. What are the weaknesses, if any, of your paper? Place an X in the margin by the parts of your essay you would like help with. Write any questions you have in the margin.
6. What did you learn from this assignment about your own writing process—about preparing to write, about writing the first draft, about revising, and about editing?

# FROM READING TO WRITING

*To read without reflecting is like eating without digesting.*

—Edmund Burke

Part IV is a collection of essays that demonstrate the rhetorical modes you are studying in this book. Each chapter focuses on a different rhetorical strategy and presents two essays that show the strategy at work with other strategies. After each essay are questions that check your understanding of the selection. By charting your correct and incorrect responses to these questions in Appendix I, you will discover your general level of understanding.

# Describing

The following essays describe their subjects through an array of sensory details. The first, "El Hoyo," was written by Mario Suarez. In it, he describes the identity of a city. The second, "Dwellings" by Linda Hogan, discusses how different dwellings suit different people and animals.

---

**Mario Suarez**

## EL HOYO

### Focusing Your Attention

1. Think of a place from your childhood that had special meaning for you as you were growing up. Where was this place? Why was it special?
2. In the essay you are about to read, the writer recounts the many sights, sounds, smells, textures, and tastes that he connects with the place where he grew up. What sights, sounds, smells, textures, and tastes do you remember about the town you grew up in? Can you describe your hometown for someone who has never been there?

### Expanding Your Vocabulary

The following words are important to your understanding of this essay.

**Tucson:** city in southeastern Arizona (paragraph 1)
**chicanos:** Mexican Americans (paragraph 1)
**padre:** father, priest (paragraph 1)
**paisanos:** countrymen (paragraph 1)
**bicker:** quarrel (paragraph 1)

**adobe:** sun-dried brick (paragraph 1)
**chavalos:** small boys (paragraph 1)
**Octavio Perea's Mexican Hour:** Spanish radio program (paragraph 2)
**"Smoke In The Eyes":** song (paragraph 2)
**solace:** comfort (paragraph 2)
**benevolent:** kind (paragraph 2)
**solicited:** asked, begged (paragraph 2)
**señora:** married woman (paragraph 2)
**chicanas:** Mexican American females (paragraph 2)
**Baja California:** peninsula along the western coast of Mexico (paragraph 2)
**boleros:** music for Spanish dances (paragraph 3)
**comadres:** gossiping women (paragraph 3)
**bloodwell:** family ancestry (paragraph 3)
**conquistador:** a Spanish conqueror (paragraph 3)
**capirotada:** Mexican bread pudding (paragraph 4)
**panocha:** corn (paragraph 4)
**Sermeños:** family name (paragraph 4)

---

From the center of downtown Tucson the ground slopes gently away to Main Street, drops a few feet, and then rolls to the banks of the Santa Cruz River. Here lies the section of the city known as El Hoyo. Why it is called El Hoyo is not very clear. In no sense is it a hole as its name would imply; it is simply the river's immediate valley. Its inhabitants are chicanos who raise hell on Saturday night and listen to Padre Estanislao on Sunday morning. While the term chicano is the short way of saying Mexicano, it is not restricted to the paisanos who came from old Mexico with the territory or the last famine to work for the railroad, labor, sing, and go on relief. Chicano is the easy way of referring to everybody. Pablo Gutíerrez married the Chinese grocer's daughter and now runs a meat department; his sons are chicanos. So are the sons of Killer Jones who threw a fight in Harlem and fled to El Hoyo to marry Cristina Mendez. And so are all of them. However, it is doubtful that all these spiritual sons of Mexico live in El Hoyo because they love each other—many fight and bicker constantly. It is doubtful they live in El Hoyo because of its scenic beauty—it is everything but beautiful. Its houses are simple affairs of unplastered adobe, wood, and abandoned car parts. Its narrow streets 1 are mostly clearings which have, in time, acquired names. Except for some tall trees which nobody has ever cared to identify, nurse, or destroy, the main things known to grow in the general area are weeds, garbage piles, dark-eyed chavalos, and dogs. And it is doubtful that the chicanos live in El Hoyo because it is safe—many times the Santa Cruz has risen and inundated the area.

2 In other respects, living in El Hoyo has its advantages. If one is born with weakness for acquiring bills, El Hoyo is where the collectors are less likely to find you. If one has acquired the habit of listening to Octavio Perea's Mexican Hour in the wee hours of the morning with the radio on at full blast, El Hoyo is where you are less likely to be reported to the authorities. Besides, Perea is very popular and sooner or later to everyone "Smoke In The Eyes" is dedicated between the pinto beans and white flour commercials. If one, for any reason whatever, comes on an extended period of hard times, where, if not in El Hoyo, are the neighbors more willing to offer solace? When Teofila Malacara's house burned to the ground with all her belongings and two children, a benevolent gentleman carried through the gesture that made tolerable her burden. He made a list of five hundred names and solicited from each a dollar. At the end of a month he turned over to the tearful but grateful señora one hundred dollars in cold cash and then accompanied her on a short vacation. When the new manager of a local store decided that no more chicanas were to work behind the counters, it was the chicanos of El Hoyo who, on taking their individually small but collectively great buying power elsewhere, drove the manager out and the girls returned to their jobs. When the Mexican Army was en route to Baja California and the chicanos found out that the enlisted men ate only at infrequent intervals, it was El Hoyo's chicanos who crusaded across town with pots of beans and trays of tortillas to meet the train. When someone gets married, celebrating is not restricted to the immediate friends of the couple. Everybody is invited. Anything calls for a celebration, and a celebration calls for anything. On Memorial Day there are no less than half a dozen good fights at the Riverside Dance Hall. On Mexican Independence Day, more than one flag is sworn allegiance to amid cheers for the queen.

3 And El Hoyo is something more. It is this something more which brought Felipe Sanchez back from the wars after having killed a score of Vietnamese with his body resembling a patchwork quilt to marry Julia Armijo. It brought Joe Zepeda, a gunner, . . . back to compose boleros. He has a metal plate for a skull. Perhaps El Hoyo is proof that those people exist, and perhaps exist best, who have as yet failed to observe the more popular modes of human conduct. Perhaps the humble appearance of El Hoyo justifies the indifferent shrug of those made aware of its existence. Perhaps El Hoyo's simplicity motivates an occasional chicano to move away from its narrow streets, babbling comadres and shrieking children to deny the bloodwell from which he springs and to claim the blood of a conquistador while his hair is straight and his face beardless. Yet El Hoyo is not

an outpost of a few families against the world. It fights for no causes except those which soothe its immediate angers. It laughs and cries with the same amount of passion in times of plenty and of want.

Perhaps El Hoyo, its inhabitants, and its essence can best be explained by telling a bit about a dish called capirotada. Its origin is uncertain. But, according to the time and the circumstance, it is made of old, new, or hard bread. It is softened with water and then cooked with peanuts, raisins, onions, cheese, and panocha. It is fired with sherry wine. Then it is served hot, cold, or just "on the weather" as they say in El Hoyo. The Sermeños like it one way, the Garcias another, and the Ortegas still another. While it might differ greatly from one home to another, nevertheless it is still capirotada. And so it is with El Hoyo's chicanos. While being divided from within and from without, like the capirotada, they remain chicanos. 4

### Thinking Critically About Content

1. What does *el hoyo* mean, according to the author?
2. List two details from this essay for each of the five senses: seeing, hearing, touching, tasting, and smelling. How do these details *show* rather than tell the readers the writer's impressions of El Hoyo?
3. What is the main reason people choose to live in El Hoyo?

### Thinking Critically About Purpose and Audience

4. What dominant impression does the writer create in this description? Explain your answer in detail.
5. Do you think readers who have never been to this place can appreciate and enjoy this essay? Why or why not?
6. What details about El Hoyo are most interesting to you? Why do you find them interesting?

### Thinking Critically About Essays

7. If an essay is unified, all of its paragraphs are related to one central idea. Based on this explanation, is this essay unified? Explain your answer.
8. How does Suarez organize his ideas and observations in this essay? (Refer to pages 46–58 for information on organization.) Make a rough outline of the essay.
9. Suarez ends his essay with an analogy that compares El Hoyo to a dish called *capirotada*. Is this an effective end for his essay? Why or why not?

10. Describe as fully as possible the inner feelings of the narrator from inside El Hoyo on a typical day.

**Linda Hogan**

## DWELLINGS

### Focusing Your Attention

1. Think about the place you currently live. Does it serve your purposes? In what ways?
2. The essay you are about to read describes different habitats that suit different animals and humans. If you could move to a new "dwelling," where would you go? Why?

### Expanding Your Vocabulary

The following words are important to your understanding of this essay.

**eroded:** worn down (paragraph 1)
**dwelling:** residence (paragraph 1)
**Anasazi:** Indian tribe (paragraph 1)
**excavations:** caves, holes in the earth (paragraph 1)
**beetle:** jut, project (paragraph 1)
**catacombs:** tunnels, hollowed-out passageways (paragraph 2)
**droning:** monotonous (paragraph 3)
**pollen:** dustlike plant spores (paragraph 3)
**sanctuary:** safe place (paragraph 6)
**troglodite:** caveman (paragraph 7)
**utopia:** ideal place (paragraph 7)
**scurrying:** moving fast (paragraph 7)
**felled:** cut down (paragraph 8)
**harmoniously:** in harmony, peacefully (paragraph 8)
**spired:** rising like a church steeple (paragraph 9)
**cathedrals:** large Catholic churches (paragraph 9)
**fledglings:** baby birds just learning to fly (paragraph 9)
**arid:** dry (paragraph 10)

**barn swallows:** birds that live in dark, hidden areas (paragraph 10)
**pellets:** animal droppings (paragraph 13)
**fetal:** newborn (paragraph 13)
**nestled:** snuggled together (paragraph 13)
**downy:** soft (paragraph 14)
**rafter:** roof beam (paragraph 14)
**Zia Pueblo:** an Indian village (paragraph 15)
**shards:** broken pieces (paragraph 15)
**sage:** an herb (paragraph 16)
**remnants:** scraps left behind (paragraph 17)
**burrowing:** cave-digging (paragraph 17)

Not far from where I live is a hill that was cut into by the moving water of a creek. Eroded this way, all that's left of it is a broken wall of earth that contains old roots and pebbles woven together and exposed. Seen from a distance, it is only a rise of raw earth. But up close it is something wonderful, a small cliff dwelling that looks almost as intricate and well made as those the Anasazi left behind when they vanished mysteriously centuries ago. This hill is a place that could be the starry skies at night turned inward into the thousand round holes where solitary bees have lived and died. It is a hill of tunneling rooms. At the mouths of some of the excavations, half-circles of clay beetle out like awnings shading a doorway. It is earth that was turned to clay in the mouths of the bees and spit out as they mined deeper into their dwelling places. 1

This place is where the bees reside at an angle safe from rain. It faces the southern sun. It is a warm and intelligent architecture of memory, learned by whatever memory lives in the blood. Many of the holes still contain gold husks of dead bees, their faces dry and gone, their flat eyes gazing out from death's land toward the other uninhabited half of the hill that is across the creek from the catacombs. 2

The first time I found the residence of the bees, it was dusty summer. The sun was hot, and land was the dry color of rust. Now and then a car rumbled along the dirt road and dust rose up behind it before settling back down on older dust. In the silence, the bees made a soft droning hum. They were alive then, and working the hill, going out and returning with pollen, in and out through the holes, back and forth between daylight and the cooler, darker regions of the inner earth. They were flying an invisible map through air, a map charted by landmarks, the slant of light, and a circling story they told one another about the direction of food held inside the center of yellow flowers. 3

4 Sitting in the hot sun, watching the small bees fly in and out around the hill, hearing the summer birds, the light breeze, I felt right in the world. I belonged there. I thought of my own dwelling places, those real and those imagined. Once I lived in a town called Manitou, which means "Great Spirit," and where hot mineral springwater gurgled beneath the streets and rose into open wells. I felt safe there. With the underground movement of water and heat a constant reminder of other life, of what lives beneath us, it seemed to be the center of the world.

5 A few years after that, I wanted silence. My daydreams were full of places I longed to be, shelters and solitudes. I wanted a room apart from others, a hidden cabin to rest in. I wanted to be in a redwood forest with trees so tall the owls called out in the daytime. I daydreamed of living in a vapor cave a few hours away from here. Underground, warm, and moist, I thought it would be the perfect world for staying out of cold winter, for escaping the noise of living.

6 And how often I've wanted to escape to a wilderness where a human hand has not been in everything. But those were only dreams of peace, of comfort, of a nest inside stone or woods, a sanctuary where a dream or life wouldn't be invaded.

7 Years ago, in the next canyon west of here, there was a man who followed one of those dreams and moved into a cave that could only be reached by climbing down a rope. For years he lived there in comfort, like a troglodite. The inner weather was stable, never too hot, too cold, too wet, or too dry. But then he felt lonely. His utopia needed a woman. He went to town until he found a wife. For a while after the marriage, his wife climbed down the rope along with him, but before long she didn't want the mice scurrying about in the cave, or the untidy bats that wanted to hang from the stones of the ceiling. So they built a door. Because of the closed entryway, the temperature changed. They had to put in heat. Then the inner moisture of earth warped the door, so they had to have air-conditioning, and after that the earth wanted to go about life in its own way and it didn't give in to the people.

8 In other days and places, people paid more attention to the strong-headed will of earth. Once homes were built of wood that had been felled from a single region in a forest. That way, it was thought, the house would hold together more harmoniously, and the family of walls would not fall or lend themselves to the unhappiness or arguments of the inhabitants.

9 An Italian immigrant to Chicago, Aldo Piacenzi, built birdhouses that were dwellings of harmony and peace. They were the incredible spired shapes of cathedrals in Italy. They housed not only the birds, but also his memories, his own past. He painted them the watery blue of his Mediterranean, the wild rose

of flowers in a summer field. Inside them was straw and the droppings of lives that laid eggs, fledglings who grew there. What places to inhabit, the bright and sunny birdhouses in dreary alleyways of the city.

One beautiful afternoon, cool and moist, with the kind of yellow light that falls 10
on earth in these arid regions, I waited for barn swallows to return from their daily work of food gathering. Inside the tunnel where they live, hundreds of swallows had mixed their saliva with mud and clay, much like the solitary bees, and formed nests that were perfect as a potter's bowl. At five in the evening, they returned all at once, a dark, flying shadow. Despite their enormous numbers and the crowding together of nests, they didn't pause for even a moment before entering the nests, nor did they crowd one another. Instantly they vanished into the nests. The tunnel went silent. It held no outward signs of life.

But I knew they were there, filled with the fire of living. And what a marriage 11
of elements was in those nests. Not only mud's earth and water, the fire of sun and dry air, but even the elements contained one another. The bodies of prophets and crazy men were broken down in that soil.

I've noticed often how when a house is abandoned, it begins to sag. Without 12
a tenant, it has no need to go on. If it were a person, we'd say it is depressed or lonely. The roof settles in, the paint cracks, the walls and floorboards warp and slope downward in their own natural ways, telling us that life must stay in everything as the world whirls and tilts and moves through boundless space.

One summer day, cleaning up after long-eared owls where I work at a reha- 13
bilitation facility for birds of prey, I was raking the gravel floor of a flight cage. Down on the ground, something looked like it was moving. I bent over to look into the pile of bones and pellets I'd just raked together. There, close to the ground, were two fetal mice. They were new to the planet, pink and hairless. They were so tenderly young. Their faces had swollen blue-veined eyes. They were nestled in a mound of feathers, soft as velvet, each one curled up smaller than an infant's ear, listening to the first sounds of earth. But the ants were biting them. They turned in agony, unable to pull away, not yet having the arms or legs to move, but feeling, twisting away from the pain of the bites. I was horrified to see them bitten out of life that way. I dipped them in water, as if to take away the sting, and let the ants fall in the bucket. Then I held the tiny mice in the palm of my hand. Some of the ants were drowning in the water. I was trading one life for another, exchanging the lives of the ants for those of mice, but I hated their suffering, and hated even more that they had not yet grown to a life, and already they inhabited the miserable world of pain. Death and life feed each other. I know that.

14 Inside these rooms where birds are healed, there are other lives besides those of mice. There are fine gray globes the wasps have woven together, the white cocoons of spiders in a corner, the downward tunneling anthills. All these dwellings are inside one small walled space, but I think most about the mice. Sometimes the downy nests fall out of the walls where their mothers have placed them out of the way of their enemies. They are so well made and soft, woven mostly from the chest feathers of birds. Sometimes the leg of a small quail holds the nest together like a slender cornerstone with dry, bent claws. The mice have adapted to life in the presence of their enemies, adapted to living in the thin wall between beak and beak, claw and claw. They move their nests often, as if a new rafter or wall will protect them from the inevitable fate of all our returns home to the deeper, wider nests of earth that houses us all.

15 One August at Zia Pueblo during the corn dance, I noticed tourists picking up shards of all the old pottery that had been made and broken there. The residents of Zia know not to take the bowls and pots left behind by the older ones. They know that the fragments of those earlier lives need to be smoothed back to earth, but younger nations, travelers from continents across the world who have come to inhabit this land, have little of their own to grow on. The pieces of earth that were formed into bowls, even on their way home to dust, provide the new people a lifeline to an unknown land, help them remember that they live in the old nest of earth.

16 It was in early February, during the mating season of the great horned owl. It was dusk, and I hiked up the back of a mountain to where I'd heard the owls a year before. I wanted to hear them again, the voices so tender, so deep, like a memory of comfort. I was halfway up the trail when I found a soft, round nest. It had fallen from one of the bare-branched trees. It was a delicate nest, woven together of feathers, sage, and strands of wild grass. Holding it in my hand in the rosy twilight, I noticed that a blue thread was entwined with the other gatherings there. I pulled at the thread a little, and then I recognized it. It was a thread from one of my skirts. It was blue cotton. It was the unmistakable color and shape of a pattern I knew. I liked it, that a thread of my life was in an abandoned nest, one that had held eggs and new life. I took the nest home. At home, I held it to the light and looked more closely. There, to my surprise, nestled into the gray-green sage, was a gnarl of black hair. It was also unmistakable. It was my daughter's hair, cleaned from a brush and picked up out in the sun beneath the maple tree, or the pit cherry where the birds eat from the overladen, fertile branches until only the seeds remain on the trees.

17 I didn't know what kind of nest it was, or who had lived there. It didn't matter. I thought of the remnants of our lives carried up the hill that way and turned into

shelter. That night, resting inside the walls of our home, the world outside weighed so heavily against the thin wood of the house. The sloped roof was the only thing between us and the universe. Everything outside of our wooden boundaries seemed so large. Filled with the night's citizens, it all came alive. The world opened in the thickets of the dark. The wild grapes would soon ripen on the vines. The burrowing ones were emerging. Horned owls sat in treetops. Mice scurried here and there. Shunks, fox, the slow and holy porcupine, all were passing by this way. The young of the solitary bees were feeding on the pollen in the dark. The whole world was a nest on its humble tilt, in the maze of the universe, holding us.

### Thinking Critically About Content

1. How do the dwellings Hogan describes suit their inhabitants? Refer to two specific dwellings to answer this question.
2. Find a least one detail for each of the five senses: seeing, hearing, touching, tasting, and smelling. Does Hogan draw on any one sense more than the others?
3. In paragraph 4, what is Hogan referring to as "the center of the world?" Explain your answer.

### Thinking Critically About Purpose and Audience

4. What dominant impression does Hogan create in this essay?
5. Who do you think Hogan's primary audience is?
6. Explain your understanding of this essay's title.

### Thinking Critically About Essays

7. Each section of Hogan's essay is about a different dwelling. Is each section unified? Look at the topic sentence of paragraph 7. Do all the sentences in this paragraph relate to its topic sentence? Explain your answer.
8. If a paragraph is coherent, it is considered logical and easy to read. Often, well-chosen transitions help a writer achieve coherence. (Refer to page 84 for a list of transitions.) Underline the words, phrases, and clauses Hogan uses as transitions in paragraph 13. How do these transitions help this paragraph read smoothly? Explain your answer.
9. Look at Hogan's conclusion. Is it effective for this essay? How does the last sentence ("The whole world was a nest on its humble tilt, in the maze of the universe, holding us") tie the whole essay together?
10. Describe in detail what you think the secret to a perfect dwelling is.

### *Writing Topics: Describing*

Before you begin to write, you might want to review the writing process in Part I.

1. In the first descriptive essay, Mario Suarez draws on impressions from all the senses to describe this *barrio*. Think of a place that is very important to you, a place that is a part of your life now or that was a part of your life in the past. Write a description of that place, drawing on as many of the senses as possible—seeing, hearing, smelling, touching, and tasting—so that your reader can experience it the way you did.
2. How well suited to you is the place where you live now? Write a description of the features of your house or apartment that make it most suitable or unsuitable for you.
3. What do you think are the most important features of a good description? Why are they important? What effect do they have on you?

CHAPTER 26

# Narrating

So that you can understand more clearly how to write narrative essays, two are included here for you to read. In "The Sanctuary of School," author Lynda Barry recalls an event that occurred during a particularly painful period of her life. In the second essay, "Writer's Retreat" by Stan Higgins, the author tells a story about writing from a prison cell.

---

**Lynda Barry**

## THE SANCTUARY OF SCHOOL

### Focusing Your Attention

1. Can you recall a time in your life when you felt particularly lonely or afraid? Write down as many facts, impressions, and memories as you can recall about that period of your life.
2. In the essay you are about to read, the writer describes a person who had a lasting impact on her. Do you think you have ever had such an important impact on someone that he or she would write an essay about you? Have you had such an impact on more than one person? Who are these people? What would they say about you in their recollections?

### Expanding Your Vocabulary

The following words are important to your understanding of this essay.

**sanctuary:** safe place (title)

**nondescript:** not distinctive (paragraph 7)

**monkey bars:** playground equipment (paragraph 8)

**breezeway:** covered passage between two buildings (paragraph 13)

---

1 I was 7 years old the first time I snuck out of the house in the dark. It was winter, and my parents had been fighting all night. They were short on money and long on relatives who kept "temporarily" moving into our house because they had nowhere else to go.

2 My brother and I were used to giving up our bedroom. We slept on the couch, something we actually liked because it put us that much closer to the light of our lives, our television.

3 At night when everyone was asleep, we lay on our pillows watching it with the sound off. We watched Steve Allen's mouth moving. We watched Johnny Carson's mouth moving. We watched movies filled with gangsters shooting machine guns into packed rooms, dying soldiers hurling a last grenade, and beautiful women crying at windows. Then the sign-off finally came, and we tried to sleep.

4 The morning I snuck out, I woke up filled with a panic about needing to get to school. The sun wasn't quite up yet, but my anxiety was so fierce that I just got dressed, walked quietly across the kitchen, and let myself out the back door.

5 It was quiet outside. Stars were still out. Nothing moved, and no one was in the street. It was as if someone had turned the sound off on the world.

6 I walked the alley, breaking thin ice over the puddles with my shoes. I didn't know why I was walking to school in the dark. I didn't think about it. All I knew was the feeling of panic, like the panic that strikes kids when they realize they are lost.

7 That feeling eased the moment I turned the corner and saw the dark outline of my school at the top of the hill. My school was made up of about 15 nondescript portable classrooms set down on a fenced concrete lot in a rundown Seattle neighborhood, but it had the most beautiful view of the Cascade Mountains. You could see them from anywhere on the playfield, and you could see them from the windows of my classroom—Room 2.

8 I walked over to the monkey bars and hooked my arms around the cold metal. I stood for a long time just looking across Rainier Valley. The sky was beginning to whiten, and I could hear a few birds.

9 In a perfect world, my absence at home would not have gone unnoticed. I would have had two parents in a panic to locate me, instead of two parents in a panic to locate an answer to the hard question of survival during a deep financial and emotional crisis.

10 But in an overcrowded and unhappy home, it's incredibly easy for any child to slip away. The high levels of frustration, depression, and anger in my house made my brother and me invisible. We were children with the sound turned off. And for us, as for the steadily increasing number of neglected children in this country, the only place where we could count on being noticed was at school.

"Hey there, young lady. Did you forget to go home last night?" It was Mr. Gunderson, our janitor, whom we all loved. He was nice and he was funny and he was old with white hair, thick glasses, and an unbelievable number of keys. I could hear them jingling as he walked across the playfield. I felt incredibly happy to see him. 11

He let me push his wheeled garbage can between the different portables as he unlocked each room. He let me turn on the lights and raise the window shades, and I saw my school slowly come to life. I saw Mrs. Holman, our school secretary, walk into the office without her orange lipstick on yet. She waved. 12

I saw the fifth-grade teacher, Mr. Cunningham, walking under the breezeway eating a hard roll. He waved. 13

And I saw my teacher, Mrs. Claire LeSane, walking toward us in a red coat and calling my name in a very happy and surprised way, and suddenly my throat got tight and my eyes stung and I ran toward her crying. It was something that surprised both of us. 14

It's only thinking about it now, 28 years later, that I realize I was crying from relief. I was with my teacher, and in a while I was going to sit at my desk, with my crayons and pencils and books and classmates all around me, and for the next six hours I was going to enjoy a thoroughly secure, warm, and stable world. It was a world I absolutely relied on. Without it, I don't know where I would have gone that morning. 15

Mrs. LeSane asked me what was wrong, and when I said, "Nothing," she seemingly left it at that. But she asked me if I would carry her purse for her, an honor above all honors, and she asked if I wanted to come into Room 2 early and paint. 16

She believed in the natural healing power of painting and drawing for troubled children. In the back of her room there was always a drawing table and an easel with plenty of supplies, and sometimes during the day she would come up to you for what seemed like no good reason and quietly ask if you wanted to go to the back table and "make some pictures for Mrs. LeSane." We all had a chance at it—to sit apart from the class for a while to paint, draw, and silently work out impossible problems on 11 × 17 sheets of newsprint. 17

Drawing came to mean everything to me. At the back table in Room 2, I learned to build myself a life preserver that I could carry into my home. . . . 18

By the time the bell rang that morning, I had finished my drawing, and Mrs. LeSane pinned it up on the special bulletin board she reserved for drawings from the back table. It was the same picture I always drew—a sun in the corner of a blue sky over a nice house with flowers all around it. 19

## Thinking Critically About Content

1. Notice the way in which the writer describes herself and her brother as "children with the sound turned off" (paragraph 10) and their

environment "as if someone had turned the sound off on the world" (paragraph 5). Is this an effective image? Why? What effect does it have on you? What does it tell you about Lynda Barry's childhood?

2. Why do you think the writer used warm and vivid details to describe the arrival of school employees (paragraphs 11 through 16)? What effect does this description have on you, compared with the description of her home life?
3. Did this essay make you compare your own childhood to Lynda Barry's?

### Thinking Critically About Purpose and Audience

4. What do you think Barry's purpose is in writing this narrative essay? Explain your answer.
5. What readers do you think would most understand and appreciate this recollection?
6. In your opinion, why doesn't the writer tell us more about her parents' problems?

### Thinking Critically About Essays

7. Describe in a complete sentence the writer's point of view in this essay.
8. How does Barry organize the details in this essay? Is this an effective order?
9. Explain Barry's title for this essay.
10. Explain in detail how this essay would be different if it were written by Lynda Barry's parents.

---

**Stan Higgins**

## WRITER'S RETREAT

### Focusing Your Attention

1. Can you remember a time in your life when you were frustrated trying to meet a goal you set for yourself? Write down as many facts, impressions, and memories as you can about this feeling.
2. In the essay you are about to read, the writer describes a person who is trying to write in prison. What do you think is his motivation? Have you ever wanted to do something so much you would even do it in prison? Explain your answer.

### Expanding Your Vocabulary

The following words are important to your understanding of this essay.

**within a pole vault:** a few yards away (paragraph 1)
**Vocational Training:** training for a job (paragraph 2)
**portable:** portable typewriter (paragraph 2)
**the Muse:** inspiration (paragraph 2)
**staccato:** consisting of short, sharp sounds (paragraph 2)
**ransacked:** torn apart (paragraph 3)
**confiscated:** taken away (paragraph 3)
**contraband:** prohibited items (paragraph 3)
**lock down:** lock all prisoners in their cells (paragraph 4)
**Bugler:** brand of tobacco (paragraph 7)
**mud:** coffee (paragraph 16)
**tier:** row of prison cells (paragraph 23)
**persevere:** continue (paragraph 30)
**tantamount:** equal (paragraph 32)
**misdemeanors:** minor crimes (paragraph 32)
**accumulation:** collection (paragraph 32)
**pop cans:** soda cans (paragraph 33)
**subsides:** decreases (paragraph 34)
**blissfully:** very happily (paragraph 34)
**nebulous:** vague, uncertain (paragraph 34)
**girth:** size (paragraph 41)
**obscenities:** offensive comments (paragraph 42)

---

Sandwiched between mountain snow and desert sand, hidden by sandstone walls 150 years old within a pole vault of the Arkansas River, it just doesn't get any better than this writer's retreat I call home. I write from a Colorado prison cell. 1

During the day I wash dishes, clean tables, and mop floors. They call it Vocational Training. And today, as every day at three P.M., I return to my cozy, bathroom-size suite and drag out my tiny portable. We've all night, just the two of us, my blue typewriter that has been my steady cell-mate for six years, through seven facilities across two states, and I. Today's goal is three pages. I blow dust 2 from the cover and clean the keys. The Muse calls. *Tack-tack. Tack. Tack-tack-tack.* My typewriter sings its staccato song as I search for a fertile word or idea, some harmonious junction of thought and paper. Locked in solitary combat with my machine, nothing exists outside my cell, or so I pretend. I type a line. My door opens. Two blue-uniformed guards stand there grinning. "Guess what?" one says. "Your number came up."

3 Somehow I know he doesn't mean the Lottery. One begins searching my cell. The other pats me down as I leave. I return twenty minutes later to find my house ransacked, my bed torn up, papers scattered, pencils and pens strewn about, sox, shorts, and typewriter piled in a heap on the floor. Taped to the shelf above my desk is a slip of yellow paper with a fancily scrawled list of books, magazines, and other confiscated contraband. I can't help but question their appreciation for the written word.

4 I put my house back in order. We lock down and the guards count us. After ten minutes the Count is cleared. My hands tremble. I can't write, not now. It's time for the ultimate challenge to a prisoner's courage . . . Chow!

5 Buoyed at having survived another meal, I return to my cell and begin anew. *Tack-tack-tack.*

6 "Hey, Bro," a green-uniformed inmate named O'Neil hollers from my doorway. "Think I can get a pinch of tobacco?"

7 This, too, is part of the territory. I pause to hand him a can of Bugler. My attention returns to writing as I study the list of disjointed, unrelated words I have accumulated, but I see out of the corner of my eye that I still have company.

8 "Think I can get a rolling paper?" O'Neil asks as he pops the lid off the can.

9 With a deep breath I fish him a pack of papers from my pocket and hand them over. He fumbles with the paper as I reread my typed words.

10 "Think you could roll it for me, Bro?"

11 "What else, O'Neil?" I say whisking the paper and tobacco from his hands and rolling him a quick, crooked cigarette. He asks for a light as I usher him to the door.

12 *Tack-tack-tack-tack,* I resume. Just more words. I pinch my lips and study the nearly blank sheet of paper. *Write what you know,* memories of books past suggest. What do I know? Steel and concrete, jingling keys, and slamming doors. *Tack-tack-tack. Tack-tack.*

13 "M-m-Mr. Higgins?" another prisoner interrupts. It's a skinny kid in oversize greens, and his voice squeaks. "W-would you maybe have a dictionary I could, you know, sorta read, please?" He hesitates at the door in his stiff, fresh-out-of-the-package uniform that reminds me of pajamas, eyeing my bookshelf from a safe distance until I stand. I pull a *Webster's New Collegiate Dictionary* from my shelf above the desk and sit down again as he thumbs through it. He clears his throat. "Uh, excuse me, how do you spell *the*?"

"With two *r*'s instead of one," I tell him, shooing him away with the back of 14
my hand.

*Tack-tack. Tack-tack, tack-tack-tack, tack.* Bones of steel, concrete skin, I 15
type, and a soul as slippery as time.

Digger B. struts into my house. "Ya got a cup a mud I can get or what?" He 16
pushes his empty cup in front of me, and as I fill it, he peers over my shoulder. "So what ya doin'?"

"Trying to write about trying to write." 17

"Man," he says and slurps coffee from his cup. "Whyn't ya write about some- 18
thin' interestin', know what I mean? Murder, war, sex, ya know—interestin'!"

I love encouragement. He wanders out. 19

I stare at my typewriter. I wait a few minutes. Nothing. My fingers creep back 20
into place. *Tack-tack-tack.*

"Got a weed?" asks a gruff voice. It's Thunder. Six-foot-six and almost as 21
wide, 300 pounds of beard and tattoo, he slides sideways into my cell. I quickly roll him a cigarette and light it.

"Anything else, Mr. Thunder?" 22

"Heared you typing clean down the tier," he grumbles. "What you doing?" 23

"Typing. Trying to type. Trying to write, I guess." 24

"You ain't writing 'bout me, are you?" He stares at me with eyes like rocks. 25

"No, sir, Mr. Thunder," I assure him, pointing to my almost blank paper. 26
"Check it out."

He squints at it. "Don't like people writing 'bout me 'hind my back." 27

"I wouldn't do that, Mr. Thunder." 28

"Just so you ain't. 'At's all I care." He turns and sidles out the doorway. Thun- 29
der is unpredictable. Thunder hears voices. Thunder caught a guy in the shower once and stabbed him 53 times with a sharpened Number 2 pencil; he thought the man was talking about him. All in all, I figure it's not a bad idea to get along with Mr. Thunder.

The sun is setting. I've completed three sentences. My goal of three pages for 30
the day is becoming as gray as my cell. At this rate I'm confident I can finish an 800-word article by my 2006 discharge date. *Persevere!* I get up and flip on the light.

Back to my typewriter; back on track. *Tack-tack-tack. Tack-tack, tack-* 31
*tackity-tack.* I'm into it finally, my head is there, I'm on the verge of something . . . when Thunder stops at my door and pokes his woolly head in. "You sure you ain't writing things 'bout me?"

In prison, opening a can of tobacco, a bag of potato chips, or brewing a pot of 32
coffee—like trying to type—is tantamount to throwing a side of beef into shark-infested waters. But these are minor distractions . . . misdemeanors. Prison overcrowding being what it is, Colorado officials have on several occasions

sent inmates to faraway places for temporary storage. Two years ago guards came to my door with a green duffel bag and ordered me to pack up. I surveyed my four-year accumulation of books, magazines, and notes that converted my six-by-ten-foot cell into a private classroom. Each book and magazine, then highlighted for frequent reference, had been a hard-collected treasure. There were works-in-progress scattered on my desk. "Now!" a guard encouraged. "You're going to Washington state. If your stuff don't all fit . . . ," he reassured me with a glint in his eye and a broad sweep of his arm, ". . . you don't need it!" A year later I was returned to sender. Back in Colorado, I set up housekeeping, mailed out another batch of address changes.

33 An aluminum trash can falls to the floor from an upper tier, perhaps with a little help. I try to type. The cell block explodes in cheering and clapping. Pop cans rain from above. I hesitate at the keyboard. It might be boredom, it might be a fight, or a stabbing. It might be a riot. Then again, it might be they just discovered what was for breakfast tomorrow.

34 It is dark outside. The noise subsides. I sit for a few minutes blissfully alone, rescuing my thoughts, pondering my last sentence, imagining some nebulous, faraway, fairy tale future where everything is happily-ever-after. I imagine a steak dinner, the meat still sizzling, its pink and brown juice puddling the plate beneath a twice-baked potato and fresh asparagus, steam rising. . . .

35 "You ain't writing 'bout me!?" Thunder startles me. This time I didn't hear or see him fill my doorway.

36 "No, sir," I tell him, cigarette smoke replacing the scent of steak. "Not one word, Mr. Thunder."

37 He scratches his beard and stares. He steps in and looks over my shoulder. When he speaks again, after some moments, his voice is uncharacteristically soft and plaintive. "Not one word?"

38 I shake my head.

39 "Ain't I good enough to be in your stories?"

40 For a minute I think he is about to cry. I tell him I'll write something about him if he likes. He reaches across the desk for the can of Bugler, rolls a cigarette, pats me on the back, and leaves.

41 I sigh into the typewriter keys and look up in time to see a couple of guards making the rounds, parading their girth like badges of authority, jingling keys. "Attention on the Block! Attention on the Block!" blares the loudspeaker. "Five minutes to Count! Lock up now!"

42 Inmates shout obscenities, but they are just pretending. They filter off to their cells. Visions of solitude dance in my head. Alone! Just me and my typewriter! Now I'll get something done. But maybe I am pretending also. Maybe we are all just pretending.

43 I get up and stretch, close my door, return to my desk, and wait.

44 "Count!" the loudspeaker squawks. "Count!"

Doors slam shut. Suddenly it is quiet. I pause to savor the silence. A plastic Salvation Army cup rests next to my typewriter, its contents cold, thick, and dark, but it is the best cup I've had all day. For a moment I think I hear crickets, distant, anonymous traffic, dogs barking, the hum of street lights. 45

*Ticktickticktick* . . . complains my clock, its face turned away, hiding time. 46

This is it. I'm either going to write, or I'm not. I remove a three-by-five-inch wire-bound notebook: musings for the day, observations carried with me through the day. Flipped open and set on the desk beside my typewriter, it reminds me that place can also be irrelevant. I turn a page and begin typing. *Tack-tack, tack-tack, tack-tackity-tack. Tack-tack.* What is it like to write from a prison cell? I write. *Tack-tack.* 47

The glare of a flashlight hits me in the eyes. There is a pounding at my door. A guard is aiming his light in my face. "What're ya doing this time of night?" he asks. 48

I take a deep breath and count to ten before answering. Writing from prison, I tell myself, just ain't what it used to be. Maybe it never was. I count to twenty. 49

"Baking a cake," I finally answer. 50

He grins. "Yeah? Is it fun?" 51

"I don't know," I say. "I'll tell you when it's done." 52

## Thinking Critically About Content

1. What characterizes this "writer's retreat"?
2. What is Higgins writing about on his typewriter?
3. How does Higgins deal with all the interruptions? In what ways are these incidents part of his writing process?

## Thinking Critically About Purpose and Audience

4. Explain your understanding of the writer's main point in this essay.
5. Who do you think Higgins's primary audience is?
6. Why was Higgins frustrated trying to meet his goal of three pages of writing for the day?

## Thinking Critically About Essays

7. Describe Higgins's point of view in this essay. Does it change throughout the essay? If so, in what ways?
8. Higgins uses many details to illustrate his frustration as he tries to write. Which details communicate his frustration most clearly to you?
9. Higgins talks about baking a cake in his conclusion. Is this an effective ending? Why or why not?
10. Tell this same story from Mr. Thunder's perspective.

### *Writing Topics: Narrating*

Before you begin to write, you might want to review the writing process in Part I.

1. In "The Sanctuary of School," Lynda Barry recalls the way her school and her teachers provided a sanctuary, a place where she could escape from the problems of home. Write an essay in which you recall a place, a person, or an event that made you feel safe, secure, and welcome.
2. We all deal with frustration in different ways. Explain the coping strategies you have observed in friends and relatives. Do they work? Are they effective? Write a narrative essay focusing on various coping strategies that you have seen in action.
3. What do you think are the most important features of a good story? Why are they important? What effect do they have on you?

CHAPTER 27

# Illustrating

The two essays in this chapter show how the authors use examples, along with other strategies, to explain their main idea. The first essay, "I Just Wanna Be Average," written by Mike Rose, relates the author's experiences growing up labeled as a slow learner. The second essay, written by a 16-year-old high school student from Maryland named Chana Schoenberger, was published in *Newsweek* magazine. Chana discusses a problem with prejudice that she recognized while participating in a National Science Foundation program with other high school students.

---

**Mike Rose**

## I JUST WANNA BE AVERAGE

### Focusing Your Attention

1. What do you think about tracking, or separating students by ability level, in high school? What are the advantages and disadvantages of this system of teaching? Did your high school track its students?
2. In the essay you are about to read, the writer claims that students use sophisticated defense mechanisms to get through high school. Have you ever used any defenses in school? How did these defenses make you act?

### Expanding Your Vocabulary

The following words are important to your understanding of this essay.

**vocational:** focused on training for a job (paragraph 1)

***Horace's Compromise:*** a novel by Theodore R. Sizer (paragraph 1)

**hypotheses:** educated guesses (paragraph 1)
**disaffected:** rebellious, uncooperative (paragraph 1)
**skeletal:** very basic (paragraph 1)
**scuttling:** moving quickly (paragraph 1)
**mediocre:** not very good, of moderate ability (paragraph 2)
**somnambulant:** walking while asleep (paragraph 2)
**wherewithal:** ability (paragraph 2)
**indifferently:** without paying attention (paragraph 2)
**prowess:** strength (paragraph 3)
**clique:** social group (paragraph 3)
**could care less:** *slang for* could not care less (paragraph 3)
**testament to:** proof of (paragraph 3)
**dearth:** lack (paragraph 3)
**one-liners:** jokes (paragraph 3)
**much-touted:** repeatedly praised (paragraph 4)
**eerie:** strange, mysterious (paragraph 4)
**salubrious:** socially or morally acceptable (paragraph 4)
**equivocal:** having two or more meanings (paragraph 4)
**hit a chuckhole:** stumbled (paragraph 4)
***Argosy:*** a science-fiction magazine (paragraph 4)
***Field and Stream:*** a hunting and fishing magazine (paragraph 4)
***Daily Worker:*** a Socialist newspaper (paragraph 4)
***The Old Man and the Sea:*** a novel by Ernest Hemingway (paragraph 4)
**rough-hewn:** unsophisticated, unpolished (paragraph 4)
**apocryphal:** a story that is not true but is believed by some people anyway (paragraph 4)
**ducktail:** a hairstyle in which the hair is swept back at the sides to meet in an upturned point at the back (paragraph 5)
**parable of the talents:** a story from the New Testament (paragraph 5)
**restive:** restless, fidgety (paragraph 5)
**affect:** emotion (paragraph 5)
**laryngectomize:** surgically remove a person's larynx (paragraph 5)
**platitudinous:** dull, boring, full of unoriginal thoughts (paragraph 5)

**melee:** battle (paragraph 5)
**dissonant:** nonconforming, disagreeing (paragraph 6)
**curriculum:** course of study (paragraph 6)
**elite:** privileged individuals (paragraph 6)
**constrained:** kept within limits (paragraph 6)
**liberate:** free (paragraph 6)
**with a vengeance:** enthusiastically (paragraph 6)
**gray matter:** brain (paragraph 7)
**diffuse:** scatter (paragraph 7)
**cultivate:** encourage (paragraph 7)
**malady:** illness (paragraph 7)
**flaunt:** show proudly (paragraph 7)

---

Students will float to the mark you set. I and the others in the vocational classes 1
were bobbing in pretty shallow water. Vocational education was aimed at increasing the economic opportunities of students who do not do well in our schools. Some serious programs succeed in doing that, and through exceptional teachers—like Mr. Gross in *Horace's Compromise*—students learn to develop hypotheses and troubleshoot, reason through a problem, and communicate effectively—the true job skills. The vocational track, however, is most often a place for those who are just not making it, a dumping ground for the disaffected. There were a few teachers who worked hard at education; young Brother Slattery, for example, combined a stern voice with weekly quizzes to try to pass along to us a skeletal outline of world history. But mostly the teachers had no idea of how to engage the imaginations of us kids who were scuttling along at the bottom of the pond.

And the teachers would have needed some inventiveness, for none of us was 2
groomed for the classroom. It wasn't just that I didn't know things—didn't know how to simplify algebraic fractions, couldn't identify different kinds of clauses, bungled Spanish translations—but that I had developed various faulty and inadequate ways of doing algebra and making sense of Spanish. Worse yet, the years of defensive tuning out in elementary school had given me a way to escape quickly while seeming at least half alert. During my time in Voc. Ed., I developed further into a mediocre student and a somnambulant problem solver, and that affected the subjects I did have the wherewithal to handle: I detested Shakespeare; I got bored with history. My attention flitted here and there. I fooled around in

class and read my books indifferently—the intellectual equivalent of playing with your food. I did what I had to do to get by, and I did it with half a mind.

3 But I did learn things about people and eventually came into my own socially. I liked the guys in Voc. Ed. Growing up where I did, I understood and admired physical prowess, and there was an abundance of muscle here. There was Dave Snyder, a sprinter and halfback of true quality. Dave's ability and his quick wit gave him a natural appeal, and he was welcome in any clique, though he always kept a little independent. He enjoyed acting the fool and could care less about studies, but he possessed a certain maturity and never caused the faculty much trouble. It was a testament to his independence that he included me among his friends—I eventually went out for track, but I was no jock. Owing to the Latin alphabet and a dearth of *R*'s and *S*'s, Snyder sat behind Rose, and we started exchanging one-liners and became friends.

4 There was Ted Richard, a much-touted Little League pitcher. He was chunky and had a baby face and came to Our Lady of Mercy as a seasoned street fighter. Ted was quick to laugh and he had a loud, jolly laugh, but when he got angry he'd smile a little smile, the kind that simply raises the corner of the mouth a quarter of an inch. For those who knew, it was an eerie signal. Those who didn't found themselves in big trouble, for Ted was very quick. He loved to carry on what we would come to call philosophical discussions: What is courage? Does God exist? He also loved words, enjoyed picking up big ones like *salubrious* and *equivocal* and using them in our conversations—laughing at himself as the word hit a chuckhole rolling off his tongue. Ted didn't do all that well in school—baseball and parties and testing the courage he'd speculated about took up his time. His textbooks were *Argosy* and *Field and Stream,* whatever newspapers he'd find on the bus stop—from the *Daily Worker* to pornography—conversations with uncles or hobos or businessmen he'd meet in a coffee shop, *The Old Man and the Sea.* With hindsight, I can see that Ted was developing into one of those rough-hewn intellectuals whose sources are a mix of the learned and the apocryphal, whose discussions are both assured and sad.

5 And then there was Ken Harvey. Ken was good-looking in a puffy way and had a full and oily ducktail and was a car enthusiast. . . . One day in religion class, he said the sentence that turned out to be one of the most memorable of the hundreds of thousands I heard in those Voc. Ed. years. We were talking about the parable of the talents, about achievement, working hard, doing the best you can do, blah-blah-blah, when the teacher called on the restive Ken Harvey for an opinion. Ken thought about it, but just for a second, and said (with studied, minimal affect), "I just wanna be average." That woke me up. Average?! Who wants to be average? Then the athletes chimed in with the clichés that make you want to laryngectomize them, and the exchange became a platitudinous melee. At the time, I thought Ken's assertion was stupid, and I wrote

him off. But his sentence has stayed with me all these years, and I think I am finally coming to understand it.

Ken Harvey was gasping for air. School can be a tremendously disorienting 6
place. No matter how bad the school, you're going to encounter notions that don't fit with the assumptions and beliefs that you grew up with—maybe you'll hear these dissonant notions from teachers, maybe from the other students, and maybe you'll read them. You'll also be thrown in with all kinds of kids from all kinds of backgrounds, and that can be unsettling—this is especially true in places of rich ethnic and linguistic mix, like the L.A. basin. You'll see a handful of students far excel you in courses that sound exotic and that are only in the curriculum of the elite: French, physics, trigonometry. And all this is happening while you're trying to shape an identity, your body is changing, and your emotions are running wild. If you're a working-class kid in the vocational track, the options you'll have to deal with this will be constrained in certain ways: You're defined by your school as "slow"; you're placed in a curriculum that isn't designed to liberate you but to occupy you, or, if you're lucky, train you, though the training is for work the society does not esteem; other students are picking up the cues from your school and your curriculum and interacting with you in particular ways. If you're a kid like Ted Richard, you turn your back on all this and let your mind roam where it may. But youngsters like Ted are rare. What Ken and so many others do is protect themselves from such suffocating madness by taking on with a vengeance the identity implied in the vocational track. Reject the confusion and frustration by openly defining yourself as the Common Joe. Champion the average. Rely on your own good sense. Fuck this bullshit. Bullshit, of course, is everything you—and the others—fear is beyond you: books, essays, tests, academic scrambling, complexity, scientific reasoning, philosophical inquiry.

The tragedy is that you have to twist the knife in your own gray matter to 7
make this defense work. You'll have to shut down, have to reject intellectual stimuli or diffuse them with sarcasm, have to cultivate stupidity, have to convert boredom from a malady into a way of confronting the world. Keep your vocabulary simple, act stoned when you're not or act more stoned than you are, flaunt ignorance, materialize your dreams. It is a powerful and effective defense—it neutralizes the insult and the frustration of being a vocational kid and, when perfected, it drives teachers up the wall, a delightful secondary effect. But like all strong magic, it exacts a price.

## Thinking Critically About Content

1. What was vocational education aimed at in Rose's school? Who is this track for?
2. What examples from this essay illustrate most clearly what Rose's academic life involved?

3. Rose says the Voc. Ed. students "were bobbing in pretty shallow water" and then refers to them "scuttling along at the bottom of the pond" (paragraph 1). In these examples, he is comparing people trying to swim and stay above water to students on a vocational track in high school. This comparison is called a *metaphor*. Find another comparison like this in paragraph 7.

### Thinking Critically About Purpose and Audience

4. What do you think Rose's purpose is in this essay? Explain your answer.
5. What type of audience do you think would most understand and appreciate this essay?
6. What do you think Ken Harvey meant when he said, "I just wanna be average" (paragraph 5)?

### Thinking Critically About Essays

7. Does Rose give you enough examples to understand his learning environment in high school? Explain your answer.
8. Is this essay unified? Does each of the author's topic sentences support the essay's thesis statement? Explain your answer.
9. What is Rose's thesis in this essay? Where is it located?
10. Explain your opinion about tracking students. Is tracking a good idea? Does it help some students? Does it hurt anyone? Can you think of any alternatives to tracking? Respond to these questions in detail.

**Chana Schoenberger**

## GETTING TO KNOW ABOUT YOU AND ME

### Focusing Your Attention

1. Think about a problem that you recently solved. How did you go about solving the problem? Did you have to change your lifestyle or behavior in some way, or did you have to convince other people to behave or think differently? Were you happy with the solution, or was it not as satisfying as you expected it to be?
2. In the essay you are about to read, the writer describes an experience she had at a camp where she found herself living with people who did

not know very much about her religion. Have you ever been in a situation in which you were misunderstood because of your race, your ethnic background, your religion, your gender, your age, or your appearance? Did this create a problem for you?

### Expanding Your Vocabulary

The following words are important to your understanding of this essay.

**diversity:** variety of ethnic types (paragraph 1)
**anti-Semitic:** prejudiced against Jewish people (paragraph 7)
**benign:** harmless (paragraph 8)
**EPA:** Environmental Protection Agency (paragraph 8)
**doctorate:** highest academic degree (paragraph 9)
**malignantly:** with bad intent (paragraph 10)
**assimilate:** blend into a larger group (paragraph 11)
**flawed:** incorrect or illogical (paragraph 13)

---

As a religious holiday approaches, students at my high school who will be celebrating the holiday prepare a presentation on it for an assembly. The Diversity Committee, which sponsors the assemblies to increase religious awareness, asked me last spring if I would help with the presentation on Passover, the Jewish holiday that commemorates the Exodus from Egypt. I was too busy with other things, and I never got around to helping. I didn't realize then how important those presentations really are, or I definitely would have done something. 1

This summer I was one of 20 teens who spent five weeks at the University of Wisconsin at Superior studying acid rain with a National Science Foundation Young Scholars program. With such a small group in such a small town, we soon became close friends and had a good deal of fun together. We learned about the science of acid rain, went on field trips, found the best and cheapest restaurants in Superior, and ate in them frequently to escape the lousy cafeteria food. We were a happy, bonded group. 2

Represented among us were eight religions: Jewish, Roman Catholic, Muslim, Hindu, Methodist, Mormon, Jehovah's Witness, and Lutheran. It was amazing, given the variety of backgrounds, to see the ignorance of some of the smartest young scholars on the subject of other religions. 3

On the first day, one girl mentioned that she had nine brothers and sisters. "Oh, are you Mormon?" asked another girl, who I knew was a Mormon herself. 4

The first girl, shocked, replied, "No, I dress normal!" She thought Mormon was the same as Mennonite, and the only thing she knew about either religion was that Mennonites don't, in her opinion, "dress normal."

5 My friends, ever curious about Judaism, asked me about everything from our basic theology to food preferences. "How come, if Jesus was a Jew, Jews aren't Christian?" my Catholic roommate asked me in all seriousness. Brought up in a small Wisconsin town, she had never met a Jew before, nor had she met people from most of the other "strange" religions (anything but Catholic or mainstream Protestant). Many of the other kids were the same way.

6 "Do you all still practice animal sacrifices?" a girl from a small town in Minnesota asked me once. I said no, laughed, and pointed out that this was the 20th century, but she had been absolutely serious. The only Jews she knew were the ones from the Bible.

7 Nobody was deliberately rude or anti-Semitic, but I got the feeling that I was representing the entire Jewish people through my actions. I realized that many of my friends would go back to their small towns thinking that all Jews liked Dairy Queen Blizzards and grilled cheese sandwiches. After all, that was true of all the Jews they knew (in most cases, me and the only other Jewish young scholar, period).

8 The most awful thing for me, however, was not the benign ignorance of my friends. Our biology professor had taken us on a field trip to the EPA field site where he worked, and he was telling us about the project he was working on. He said that they had to make sure the EPA got its money's worth from the study—he "wouldn't want them to get Jewed."

9 I was astounded. The professor had a doctorate and various other degrees and seemed to be a very intelligent man. He apparently had no idea that he had just made an anti-Semitic remark. The other Jewish girl in the group and I debated whether or not to say something to him about it, and although we agreed we would, neither of us ever did. Personally, it made me feel uncomfortable. For a high-shcool student to tell a professor who taught her class that he was a bigot seemed out of place to me, even if he was one.

10 What scares me about that experience, in fact about my whole visit to Wisconsin, was that I never met a really vicious anti-Semite or a malignantly prejudiced person. Many of the people I met had been brought up to think that Jews (or Mormons or members of any other religion that's not mainstream Christian) were different and that difference was not good.

11 Difference, in America, is supposed to be good. We are expected—at least, I always thought we were expected—to respect each other's traditions. Respect requires some knowledge about people's backgrounds. Singing Christmas carols as a kid in school did not make me Christian, but it taught me to appreciate

beautiful music and someone else's holiday. It's not necessary or desirable for all ethnic groups in America to assimilate into one traditionless mass. Rather, we all need to learn about other cultures so that we can understand one another and not feel threatened by others.

In the little multicultural universe that I live in, it's safe not to worry about explaining the story of Passover, because if people don't hear it from me, they'll hear it some other way. Now I realize that's not true everywhere. 12

Ignorance was the problem I faced this summer. By itself, ignorance is not always a problem, but it leads to misunderstandings, prejudice, and hatred. Many of today's problems involve hatred. If there weren't so much ignorance about other people's backgrounds, would people still hate each other as badly as they do now? Maybe so, but at least that hatred would be based on facts and not flawed beliefs. 13

I'm now back at school, and I plan to apply for the Diversity Committee. I'm going to get up and tell the whole school about my religion and the tradition I'm proud of. I see now how important it is to celebrate your heritage and to educate others about it. I can no longer take for granted that everyone knows about my religion or that I know about theirs. People who are suspicious when they find out I'm Jewish usually don't know much about Judaism. I would much prefer them to hate or distrust me because of something I've done, instead of them hating me on the basis of prejudice. 14

### Thinking Critically About Content

1. Why do you think the writer stated that the people she attended the program with were "some of the smartest young scholars" (paragraph 3)?
2. What do you think the writer means when she says, "Nobody was deliberately rude or anti-Semitic" (paragraph 7)? Explain your answer.
3. Why does Schoenberger think that ignorance is dangerous? What does she propose to do about people's ignorance regarding her religion?

### Thinking Critically About Purpose and Audience

4. What do you think Chana Schoenberger's purpose is in this essay?
5. Do you think this essay should be read by all students? What other groups would benefit from reading this essay? Why?
6. Why do you think the writer chose to send her essay to *Newsweek* magazine rather than to her school newspaper?

### Thinking Critically About Essays

7. Why do you think the writer explained people's prejudice and ignorance in reference to other religions as well as toward Judaism?
8. How do you think the biology professor mentioned in the essay would respond to Schoenberger's explanation of prejudice? Explain your answer.
9. How does the writer organize her main points? Is this an effective order? Why or why not?
10. Were your views on religion or on society's ignorance about some religions changed as a result of reading this essay? If so, in what way? Explain your answer in detail.

### *Writing Topics: Illustrating*

Before you begin to write, you might want to review the writing process in Part I.

1. Contemporary American society rewards students who fit into the educational system and can keep up. But some people just can't keep up with a course for a variety of reasons. Have you ever felt the way Mike Rose says he felt in his essay? What was your reason for not keeping up? Discuss any similarities you see between yourself and Mike Rose.
2. How do you think the generation that is currently in high school handles ethnic and religious differences? Explain how you think these young people will change as they grow up.
3. What do you think writers should consider first when choosing examples in an essay? How should the examples be related to the thesis statement? Why are these criteria important when working with examples?

CHAPTER 28

# Analyzing a Process

The essays in this chapter explain different events or processes. In other words, they tell you how to do something or why something happened the way it did. The first essay, "Don't Be Cruel" by Roger Flax, offers some guidelines for criticizing and motivating at the same time—at work, at home, at school. "Access Activism," written by Geeta Dardick in 1992 just after the Americans with Disabilities Act (ADA) was passed, explains how that law got its start.

**Roger Flax**

## DON'T BE CRUEL

### Focusing Your Attention

1. Think of a time when you had to explain to someone how to do something. Was it an easy or a difficult task? Did the person understand you? Was the person able to follow your directions?
2. In the process analysis essay you are about to read, the writer tells us how to criticize other people effectively. Have you ever wanted to tell someone about something he or she did wrong without ruining the relationship? What did you do to solve the problem?

### Expanding Your Vocabulary

The following words are important to your understanding of this essay.

**coronary:** heart attack (paragraph 1)

**mercilessly:** cruelly (paragraph 1)

**humiliation:** shame (paragraph 3)

**reprimands:** expressions of disapproval (paragraph 4)

**manager-subordinate scenarios:** boss-employee situations (paragraph 4)

**Project Management Work Teams:** groups of individuals who work together in the workforce to improve their management style (paragraph 7)

**rapport:** sense of trust (paragraph 10)

**repercussions:** results or effects (paragraph 14)

**malice:** desire to cause harm or suffering (paragraph 16)

**exploiting:** using (paragraph 16)

**facilitate:** guide (paragraph 20)

**implementation:** the act of putting something into practice (paragraph 21)

**misconstrues:** misunderstands (paragraph 21)

**stroke:** flatter, compliment (paragraph 22)

**perennial:** constant (paragraph 29)

**belittle:** say negative things about a person (paragraph 31)

---

1 Picture this scenario: Seymour Axshun (we'll call him), a terrific manager who has been a loyal employee for several years, messes up on an assignment. He misses a deadline on a proposal and that three-day delay costs the company $9,100. Seymour's boss, Sy Kottick, has a near coronary over the incident, lashes out at Seymour and criticizes him mercilessly. In front of four of Seymour's co-workers, Kottick shouts, "Axshun, how many times do I have to tell you to be more efficient with your planning? You blew it, and your mistake will cost us almost $10,000. I don't know what it takes to drill into your head that you must meet deadlines. It's disgusting, and I'm fed up. If you treated the money as if it were your own, you wouldn't be so careless."

2 "Incidentally, Seymour, on another issue, don't you think you should come to work dressed a bit more professionally? That suit you wore yesterday was a bit outdated, especially since we had our big client, Meyer Fivis, here. And one more thing, while we're at it Seymour . . ."

3 Seymour shrinks from humiliation. He wishes he could push a button and disappear. He looks around him and sees four embarrassed colleagues. His boss storms out of the room and slams the door.

4 This thoughtless, but real-life managerial scenario happens every minute of every day, in every city of every state. People insensitively and ruthlessly come

down on others with reprimands and criticisms that leave permanent scars. And it happens not only in manager-subordinate scenarios, but in parent-child relationships, teacher-student interfaces, sports coach–player affairs and friendships.

It's called *unconstructive, unmotivational criticism* or in better words, *relationship breaking*. 5

Put yourself in Seymour Axshun's shoes. Would you ever want to work for that jerk again? And if you did, how dedicated would you really be? How motivated would you be to make him look good? 6

The two most critical assets of companies are people and time. Valuable people are hard to replace, and time is irreplaceable. With the evolution of Project Management Work Teams in companies throughout the world, it's absolutely imperative that team leaders and managers master the art of giving constructive, tactful, motivational criticism. After all, if the goal of the project group is to work as a team to attain a goal, unconstructive criticism can destroy the group quickly. *Motivation magic,* as I call it, can only enhance the team. 7

You shouldn't be a robot when giving constructive criticism, but there is a human-relations approach that does work. Here's a several-step process to follow the next time you have to reprimand another person, but truly want to motivate that person and enhance the relationship. 8

1. *Always begin constructive criticism with a positive statement.* Open with an energizing comment that builds up the person's esteem and sincerely expresses your approval and support on a specific item. For example, in the Seymour Axshun incident, why not begin with: "Seymour, you've done an outstanding job in the Quality Improvement Program, and the results are quickly having an impact on our operation. Many people have commented to me about your great work." 9

2. *Never follow that complimentary opening remark with "but" or "however."* Those words immediately eliminate the good feeling and rapport initiated by the compliment. The person will quickly surmise that the opening statement was merely lip service—a manipulative tool geared to set up the reprimand or criticism. It's very natural, and even habitual, to say "but" or "however" after you open with a positive statement, but it will destroy the initial goodwill created and result in perceived insincerity. 10

3. *Use the acronym PEN to plan and verbalize the actual criticism.* 11

*P—Problem.* State the problem that exists. Be concise and to the point. Remember: Don't begin expressing the problem with "but" or "however."

*E—Example.* Give an example or two that clearly supports the problem or reason for criticism. Get your facts straight, and keep them brief. The lengthier the criticism is, the more painful it becomes.

*N—Negative Impact.* Let the person know what negative effects have resulted from the problem or action. It's important to do some planning before the criticism session. Think through your PEN before giving it. It will come across more concisely, smoothly and convincingly.

12 4. *Avoid using the word "you" when giving the actual criticism.* This is definitely the most important rule to remember. Discipline yourself to criticize the object or the problem, not the person. Don't let yourself say "you"—it's accusatory, threatening and puts the criticism on a personal, emotional, confrontational level.

13 Example: "Seymour, you've done an outstanding job in the Quality Improvement Program, and the results are quickly having an impact on our operation. There's one situation that could be improved upon and that is meeting deadlines. On one occasion this month, a deadline was missed by three days and that has cost our company several thousand dollars. The negative effects not only include a large dollar loss, but a potential loss in credibility for future dealings."

14 Now go back and read the opening example—the confrontational, insensitive way of criticizing. Notice in the second example that the criticizer avoided the word "you" (except for the opening praise) and dealt with the problem, not the person. You need to practice this technique over and over again. Don't just use it at work, but also use it with your spouse, children, friends, relatives—everyone. It goes a long way in relationship building and effective human relations, and it reduces the enormous repercussions that can occur from giving cutthroat criticism.

15 Of course, it's okay to use "you" when you're praising the person or engaging in a subsequent dialogue after the initial criticism has been communicated. However, the word "you" should be avoided when the actual bad news is being stated.

16 If husbands and wives disciplined themselves to avoid the word "you" during potential emotional outbursts, they wouldn't build up years of frustration and marital malice. If coaches stopped publicly criticizing their players and saying "you" every time the players made a mistake, there'd be many more motivated athletes exploiting and reaching their fullest potential.

17 5. *Ask for feedback.* After "PEN-ning" people, find out what their feelings or opinions are on the matter. Let them talk. Let them express their emotions, and don't interrupt. If they're looking to save a little face, go ahead and let them. Lose the battle, but win the war. Open the window of communication, and let the air flow in.

18 6. *Actively listen to their response.* Instead of just gazing at them as they speak, be an active, nonverbal listener. Show facial expressions, nod, react

with sounds, such as "hmmm," "oh, I see" or "really." Show a genuine, caring interest.

When someone has a problem, active listening helps reduce the pain. That's what psychologists do every day. The client reveals painful experiences to the psychologist, and the psychologist uses active listening techniques to show support, concern and empathy. It's also a technique used by successful sales pros who strive to develop relationships with customers. 19

7. *Discuss the situation in a low-key manner.* Your two-way communication, although unstructured, should remain focused on the problem. Facilitate the discussion to an agreed-upon action or solution. Clearly state what you want the person to do, if it's not clear, and make sure you obtain a mutual understanding. Don't dominate the communication. If the other person raises his or her voice, keep yours down. That will keep the discussion less emotional and more low-key. 20

8. *Mutually agree upon an action or next step.* It's always better this way. Forcing a person to do something usually produces substantially less long-term growth and relationship building. Both parties should agree upon an action, set a date for its implementation, and end with a handshake. Try getting the person to verbalize what the action steps will be, thereby ensuring that both people are in sync. You'd be surprised how many times the criticized person misconstrues the next action step. 21

9. *End with a positive.* Now that the hard work is completed (and nobody likes giving criticism), go back and stroke the person a bit. Remind him or her that you greatly appreciate the person's effort and dedication and are very supportive of his or her performance. Make sure that no negative feelings exist, and if they do, probe and uncover them. You want to assure the person that this is a very correctable problem and that, in the big picture, you're a very satisfied manager. 22

Example: "Seymour, remember, I am extremely pleased with your performance. You are a valuable asset to our department." 23

A few musts to keep in mind when giving constructive, motivational criticism: 24

First, *always do it in private.* Nobody is proud of reprimands, so do it when you're alone with the person. It's humiliating when done in public. 25

Second, *limit the criticism session to one act.* If you bring up things from the past, you're turning the knife and potentially destroying the relationship. You should communicate criticism within a day or two of the occurrence; otherwise, drop it. Some people bring up events that occurred six months or even six years ago. That's a no-no. 26

Third, *criticize face-to-face, never over the phone.* You never know how the person is reacting. If you're criticizing over the phone, the other person might be 27 dying inside, and you'll never know it. Even if it's timely to do it over the phone, hold it in. Set up an immediate meeting with the person.

28 Finally, *don't dig it in.* Statements such as "you see," "I told you so" or "you don't listen" are worthless. They might make you feel good, but they ruin relationships.

29 A great example of how *not* to criticize can be seen during a sports event—basketball, baseball or football. How many times does a basketball coach yell at his point guard for missing the play and use the accusatory "you" over and over again? The coach raises his voice in frustration and does it in front of teammates and fans. The player feels abused, his confidence is shaken, and his motivation is drained from within. It's no wonder certain professional coaches go from team to team but continue to lose year after year. They might know the sport, but they know little about human motivation. A little motivational psychology would go a long way for these perennial losers.

30 How do you tie all these points together the next time you must criticize a person? Remember: The goal of motivational criticism should be to leave the person feeling helped, not hurt. So, the next time you're about to criticize a person, think it through before you do. Be tactful, firm, empathetic and concise.

31 After all, you have to be little to belittle. *You* hold the key to motivational magic.

### Thinking Critically About Content

1. What does Roger Flax mean by "motivation magic" (paragraph 7)?
2. What are the nine main steps of Flax's method?
3. What does Flax say the main goal of motivational criticism is?

### Thinking Critically About Purpose and Audience

4. What do you think Flax's purpose is in this essay?
5. Do you think that only businesspeople can benefit from this essay? Why? Explain your answer.
6. Which piece of Flax's advice do you find most useful for your own life?

### Thinking Critically About Essays

7. Describe in a complete sentence Flax's point of view in his last paragraph.
8. How does Flax organize this essay? Write a rough outline to show his method of organization.
9. Choose a paragraph from his essay, and explain how it is developed.

10. Explain in detail whether or not you agree with Flax when he says that using "you" to criticize people makes them feel like they are being attacked.

## Geeta Dardick

# ACCESS ACTIVISM

### Focusing Your Attention

1. Think of a problem you frequently face. Make a list of ways you might solve that problem, or freewrite about various solutions to the problem.
2. In the essay you are about to read, the writer describes the enormous amount of time she and her husband devoted to improving the lives of disabled people. Sometimes solving a big problem, such as improving the quality of life of disabled people, requires more energy, hard work, dedication, and expense than we are willing to give. Have you ever avoided attempting to solve a problem for these reasons? What was the problem? Was it easier to live with the problem than do what was required to solve it? Explain why.

### Expanding Your Vocabulary

The following words are important to your understanding of this essay.

**ardor:** passion, love (paragraph 1)

**dormant:** sleeping, not active (paragraph 5)

**innumerable:** too many to count (paragraph 10)

**inaccessible:** denying access (paragraph 10)

**busted:** broke into (paragraph 11)

**gusto:** enthusiasm (paragraph 11)

**caveat:** warning (paragraph 11)

**auxiliary:** supplementary, additional (paragraph 17)

**implementation:** the act of putting something into practice (paragraph 21)

**succinctly:** briefly (paragraph 21)

1 In 1963 I fell in love with Sam Dardick, a man who happened to have a disability. After I announced my engagement to Sam, some narrow-minded "friends" tried to convince me that I shouldn't choose a wheelchair user for a husband, but I ignored their negative comments. To me, Sam Dardick was a charming and sexy guy, and the fact that he'd had polio as a kid didn't dampen my ardor for him.

2 Still, during the early years of our marriage, when we lived in St. Louis, Sam's wheelchair was a problem for both of us. We'd try to rent an apartment, and find that 100 percent of them had stairs. We'd go to the movies: stairs again. We'd plan to take the bus . . . more stairs. It soon became obvious that architects, builders, and designers did not take Sam's and my needs into consideration (ironic, since Sam was a graduate of Washington University's School of Architecture).

3 I felt extremely annoyed every time we encountered an architectural barrier, but I had no way to vent my anger. There weren't any disability laws in Missouri at that time. All I could do was stuff my feelings about the lack of wheelchair access and move on with my life.

4 In the early 1970s, we gave up our urban lifestyle, bought land on the San Juan Ridge in Nevada County, California, and became back-to-the-land farmers. Now I worried about the simple things in life, like keeping the woodstove burning so the cabin would be warm enough for the whole-wheat bread to rise. Access seemed irrelevant, since we rarely left our land.

5 My feelings about accessibility issues remained dormant for many years; then one sunny day in the spring of 1984, like Rip Van Winkle, I woke up. Sam and I were celebrating his birthday by lunching together at the Posh Nosh Restaurant in Nevada City. After we paid for our beers and pastrami-on-rye sandwiches, Sam suddenly felt an urgent call of nature.

6 He wheeled his wheelchair over to the bathroom and discovered that the door was two feet wide. His wheelchair measured two and one-half feet wide. There was no way his chair was going to pass through that door.

7 Sam wheeled back to our table, about 20 feet from the bathroom door. Without telling me what he intended to do, Sam jumped out of his wheelchair and dropped himself onto the floor of the restaurant. And then he started crawling rapidly toward the bathroom door.

8 Paraplegics like Sam can use their arms, but not their legs. Sam's crawl was a two-handed movement in which he dragged himself across the room like a caterpillar. I sat there watching him in disbelief. Here was the man who was my lover, my husband, the father of my three children, the president of the San Juan Ridge School Board, a guy with graduate degrees in architecture and city planning; here he was, being forced to crawl across the floor of the Posh Nosh Restaurant to use the bathroom. As I watched Sam crawling, I pledged that I was going

to do something, to help make sure that neither my husband nor anyone else would be forced to crawl to a bathroom again.

The following day I started making phone calls. I found out that California already had laws requiring wheelchair accessibility. I also found out that Sam and I could join a state-sponsored program, called the Community Access Network (CAN), that would teach us the state's accessibility codes and then send us back into Nevada County to enforce them. 9

That summer, I trained as a CAN volunteer; from that moment on, I became an access cop, with my evil eye turned on the county's innumerable inaccessible structures. Rather than act alone, Sam and I networked with persons from all disability groups and formed a broad-based local access committee to raise community awareness of the need for accessibility and to police new construction projects. 10

During the next few years, Sam and I volunteered thousands of hours for disability causes throughout California. We marched for access to public transportation in San Francisco, testified for accessible apartments in Sacramento, busted inaccessible city-council meetings in Nevada City, and started an Independent Living Center in Grass Valley. Every victory was celebrated with gusto, but there was always one caveat. We realized that the state of California, with its progressive legislation promoting architectural accessibility, was more advanced on disability issues than most other states. Would the fight for accessibility have to be fought over and over again in every state in the nation? Wasn't there ever going to be a national disability policy? 11

We didn't have long to wait. Back in 1984, then-president Ronald Reagan directed the National Council on the Handicapped to prepare a special report that would present legislative recommendations for enhancing the productivity and quality of life of Americans with disabilities. 12

The council's report, submitted to President Reagan in 1986, was entitled *Toward Independence,* and it was much more hard hitting than might have been expected. It recommended "enactment of a comprehensive law requiring equal opportunity for individuals with disabilities, with broad coverage and setting clear, consistent, and enforceable standards prohibiting discrimination on the basis of handicap." That bold recommendation was the seed that resulted in the development of legislation for the Americans with Disabilities Act (ADA), the first national civil-rights bill for people with disabilities. 13

Opposition to the ADA from business and transportation interests forced disability leaders to wheel and deal. The right to universal health-insurance coverage was bartered away for support from some key legislators. After a great deal of behind-the-scenes negotiation, the ADA passed the House of Representatives 377–28 and the Senate 91–6, with its most important provisions still intact. 14

The ADA is a comprehensive piece of legislation. The regulations of the ADA (which went into effect on January 26, 1991) will eventually eliminate many of the 15 barriers faced by people with disabilities. All "public accommodations," such as restaurants, hotels, medical offices, and retail stores, will need to be built with full accessibility. (Adding accessibility to a new structure increases the total cost by 1 percent or less.) Typical accessibility features include ramps, bathrooms with ample space for wheelchairs to turn around, and lightweight doors that are easy to open.

16 Businesses that decide to remodel will have to make the remodeled area accessible, as well as the path of travel to the area. In existing buildings, inaccessible features must be eliminated if such changes are "readily achievable" without much difficulty or expense. An example would be placing a ramp over one or two steps leading into a store or office.

17 Businesses must provide auxiliary aids to enable a person with a disability to use available materials and services. For example, any video presentations about products would need to be closed-captioned for the deaf, and brochures would need large print so that those with low vision could read them. Another example: providing special pens that have large, spongy, easy-to-hold grips—helpful for many people with arthritis.

18 The ADA also makes major changes in employment criteria. Under the ADA, an employer cannot refuse to hire a qualified applicant with a disability, just because of the person's disability. An employer does not, however, have to give preference to a qualified applicant with a disability over other applicants. An employer must also make "reasonable accommodations" for a person with a disability so he or she can perform the job. This might mean putting an amplifier on a telephone, lowering a desk, or establishing a flexible work schedule. And in new or remodeled facilities, all employee areas including sales and service areas must be made fully accessible. If the accommodations would impose an "undue hardship" (be too costly), however, they will not be required.

19 There are many incentives written into the law to encourage businesses to comply with the ADA. Businesses can receive tax deductions of up to $15,000 for the removal of architectural barriers (if it costs $12,000 to replace stairs with a ramp, for example, the entire amount is tax-deductible). Businesses can receive tax credits equal to 50 percent of all costs of meeting the Americans with Disabilities Act, providing those costs are over $250 and under $10,250. If, for instance, you hired a sign-language interpreter to be present for the signing of contracts with deaf buyers, or if you made a workstation accessible for an employee who uses a wheelchair, you could deduct half of the cost.

20 Public services also come under the ADA umbrella. All new public buildings and all new buses and rail vehicles must be accessible. By 1993, telephone companies must provide telecommunications relay services for hearing-impaired and speech-impaired individuals, 24 hours a day.

Of course, passing a law is only a first step to full equality. Implementation is the second step, and it is just as important. Congressman Steny Hoyer put it most succinctly when he said, "Passing ADA was incredibly historic. Now every day we must fight to make sure that the words in the law, the words on the White House lawn, the words in the House, and the words in the Senate become reality for 43 million Americans with disabilities and millions more around the world who are looking to American leadership for the rights of the disabled." 21

### Thinking Critically About Content

1. Writers often use personal stories to get the reader's attention, sympathy, or understanding. What does Dardick use in this essay that is particularly effective in helping her readers understand the problem?
2. What steps does Dardick take to change accessibility laws in this country?
3. According to Dardick, what are the two steps toward "full equality" (paragraph 21)?

### Thinking Critically About Purpose and Audience

4. What do you think the purpose of this essay is?
5. How do you think a general audience would respond to the author's description of the many incentives offered to businesses for complying with the laws that were written to help people with disabilities?
6. We often think that some problems are just too big for one person to solve, especially if bureaucracies like state or federal governments are involved. In what ways might Dardick's essay inspire others who face problems that can't be solved very quickly or easily?

### Thinking Critically About Essays

7. Describe in a complete sentence the writer's point of view.
8. Why do you think Dardick devotes the second half of her essay to an explanation of the rules and regulations required by the Americans with Disabilities Act?
9. How does Dardick organize her essay?
10. If Dardick were writing this essay for a publication to be read only by people with disabilities, how might it be different? How might it be the same? Rewrite the introduction or the conclusion for an audience of people with disabilities.

*Writing Topics: Analyzing a Process*

Before you begin to write, you might want to review the writing process in Part I.

1. In the first essay, Flax talks about motivating people by criticizing without using the word "you." Are you usually aware of your word choice as you talk? How can careful use of words help you get what you want in life? Explain a process that involved getting something you wanted by using words carefully.
2. Think of something in life that you want to change as much as Dardick wanted to change the laws for the disabled. Then explain your plan for achieving this goal or accomplishing this mission you have set for yourself.
3. Which type of process analysis do you find most interesting—the how-to essays or the background explanations? Explain your answer.

CHAPTER 29

# Comparing and Contrasting

The following essays use comparison and contrast to communicate their main ideas. The first, written by Stephanie Coontz, was originally published in *Life* magazine; it compares the family at the end of the twentieth century with that at the beginning of the century. The second essay, "Venus Envy" by Patricia McLaughlin, compares and contrasts men's and women's outward appearance.

---

**Stephanie Coontz**

## THE AMERICAN FAMILY

### Focusing Your Attention

1. What do you think are the good qualities of the American family today? What were the good qualities of the family when your parents were children?
2. In the essay you are about to read, the writer compares and contrasts the American family at the turn of the twenty-first century with the family at the turn of the twentieth century. What do you think are some of the differences in family life at these two times? Some of the similarities?

### Expanding Your Vocabulary

The following words are important to your understanding of this essay.

**epidemic:** a widespread outbreak of an infectious disease (paragraph 2)

**litany:** list (paragraph 3)

**nuclear family:** parents and their children, living in the same household (paragraph 5)

**consensus:** widespread agreement (paragraph 5)

**nostalgia:** a feeling of pleasure and sadness about the past (paragraph 6)

**GI Bill:** a series of laws passed after World War II providing low-cost government loans to veterans (paragraph 6)

**subsidized:** supported by government money (paragraph 6)

**amnesia:** forgetting (paragraph 7)

**coercion:** force (paragraph 7)

**arbitrary:** on a whim, for no clear reason (paragraph 7)

**ostracized:** excluded, left out (paragraph 7)

***Leave It to Beaver*:** television series of the 1950s featuring the fictional Cleaver family and presenting an idealized picture of family life (paragraph 8)

**juvenile delinquency:** serious troublemaking by teenagers (paragraph 10)

**barbiturate:** a drug that calms and relaxes people (paragraph 10)

**disparaged:** put down, treated unkindly (paragraph 11)

**gonorrhea:** a sexually transmitted disease (paragraph 12)

**syphilis:** a sexually transmitted disease (paragraph 12)

**Oedipal fantasies:** sexual attraction that a child feels for the parent of the opposite sex (paragraph 12)

**spousal:** of one's husband or wife (paragraph 13)

**in flux:** changing (paragraph 17)

**breadwinner:** person who earns the money on which a family lives (paragraph 19)

**impoverished:** made poor (paragraph 26)

**incapacitated:** disabled (paragraph 26)

**noncustodial:** not having legal authority over one's own child (paragraph 27)

**stepfamilies:** nuclear families in which one parent is not the original parent of one or more of the children (paragraph 27)

**debilitating:** causing weakness or loss of strength (paragraph 29)

As the century comes to an end, many observers fear for the future of America's families. Our divorce rate is the highest in the world, and the percentage of unmarried women is significantly higher than in 1960. Educated women are having fewer babies, while immigrant children flood the schools, demanding to be taught in their native language. Harvard University reports that only 4 percent of its applicants can write a proper sentence. 1

There's an epidemic of sexually transmitted diseases among men. Many streets in urban neighborhoods are littered with cocaine vials. Youths call heroin "happy dust." Even in small towns, people have easy access to addictive drugs, and drug abuse by middle-class wives is skyrocketing. Police see 16-year-old killers, 12-year-old prostitutes, and gang members as young as 11. America at the end of the 1990s? No, America at the end of the 1890s. 2

The litany of complaints may sound familiar, but the truth is that many things were worse at the start of the 20th century than they are today. Then, thousands of children worked full-time in mines, mills and sweatshops. Most workers labored 10 hours a day, often six days a week, which left them little time or energy for family life. Race riots were more frequent and more deadly than those experienced by recent generations. Women couldn't vote, and their wages were so low that many turned to prostitution. 3

In 1900 a white child had one chance in three of losing a brother or sister before age 15, and a black child had a fifty-fifty chance of seeing a sibling die. Children's-aid groups reported widespread abuse and neglect by parents. Men who deserted or divorced their wives rarely paid child support. And only 6 percent of the children graduated from high school, compared with 88 percent today. 4

Why do so many people think American families are facing worse problems now than in the past? Partly it's because we compare the complex and diverse families of the 1990s with the seemingly more standard-issue ones of the 1950s, a unique decade when every long-term trend of the 20th century was temporarily reversed. In the 1950s, for the first time in 100 years, the divorce rate fell while marriage and fertility rates soared, creating a boom in nuclear-family living. The percentage of foreign-born individuals in the country decreased. And the debates over social and cultural issues that had divided Americans for 150 years were silenced, suggesting a national consensus on family values and norms. 5

Some nostalgia for the 1950s is understandable: Life looked pretty good in comparison with the hardships of the Great Depression and World War II. The GI Bill gave a generation of young fathers a college education and a subsidized mortgage on a new house. For the first time, a majority of men could support a family and buy a home without pooling their earnings with those of other family members. Many Americans built a stable family life on these foundations. 6

But much nostalgia for the 1950s is a result of selective amnesia—the same process that makes childhood memories of summer vacations grow sunnier with 7 each passing year. The superficial sameness of 1950s family life was achieved through censorship, coercion and discrimination. People with unconventional beliefs faced governmental investigation and arbitrary firings. African Americans and Mexican Americans were prevented from voting in some states by literacy tests that were not administered to whites. Individuals who didn't follow the rigid gender and sexual rules of the day were ostracized.

8 *Leave It to Beaver* did not reflect the real-life experience of most American families. While many moved into the middle class during the 1950s, poverty remained more widespread than in the worst of our last three recessions. More children went hungry, and poverty rates for the elderly were more than twice as high as today's.

9 Even in the white middle class, not every woman was as serenely happy with her lot as June Cleaver was on TV. Housewives of the 1950s may have been less rushed than today's working mothers, but they were more likely to suffer anxiety and depression. In many states, women couldn't serve on juries or get loans or credit cards in their own names.

10 And not every kid was as wholesome as Beaver Cleaver, whose mischievous antics could be handled by Dad at the dinner table. In 1955 alone, Congress discussed 200 bills aimed at curbing juvenile delinquency. Three years later, *Life* reported that urban teachers were being terrorized by their students. The drugs that were so freely available in 1900 had been outlawed, but many children grew up in families ravaged by alcohol and barbiturate abuse.

11 Rates of unwed childbearing tripled between 1940 and 1958, but most Americans didn't notice because unwed mothers generally left town, gave their babies up for adoption and returned home as if nothing had happened. Troubled youths were encouraged to drop out of high school. Mentally handicapped children were warehoused in institutions like the Home for Idiotic and Imbecilic Children in Kansas, where a woman whose sister had lived there for most of the 1950s once took me. Wives routinely told pollsters that being disparaged or ignored by their husbands was a normal part of a happier-than-average marriage.

12 Denial extended to other areas of life as well. In the early 1900s, doctors refused to believe that the cases of gonorrhea and syphilis they saw in young girls could have been caused by sexual abuse. Instead, they reasoned, girls could get these diseases from toilet seats, a myth that terrified generations of mothers and daughters. In the 1950s, psychiatrists dismissed incest reports as Oedipal fantasies on the part of children.

13 Spousal rape was legal throughout the period, and wife beating was not taken seriously by authorities. Much of what we now label child abuse was accepted as a normal part of parental discipline. Physicians saw no reason to question parents who claimed that their child's broken bones had been caused by a fall from a tree.

There are plenty of stresses in modern family life, but one reason they seem worse is that we no longer sweep them under the rug. Another is that we have higher expectations of parenting and marriage. That's a good thing. We're right to be concerned about inattentive parents, conflicted marriages, antisocial values, teen violence and child abuse. But we need to realize that many of our worries reflect how much better we *want* to be, not how much better we *used* to be. 14

Fathers in intact families are spending more time with their children than at any other point in the past 100 years. Although the number of hours the average woman spends at home with her children has declined since the early 1900s, there has been a decrease in the number of children per family and an increase in individual attention to each child. As a result, mothers today, including working moms, spend almost twice as much time with each child as mothers did in the 1920s. People who raised children in the 1940s and 1950s typically report that their own adult children and grandchildren communicate far better with their kids and spend more time helping with homework than they did—even as they complain that other parents today are doing a worse job than in the past. 15

Despite the rise in youth violence from the 1960s to the early 1990s, America's children are also safer now than they've ever been. An infant was four times more likely to die in the 1950s than today. A parent then was three times more likely than a modern one to preside at the funeral of a child under the age of 15, and 27 percent more likely to lose an older teen to death. 16

If we look back over the last millennium, we can see that families have always been diverse and in flux. In each period, families have solved one set of problems only to face a new array of challenges. What works for a family in one economic and cultural setting doesn't work for a family in another. What's helpful at one stage of a family's life may be destructive at the next stage. If there is one lesson to be drawn from the last millennium of family history, it's that families are always having to play catch-up with a changing world. 17

Take the issue of working mothers. Families in which mothers spend as much time earning a living as they do raising children are nothing new. They were the norm throughout most of the last two millennia. In the 19th century, married women in the United States began a withdrawal from the workforce, but for most families this was made possible only by sending their children out to work instead. When child labor was abolished, married women began reentering the workforce in ever larger numbers. 18

For a few decades, the decline in child labor was greater than the growth of women's employment. The result was an aberration: the male-breadwinner family. In the 1920s, for the first time, a bare majority of American children grew up in families where the husband provided all the income, the wife stayed home full-time, and they and their siblings went to school instead of work. During the 1950s, almost two thirds of children grew up in such families, an all-time high. 19

Yet that same decade saw an acceleration of workforce participation by wives and mothers that soon made the dual-earner family the norm, a trend not likely to be reversed in the next century.

20 What's new is not that women make half their families' living, but that for the first time they have substantial control over their own income, along with the social freedom to remain single or to leave an unsatisfactory marriage. Also new is the declining proportion of their lives that people devote to rearing children, both because they have fewer kids and because they are living longer. Until about 1940, the typical marriage was broken by the death of one partner within a few years after the last child left home. Today, couples can look forward to spending more than two decades together after the children leave.

21 The growing length of time partners spend with only each other for company has made many individuals less willing to put up with an unhappy marriage, while women's economic independence makes it less essential for them to do so. It is no wonder that divorce has risen steadily since 1900. Disregarding a spurt in 1946, a dip in the 1950s and another peak around 1980, the divorce rate is just where you'd expect to find it, based on the rate of increase from 1900 to 1950. Today, 40 percent of all marriages will end in divorce before a couple's 40th anniversary. Yet despite this high divorce rate, expanded life expectancies mean that more couples are reaching that anniversary than ever before.

22 Families and individuals in contemporary America have more life choices than in the past. That makes it easier for some to consider dangerous or unpopular options. But it also makes success easier for many families that never would have had a chance before—interracial, gay or lesbian, and single-mother families, for example. And it expands horizons for most families.

23 Women's new options are good not just for themselves but for their children. While some people say that women who choose to work are selfish, it turns out that maternal self-sacrifice is not good for children. Kids do better when their mothers are happy with their lives, whether their satisfaction comes from being a full-time homemaker or from having a job.

24 Largely because of women's new roles at work, men are doing more at home. Although most men still do less housework than their wives, the gap has been halved since the 1960s. Today, 49 percent of couples say they share childcare equally, compared with 25 percent in 1985.

25 Men's greater involvement at home is good for their relationships with their partners and also good for their children. Hands-on fathers make better parents than men who let their wives do all the nurturing and childcare: They raise sons who are more expressive and daughters who are more likely to do well in school, especially in math and science.

26 In 1900, life expectancy was 47 years, and only 4 percent of the population was 65 or older. Today, life expectancy is 76 years, and by 2025, about 20 percent of Americans will be 65 or older. For the first time, a generation of adults must

plan for the needs of both their parents and their children. Most Americans are responding with remarkable grace. One in four households gives the equivalent of a full day a week or more in unpaid care to an aging relative, and more than half say they expect to do so in the next 10 years. Older people are less likely to be impoverished or incapacitated by illness than in the past, and they have more opportunity to develop a relationship with their grandchildren.

Even some of the choices that worry us the most are turning out to be manageable. Divorce rates are likely to remain high, but more noncustodial parents are staying in touch with their children. Child-support receipts are up. And a lower proportion of kids from divorced families are exhibiting problems than in earlier decades. Stepfamilies are learning to maximize children's access to supportive adults rather than cutting them off from one side of the family. 27

Out-of-wedlock births are also high, however, and this will probably continue because the age of first marriage for women has risen to an all-time high of 25, almost five years above what it was in the 1950s. Women who marry at an older age are less likely to divorce, but they have more years when they are at risk—or at choice—for a nonmarital birth. 28

Nevertheless, births to teenagers have fallen from 50 percent of all nonmarital births in the late 1970s to just 30 percent today. A growing proportion of women who have a nonmarital birth are in their twenties and thirties and usually have more economic and educational resources than unwed mothers of the past. While two involved parents are generally better than one, a mother's personal maturity, along with her educational and economic status, is a better predictor of how well her child will turn out than her marital status. We should no longer assume that children raised by single parents face debilitating disadvantages. 29

As we begin to understand the range of sizes, shapes and colors that today's families come in, we find that the differences *within* family types are more important than the differences *between* them. No particular family form guarantees success, and no particular form is doomed to fail. How a family functions on the inside is more important than how it looks from the outside. 30

The biggest problem facing most families is not that our families have changed too much but that our institutions have changed too little. America's work policies are 50 years out of date, designed for a time when most moms weren't in the workforce and most dads didn't understand the joys of being involved in childcare. Our school schedules are 150 years out of date, designed for a time when kids needed to be home to help with the milking and haying. And many political leaders feel they have to decide whether to help parents stay home longer with their kids or invest in better childcare, preschool and afterschool programs, when most industrialized nations have long since learned it's possible to do both. 31

So America's social institutions have some bugs to iron out. But for the most part, our families are ready for the new millennium. 32

### Thinking Critically About Content

1. Explain four differences between the American family now and 100 years ago.
2. What difference between family life is most interesting to you? Why?
3. According to Coontz, in what ways are families "always having to play catch-up with a changing world" (paragraph 17)?

### Thinking Critically About Purpose and Audience

4. Why do you think Coontz wrote this essay?
5. Who do you think is her main audience?
6. What is Coontz's general opinion about the American family today?

### Thinking Critically About Essays

7. What is Coontz's thesis statement? How does she lead up to this thesis?
8. Explain how the topic sentence works in paragraph 5. Does it supply the controlling idea for the entire paragraph?
9. Are the statistics and facts that Coontz cites in this essay effective? Which are most effective in proving her thesis?
10. Do you agree or disagree with her general conclusions about the American family today? Write a detailed response to some of Coontz's observations.

**Patricia McLaughlin**

## VENUS ENVY

### Focusing Your Attention

1. What messages do men receive from the media about their looks? What messages do women receive? How are these messages the same? How are they different?
2. In the essay you are about to read, the author compares and contrasts the various expectations men and women have of each other. What do you think these expectations are? What do you think is the source of these expectations?

### Expanding Your Vocabulary

The following words are important to your understanding of this essay.

**Great Seesaw of Being:** a joke on the Great Chain of Being, which portrays the universe with God at the top and humans somewhere in the middle (paragraph 2)

**love handles:** rolls of fat around the waist (paragraph 2)

**wince:** cringe (paragraph 2)

**vertiginous:** feeling dizzy from being up high (paragraph 3)

**anorexia:** disorder caused by an individual eating too little out of fear of gaining weight (paragraph 5)

**bulimia:** disorder caused by an individual eating large amounts of food and then vomiting to prevent it from being digested (paragraph 5)

**dermatologists:** skin doctors (paragraph 6)

**plastic surgeons:** physicians who perform surgery to reshape body parts (paragraph 6)

**ogle:** stare (paragraph 7)

**Ken:** a children's doll (paragraph 8)

**Barbie:** a children's doll (paragraph 8)

**electric broom:** vacuum cleaner (paragraph 10)

---

It used to be that what mattered in life was how women looked and what men did—which, to many women and other right-thinking people, didn't seem fair. Now, thanks to the efforts of feminists (and a lot of social and economic factors beyond their control), what women do matters more. 1

Meanwhile, in a development that's almost enough to make you believe in the Great Seesaw of Being, how men look is also beginning to carry more weight. Men are having plastic surgery to get rid of their love handles and tighten their eye bags and beef up their chins and flatten their bellies and even (*major wince*) bulk up their penises. They're dyeing their hair to hide the gray. They're buying magazines to find out how to lose those pesky last five pounds. 2

Naturally, women who always envied the way men never had to suffer to be beautiful think they're making a big mistake. (What next: too-small shoes with vertiginous heels?) But maybe they don't exactly have a choice. 3

The key to how men feel about how they look, says Michael Pertschuk, who's writing a book about it, is social expectation: What do they think folks expect them to look like? And how far do folks expect them to go to look that way? 4

5 You think of anorexia and bulimia as disorders that strike teenage girls, but men get them, too—not many, but "a bit more" than used to, according to Pertschuk, a psychiatrist who sees patients (including men) with eating disorders. Because eating disorders virtually always start with a "normal" desire to lose weight and look slimmer, the increase among men suggests that men are worrying about their looks more than they used to.

6 Pertschuk has also worked with the dermatologists and plastic surgeons at the Center for Human Appearance at the University of Pennsylvania to screen candidates for cosmetic surgery, and he says "there are certainly more male plastic surgery patients," which suggests the same thing: "It's become more culturally accepted or expected for men to be concerned about their appearance."

7 And no wonder, when you look at the media. Stephen Perrine, articles editor at *Men's Health,* a magazine that in the last six years has built a circulation as big as *Esquire's* and *GQ*'s put together, says the mass media "in the last five to seven years has really changed the way it portrays men." Whether you look at Calvin Klein's underwear ads or that Diet Coke commercial where the girls in the office ogle the shirtless construction hunk, "men are more and more portrayed as sex objects. . . . So they're feeling the way women have for many, many years: 'Oh, *that's* what's expected of me? *That's* what I'm supposed to look like?'" And they—some of them, anyway—rush to live up to those expectations.

8 Which—wouldn't you know?—turns out to be a heck of a lot easier for them than it ever was for women: "It's easier for men to change their bodies," Perrine says, "easier to build muscle, easier to burn fat." Besides, the male physical ideal is more realistic to begin with: A man "who's healthy and works out . . . *will* look like Ken, but a woman can exercise till she's dead, and she's not going to look like Barbie," Perrine says.

9 Ken? Is that really what women want?

10 Maybe some women. Me, I get all weak in the knees when I see a guy running a vacuum, or unloading a dishwasher without being asked. Not that Calvin Klein is ever going to advertise his underwear on a cute guy with a nice big electric broom.

11 But what women want isn't the point.

12 Used to be, Pertschuk says, men who had plastic surgery said they were doing it for their careers: They wouldn't get promoted if they looked old and fat and tired. Now they say the same thing women do: "I want to feel better about myself." In other words, they look at their love handles or eyebags or pot bellies or saggy chins and feel inadequate and ugly and unworthy, just the way women have been feeling all along about their hips, stomachs, thighs, breasts, wrinkles, etc.

13 That's new: For more men, self-regard has come to hinge not just on what they do, but on what they see in the mirror. And it's easier to change *that* than the values that make them feel bad about it.

### Thinking Critically About Content

1. What do you think is McLaughlin's main point in this essay?
2. What activities suggest that men are worrying more about their looks than they used to?
3. What does McLaughlin mean by "social expectation" in paragraph 4? What other words in the sentence help you figure out this reference?

### Thinking Critically About Purpose and Audience

4. Why do you think McLaughlin wrote this essay?
5. Who would be most interested in this essay?
6. How does this essay make you feel about the role of the media in our society?

### Thinking Critically About Essays

7. Name four points of comparison and four points of contrast in this essay.
8. How are most of the paragraphs in this essay organized? Use one paragraph to explain your answer.
9. Is McLaughlin's title effective? Explain your answer.
10. Write a short fable about a similarity or difference between men and women.

### *Writing Topics: Comparing and Contrasting*

Before you begin to write, you might want to review the writing process in Part I.

1. In the first essay, Stephanie Coontz talks about the changes she sees in the past century in the role of the family in American society, but there are also differences between families today. Compare and contrast your family's values with those of another family. What is the same between the two? What is different?
2. Expand the fable you wrote in response to question 10 after Patricia McLaughlin's essay by adding more characters and more points.
3. What process do you have to go through to come up with an interesting comparison or contrast? How is it different from the process you go through for other rhetorical modes?

# Dividing and Classifying

The essays in this chapter show division and classification at work. The first, "Black Music in Our Hands," written by Bernice Reagon, divides and classifies the role of music in her life. The second essays, "What Are Friends For?" by Marion Winik, divides and classifies various types of friends.

**Bernice Reagon**

## BLACK MUSIC IN OUR HANDS

### Focusing Your Attention

1. What are some of your main interests in life? Have any of these interests been part of your life for a long time? How have they changed over time?
2. In the essay you are about to read, the writer divides and classifies music from a number of different perspectives. What role does music play in your life? Has it always played this role? How has it changed in your life over the years?

### Expanding Your Vocabulary

The following words are important to your understanding of this essay.

**Albany State:** college in Albany, Georgia (paragraph 1)

**contralto soloist:** a woman singer with a very low voice (paragraph 1)

**arias:** songs in an opera (paragraph 1)

**lieder:** traditional German songs (paragraph 1)

**Nathaniel Dett:** 1882–1943, American composer and pianist (paragraph 1)

**William Dawson:** 1899–1990, African American composer (paragraph 1)

**unaccompanied:** without musical instruments (paragraph 2)

**ornate:** complex (paragraph 2)

**congregational responses:** singing by the people in the pews in reply to someone at the front of the church (paragraph 2)

**Civil Rights Movement:** push for equal rights for African Americans in the 1950s and 1960s (paragraph 5)

**march:** organized movement of demonstrators (paragraph 5)

**integrative:** uniting (paragraph 5)

**segregated:** separated according to race (paragraph 7)

**Albany Movement:** a movement started in Albany, Georgia, and led by Rev. Martin Luther King, Jr. that hoped to gain more freedom for African Americans but ended up in racial violence (paragraph 8)

**Freedom Singers:** African Americans who sang about civic rights during the Civil Rights Movement (paragraph 12)

**Georgia Sea Island Singers:** international performing artists who sing about African American culture (paragraph 13)

**Newport Festival:** summer music festival held in Newport, Rhode Island (paragraph 13)

**repertoire:** collection of songs that an artist can perform (paragraph 13)

**casings:** coverings (paragraph 16)

**sit-in:** an act of protest in which demonstrators sit down and refuse to leave the premises (paragraph 17)

**Wallace:** George Wallace, the segregationist governor of Alabama (paragraph 17)

**Freedom Rides:** rides taken by civil rights activists to ensure that public facilities had been desegregated (paragraph 17)

**ensemble:** a group of musicians who perform together (paragraph 17)

**Thelonious Monk:** 1917–1982, composer and pianist who created a new type of jazz known as bebop (paragraph 18)

**Charlie Mingus:** 1922–1979, jazz performer on bass and piano, hailed as a composer and a poet (paragraph 18)

**SNCC:** Student Nonviolent Coordinating Committee, a group of black and white students that promoted peace between races (paragraph 18)

**Coltrane:** John Coltrane, 1926–1967, jazz saxophonist who also played the flute (paragraph 18)

**Charlie Parker:** 1920–1955, a bebop jazz artist who played the alto saxophone (paragraph 18)

**Coleman Hawkins:** 1901–1969, known as the father of the jazz tenor saxophone (paragraph 18)

**compost:** mixture (paragraph 20)

---

1 In the early 1960s, I was in college at Albany State. My major interests were music and biology. In music I was a contralto soloist with the choir, studying Italian arias and German lieder. The black music I sang was of three types: (1) Spirituals sung by the college choir. These were arranged by such people as Nathaniel Dett and William Dawson and had major injections of European musical harmony and composition. (2) Rhythm 'n' Blues, music done by and for Blacks in social settings. This included the music of bands at proms, juke boxes, and football game songs. (3) Church music; gospel was a major part of Black church music by the time I was in college. I was a soloist with the gospel choir.

2 Prior to the gospel choir, introduced in my church when I was twelve, was many years' experience with unaccompanied music—Black choral singing, hymns, lined out by strong song leaders with full, powerful, richly ornate congregational responses. These hymns were offset by upbeat, clapping call-and-response songs.

3 I saw people in church sing and pray until they shouted. I knew *that* music as a part of a cultural expression that was powerful enough to take people from their conscious selves to a place where the physical and intellectual being worked in harmony with the spirit. I enjoyed and needed that experience. The music of the church was an integral part of the cultural world into which I was born.

4 Outside of church, I saw music as good, powerful sounds you made or listened to. Rhythm and blues—you danced to; music of the college choir—you clapped after the number was finished.

5 The Civil Rights Movement changed my view of music. It was after my first march. I began to sing a song and in the course of singing changed the song so that it made sense for that particular moment. Although I was not consciously aware of it, this was one of my earliest experiences with how my music was supposed to *function*. This music was to be integrative of and consistent with

everything I was doing at that time; it was to be tied to activities that went beyond artistic affairs such as concerts, dances, and church meetings.

The next level of awareness came while in jail. I had grown up in a rural area outside the city limits, riding a bus to public school or driving to college. My life had been a pretty consistent, balanced blend of church, school, and proper upbringing. I was aware of a Black educated class that taught me in high school and college, of taxi cabs I never rode in, and of people who used buses I never boarded. I went to school with their children. 6

In jail with me were all these people. All ages. In my section were women from about thirteen to eighty years old. Ministers' wives and teachers and teachers' wives who had only nodded at me or clapped at a concert or spoken to my mother. A few people from my classes. A large number of people who rode segregated city buses. One or two women who had been drinking along the two-block stretch of Little Harlem as the march went by. Very quickly, clashes arose: around age, who would have authority, what was proper behavior? 7

The Albany Movement was already a singing movement, and we took the songs to jail. There the songs I had sung because they made me feel good or because they said what I thought about a specific issue did something. I would start a song and everybody would join in. After the song, the differences among us would not be as great. Somehow, making a song required an expression of that which was common to us all. The songs did not feel like the same songs I had sung in college. This music was like an instrument, like holding a tool in your hand. 8

I found that although I was younger than many of the women in my section of the jail, I was asked to take on leadership roles. First as a song leader and then in most other matters concerning the group, especially in discussions, or when speaking with prison officials. 9

I fell in love with that kind of music. I saw that to define music as something you listen to, something that pleases you, is very different from defining it as an instrument with which you can drive a point. In both instances, you can have the same song. But using it as an instrument makes it a different kind of music. 10

The next level of awareness occurred during the first mass meeting after my release from jail. I was asked to lead the song that I had changed after the first march. When I opened my mouth and began to sing, there was a force and power within myself I had never heard before. Somehow this music—music I could use as an instrument to do things with, music that was mine to shape and change so that it made the statement I needed to make—released a kind of 11 power and required a level of concentrated energy I did not know I had. I liked the feeling.

12 For several years, I worked with the Movement eventually doing Civil Rights songs with the Freedom Singers. The Freedom Singers used the songs, interspersed with narrative, to convey the story of the Civil Rights Movement's struggles. The songs were more powerful than spoken conversation. They became a major way of making people who were not on the scene feel the intensity of what was happening in the South. Hopefully, they would move the people to take a stand, to organize support groups or participate in various projects.

13 The Georgia Sea Island Singers, whom I first heard at the Newport Festival, were a major link. Bessie Jones, coming from within twenty miles of Albany, Georgia, had a repertoire and song-leading style I recognized from the churches I had grown up in. She, along with John Davis, would talk about songs that Black people had sung as slaves and what those songs meant in terms of their struggle to be free. The songs did not sound like the spirituals I had sung in college choirs; they sounded like the songs I had grown up with in church. There I had been told the songs had to do with worship of Jesus Christ.

14 The next few years I spent focusing on three components: (1) The music I had found in the Civil Rights Movement. (2) Songs of the Georgia Sea Island Singers and other traditional groups, and the ways in which those songs were linked to the struggles of Black peoples at earlier times. (3) Songs of the church that now sounded like those traditional songs and came close to having, for many people, the same kind of freeing power.

15 There was another experience that helped to shape my present-day use of music. After getting out of jail, the mother of the church my father pastored was at the mass meeting. She prayed, a prayer I had heard hundreds of times. I had focused on its sound, tune, rhythm, chant, whether the moans came at the proper pace and intensity. That morning I heard every word that she said. She did not have to change one word of prayer she had been praying for much of her Christian life for me to know she was addressing the issues we were facing at that moment. More than her personal prayer, it felt like an analysis of the Albany, Georgia, Black community.

16 My collection, study, and creation of Black music has been, to a large extent, about freeing the sounds and the words and the messages from casings in which they have been put, about hearing clearly what the music has to say about Black people and their struggle.

17 When I first began to search, I looked for what was then being called folk music, rather than for other Black forms, such as jazz, rhythm and blues, or gospel. It slowly dawned on me that during the Movement we had used all

those forms. When we were relaxing in the office, we made up songs using popular rhythm and blues tunes; songs based in rhythm and blues also came out of jails, especially from the sit-in movement and the march to Selma, Alabama. "Oh Wallace, You Never Can Jail Us All" is an example from Selma. "You Better Leave Segregation Alone" came out of the Nashville Freedom Rides and was based on a bit by Little Willie John, "You Better Leave My Kitten Alone." Gospel choirs became the major musical vehicle in the urban center of Birmingham, with the choir led by Carlton Reese. There was also a gospel choir in the Chicago work, as well as an instrumental ensemble led by Ben Branch.

Jazz had not been a strong part of my musical life. I began to hear it as I 18 traveled north. Thelonious Monk and Charlie Mingus played on the first SNCC benefit at Carnegie Hall. I heard of and then heard Coltrane. Then I began to pick up the pieces that had been laid by Charlie Parker and Coleman Hawkins and whole lifetimes of music. This music had no words. But, it had power, intensity, and movement under various degrees of pressure; it had vocal texture and color. I could feel that the music knew how it felt to be Black and Angry. Black and Down, Black and Loved, Black and Fighting.

I now believe that Black music exists in every place where Black people run, 19 every corner where they live, every level on which they struggle. We have been here a long while, in many situations. It takes all that we have created to sing our song. I believe that Black musicians/artists have a responsibility to be conscious of their world and to let their consciousness be heard in their songs.

And we need it all—blues, gospel, ballads, children's games, dance, rhythms, 20 jazz, lovesongs, topical songs—doing what it has always done. We need Black music that functions in relation to the people and community who provide the nurturing compost that makes its creation and continuation possible.

## Thinking Critically About Content

1. Reagon divides and classifies music in at least three different ways. What are these categories?
2. What are the main differences in these categories?
3. What does Reagon mean when she says, "It takes all that we have created to sing our song" (paragraph 19)?

## Thinking Critically About Purpose and Audience

4. What do you think Reagon's purpose is in this essay?
5. What makes this purpose both personal and social?
6. Who do you think is Reagon's main audience?

### Thinking Critically About Essays

7. Explain how the topic sentence works in paragraph 5. Does it supply the controlling idea for the entire paragraph?
8. Choose a paragraph from this essay, and explain whether or not it is unified. Be as specific as possible.
9. What do you think "in our hands" means in the title of this essay?
10. What role does music play in your life? Divide and classify its role in your life over the years.

**Marion Winik**

## WHAT ARE FRIENDS FOR?

### Focusing Your Attention

1. Who do you rely on to talk out your problems? To confide in? To tell secrets to? How do these people fit into your life? How do you fit into theirs?
2. In the essay you are about to read, the author divides and classifies the types of friends people generally have. What do you think these types are?

### Expanding Your Vocabulary

The following words are important to your understanding of this essay.

**half-slip:** undergarment worn by women (paragraph 1)

**innumerable:** too many to count (paragraph 2)

**Aquarena Springs:** a theme park in San Marcos, Texas, that is now a preservation and education center (paragraph 2)

**infallible:** error-free (paragraph 6)

**nostalgic:** a combination of pleasure and sadness (paragraph 6)

**binges:** enjoyable activities in excessive amounts (paragraph 7)

**crackerbox subdivision:** secluded neighborhood (paragraph 8)

**indispensable:** absolutely necessary (paragraph 8)

**wistful:** nostalgic (paragraph 10)

**ill-conceived:** poorly planned (paragraph 10)

**do in:** destroy (paragraph 10)
**inopportune:** not suitable (paragraph 11)
**tonic:** boost (paragraph 14)

I was thinking about how everybody can't be everything to each other, but some people can be something to each other, thank God, from the ones whose shoulder you cry on to the ones whose half-slips you borrow to the nameless ones you chat with in the grocery line. 1

Buddies, for example, are the workhorses of the friendship world, the people out there on the front lines, defending you from loneliness and boredom. They call you up, they listen to your complaints, they celebrate your successes and curse your misfortunes, and you do the same for them in return. They hold out through innumerable crises before concluding that the person you're dating is no good, and even then understand if you ignore their good counsel. They accompany you to a movie with subtitles or to see the diving pig at Aquarena Springs. They feed your cat when you are out of town and pick you up from the airport when you get back. They come over to help you decide what to wear on a date. Even if it is with that creep. 2

What about family members? Most of them are people you just got stuck with, and though you love them, you may not have very much in common. But there is that rare exception, the Relative Friend. It is your cousin, your brother, maybe even your aunt. The two of you share the same views of the other family members. Meg never should have divorced Martin. He was the best thing that ever happened to her. You can confirm each other's memories of things that happened a long time ago. Don't you remember when Uncle Hank and Daddy had that awful fight in the middle of Thanksgiving dinner? Grandma always hated Grandpa's stamp collection; she probably left the windows open during the hurricane on purpose. 3

While so many family relationships are tinged with guilt and obligation, a relationship with a Relative Friend is relatively worry-free. You don't even have to hide your vices from this delightful person. When you slip out Aunt Joan's back door for a cigarette, she is already there. 4

Then there is that special guy at work. Like all the other people at the job site, at first he's just part of the scenery. But gradually he starts to stand out from the crowd. Your friendship is cemented by jokes about co-workers and thoughtful favors around the office. Did you see Ryan's hair? Want half my bagel? Soon you know the names of his turtles, what he did last Friday night, exactly which model CD player he wants for his birthday. His handwriting is as familiar to you as your own. 5

6 Though you invite each other to parties, you somehow don't quite fit into each other's outside lives. For this reason, the friendship may not survive a job change. Company gossip, once an infallible source of entertainment, soon awkwardly accentuates the distance between you. But wait. Like School Friends, Work Friends share certain memories which acquire a nostalgic glow after about a decade.

7 A Faraway Friend is someone you grew up with or went to school with or lived in the same town as until one of you moved away. Without a Faraway Friend, you would never get any mail addressed in handwriting. A Faraway Friend calls late at night, invites you to her wedding, always says she is coming to visit but rarely shows up. An actual visit from a Faraway Friend is a cause for celebration and binges of all kinds. Cigarettes, Chips Ahoy, bottles of tequila.

8 Faraway Friends go through phases of intense communication, then may be out of touch for many months. Either way, the connection is always there. A conversation with your Faraway Friend always helps to put your life in perspective: When you feel you've hit a dead end, come to a confusing fork in the road, or gotten lost in some crackerbox subdivision of your life, the advice of the Faraway Friend—who has the big picture, who is so well acquainted with the route that brought you to this place—is indispensable.

9 Another useful function of the Faraway Friend is to help you remember things from a long time ago, like the name of your seventh-grade history teacher, what was in that really good stir-fry, or exactly what happened that night on the boat with the guys from Florida.

10 Ah, the Former Friend. A sad thing. At best a wistful memory, at worst a dangerous enemy who is in possession of many of your deepest secrets. But what was it that drove you apart? A misunderstanding, a betrayed confidence, an unrepaid loan, an ill-conceived flirtation. A poor choice of spouse can do in a friendship just like that. Going into business together can be a serious mistake. Time, money, distance, cult religions: all noted friendship killers. You quit doing drugs, you're not such good friends with your dealer anymore.

11 And lest we forget, there are the Friends You Love to Hate. They call at inopportune times. They say stupid things. They butt in, they boss you around, they embarrass you in public. They invite themselves over. They take advantage. You've done the best you can, but they need professional help. On top of all this, they love you to death and are convinced they're your best friend on the planet.

12 So why do you continue to be involved with these people? Why do you tolerate them? On the contrary, the real question is, What would you do without them? Without Friends You Love to Hate, there would be nothing to talk about with your other friends. Their problems and their irritating stunts provide a reliable source

of conversation for everyone they know. What's more, Friends You Love to Hate make you feel good about yourself, since you are obviously in so much better shape than they are. No matter what these people do, you will never get rid of them. As much as they need you, you need them too.

At the other end of the spectrum are Hero Friends. These people are better than the rest of us, that's all there is to it. Their career is something you wanted to be when you grew up—painter, forest ranger, tireless doer of good. They have beautiful homes filled with special handmade things presented to them by villagers in the remote areas they have visited in their extensive travels. Yet they are modest. They never gossip. They are always helping others, especially those who have suffered a death in the family or an illness. You would think people like this would just make you sick, but somehow they don't. 13

A New Friend is a tonic unlike any other. Say you meet her at a party. In your bowling league. At a Japanese conversation class, perhaps. Wherever, whenever, there's that spark of recognition. The first time you talk, you can't believe how much you have in common. Suddenly, your life story is interesting again, your insights fresh, your opinion valued. Your various shortcomings are as yet completely invisible. 14

It's almost like falling in love. 15

### Thinking Critically About Content

1. How many types of friends does Winik introduce? What are they?
2. On what basis does Winik create these categories?
3. In what ways is a new friend "a tonic" (paragraph 14)?

### Thinking Critically About Purpose and Audience

4. Why do you think Winik wrote this essay?
5. Who would be most interested in this essay?
6. How does this essay make you feel about the role of friends in your life?

### Thinking Critically About Essays

7. How does Winik organize her essay? Why do you think she puts her categories in this order?
8. How does the author develop each category? Use one paragraph to explain your answer.
9. Explain Winik's title.
10. Write a detailed description of one of your friends. Why is this person a friend of yours?

### *Writing Topics: Dividing and Classifying*

Before you begin to write, you might want to review the writing process in Part I.

1. In the first essay, Reagon talks about the changing role of music in her life. Divide and classify one of your interests over the years.
2. Divide and classify your friends into meaningful categories, and write an essay explaining your classification system.
3. What process do you have to go through to come up with an interesting comparison or contrast? How is it different from the process you go through for other rhetorical modes?

CHAPTER 31

# Defining

Here are two essays that show how definition works in two completely different contexts: "How to Find True Love: Or, Rather, How It Finds You" by Lois Smith Brady defines "true love" and suggests ways of finding it. The second essay, "Healing Myself with the Power of Work" by Michael Norlen, explains how work has been a form of lifesaving therapy for the author.

---

**Lois Smith Brady**

## HOW TO FIND TRUE LOVE: OR, RATHER, HOW IT FINDS YOU

### Focusing Your Attention

1. As a student, do you have any advantages over other people in the search for true love? Have you already found true love? How do you know it's "the real thing"?
2. The essay you are about to read defines love. What does "true love" mean for you? What qualities are important to you in a lifetime mate? How will you know the difference between "true love" and just plain "love"?

### Expanding Your Vocabulary

The following words are important to your understanding of this essay.

**metronomes:** devices with pendulums that produce a steady beat for musicians (paragraph 3)

**shimmied:** climbed (paragraph 3)

**powder room:** bathroom, rest room (paragraph 4)

**retreat:** private place (paragraph 4)

**tragicomic novel:** a story that combines elements of comedy and tragedy (paragraph 7)
**Upper West Side:** an area in New York City (paragraph 8)
**apparition:** ghost (paragraph 10)
**dingy:** dark (paragraph 15)
**chronic:** constant (paragraph 18)
**Filofax:** a brand of personal organizers (paragraph 21)
**evoked:** brought to mind (paragraph 21)
**stick it out:** wait patiently (paragraph 25)

1 I began to learn about love in dancing school, at age 12. I remember thinking on the first day I was going to fall madly in love with one of the boys and spend the next years of my life kissing and waltzing.

2 During class, however, I sat among the girls, waiting for a boy to ask me to dance. To my complete shock, I was consistently one of the last to be asked. At first I thought the boys had made a terrible mistake. I was so funny and pretty, and I could beat everyone I knew at tennis and climb trees faster than a cat. Why didn't they dash toward me?

3 Yet class after class, I watched boys dressed in blue blazers and gray pants head toward girls in flowered shifts whose perfect ponytails swung back and forth like metronomes. They fell easily into step with one another in a way that was completely mysterious to me. I came to believe that love belonged only to those who glided, who never shimmied up trees or even really touched the ground.

4 By the time I was 13, I knew how to subtly tilt my head and make my tears fall back into my eyes, instead of down my cheeks, when no one asked me to dance. I also discovered the "powder room," which became my softly lit, reliable retreat. Whenever I started to cry, I'd excuse myself and run in there.

5 I finally stopped crying when I met Matt, who was quiet and hung out on the edges of the room. When we danced for the first time, he wouldn't even look me in the eyes. But he was cute, and he told great stories. We became good buddies, dancing every dance together until the end of school.

6 I learned from him my most important early lesson about romance: that the potential for love exists in corners, in the most unlikely as well as the most obvious places.

7 For years my love life continued to be one long tragicomic novel. In college I fell in love with a tall English major who rode a motorcycle. He stood me up on our sixth date—an afternoon of sky diving. I jumped out of the plane alone and landed in a parking lot.

In my mid-20s, I moved to New York City where love is as hard to find as a legal parking spot. My first Valentine's Day there, I went on a date to a crowded bar on the Upper West Side. Halfway through dinner my date excused himself and never returned. 8

At the time, I lived with a beautiful roommate. Flowers piled up at our door like snowdrifts, and the light on the answering machine always blinked in a panicky way, overloaded with messages from her admirers. Limousines purred outside, with dates waiting for her behind tinted windows. 9

In my mind, love was something behind a tinted window, part apparition, part shadow, definitely unreachable. Whenever I spotted happy-looking couples, I'd wonder where they found love and want to follow them home for the answer. 10

After a few years in the city I got my dream job—writing about weddings for a magazine called *7 Days*. I had to find interesting engaged couples and write up their love stories. I got to ask total strangers the things I'd always wanted to know. 11

I found at least one sure answer to the question "How do you know it's love?" You know when the everyday things surrounding you—the leaves, the shade of light in the sky, a bowl of strawberries—suddenly shimmer with a kind of unreality. 12

You know when the tiny details about another person, ones that are insignificant to most people, seem fascinating and incredible to you. One groom told me he loved everything about his future wife, from her handwriting to the way she scratched on their apartment door like a cat when she came home. One bride said she fell in love with her fiancé because "one night, a moth was flying around a light bulb, and he caught it and let it out the window. I said, 'That's it. He's the guy.'" 13

You also know it's love when you can't stop talking to each other. Almost every couple I've ever interviewed said that on their first or second date, they talked for hours and hours. For some, falling in love is like walking into a soundproof confessional booth, a place where you can tell all. 14

Finding love can be like discovering a gilded ballroom on the other side of your dingy apartment, and at the same time like finding a pair of great old blue jeans that are exactly your size and seem as if you've worn them forever. I can't tell you how many women have told me they knew they were in love because they forgot to wear makeup around their boyfriend. Or because they felt at ease hanging around him in flannel pajamas. There's some modern truth to Cinderella's tale—it's love when you're incredibly comfortable, when the shoe fits perfectly. 15

Finally, I think you're in love if you can make each other laugh at the very worst times—when the IRS is auditing you or when you're driving a convertible in a rainstorm or when your hair is turning gray. As someone once told me, 90 percent of being in love is making each other's lives funnier and easier, all the way to the deathbed. 16

17 Seven years ago I started writing about love and weddings for the *New York Times* in a column called "Vows." And now that I have been on this beat for so long, a strange thing has happened: I'm considered an expert on love. The truth is, love is still mostly a mystery to me. The only thing I can confidently say is this: Love is as plentiful as oxygen. You don't have to be thin, naturally blond, super-successful, socially connected, knowledgeable about politics or even particularly charming to find it.

18 I've interviewed many people who were down on their luck in every way—a ballerina with chronic back problems, a physicist who had been on 112 (he counted) disastrous blind dates, a clarinet player who was a single dad and could barely pay the rent. But love, when they found it, brought humor, candlelight, home-cooked meals, fun, adventure, poetry and long conversations into their lives.

19 When people ask me where to find love, I tell a story about one of my first job interviews. It was with an editor at a famous literary magazine. I had no experience or skills, and he didn't for one second consider hiring me. But he gave me some advice I will never forget. He said, "Go out into the world. Work hard and concentrate on what you love to do, writing. If you become good, we will find you."

20 That's why I always tell people looking for love to wait for that "I won the lottery" feeling—wait, wait, wait! Don't read articles about how to trap, seduce or hypnotize a mate. Don't worry about your lipstick or your height, because it's not going to matter. Just live your life well, take care of yourself, and don't mope too much. Love will find you.

21 Eventually it even found me. At 28, I met my husband in a stationery store. I was buying a typewriter ribbon, and he was looking at Filofaxes. I remember that his eyes perfectly matched his faded jeans. He remembers that my sneakers were full of sand. He still talks about those sneakers and how they evoked his childhood—bonfires by the ocean, driving on the sand in an old Jeep—all those things that he cherished.

22 How did I know that it was true love? Our first real date lasted for nine hours; we just couldn't stop talking. I had never been able to dance in my life, but I could dance with him, perfectly in step. I have learned that it's love when you finally stop tripping over your toes.

23 A year after we met, we married.

24 I have come to cherish writing the "Vows" column. With each story I hear, I have proof that love, optimism, guts, grace, perfect partners and good luck do, in fact, exist.

25 Love, in my opinion, is not a fantasy, not the stuff of romance novels or fairy tales. It's as gritty and real as the subway, it comes around just as regularly, and as long as you can stick it out on the platform, you won't miss it.

### Thinking Critically About Content

1. Restate Brady's definition of "true love" in your own words. Does Brady's definition make sense to you?
2. How does the author say she found true love?
3. What does Brady mean when she says, "Finding love can be . . . like finding a pair of great old blue jeans that are exactly your size and seem as if you've worn them forever" (paragraph 15)?

### Thinking Critically About Purpose and Audience

4. What is Brady's purpose in writing this essay?
5. Who do you think is her primary audience?
6. Does Brady capture the essence of new love in her essay? Which details communicate this message most effectively?

### Thinking Critically About Essays

7. Brady uses similes and metaphors (comparisons of two unlike items) to help her explain what true love is. One example is at the end of the essay when she compares love to a subway: "It's as gritty and real as the subway, it comes around just as regularly, and as long as you can stick it out on the platform, you won't miss it" (paragraph 25). Explain this comparison, and find one other example of this technique.
8. How does Brady organize her definition? Is this the most effective arrangement for her supporting ideas?
9. Choose three transitions in Brady's essay that you think work well. Explain why they are effective.
10. Write a comic response to this essay titled "True Love Doesn't Exist."

---

**Michael Norlen**

## HEALING MYSELF WITH THE POWER OF WORK

### Focusing Your Attention

1. As a student or as an employee in the job market, what advantages do you get from your work? Are these rewards mostly physical or emotional?

2. The essay you are about to read defines depression. Have you ever been depressed? How did you manage your daily responsibilities? How did you pull yourself out of your depression?

### Expanding Your Vocabulary

The following words are important to your understanding of this essay.

***Kansas City Star*:** a daily newspaper published in Missouri (paragraph 1)

**Texaco:** brand of gasoline (paragraph 1)

**perfunctory:** indifferent (paragraph 2)

**indignant:** angry (paragraph 3)

**shadowed:** followed (paragraph 3)

**despondency:** sadness (paragraph 4)

**glimpses:** flashes, brief views (paragraph 5)

**night-dwellers:** people who are active at night (paragraph 6)

**Patsy Cline:** country singer who died in a plane crash at age 30 in 1963 (paragraph 6)

**insidious:** evil (paragraph 8)

**neurons:** nerve endings (paragraph 8)

**synapses:** spaces between nerve endings (paragraph 8)

**serotonin:** a substance that transmits impulses between nerves (paragraph 8)

**dopamine:** a substance that transmits impulses between nerves (paragraph 8)

**manifest:** become noticeable (paragraph 8)

**dispiriting:** depressing (paragraph 8)

**regimen:** diet (paragraph 9)

**antidepressants:** medications to fight depression (paragraph 9)

**tolerance:** resistance, lack of response (paragraph 9)

**Jim Beam:** a brand of bourbon (paragraph 10)

**Coors:** a brand of beer (paragraph 10)

**strewn:** scattered (paragraph 10)

**introverted:** focused on oneself (paragraph 10)

**psychotherapy:** professional counseling (paragraph 11)

**calluses:** hardened areas of the skin (paragraph 11)

**arsenal:** collection of weapons (paragraph 12)
**satiated:** no longer hungry (paragraph 12)

---

"The paper guy's here!" Every Monday morning a cashier at Eckerd's drugstore greets me with these words. A manager gives her a key, and she fishes $3 and change from the cash drawer and pays me for the copies of the *Kansas City Star* sold the previous week. I pick up the 10 or 12 unsold papers and throw them in my car, next to the returns from the supermarket, the doughnut shop, and the Texaco station. 1

Quite a difference from a year ago. Then, I would announce myself in response to a judge's perfunctory order: "Counsel, state your appearance." Instead of delivering papers from 1:30 a.m. to 6 a.m., I spent my nights sleeping and my days in an office, a courtroom, or a library. 2

It all changed 12 months ago. For the second time in six years, I abandoned my solo law practice. I stopped returning phone calls, forgot to pay bills, and ignored court dates. I began to sleep 16 hours a day. By July of last year, I stopped coming into the office, leaving it to fill up with unopened mail and indignant phone messages. By August I was behind on my office rent, and by October my landlord asked me to leave. I ate, but nothing tasted good. I slept, but woke up tired. I felt like a stranger around my wife and two daughters. Thoughts of suicide shadowed me. And in the midst of all this, I knew. *It* had returned. 3

Tracy Thompson, the journalist, calls *It* "The Beast." To Winston Churchill, *It* was his "Black Dog." To me, it is both of these; a nameless, faceless thing that infects me with a despondency so bleak I fear that I will never feel joy again. *It* is depression. Twice now *It* has laid me low. 4

Trying to throw me a lifeline, a friend offered me a job delivering newspapers. To my great surprise, I found myself almost enjoying the job. Contrasted to the stresses of maintaining a law practice, this mindless work of assembling and bundling papers in a dimly lit warehouse was a welcome distraction. When I left the warehouse to deliver the papers, to vending machines, gas stations, and supermarkets, I began to catch glimpses of small joys. 5

After months of hiding from people and avoiding conversation, little by little I got to know some of the night-dwellers. The clerk at the Phillip's station who plays country music and seems to have an obsession with Patsy Cline. The jogger I always pass at 4 a.m. With friendly greetings and idle conversation, these people, whose names I still don't know, began to draw me out of my darkness. 6

At the end of each night I look down at my hands, stained with ink from handling 450 newspapers. I stretch and feel a tightness in my shoulders from lifting the 40- or 50-pound bundles into and out of my car. The grime and the pain 7 serve as wake-up calls for my tired body and mind. And every Sunday morning, when my friend hands me a modest check, I begin to feel just a bit more confident.

8 Depression is an insidious disease. On one level it is about neurons and synapses, seratonin levels, and dopamine readings. On another level it is memories of trauma stashed in dusty corners of the mind that manifest years later in fear and anxiety. And on yet another level it is a crippling, dispiriting mind-set that convinces me I am worthless and helpless.

9 For almost five years I have been on a steady regimen of antidepressants, from Prozac to Serzone. When I build up a tolerance to one drug, my doctor simply switches me to another. Except for some inconvenient side effects, they have been my safety net, stopping my free fall into madness.

10 For most of the same period, I have been in individual or group therapy. I've learned how some of the difficult periods of my life have shaped me and contributed to my depression. The memories of my drunken mother and the Jim Beam and Coors bottles strewn around our rented houses help me understand why I'm so fearful of failure, so introverted and so reluctant to trust others.

11 For all the insight and help I've received from drug therapy and psychotherapy, I still have feelings of worthlessness. Every bout of depression eats away at my self-esteem, and no amount of drugs or talking can restore it. That restoration has to come through a different vehicle. For me, that vehicle is physical work. Every time I look at the calluses on my hands, I realize that this job provides me with a reason to get out of bed.

12 One day soon I'll be ready to leave this job behind, but I'll never again view work as just a paycheck or a daily obligation. It will always be a part of my therapy, my healing. I don't know where my next job will be; in the courtroom, the classroom, or the office. But wherever it is, my work will be a weapon in my arsenal against the attacks I know will come again and again, because the Beast will not be satiated, and the Dog will never be securely leashed.

### Thinking Critically About Content

1. Restate Norlen's definition of depression in your own words. Does Norlen's definition make sense to you?
2. How does the author say he is digging himself out of his depression?
3. What does Norlen mean when he says, "I'll never again view work as just a paycheck or a daily obligation" (paragraph 12)?

### Thinking Critically About Purpose and Audience

4. Why do you think Norlen wrote this essay?
5. Who do you think is his primary audience?

6. Have you ever helped someone who was depressed? What did you do? Explain your answer.

### Thinking Critically About Essays

7. Paragraph 7 ends rather than begins with its controlling idea. Explain how Norlen develops this particular paragraph.
8. How is paragraph 3 organized? Why do you think Norlen puts these facts in this particular order?
9. Choose one paragraph, and explain its tone or mood.
10. Write a summary of this essay for your English class.

### *Writing Topics: Defining*

Before you begin to write, you might want to review the writing process in Part I.

1. In the first essay, Brady defines *true love*. Write your own definition of another state of mind, such as *joy, fear, loneliness*, or *stress*.
2. Using Norlen's method of development through personal narrative, define *work* for your class.
3. Now that you have studied different approaches to the process of definition, what makes a definition effective or useful for you? Apply what you have studied about definition to your answer.

# Analyzing Causes and Effects

In the essays in this chapter, the writers analyze the causes and effects related to their topics. "A Family Dilemma: To Scout or Not to Scout?" by Michael Alvear openly discusses the relationship between boy scouts and gays. The second essay, "Happiness Is Catching" by Stacey Colino, discusses the moods in our lives.

**Michael Alvear**

## A FAMILY DILEMMA: TO SCOUT OR NOT TO SCOUT?

### Focusing Your Attention

1. Think of the last time you had a moral dilemma. What caused the dilemma? How did you handle it?
2. In the essay you are about to read, Michael Alvear looks at the effect on his family of the ruling that the Scouts have a constitutional right to fire gay Scout leaders. What has the greatest impact on your life—your family or your peers? Analyze the effect one of these groups has on your life.

### Expanding Your Vocabulary

The following words are important to your understanding of this essay.

**backlash:** strong negative reaction (paragraph 3)
**municipal:** owned and operated by the town (paragraph 3)
**unsettling:** disturbing (paragraph 5)

**ethical:** moral (paragraph 5)
**quandary:** dilemma (paragraph 7)
**ironically:** surprisingly (paragraph 10)
**inconceivable:** impossible to imagine (paragraph 11)

---

My sister constantly tells me how much her 6-year-old son Ricky (not his real name) adores me. So when he came home with a flier about joining a fun and exciting group for kids his age, she had a tough decision to make. Should she let him join a group that doesn't like his beloved uncle Michael? 1

When the Supreme Court ruled that the Boy Scouts have the constitutional right to fire Scout leaders for being gay, my sister was caught in an agonizing moral dilemma: allowing her son to become a member of America's most family-friendly group meant dishonoring part of her family. 2

The political backlash since the ruling against the Boy Scouts is clear to anyone who reads the local papers. Many cities, believing the Scouts are engaging in discrimination, have told local Scout troops that they can't use parks, schools, and other municipal sites. Companies and charities have withdrawn hundreds of thousands of dollars in support. But what isn't so easy to see is the division the Supreme Court ruling created in millions of families like mine. 3

When my sister first called to tell me she was thinking of putting Ricky in the Cub Scouts (a program run by the Boy Scouts of America), I could hear the torment in her voice. Ricky is a bright, athletic boy who suffers from a shyness so paralyzing he doesn't have any friends. The other day my sister asked who he had played with during recess. "Nobody," he mumbled, looking at the floor. "I just scratched the mosquito bites on my leg till it was time to go back to class." 4

It breaks my sister's heart to see what Ricky's shyness is doing to him. Karate, softball, and soccer leagues helped, but not nearly enough. In another age, my sister wouldn't have thought twice about letting him join the Scouts. But now the decision has taken on an unsettling ethical dimension. 5

"I don't understand why they're making me take sides in my own family," she said about the Boy Scout policy. "In order to help my son I have to abandon my brother." 6

My sister was up against some disturbing questions. Should she violate her sense of family loyalty for the social needs of her son? Or keep her values intact and deny her son the possibility of overcoming his shyness? By saying that troops have the right to fire gay leaders, the Boy Scouts created the unimaginable: a moral quandary about joining the most wholesome group in America. 7

8 My sister was afraid she'd be doing the same thing many parents did a generation ago when they joined country clubs that didn't allow blacks and Jews. They, too, must have rationalized their membership by saying the clubs' wholesome activities would be good for their kids.

9 There was one thing my sister and her husband were not conflicted about: me. "No way are we putting Ricky in the Scouts if this is an issue for you," she said. "Blood is thicker than camping." Still, she wanted to know how I'd feel if my nephew became a Scout.

10 I felt completely torn, but I answered with as much certainty as I could muster. "I am not getting in the way of what's best for a 6-year-old," I told her. Ironically, I found myself trying to persuade her to let Ricky join the Scouts. It's families that teach morality, I argued, not after-school groups. Besides, I added, it's not like the issue will come up during any of the Scouting activities.

11 Or will it? Is it really inconceivable that kids who know why the president of the United States was impeached would ask their Scout leader why gay people aren't allowed in the organization? And what would the scoutmaster's response be? I was shaken by the possibility of my nephew hearing a trusted grown-up trying to convince him that his uncle Michael is someone to be scared of.

12 One night I had a terrible dream of a Boy Scout official pointing me out to Ricky and saying, "See that guy? The one you love more than any other man except your father? He's not allowed in here."

13 I woke up feeling a kind of enraged helplessness. How could I mean so much to my family and so little to so many outside it? Ultimately, I knew I could live with the indignity of my nephew belonging to a group that discriminates against his uncle; what I couldn't live with was the guilt of denying Ricky a chance to improve his life.

14 How can Ricky's parents know what the right thing to do is in this situation? For starters, they plan to get more information before they make a decision. And so my sister, a mom torn between her devotion to her brother and concern for her son, will go to next month's Scout meeting with her husband.

15 Will they put Ricky in the Scouts? I don't know. But as the date of the meeting approaches, I can't help thinking how unfair it is that my sister will have to pass under that imaginary sign that hangs over every Scout gathering: YOUR SON IS WELCOME, BUT YOUR BROTHER IS NOT.

### Thinking Critically About Content

1. What is Alvear analyzing in this essay?
2. What are the causes and effects of the moral dilemma Alvear's sister is struggling with?
3. What is Alvear referring to when he says, "I was shaken by the possibility of my nephew hearing a trusted grown-up trying to convince

him that his uncle Michael is someone to be scared of" (paragraph 11)?

### Thinking Critically About Purpose and Audience

4. What do you think Michael Alvear's purpose is in this essay?
5. Who do you think would find this essay most interesting? Explain your answer.
6. What emotions do you think Alvear is trying to evoke in his readers as he analyzes his family's moral dilemma?

### Thinking Critically About Essays

7. Describe this writer's point of view toward this moral dilemma.
8. The author sets the scene for his essay by explaining his close relationship with his sister's son. Is this an effective beginning? Why or why not?
9. How does Alvear organize his essay? List his main points to answer this question.
10. Analyze your reactions to this situation as Ricky's dad. How would you feel? Why would you feel that way?

**Stacey Colino**

## HAPPINESS IS CATCHING: WHY EMOTIONS ARE CONTAGIOUS

### Focusing Your Attention

1. Are you easily influenced by other people's moods? How do you know this?
2. In the essay you are about to read, Stacey Colino explains how we "catch" the feelings of others. Think of someone who generally makes you happy and someone who usually makes you sad. What is the difference between these two people? How do they each approach life? How do they each relate to you?

### Expanding Your Vocabulary

The following words are important to your understanding of this essay.

**catching:** easily transmitted from one person to another (title)

**contagious:** catching (title)

**elation:** joy, happiness (paragraph 1)
**euphoria:** extreme happiness (paragraph 1)
**inoculate against:** become immune to, resist (paragraph 1)
**milliseconds:** thousandths of a second (paragraph 2)
**primitive:** natural, basic (paragraph 2)
**mimic:** copy (paragraph 2)
**synchronize:** coordinate (paragraph 2)
**extroverts:** outgoing people (paragraph 4)
**engulfed:** completely surrounded, overwhelmed (paragraph 5)
**introverts:** shy, quiet people (paragraph 5)
**susceptible to:** easily influenced by (paragraph 8)
**mimicry:** copying (paragraph 9)

---

1 Researchers have found that emotions, both good and bad, are nearly as contagious as colds and flus. You can catch elation, euphoria, sadness, and more from friends, family, colleagues, even strangers. And once you understand how to protect yourself, you can inoculate yourself against the bad.

2 Mood "infection" happens in milliseconds, says Elaine Hatfield, Ph.D., a professor of psychology at the University of Hawaii in Honolulu and coauthor of *Emotional Contagion* (Cambridge University Press, 1994). And it stems from a primitive instinct: During conversation, we naturally tend to mimic and synchronize our facial expressions, movements, and speech rhythms to match the other person's. "Through this, we come to feel what the person is feeling," explains Dr. Hatfield. In other words, it puts us in touch with their feelings and affects our behavior.

3 Not surprisingly, spouses are especially likely to catch each other's moods, but so are parents, children, and good friends. In fact, a recent study at the University of Texas Medical Branch at Galveston found that depression was highly contagious among college roommates. "The same thing can occur with a spouse or co-worker, where one person is moderately depressed," says study author Thomas E. Joiner Jr., Ph.D., assistant professor of psychiatry and behavioral sciences.

4 Dr. Hatfield's research shows that extroverts and emotionally expressive people tend to transmit their feelings more powerfully. There's also a breed of people who, consciously or not, may want or need you to feel what they feel; they're the ones who live by the adage "misery loves company." They manipulate other

people's moods—perhaps without even realizing it—to gain the upper hand or to feel better about themselves. "They express emotion to get a response—perhaps attention or sympathy," says Ross Buck, Ph.D., professor of communication sciences and psychology at the University of Connecticut.

On the other hand, some personality types are more likely to be engulfed by others' moods. Introverts are vulnerable because they're easily aroused. So are highly sensitive individuals who react physically to emotionally charged situations—their hearts flutter before giving a speech, for example. 5

If anyone knows how quickly moods spread, it's Ginny Graves, 33, a San Francisco writer. Last year, when she was pregnant with her first child, her mood took a nosedive every time she saw a particular friend. 6

"Basically nothing good was going on in her life—she didn't like her job and she was obsessed with her weight," recalls Ginny. "I tried to bolster her up, but whenever I talked to her, I'd feel tense and tired." Afterward, Ginny was left with a case of the moody blues that lingered a day or so. 7

Indeed, there's some evidence that women may be particularly susceptible to catching moods, perhaps because we're better able to read other people's emotions and body language, according to psychologist Judith Hall, Ph.D., professor of psychology at Northeastern University in Boston. 8

Since women perceive facial expressions so readily, we may be more likely to mimic them—and wind up sharing the feeling. Just how mimicry leads to catching a mood is not known, notes John T. Cacioppo, Ph.D., professor of psychology at Ohio State University and coauthor of *Emotional Contagion.* One theory holds that when you frown or smile, the muscular movements in your face alter blood flow to the brain, which in turn affects mood; another theory maintains that the sensations associated with specific facial expressions trigger emotional memories—and hence the feelings—linked with those particular expressions. 9

With any luck, we catch the happy moods—infectious laughter at a dinner party or a colleague's enthusiasm for a project, for instance. Some psychologists suspect, however, that negative emotions—especially depression and anxiety—may be the most infectious of all. "For women, stress and depression are like emotional germs—they jump from one person to the next," notes Ellen McGrath, Ph.D., a psychologist in Laguna Beach, California, and author of *When Feeling Bad Is Good* (Bantam, 1994). 10

Being susceptible to other people's moods does make for a rich emotional life. But let's face it: When you catch a happy mood, you don't want to change it. Downbeat emotions are harder to deal with. And who wants her life to be ruled by other people's bad moods? 11

Fortunately, there are ways to protect yourself from unpleasant emotions, while letting yourself catch the good ones. For starters, pay attention to how you feel around different people, suggests Dr. McGrath. Then label your emotions—noting, 12 for example, whether you feel optimistic around your best friend or gloomy after seeing your aunt. Then ask yourself if you're feeling what you do because *you* actually feel that way or because you've caught a mood from the other person. Just recognizing that an emotion belongs to someone else, not you, can be enough to short-circuit its transmission.

13 Once you know how people affect you, you can be more selective about whom you spend time with. Instead of going on an all-day outing with family members who bring you down, for instance, try spending shorter periods of time with them. Another solution is to give yourself a time-out: It could be as simple as a restroom break during an intense dinner.

14 Putting up emotional barriers is not the answer, though. If the channels are open, both positive and negative influences flow in. Shutting out the bad precludes you from catching joyful moods, too. Instead, it's better to monitor the floodgates—and to come to your own rescue when you feel yourself catching other people's negativity. And if you get swept up in another person's excitement? Sit back and enjoy the ride.

### Thinking Critically About Content

1. What is Colino analyzing in this essay? How does her title help focus her analysis?
2. Name two causes and two effects of people's moods.
3. How does Colino suggest that you can protect yourself from unpleasant emotions?

### Thinking Critically About Purpose and Audience

4. Why do you think Colino wrote this essay?
5. Considering that this essay was originally published in a magazine called *Family Circle*, who do you think Colino's intended audience is? Explain your answer.
6. Are you susceptible to other people's moods? Why or why not?

### Thinking Critically About Essays

7. The author of this essay quotes many authorities in the field of psychology. Are these quotations convincing to you? Explain your answer.
8. Which of Colino's paragraphs deal primarily with causes? Which with effects? Do you think this is a good balance? Explain your answer.
9. Find five transitions in Colino's essay that work well, and explain why they are effective.

10. Discuss the emotional climate in the place where you live. Are you able to separate your emotions from those of the people you live with? Are you affected by the emotions of roommates, friends, family? How will you manage emotional swings after reading this essay?

### *Writing Topics: Analyzing Causes and Effects*

Before you begin to write, you might want to review the writing process in Part I.

1. Are you currently dealing with any moral dilemmas? What are they? Does one bother you more than the others? Write an essay analyzing the causes and effects of this particular dilemma.
2. In "Happiness is Catching," Stacey Colino talks about how contagious moods are. Have you ever been responsible for giving a good or bad mood to someone? What were the circumstances? How did someone "catch" your mood? Write an essay analyzing the causes and effects of the situation.
3. How would looking closely at causes and effects help you live a better life? How would the process of discovering causes and effects help you think through your decisions and problems more logically? Explain your answer.

# Arguing

In all three essays in this chapter, the writers state their evidence clearly and convincingly. In the first essay, "The Neglected Heart," Thomas Lickona, a psychologist and educator at the State University of New York at Cortland, tries to persuade his readers that sexual relationships can harm people emotionally if they are not ready for the consequences. The small numbers printed throughout the essay refer to the endnotes that follow the essay, where the writer lists the books and articles he quotes throughout the essay.

The next two essays in this chapter deal with a topic that has been a part of American society for a long time—controlling gang violence. They present two different sides of the issue. The first essay, written by Richard Willard and published in February 1999 in *Supreme Court Debates*, claims that anti-loitering laws can reduce gang violence. The second essay, written by David Cole, argues that anti-loitering laws are not effective. It was first published in February 1999 in *The Nation*.

**Thomas Lickona**

## THE NEGLECTED HEART

**Focusing Your Attention**

1. At what age or in what situation do you think two people are ready to engage in sexual relations?
2. In the essay you are about to read, the writer explains that many emotional problems are caused when people who are too young engage in sexual relations. What do you think some of these emotional problems are?

### Expanding Your Vocabulary

The following words are important to your understanding of this essay.

**hazards:** dangers (paragraph 1)
**ironic:** surprising (paragraph 4)
**self-recrimination:** blaming oneself (heading above paragraph 10)
**interlude:** brief experience (paragraph 13)
**reluctant:** hesitant (paragraph 14)
**persistent:** insistent (paragraph 14)
**IUD:** intrauterine device, a contraceptive used by women (paragraph 16)
**steeled:** hardened (paragraph 16)
**promiscuous:** sexually active with many partners (paragraph 16)
**sexual liberation:** freedom to engage in sex without guilt (paragraph 23)
**hypocrites:** people who pretend to be pure but are not (paragraph 25)
**self-loathing:** self-hatred (paragraph 28)
**debasement:** reduced value (heading above paragraph 32)
**Freud:** Sigmund Freud, 1856–1939, founder of the field of psychoanalysis (paragraph 33)
**restraint:** self-control (paragraph 35)
**Tailhook:** a scandal involving sexual assaults that took place during a 1991 U.S. Navy convention (paragraph 36)
**egregious:** extremely bad (paragraph 36)
**mimic:** copy (paragraph 37)
**undermines:** weakens (paragraph 39)
**subverting:** damaging, destroying (paragraph 39)
**unchecked:** uncontrolled (paragraph 39)
**run amok:** go wild (paragraph 39)
**hedonism:** selfish pleasure (paragraph 39)
**trivialized:** made to seem unimportant (paragraph 39)
**degraded:** reduced in value (paragraph 39)
**demeaning:** degrading, cheapening (paragraph 41)
**ruptured:** broken, cut (paragraph 46)
**turmoil:** confusion (paragraph 47)

**aftermath:** consequence, result (paragraph 49)
**stunting:** stopping at too early a stage of development (heading above paragraph 53)
**thwarted:** prevented (paragraph 57)
**desolation:** despair, feelings of emptiness (paragraph 58)
**amply:** very (paragraph 59)

---

You didn't get pregnant. You didn't get AIDS. So why do you feel so bad?
—LESLEE UNRUH, ABSTINENCE EDUCATOR

There is no condom for the heart.
—SIGN AT A SEX EDUCATION CONFERENCE

1 In discussions of teen sex, much is said about the dangers of pregnancy and disease—but far less about the emotional hazards. And that's a problem, because the destructive psychological consequences of temporary sexual relationships are very real. Being aware of them can help a young person make and stick to the decision to avoid premature sexual involvement.

2 That's not to say we should downplay the physical dangers of uncommitted sex. Pregnancy is a life-changing event. Sexually transmitted disease (STD)—and there are now more than 20 STDs—can rob you of your health and even your life. Condoms don't remove these dangers. Condoms have an annual failure rate of 10 percent to 30 percent in preventing pregnancy because of human error in using them and because they sometimes leak, break, or slip off. Condoms reduce but by no means eliminate the risk of AIDS. In a 1993 analysis of 11 different medical studies, condoms were found to have a 31 percent average failure rate in preventing the sexual transmission of the AIDS virus.[1] Finally, condoms do little or nothing to protect against the two STDs infecting at least one-third of sexually active teenage girls: human papilloma virus (the leading cause of cervical cancer) and chlamydia (the leading cause of infertility), both of which can be transmitted by skin-to-skin contact in the entire genital area, only a small part of which is covered by the condom.[2]

3 Why is it so much harder to discuss sex and emotional hurt—to name and talk about the damaging psychological effects that can come from premature sexual involvement? For one thing, most of us have never heard this aspect of sex discussed. Our parents didn't talk to us about it. The media don't talk about it. And the heated debate about condoms in schools typically doesn't say much about the fact that condoms do nothing to make sex emotionally safe. When it comes to trying to explain to their children or students how early sexuality can do

harm to one's personality and character as well as to one's health, many adults are simply at a loss for words, or reduced to vague generalities such as "You're too young" or "You're not ready" or "You're not mature enough."

This relative silence about the emotional side of sex is ironic, because the emotional dimension of sex is what makes it distinctively human. 4

What in fact are the emotional or psychological consequences of premature, uncommitted sex? These consequences vary among individuals. Some emotional consequences are short-term but still serious. Some of them last a long time, sometimes even into marriage and parenting. Many of these psychological consequences are hard to imagine until they've been experienced. In all cases, the emotional consequences of sexual experiences are not to be taken lightly. A moment's reflection reminds us that emotional problems can have damaging, even crippling, effects on a person's ability to lead a happy and productive life. 5

Let's look at 10 negative psychological consequences of premature sexual involvement. 6

## 1. Worry About Pregnancy and AIDS

For many sexually active young people, the fear of becoming pregnant or getting AIDS is a major emotional stress. 7

Russell Henke, health education coordinator in the Montgomery County (Maryland) Public Schools, says, "I see kids going to the nurses in schools, crying a day after their first sexual experience, and wanting to be tested for AIDS. They have done it, and now they are terrified. For some of them, that's enough. They say, 'I don't want to have to go through that experience anymore.'"[3] 8

A high school girl told a nurse: "I see some of my friends buying home pregnancy tests, and they are so worried and so distracted every month, afraid that they might be pregnant. It's a relief to me to be a virgin." 9

## 2. Regret and Self-Recrimination

Girls, especially, need to know in advance the sharp regret that so many young women feel after becoming sexually involved. 10

Says one high school girl: "I get upset when I see my friends losing their virginity to some guy they've just met. Later, after the guy's dumped them, they come to me and say, 'I wish I hadn't done it.'"[4] A ninth-grade girl who slept with eight boys in junior high says, "I'm young, but I feel old." 11

Girls are more vulnerable than boys because girls are more likely to think of sex as a way to "show you care." They're more likely to see sex as a sign of commitment in the relationship. 12

If a girl expects a sexual interlude to be loving, she may very well feel cheated and used when the boy doesn't show a greater romantic interest after the event. As one 15-year-old girl describes her experience: "I didn't expect the guy to marry me, but I never expected him to avoid me in school." 13

14 Bob Bartlett, who teaches a freshman sexuality class in a Richfield, Minnesota, high school, shares the following story of regret on the part of one of his students (we'll call her Sandy):

> Sandy, a bright and pretty girl, asked to see Mr. Bartlett during her lunch period. She explained that she had never had a boyfriend, so she was excited when a senior asked her out.
>
> After they dated for several weeks, the boy asked her to have sex with him. She was reluctant; he was persistent. She was afraid of appearing immature and losing him, so she consented.
>
> "Did it work?" Mr. Bartlett asked gently. "Did you keep him?"
>
> Sandy replied: "For another week. We had sex again, and then he dropped me. He said I wasn't good enough. There was no spark.
>
> "I know what you're going to say. I take your class. I know now that he didn't really love me. I feel so stupid, so cheap."[5]

15 Sandy hoped, naively, that sex would keep the guy. Here is another high school girl, writing to an advice column about a different kind of regret. She wishes she could lose the guy she's involved with, but she feels trapped by their sexual relationship.

> I am 16, a junior in high school, and like nearly all the other girls here, I have already lost my virginity. Although most people consider this subject very personal, I feel the need to share this part of my life with girls who are trying to decide whether to have sex for the first time.
>
> Sex does not live up to the glowing reports and hype you see in the movies. It's no big deal. In fact, it's pretty disappointing.
>
> I truly regret that my first time was with a guy that I didn't care that much about. I am still going out with him, which is getting to be a problem. I'd like to end this relationship and date others, but after being so intimate, it's awfully tough.
>
> Since that first night, he expects sex on every date, like we are married or something. When I don't feel like it, we end up in an argument. It's like I owe it to him. I don't think this guy is in love with me, at least he's never said so. I know deep down that I am not in love with him either, and this makes me feel sort of cheap.
>
> I realize now that this is a very big step in a girl's life. After you've done it, things are never the same. It changes everything.
>
> My advice is, don't be in such a rush. It's a headache and a worry. (Could I be pregnant?) Sex is not for entertainment. It should be a commitment. Be smart and save yourself for someone you wouldn't mind spending the rest of your life with.
>
> —Sorry I Didn't and Wish I Could Take It Back[6]

Regret over uncommitted sexual relationships can last for years. I recently received a letter from a 33-year-old woman, now a psychiatrist, who is very much concerned about the sexual pressures and temptations facing young people today. She wanted to share the lessons she had learned about sex the hard way. After high school, she says, she spent a year abroad as an exchange student. 16

> I was a virgin when I left, but I felt I was protected. I had gotten an IUD so I could make my own decisions if and when I wanted. I had steeled myself against commitment. I was never going to marry or have children; I was going to have a career. During that year abroad, from 17½ to 18½, I was very promiscuous.
>
> But the fact is, it cost me to be separated from myself. The longest-standing and deepest wound I gave myself was heartfelt. That sick, used feeling of having given a precious part of myself—my soul—to so many and for nothing, still aches. I never imagined I'd pay so dearly and for so long.

This woman is happily married now, she says, and has a good sexual relationship with her husband. But she still carries the emotional scar of those early sexual experiences. She wants young people to know that "sex without commitment is very risky for the heart." 17

### 3. Guilt

Guilt is a special form of regret—a strong sense of having done something morally wrong. Guilt is a normal and healthy moral response, a sign that one's conscience is working. 18

In his book for teenagers, *Love, Dating, and Sex,* George Eager tells the story of a well-known speaker who was addressing a high school assembly. The speaker was asked, "What do you most regret about your high school days?" 19

He answered, "The thing I most regret about high school is the time I single-handedly destroyed a girl." 20

Eager offers this advice to young men: "When the breakup comes, it's usually a lot tougher on the girls than it is on the guys. It's not something you want on your conscience—that you caused a girl to have deep emotional problems." 21

One 16-year-old boy says he stopped having sex with girls when he saw and felt guilty about the pain he was causing: "You see them crying and confused. They say they love you, but you don't love them." 22

Even in an age of sexual liberation, a lot of people who are having sex nevertheless have a guilty conscience about it. The guilt may come, as in the case of the young man just quoted, from seeing the hurt you've caused other people. 23

The guilt may come from knowing that your parents would be upset if they knew you were having sex. Or it may stem from your religious convictions. Christianity, Judaism, and Islam, for example, all teach that sex is a gift from God reserved for marriage and that sexual relations outside marriage are morally wrong. 24

25 Sometimes guilt about their sexual past ends up crippling people when they become parents by keeping them from advising their own children not to become sexually involved. According to counselor Dr. Carson Daly: "Because these parents can't bear to be considered hypocrites, or to consider themselves hypocrites, they don't give their children the sexual guidance they very much need."[8]

### 4. Loss of Self-Respect and Self-Esteem

26 Many people suffer a loss of self-esteem when they find out they have a sexually transmitted disease. For example, according to the Austin, Texas–based Medical Institute for Sexual Health, more than 80 percent of people with herpes say they feel "less confident" and "less desirable sexually."[9]

27 But even if a person is fortunate enough to escape sexually transmitted disease, temporary sexual relationships can lower the self-respect of both the user and the used.

28 Sometimes casual sex lowers self-esteem, leading a person into further casual sex, which leads to further loss of self-esteem in an oppressive cycle from which it may be hard to break free. This pattern is described by a college senior, a young woman who works as a residence hall director:

> There are girls in our dorm who have had multiple pregnancies and multiple abortions. They tend to be filled with self-loathing. But because they have so little self-esteem, they will settle for any kind of attention from guys. So they keep going back to the same kind of destructive situations and relationships that got them into trouble in the first place.

29 On both sides of dehumanized sex, there is a loss of dignity and self-worth. One 20-year-old college male confides: "You feel pretty crummy when you get drunk at a party and have sex with some girl, and then the next morning you can't even remember who she was."

30 Another college student describes the loss of self-respect that followed his first sexual "conquest":

> I finally got a girl into bed—actually it was in a car—when I was 17. I thought it was the hottest thing there was, but then she started saying she loved me and getting clingy.
>
> I figured out that there had probably been a dozen guys before me who thought they had "conquered" her, but who were really just objects of her need for security. That realization took all the wind out of my sails. I couldn't respect someone who gave in as easily as she did.
>
> I was amazed to find that after four weeks of having sex as often as I wanted, I was tired of her. I didn't see any point in continuing the

relationship. I finally dumped her, which made me feel even worse, because I could see that she was hurting. I felt pretty low.[10]

People aren't things. When we treat them as if they were, we not only hurt them; we lose respect for ourselves. 31

## 5. The Corruption of Character and the Debasement of Sex

When people treat others as sexual objects and exploit them for their own pleasure, they not only lose self-respect, they corrupt their characters and debase their sexuality in the process. 32

Good character consists of virtues such as respect, responsibility, honesty, fairness, caring, and self-control. With regard to sex, the character trait of self-control is particularly crucial. The breakdown of sexual self-control is a big factor in many of the sex-related problems that plague our society: rape, promiscuity, pornography, addiction to sex, sexual harassment, the sexual abuse of children, sexual infidelity in marriage, and the serious damage to families many of these problems cause. It was Freud who said—and it is now obvious how right he was—that sexual self-control is essential for civilization. 33

Sex frequently corrupts character by leading people to tell lies in order to get sex. The Medical Institute for Sexual Health reports: "Almost all studies show that many sexually active people will lie if they think it will help them have sex."[11] Common lies: "I love you" and "I've never had a sexually transmitted disease." 34

Because sex is powerful, once sexual restraint is set aside, it easily takes over individuals and relationships. Consider the highly sexualized atmosphere that now characterizes many high schools. A high school teacher in Indiana says, "The air is thick with sex talk. Kids in the halls will say—boy to girl, girl to boy—'I want to f--- you.'" 35

In a 1993 study by the American Association of University Women, four out of five high school students—85 percent of girls and 75 percent of boys—said they have experienced "unwelcome sexual behavior that interferes with my life" in school.[12] An example: A boy backs a 14-year-old girl up against her locker, day after day. Says Nan Stein, a Wellesley College researcher: "There's a Tailhook happening in every school. Egregious behavior is going on." 36

Another recently reported example of this corruption of character is the Spur Posse club at Lakewood High School in suburban Los Angeles. Members of this club competed to see how many girls they could sleep with; one claimed he had slept with 63. Sadly, elementary school–age children are beginning to mimic such behavior. In a suburb of Pittsburgh, an assistant superintendent reports that sixth-grade boys were found playing a sexual contact game; the object of the game was to earn points by touching girls' private parts, the most points being awarded for "going all the way." 37

38 In this sex-out-of-control environment, even rape is judged permissible by many young people. In a 1988 survey of students in grades six through nine, the Rhode Island Rape Crisis Center found that two out of three boys and 49 percent of the girls said it was "acceptable for a man to force sex on a woman if they have been dating for six months or more."[13] In view of attitudes like these, it's easy to understand why date rape has become such a widespread problem.

39 In short, sex that isn't tied to love and commitment undermines character by subverting self-control, respect, and responsibility. Unchecked, sexual desires and impulses easily run amok and lead to habits of hedonism and using others for one's personal pleasure. In the process, sexual intercourse loses its meaning, beauty, and specialness; instead of being a loving, uniquely intimate expression of two people's commitment to each other, sex is trivialized and degraded.

## 6. Shaken Trust and Fear of Commitment

40 Young people who feel used or betrayed after the break-up of a sexual relationship may experience difficulty in future relationships.

41 Some sexually exploited people, as we've seen, develop such low self-esteem that they seek any kind of attention, even if it's another short-lived and demeaning sexual relationship. But other people, once burned, withdraw. They have trouble trusting; they don't want to get burned again.

42 Usually, this happens to the girl. She begins to see guys as interested in just one thing: sex. Says one young woman: "Besides feeling cheap [after several sexual relationships], I began to wonder if there would ever be anyone who would love and accept me without demanding that I do something with my body to earn that love."[14]

43 However, boys can also experience loss of trust and fear of commitment as a result of a broken relationship that involved sex. Brian, a college senior, tells how this happened to him:

> I first had intercourse with my girlfriend when we were 15. I'd been going with her for almost a year, and I loved her very much. She was friendly, outgoing, charismatic. We'd done everything but have intercourse, and then one night she asked if we could go all the way.
>
> A few days later, we broke up. It was the most painful time of my life. I had opened myself up to her more than I had to anybody, even my parents.
>
> I was depressed, moody, nervous. My friends dropped me because I was so bummed out. I felt like a failure. I dropped out of sports. My grades weren't terrific.
>
> I didn't go out again until I got to college. I've had mostly one-night stands in the last couple of years.
>
> I'm afraid of falling in love.[15]

## 7. Rage over Betrayal

Sometimes the emotional reaction to being "dumped" isn't just a lack of trust or fear of commitment. It's rage. 44

Every so often, the media carry a story about a person who had this rage reaction and then committed an act of violence against the former boyfriend or girlfriend. Read these accounts, and you'll find that sex was almost always a part of the broken relationship. 45

Of course, people often feel angry when somebody breaks up with them, even if sex has not been involved. But the sense of betrayal is usually much greater if sex has been part of the relationship. Sex can be emotional dynamite. It can lead a person to think that the relationship is really serious, that both people really love each other. It can create a very strong emotional bond that hurts terribly when it's ruptured—especially if it seems that the other person never had the same commitment. And the resulting sense of betrayal can give rise to rage, even violence. 46

## 8. Depression and Suicide

In *Sex and the Teenager,* Kieran Sawyer writes: "The more the relationship seems like real love, the more the young person is likely to invest, and the deeper the pain and hurt if the relationship breaks up."[16] Sometimes the emotional turmoil caused by the rupture of a sexual relationship leads to deep depression. The depression, in turn, may lead some people to take their own lives. 47

In the past 25 years, teen suicide has tripled. In a 1988 survey by the U.S. Department of Health and Human Services, one in five adolescent girls said they have tried to kill themselves (the figure for boys was one in 10). 48

This is the same period during which the rate of teenage sexual activity has sharply increased, especially for girls. No doubt, the rise in youth suicide has multiple causes, but given what we know about the emotional aftermath of broken sexual relationships, it is reasonable to suspect that the pain from such break-ups is a factor in the suicide deaths of some young people. 49

## 9. Ruined Relationships

Sex can have another kind of emotional consequence: It can turn a good relationship bad. Other dimensions of the relationship stop developing. Pretty soon, negative emotions enter the picture. Eventually, they poison the relationship, and what had been a caring relationship comes to a bitter end. 50

One young woman shares her story, which illustrates the process: 51

> With each date, my boyfriend's requests for sex became more convincing. After all, we did love each other. Within two months, I gave in, because I had justified the whole thing. Over the next six months, sex became the center of our relationship. . . .

> At the same time, some new things entered our relationship—things like anger, impatience, jealousy, and selfishness. We just couldn't talk anymore. We grew very bored with each other. I desperately wanted a change.[17]

52 A young man who identified himself as a 22-year-old virgin echoes this warning about the damage premature sex can do to a relationship:

> I've seen too many of my friends break up after their relationships turned physical. The emotional wreckage is horrendous because they have already shared something so powerful. When you use sex too early, it will block other means of communicating love and can stunt the balanced growth of a relationship.[18]

### 10. Stunting Personal Development

53 Premature sexual involvement not only can stunt the development of a relationship but also can stunt one's development as a person.

54 Just as some young people handle anxieties by turning to drugs and alcohol, others handle them by turning to sex. Sex becomes an escape. They aren't learning how to cope with life's pressures.

55 Teenagers who are absorbed in an intense sexual relationship are turning inward on one thing at the very time in their lives when they should be reaching out—forming new friendships, joining clubs and teams, developing their interests and skills, taking on bigger social responsibilities.

56 All of these are important nutrients for a teenager's development as a person. And this period of life is special because young people have both the time and the opportunities to develop their talents and interests. The growing they do during these years will affect them all their lives. If young people don't put these years to good use, they may never develop their full potential.

57 The risk appears to be greater for girls who get sexually involved and in so doing close the door on other interests and relationships. Says New York psychiatrist Samuel Kaufman:

> A girl who enters into a serious relationship with a boy very early in life may find out later that her individuality was thwarted. She became part of him and failed to develop her own interests, her sense of independent identity.[19]

58 Reflecting on her long experience in counseling college students and others about sexual matters, Dr. Carson Daly comments:

> I don't think I ever met a student who was sorry he or she had postponed sexual activity, but I certainly met many who deeply regretted their sexual

> involvements. Time and time again, I have seen the long-term emotional and spiritual desolation that results from casual sex and promiscuity.
>
> No one tells students that it sometimes takes years to recover from the effects of these sexual involvements—if one every fully recovers.

Sex certainly can be a source of great pleasure and joy. But as should be 59 amply clear—and youngsters need our help and guidance in understanding this—sex also can be the source of deep wounds and suffering. What makes the difference is the relationship within which it occurs. Sex is most joyful and fulfilling—most emotionally safe as well as physically safe—when it occurs within a loving, total, and binding commitment. Historically, we have called that marriage. Sexual union is then part of something bigger—the union of two persons' lives.

## Notes

1. Susan Weller, "A Meta-Analysis of Condom Effectiveness in Reducing Sexually Transmitted HIV," *Social Science and Medicine*, June 1993, p. 12.
2. See, for example, Kenneth Noller, *OB/GYN Clinical Alert*, September 1992; for a thorough discussion of the dangers of human papilloma virus, see "Condoms Ineffective Against Human Papilloma Virus," *Sexual Health Update*, April 1994, a publication of the Medical Institute for Sexual Health, P.O. Box 4919, Austin, TX 78765.
3. "Some Teens Taking Vows of Virginity," *Washington Post*, November 21, 1993.
4. William Bennett, "Sex and the Education of Our Children," *America*, February 14, 1987, p. 124.
5. Bob Bartlett, "Going All the Way," *Momentum*, April–May 1993, p. 36.
6. Abridged from Ann Landers, "A Not-So-Sweet Sexteen Story," *Daily News*, September 23, 1991, p. 20.
7. Eager's book is available from Mailbox Club Books, 404 Eager Rd., Valdosta, GA 31602.
8. Carson Daly, personal communication.
9. *Safe Sex: A Slide Program*. Austin, TX: Medical Institute for Sexual Health, 1992.
10. Josh McDowell and Dick Day, *Why Wait? What You Need to Know About the Teen Sexuality Crisis*. San Bernardino, CA: Here's Life Publishers, 1987.
11. Medical Institute for Sexual Health, P.O. Box 4919, Austin, TX 78765.
12. *American Association of University Women Report on Sexual Harassment*, June 1993.
13. J. Kikuchi, "Rhode Island Develops Successful Intervention Program for Adolescents," *National Coalition Against Sexual Assault Newsletter*, Fall 1988.

14. McDowell and Day, *Why Wait?*
15. Abridged from *Choosing the Best: A Values-Based Sex Education Curriculum*, 1993; available from 5500 Interstate North Parkway, Suite 515, Atlanta, GA 30328.
16. Kieran Sawyer, *Sex and the Teenager*. Notre Dame, IN: Ave Maria Press, 1990.
17. McDowell and Day, *Why Wait?*
18. Ann Landers, "Despite Urgin', He's a Virgin," *Daily News*, January 15, 1994.
19. Quoted in Howard Lewis and Martha Lewis, *The Parent's Guide to Teenage Sex and Pregnancy*. New York: St. Martin's Press, 1980.

### Thinking Critically About Content

1. According to Lickona, what makes sex "distinctively human" (paragraph 4)?
2. What are the 10 consequences of premature sexual involvement that Lickona lists?
3. Why do you think the writer includes so many quotes from teenagers about their sexual experiences?

### Thinking Critically About Purpose and Audience

4. What do you think Lickona's purpose is in this essay?
5. Although this essay was published in a magazine for teachers, do you think other groups of people could benefit from reading it? Explain your answer.
6. What effect do you think this essay will have on teenagers who have already had sexual relationships?

### Thinking Critically About Essays

7. Describe in a complete sentence the writer's point of view.
8. Why do you think the writer presents the negative consequences of premature sex by numbering them 1 through 10 and giving each consequence a heading instead of presenting them in paragraph form? What effect does this strategy have in the essay?
9. Explain the title of this essay.
10. This essay was written for teachers. If you were writing an essay about the same topic for students, how would it be different? How would it be the same? Rewrite the introduction and conclusion of this essay for a student audience.

## ARGUING A POSITION

### Focusing Your Attention

1. If you were asked to take a position for or against a topic of great importance to you or to society, what are some of the topics you would consider?
2. In the two essays that you will be reading, one writer claims that if we control loitering, we can control gang activity. The other writer claims loitering is not related to gang activity. Before you read these essays, try to predict some of the arguments each author will make.

**Richard Willard**

## ANTI-LOITERING LAWS CAN REDUCE GANG VIOLENCE

### Expanding Your Vocabulary

The following words are important to your understanding of this essay.

**anti-loitering:** trying to prevent people from hanging around in a public place without an obvious reason (title)

**innovative:** clever, original (paragraph 1)

**curfew:** time by which individuals must be off the public streets (paragraph 1)

**statutes:** laws (paragraph 1)

**court injunctions:** orders issued by the courts (paragraph 1)

**deterrence:** avoidance (paragraph 1)

**sanctions:** punishments (paragraph 1)

**constrained:** limited (paragraph 1)

**discretion:** personal judgment (paragraph 1)

**gang-loitering ordinances:** laws against gangs hanging around public places without reason (paragraph 2)

**implemented:** used, enforced (paragraph 2)

**pervasiveness:** extent (paragraph 2)

**engenders:** produces, causes (paragraph 3)

**vandalism:** damaging property (paragraph 5)
**panhandling:** begging for money (paragraph 5)
**vending:** the selling of merchandise (paragraph 5)
**commons:** open public areas such as parks and squares (paragraph 6)
**prevalent:** widespread (paragraph 7)
**skewed:** distorted (paragraph 7)
**augment:** increase (paragraph 10)
**condemnation:** blame (paragraph 10)
**suppression:** control (paragraph 11)
**abatement:** decrease (paragraph 11)

1 Chicago is not alone in seeking to resist the devastating effects of gang violence. Having witnessed the failure of more traditional policing methods, many other threatened localities—from Los Angeles to Washington, D.C.—have reacted by passing a variety of innovative laws, which range from curfew measures to anti-loitering statutes to court injunctions against specific gang members. All of these measures emphasize prevention and deterrence strategies over increased criminal sanctions. In order to meet the particular challenges of increased gang violence, communities have also strongly supported constrained expansions of police discretion to help communities reassert their own law-abiding norms.

2 Residents of high-crime communities are much more likely to support gang-loitering ordinances, curfews, and other order-maintenance policies, which they perceive to be appropriately moderate yet effective devices for reducing crime. Communities have implemented these policies in various ways, tailored to their particular needs and depending on the pervasiveness of the problem.

## Maintaining Order

3 Just as community disorder engenders increasing disorder and crime, reinforcement of [existing] community law-abiding norms engenders increasing social order and prevents more serious crime. Modern policing theory has undergone a "quiet revolution" to learn that, in cooperation with community efforts, enforcing community public order norms is one of the most effective means of combating all levels of crime. By focusing on order maintenance and prevention, advocating a more visible presence in policed areas, and basing its legitimacy on the consent of policed populations, police can most effectively prevent the occurrence of more serious crime.

New York City's experience confirms this. Today, that city has much less crime than it did five years ago. From 1993 to 1996, the murder rate dropped by 40 percent, robberies dropped by 30 percent, and burglary dropped by more than 25 percent, more than double the national average. 4

These drops are not the result of increased police resources, but rather more effectively applied resources. While New York has not increased its law enforcement expenditures substantially more than other cities, since 1993, the city began to focus intensively on "public order" offenses, including vandalism, aggressive panhandling, public drunkenness, unlicensed vending, public urination, and prostitution. This focus on order maintenance is credited for much of the crime reduction. 5

Anti-loitering ordinances implement community-driven order maintenance policing citywide—appropriate to the extreme pervasiveness of Chicago's gang problem—but on a neighborhood scale. Preservation of neighborhood commons is essential to ensuring healthy and vital cities. 6

## Ineffective Strategies

Gang loitering works to increase disorder. Order-maintenance policing strikes a reasonable intermediate balance between harsh criminal penalties and inaction. Conventional suppression strategies are ineffective in gang-threatened communities. Where gang activity is prevalent, individuals are more likely to act in an aggressive manner in order to conform to gang norms of behavior. When numerous youths act according to these skewed norms, more are likely to turn to crime: Widespread adoption of aggressive mannerisms sends skewed signals about public attitudes toward gang membership and creates barriers to mainstream law-abiding society, which strongly disfavors aggression. 7

Accordingly, policies that "raise the price" of gang activity can sometimes function at cross-purposes. If juveniles value willingness to break the law, delinquency may be seen as "status-enhancing." As penalties grow more severe, lawbreaking gives increasing status. More severe punishments may also provoke unintended racist accusation, if community minorities view harsher penalties as unfairly applied to their particular groups. Thus, any strategy dependent on harsh penalties may in fact be "at war with itself." 8

## Why Anti-Loitering Laws Work

Strategies that instead attack public signals to juveniles' peers about the value of gang criminality are more effective. Gang anti-loitering laws do this, for example, by "authorizing police to disperse known gang members when they congregate in public places," or by "directly prohibiting individuals from displaying gang allegiance through distinctive gestures or clothing." By preventing 9 gangs from flaunting their authority, such laws establish community authority while combating the perception that gangs have high status. As that perception weakens, so does the pressure to join gangs that youths might otherwise perceive.

10 Such strategies also positively influence law-abiding adults. Gang-loitering laws augment law-abiders' confidence so that they can oppose gangs. When public deterrence predominates, individuals are much less likely to perceive that criminality is widespread and much more likely to see private precautions as worthwhile. When the community as a whole is again able to express its condemnation, gang influence quickly wanes.

11 The most successful anti-gang programs combine effective gang suppression programs with targeted community aid efforts: increased social services, job placement, and crisis intervention. Civil gang abatement, together with other government and community-based efforts, has reduced crime and visibly improved the neighborhood's quality of life.

12 Chicago has also implemented alternative community aid programs. Since 1992, for example, the Gang Violence Reduction Project has targeted Little Village to serve as a model gang violence reduction program.

13 The program coordinates increased levels of social services—the carrot—in conjunction with focused suppression strategies—the stick. The result has been a lower level of serious gang violence among the targeted gangs than among comparable gangs in the area. The project also noted improvement in residents' perceptions of gang crime and police effectiveness in dealing with it. Chicago's anti-loitering ordinance is the necessary "stick" of an effective gang violence reduction equation.

---

**David Cole**

## ANTI-LOITERING LAWS ARE INEFFECTIVE AND BIASED

### Expanding Your Vocabulary

The following words are important to your understanding of this essay.

**anti-loitering:** trying to prevent people from hanging around in a public place without an obvious reason (title)

**starkly:** boldly (paragraph 1)

**ordinance:** law (paragraph 1)

**due process:** the requirement that laws treat all individuals fairly (paragraph 1)

**discretion:** personal judgment (paragraph 3)
**empirical:** theoretical (paragraph 4)
**aldermen:** members of the town council or governing board (paragraph 4)
**apartheid regime:** political system in which people of different races were separated (paragraph 4)
**disparities:** differences (paragraph 4)
**invalidated:** canceled (paragraph 5)
**unfettered:** free, unlimited (paragraph 6)
**mores:** moral attitudes (paragraph 6)
**strictures:** restraints and limits (paragraph 6)
**discriminatory:** biased, unfair (paragraph 6)
**legitimacy:** acceptance as lawful (paragraph 6)
**cynicism:** doubt, distrust (paragraph 6)
**alienation:** sense of not belonging (paragraph 6)
**Kerner Commission:** task force established by President Lyndon Johnson to investigate the causes of race riots (paragraph 7)
**street sweeps:** stopping and searching everyone on the street as if guilty of a crime (paragraph 7)
**antithetical:** opposing (paragraph 7)
**carte blanche:** complete freedom (paragraph 7)
**impeding:** blocking, obstructing (paragraph 7)

---

Do "quality of life" policing and "community" policing, the law enforcement watchwords of the nineties, require the abandonment or dilution of civil rights and civil liberties? On December 9, 1998, the Supreme Court heard arguments in a case that starkly poses that question. At issue is a sweeping Chicago ordinance that makes it a crime for gang members or anyone associated with them merely to stand in public "with no apparent purpose." Chicago calls the offense "gang loitering," but it might more candidly be termed "standing while black." Sixty-six of the more than 45,000 Chicago citizens arrested for this offense in the three years that the law was on the books challenged its constitutionality, and in 1997 the Illinois Supreme Court unanimously ruled that it violated due process. 1

But the Supreme Court agreed to review that decision, and lined up in defense of the ordinance is not only the city of Chicago but also the United States, 2 the attorneys general of thirty-one states, the National District Attorneys Association, the International Association of Chiefs of Police, the U.S. Conference of Mayors and, perhaps most interesting, a pair of otherwise liberal University of Chicago law professors representing several Chicago neighborhood groups.

## Disputing the Arguments for Loitering Laws

3 The ordinance's advocates argue that it played a critical role in making Chicago's high-crime neighborhoods safe and therefore served the interests of the minority poor who live there. They suggest that strict constitutional standards need to be loosened in order to give police the discretion to engage in the day-to-day encounters of "quality of life" or "community" policing. Most astounding, they argue that criminal laws no longer must be clear in places where minority groups have a voice in the political process and can protect themselves. These arguments resonate with one commonly heard these days, particularly but not exclusively in Mayor Rudolph Giuliani's New York City—namely, that heavy-handed police efforts directed at the inner city benefit minority residents by making their neighborhoods safer places in which to grow up, work, and live.

4 The arguments fail. First, as an empirical matter it is far from clear that the minority community in Chicago supported the law or that minority communities generally favor "quality of life" policing efforts that send so many of their residents to jail. The majority of Chicago's African-American aldermen voted against the ordinance; one representative, predicting that the law would be targeted at young black men, compared it to South Africa's apartheid regime. And voter turnout rates are so low in the inner city that it is difficult to say whether any elected official speaks for that community. The notion that minorities no longer need the protection of constitutional law simply ignores the racial disparities evident at every stage of the criminal justice system.

5 It is also not clear that the antigang law actually benefited anyone, much less Chicago's minority communities. Chicago did experience a falling crime rate while the law was in effect, but so did the rest of the nation. And the crime rate continued to fall after the ordinance was invalidated. So it is far from proven that arresting tens of thousands for standing in public had any positive effects.

## Law Enforcement Must Build Trust

6 Most important, giving the police unfettered discretion to sweep the city streets of "undesirable" youth probably undermines safety by incurring distrust among those community members whose trust the police need most. The law's most powerful tool is its legitimacy. The more people believe the law is legitimate, the more likely they are to internalize its mores, obey its strictures, and cooperate with police. When laws are enforced in discriminatory ways, they lose their legitimacy. Cynicism and alienation about the criminal law are nowhere higher

than among minorities and the urban poor, and laws like Chicago's only feed the alienation by inviting selective enforcement.

Indeed, law enforcement authorities and experts have long understood the importance of maintaining the community's faith and trust. Thirty years ago, the Kerner Commission reported that such support "will not be present when a substantial segment of the community feels threatened by the police and regards the police as an occupying force." The father of "quality of life" policing, George Kelling, has argued that street sweeps are antithetical to its goals precisely because they foster enmity, not community. And Attorney General Janet Reno has written that effective crime control requires "a greater sense of community and trust between law enforcement and the minority community." Yet her Justice Department, the City of Chicago, and the majority of our nation's state attorneys general fail to understand that you don't build trust by unleashing the police on minority communities with carte blanche to arrest anyone standing in public without an apparent purpose. Civil rights and civil liberties, far from impeding law enforcement, are critical to preserving its legitimacy. 7

### Thinking Critically About Content

1. Make a list of the reasons, evidence, and statistics each writer uses to convince the reader of his position.
2. Explain how both writers use the anti-loitering laws in Chicago to argue different positions.
3. Which essay contains the most convincing evidence in your opinion? Why is it so convincing to you?

### Thinking Critically About Purpose and Audience

4. What do you think the writers' purposes are in these essays?
5. What type of audience would be most interested in the subject of these two essays? Explain your answer.
6. If you changed your mind as a result of reading one of these essays, what in the essay caused the change?

### Thinking Critically About Essays

7. State each writer's point of view in a single sentence.
8. How do both writers organize their essays? Make a rough outline of each essay to demonstrate your answer.
9. Which points do the two writers agree on? Which points do they disagree on? Explain your answer.
10. Write your own argument about the relationship between loitering and gang activity.

### *Writing Topics: Arguing and Persuading*

Before you begin to write, you might want to review the writing process in Part I.

1. In "The Neglected Heart," Lickona tries to convince his readers of the serious emotional side effects of premature sex. Choose another activity that can be harmful if done prematurely, and try to persuade someone not to do this activity.
2. These pro and con essays deal mainly with loitering as it relates to gang activity. Think of another strategy for fighting gang activity, and attempt to convince a group in authority to try your solution to the problem. Gather as much evidence as you can before you begin to write.
3. How can being able to develop good arguments and persuade people of your point of view help you in life? How might this ability give you the edge over other people on the job market?

# THE HANDBOOK

This part of *Mosaics* provides you with a complete handbook for editing your writing. You can use it as a reference tool as you write or as a source of instruction and practice in areas where you need work.

This handbook consists of an Introduction and eight units:

The chapters in each unit start with a self-test to help you identify your strengths and weaknesses in that area. Then the chapter teaches those sentence skills and provides exercises so you can practice what you have learned. Each chapter periodically asks you to write your own sentences and then work with another student to edit each other's sentences. At the end of each unit, you are asked to write a short paragraph and apply what you learned in the chapter to that paragraph.

The Editing Symbols on the inside back cover will give you marks for highlighting errors in your papers. In addition, the Error Log (Appendix 6) and Spelling Log (Appendix 7) will help you tailor the instruction to your own needs and keep track of your progress.

# Introduction

This handbook uses very little terminology. But sometimes talking about the language and the way it works is difficult without a shared understanding of certain basic grammar terms. For that reason, your instructor may ask you to study parts of this introduction to review basic grammar—parts of speech, phrases, and clauses. You might also use this Introduction for reference.

This section has three parts:

Parts of Speech
Phrases
Clauses

## PARTS OF SPEECH

### Test Yourself

In the following paragraph, label the parts of speech listed here:

| | |
|---|---|
| 2 verbs (v) | 2 adverbs (adv) |
| 2 nouns (n) | 2 prepositions (prep) |
| 2 pronouns (pro) | 2 conjunctions (conj) |
| 2 adjectives (adj) | 2 interjections (int) |

Professional basketball is definitely this nation's best spectator sport. The talented players move around the court so quickly that the audience never has a chance to become bored. Boy, I'll never forget that Saturday night last February when my favorite uncle took me to see the Spurs game against the Trailblazers. It was an important home game for San Antonio, so the arena was packed. The Spurs were behind throughout most of the game, but they pulled through and won with a three-pointer in the last few seconds.

Wow! I have never seen so many people on their feet and screaming at the top of their lungs.

(Answers are in Appendix 4.)

---

Every sentence is made up of a variety of words that play different roles. Each word, like each part of a coordinated outfit, serves a distinct function. These functions fall into eight categories:

1. Verbs
2. Nouns
3. Pronouns
4. Adjectives
5. Adverbs
6. Prepositions
7. Conjunctions
8. Interjections

Some words, such as *is*, can function in only one way—in this case, as a verb. Other words, however, can serve as different parts of speech depending on how they are used in a sentence. For example, look at the different ways the word *show* can be used:

**Verb:** The artists **show** their work at a gallery.
(*Show* is a verb here, telling what the artists do.)

**Noun:** The **show** will start in 10 minutes.
(*Show* functions as a noun here, telling what will start in 10 minutes.)

**Adjective:** The little boy loves to sing **show** tunes.
(*Show* is an adjective here, modifying the noun *tunes*.)

## Verbs

The **verb** is the most important word in a sentence because every other word depends on it in some way. Verbs tell what's going on in the sentence.

There are three types of verbs: action, linking, and helping. An **action verb** tells what someone or something is doing. A **linking verb** tells what someone or something is, feels, or looks like. Sometimes an action or linking verb has **helping verbs**—words that add information, such as when an action is taking place. A **complete verb** consists of an action or linking verb and all the helping verbs.

**Action:** The girl **wandered** too far from the campsite.

**Action:** Luca **ran** to the bus stop.

| | |
|---|---|
| **Linking:** | He **looks** very tired. |
| **Linking:** | It **was** a real surprise to see you. |
| **Helping:** | My aunt and uncle **will be** arriving tomorrow. |
| **Helping:** | My grandmother **has** been very ill lately. |
| **Complete Verb:** | My aunt and uncle **will be arriving** tomorrow. |
| **Complete Verb:** | My grandmother **has been** very ill lately. |

### Reviewing Verbs

***Define each of the following types of verbs, and give an example of each.***

*Action:* ______________________________

*Linking:* ______________________________

*Helping:* ______________________________

***What is a complete verb? Give an example with your definition.***

______________________________

______________________________

**Practice 1 Identifying** In each of the following sentences, underline the complete verbs. Some sentences have more than one verb.

1. I read *Moby Dick* for my literature class.
2. The attorney arrived late for his meeting.
3. The best place for inexpensive fast food is Taco Bell.
4. You seem tired.
5. I wonder if Chad was going to be attending.
6. Martin feels confident in his tennis skills.
7. The people in that boat were learning to water-ski.
8. Jennifer wanted Nathan to marry her.
9. How many chickens can I purchase if I have only five dollars?
10. The teenager climbed to the top of the mountain before he stopped for lunch.

**Practice 2 Completing** Fill in each blank in the following paragraph with a verb.

This year my sister (1) ____________ to get married. She and her fiancé (2) ____________ in Dallas, Texas, so I had to buy a plane ticket from Los Angeles. First, I tried the computer and (3) ____________ all of the Web sites that people talk about, but I couldn't find any good deals. Finally, I (4) ____________ a travel agent and asked her to tell me what my best options were. The best deal she (5) ____________ was $280 round-trip, so I charged it to a credit card. I guess my sister is worth it.

**Practice 3 Writing Your Own** Write a sentence of your own for each of the following verbs.

1. was sitting ____________________________________________
2. handled ____________________________________________
3. seems ____________________________________________
4. had been taking ____________________________________________
5. buy ____________________________________________

## Nouns

People often think of **nouns** as "naming words" because they identify—or name—people (*student, Susan, mom, server*), places (*city, ocean, Thomasville*), or things (*bush, airplane, chair, shirt*). Nouns also name ideas (*liberty, justice*), qualities (*bravery, patience*), emotions (*sadness, happiness*), and actions (*challenge, compromise*). A **common noun** names something general (*singer, hill, water, theater*). A **proper noun** names something specific (*Nicole Kidman, Angel Falls, Coke, McDonald's*).

**Hint:** To test whether a word is a noun, try putting *a*, *an*, or *the* in front of it:

**Nouns:** a squirrel, an orange, the hope
**NOT Nouns:** a funny, an over, the eat

This test does not work with proper nouns:

**NOT** a Natalie, the New York

### Reviewing Nouns

***What is a noun?***

______________________________________________

***What is the difference between a common noun and a proper noun? Give an example of each.***

***Common noun:*** ______________________________

***Proper noun:*** ______________________________

**Practice 4 Identifying** Underline all the nouns in the following sentences.

1. The Golden Gate Bridge is a popular tourist attraction in San Francisco.
2. Collectors will spend lots of money on limited-edition coins.
3. My son is wearing my favorite shirt.
4. In October, we are planning a trip to Seattle.
5. *Emeril Live* was voted the most popular TV cooking show.
6. The weather in this area has been very unpredictable.
7. Their chocolate chip cookies have won many awards.
8. Baseball is entertaining to watch, but it is more fun to play.
9. Grant wrote a very good essay on *Gulliver's Travels* by Jonathan Swift.
10. Can you tell me how far it is to Salt Lake City?

**Practice 5 Completing** Fill in each blank in the following paragraph with a noun that will make each sentence complete.

Last May, I joined a volunteer organization called (1) ________. Within a month, the secretary left, and I was nominated to take his place. I had to put all of the (2) ____________ about the organization and its members into my computer and then create a mail merge. With this database, I was able to make labels and (3) ____________ very easily. My first assignment was to create a form letter and send it to all of the (4) ____________ who promised to send money to the group. I finally saw the (5) ____________ of all the grammar lessons I had in my English classes, and I learned that writing good letters is harder than I thought.

**Practice 6 Writing Your Own** Write a sentence of your own for each of the following nouns.

1. pastor ______________________________________________
2. Sea World ___________________________________________
3. strength ____________________________________________
4. audience ____________________________________________
5. actions _____________________________________________

## Pronouns

Pronouns can do anything nouns can do. In fact, **pronouns** can take the place of nouns. Without pronouns, you would find yourself repeating nouns and producing boring sentences. Compare the following sentences, for example:

> **George** drove **George's** car very fast to **George's** house because **George** had to get home early.
>
> **George** drove **his** car very fast to **his** house because **he** had to get home early.

There are many different types of pronouns, but you need only focus on the following four types for now.

### Most Common Pronouns

**Personal (refer to people or things)**

| | | |
|---|---|---|
| **Singular:** | First person: | *I, me, my, mine* |
| | Second person: | *you, your, yours* |
| | Third person: | *he, she, it, him, her, hers, his, its* |
| **Plural:** | First person: | *we, us, our, ours* |
| | Second person: | *you, your, yours* |
| | Third person: | *they, them, their, theirs* |

**Demonstrative (point out someone or something)**

**Singular:** *this, that*

**Plural:** *these, those*

**Relative (introduce a dependent clause)**

*who, whom, whose, which, that*

**Indefinite (refer to someone or something general, not specific)**

| | |
|---|---|
| **Singular:** | *another, anybody, anyone, anything, each, either, everybody, everyone, everything, little, much, neither, nobody, none, no one, nothing, one, other, somebody, someone, something* |
| **Plural:** | *both, few, many, others, several* |
| **Either Singular or Plural:** | *all, any, more, most, some* |

**Hint:** When any of these words are used with nouns, they become adjectives instead of pronouns.

**Adjective:** He can have **some candy.**
**Pronoun:** He can have **some.**

**Adjective:** The baby wants **that toy.**
**Pronoun:** The baby wants **that.**

Reviewing Pronouns

*What is a pronoun?*

______________________________________________

***Define the four most common types of pronouns, and give two examples of each.***

***Personal:*** ______________________________________________

***Demonstrative:*** ______________________________________________

***Relative:*** ______________________________________________

***Indefinite:*** ______________________________________________

**Practice 7 Identifying** Underline all the pronouns in the following sentences. Don't underline pronouns that are really adjectives.

1. Some of the wedding guests were vegetarians.
2. Those are the biggest shoes I have ever seen.
3. You may think you know them, but I think they have everyone fooled.
4. Somebody had better admit to this.
5. Is that the movie several of our friends are seeing tonight?
6. After his car was stolen, everything else seemed to go wrong for him too.
7. She didn't know that her cat was under the couch until she sat down.
8. Does anyone else need anything while I'm up?
9. I think these are my new glasses.
10. If many people forget to send in their reply cards, planning the party will be difficult for me.

**Practice 8 Completing** Rewrite the following paragraph, replacing the nouns in parentheses with pronouns.

Mike first tried rollerblading when (1) ______________ (Mike) was 19. It was pretty funny to watch (2) ______________ (Mike) buy the shin guards and wrist guards, put (3) ______________ (the shin and wrist guards) on, and then roll down the sidewalk out of control. (4) ______________ (Mike's) two best friends, Carl and Luis, wanted to learn also, but when they saw the hard time Mike was having,

(5) ______________ (Carl and Luis) were too afraid.

**Practice 9 Writing Your Own** Write a sentence of your own for each of the following pronouns.

1. anyone ______________________________
2. these ______________________________
3. who ______________________________
4. many ______________________________
5. our ______________________________

## Adjectives

**Adjectives** modify—or describe—nouns or pronouns. Adjectives generally make sentences clear and vivid.

**Without Adjectives:** She brought an umbrella, a towel, and a Walkman to the beach.

**With Adjectives:** She brought a **bright orange** umbrella, a **striped blue** towel, and a **waterproof** Walkman to the beach.

REVIEWING ADJECTIVES

***What is an adjective?***

______________________________

***Give three examples of adjectives.***

______________ ______________ ______________

**Practice 10 Identifying** Underline all the adjectives in the following sentences.

1. His long black goatee was formed into two sharp points.
2. The talented musicians gave a two-hour concert for an excited audience.

3. Grisham's best-selling novel, *Runaway Jury*, is about a strange man and his intelligent girlfriend.
4. Getting a good parking place is sometimes impossible.
5. One cold day, I saw a long brown leaf in my swimming pool that reminded me of the sinking Titanic.
6. Steve's homemade burger was especially good with two slices of melted cheese on it.
7. The child's loud cry made the hair on my neck stand up.
8. Seeing the steam rise from her hot chocolate made me thirsty and jealous.
9. The dark green grass in the park looked like shag carpet.
10. Matthew signed his name using a smooth ballpoint pen.

**Practice 11 Completing** Fill in each blank in the following paragraph with an adjective.

My girlfriend and I went to a (1) ____________ baseball game at the Anaheim Stadium last weekend. The Angels were playing the Texas Rangers, and the Rangers were much more (2) ____________. This year, the Rangers have (3) ____________ infielders, and their batters are pretty (4) ____________ also. Overall, the teams were unequally matched, and it was (5) ____________ that one of them was going to lose pretty badly.

**Practice 12 Writing Your Own** Write a sentence of your own for each of the following adjectives.

1. gorgeous ____________________________________________
2. dark ____________________________________________
3. tempting ____________________________________________

4. thrifty ______________________________

5. sixth ______________________________

## Adverbs

**Adverbs** modify—or describe—adjectives, verbs, and other adverbs. They do *not* modify nouns. Adverbs also answer the following questions:

| | |
|---|---|
| **How?** | thoughtfully, kindly, briefly, quietly |
| **When?** | soon, tomorrow, late, now |
| **Where?** | inside, somewhere, everywhere, there |
| **How often?** | daily, always, annually, rarely |
| **To what extent?** | generally, specifically, exactly, very |

**Hint:** Notice that adverbs often end in *-ly*. That might help you recognize them.

### Reviewing Adverbs

***What is an adverb?***

______________________________

***What are the five questions that adverbs answer?***

__________ __________ __________ __________ __________

***Give one example of an adverb that answers each question.***

__________ __________ __________ __________ __________

**Practice 13 Identifying** Underline all the adverbs in the following sentences.

1. I definitely won't go to that pizza parlor again.
2. He almost passed Stephanie when he was running aimlessly down the hall.
3. Jan is going to the library tomorrow and gladly volunteered to return my books.

4. That was the very last time George Clooney was on television.
5. If you read it too fast, you'll surely miss the point of the essay.
6. It was quite disappointing to lose after nearly six months of training.
7. Samantha walked quickly to avoid the rain.
8. Are you absolutely sure that you remembered to set the alarm?
9. Casually strolling down Main Street, the two oddly dressed women didn't seem to care when a child suddenly stopped and pointed at them.
10. I try to buy groceries weekly so that we are never missing the basic necessities.

**Practice 14 Completing** Fill in each blank in the following paragraph with an adverb.

When Shanika (1) ____________ lost her job at the grocery store, she felt desperate. She (2) ____________ began calling her friends and relatives, asking if they knew of any job openings. (3) ____________ for Shanika, her aunt Betsy owned a hair salon that needed a receptionist. Shanika didn't know anything about beauty parlors, but she (4) ____________ agreed to work there because she needed the money. After only three weeks, Shanika became very interested in the salon, and she (5) ____________ decided to take classes at a local beauty college and earned a license in cosmetology.

**Practice 15 Writing Your Own** Write a sentence of your own for each of the following adverbs.

1. sometimes ________________________________________
2. hardly ________________________________________
3. gently ________________________________________

4. too ____________________

5. tomorrow ____________________

## Prepositions

**Prepositions** indicate relationships among the ideas in a sentence. Something is *at, in, by, next to, behind, around, near,* or *under* something else. A preposition is always followed by a noun or a pronoun called the **object of the preposition.** Together, they form a **prepositional phrase.**

| **Preposition + Object** | | **= Prepositional Phrase** |
|---|---|---|
| near | the beach | near the beach |
| for | the party | for the party |

Here is a list of some common prepositions.

**Common Prepositions**

| | | | |
|---|---|---|---|
| *about* | *beside* | *into* | *since* |
| *above* | *between* | *like* | *through* |
| *across* | *beyond* | *near* | *throughout* |
| *after* | *by* | *next to* | *to* |
| *against* | *despite* | *of* | *toward* |
| *among* | *down* | *off* | *under* |
| *around* | *during* | *on* | *until* |
| *as* | *except* | *on top of* | *up* |
| *at* | *for* | *out* | *upon* |
| *before* | *from* | *out of* | *up to* |
| *behind* | *in* | *outside* | *with* |
| *below* | *in front of* | *over* | *within* |
| *beneath* | *inside* | *past* | *without* |

**HINT:** *To* + a verb (as in *to go, to come, to feel*) is not a prepositional phrase. It is a verb phrase, which we will deal with later in this unit.

### REVIEWING PREPOSITIONS

***What is a preposition?***

____________________

*Give two examples:* ______________ ______________

*What is a prepositional phrase?*

______________________________________________

*Give two examples:* ______________ ______________

**Practice 16 Identifying** Underline all the prepositions in the following sentences.

1. When I stepped off the bus, I looked down the street and saw an old man in a white hat.
2. The cabin is over the big hill, past the creek, and down a winding dirt path.
3. If you go to Maui, stay in Kaanapali at a resort hotel beside the ocean.
4. The paper in my printer is jammed, so the light on the top won't stop blinking.
5. After the party, I found confetti in my hair, on the carpet, behind the sofa, and in all four corners of the room.
6. Between the two of us, we'll be finished with this project in no time.
7. After Seth took all of the crayons out of the box, he spread them across the floor.
8. Michelle left her wallet on top of the bench under the tree.
9. The temperature in the room was below 50 degrees.
10. Our season seats are on the 50-yard line, three rows below the announcers' booth.

**Practice 17 Completing** Fill in each blank in the following paragraph with a preposition.

I was so surprised when I saw Carlos walking (1) ______________ campus toward me. The last time we talked was eight months ago, when he was still living (2) ______________ Kendra. He decided to take some time (3) ____________ work to finish his degree, and he was hoping to have it completed (4) ____________ the next year. I was very proud (5) ____________ him for setting his priorities straight.

**Practice 18 Writing Your Own** Write a sentence of your own for each of the following prepositions.

1. with ______________________________
2. beside ______________________________
3. on top of ______________________________
4. until ______________________________
5. against ______________________________

## Conjunctions

**Conjunctions** connect groups of words. Without conjunctions, most of our writing would be choppy and boring. The two types of conjunctions are easy to remember because their names state their purpose: *Coordinating* conjunctions link equal ideas, and *subordinating* conjunctions make one idea subordinate to—or dependent on—another.

**Coordinating conjunctions** connect parts of a sentence that are of equal importance or weight. Each part of the sentence is an **independent clause,** a group of words with a subject and verb that can stand alone as a sentence (see page 524). There are only seven coordinating conjunctions:

**Coordinating Conjunctions**

*and, but, for, nor, or, so, yet*

**Coordinating:** My sister wanted to go shopping, **and** I wanted to go to the museum.

**Coordinating:** The teacher was very demanding, **but** I learned a lot from him.

**Subordinating conjunctions** join two ideas by making one dependent on the other. The idea introduced by the subordinating conjunction becomes a **dependent clause,** a group of words with a subject and a verb that cannot stand alone as a sentence (see page 524). The other part of the sentence is an independent clause.

Dependent Clause

**Subordinating:** I won't leave **until** he comes home.

Dependent Clause

**Subordinating:** **Unless** you study more, you won't be accepted to college.

**Common Subordinating Conjunctions**

| | | | |
|---|---|---|---|
| *after* | *because* | *since* | *until* |
| *although* | *before* | *so* | *when* |
| *as* | *even if* | *so that* | *whenever* |
| *as if* | *even though* | *than* | *where* |
| *as long as* | *how* | *that* | *wherever* |
| *as soon as* | *if* | *though* | *whether* |
| *as though* | *in order that* | *unless* | *while* |

REVIEWING CONJUNCTIONS

***What is a coordinating conjunction?***

______________________________________________

______________________________________________

***Name the seven coordinating conjunctions.***

_______ _______ _______ _______ _______ _______ _______

***What is a subordinating conjunction?***

______________________________________________

***Write a sentence using a subordinating conjunction.***

______________________________________________

**Practice 19 Identifying** Underline all the conjunctions in the following sentences.

1. My best personality trait is my sense of humor, but people also say that I'm a good listener.
2. As soon as Mark gets home, he turns on the television.
3. The homecoming game was a lot of fun, yet I didn't see anyone I knew.
4. While the other people were touring the city, Thomas stayed in the hotel room and took a nap.
5. This weekend has to be spent studying, for the midterm on Monday will be very difficult.
6. Even though I don't believe in Santa Claus anymore, I still feel more generous during the holiday season.
7. Carmen will be in our study group as long as we meet at her house.
8. Shane volunteered to take us to the airport even though his car seats only four people.
9. My grandma knows that her cookies are my favorite, so she sent some to me while I was at summer camp.
10. Whenever you decide what we are doing for dinner, call me.

**Practice 20 Completing** Fill in each blank in the following paragraph with a conjunction.

Babysitting is definitely not an easy job, (1) ______________ it is a fast way to make money. One couple I babysit for has two children, and (2) ______________ one of them is a perfect angel, the other one is constantly getting into trouble. Michael is the troublemaker, (3) ______________ he is 6 years old. (4) ______________ I arrive at his house, he runs to his room and begins pulling everything off of his bookshelves. Of course, I clean everything up (5) ______________ his parents get home, so they never see how messy it is.

**Practice 21 Writing Your Own** Write a sentence of your own for each of the following conjunctions.

1. or ______________________________
2. even if ______________________________
3. whether ______________________________
4. yet ______________________________
5. since ______________________________

## Interjections

**Interjections** are words that express strong emotion, surprise, or disappointment. An interjection is usually followed by an exclamation point or a comma.

> **Interjection:** **Whoa!** You're going too fast.
>
> **Interjection:** **Ouch,** that hurt!

Other common interjections include *aha*, *alas*, *great*, *hallelujah*, *neat*, *oh*, *oops*, *ouch*, *well*, *whoa*, *yeah*, and *yippee*.

REVIEWING INTERJECTIONS

***What is an interjection?***

______________________________

***Write a sentence using an interjection.***

______________________________

**Practice 22 Identifying** Underline all the interjections in the following sentences.

1. My goodness! This wind is going to blow down my fence!
2. The tide, alas, has swept our picnic basket out into the ocean.

3. Hooray! Our team is winning the playoff game!
4. Wow, are you going to eat all that food?
5. I just won the lottery! Hallelujah!
6. Boy, I'm beat—I can't walk another step.
7. Oh, I almost forgot to tell you the big news!
8. Yeah! We made it in time for the parade!
9. We just got a new car! Cool!
10. Good grief! Am I the only one working today?

**Practice 23 Completing** Fill in each blank in the following paragraph with an interjection.

(1) ______________, I thought that was the easiest test this professor has ever given. (2) ______________! I was really worried about this test. (3) ______________, it's over! I spent two weeks solid studying for this test. For the last two nights, I've slept only four hours. (4) ______________, am I ever tired. But at least the test is behind me, (5) ______________!

**Practice 24 Writing Your Own** Write a sentence of your own for each of the following interjections.

1. help ______________________________________________
2. mercy ______________________________________________
3. wow ______________________________________________
4. yippee ______________________________________________
5. ouch ______________________________________________

# PHRASES

**Test Yourself**

Define a phrase.

___

Give two examples of a phrase.

___

___

(Answers are in Appendix 4.)

A **phrase** is a group of words that function together as a unit. Phrases cannot stand alone, however, because they are missing a subject, a verb, or both.

**Phrases:** the silver moon, a boneless fish
**Phrases:** threw out the trash, navigated the river, floated to the top
**Phrases:** after piano lessons, in the crowded boat, by the beach
**Phrases:** jumping into the water, to be smart

Notice that all these groups of words are missing a subject, a verb, or both.

REVIEWING PHRASES

***What is a phrase?***

___

***Give two examples of phrases.***

___ ___

**Practice 25 Identifying** Underline 12 phrases in the following sentences.

1. Walking to the store, I saw two small boys riding bicycles.
2. My favorite hobbies are mountain biking and snow skiing.

3. If you want something to snack on, look in the cabinet above the refrigerator.
4. The grocery store clerk scanned the items and pointed to the total at the bottom of the register tape.
5. I bought a few antiques at the little store in downtown McKinley.
6. Tess is going to be a professional ballerina when she gets older.
7. Using the computer, I got most of the research done for my report.
8. To be totally confident, I checked for spelling and grammar errors twice.
9. Susan lives in the gray house at the end of Maple Avenue, behind the bank and the 7-Eleven.
10. Do you want to join us for dinner this evening?

**Practice 26 Completing** Fill in each blank in the following paragraph with a phrase.

Marci, my roommate, drove (1) ______________ this weekend because she wanted to visit her relatives there. She also mentioned that there is an outlet mall in the city, where she plans to (2) ______________ for some (3) ______________. She said the drive is only about two hours, and she listens to the radio (4) ______________. I think her relatives are in the food industry, so maybe she'll come home (5) ______________.

**Practice 27 Writing Your Own** Write a sentence of your own for each of the following phrases.

1. the brave contestant ____________________________________________
2. hoping to be chosen ____________________________________________
3. on the blackboard ____________________________________________

4. to make a point ______________________________

5. encouraged by the reward money ______________________________

## CLAUSES

**Test Yourself**

Define a clause.

______________________________

How is a clause different from a phrase?

______________________________

Give an example of a clause.

______________________________

(Answers are in Appendix 4.)

Like phrases, clauses are groups of words. But unlike phrases, a **clause** always contains a subject and a verb. There are two types of clauses: *independent* and *dependent*.

An **independent clause** contains a subject and a verb and can stand alone and make sense by itself. Every complete sentence must have at least one independent clause.

**Independent Clause:** The doctor held the baby very gently.

Now look at the following group of words. It is a clause because it contains a subject and a verb. But it is a **dependent clause** because it is introduced by a word that makes it dependent, *because*.

**Dependent Clause:** **Because** the doctor held the baby very gently.

This clause cannot stand alone. It must be connected to an independent clause to make sense. Here is one way to complete the dependent clause and form a complete sentence.

Dependent Independent

**Because** the doctor held the baby very gently, the baby stopped crying.

**HINT:** Subordinating conjunctions (such as *since*, *although*, *because*, *while*) and relative pronouns (*who*, *whom*, *whose*, *which*, *that*) make clauses dependent. (For more information on subordinating conjunctions, see page 518, and on relative pronouns, see page 509.)

### Reviewing Clauses

***For a group of words to be a clause, it must have a _____________ and a _____________.***

***What is an independent clause?***

______________________________________________

______________________________________________

***What is a dependent clause?***

______________________________________________

***Name the two kinds of words that can begin a dependent clause.***

______________________ ______________________

***Name five subordinating conjunctions.***

________ ________ ________ ________ ________

***Name the five relative pronouns.***

________ ________ ________ ________ ________

**Practice 28 Identifying** Each of the following sentences is made up of two clauses. Circle the coordinating or subordinating conjunctions and relative pronouns. Then label each clause either independent (Ind) or dependent (Dep).

1. As soon as Vanessa arrived, she began telling the others what to do.
2. When the car approached, the driver turned off the headlights.

3. We wanted to invite you to join us, as long as you pay your own way.
4. Tomas can turn in his paper late, but he will not receive full credit.
5. Magdalena will be a great attorney because she argues so well.
6. You don't understand the math concept, so I will keep going over it with you.
7. Mr. Johnson was the teacher who influenced my life the most.
8. If Shane is going to drive, he should have car insurance.
9. We finished the big test, and then we all went out for pizza.
10. I enjoyed the vacation even though I had one really bad seafood dinner.

**Practice 29 Completing** Add an independent or dependent clause that will complete each sentence and make sense.

Steven, who (1) ______________, takes his textbooks to the beach to study. He says that whenever (2) ______________, the sound of the ocean relaxes him. Of course, he also enjoys the view. One night he stayed out until (3) ______________, and his parents were afraid that something bad had happened to him. I'm sure he just lost track of time, unless (4) ______________. He is definitely a "beach bum" because (5) ______________.

**Practice 30 Writing Your Own** Write five independent clauses. Then add at least one dependent clause to each independent clause.

## REVIEW

You might want to reread your answers to the questions in the review boxes before you do the following exercises.

**Review Practice 1 Identifying** Use the following abbreviations to label the underlined words in these sentences.

| | | | |
|---|---|---|---|
| v | Verb | adv | Adverb |
| n | Noun | prep | Preposition |
| pro | Pronoun | conj | Conjunction |
| adj | Adjective | int | Interjection |
| ph | Phrase | cl | Clause |

1. Wow, that man looks just like my uncle Bob.
2. Tiffany is going shopping at the new mall on Harbor Boulevard tomorrow.
3. Frank is truly my best friend, but sometimes he can't keep a secret.
4. Whenever Lindsay feels sad, she drives into the mountains and looks at the stars.
5. The most popular music artist of the 1960s was definitely Elvis Presley.
6. Gee, are you sure we had to read the entire novel before class today?
7. Ryan wants to take piano lessons, so he can compose music for the poetry he has written.
8. Mikella took her dog to the vet and found out it has a lung infection.
9. Though I didn't want to accept the job, I felt pressured by my mother.
10. This morning was dark and cloudy, so I stayed in bed until noon.

**Review Practice 2 Completing** Fill in each blank in the following paragraph with an appropriate word, phrase, or clause, as indicated.

The most foolish purchase I ever made was a new (1) __________ (noun) for my computer. When I went to the (2) ______________ (adjective) store, the salesman (3) ______________ (verb) that I needed this thing. I asked him what the part would do (4) ________ (preposition) my computer, and he promised it would make a big difference in the way the computer operated. (5) ______________

(interjection), did I believe him! I knew my computer was pretty old, (6) ______________ (conjunction) I really didn't want to spend a lot of money on it. Still, I (7) ______________ (adverb) bought the part and took (8) ______________ (pronoun) home to try it out. After (9) ________________ (clause), I turned on the computer and it began to heat up. Suddenly, smoke began coming (10) ______________ (phrase), and I realized the computer had just died.

**Review Practice 3 Writing Your Own** Write your own paragraph about your favorite pet. What did you name it? What kind of animal was it?

## Editing Through Collaboration

Exchange paragraphs from Review Practice 3 with a classmate, and do the following:

1. Circle any words that are used incorrectly.
2. Underline any phrases that do not read smoothly.
3. Put an X in the margin where you find a dependent clause that is not connected to an independent clause.

Then return the paragraph to its writer, and use the information in the Introduction to edit your own paragraph. Record your errors on the Error Log in Appendix 6.

# Subjects and Verbs

## Checklist for Identifying Subjects and Verbs

- ✔ Does each of your sentences contain a subject?
- ✔ Does each of your sentences contain a verb?

**Test Yourself**

Underline the subjects once and the verbs twice in the following sentences.

- You are my best friend.
- Hang up your clothes.
- They really wanted to be here tonight.
- He made a sandwich and put it in a brown paper bag.
- Susie and Tom went to the dance.
- The insurance agent never called me today.

(Answers are in Appendix 4.)

---

A sentence has a message to communicate, but for that message to be meaningful, the sentence must have a subject and a verb. The subject is the topic of the sentence, what the sentence is about. The verb is the sentence's motor. It moves the message forward to its destination. Without these two parts, the sentence is not complete.

## SUBJECTS

To be complete, every sentence must have a subject. The **subject** tells who or what the sentence is about.

Subject

**He** always came home on time.
Action **movies** appeal to teenagers.

## Compound Subjects

When two or more separate words tell what the sentence is about, the sentence has a **compound subject.**

**Compound Subject:** **Painting** and **sewing** are my hobbies.
**Compound Subject:** My **brother** and **I** live with my grandmother.

HINT: Note that *and* is not part of the compound subject.

## Unstated Subjects

Sometimes a subject does not actually appear in a sentence but is understood. This occurs in commands and requests. The understood subject is always *you*, meaning either someone specific or anyone in general.

**Command:** Get up now or you'll be late.

S
**Unstated Subject:** (**You**) get up now or you'll be late.
**Request:** Write me an e-mail soon, please.

S
**Unstated Subject:** (**You**) write me an e-mail soon, please.

## Subjects and Prepositional Phrases

The subject of a sentence cannot be part of a prepositional phrase. A **prepositional phrase** is a group of words that begins with a **preposition,** a word like *in, on, under, after,* or *from.* Here are some examples of prepositional phrases:

| | | |
|---|---|---|
| **in** the yard | **next to** it | **before** supper |
| **on** the plane | **behind** the chair | **instead of** me |
| **under** the rug | **around** the circle | **across** the road |
| **after** school | **into** the boat | **for** the family |
| **from** the White House | **during** the storm | **at** college |

(See page 515 for a more complete list of prepositions.)

If you are looking for the subject of a sentence, first cross out all the prepositional phrases. Then figure out what the sentence is about.

                    s                    s
~~During the game~~, the coaches and the players had a fight ~~with the other team~~.

        s
The new store ~~around the corner~~ sells designer jeans.

s
Some ~~of our luggage~~ was lost ~~on the trip~~.

### Reviewing Subjects

***What is a subject?***

______________________________________________

***What is a compound subject?***

______________________________________________

______________________________________________

***What is an unstated subject?***

______________________________________________

***How can you find the subject of a sentence?***

______________________________________________

______________________________________________

**Practice 1 Identifying** Cross out the prepositional phrases in each of the following sentences, and then underline the subjects.

1. The golfer stood quietly in front of the ball.
2. Marty and Mike gave a presentation at the big convention.
3. Two of the graduates had perfect grade point averages.

4. Before I go to the store, I need to balance my checkbook.
5. Get the mayonnaise out of the refrigerator.
6. Greta told most of her friends about her engagement.
7. All of the biology students are responsible for their own lab work.
8. The cars and buses were stuck in traffic for two hours.
9. Loan me two dollars, so I can get a cup of coffee.
10. Fortunately, Stan didn't have the car for the day.

**Practice 2 Completing** Fill in each blank in the following sentences with a subject without using a person's name.

1. ______________ was voted the best restaurant in this area.
2. Walking to class, ______________ considered whether or not to change his major.
3. Sometimes, ______________ is a great bargain.
4. ______________ and ______________ are two very positive personality traits.
5. ______________ was late to work again.

**Practice 3 Writing Your Own** Write five sentences of your own, and underline the subjects.

## Verbs

To be complete, a sentence must have a verb as well as a subject. A **verb** tells what the subject is doing or what is happening.

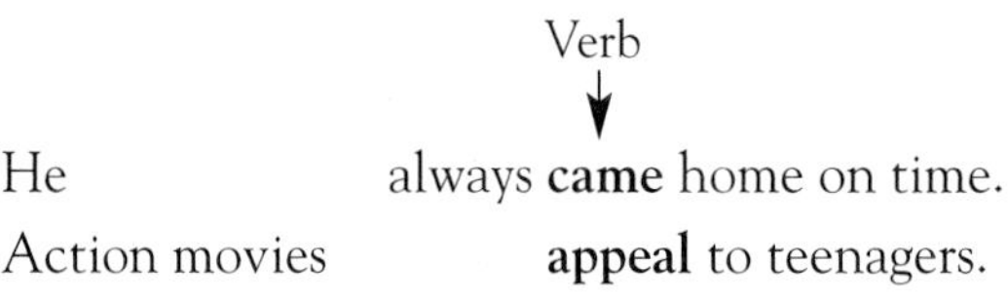

Verb
He always **came** home on time.
Action movies **appeal** to teenagers.

## Action Verbs

An **action verb** tells what a subject is doing. Some examples of action verbs are *skip*, *ski*, *stare*, *flip*, *breathe*, *remember*, *restate*, *sigh*, *cry*, *decrease*, *write*, and *pant*.

**Action Verb:** The children **laughed** at the clown.

**Action Verb:** The car **crashed** into the tree.

## Linking Verbs

A **linking verb** connects the subject to other words in the sentence that say something about it. Linking verbs are also called **state-of-being verbs** because they do not show action. Rather, they say that something "is" a particular way. The most common linking verb is *be* (*am*, *are*, *is*, *was*, *were*).

**Linking Verb:** The horses **are** in the stable.

**Linking Verb:** I **am** unhappy with the results.

Other common linking verbs are *remain*, *act*, *look*, *grow*, and *seem*.

**Linking Verb:** Darnell **remains** enthusiastic about school.

**Linking Verb:** I **act** happy even when I'm not.

**Linking Verb:** The yard **looks** neglected.

**Linking Verb:** She **grew** fonder of her aunt.

**Linking Verb:** Lupe **seems** happy with her new house.

Some words, like *smell* and *taste*, can be either action verbs or linking verbs.

**Action Verb:** I **smell** smoke.

**Linking Verb:** This house **smells** like flowers.

**Action Verb:** She **tasted** the soup.

**Linking Verb:** It **tasted** too salty.

## Compound Verbs

Just as a verb can have more than one subject, some subjects can have more than one verb. These are called **compound verbs.**

**Compound Verb:** She **cooks** and **cleans** every day.

**Compound Verb:** He **runs** and **swims** twice a week in the summer.

HINT: A sentence can have both a compound subject and a compound verb.

S S V V
**Joe** and **Mitchell** **jumped** into the boat and **started** the motor.

## Helping Verbs

Often the **main verb** (the action verb or linking verb) in a sentence needs help to convey its meaning. **Helping verbs** add information, such as when an action took place. The **complete verb** consists of a main verb and all its helping verbs.

**Complete Verb:** The children **will** return tomorrow.
**Complete Verb:** You **should** not go home with him.
**Complete Verb:** It **might** rain tomorrow.
**Complete Verb:** We **should have** gone to the concert.
**Complete Verb:** My uncle **has** given me money for Christmas.
**Complete Verb:** My sister **will be** coming for my wedding.

HINT: Note that *not* isn't part of the helping verb. Similarly, *never, always, only, just,* and *still* are never part of the verb.

**Complete Verb:** I **have** always **liked** history classes.

The most common helping verbs are

*be, am, is, are, was, were*
*have, has, had*
*do, did*

Other common helping verbs are

*may, might*
*can, could*
*will, would*
*should, used to, ought to*

REVIEWING VERBS

***What is a verb?***

___________________________________________

***What is the difference between action and linking verbs?***

______________________________________________

______________________________________________

***Give an example of a compound verb.*** ____________________

***Give an example of a helping verb.*** ____________________

***What is the difference between a subject and a verb?***

______________________________________________

______________________________________________

**Practice 4 Identifying** Underline the complete verbs in each of the following sentences.

1. The students seemed tired in class Monday morning.
2. One of my professors is a popular public speaker.
3. High school students must read *The Scarlet Letter*.
4. Timothy will go to the championships.
5. Every week we write a new essay.
6. Get out of the rain.
7. Right now, Albert is fishing in Alaska.
8. He feels like a failure because he did not pass the midterm.
9. We are going to climb Mount Everest in July.
10. Dora and Robert bought souvenirs for all of their relatives.

**Practice 5 Completing** Fill in each blank in the following sentences with a verb. Avoid using *is*, *are*, *was*, and *were* except as helping verbs.

1. Chad ______________ extreme pain after falling from the ladder and landing on his back.

2. The specialist ____________ her client about the different options.
3. Both the parents and the teachers ____________ about the need for more meetings.
4. My ill child ____________ throughout the night.
5. Red stickers on the price tags ____________ the sale items.

**Practice 6 Writing Your Own** Write five sentences of your own, and underline all the verbs in each.

## CHAPTER REVIEW

You might want to reread your answers to the questions in the review boxes before you do the following exercises.

**Review Practice 1 Identifying** Underline the subjects once and the verbs twice in each of the following sentences. Cross out the prepositional phrases first.

1. The horses in the corral are being trained for racing.
2. Matilda received a scholarship for her biology research.
3. Salespeople can earn thousands of dollars in commissions every year.
4. Each month, my office pays us for overtime.
5. The bikes and the helmets are on sale right now.
6. I am going to the grocery store for dinner.
7. Tonya's computer crashed the other day, and she used mine for her homework.
8. Grandma cannot see very well.
9. Joe and Christine are building a new house.
10. The baby played with the blocks and stacked them on top of each other.

**Review Practice 2 Completing** Fill in the missing subjects or verbs in each of the following sentences.

1. Tonight's dinner ______________ like leftovers.
2. ______________ can't remember where we said we would meet.
3. Taking that midterm ______________ my hardest challenge last week.
4. The catcher and the pitcher ______________ with the referee.
5. If you want to go with us, you ______________ to come along.
6. When Tiffany left this morning, ______________ didn't know when she would be back.
7. ______________ wear lab coats to set them apart from students.
8. Yesterday I ______________ an old box of letters from my friends in high school.
9. (You) ______________ your room before we leave.
10. ______________ was the best entertainment of the evening.

**Review Practice 3 Writing Your Own** Write a paragraph about a major decision you made within the past three years. How has it affected your life? What did you learn from the process?

## Editing Through Collaboration

Exchange paragraphs from Review Practice 3 with another student, and do the following:

1. Underline the subjects once.
2. Underline the verbs twice.

Then return the paragraph to its writer, and edit any sentences in your own paragraph that do not have both a subject and a verb. Record your errors on the Error Log in Appendix 6.

# Fragments

## Checklist for Identifying and Correcting Fragments

✔ Does each sentence have a subject?
✔ Does each sentence have a verb?

**Test Yourself**

Put an X by the sentences that are fragments.

- _____ I wanted to go to the gym yesterday.
- _____ Whose tie doesn't match his suit.
- _____ Giving up his seat for an elderly woman.
- _____ Paul asked for the most popular menu item.
- _____ While the captain was away from the cockpit.

(Answers are in Appendix 4.)

One of the most common errors in college writing is the fragment. A fragment is a piece of a sentence that is punctuated as a complete sentence. But it cannot stand alone. Once you learn how to identify fragments, you can avoid them in your writing.

## ABOUT FRAGMENTS

A complete sentence must have both a subject and a verb. If one or both are missing or if the subject and verb are introduced by a dependent word, you have only part of a sentence, a **fragment.** Even if it begins with a capital letter and ends with a period, it cannot stand alone and must be corrected in your writing. The five most common types of fragments are explained in this chapter.

**Type 1: Afterthought Fragment**

He goes to school during the day. **And works at night.**

**Type 2: *-ing* Fragment**

**Finding no one at the house.** Kenny walked back home.

**Type 3: *to* Fragment**

The school started a tutoring program. **To help improve SAT scores.**

**Type 4: Dependent-Clause Fragment**

**Because I decided to go back to school.** My boss fired me.

**Type 5: Relative-Clause Fragment**

Last summer I visited Rome. **Which is a beautiful city.**

Once you have identified a fragment, you have two options for correcting it. You can connect the fragment to the sentence before or after it or make the fragment into an independent clause.

### Ways to Correct Fragments

**Correction 1:** *Connect the fragment to the sentence before or after it.*

**Correction 2:** *Make the fragment into an independent clause:*
either *add the missing subject and/or verb,*
or *drop the subordinating word before the fragment.*

---

### Reviewing Fragments

*What is a sentence fragment?*

______________________________________________

______________________________________________

*What are the five types of fragments?*

______________________________________________

______________________________________________

______________________________________________

______________________________________________

______________________________________________

*What are the two ways to correct a fragment?*

*1.* ____________________ *2.* ____________________

## IDENTIFYING AND CORRECTING FRAGMENTS

The rest of this chapter discusses the five types of fragments and the corrections for each type.

### Type 1: Afterthought Fragments

Afterthought fragments occur when you add an idea to a sentence but don't punctuate it correctly.

**Fragment:** He goes to school during the day. **And works at night.**

The phrase *And works at night* is punctuated and capitalized as a complete sentence. Because this group of words lacks a subject, however, it is a fragment.

**Correction 1:** He goes to school during the day **and** works at night.

**Correction 2:** He goes to school during the day. **He** works at night.

#### Reviewing Afterthought Fragments

*What is an afterthought fragment?*

______________________________________________

*Give an example of an afterthought fragment.*

______________________________________________

*What are the two ways to correct an afterthought fragment?*

*1.* ______________________________________________

*2.* ______________________________________________

**Practice 1A Identifying** Underline the afterthought fragments in each of the following sentences.

1. The men on the opposing team were very strong. Everyone was scared to play them. Including me.
2. Mark peered into the window of his locked car and saw his keys. Stuck in the ignition.
3. Sharla is sleeping in class today because she stayed up late. On the telephone with her boyfriend.
4. Spring is my favorite time of year. Flowers and trees in bloom. Lovers holding hands in the park. New parents pushing babies in strollers.
5. Carlene turned in her paper on time and knew she would get a good grade. Because she really liked her topic.
6. When Aiko went to her first job interview, she was very nervous. So nervous she began biting her nails.
7. I applied for a credit card and was turned down. Even though I have four other credit cards.
8. A free lunch was served. To those who attended the seminar.
9. I used to drink whole milk, but my doctor told me to begin drinking nonfat milk. Better for my diet.
10. "Keeping up with the Joneses" is an expression. That my mother uses a lot.

**Practice 1B Correcting** Correct the fragments in Practice 1A by rewriting each sentence.

**Practice 2 Completing** Correct the following afterthought fragments using both correction 1 and correction 2. Rewrite any corrected sentences that you think could be smoother.

1. The child drew in a coloring book. With brand new crayons.
2. I bought two new books at the bookstore. Also some fashion magazines.
3. Jennifer usually drives very fast. Sometimes running stop signs.
4. My friends are going to the beach. In Santa Barbara for the weekend.
5. He walked over to my desk very slowly. Smiled in a playful way.

**Practice 3 Writing Your Own** Write five afterthought fragments of your own, and correct them.

## Type 2: *-ing* Fragments

Words that end in *-ing* are formed from verbs but cannot be the main verbs in their sentences. For an *-ing* word to function as a verb, it must have a helping verb with it (*be, do,* or *have;* see pages 582–588).

**Fragment:** **Finding no one at the house.** Kenny walked back home.

*Finding* is not a verb in this sentence because it has no helping verb. Also, this group of words is a fragment because it has no subject.

**Correction 1:** **Finding no one at the house,** Kenny walked home.
**Correction 2:** **He found no one at the house.** Kenny walked home.

HINT: When you connect an *-ing* fragment to a sentence, insert a comma between the two sentence parts. You should insert the comma whether the *-ing* part comes at the beginning or the end of the sentence.

Kenny walked home**, finding no one at the house.**
**Finding no one at the house,** Kenny walked home.

REVIEWING *-ing* FRAGMENTS

***How can you tell if an -ing word is part of a fragment or is a main verb?***

______________________________

______________________________

*Give an example of an -ing fragment.*

______________________________________________

*What are the two ways to correct an -ing fragment?*

*1.* ______________________________________________

*2.* ______________________________________________

*What kind of punctuation should you use when you join an -ing fragment to another sentence?*

______________________________________________

**Practice 4A Identifying** Underline the *-ing* fragments in each of the following sentences.

1. Driving to the store. I thought about all of the things I needed to buy.
2. The baseball player dropped the ball. Tripping over his shoelace while running to make the catch.
3. Mr. Holland was the best music teacher I ever had. Treating everyone with respect.
4. I plan to read at least one book each month. Challenging my brother to do the same.
5. Wanting to leave her parents' house. Marissa got married when she was 18 years old.
6. Raining every day. The weather is keeping me from getting yard work done.
7. The transfer papers have been approved for Tim. Moving to an office in San Francisco.
8. Her parents made her feel important and special. Attending every one of her soccer games.
9. Listening to Tamara's problems. Jeff wondered if he really wanted to date her anymore.
10. They paid the bill when we went out to dinner. Telling us that was our anniversary gift.

**Practice 4B Correcting** Correct the fragments in Practice 4A by rewriting each sentence.

**Practice 5 Completing** Correct each of the following *-ing* fragments using both methods. Remember to insert a comma when using correction 1.

1. Making the best grade in the class. Carlos was excited to tell his parents about it.
2. I think I hurt my back. Trying to move the sofa.
3. Looking back at my senior year in high school. I can't believe I dated that guy.
4. Wondering whether he left his car windows down. Shawn saw the rain begin to fall.
5. Jamar was glad he survived the accident. Seeing the damage to his car.

**Practice 6 Writing Your Own** Write five *-ing* fragments of your own, and correct them.

## Type 3: *to* Fragments

When *to* is added to a verb (*to see*, *to hop*, *to skip*, *to jump*), the combination cannot be a main verb in its sentence. As a result, this group of words is often involved in a fragment.

**Fragment:** The school started a tutoring program. **To improve SAT scores.**

Because *to* + a verb cannot function as the main verb of its sentence, *to improve SAT scores* is a fragment as it is punctuated here.

**Correction 1:** The school started a tutoring program **to improve SAT scores.**

**Correction 2:** The school started a tutoring program. **It wanted to improve SAT scores.**

HINT: A *to* fragment can also occur at the beginning of a sentence. In this case, insert a comma between the two sentence parts when correcting the fragment.

**To improve SAT scores,** the school started a tutoring program.

### Reviewing *to* Fragments

***What does a* to *fragment consist of?***

______________________________________________

***Give an example of a* to *fragment.***

______________________________________________

***What are the two ways to correct a* to *fragment?***

1. ______________________________________________

2. ______________________________________________

**Practice 7A Identifying** Underline the *to* fragments in each of the following sentences.

1. To make the crowd more excited. The rodeo clown came out and chased the bull around the arena.
2. To grow perfect roses. You should attend free classes at Home Depot.
3. The baby screamed loudly. To tell his parents he was hungry.
4. We stopped eating fried foods and sweets. To lose weight before summer.
5. To improve their chances at winning the World Series. The Texas Rangers signed Alex Rodriguez.
6. Gerry called me this afternoon. To say he won't be at the meeting.
7. To be selected for the scholarship. An applicant must be interviewed by the scholarship committee.
8. Come with me to the mall. To pick out a new dress for the dance.
9. The secretary held his boss's telephone calls. To give her time to finish her meeting.
10. To feel like a princess. Every woman should get a pedicure.

**Practice 7B Correcting** Correct the fragments in Practice 7A by rewriting each sentence.

**Practice 8 Completing** Correct the following *to* fragments using both correction 1 and correction 2. Try putting the fragment at the beginning of the sentence instead of always at the end. Remember to insert a comma when you add the *to* fragment to the beginning of a sentence.

1. Avoid driving faster than the posted speed limit. To get the best gas mileage.
2. He wanted to buy a new suit. To impress his boss.
3. Suzanne told Warren that she had a boyfriend. To avoid hurting his feelings.
4. The bank is closed on Labor Day. To give the employees time with their families.
5. I put the names and addresses in a mail merge. To make it easier to print labels.

**Practice 9 Writing Your Own** Write five *to* fragments of your own, and correct them.

## Type 4: Dependent-Clause Fragment

A group of words that begins with a **subordinating conjunction** (see the list) is called a **dependent clause** and cannot stand alone. Even though it has a subject and a verb, it is a fragment because it depends on an independent clause to complete its meaning. An **independent clause** is a group of words with a subject and a verb that can stand alone. (See pages 524–528 for help with clauses.)

Here is a list of some commonly used subordinating conjunctions that create dependent clauses.

**Subordinating Conjunctions**

| | | | |
|---|---|---|---|
| *after* | *because* | *since* | *until* |
| *although* | *before* | *so* | *when* |
| *as* | *even if* | *so that* | *whenever* |
| *as if* | *even though* | *than* | *where* |
| *as long as* | *how* | *that* | *wherever* |
| *as soon as* | *if* | *though* | *whether* |
| *as though* | *in order that* | *unless* | *while* |

**Fragment:** **<u>Because</u> I decided to go back to school.** My boss fired me.

This sentence has a subject and a verb, but it is introduced by a subordinating conjunction, *because*. As a result, this sentence is a dependent clause and cannot stand alone.

**Correction 1:** Because I decided to go back to school**, m**y boss fired me.

**Correction 2:** ~~**Because**~~ **I** decided to back to school. My boss fired me.

**HINT:** If the dependent clause comes first, put a comma between the two parts of the sentence. If the dependent clause comes second, the comma is not necessary.

**Because I decided to go back to school,** my boss fired me.

My boss fired me **because I decided to go back to school.**

## Reviewing Dependent-Clause Fragments

***What is a dependent-clause fragment?***

______________________________________________

***What type of conjunction makes a clause dependent?***

______________________________________________

***What is an independent clause?***

______________________________________________

***Give an example of a dependent-clause fragment.***

______________________________________________

***What are the two ways to correct a dependent-clause fragment?***

1. ______________________________________________

2. ______________________________________________

**Practice 10A Identifying** Underline the dependent-clause fragments in each of the following sentences.

1. I love to eat sushi. Although it's sometimes very expensive.
2. It is good to know some trivia. So that you can participate in lots of conversations.
3. After the child finished riding on it. The rocking horse stood in the corner.
4. I will have Thanksgiving dinner at my house again. As long as my parents get along with my in-laws.
5. Before she goes to work in the morning. Margaret takes her children to school.
6. The deaf child gets her hearing checked. While she attends a special school to learn sign language.
7. So that we'll have a retirement fund. The financial consultant told us to start an IRA.
8. Cheyenne went to the circus with her son. Since she had the day off work.
9. Even if it's snowing outside. Maurice exercises at the gym every Monday.
10. We're going to watch the Emmy Awards tonight. Unless the Lakers game is on at the same time.

**Practice 10B Correcting** Correct the fragments in Practice 10A by rewriting each sentence.

**Practice 11 Completing** Correct the following dependent-clause fragments using both correction 1 and correction 2. When you use correction 1, remember to add a comma if the dependent clause comes first.

1. Manny takes his basketball with him. Wherever he goes.
2. While I'm out of town. My mother will take care of my house.
3. The power bill is higher this month. Though we didn't run the air conditioner very often.
4. When she got home from work. Jamie made green beans for dinner.
5. Russ always watches TV for an hour. After he finishes studying.

**Practice 12 Writing Your Own** Write five dependent-clause fragments of your own, and correct them.

## Type 5: Relative-Clause Fragment

A **relative clause** is a dependent clause that begins with a **relative pronoun:** *who, whom whose, which,* or *that.* When a relative clause is punctuated as a sentence, the result is a fragment.

**Fragment:** Last summer I visited Rome. **Which is a beautiful city.**

*Which is a beautiful city* is a clause fragment that begins with the relative pronoun *which.* This word automatically makes the words that follow it a dependent clause, so they cannot stand alone as a sentence.

**Correction 1:** Last summer I visited Rome**, which is a beautiful city.**

**Correction 2:** Last summer I visited Rome. **It is a beautiful city.**

### Reviewing Relative-Clause Fragments

***How is a relative-clause fragment different from a dependent-clause fragment?***

______________________________________________

______________________________________________

***Give an example of a relative-clause fragment.***

______________________________________________

***What are the two ways to correct a relative-clause fragment?***

1. ______________________________________________

2. ______________________________________________

**Practice 13A Identifying** Underline the relative-clause fragments in the following sentences.

1. I made an appointment with the doctor. Whom my cousin recommended.

2. The child ate the pills. That the father left on the bathroom counter.
3. The station got a new captain. Who transferred from another department.
4. I talked to the man at the car wash. Whose nametag said "Sylvester."
5. Karen got a job at the bakery. Which makes fresh donuts every morning.
6. The patient talked to the police detectives. Who came to investigate his accident.
7. I rented a Nissan Maxima. That had leather seats.
8. Grant told me the good news. Which made me very happy.
9. Michele finished scheduling the employees. Who asked for vacation days in December.
10. My dentist is a man from Sweden. Whose last name is Hanson.

**Practice 13B Correcting** Correct the fragments in Practice 13A by rewriting each sentence.

**Practice 14 Completing** Correct the following relative-clause fragments using both correction 1 and correction 2.

1. Paul studied for the midterm with Charlotte. Who scored the highest on the first exam.
2. My girlfriend works at the bank. That is located on the corner of F Street and Market Avenue.
3. I put more memory in my computer. Which cost me about $70.
4. My boss is the man with the goatee. Whose ties are usually very colorful.
5. Penny shops only at grocery stores. That offer double coupons.

**Practice 15 Writing Your Own** Write five relative clause fragments of your own, and correct them.

## CHAPTER REVIEW

You might want to reread your answers to the questions in the review boxes before you do the following exercises.

**Review Practice 1 Identifying** Underline the fragments in the following paragraph.

> Buying an old home can be a good experience. If the house is inspected thoroughly before any papers are signed. Thinking we were getting an incredible deal. We rushed into buying a thirty-year-old house in an established neighborhood. The house had lots of personality and big living rooms. To make it perfect for entertaining. Unfortunately, there were several things about the house that we didn't see right away. Plumbing problems. Faulty wiring. Not enough insulation. We put thousands of dollars into repairs. Before we could even invite our friends over for dinner. Even though the house wasn't expensive to buy. It became very expensive for us to maintain. Eventually, we had to sell it. To keep from losing more money. The man who bought it was a contractor. Who could do most of the repairs. himself. Which is a big advantage that we didn't have.

**Review Practice 2 Correcting** Correct all the fragments you underlined in Review Practice 1 by rewriting the paragraph.

**Review Practice 3 Writing Your Own** Write a paragraph about your dream vacation. Where would you go? How long would you stay? Who would go with you, or would you go alone?

## Editing Through Collaboration

Exchange paragraphs from Review Practice 3 with another student, and do the following:

1. Put brackets around any fragments that you find.
2. Identify the types of fragments that you find.

Then return the paper to its writer, and use the information in this chapter to correct any fragments in your own paragraph. Record your errors on the Error Log in Appendix 6.

# Run-Ons

## Checklist for Identifying and Correcting Run-Ons

- ✔ Are any sentences run together without punctuation?
- ✔ Are any sentences incorrectly joined with only a comma?

**Test Yourself**

Mark any run-on sentences here with a slash between the independent clauses that are not joined correctly.

- The rainstorm washed out my garden, I had just planted spring bulbs.
- When we cleaned the house, we found the TV remote control it was between the sofa cushions.
- People in authority are often criticized and seldom thanked.
- The kids didn't find all of the Easter eggs during the hunt, when we finally found them, they were rotten.
- You should ask Aubri to cut your hair she's been cutting mine for four years.

(Answers are in Appendix 4.)

---

When we cram two separate statements into a single sentence, we create what is called a *run-on*. Run-on sentences generally distort our message and cause problems for our readers. In this chapter, you will learn how to identify and avoid run-ons in your writing.

## IDENTIFYING RUN-ON SENTENCES

Whereas a fragment is a piece of a sentence, a **run-on** is two sentences written as one. A run-on just runs on—the first sentence runs into the next without the proper punctuation between the two. There are two types of run-ons: *fused sentences* and *comma splices*.

**Fused Sentence:** The bus stopped we got off.

**Comma Splice:** The bus stopped, we got off.

Both of these sentences are run-ons. The difference between them is one comma.

A **fused sentence** is two sentences "fused" or jammed together without any punctuation. Look at these examples of run-on sentences:

**Fused Sentence:** Rosa's favorite subject is math she always does very well on her math tests.

This example consists of two independent clauses with no punctuation between them:

1. Rosa's favorite subject is math.
2. She always does very well on her math tests.

**Fused Sentence:** My grandfather likes to cook his own meals he doesn't want anyone to do it for him.

This run-on also consists of two independent clauses with no punctuation between them:

1. My grandfather likes to cook his own meals.
2. He doesn't want anyone to do it for him.

Like a fused sentence, a **comma splice** incorrectly joins two independent clauses. However, a comma splice puts a comma between the two independent clauses. The only difference between a fused sentence and a comma splice is the comma. Look at the following examples:

**Comma Splice:** Rosa's favorite subject is math, she always does very well on her math tests.

**Comma Splice:** My grandfather likes to cook his own meals, he doesn't want anyone to do it for him.

Both of these sentences consist of two independent clauses. But a comma is not the proper punctuation to separate these two clauses.

### Reviewing Run-On Sentences

***What are the two types of run-on sentences?***

____________________ ____________________

***What is the difference between them?***

________________________________________

________________________________________

**Practice 1 Identifying** Put a slash between the independent clauses that are not joined correctly.

1. Paul plays hockey every Thursday he usually gets home after dark.
2. My mom always tucked me into bed at night, that's what I remember most about her.
3. Toni borrowed my pencil yesterday then she lost it.
4. My boyfriend made my favorite cake for my birthday, I had to eat the whole thing.
5. The child needed a bone marrow transplant, we raised $10,000 last night for her cause.
6. The scoreboard says there are two outs that must be a mistake.
7. Nick sealed the envelope, and he put it in the mail, then he realized he forgot to enclose the check.
8. I got tickets to *Les Misérables* in Los Angeles I have wanted to see that play for years.
9. Stacy went off her diet this afternoon she ate fast food.
10. Kari Kruise has a morning show on my favorite radio station, I listen to her religiously.

**Practice 2 Identifying** In each run-on sentence in the following paragraph, put a slash between the independent clauses that are not joined correctly.

The fitness craze is sweeping across America, it seems like everyone has a gym membership. The best-selling food items have "light," "lite," or "fat free" on the packaging, and people are watching their cholesterol and counting calories. Only the thinnest models are shown in food advertisements they symbolize good health, responsible eating habits, and overall physical attractiveness. Ironically, thin people are even used in ads for unhealthy food items, like candy and soft drinks, this sends a very confusing message to the consumer. The stereotypes are not fair not everyone can have the "perfect" body seen in the ads. Some people are just born with bigger body shapes, and there is nothing wrong or unattractive about that. These people should learn to eat healthy foods, they should not try to be unnaturally thin.

**Practice 3 Writing Your Own** Write five fused sentences. Then write the same sentences as comma splices.

## CORRECTING RUN-ON SENTENCES

You have four different options for correcting your run-on sentences.

1. Separate the two sentences with a period, and capitalize the next word.
2. Separate the two sentences with a comma, and add a coordinating conjunction (*and*, *but*, *for*, *nor*, *or*, *so*, or *yet*).
3. Change one of the sentences into a dependent clause with a subordinating conjunction (such as *if*, *because*, *since*, *after*, or *when*) or a relative pronoun (*who*, *whom*, *whose*, *which*, or *that*).
4. Separate the two sentences with a semicolon.

### Correction 1: Use a Period

Separate the two sentences with a period, and capitalize the next word.

Rosa's favorite subject is math**. She** always does very well on her math tests.

> My grandfather likes to cook his own meals. **He** doesn't want anyone to do it for him.

**Practice 4 Correcting** Correct all the sentences in Practice 1 using correction 1.

**Practice 5 Correcting** Correct the paragraph in Practice 2 using correction 1.

**Practice 6 Writing Your Own** Correct the run-on sentences you wrote in Practice 3 using correction 1.

## Correction 2: Use a Coordinating Conjunction

Separate the two sentences with a comma, and add a coordinating conjunction (*and*, *but*, *for*, *nor*, *or*, *so*, or *yet*).

> Rosa's favorite subject is math**, so** she always does very well on her math tests.
>
> My grandfather likes to cook his own meals**, and** he doesn't want anyone to do it for him.

**Practice 7 Correcting** Correct all the sentences in Practice 1 using correction 2.

**Practice 8 Correcting** Correct the paragraph in Practice 2 using correction 2.

**Practice 9 Writing Your Own** Correct the run-on sentences you wrote in Practice 3 using correction 2.

## Correction 3: Create a Dependent Clause

Change one of the sentences into a dependent clause with a subordinating conjunction (such as *if*, *because*, *since*, *after*, or *when*) or a relative pronoun (*who*, *whom*, *whose*, *which*, or *that*).

Rosa's favorite subject is math **because** she always does very well on her math tests.

**Since** my grandfather likes to cook his own meals, he doesn't want anyone to do it for him.

For a list of subordinating conjunctions, see page 518.

**HINT:** If you put the dependent clause at the beginning of the sentence, add a comma between the two sentence parts.

**Because** she always does very well on her math tests**,** Rosa's favorite subject is math.

**Practice 10 Correcting** Correct all the sentences in Practice 1 using correction 3.

**Practice 11 Correcting** Correct the paragraph in Practice 2 using correction 3.

**Practice 12 Writing Your Own** Correct the run-on sentences you wrote in Practice 3 using correction 3.

## Correction 4: Use a Semicolon

Separate the two sentences with a semicolon.

Rosa's favorite subject is math**;** she always does very well on her math tests.

My grandfather likes to cook his own meals**;** he doesn't want anyone to do it for him.

You can also use a **transition,** a word or an expression that indicates how the two parts of the sentence are related, with a semicolon. A transition often makes the sentence smoother. It is preceded by a semicolon and followed by a comma.

Rosa's favorite subject is math**; as a result,** she always does very well on her math tests.

My grandfather likes to cook his own meals**; therefore,** he doesn't want anyone to do it for him.

Here are some transitions commonly used with semicolons.

### Transitions Used with a Semicolon Before and a Comma After

| | | | |
|---|---|---|---|
| *also* | *however* | *furthermore* | *instead* |
| *meanwhile* | *consequently* | *for example* | *similarly* |
| *in contrast* | *therefore* | *for instance* | *otherwise* |
| *of course* | *finally* | *in fact* | *nevertheless* |

**Practice 13 Correcting** Correct all the sentences in Practice 1 using correction 4.

**Practice 14 Correcting** Correct the paragraph in Practice 2 using correction 4.

**Practice 15 Writing Your Own** Correct the run-on sentences you wrote in Practice 3 using correction 4.

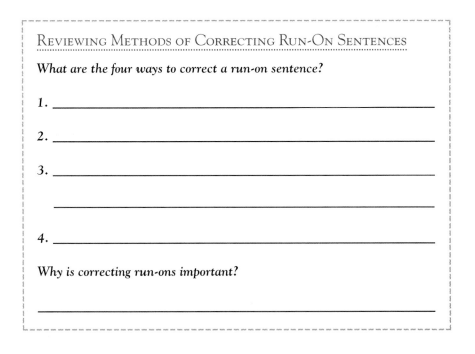

#### Reviewing Methods of Correcting Run-On Sentences

***What are the four ways to correct a run-on sentence?***

1. ______________________________

2. ______________________________

3. ______________________________

______________________________

4. ______________________________

***Why is correcting run-ons important?***

______________________________

## CHAPTER REVIEW

You might want to reread your answers to the questions in the review boxes before you do the following exercises.

**Review Practice 1 Identifying** Label each of the following sentences as fused (F), comma splice (CS), or correct (C).

1. _____ My sister woke up late this morning, she made us late for school.

2. _____ River rafting can be dangerous you need an experienced guide.

3. _____ When I dyed my hair black, I didn't know it might turn my scalp black too, it did.

4. _____ People who compete in triathlons are excellent athletes because the events are very difficult.

5. _____ Mike made an ice sculpture in his art class it was a penguin with a fish in its mouth.

6. _____ Terry needed to mow his lawn, the grass was very high, and the neighbors were complaining.

7. _____ I drove my car without engine oil, and the repairs were incredibly expensive.

8. _____ The big earthquake was on the front page of the newspaper many homes and businesses were destroyed.

9. _____ We had the perfect beach vacation planned, but then it rained the whole time we were so disappointed.

10. _____ If you stay out in the sun very long, you should use sunblock, skin cancer is a horrible thing.

**Review Practice 2 Completing** Correct the run-on sentences in Review Practice 1.

**Review Practice 3 Writing Your Own** Write a paragraph about your favorite season of the year. Why do you enjoy it? What do you do during this time of year?

## Editing Through Collaboration

Exchange paragraphs from Review Practice 3 with another student, and do the following:

1. Put brackets around any sentences that have more than one independent clause.
2. Circle the words that connect these clauses.

Then return the paper to its writer, and use the information in this chapter to correct any run-ons in your own paragraph. Record your errors on the Error Log in Appendix 6.

# Regular and Irregular Verbs

## Checklist for Using Regular and Irregular Verbs

- ✔ Are regular verbs in their correct forms?
- ✔ Are irregular verbs in their correct forms?

### Test Yourself

Underline the complete verb in each of the following sentences. Then mark an X if the form of the verb is incorrect.

- ______ The pipe has bursted.
- ______ Sim reacted to the scene calmly.
- ______ I bought my car at an auction.
- ______ We had hid in the basement.
- ______ Sorry, I eated all the cookies.

(Answers are in Appendix 4.)

All verbs are either regular or irregular. *Regular verbs* form the past and past participle by adding *-d* or *-ed* to the present tense. If a verb does not form its past tense and past participle this way, it is called an *irregular verb*.

## REGULAR VERBS

Here are the present, past, and past participle forms of some regular verbs. **Regular verbs** form the past tense and past participle by adding *-d* or *-ed*. The past participle is the verb form often used with helping verbs like *have*, *has*, or *had*.

**Some Regular Verbs**

| Present Tense | Past Tense | Past Participle (used with helping words like *have, has, had*) |
|---|---|---|
| *talk* | *talked* | *talked* |
| *sigh* | *sighed* | *sighed* |
| *drag* | *dragged* | *dragged* |
| *enter* | *entered* | *entered* |
| *consider* | *considered* | *considered* |

The different forms of a verb tell when something happened—in the *present* (I *talk*) or in the *past* (I *talked*, I *have talked*, I *had talked*).

### Reviewing Regular Verbs

***What is a regular verb?***

______________________________

***Identify three forms of a regular verb.***

__________ __________ __________

**Practice 1 Identifying** Put an X to the left of the incorrect verb forms in the following chart.

| | Present Tense | Past Tense | Past Participle |
|---|---|---|---|
| 1. | ______ clap | ______ clapped | ______ clapped |
| 2. | ______ help | ______ helpt | ______ helped |
| 3. | ______ watched | ______ watched | ______ watched |
| 4. | ______ point | ______ pointed | ______ pointd |
| 5. | ______ suggestd | ______ suggested | ______ suggested |
| 6. | ______ scream | ______ screamt | ______ screamed |
| 7. | ______ ski | ______ skid | ______ skied |
| 8. | ______ bake | ______ baken | ______ baked |
| 9. | ______ gaze | ______ gazed | ______ gazd |
| 10. | ______ reclined | ______ reclined | ______ reclined |

**Practice 2 Completing** Write the correct forms of the following regular verbs.

| | Present Tense | Past Tense | Past Participle |
|---|---|---|---|
| 1. smoke | ______________ | ______________ | ______________ |
| 2. create | ______________ | ______________ | ______________ |
| 3. paste | ______________ | ______________ | ______________ |
| 4. buzz | ______________ | ______________ | ______________ |
| 5. pick | ______________ | ______________ | ______________ |

**Practice 3 Writing Your Own** Write five sentences using at least five of the words from Practice 1.

## IRREGULAR VERBS

**Irregular verbs** do not form their past tense and past participle with *-d* or *-ed*. That is why they are irregular. Some follow certain patterns (*spring, sprang, sprung; ring, rang, rung; drink, drank, drunk; sink, sank, sunk*). But the only sure way to know the forms of an irregular verb is to spend time learning them. As you write, you can check a dictionary or the following list.

**Irregular Verbs**

| Present | Past | Past Participle (used with helping words like *have, has, had*) |
|---|---|---|
| *am* | *was* | *been* |
| *are* | *were* | *been* |
| *be* | *was* | *been* |
| *bear* | *bore* | *borne, born* |
| *beat* | *beat* | *beaten* |
| *begin* | *began* | *begun* |
| *bend* | *bent* | *bent* |
| *bid* | *bid* | *bid* |
| *bind* | *bound* | *bound* |
| *bite* | *bit* | *bitten* |
| *blow* | *blew* | *blown* |
| *break* | *broke* | *broken* |
| *bring* | *brought* (not *brang*) | *brought* (not *brung*) |
| *build* | *built* | *built* |
| *burst* | *burst* (not *bursted*) | *burst* |
| *buy* | *bought* | *bought* |
| *choose* | *chose* | *chosen* |
| *come* | *came* | *come* |
| *cost* | *cost* (not *costed*) | *cost* |
| *cut* | *cut* | *cut* |
| *deal* | *dealt* | *dealt* |

| | | |
|---|---|---|
| *do* | *did* (not *done)* | *done* |
| *draw* | *drew* | *drawn* |
| *drink* | *drank* | *drunk* |
| *drive* | *drove* | *driven* |
| *eat* | *ate* | *eaten* |
| *fall* | *fell* | *fallen* |
| *feed* | *fed* | *fed* |
| *feel* | *felt* | *felt* |
| *fight* | *fought* | *fought* |
| *find* | *found* | *found* |
| *flee* | *fled* | *fled* |
| *fly* | *flew* | *flown* |
| *forget* | *forgot* | *forgotten* |
| *forgive* | *forgave* | *forgiven* |
| *freeze* | *froze* | *frozen* |
| *get* | *got* | *got, gotten* |
| *go* | *went* | *gone* |
| *grow* | *grew* | *grown* |
| *hang*[1] *(a picture)* | *hung* | *hung* |
| *has* | *had* | *had* |
| *have* | *had* | *had* |
| *hide* | *hid* | *hidden* |
| *hear* | *heard* | *heard* |
| *hurt* | *hurt* (not *hurted)* | *hurt* |
| *is* | *was* | *been* |
| *know* | *knew* | *known* |
| *lay* | *laid* | *laid* |
| *lead* | *led* | *led* |
| *leave* | *left* | *left* |
| *lend* | *lent* | *lent* |
| *lie*[2] | *lay* | *lain* |
| *lose* | *lost* | *lost* |
| *meet* | *met* | *met* |
| *pay* | *paid* | *paid* |

| | | |
|---|---|---|
| *prove* | *proved* | *proved, proven* |
| *put* | *put* | *put* |
| *read [rēd]* | *read [rěd]* | *read [rěd]* |
| *ride* | *rode* | *ridden* |
| *ring* | *rang* | *rung* |
| *rise* | *rose* | *risen* |
| *run* | *ran* | *run* |
| *say* | *said* | *said* |
| *see* | *saw* (not *seen*) | *seen* |
| *set* | *set* | *set* |
| *shake* | *shook* | *shaken* |
| *shine*[3] *(a light)* | *shone* | *shone* |
| *shrink* | *shrank* | *shrunk* |
| *sing* | *sang* | *sung* |
| *sink* | *sank* | *sunk* |
| *sit* | *sat* | *sat* |
| *sleep* | *slept* | *slept* |
| *speak* | *spoke* | *spoken* |
| *spend* | *spent* | *spent* |
| *spread* | *spread* | *spread* |
| *spring* | *sprang* (not *sprung*) | *sprung* |
| *stand* | *stood* | *stood* |
| *steal* | *stole* | *stolen* |
| *stick* | *stuck* | *stuck* |
| *stink* | *stank* (not *stunk*) | *stunk* |
| *strike* | *struck* | *struck, stricken* |
| *strive* | *strove* | *striven* |
| *swear* | *swore* | *sworn* |
| *sweep* | *swept* | *swept* |
| *swell* | *swelled* | *swelled, swollen* |
| *swim* | *swam* | *swum* |
| *swing* | *swung* | *swung* |
| *take* | *took* | *taken* |
| *teach* | *taught* | *taught* |

| | | |
|---|---|---|
| *tear* | *tore* | *torn* |
| *tell* | *told* | *told* |
| *think* | *thought* | *thought* |
| *throw* | *threw* | *thrown* |
| *understand* | *understood* | *understood* |
| *wake* | *woke* | *woken* |
| *wear* | *wore* | *worn* |
| *weave* | *wove* | *woven* |
| *win* | *won* | *won* |
| *wring* | *wrung* | *wrung* |
| *write* | *wrote* | *written* |

1. *Hang* meaning "execute by hanging" is regular: *hang, hanged, hanged.*
2. *Lie* meaning "tell a lie" is regular: *lie, lied, lied.*
3. *Shine* meaning "brighten by polishing" is regular: *shine, shined, shined.*

### Reviewing Irregular Verbs

***What is the difference between regular and irregular verbs?***

______________________________________________________________________

***What is the best way to learn how irregular verbs form their past tense and past participle?***

______________________________________________________________________

**Practice 4 Identifying** Put an X to the left of the incorrect verb forms in the following chart.

| | Present Tense | Past Tense | Past Participle |
|---|---|---|---|
| 1. | _____ bear | _____ beared | _____ borne |
| 2. | _____ shrink | _____ shrank | _____ shrank |
| 3. | _____ swing | _____ swung | _____ swang |

4. ______ deal ______ dealed ______ dealt

5. ______ chose ______ chose ______ chosen

6. ______ freeze ______ freezen ______ frozen

7. ______ drive ______ drove ______ drived

8. ______ forget ______ forgotten ______ forgotten

9. ______ hurt ______ hurted ______ hurt

10. ______ bent ______ bent ______ bent

**Practice 5 Completing** Write the correct forms of the following irregular verbs.

| | Present Tense | Past Tense | Past Participle |
|---|---|---|---|
| 1. am | ____________ | ____________ | ____________ |
| 2. write | ____________ | ____________ | ____________ |
| 3. sweep | ____________ | ____________ | ____________ |
| 4. fall | ____________ | ____________ | ____________ |
| 5. swell | ____________ | ____________ | ____________ |

**Practice 6 Writing Your Own** Write five sentences using at least five of the words from the chart in Practice 5.

## USING *LIE/LAY* AND *SIT/SET* CORRECTLY

Two pairs of verbs are often used incorrectly—*lie/lay* and *sit/set*.

### *Lie/Lay*

| | Present Tense | Past Tense | Past Participle |
|---|---|---|---|
| **lie** (recline or lie down) | lie | lay | (have, has, had) lain |
| **lay** (put or place down) | lay | laid | (have, has, had) laid |

The verb *lay* always takes an object. You must lay something down:

Lay down *what?*

Lay down *your books*.

## *Sit/Set*

| | Present Tense | Past Tense | Past Participle |
|---|---|---|---|
| **sit** (get into a seated position) | sit | sat | (have, has, had) sat |
| **set** (put or place down) | set | set | (have, has, had) set |

Like the verb *lay*, the verb *set* must always have an object. You must set something down:

Set *what?*

Set *the presents* over here.

REVIEWING *Lie/Lay* AND *Sit/Set*

***What do* lie *and* lay *mean?***

______________________________

***What are the principal parts of* lie *and* lay*?***

______________________________

***What do* sit *and* set *mean?***

______________________________

***What are the principal parts of* sit *and* set*?***

______________________________

***Which of these verbs always take an object?***

______________________________

**Practice 7 Identifying** Choose the correct verb in the following sentences.

1. After I (sat, set) down, I felt much better.
2. All day I have (lain, laid) in my room watching TV.
3. He has (lay, laid) the blanket down for our picnic.
4. We had to (sat, set) our watches to exactly the same time.
5. (Laid, Lay) the pieces of the puzzle out on the table, please.
6. Dennis has (sat, set) in that chair for so long that his legs have gone numb.
7. I love to (lie, lay) in the sun while listening to music.
8. (Sit, Set) beneath the tree, and I will take your picture.
9. I (lay, laid) my keys down on the counter.
10. "(Lie, Lay) back and relax," said the dentist.

**Practice 8 Completing** Fill in each blank in the following sentences with the correct form of *lie/lay* or *sit/set.*

1. Suzy has ______________ in the bathtub for so long that her skin has wrinkled.
2. I could have ______________ in the moonlight looking at the stars all night.
3. The cook ______________ out all the ingredients.
4. Please ______________ those heavy boxes down before you strain your back.
5. I think I will go and ______________ down for a while.

**Practice 9 Writing Your Own** Write five sentences using variations of *lie/lay* or *sit/set.*

## CHAPTER REVIEW

You might want to reread your answers to the questions in the review boxes before you do the following exercises.

**Review Practice 1 Identifying** Write out the past tense and past participle of each verb listed here and then identify the verb as either regular or irregular.

| Present Tense | Past Tense | Past Participle | Type of Verb |
|---|---|---|---|
| 1. brush | __________ | __________ | __________ |
| 2. fix | __________ | __________ | __________ |
| 3. wear | __________ | __________ | __________ |
| 4. buy | __________ | __________ | __________ |
| 5. suffer | __________ | __________ | __________ |
| 6. have | __________ | __________ | __________ |
| 7. type | __________ | __________ | __________ |
| 8. feel | __________ | __________ | __________ |
| 9. touch | __________ | __________ | __________ |
| 10. teach | __________ | __________ | __________ |

**Review Practice 2 Completing** Fill in each blank in the following sentences with a regular or irregular verb that makes sense.

1. Yesterday, I __________ at my computer and tried to write my essay.
2. Tilda __________ over to my house last night.
3. I always smile and __________ my hand to the people on the Mardi Gras floats.
4. Geraldo has __________ his drink all over the waitress.
5. Carlos and Tom have __________ class again.
6. You should never __________ an infant; doing so can cause brain damage and death.

7. The groom smiled at his bride and ____________ the ring on her third finger.
8. The plumbing in the house has ____________ a leak.
9. Mary Ann ____________ the picture in her bedroom.
10. All cozy in my bed, I ____________ right through the earth quake.

**Review Practice 3 Writing Your Own** Write a paragraph explaining the most important parts of your daily routine. Be sure to explain why each activity is important.

## Editing Through Collaboration

Exchange paragraphs from Review Practice 3 with another student, and do the following:

1. Circle any verb forms that are not correct.
2. Suggest a correction for these incorrect forms.

Then return the paper to its writer, and use the information in this chapter to correct the verb forms in your own paragraph. Record your errors on the Error Log in Appendix 6.

# Verb Tense

## Checklist for Correcting Tense Problems

- ✔ Are present-tense verbs in the correct form?
- ✔ Are past-tense verbs in the correct form?
- ✔ Are *-ing* verbs used with the correct helping verbs?
- ✔ Are the forms of *be*, *do*, and *have* used correctly?

### Test Yourself

Underline the complete verb in each sentence. Then mark an X if the form of the verb is incorrect.

- ______ Jean always laugh when I tell that joke.
- ______ Mark jumped over the hurdle and crossed the finish line.
- ______ I had spoke to the salesclerk about a discount.
- ______ Students ain't allowed to bring food and drink into the computer lab.
- ______ My two cats be playing in the sunshine.

(Answers are in Appendix 4.)

---

When we hear the word "verb," we often think of action. We also know that action occurs in time. We are naturally interested in whether something happened today or yesterday or if it will happen at some time in the future. The time of an action is indicated by the **tense** of a verb, and the ending of a verb shows its tense. This chapter discusses the most common errors in using verb tense.

## PRESENT TENSE

One of the most common errors in college writing is reversing the present-tense endings—adding an *-s* where none is needed and omitting the *-s* where it is required. Make sure you understand this mistake, and then proofread carefully to avoid it in your writing.

**Present Tense**

| **Singular** | | **Plural** | |
|---|---|---|---|
| INCORRECT | CORRECT | INCORRECT | CORRECT |
| *NOT I walks* | *I walk* | *NOT we walks* | *we walk* |
| *NOT you walks* | *you walk* | *NOT you walks* | *you walk* |
| *NOT he, she, it walk* | *he, she, it walks* | *NOT they walks* | *they walk* |

You also need to be able to spot these same errors in sentences.

| | Error | Correction |
|---|---|---|
| NOT | **That car run** me off the road. | **That car ran** me off the road. |
| NOT | **My mother hate** my boyfriend. | **My mother hates** my boyfriend. |
| NOT | **You speaks** too fast. | **You speak** too fast. |
| NOT | **They trims** the trees once a year. | **They trim** the trees once a year. |

### Reviewing Present-Tense Errors

***What is the most common error in using the present tense?***

______________________________________________

______________________________________________

***How can you prevent this error?***

______________________________________________

**Practice 1A Identifying** Underline the present-tense errors in each of the following sentences.

1. I loves to sit in a cool theater on a hot summer day.
2. You babbles too much.
3. John is going to the mall so he cans shop for my birthday present.
4. My baby sister play well with her cousin.
5. She grow tulips every spring.
6. The car is broken; it need a new starter.
7. We seems to be lost.
8. They plans on going to the party after the show.
9. On Sundays, he get to choose where we go.
10. The little boy losts all his money.

**Practice 1B Correcting** Correct the present-tense errors in Practice 1A by rewriting each sentence.

**Practice 2 Completing** Fill in each blank in the following paragraph with the correct present-tense verbs.

My brother always (1) ______________ me to help him with his paper route. Usually I don't mind because he (2) ______________ me money and we (3) ______________ to work together. It's strange, too, because I actually (4) ______________ rolling up the papers. But lately my brother has been sleeping late while I do all the work. So I told him I was going on strike until I got either more money or more help. Do you know what he did? He fired me! Can you (5) ______________ that?

**Practice 3 Writing Your Own** Write a sentence of your own for each of the following present-tense verbs.

1. relieve ______________________________

2. feels ______________________________

3. skates ______________________________

4. asks ______________________________

5. skip ______________________________

## PAST TENSE

Just as we know that a verb is in the present tense by its ending, we see that a verb is in the past tense by its ending. Regular verbs form the past tense by adding *-d* or *-ed*. But some writers forget the ending when they are writing the past tense. Understanding this problem and then proofreading carefully will help you catch this error.

**Past Tense**

| **Singular** | | **Plural** | |
|---|---|---|---|
| INCORRECT | CORRECT | INCORRECT | CORRECT |
| NOT *I walk* | *I walked* | NOT *we walk* | *we walked* |
| NOT *you walk* | *you walked* | NOT *you walk* | *you walked* |
| NOT *he, she, it walk* | *he, she, it walked* | NOT *they walk* | *they walked* |

You also need to be able to spot these same errors in sentences.

| | **Error** | **Correction** |
|---|---|---|
| **NOT** | **She run** fast. | **She ran** fast. |
| **NOT** | **He see** the game. | **He saw** the game. |
| **NOT** | **The girl study** hard. | **The girl studied** hard. |
| **NOT** | Yes, **we learn** a lot. | Yes, **we learned** a lot. |

REVIEWING PAST-TENSE ERRORS

***What is the most common sentence error made with the past tense?***

______________________________

*How can you prevent this error?*

______________________________________________

**Practice 4A Identifying** Underline the past-tense errors in the following sentences.

1. When we were in high school, we talk on the phone for hours.
2. The radio station play the song over and over again.
3. Yesterday you edit your work.
4. She close all the windows when she left.
5. I just realize that I have already done these exercises.
6. Fernando almost kill himself on his motorcycle.
7. We follow the road to Grandmother's house.
8. I type that report a couple of weeks ago.
9. Last year, we watch the Fourth of July fireworks from our house.
10. Julie and Scarlet laugh at the joke.

**Practice 4B Correcting** Correct the past-tense errors in Practice 4A by rewriting each sentence.

**Practice 5 Completing** Fill in each blank in the following paragraph with the correct past-tense verb.

Yesterday, it was so hot that several of my friends (1) ____________ to go to the beach. They (2) ____________ a lunch, put on their swimsuits, and (3) ____________ into the car. Sadly, I had a cold, so I (4) ____________ home. Boy, am I glad I did. My friends were stuck in traffic for two hours with no air conditioning. This is the one time I (5) ____________ my lucky stars for a cold.

**Practice 6 Writing Your Own** Write a sentence of your own for each of the following past-tense verbs.

1. rained ______________________________

2. fixed ______________________________

3. sipped ______________________________

4. lifted ______________________________

5. visited ______________________________

## USING HELPING WORDS WITH PAST PARTICIPLES

Helping words are used only with the past participle form, *not* with the past-tense form. It is therefore incorrect to use a helping verb (such as *is*, *was*, *were*, *have*, *has*, or *had*) with the past tense. Make sure you understand how to use helping words with past participles, and then proofread your written work to avoid making errors.

| | Error | Correction |
|---|---|---|
| **NOT** | They **have went.** | They **have come.** |
| **NOT** | She **has decide** to get married. | She **has decided** to get married. |
| **NOT** | I **have ate** breakfast already. | I **have eaten** breakfast already. |
| **NOT** | We **had took** the test early. | We **had taken** the test early. |

### Reviewing Errors with Helping Words and Past Participles

***What is the most common sentence error made with past participles?***

______________________________

***How can you prevent this error?***

______________________________

**Practice 7A Identifying** Underline the incorrect helping words and past participles in each of the following sentences.

1. I have sang that song in French.
2. Kendra and Misty have hid all the Easter eggs.

3. The plane has flew over the ocean.
4. We have did all the necessary repairs to the fence.
5. She has forget the phone number.
6. You have sank the golf ball.
7. Ken had forgive her for her unkind words.
8. If I had knew you weren't coming, I wouldn't have cooked so much food.
9. Everyone has rode this horse trail before.
10. Mr. and Mrs. Titus have spoke to the person in charge.

**Practice 7B Correcting** Correct the helping verb and past participle errors in Practice 7A by rewriting each sentence.

**Practice 8 Completing** Fill in each blank in the following paragraph with helping verbs and past participles that make sense.

It all started in elementary school. I was a new student and didn't know a single person. For two weeks, I (1) ______________ my lunch alone. No one would play or even talk to me. Even though I didn't show it, my classmates' neglect really (2) ______________ my feelings. My little heart (3) ______________. But one day, a wonderful boy named John happened to notice me. I (4) ______________ my lunch, so he decided to share his with me. From that day forward, we (5) ______________ the best of friends.

**Practice 9 Writing Your Own** Write a sentence of your own for each of the following helping words and past participles.

1. have drunk ______________________________________________
2. has seen ______________________________________________
3. had woven ______________________________________________

4. has risen ______________________________

5. have hidden ______________________________

## USING *-ing* VERBS CORRECTLY

Verbs ending in *-ing* describe action that is going on or that was going on for a while. To be a complete verb, an *-ing* verb is always used with a helping verb. Two common errors occur with *-ing* verbs:

1. Using *be* or *been* instead of the correct helping verb
2. Using no helping verb at all

Learn the correct forms, and proofread carefully to catch these errors.

| | Error | Correction |
|---|---|---|
| **NOT** | The car **be going** too fast. | The car **is going** too fast.<br>The car **was going** too fast. |
| **NOT** | The car **been going** too fast. | The car **has been going** too fast.<br>The car **had been going** too fast. |
| **NOT** | We **watching** a movie. | We **are watching** a movie.<br>We **have been watching** a movie.<br>We **were watching** a movie.<br>We **had been watching** a movie. |

### Reviewing *-ing* Verb Errors

***What two kinds of errors occur with* -ing *verbs?***

______________________________

______________________________

***How can you prevent these errors?***

______________________________

**Practice 10A Identifying** Underline the incorrect helping verbs and *-ing* forms in each of the following sentences.

1. The cat be chasing the dog!
2. The patient been waiting for the doctor for over an hour.

3. That building be leaning to the side for over 20 years.
4. I feeling sick because I ate an entire pizza by myself.
5. We be driving down Sunset Boulevard.
6. If you be going to the concert, then so am I.
7. He been inviting the most famous people to the banquet.
8. The cooler be working again.
9. Alyssa needs a glass of milk since she eating peanut butter cookies.
10. The guests been signing in all morning.

**Practice 10B Correcting** Correct the verb form errors in Practice 10A by rewriting each sentence.

**Practice 11 Completing** Fill in each blank in the following paragraph with the correct helping verb and *-ing* form.

I (1) ____________ one of the best days of my life. It started while I (2) ____________ my clothes and found $20 in my pocket. Then on my way to work, I was pulled over by a police offer. While he (3) ____________ out the ticket, I made him laugh so hard that he tore it up and let me go with a warning. But the best part of my day happened while I was at work. I (4) ____________ to the radio when I heard my name announced. I had just won a trip to Hawaii! I (5) ____________ up and down and screaming. My boss was so happy for me that he gave me the rest of the day off.

**Practice 12 Writing Your Own** Write a sentence of your own for each of the following verbs.

1. is wishing ________________________________________
2. has been writing ____________________________________

3. were laying ______________________________

4. was driving ______________________________

5. had been sailing ______________________________

## PROBLEMS WITH *be*

The verb *be* can cause problems in both the present tense and the past tense. The following chart demonstrates these problems. Learn how to use these forms correctly, and then always proofread your written work carefully to avoid errors.

### The Verb *be*

**Present Tense**

| **Singular** | | **Plural** | |
|---|---|---|---|
| INCORRECT | CORRECT | INCORRECT | CORRECT |
| NOT *I be/ain't* | *I* **am/am not** | NOT *we be/ain't* | *we* **are/are not** |
| NOT *you be/ain't* | *you* **are/are not** | NOT *you be/ain't* | *you* **are/are not** |
| NOT *he, she, it be/ain't* | *he, she, it* **is/is not** | NOT *they be/ain't* | *they* **are/are not** |

**Past Tense**

| **Singular** | | **Plural** | |
|---|---|---|---|
| INCORRECT | CORRECT | INCORRECT | CORRECT |
| NOT *I were* | *I* **was** | NOT *we was* | *we* **were** |
| NOT *you was* | *you* **were** | NOT *you was* | *you* **were** |
| NOT *he, she, it were* | *he, she, it* **was** | NOT *they was* | *they* **were** |

Reviewing Problems with *be*

***What are two common errors made with* be*?***

______________________________

______________________________

***How can you prevent these errors?***

______________________________________________________________

**Practice 13A Identifying** Underline the incorrect forms of *be* in each of the following sentences.

1. I ain't going to travel by plane.
2. I were sitting in the seat next to the window.
3. You is going to have to study for this exam.
4. He be the person you need to talk to about enrollment.
5. We be having so much fun that we don't want to go home.
6. Since Toby forgot the handouts, we was going to look up the information on the Internet.
7. You ain't allowed to take pictures in the museum.
8. She were so tired that she took a nap.
9. You was supposed to take your clothes off before you ironed them.
10. They was not having any fun.

**Practice 13B Correcting** Correct the incorrect forms of *be* in Practice 13A by rewriting each sentence.

**Practice 14 Completing** Fill in each blank in the following paragraph with the correct form of *be*.

Crystal (1) ______________ an adventurous person. She (2) ______________ willing to try just about anything, and she usually talks me into going along with her. We have jumped out of a plane, off a bridge, and off a mountain—with a parachute or a bungee cord, of course. But when she decided we should have our belly buttons pierced, I panicked. Now, I (3) ______________ not a coward, but I knew this little adventure (4) ______________ going to hurt. Danger

I like, but pain—well, that's a different story. This (5) ______________ one adventure I had to say no to.

**Practice 15 Writing Your Own** Write a sentence of your own for each of the following verbs.

1. am not ______________________________
2. is ______________________________
3. was ______________________________
4. are ______________________________
5. were ______________________________

## PROBLEMS WITH *do*

Another verb that causes sentence problems in the present and past tenses is *do*. The following chart shows these problems. Learn the correct forms, and proofread to avoid errors.

### The Verb *do*

**Present Tense**

| **Singular** | | **Plural** | |
|---|---|---|---|
| INCORRECT | CORRECT | INCORRECT | CORRECT |
| NOT *I does* | *I* ***do*** | NOT *we does* | *we* ***do*** |
| NOT *you does* | *you* ***do*** | NOT *you does* | *you* ***do*** |
| NOT *he, she, it do* | *he, she, it* ***does*** | NOT *they does* | *they* ***do*** |

**Past Tense**

| **Singular** | | **Plural** | |
|---|---|---|---|
| INCORRECT | CORRECT | INCORRECT | CORRECT |
| NOT *I done* | *I* ***did*** | NOT *we done* | *we* ***did*** |
| NOT *you done* | *you* ***did*** | NOT *you done* | *you* ***did*** |
| NOT *he, she, it done* | *he, she, it* ***did*** | NOT *they done* | *they* ***did*** |

### Reviewing Problems with *do*

***What are two common errors made with* do?**

______________________________________________

______________________________________________

***How can you prevent these errors?***

______________________________________________

**Practice 16A Identifying** Underline the incorrect forms of *do* in each of the following sentences.

1. He really do believe in ghosts.
2. We always does the prewriting exercises before organizing our essays.
3. She done it again.
4. You does a good job even when you don't have to.
5. I done forgot the question.
6. Those machines does the work of a dozen men.
7. Yes, that computer certainly do need a new modem.
8. Henry, you done let the cat out!
9. I does all the work while you sit there and watch me.
10. Since he does the housework, I does the cooking.

**Practice 16B Correcting** Correct the incorrect forms of *do* in Practice 16A by rewriting each sentence.

**Practice 17 Completing** Fill in each blank in the following paragraph with the correct form of *do*.

I (1) ____________ believe it was love at first sight. She had the prettiest brown eyes and the silkiest blonde hair I had ever seen.

My friends warned me that she wasn't right for me, but they (2) ____________n't understand—we were made for each other. Now, I admit that she (3) ____________ slobber a bit and her hair (4) ____________ shed in the summer, but she's always happy to see me and doesn't mind my stupid mistakes. Adopting Porsche, my golden retriever, was the best thing I ever (5) ____________.

**Practice 18 Writing Your Own** Write a sentence of your own for each of the following verbs.

1. do ________________________________
2. does ________________________________
3. did ________________________________
4. does ________________________________
5. do ________________________________

## PROBLEMS WITH *have*

Along with *be* and *do*, the verb *have* causes sentence problems in the present and past tenses. The following chart demonstrates these problems. Learn the correct forms, and proofread to avoid the errors with *have*.

### The Verb *have*

**Present Tense**

| Singular | | Plural | |
|---|---|---|---|
| INCORRECT | CORRECT | INCORRECT | CORRECT |
| NOT *I has* | *I* **have** | NOT *we has* | *we* **have** |
| NOT *you has* | *you* **have** | NOT *you has* | *you* **have** |
| NOT *he, she, it have* | *he, she, it* **has** | NOT *they has* | *they* **have** |

### Past Tense

| Singular | | Plural | |
|---|---|---|---|
| INCORRECT | CORRECT | INCORRECT | CORRECT |
| NOT *I has* | *I* ***had*** | NOT *we has* | *we* ***had*** |
| NOT *you have* | *you* ***had*** | NOT *you has* | *you* ***had*** |
| NOT *he, she, it have* | *he, she, it* ***had*** | NOT *they has* | *they* ***had*** |

### Reviewing Problems with *have*

***What are two common errors made with* have*?***

______________________________________________________________________

______________________________________________________________________

***How can you prevent these errors?***

______________________________________________________________________

**Practice 19A Identifying** Underline the incorrect forms of *have* in each of the following sentences.

1. She have sewn that hem for over a week.
2. We has already taken up too much space.
3. Yesterday, I has money in my account; today I has none.
4. You has a great deal of courage when dealing with angry customers.
5. If George is late, then he have to come in through the back entrance.
6. Since there are no vacancies at the hotel, we has nowhere to go.
7. Sabine and Jackie has taken the rest of the afternoon off.
8. I has faith that you can graduate college.
9. You have better tell the truth, or you're going to get in trouble.
10. Areceli and Abigail has better get here soon.

**Practice 19B Correcting** Correct the incorrect forms of *have* in Practice 19A by rewriting each sentence.

**Practice 20 Completing** Fill in each blank in the following paragraph with the correct form of *have*.

"I (1) ______________ a secret," said my little brother Bubba, "but you (2) ______________ to promise not to tell." Now Bubba (3) ______________ the most wonderful imagination, and I knew to expect the unexpected since we (4) ______________ shared many secrets in the past. So I said, "OK, what is it?" He leaned closer, cupped his hand to my ear, and whispered, "Babies don't really come from the stork." "No!" I exclaimed, pretending shock. "Where do they come from?" I asked. "Why, they come from eggs," he proudly said. I (5) ______________ the hardest time keeping a straight face.

**Practice 21 Writing Your Own** Write a sentence of your own for each of the following verbs.

1. have ______________________________________________
2. has ______________________________________________
3. had ______________________________________________
4. has ______________________________________________
5. have ______________________________________________

## CHAPTER REVIEW

You might want to reread your answers to the questions in the review boxes before you do the following exercises.

**Review Practice 1 Identifying** Underline the incorrect verb forms in the following sentences. Check problem areas carefully: Is an *-s* needed, or is there an unnecessary *-s* ending? Do all past-tense regular verbs end in *-d* or *-ed*? Is the past participle used with helping words? Is the correct helping verb used with *-ing* verbs? Are the forms of *be*, *do*, and *have* correct?

1. Janet and Henry likes to go for long drives in the mountains.
2. Our high school band has strove to be the best in the nation.
3. I be sorry for your troubles.
4. I enjoys a hot cup of coffee while I work.
5. You done a wise thing when you signed up for classes early.
6. The birds be flying south for the winter.
7. I have wove the tapestry threads back together.
8. That fat cat been sleeping in the sun all day.
9. Those two girls think they has all the answers.
10. Last Christmas, we bake most of our gifts.

**Review Practice 2 Completing** Correct the errors in Review Practice 1 by rewriting each sentence.

**Review Practice 3 Writing Your Own** Write a short paragraph describing your favorite pet. Be careful to use all verbs in the correct tense. Check in particular for errors with *be*, *do*, and *have*.

## Editing Through Collaboration

Exchange paragraphs from Review Practice 3 with another student, and do the following:

1. Underline any incorrect tenses.
2. Circle any incorrect verb forms.

Then return the paper to its writer, and use the information in this chapter to correct any verb errors in your own paragraph. Record your errors on the Error Log in Appendix 6.

# Subject-Verb Agreement

## Checklist for Correcting Subject-Verb Agreement Problems

✔ Do all subjects agree with their verbs?

**Test Yourself**

Underline the subjects once and the complete verbs twice in the following sentences. Put an X by the sentence if its subject and verb do not agree.

- _____ Neither the shorts nor the shirt fit me.
- _____ Chips and dip is my favorite snack.
- _____ There were a large storm last night.
- _____ Some of the soil along with the fertilizer are for the orchard.
- _____ Cotton and silk is more comfortable than wool.

(Answers are in Appendix 4.)

---

Almost every day, we come across situations that require us to reach an agreement with someone. For example, you and a friend might have to agree on which movie to see, or you and your manager at work might have to agree on how many hours you'll work in the coming week. Whatever the issue, agreement is essential in most aspects of life—including writing. In this chapter, you will learn how to resolve conflicts in your sentences by making sure your subjects and verbs agree.

## SUBJECT-VERB AGREEMENT

**Subject-verb agreement** simply means that singular subjects must be paired with singular verbs and plural subjects with plural verbs. Look at this example:

**Singular:** **She works** in Baltimore.

The subject *she* is singular because it refers to only one person. The verb *works* is singular and matches the singular subject. Here is the same sentence in plural form:

**Plural:** **They work** in Baltimore.

The subject *they* is plural, more than one person, and the verb *work* is also plural.

### Reviewing Subject-Verb Agreement

***What is the difference between singular and plural?***

______________________________________________

***What kind of verb goes with a singular subject?***

______________________________________________

***What kind of verb goes with a plural subject?***

______________________________________________

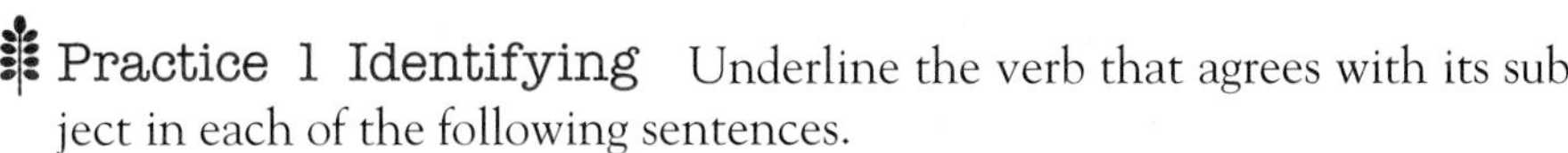

**Practice 1 Identifying** Underline the verb that agrees with its subject in each of the following sentences.

1. In her free time, Cassie (be, is) a volunteer nurse.
2. The girls usually (store, stores) their gear in the lockers.
3. Mrs. Turner always (smile, smiles) whenever she sees me.
4. Rocky, my 80-pound dog, (eat, eats) more food in a day than I do.
5. I (do, does) all of my reading for my classes at least one week ahead of time.
6. Those boys constantly (tinker, tinkers) with anything electrical.

7. You (has, have) something green in your hair.
8. At Halloween, my cousin Benjamin (get, gets) all the best candy.
9. The stars (appear, appears) brighter in the mountains.
10. He (work, works) at a very fast pace.

**Practice 2 Completing** Fill in each blank in the following sentences with a present-tense verb that agrees with its subject.

1. Every evening, Michael ______________ by the fire.
2. They ______________ many questions.
3. Neil ______________ everything chocolate.
4. We rarely ______________ down that path, for it is always dark and eerie.
5. He ______________ to only classical music.

**Practice 3 Writing Your Own** Write five sentences of your own, and underline the subjects and verbs.

## WORDS SEPARATING SUBJECTS AND VERBS

With sentences that are as simple and direct as *She works in Baltimore,* it is easy to check that the subject and verb agree. But problems can arise when words come between the subject and the verb. Often the words between the subject and verb are prepositional phrases. If you follow the advice given in Chapter 30, you will be able to find the subject and verb: *Cross out all the prepositional phrases in a sentence. The subject and verb will be among the words that are left.* Here are some examples:

S V

**Prepositional Phrases:** The **notebook** ~~for history class~~ **is** ~~in my backpack~~.

When you cross out the prepositional phrases, you can tell that the singular subject, *notebook,* and the singular verb, *is,* agree.

S V

**Prepositional Phrases:** The **roses** ~~in my garden~~ **bloom** ~~in April~~.

When you cross out the prepositional phrases, you can tell that the plural subject, *roses*, and the plural verb, *bloom*, agree.

### Reviewing Words Separating Subjects and Verbs

***What words often come between subjects and verbs?***

______________________________________________

***What is an easy way to identify the subject and verb in a sentence?***

______________________________________________

**Practice 4 Identifying** Underline the subject once and the verb twice in each of the following sentences. Cross out the prepositional phrases first. Put an X to the left of any sentence in which the subject and verb do not agree.

1. ______ Cindy, unlike many people today, do so much for others.
2. ______ That man in the red suit think a lot about his social life.
3. ______ Frog legs, in spite of what most people say, tastes like frog legs.
4. ______ The flowers in the garden smell nice.
5. ______ The economy in America seem to be getting stronger.
6. ______ My grandparents in New England likes to sit on the front porch in the summer time.
7. ______ Parents with small children finds it hard to spend quiet time together.
8. ______ All the folders on the table belong to me.
9. ______ The monkey near the front of the zoo watch people all day long.
10. ______ That movie on television looks interesting.

**Practice 5 Completing** Fill in each blank in the following sentences with a present-tense verb that agrees with its subject.

1. My little brother, despite being told otherwise, still ____________ in Santa Claus.
2. The train for San Francisco ____________ in the station at 7:45 p.m.
3. MTV, unlike VH1, ____________ to air more music videos.
4. The boxes in the hallway ____________ in the moving van.
5. The wind and the rain during a thunderstorm always ____________ me.

**Practice 6 Writing Your Own** Write five sentences of your own with at least one prepositional phrase in each, and underline the subjects and verbs.

## MORE THAN ONE SUBJECT

Sometimes a subject consists of more than one person, place, thing, or idea. These subjects are called **compound** (as discussed in Chapter 30). Follow these three rules when matching a verb to a compound subject:

1. **When compound subjects are joined by *and*, use a plural verb.**

**Plural:** **Thursday** and **Friday were** hot days.

The singular words *Thursday* and *Friday* together make a plural subject. Therefore, the plural verb *were* is needed.

2. **When the subject appears to have more than one part but the parts refer to a single unit, use a singular verb.**

**Singular:** **Macaroni and cheese is** Eli's favorite food.

*Macaroni* is one item and *cheese* is one item, but Eli does not eat one without the other, so they form a single unit. Because they are a single unit, they require a singular verb—*is*.

3. **When compound subjects are joined by *or* or *nor*, make the verb agree with the subject closest to it.**

**Singular:** Neither **hot dogs** nor **chicken was** on the menu.

The compound subject closest to the verb is *chicken*, which is singular. Therefore, the verb must be singular—*was*.

**Plural:** Neither **chicken** nor **hot dogs were** on the menu.

This time, the compound subject closest to the verb is *hot dogs*, which is plural. Therefore, the verb must be plural—*were*.

### Reviewing Subject-Verb Agreement with More than One Subject

***Do you use a singular or plural verb with compound subjects joined by*** **and?**

______________________________________________

***Why should you use a singular verb with a subject like*** **macaroni and cheese?**

______________________________________________

***If one part of a compound subject joined by*** **or** ***or*** **nor** ***is singular and the other is plural, how do you decide whether to use a singular or plural verb?***

______________________________________________

**Practice 7 Identifying** Underline the verb that agrees with its subject in each of the following sentences. Cross out the prepositional phrases first.

1. You and I (was, were) going the wrong way down a one-way street.
2. Mashed potatoes and gravy (taste, tastes) better with a little salt and pepper.
3. Either the mosquitoes or the wind (cause, causes) my skin problems.
4. Your tuition and parking fees (is, are) due at the beginning of school.
5. Celery and peanut butter (is, are) my favorite snack.
6. Neither the professor nor the students (knows, know) the answer to this question.
7. Either the gardener or I (weed, weeds) the front flowerbed.

8. Neither the steak nor the hamburgers (need, needs) seasoning on the grill.
9. Marcy and I (do, does) wish we could go to the Huntington Library.
10. Jack's Crab Shack and Papa Joe's (have, has) some of the best crawfish.

**Practice 8 Completing** Fill in each blank in the following sentences with a present-tense verb that agrees with its subject. Avoid *is*, *are*, *was*, and *were*. Cross out the prepositional phrases first.

1. Either lilies or tulips ______________ well in the spring.
2. Pie and ice cream ______________ the best dessert.
3. The ants and flies in the house ______________ me.
4. The train and the passengers ______________ sometime this evening.
5. Neither the entrees nor the dessert ______________ appetizing tonight.

**Practice 9 Writing Your Own** Write a sentence of your own for each of the following compound subjects.

1. either the handouts or the manuscript ______________________________
2. brooms and brushes ______________________________
3. neither the nurses nor the doctor ______________________________
4. ham and cheese ______________________________
5. the horse and her foal ______________________________

## VERBS BEFORE SUBJECTS

When the subject follows its verb, the subject may be hard to find, which makes the process of agreeing subjects and verbs difficult. Subjects come after verbs in two particular situations—when the sentence begins with *here* or *there* and when a question begins with *who*, *what*, *where*, *when*, *why*, or *how*. Here are some examples:

**Verb Before Subject:** Here **are** the **decorations** ~~for the party~~.

**Verb Before Subject:** There **is** iced **tea** ~~in the refrigerator~~.

In sentences that begin with *here* or *there*, the verb always comes before the subject. Don't forget to cross out prepositional phrases to help you identify the subject. One of the words that's left will be the subject, and then you can check that the verb agrees with it.

v s

**Verb Before Subject:** Who **is** that attractive **man** ~~in the blue suit~~?

v s

**Verb Before Subject:** Where **are** the valuable **paintings** kept?

v s v

**Verb Before Subject:** When **are you flying** ~~to Rome~~?

In questions that begin with *who*, *what*, *when*, *where*, *why*, and *how*, the verb comes before the subject or is split by the subject, as in the last example.

### Reviewing Verbs Before Subjects

***Where will you find the verb in sentences that begin with* here *or* there?**

______________________________________________

***Where will you find the verb in questions that begin with* who, what, where, when, why, *and* how?**

______________________________________________

**Practice 10 Identifying** Underline the subject once and the verb twice in each of the following sentences. Cross out the prepositional phrases first.

1. Here lies the cause of the problem despite the evidence.
2. Who is the leader of your group?

3. How do you feel after your recent operation?
4. Where in the world are my keys?
5. When does the first act of the second play begin?
6. There on the table are your books.
7. What was the name of the band?
8. Why did Jamie lie on her questionnaire?
9. There goes my dog down the street again.
10. Here is the house with the blue roof.

**Practice 11 Completing** Fill in each blank in the following sentences with a verb that agrees with its subject. Cross out the prepositional phrases first.

1. Where ______________ the rest of the apricot pie?
2. Over the hill, there ______________ a great swimming hole.
3. Why ______________ their dirty clothes on the bathroom floor?
4. How many times ______________ your sister asked you to fix that hair dryer?
5. What ______________ this mess in the front yard?

**Practice 12 Writing Your Own** Write a sentence of your own for each of the following words and phrases.

1. there may be ______________________________________________
2. who paints ______________________________________________
3. how did he ______________________________________________
4. when is ______________________________________________
5. here is ______________________________________________

## COLLECTIVE NOUNS

**Collective nouns** name a group of people or things. Examples include such nouns as *army*, *audience*, *band*, *class*, *committee*, *crew*, *crowd*, *family*, *flock*, *gang*, *jury*, *majority*, *minority*, *orchestra*, *senate*, *team*, and *troop*. Collective nouns can be singular or plural. They are singular when they refer to a group as a single unit. They are plural when they refer to the individual actions or feelings of the group members.

S V
**Singular:** The string **quartet performs** three times a year.

*Quartet* refers to the entire unit or group. Therefore, it requires the singular verb *performs*.

S V
**Plural:** The string **quartet get** their new instruments on Monday.

Here *quartet* refers to the individual members, who will each get a new instrument, so the plural verb *get* is used.

### Reviewing Collective Nouns

***When is a collective noun singular?***

______________________________

***When is a collective noun plural?***

______________________________

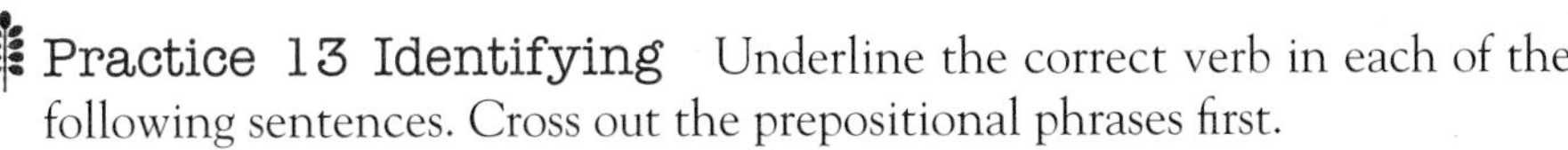

**Practice 13 Identifying** Underline the correct verb in each of the following sentences. Cross out the prepositional phrases first.

1. The audience (listen, listens) intently to the guest speaker.
2. The majority (have, has) voted at different polling booths.
3. The orchestra (play, plays) different selections, depending on the concert.

4. Our high school cheerleading squad (is, are) all going to different colleges.
5. The litter of puppies (get, gets) a bath today.
6. Our team (win, wins) the state championship every year.
7. My family (love, loves) one another very much.
8. The jury (were, was) undecided about the case.
9. The army (march, marches) through the snow and rain.
10. The police crew routinely (stop, stops) drivers on the road to test for drunk driving.

**Practice 14 Completing** Fill in each blank in the following sentences with a present-tense verb that agrees with its subject. Cross out the prepositional phrases first.

1. A flock of geese always ______________ south for the winter.
2. The crew ______________ trouble making sure everyone has a good time.
3. The school orchestra ______________ this competition every year.
4. The army ______________ students who have degrees as officers.
5. The senate ______________ according to individual beliefs.

**Practice 15 Writing Your Own** Write a sentence of your own using each of the following words as a plural subject.

1. committee ______________________________________________
2. gang ______________________________________________
3. class ______________________________________________
4. minority ______________________________________________
5. group ______________________________________________

## INDEFINITE PRONOUNS

**Indefinite pronouns** do not refer to anyone or anything specific. Some indefinite pronouns are always singular, and some are always plural. A few can be either singular or plural, depending on the other words in the sentence. When an indefinite pronoun is the subject of a sentence, the verb must agree with the pronoun. Here is a list of indefinite pronouns.

**Indefinite Pronouns**

| Always Singular | | Always Plural | Either Singular or Plural |
|---|---|---|---|
| *another* | *neither* | *both* | *all* |
| *anybody* | *nobody* | *few* | *any* |
| *anyone* | *none* | *many* | *more* |
| *anything* | *no one* | *others* | *most* |
| *each* | *nothing* | *several* | *some* |
| *either* | *one* | | |
| *everybody* | *other* | | |
| *everyone* | *somebody* | | |
| *everything* | *someone* | | |
| *little* | *something* | | |
| *much* | | | |

**Singular:** **No one** (S) ever **changes** (V) at work.

**Everybody** (S) **refuses** (V) to work harder.

**Plural:** **Many** (S) **take** (V) long lunches and **go** (V) home early.

**Others** (S) **stay** (V) late but are **tired** (V) and unmotivated.

The pronouns that can be either singular or plural are singular when they refer to singular words and plural when they refer to plural words.

S V
**Singular:** **Some** of Abby's *day* **was** hectic.

*Some* is singular because it refers to *day*, which is singular. The singular verb *was* agrees with the singular subject *some*.

S V
**Plural:** **Some** of Abby's *co-workers* **were** late.

*Some* is plural because it refers to *co-workers*, which is plural. The plural verb *were* agrees with the plural subject *some*.

REVIEWING INDEFINITE PRONOUNS

***What is an indefinite pronoun?***

_______________________________________________

*When are* **all, any, more, most,** *and* **some** *singular or plural?*

_______________________________________________

_______________________________________________

**Practice 16 Identifying** Underline the verb that agrees with its subject in each of the following sentences. Cross out the prepositional phrases first.

1. All of my money (is, are) gone.
2. Both of the pools (was, were) treated with chlorine.
3. No one (do, does) more work than she.
4. Something (fly, flies) into my window every night and (buzz, buzzes) around my head.
5. Most of Omar's friends (seem, seems) friendly.
6. Everybody (stand, stands) at attention when the general is speaking.
7. Several of the workers (is, are) on strike.
8. Everything always (go, goes) wrong on Friday the thirteenth.

9. None of the appointments (fit, fits) my schedule this week.
10. Few actually (read, reads) the instructions before putting the machine together.

**Practice 17 Completing** Fill in each blank in the following sentences with a present-tense verb that agrees with its subject. Cross out the prepositional phrases first.

1. Most of the people ______________ to work in the mornings.
2. No one really ______________ if he will accept the job.
3. Both ______________ the consequences of their actions.
4. None of the fake contestants ______________ it was a joke.
5. Somebody ______________ moving my things off my desk.

**Practice 18 Writing Your Own** Write a sentence of your own using each of the following words as a subject, combined with one of the following verbs: *is*, *are*, *was*, *were*. Check that the subject and verb agree.

1. anything ______________________________________________
2. others ______________________________________________
3. some ______________________________________________
4. any ______________________________________________
5. several ______________________________________________

## CHAPTER REVIEW

You might want to review your answers to the questions in the review boxes before you do the following exercises.

**Review Practice 1 Identifying** Underline the subject once and the verb twice in each of the following sentences. Cross out the prepositional phrases first. Then put an X to the left of each sentence in which the subject and verb do not agree. Correct the subjects and verbs that don't agree by rewriting the incorrect sentences.

1. ______ There sit the man who will be the next president of the United States.
2. ______ The moon and the stars in the evening sky shines brightly.
3. ______ The team usually practice off the track every Tuesday.
4. ______ Some of the fish in that tank appear to be sick.
5. ______ Doctor, how is the patient in room 204?
6. ______ Something rather sharp keep pinching me on my back.
7. ______ Sour cream and onion are my favorite type of dip.
8. ______ Here are the recipe from my grandmother.
9. ______ Neither the chairs nor the table match the décor in this room.
10. ______ My gang of artistic friends finds the new trends exciting.

**Review Practice 2 Completing** Fill in each blank in the following sentences with a present-tense verb that agrees with its subject.

1. My gang ______________ late for the show.
2. Neither wind nor rain nor snow ______________ us from going outside.
3. Here ______________ where Eugene's great-grandmother built her first house.
4. Several of the guests ______________ the secret code to the room back stage.
5. None of the water ______________ safe for drinking.
6. Where ______________ the tourists go for information about hotels?

7. Nothing ____________ to be wrong with the car.

8. The track team ____________ 5 miles every day, regardless of the weather.

9. Steven's mother and father ____________ planning a vacation to Paris.

10. There in that apartment building ____________ my former high school principal.

**Review Practice 3 Writing Your Own** Write a paragraph explaining why you did or did not join a committee, team, or other group. Make sure all your subjects and verbs agree.

## Editing Through Collaboration

Exchange paragraphs from Review Practice 3 with another student, and do the following:

1. Underline the subject once in each sentence.
2. Underline the verbs twice.
3. Put an X by any verbs that do not agree with their subjects.

Then return the paper to its writer, and use the information in this chapter to correct any subject-verb agreement errors in your own paragraph. Record your errors on the Error Log in Appendix 6.

# More on Verbs

## Checklist for Correcting Tense and Voice Problems

- ✔ Are verb tenses consistent?
- ✔ Are sentences written in the active voice?

**Test Yourself**

Label each sentence I if the verb tenses are inconsistent or P if it uses the passive voice.

- _____ George raced across the field and the ball was caught.
- _____ The old record was broken by Justin.
- _____ That painting was done by a famous artist.
- _____ In the future, we may live on Mars, and we have produced our food in greenhouses.
- _____ First, the baker prepares the dough, and then she will cut out the cookies.

(Answers are in Appendix 4.)

Verbs communicate the action and time of each sentence. So it is important that you use verb tense consistently. Also, you should strive to write in the active, not the passive, voice. This chapter provides help with both of these sentence skills.

## CONSISTENT VERB TENSE

Verb tense refers to the time an action takes place—in the present, the past, or the future. The verb tenses in a sentence should be consistent. That is, if you start out using one tense, you should not switch tenses unless absolutely necessary. Switching tenses can be confusing. Here are some examples:

Present Present
**Inconsistent:** When the sun **sinks** into the bay, and the moon **rises**

Past
from behind the trees, the pelicans **flew** away to the south.

Present Present
**Consistent:** When the sun **sinks** into the bay, and the moon **rises**

Present
from behind the trees, the pelicans **fly** away to the south.

Past Present
**Inconsistent:** They **skidded** off the road yesterday when the rain **is** heavy.

Past Past
**Consistent:** They **skidded** off the road yesterday when the rain **was** heavy.

Future
**Inconsistent:** My brother **will receive** his degree in June, and then

Present
he **moves** to Boston.

Future
**Consistent:** My brother **will receive** his degree in June, and then

Future
he **will move** to Boston.

### Reviewing Consistent Verb Tenses

***Why should verb tenses be consistent?***

______________________________________________

***What problem do inconsistent verb tenses create?***

______________________________________________

**Practice 1A Identifying** In the following sentences, write C if the verb tense is consistent or I if it is inconsistent.

1. _____ Scott walked to the store and buy some milk.
2. _____ Last evening, Charles waited at the park for his friends, but they never make it.
3. _____ According to the instructor, we will need to bring a change of clothes, and we have to get all of our medical records updated.
4. _____ They grilled fresh fish over the fire and sleep under the stars.
5. _____ The salesclerk was rude to me, yet I thanked her anyway.
6. _____ When the surf breaks through the reef, it gushes into our backyard and flooded the deck.
7. _____ The judge will be sentencing the criminal this week, but he wouldn't hear any new testimony.
8. _____ The firefighters periodically check their equipment and will run routine drills.
9. _____ That cottage used to belong to Jay's uncle, and Jay used to spend his summers there.
10. _____ Next year, I will finish all my coursework and will graduate with honors.

**Practice 1B Correcting** Correct the verb tense errors in Practice 1A by rewriting the inconsistent sentences.

**Practice 2 Completing** Fill in each blank in the following sentences with consistent verbs.

1. During Kendra's vacation, she ____________ along the beach and ____________ souvenirs for her friends and family.
2. Out of the box ____________ the cat, and then he ____________ under the table.
3. Oh, no, I ____________ to bring the decorations for the prom, and I ____________ the invitations sitting on my kitchen counter.
4. Actors and singers generally ____________ a lot of media coverage and ____________ featured on many special television shows.
5. Madonna's music and videos ____________ many people, but her loyal fans ____________ her.

**Practice 3 Writing Your Own** Write five sentences of your own with at least two verbs in each. Make sure your tenses are consistent.

## USING THE ACTIVE VOICE

In the **active voice,** the subject performs the action. In the **passive voice,** the subject receives the action. Compare the following two examples:

**Passive Voice:** The mayor **was accused** of stealing **by the police.**

**Active Voice:** **The police accused** the mayor of stealing.

The active voice adds energy to your writing. Here is another example. Notice the difference between active and passive.

**Passive Voice:** The cake **was baked** for Tim's birthday **by my grandmother.**

**Active Voice:** **My grandmother baked the cake** for Tim's birthday.

### Reviewing Active and Passive Voice

***What is the difference between the active and passive voice?***

______________________________________________

______________________________________________

***Why is the active voice usually better than the passive?***

______________________________________________

**Practice 4A Identifying** Write A if the sentence is in the active voice and P if it is in the passive voice.

1. ______ The water was spilled on the floor by you.
2. ______ All of our belongings burned in the fire.
3. ______ Knives and swords were juggled by the entertainer.
4. ______ Those gifts were bought as a joke.
5. ______ Alisha's ankle was twisted while skiing.
6. ______ The astronauts landed on the moon and planted a flag.
7. ______ Flowers are being sent to the funeral home.
8. ______ Jordan hit the ball over the fence into the neighbor's yard.
9. ______ The experimental medicines were shipped to the laboratory for further testing.
10. ______ People who heckle the politicians will be escorted from the building.

**Practice 4B Correcting** Rewrite the passive sentences in Practice 4A in the active voice.

**Practice 5 Completing** Complete the following sentences in the active voice.

1. Many boxes of clothes ________________________________________.

2. A can of hairspray ________________________________________.

3. A plate of food ________________________________________.

4. The boy's ball ________________________________________.

5. The trip ________________________________________.

**Practice 6 Writing Your Own** Write five sentences in the passive voice. Then rewrite them in the active voice.

## CHAPTER REVIEW

You might want to reread your answers to the questions in the review boxes before you do the following exercises.

**Review Practice 1A Identifying** Label each sentence I if the verb tenses are inconsistent, P if it is in the passive voice, or C if it is correct. Then correct the inconsistent and passive sentences by rewriting them.

1. ______ You should pick up the trash in the yard.

2. ______ The yacht keeps listing to the left and will need to be fixed before anyone can board her.

3. ______ The ornaments sitting above the fireplace were given to my grandmother by famous people and were some of her favorite belongings.

4. ______ Tomorrow, you and I will go to the lake and fished for trout.

5. ______ I drank the Sprite and eat all the cookies.

6. ______ Ken wished he had remembered his girlfriend's birthday and prays that she will forgive him.

7. ______ The wad of gum was placed under the desk by a naughty boy.

8. ______ The piano is played by Jeannie, and the songs are sung by Mark.

9. _____ Your purchases will be sent to you later this week.

10. _____ A caring individual thinks of others before themselves and performs unselfish acts.

**Review Practice 2 Completing** Fill in each blank with consistent, active verbs.

1. Mike ____________ the house on time but ____________ stuck in traffic.

2. I ____________ the hot coffee too quickly and ____________ my tongue.

3. The pebble in my shoe ____________ my foot, so I ____________ down.

4. The bird ____________ out the window.

5. Clare still ____________ in the Easter Bunny, but then she ____________ only 3 years old.

**Review Practice 3 Writing Your Own** Write a paragraph about a recent, difficult decision you have made. Be sure to give the reasons for your decision. Stay in the present tense, and use the active voice.

## Editing Through Collaboration

Exchange paragraphs from Review Practice 3 with another student, and do the following:

1. Circle all verbs that are not consistent in tense.
2. Underline any verbs in the passive voice.

Then return the paper to its writer, and use the information in this chapter to correct any verb consistency or voice errors in your own paragraph. Record your errors on the Error Log in Appendix 6.

CHAPTER 41

# Pronoun Problems

## Checklist for Using Pronouns

- ✔ Are all subject pronouns used correctly?
- ✔ Are all object pronouns used correctly?
- ✔ Are all possessive pronouns used correctly?
- ✔ Are pronouns used in *than* or *as* comparisons in the correct form?
- ✔ Are the pronouns *this*, *that*, *these*, and *those* used correctly?

**Test Yourself**

Correct the pronoun errors in the following sentences.

- The shirt was mines' to begin with.
- Tom told Valerie and I the most exciting story.
- James can type a lot faster than me.
- Those there running shoes are Kim's.
- Becca and me are going to the movies tonight.

(Answers are in Appendix 4.)

---

**Pronouns** are words that take the place of nouns. They help us avoid repeating nouns. In this chapter, we'll discuss five types of pronoun problems: (1) using the wrong pronoun as a subject, (2) using the wrong pronoun as an object, (3) using an apostrophe with a possessive pronoun, (4) misusing pronouns in comparisons, and (5) misusing demonstrative pronouns.

## PRONOUNS AS SUBJECTS

Single pronouns as subjects usually don't cause problems.

| | |
|---|---|
| **Subject Pronoun:** | **I** attended the opera with my aunt and uncle. |
| **Subject Pronoun:** | **They** relocated to New York. |

You wouldn't say "*Me* attended the game" or "*Them* went to Los Angeles." But an error often occurs when a sentence has a compound subject and one or more of the subjects is a pronoun.

| | Error | Correction |
|---|---|---|
| NOT | The boys and **us** competed for the trophy. | The boys and **we** competed for the trophy. |
| NOT | **Her** and **me** decided to go to Paris. | **She** and **I** decided to go to Paris. |

To test whether you have used the correct form of the pronoun in a compound subject, try each subject alone:

| | |
|---|---|
| **Subject Pronoun?** | **The boys** and **us** competed for the trophy. |
| **Test:** | **The boys** competed for the trophy. **YES** |
| **Test:** | **Us** competed for the trophy. **NO** |
| | **We** competed for the trophy. **YES** |
| **Correction:** | **The boys** and **we** competed for the trophy. |

Here is a list of subject pronouns.

**Subject Pronouns**

| **Singular** | **Plural** |
|---|---|
| *I* | *we* |
| *you* | *you* |
| *he, she, it* | *they* |

### Reviewing Pronouns as Subjects

***Name two subject pronouns.***

___

***How can you test whether you are using the correct pronoun as the subject of a sentence?***

___

**Practice 1 Identifying** Underline the pronouns used as subjects in each of the following sentences.

1. Diane and he will be gone for at least a week.
2. He is going to have to work faster if he wants to meet the deadline.
3. Dean quit his job after he received a better offer.
4. They are going to have to take a different route.
5. Simon went to the chiropractor because he was having back problems.
6. You can take your turn after Joey has his.
7. "I really don't want to go," he said.
8. We cannot use the elevator because it is not working.
9. During the interview, Laura presented herself in a professional manner, so she got the job.
10. She and I have been best friends since I can remember.

**Practice 2 Completing** Fill in each blank in the following paragraph with a subject pronoun.

At first, my friends had me convinced that (1) ______________ should go on the annual deep-sea fishing trip. (2) ______________ spoke on and on about how much fun the last trip was. But before long, Brian admitted that (3) ______________ got sick once the boat was out at sea. Then Misty explained how the captain of the boat cut off the heads of the fish and gutted them. (4) ______________ found the whole process exciting. (5) ______________ can just imagine my reaction! I don't think I'll be joining my friends on their fishing trip.

**Practice 3 Writing Your Own** Write a sentence of your own for each of the following subject pronouns.

1. they ______________________

2. you ______________________

3. he ______________________

4. it ______________________

5. I ______________________

## PRONOUNS AS OBJECTS

One of the most frequent pronoun errors is using a subject pronoun when the sentence calls for an object pronoun. The sentence may require an object after a verb, showing that someone or something receives the action of the verb. Or it may be an object of a preposition that is required (see page 515 for a list of prepositions).

| | Error | Correction |
|---|---|---|
| **NOT** | She gave Kenisha and **I** some money. | She gave Kenisha and **me** some money. |
| **NOT** | The secret is between you and **I.** | The secret is between you and **me.** |

Like the subject pronoun error, the object pronoun error usually occurs with compound objects. Also like the subject pronoun error, you can test whether you are using the correct pronoun by using each object separately.

| | |
|---|---|
| **Object Pronoun?** | She gave **Kenisha** and **I** some money. |
| **Test:** | She gave **Kenisha** some money. **YES** |
| **Test:** | She gave **I** some money. **NO** |
| | She gave **me** some money. **YES** |
| **Correction:** | She gave **Kenisha** and **me** some money. |

Here is a list of object pronouns:

**Object Pronouns**

| **Singular** | **Plural** |
|---|---|
| *me* | *us* |
| *you* | *you* |
| *him, her, it* | *them* |

### Reviewing Pronouns as Objects

***In what two places are pronouns used as objects?***

______________________________________________

***How can you test whether you have used the correct pronoun as the object in a sentence?***

______________________________________________

**Practice 4 Identifying** Underline the correct object pronoun in each of the following sentences.

1. Issa's grandmother raised (her, she) since she was 5.
2. The nurse gave (I, me) a vaccine for measles.
3. The wonderful neighbors welcomed (we, us) Wilsons to the community with a cake.
4. Corrina accidentally sprayed my sister and (I, me) with the hose.
5. Hey, that bully took the ball from (them, they).
6. All are going on the trip except for you and (him, he).
7. We froze because behind (we, us) was a large bear.
8. Jimmy threw the ball to (him, he), and he caught it.
9. For (her, she), I will sit through this awful movie.
10. The crowd was cheering so enthusiastically that the band had to play one more song for (them, they).

**Practice 5 Completing** Fill in each blank in the following sentences with an object pronoun.

1. Between the two of ______________, we should be able to fix the problem.
2. He asked you and ______________ to the same dance.
3. Unlike ______________, I am going to take emergency gear on this hiking trip.

4. According to you and ____________, the test will take one hour.

5. The priest took ____________ on a tour of the temple.

**Practice 6 Writing Your Own** Write a sentence of your own for each of the following object pronouns.

1. us ______________________________
2. him ______________________________
3. me ______________________________
4. them ______________________________
5. her ______________________________

## POSSESSIVE PRONOUNS

**Possessive pronouns** show ownership (*my* house, *her* baseball, *our* family). (See page 509 for a list of pronouns.) An apostrophe is used with *nouns* to show ownership (*Jack's* dog, the *farmer's* tractor, the *people's* opinions). But an apostrophe is *never* used with possessive pronouns.

**Possessive Pronouns**

| Singular | Plural |
|---|---|
| *my, mine* | *our, ours* |
| *your, yours* | *you, yours* |
| *his, her, hers* | *their, theirs* |

| | Error | Correction |
|---|---|---|
| NOT | That house is **their's.** | That house is **theirs.** |
| NOT | The book on the table is **yours'.** | The book on the table is **yours.** |
| NOT | The dog chased **it's** tail. | The dog chased **its** tail. |

### Reviewing Possessive Pronouns

***When do you use an apostrophe with a noun?***

_______________________________________________

***Do possessive pronouns take apostrophes?***

_______________________________________________

**Practice 7 Identifying** Underline the correct possessive pronoun in each of the following sentences.

1. The computer needs its monitor fixed.
2. Both of my aunts live in New Mexico.
3. That piece of cake on the counter is hers.
4. The children left their toys in the driveway.
5. Hey! That was his.
6. When the hurricane hit, we knew our vacation was over.
7. These are her published stories, though she will not admit it.
8. Of all the science entries, we thought ours was the best.
9. That front-row seat was supposed to be mine.
10. These clothes are too outrageous to be mine; they must be yours.

**Practice 8 Completing** Fill in each blank in the following sentences with a possessive pronoun.

1. These books aren't ______________, so they must be ______________.
2. ____________ dogs bothered the neighbors so much that we had to move.
3. The filming crew left ______________ equipment on the set.
4. Look at John's dog carrying ______________ bowl in his mouth.
5. The copy machine won't work because ______________ ink cartridge is empty.

**Practice 9 Writing Your Own** Write a sentence of your own for each of the following possessive pronouns.

1. mine ________________________________________

2. theirs ________________________________________

3. his ________________________________________

4. its ________________________________________

5. our ________________________________________

## PRONOUNS IN COMPARISONS

Sometimes pronoun problems occur in comparisons with *than* or *as*. An object pronoun may be mistakenly used instead of a subject pronoun. To find out if you are using the right pronoun, you should finish the sentence as shown here.

| | Error | Correction |
|---|---|---|
| **NOT** | She can analyze poems better than **me.** | She can analyze poems better than **I** [can analyze poems]. |
| **NOT** | Lilly is not as good a piano player as **him.** | Lilly is not as good a piano player as **he** [is]. |

HINT: Sometimes an object pronoun is required in a *than* or *as* comparison. But errors rarely occur in this case because the subject pronoun sounds so unnatural.

| | Error | Correction |
|---|---|---|
| **NOT** | Kay dislikes him more that she dislikes **I.** | Kay dislikes him more than she dislikes **me.** |

### REVIEWING PRONOUNS IN COMPARISONS

***What causes pronoun problems in comparisons?***

________________________________________

________________________________________

***How can you test whether to use a subject pronoun or an object pronoun in a* than *or* as *comparison?***

_______________________________________________

**Practice 10 Identifying** Underline the correct pronoun in each of the following comparisons.

1. Mark is much neater than (I, me).
2. Cindy, the head majorette at our high school, can twirl a baton as well as (we, us).
3. Simone is not as talented an artist as (him, he).
4. Those other puppies are much fatter than (they, them).
5. Carlos is just as happy as (she, her).
6. Brenda can sew better than (we, us).
7. We laughed just as loud as (they, them).
8. He can hold his breath under water longer than (she, her) can.
9. With a bit more practice, you will be just as good at these video games as (I, me).
10. I do not talk as much as (him, he).

**Practice 11 Completing** Fill in each blank in the following sentences with an appropriate pronoun for comparison.

1. After he appeared in *Star Wars*, Harrison Ford became a bigger star than ______________.
2. Joey can throw a ball as far as ______________.
3. My friends managed to stay longer in the haunted house than ______________ did.
4. He makes you just as mad as he makes ______________.

5. Julia, whose parents are well-known artists, is a more talented painter than ____________.

**Practice 12 Writing Your Own** Write a sentence of your own using each of the following pronouns in *than* or *as* comparisons.

1. I ____________________________________
2. she ____________________________________
3. they ____________________________________
4. we ____________________________________
5. he ____________________________________

## DEMONSTRATIVE PRONOUNS

There are four demonstrative pronouns: *this*, *that*, *these*, and *those*. **Demonstrative pronouns** point to specific people or objects. Use *this* and *these* to refer to items that are near and *that* and *those* to refer to items farther away. Look at the following examples.

| | |
|---|---|
| **Demonstrative (near):** | **This** is my room. |
| **Demonstrative (near):** | **These** are yesterday's notes. |
| **Demonstrative (farther):** | **That** is the town hall. |
| **Demonstrative (farther):** | **Those** are the cheerleaders for the other team. |

Sometimes demonstrative pronouns are not used correctly.

| | Error | Correct |
|---|---|---|
| **NOT** | this here, that there | this, that |
| **NOT** | these here, these ones | these |
| **NOT** | them, those there, those ones | those |

| | Error | Correction |
|---|---|---|
| **NOT** | **Them** are the clothes she bought. | **Those** are the clothes she bought. |

| | | |
|---|---|---|
| **NOT** | I'd like to have **these here** books. | I'd like to have **these** books. |
| **NOT** | I found **those ones** in the attic. | I found **those** in the attic. |
| **NOT** | **Those there** are the ones I like. | **Those** are the ones I like. |

When demonstrative pronouns are used with nouns, they become adjectives.

**Pronoun:** **That** is mine.
**Adjective:** **That computer** is hers.

**Pronoun:** **Those** are actions you may regret.
**Adjective:** You may regret **those actions.**

The problems that occur with demonstrative pronouns can also occur when these pronouns act as adjectives.

| | Error | Correction |
|---|---|---|
| **NOT** | Please give me **that there** paper. | Please give me **that** paper. |

### Reviewing Demonstrative Pronouns

*Name the four demonstrative pronouns.*

________ ________ ________ ________

*Give two examples of errors with demonstrative pronouns.*

________________________________

________________________________

**Practice 13A Identifying** Underline the demonstrative pronoun errors in each of the following sentences.

1. The babies usually play with those there toys.
2. This here test is just too difficult.

3. I believe that there pair of shoes will do nicely for this outfit.
4. These ones should be brought in out of the rain.
5. I can carry this here if you'll take that there.
6. During the earthquake, those there shelves shook loose.
7. Marcy placed those ones there for a reason.
8. These here mosquitoes are about to drive me crazy.
9. Yes, you may take those there on the table.
10. These is the groceries I ordered.

**Practice 13B Correcting** Correct the demonstrative pronoun errors in Practice 13A by rewriting the incorrect sentences.

**Practice 14 Completing** Fill in each blank in the following sentences with a logical demonstrative pronoun.

1. ______________ are the skates he wanted.
2. Would you like ______________ curtains for your house?
3. ______________ Corvette belongs to my uncle.
4. She baked ______________ cookies herself.
5. I want ______________ candle for my bathroom.

**Practice 15 Writing Your Own** Write four sentences of your own, one using each demonstrative pronoun. Be sure you don't use these pronouns as adjectives in your sentences.

## CHAPTER REVIEW

You might want to reread your answers to the questions in the review boxes before you do the following exercises.

**Review Practice 1 Identifying** Underline the pronoun errors in each of the following sentences.

1. The football team and us went out for pizza after the game.
2. I think the fish is trying to tell you its' tank needs to be cleaned.
3. That secret was supposed to remain between you and I.
4. My brother at age 4 was as big as him at age 6.
5. These here tarts are the best I've ever tasted.
6. Due to the power outage, him and me had dinner by candlelight.
7. I do believe you are stronger than him.
8. Hers' money is already spent even though she started out with $100.
9. One of my high school teachers taught me and she how to fly a plane.
10. I know that those there CDs belong to me.

**Review Practice 2 Completing** Correct the pronoun errors in Review Practice 1 by rewriting the incorrect sentences.

**Review Practice 3 Writing Your Own** Write a short paragraph about your most treasured object. Why is it one of your favorite possessions?

## Editing Through Collaboration

Exchange paragraphs from Review Practice 3 with another student, and do the following:

1. Circle all pronouns.
2. Put an X through any that are not in the correct form: Check that all the subject and object pronouns are used correctly. Also check that possessive pronouns, pronouns used in comparisons, and demonstrative pronouns are used correctly.

Then return the paper to its writer, and use the information in this chapter to correct the pronoun errors in your own paragraph. Record your errors on the Error Log in Appendix 6.

# Pronoun Reference and Point of View

## Checklist for Correcting Problems with Pronoun Reference and Point of View

- ✔ Does every pronoun have a clear antecedent?
- ✔ Are pronouns as close as possible to the words they refer to?
- ✔ Do you maintain a single point of view?

**Test Yourself**

Underline the pronouns in these sentences. Then put an X over any pronouns that are confusing or unclear.

- It says to schedule your own appointments.
- Millie and Tanya were going to go to Las Vegas, but her car broke.
- I created a backup plan because you should always be prepared for the unexpected.
- You know they are covering up evidence of alien beings.
- Jimmy forgot the answer to questions 1 and 10, but he remembered it the next day.

(Answers are in Appendix 4.)

---

Anytime you use a pronoun, it must clearly refer to a specific word in the sentence. The word it refers to is called its **antecedent.** Two kinds of problems occur with pronoun references: The antecedent may be unclear, or the antecedent may be missing altogether. You should also be careful to stick to the same point of view in your writing. If, for example, you start out talking about "I," you should not shift to "you" in the middle of the sentence.

## PRONOUN REFERENCE

Sometimes a sentence is confusing because the reader can't tell what a pronoun is referring to. The confusion may occur because the pronoun's antecedent is unclear or is completely missing.

### Unclear Antecedents

In the following examples, the word each pronoun is referring to is unclear.

**Unclear:** A bucket and an oar lay in the boat. As Rachel reached for **it,** the boat began to move forward.

(Was Rachel reaching for the bucket or the oar? Only Rachel knows for sure.)

**Clear:** A bucket and an oar lay in the boat. As Rachel reached for **the bucket,** the boat began to move forward.

**Clear:** A bucket and an oar lay in the boat. As Rachel reached for **the oar**, the boat began to move forward.

**Unclear:** Michael told Oliver that **he** should change jobs.

(Does *he* refer to Michael or Oliver? Only the writer knows.)

**Clear:** Michael told Oliver that **Oliver** should change jobs.

**Clear:** Talking with Michael, **Oliver** promised that **he** would change jobs.

How can you be sure that every pronoun you use has a clear antecedent? First, you can proofread carefully. Probably an even better test, though, is to ask a friend to read what you have written and tell you if your meaning is clear or not.

### Missing Antecedents

Every pronoun should have a clear antecedent, the word it refers to. But what happens when there is no antecedent at all? The writer's message is not communicated. Two words in particular should alert you to the possibility of missing antecedents: *it* and *they*.

The following sentences have missing antecedents:

**Missing Antecedent:** In a recent political poll, **it** shows that most people consider themselves Independents.

(What does *it* refer to? It has no antecedent.)

**Clear:** **A recent political poll** shows that most people consider themselves Independents.

**Missing Antecedent:** **They** say that a fool and his money are soon parted.

(Who is *they*?)

**Clear:** **An old saying** states that a fool and his money are soon parted.

REVIEWING PRONOUN REFERENCE

***What is an antecedent?***

______________________________________________

***How can you be sure every pronoun you use has a clear antecedent?***

______________________________________________

______________________________________________

***What two words warn you that an antecedent may be missing?***

____________________ ____________________

**Practice 1A Identifying** Underline the pronouns in each of the following sentences. Then put an X next to any sentences with missing or unclear antecedents.

1. _______ According to recent surveys, it says that more people are getting a college education.
2. _______ My red pen should be in my purse, but I can't find it.
3. _______ The sitting room must have its baseboards cleaned.
4. _______ Talking with Kesha and Mindy, I learned that she is moving to Texas!
5. _______ They say you can catch more flies with honey than with vinegar.
6. _______ Emma and Candace have gone to the beach for the weekend, but she is going to have to return home sooner than expected.

7. _______ The apple pie and the chocolate cake are on the counter, but it's still too hot to eat.

8. _______ Nick and Ben believed the weather announcer when he predicted rain, so he brought his umbrella.

9. _______ Between Becca and Valerie, she should be able to finish the work on time.

10. _______ Debbie doesn't agree with Tom that he should be the first to go.

**Practice 1B Correcting** Correct the sentences with pronoun errors in Practice 1A by rewriting them.

**Practice 2 Completing** Correct the unclear or missing pronoun references in the following sentences by rewriting them. Pronouns that should be corrected are underlined.

1. <u>It</u> says that we are all required to be at the meeting.
2. <u>They</u> always told me to treat people the way I want to be treated.
3. According to Sue and Hanna, <u>she</u> has been accepted into Yale.
4. We have chocolate and vanilla ice cream, but <u>it</u> tastes better.
5. <u>It</u> indicates that we should have turned left at the first light.

**Practice 3 Writing Your Own** Write five sentences of your own using pronouns with clear antecedents.

## SHIFTING POINT OF VIEW

**Point of view** refers to whether a statement is made in the first person, the second person, or the third person. Each person—or point of view—requires different pronouns. The following chart lists the pronouns for each point of view.

| **Point of View** | |
|---|---|
| *First Person:* | *I, we* |
| *Second Person:* | *you, you* |
| *Third Person:* | *he, she, it, they* |

If you begin writing from one point of view, you should stay in that point of view. Do not shift to another point of view. For example, if you start out writing "I," you should continue with "I" and not shift to "you." Shifting point of view is a very common error in college writing.

**Shift:** If **a person** doesn't study, **you** will not do well in school.
**Correct:** If **a person** doesn't study, **he or she** will not do well in school.

**Shift:** **I** changed jobs because **you** have more opportunities here.
**Correct:** **I** changed jobs because **I** have more opportunities here.

### Reviewing Point of View

***What is point of view?***

___

***What does it mean to shift point of view?***

___

**Practice 4A Identifying** Underline the pronouns that shift in point of view in the following sentences.

1. If you don't eat a good diet, they may find their health suffering.
2. The students decided to protest the new rules, so you will walk out of class at noon.
3. One can always find unique merchandise at the more exclusive stores, but you have to be willing to pay the price.
4. I hinted that I didn't want to take part in the play, but you never know if you've gotten the message across.
5. I see a couple of concerts a year because everyone needs a little culture in his or her life.
6. You try to be nice to strangers because we never know when we might need help.
7. A body can only take on so much before you suffer from stress.
8. You can always seek help from the counselors if someone has questions.

9. I've already started writing my research paper because you should never wait until the last minute.
10. A person should be left alone occasionally because you have a right to your privacy.

**Practice 4B Correcting** Correct the point-of-view errors in Practice 4A by rewriting the incorrect sentences.

**Practice 5 Completing** Complete the following sentences with pronouns that stay in the same point of view.

1. I decided to pack lightly and carry my luggage on board the airplane, so ______ know my luggage will arrive when I do.
2. I should taste these dishes since ______ never know if I'm going to like them until I try them.
3. A person is expected to follow the rules of the road; otherwise, ______ may cause an accident.
4. I always wear a smile on my face since ______ never know who might be around.
5. One should pay attention; then ______ might not feel so confused.

**Practice 6 Writing Your Own** Write a sentence of your own for each of the following pronouns. Be sure the pronouns have clear antecedents and do not shift point of view.

1. they ________________________________________
2. you ________________________________________
3. I ________________________________________
4. it ________________________________________
5. we ________________________________________

## CHAPTER REVIEW

You might want to reread your answers to the questions in the review boxes before you do the following exercises.

**Review Practice 1 Identifying** Label the following sentences U if the antecedent is unclear, M if the antecedent is missing, or S if the sentence shifts point of view. Then correct the pronoun errors by rewriting the incorrect sentences.

1. ______ If one forgets the answer, then you should look it up.
2. ______ They say you should never accept rides from strangers.
3. ______ Janie bought milk, bread, cheese, and lettuce at the grocery store, but she left it in the car.
4. ______ A person should always look both ways before crossing the street; otherwise, you might get hit by a car.
5. ______ Stacy and Myra have already left for the show, but she forgot her wallet.
6. ______ It explains that the majority of the citizens are in favor of the proposed freeway.
7. ______ I asked my friends about my decision because you always value your friends' advice.
8. ______ It pointed out that "every cloud has a silver lining."
9. ______ Steven told Jason that he was going to be late.
10. ______ I ordered two pairs of jeans, a pair of shorts, and a pair of shoes from a catalog. I received it one week later.

**Review Practice 2 Completing** Correct the pronoun errors in the following sentences by rewriting each incorrect sentence.

1. I am going to purchase the most expensive champagne I can find, for you know that will impress the guests.

2. According to this announcement, it says we need to arrive no later than 2:00 p.m.
3. Jake and Dean will probably get into good colleges, even though he has a higher GPA.
4. A person should manage time wisely since you only have 24 hours in a day.
5. They are always carrying on about how bad the humidity is in the South.
6. Before Carla and Trisha left town, she bought a new swimsuit.
7. We were gossiping about Jarrett and Jeremy when he walked right by us.
8. One should study for the test if you want to pass it.
9. I had my hands full with a squirming puppy and a hissing cat until I decided to set him down.
10. You know what they say: "Never go to bed with a wet head."

**Review Practice 3 Writing Your Own** Write a paragraph about a new experience you have had. Include at least six different pronouns.

## Editing Through Collaboration

Exchange paragraphs from Review Practice 3 with another student, and do the following:

1. Underline all pronouns.
2. Draw arrows to the words they modify.
3. Put an X through any pronouns that do not refer to a clear antecedent or that shift point of view.

Then return the paper to its writer, and use the information in this chapter to correct any pronoun reference and point-of-view errors in your own paragraph. Record your errors on the Error Log in Appendix 6.

# Pronoun Agreement

## Checklist for Correcting Pronoun Agreement Problems

- ✔ Do all pronouns and their antecedents agree in number (singular or plural)?
- ✔ Do any pronouns that refer to indefinite pronouns agree in number?
- ✔ Are any pronouns used in a sexist way?

**Test Yourself**

Underline the pronoun in each sentence, and draw an arrow to its antecedent. Put an X over any pronouns that do not agree with their antecedents.

- Somebody left his lights on in his car.
- A judge must put aside her bias.
- Each of the children needs their permission slip signed.
- None of the fans could keep their voices quiet.
- A motorcyclist must take care of her gear.

(Answers are in Appendix 4.)

As you learned in Chapter 35, subjects and verbs must agree to communicate clearly. If the subject is singular, the verb must be singular; if the subject is plural, the verb must be plural. The same holds true for pronouns and the words they refer to—their *antecedents*. They must agree in number—both singular or both plural. Usually, pronoun agreement is not a problem, as these sentences show:

**Singular:** **Dr. Gomez** told **his** patient to stop smoking.

**Plural:** **Carlos** and **Gina** took **their** children to Disney World.

## INDEFINITE PRONOUNS

Pronoun agreement may become a problem with indefinite pronouns. Indefinite pronouns that are always singular give writers the most trouble.

NOT **One** of the students finished **their** test early.

(How many students finished early? Only one, so use a singular pronoun.)

**Correct:** **One** of the students finished **her** test early.

**Correct:** **One** of the students finished **his** test early.

NOT **Somebody** just drove **their** new car into a ditch.

(How many people just drove a car into a ditch? One person, so use a singular pronoun.)

**Correct:** **Somebody** just drove **her** new car into a ditch.

**Correct:** **Somebody** just drove **his** new car into a ditch.

Here is a list of indefinite pronouns that are always singular.

**Singular Indefinite Pronouns**

| | | | |
|---|---|---|---|
| *another* | *everybody* | *neither* | *one* |
| *anybody* | *everyone* | *nobody* | *other* |
| *anyone* | *everything* | *none* | *somebody* |
| *anything* | *little* | *no one* | *someone* |
| *each* | *much* | *nothing* | *something* |
| *either* | | | |

HINT: A few indefinite pronouns can be either singular or plural, depending on their meaning in the sentence. These pronouns are *any*, *all*, *more*, *most*, and *some*.

**Singular:** **Some** of the money was left over, so we gave **it** to charity.

**Plural:** **Some** of the donations were left over, so we gave **them** to charity.

In the first sentence, *money* is singular, so the singular pronoun *it* is used. In the second sentence, *donations* is plural, so the plural pronoun *them* is used.

### Reviewing Indefinite Pronouns

***Why should a pronoun agree with the word it refers to?***

______________________________________________

***Name five indefinite pronouns that are always singular.***

________ ________ ________ ________ ________

**Practice 1 Identifying** Underline the correct pronoun from the choices in parentheses, and be prepared to explain your choices.

1. All of the infants had (his or her, their) footprints and handprints recorded at the hospital.
2. The parents and the children want (his or her, their) voices to be heard.
3. Anyone can get (his or her, their) high school diploma.
4. Neither of the doctors could diagnose (his or her, their) patient's illness.
5. None of the cars needs (its, their) tires changed.
6. Before anybody can join the club, (he or she, they) must fill out an enrollment form.
7. The farmers and the farmworkers need (his or her, their) work hours shortened.
8. Each of the girls needs to have (her, their) hair cut.
9. Most of the stories need (its, their) titles rewritten.
10. No one should harm (his or her, their) body.

**Practice 2 Completing** Fill in each blank in the following sentences with a pronoun that agrees with its antecedent.

1. Fabiola and Fabian asked ____________ questions at the same time.
2. Everyone should listen more closely to ____________ teacher.

3. Matt lost ____________ backpack at the park.

4. Someone who could do a thing like that should have ____________ head examined.

5. Something in the car leaked all ____________ fluids onto the driveway.

**Practice 3 Writing Your Own** Write a sentence of your own for each of the following pronouns.

1. none ____________________________________________

2. other ____________________________________________

3. no one ____________________________________________

4. everything ____________________________________________

5. someone ____________________________________________

## AVOIDING SEXISM

In the first section of this chapter, you learned that you should use singular pronouns to refer to singular indefinite pronouns. For example, the indefinite pronoun *someone* requires a singular pronoun, *his* or *her*, not the plural *their*. But what if you don't know whether the person referred to is male or female? Then you have a choice: (1) You can say "he or she" or "his or her," or (2) you can make the sentence plural. What you should not do is ignore half the population by referring to all humans as males.

NOT If **anyone** wants to go, **they** are welcome to do so.
NOT If **anyone** wants to go, **he** is welcome to do so.
Correct: If **anyone** wants to go, **he or she** is welcome to do so.
Correct: **People** who want to go are welcome to do so.

NOT **Everyone** remembered to bring **their** lunch.
NOT **Everyone** remembered to bring **his** lunch.
Correct: **Everyone** remembered to bring **his or her** lunch.
Correct: **All the students** remembered to bring **their** lunch.

Sexism in writing can also occur in ways other than with indefinite pronouns. We often assume that doctors, lawyers, and bank presidents are men and that nurses, schoolteachers, and secretaries are women. But that is not very accurate.

**NOT** Ask a **fireman** if **he** thinks the wiring is safe.

(Why automatically assume that the person fighting fires is a male instead of a female?)

**Correct:** Ask a **firefighter** if **he or she** thinks the wiring is safe.

**NOT** The **mailman** delivered my neighbor's mail to my house by mistake.

(Since both men and women deliver mail, the more correct term is *mail carrier.*)

**Correct:** The **mail carrier** delivered my neighbor's mail to my house by mistake.

**NOT** A **secretary** cannot reveal **her** boss's confidential business.

(Why leave the men who are secretaries out of this sentence?)

**Correct:** A **secretary** cannot reveal **his or her** boss's confidential business.

**Correct:** **Secretaries** cannot reveal **their** boss's confidential business.

### Reviewing Sexism in Writing

***What is sexism in writing?***

______________________________

***What are two ways to get around the problem of using male pronouns to refer to both women and men?***

______________ ______________

***Give two other examples of sexism in writing.***

______________ ______________

**Practice 4A Identifying** Underline the sexist references in the following sentences.

1. The chairperson should keep his board informed of new developments.
2. A nurse gives her time and patience freely.
3. Each person is responsible if they miss an assignment.
4. At least one instructor forgot her uniform.
5. A plumber usually leaves something of his behind.
6. Everybody must bring food if they plan to eat.
7. A good sailor knows his knots.
8. Another person must have left her books in class.
9. A parent needs to pick up her child from school.
10. Everyone loves to laugh until they start crying.

**Practice 4B Correcting** Correct the sexist pronouns in Practice 4A by rewriting the incorrect sentences.

**Practice 5 Completing** Fill in each blank in the following sentences with an appropriate pronoun.

1. A technician might become frustrated with ______________ job.
2. A hairdresser who attracts celebrity customers can name ______________ price.
3. An accountant needs help with ______________ accounts.
4. Somebody wrote ______________ phone number on the bathroom wall.
5. Another child has forgotten ______________ lunch.

**Practice 6 Writing Your Own** Write a sentence of your own for each of the following antecedents. Include at least one pronoun in each sentence.

1. doctor ______________________________

2. politician ______________________________

3. police officer ______________________________

4. spokesperson ______________________________

5. FBI agent ______________________________

## CHAPTER REVIEW

You might want to reread your answers to the questions in the review boxes before you do the following exercises.

**Review Practice 1 Identifying** Underline and correct the pronoun errors in the following sentences.

1. Anyone who wants their book signed should stand in this line.
2. A good secretary keeps her dictionary within easy reach.
3. A surfer can lose his wave.
4. Only one of the contestants turned in their enrollment form on time.
5. The politician who cares about his people will win the election.
6. Each of the photographers has their own camera.
7. Everyone needs their funny bone tickled every now and then.
8. A tattoo artist should always clean her equipment before each new client.
9. A teacher should always ask her students if they understand the assignment.
10. Someone that messy should clean their room more often.

**Review Practice 2 Completing** Fill in each blank in the following sentences with an appropriate pronoun.

1. Neither of the criminals wanted ______________ picture taken.
2. A racecar driver depends on ______________ car and skill to win the race.

3. A housecleaner brings ______________ own supplies.

4. Each of the boys can do ______________ own work.

5. None of the students wanted to disappoint ______________ teacher.

6. At the reunion, everyone talked to ______________ friends.

7. Another person left ______________ homework behind.

8. Somebody needs to water ______________ lawn.

9. Everyone should be nice to ______________ neighbors.

10. Nobody should park ______________ car in a no-parking zone.

**Review Practice 3 Writing Your Own** Write a paragraph describing your favorite type of music. Why is it your favorite?

## Editing Through Collaboration

Exchange paragraphs from Review Practice 3 with another student, and do the following:

1. Underline any pronouns.
2. Circle any pronouns that do not agree with the words they refer to.

Then return the paper to its writer, and use the information in this chapter to correct any pronoun agreement errors in your own paragraph. Record your errors on the Error Log in Appendix 6.

# Adjectives

## Checklist for Using Adjectives Correctly

✔ Are all adjectives that show comparison used correctly?
✔ Are the forms of *good* and *bad* used correctly?

**Test Yourself**

Underline the adjectives in the following sentences. Then put an X over the adjectives that are used incorrectly.

- The kites were very colorful.
- She has the worstest hair color.
- We were more busier this week than last week.
- He is the oldest of the two brothers.
- The Ford Mustang is more better than the Nissan Sentra.

(Answers are in Appendix 4.)

Adjectives are modifiers. They help us communicate more clearly (I have a *green* car; I want a *red* one) and vividly (the movie was *funny* and *romantic*). Without adjectives, our language would be drab and boring.

## USING ADJECTIVES

**Adjectives** are words that modify—or describe—nouns or pronouns. Adjectives tell how something or someone looks: *dark, light, tall, short, large, small.* Most adjectives come before the words they modify, but with linking verbs (such as *is, are, look, become,* and *feel*), adjectives follow the words they modify.

**Adjectives Before a Noun:** We felt the **cold, icy** snow.
**Adjectives After a Linking Verb:** The snow was **cold** and **icy.**

REVIEWING ADJECTIVES

*What are adjectives?*

______________________________________________

*Where can you find adjectives in a sentence?*

______________________________________________

**Practice 1 Identifying** In the following sentences, underline the adjectives, and circle the words they modify.

1. Michael left a shiny red apple on the teacher's desk on Monday morning.
2. I wore my long-sleeved sweater today because it was very cold outside.
3. Mrs. Johnson gave the 2-year-old boy a piece of hard candy.
4. Our family doctor wants us to come in for our annual checkups.
5. I read a great book by John Grisham last week.
6. Sarah's marriage was failing, so she spent lots of money on family counseling.
7. Grandma's beautiful garden is a quiet place for me to read, draw, or take a quick nap.
8. Traffic was heavy today because of a large, messy accident.
9. I bought a delicious cup of coffee this morning at the corner coffeehouse.
10. Steven was running down the steep stairs when he lost his balance and had a scary fall.

**Practice 2 Completing** Fill in each blank in the following sentences with logical adjectives.

During my (1) ______________ year of high school, I asked the head cheerleader to go to the prom with me. I was

(2) ____________ when she agreed to be my date, and I really wanted to impress her. I rented an expensive tuxedo, bought a (3) ____________ corsage for her to wear on her wrist, and made sure to pick her up on time. The (4) ____________ price was worth it because when we arrived at the dance, all of my buddies patted me on the back and said, "You two look (5) ____________ together!"

**Practice 3 Writing Your Own** Write a sentence of your own for each of the following adjectives.

1. curious ____________________________________________
2. durable ____________________________________________
3. thirteen ____________________________________________
4. helpful ____________________________________________
5. short-tempered ______________________________________

## COMPARING WITH ADJECTIVES

Most adjectives have three forms: a **basic** form, a **comparative** form (used to compare two items), and a **superlative** form (used to compare three or more items).

For positive comparisons, adjectives form the comparative and superlative in two different ways.

1. For one-syllable adjectives and some two-syllable adjectives, use *-er* to compare two items and *-est* to compare three or more items.

| Basic | Comparative (used to compare two items) | Superlative (used to compare three or more items) |
|---|---|---|
| bold | bolder | boldest |
| warm | warmer | warmest |

| | | |
|---|---|---|
| foggy | foggier | foggiest |
| cozy | cozier | coziest |

2. For some two-syllable adjectives and all longer adjectives, use *more* to compare two items and *most* to compare three or more items.

| **Basic** | **Comparative (used to compare two items)** | **Superlative (used to compare three or more items)** |
|---|---|---|
| friendly | more friendly | most friendly |
| peaceful | more peaceful | most peaceful |
| wonderful | more wonderful | most wonderful |
| appropriate | more appropriate | most appropriate |

For negative comparisons, use *less* to compare two items and *least* to compare three or more items.

| **Basic** | **Comparative (used to compare two items)** | **Superlative (used to compare three or more items)** |
|---|---|---|
| loud | less loud | least loud |
| funny | less funny | least funny |
| popular | less popular | least popular |

**Hint:** Some adjectives are not usually compared. For example, one person cannot be "more dead" than another. Here are some more examples.

| | | |
|---|---|---|
| *broken* | *final* | *square* |
| *empty* | *impossible* | *supreme* |
| *equal* | *singular* | *unanimous* |

### Reviewing Adjective Forms

***When do you use the comparative form of an adjective?***

______________________________________________

*When do you use the superlative form of an adjective?*

_______________________________________________

*How do one-syllable and some two-syllable adjectives form the comparative and superlative in positive comparisons?*

_______________________________________________

*How do some two-syllable adjectives and all longer adjectives form the comparative and superlative in positive comparisons?*

_______________________________________________

*How do you form negative comparisons?*

_______________________________________________

**Practice 4 Identifying** Underline the adjectives, and note whether they are basic (B), comparative (C), or superlative (S).

1. ______ He is the most stubborn of all the men I've ever dated.
2. ______ If you want to see an even nicer neighborhood, drive about four miles farther on Stockdale Avenue.
3. ______ I just heard that the biggest raise is going to the most worthy employee.
4. ______ Jeff ran five miles at the charity jog-a-thon.
5. ______ I think a meal of rice and beans is healthier than a meal of macaroni and cheese.
6. ______ The most logical decision would be to appoint Sam to the position.
7. ______ Today the students showed how dedicated they can be.
8. ______ Tiffany was happier about the engagement than her father was.

9. ______ The strongest students always score the highest on the exam.

10. ______ The food Nora and Richard ate on vacation was less healthy than what they eat at home.

**Practice 5 Completing** Fill in each blank in the following paragraph with the correct comparative or superlative form of the adjective in parentheses.

One summer afternoon, I was hiking high in the mountains when the skies above me grew suddenly (1) ________________ (dark). It looked like rain was going to fall soon, and I happened to be in the (2) ________________ (unsheltered) place on the mountain. I looked around to find the (3) ________________ (suitable) tree to sit under, but there weren't any that would protect me. Even the (4) ________________ (thick) tree was very puny and wouldn't keep the rain off of my head. Quickly, I realized I had no option but to run (5) ________________ (fast) than the rain to find shelter farther down the hill.

**Practice 6 Writing Your Own** Write a sentence of your own for each of the following adjectives.

1. the superlative form of *pretty* ________________________________
2. the positive form of *sensible* ________________________________
3. the comparative form of *talented* ________________________________
4. the superlative form of *disgusting* ________________________________
5. the comparative form of *shy* ________________________________

## COMMON ADJECTIVE ERRORS

Two types of problems occur with adjectives used in comparisons.

1. Instead of using one method for forming the comparative or superlative, both are used. That is, both *-er* and *more* or *less* are used to compare two items or both *-est* and *most* or *least* are used to compare three or more items.

   **NOT** My youngest son is **more taller** than his brothers.
   **Correct:** My youngest son is **taller** than his brothers.

   **NOT** This is the **most happiest** day of my life.
   **Correct:** This is the **happiest** day of my life.

2. The second type of error occurs when the comparative or superlative is used with the wrong number of items. The comparative form should be used for two items and the superlative for three or more items.

   **NOT** Marina is the **smartest** of the two sisters.
   **Correct:** Marina is the **smarter** of the two sisters.

   **NOT** History is the **harder** of my three classes this semester.
   **Correct:** History is the **hardest** of my three classes this semester.

### Reviewing Common Adjective Errors

***Can you ever use* -er + more *or* -est + most?**

______________________________________________

***When do you use the comparative form of an adjective?***

______________________________________________

***When do you use the superlative form of an adjective?***

______________________________________________

**Practice 7A Identifying** Underline the adjectives in the following sentences that are used incorrectly in comparisons. Mark sentences that are correct C.

1. ______ The most rudest customers are usually the ones who are trying to get something for free.

2. ______ Bob and Chad are both good-looking, but Bob is the smartest.

3. ______ This class would be more fun if we could meet outside sometimes.

4. ______ The most rainiest day of the year was April 15.

5. ______ The bigger house in town is at 1859 Pine Street.

6. ______ I would have been more happier about Toby asking me out, but I already had plans for that weekend.

7. ______ Dr. Romano told the most funniest jokes while he was examining my broken arm.

8. ______ The most prepared of the two athletes was Kareem.

9. ______ Organic chemistry was the most hardest class of all the sciences.

10. ______ Of all my friends, Hal is the most faithful.

**Practice 7B Correcting** Correct the adjective errors in Practice 7A by rewriting the incorrect sentences.

**Practice 8 Completing** Choose the correct adjective forms in the following paragraph to complete the sentences.

Giving the dog a bath is the (1) ______________ (more difficult, most difficult) chore in our house, and somehow it always seems to be my job. My sister Stephanie and I share most of the chores, but I am definitely (2) ______________ (more responsible, most responsible) than she is. Usually, I do my chores without complaining, but bathing the dog is just unfair. We have an Australian sheepdog, and he is the

(3) ____________ (clumsiest, most clumsiest) thing alive. He seems to find every puddle of mud and sticky stuff to step in, and it quickly gets all over his fur. Unfortunately, though, he has a great disdain for baths, so the struggle to wash him is (4) ____________ (trickiest, more tricky) than it should be. And Stephanie is no help at all. While I'm fighting to hose him down, she just stands back and laughs at me, which makes me even (5) ____________ (madder, more madder).

**Practice 9 Writing Your Own** Write a sentence of your own for each of the following adjectives.

1. strongest ________________________________
2. more truthful ________________________________
3. most gracious ________________________________
4. larger ________________________________
5. most frightening ________________________________

## USING *GOOD* AND *BAD* CORRECTLY

The adjectives *good* and *bad* are irregular. They do not form the comparative and superlative like most other adjectives. Here are the correct forms for these two irregular adjectives:

| **Basic** | **Comparative (used to compare two items)** | **Superlative (used to compare three or more items)** |
|---|---|---|
| good | better | best |
| bad | worse | worst |

Problems occur with *good* and *bad* when writers don't know how to form their comparative and superlative forms.

| | |
|---|---|
| **NOT** | more better, more worse, worser, most best, most worst, bestest, worstest |
| **Correct:** | better, worse, best, worst |

These errors appear in sentences in the following ways:

| | |
|---|---|
| **NOT** | That is the **worstest** food I've ever tasted. |
| **Correct:** | That is the **worst** food I've ever tasted. |
| **NOT** | Air pollution is getting **more worse** every year. |
| **Correct:** | Air pollution is getting **worse** every year. |

### REVIEWING *Good* AND *Bad*

***What are the three forms of* good?**

______________ ______________ ______________

***What are the three forms of* bad?**

______________ ______________ ______________

**Practice 10A Identifying** In the following sentences, underline the forms of *good* and *bad* used correctly, and circle the forms of *good* and *bad* used incorrectly.

1. Both options are good, but getting a raise is more better than getting time off from work.
2. I think the most best outfit in my closet is my red shirt and black pants.
3. Giving that oral presentation in my psychology class was the worstest experience of my college career.
4. Giving your time to a charity is more good than just giving your money.
5. Sean wanted to go to Princeton, but his grades were worse than he thought.
6. David told a scary ghost story about two bestest friends getting lost in the woods.
7. You should tell your boss that you are more better at your job than he realizes.

8. I heard the most worst pickup line on TV the other day.
9. Doing the laundry is more worse than getting a root canal.
10. It's a good thing I didn't see that horror film because I would be having really bad dreams.

**Practice 10B Correcting** Correct the errors with *good* and *bad* in Practice 10A by rewriting the incorrect sentences.

**Practice 11 Completing** Using the correct forms of *good* or *bad*, complete the following paragraph.

The (1) ______________ day of my life was July 8, 2001. I remember it (2) ______________ than any other. I had just bought a brand new convertible and was taking it to the beach for a couple of days of fun in the sun. Fortunately, my (3) ______________ friend, Tara, was with me, because just 20 miles outside town, the engine of my dream car overheated! What was (4) ______________ was neither of us had a cell phone, and the closest pay phone was more than a mile away. We finally found a phone and called another friend, and then we waited and waited for a tow truck. After spending more than $3,000 in repairs, my dream car became my (5) ______________ nightmare.

**Practice 12 Writing Your Own** Write a sentence of your own for each of the following forms of *good* and *bad*.

1. best ______________________________________________
2. bad ______________________________________________
3. worse ______________________________________________
4. better ______________________________________________
5. worst ______________________________________________

## CHAPTER REVIEW

You might want to reread your answers to the questions in the review boxes before you do the following exercises.

**Review Practice 1 Identifying** Label the following adjectives basic (B), comparative (C), superlative (S), or not able to be compared (X).

1. ______ sillier
2. ______ most ridiculous
3. ______ dead
4. ______ tempting
5. ______ more stubborn
6. ______ meatiest
7. ______ most appealing
8. ______ broken
9. ______ tired
10. ______ lovelier

**Review Practice 2 Completing** Supply the comparative and superlative forms for each of the following adjectives.

| Basic | Comparative | Superlative |
|---|---|---|
| 1. welcome | ____________________ | ____________________ |
| 2. justifiable | ____________________ | ____________________ |
| 3. scary | ____________________ | ____________________ |
| 4. kind | ____________________ | ____________________ |
| 5. mystical | ____________________ | ____________________ |
| 6. strong | ____________________ | ____________________ |

7. foolish ____________ ____________
8. confusing ____________ ____________
9. extraordinary ____________ ____________
10. loving ____________ ____________

**Review Practice 3 Writing Your Own** Write a paragraph describing the first pet you ever owned. What kind of animal was it? What did it look like? How did it act? What did you name it, and why did you choose that name?

## Editing Through Collaboration

Exchange paragraphs from Review Practice 3 with another student, and do the following:

1. Underline all the adjectives.
2. Circle those that are not in the correct form.

Then return the paper to its writer, and use the information in this chapter to correct any adjective errors in your own paragraph. Record your errors on the Error Log in Appendix 6.

# Adverbs

## Checklist for Using Adverbs

- ✔ Are all adverbs that show comparison used correctly?
- ✔ Are *good/well* and *bad/badly* used correctly?

**Test Yourself**

Underline the adverbs in the following sentences. Then put an X over the adverbs that are used incorrectly.

- The pants fit me too loose, so I returned them to the store.
- When Madeline returned from Paris, she said she had a real good time.
- We happily made more ice cream when our first supply ran out.
- Tori wasn't never so happy as after she won the lottery.
- I wanted so bad to win the race, but I couldn't catch up.

(Answers are in Appendix 4.)

Like adjectives, adverbs help us communicate more clearly (she talked *slowly*) and more vividly (he sang *beautifully*). They make their sentences more interesting.

## USING ADVERBS

Adverbs modify verbs, adjectives, and other adverbs. They answer the questions *how? when? where? how often?* and *to what extent?* Look at the following examples.

| | |
|---|---|
| **How:** | My grandfather walked **slowly** up the stairs. |
| **When:** | School **always** begins after Labor Day in this state. |
| **Where:** | Music lessons are held **here.** |
| **How often:** | I shop there **regularly.** |
| **To what extent:** | The airport is **extremely** busy during the holidays. |

Some words are always adverbs, including *here*, *there*, *not*, *never*, *now*, *again*, *almost*, *often*, and *well*.

Other adverbs are formed by adding *-ly* to an adjective:

| Adjective | Adverb |
|---|---|
| dim | dimly |
| soft | softly |
| careless | carelessly |

**HINT:** Not all words that end in *-ly* are adverbs. Some, such as *friendly*, *early*, *lonely*, *chilly*, and *lively*, are adjectives.

REVIEWING ADVERBS

***What are adverbs?***

______________________________________________

***What five questions do adverbs answer?***

________ ________ ________ ________ ________

***List four words that are always adverbs.***

__________ __________ __________ __________

***How do many adverbs end?***

______________________________________________

**Practice 1 Identifying** In the following sentences, underline the adverbs, and circle the words they modify.

1. We drove quickly to Los Angeles so that we wouldn't miss the concert.
2. I never saw that girl again.
3. Dirk suddenly changed his mind and agreed to host the party.
4. Marci successfully completed the nursing program.
5. When the children became impatient during the drive, we continuously told them, "We're almost there."
6. The post office is there by the Catholic church.
7. Wilson gratefully accepted our invitation.
8. Ernie is almost always singing.
9. Tammy firmly discussed with her teenage daughter the consequences of smoking.
10. Anabel quietly tiptoed through the bedroom so she wouldn't wake the baby.

**Practice 2 Completing** Fill in each blank in the following sentences with an adverb that makes sense.

Sam's mom (1) ____________ drove him to the airport, where he caught a plane to Houston, Texas. He was going to visit his grandparents (2) ____________. Sam was only 10 years old, but he had (3) ____________ flown alone before. When the plane landed in Houston, Sam (4) ____________ grabbed his carry-on luggage and (5) ____________ ran to meet "Papa" and "Nonny."

**Practice 3 Writing Your Own** Write a sentence of your own for each of the following adverbs.

1. now ________________________________________
2. briskly ________________________________________
3. innocently ________________________________________

4. lazily ______________________________

5. often ______________________________

## COMPARING WITH ADVERBS

Like adjectives, most adverbs have three forms: a **basic** form, a **comparative** form (used to compare two items), and a **superlative** form (used to compare three or more items).

For positive comparisons, adverbs form the comparative and superlative forms in two different ways:

1. For one-syllable adverbs, use *-er* to compare two items and *-est* to compare three or more items.

| **Basic** | **Comparative (used to compare two items)** | **Superlative (used to compare three or more items)** |
|---|---|---|
| soon | sooner | soonest |
| fast | faster | fastest |

2. For adverbs of two or more syllables, use *more* to compare two items and *most* to compare three or more items.

| **Basic** | **Comparative (used to compare two items)** | **Superlative (used to compare three or more items)** |
|---|---|---|
| strangely | more strangely | most strangely |
| carefully | more carefully | most carefully |
| happily | more happily | most happily |

For negative comparisons, adverbs, like adjectives, use *less* to compare two items and *least* to compare three or more items.

| **Basic** | **Comparative (used to compare two items)** | **Superlative (used to compare three or more items)** |
|---|---|---|
| close | less close | least close |
| quickly | less quickly | least quickly |
| creatively | less creatively | least creatively |

**Hint:** Like adjectives, certain adverbs are not usually compared. Something cannot last "more eternally" or work "more invisibly." The following adverbs cannot logically be compared.

| | | |
|---|---|---|
| *endlessly* | *eternally* | *infinitely* |
| *equally* | *impossibly* | *invisibly* |

## Reviewing Adverb Forms

***When do you use the comparative form of an adverb?***

______________________________________________

***When do you use the superlative form of an adverb?***

______________________________________________

***How do one-syllable adverbs form the comparative and superlative in positive comparisons?***

______________________________________________

***How do adverbs of two or more syllables form the comparative and superlative in positive comparisons?***

______________________________________________

***How do you form negative comparisons with adverbs?***

______________________________________________

**Practice 4 Identifying** Underline the adverbs, and note whether they are basic (B), comparative (C), or superlative (S).

1. ______ When Jack joined the gym, he began to lose weight more quickly.
2. ______ The sun shone more brightly after the rain stopped.
3. ______ Valencia is the most rapidly growing city in southern California.
4. ______ There are fewer people enrolled in the morning classes than the afternoon classes.

5. _____ Priscilla rudely interrupted her mother and walked out of the room.

6. _____ The house was totally destroyed by the fire.

7. _____ Curtis got distracted, and his car drifted nearer to the center divider than it was before.

8. _____ Handle the antiques more gently than you did this morning because they are fragile.

9. _____ Shelly mowed the lawn awkwardly.

10. _____ He has the most loudly painted car I've seen.

**Practice 5 Completing** Fill in each blank in the following paragraph with the correct comparative or superlative form of the adverb in parentheses.

At one time, *Highlights* was the (1) ____________ (widely) read children's magazine. It had (2) ____________ (simply) written stories for the younger readers and (3) ____________ (intellectually) challenging games for the older kids than any other magazine. Because of the wide variety of material in each issue, *Highlights* was the (4) ____________ (highly) acclaimed publication for American youth. Now, though, *Highlights* has lots of competition, and big publishers are creating magazines for young readers (5) ____________ (often) than they used to.

**Practice 6 Writing Your Own** Write a sentence of your own for each of the following adverbs.

1. the superlative form of *readily* ______________________________

2. the comparative form of *eagerly* ______________________________

3. the positive form of *unhappily* ______________________________

4. the superlative form of *angrily* ______________________________

5. the comparative form of *honestly* ______________________________

## ADJECTIVE OR ADVERB?

One of the most common errors with modifiers is using an adjective when an adverb is called for. Keep in mind that adjectives modify nouns and pronouns, whereas adverbs modify verbs, adjectives, and other adverbs. Adverbs *do not* modify nouns or pronouns. Here are some examples.

**NOT** She spoke too **slow.** [adjective]
**Correct:** She spoke too **slowly.** [adverb]

**NOT** We were **real** sorry about the accident. [adjective]
**Correct:** We were **really** sorry about the accident. [adverb]

### Reviewing the Difference Between Adjectives and Adverbs

***How do you know whether to use an adjective or an adverb in a sentence?***

______________________________________________________________

______________________________________________________________

***Give an example of an adverb in a sentence.***

______________________________________________________________

***Give an example of an adjective in a sentence.***

______________________________________________________________

**Practice 7A Identifying** Underline the adverbs in the following sentences. Write C next to the sentences that are correct.

1. _____ Adam Sandler's character snored loud in *Little Nicky*.
2. _____ I rocked the baby gently to put her to sleep.
3. _____ Mr. Simpson talked too quick, and I didn't understand the assignment.
4. _____ Before we left the zoo, we checked the map careful to make sure we'd seen everything.
5. _____ Cook the beans slow so they don't burn.
6. _____ During the test, Professor Klump said we could talk quiet with our lab partners.
7. _____ Stephen happily accepted the position.
8. _____ Jenny walked proud across the stage at her graduation.
9. _____ In the 1800s, women wore girdles laced up tight to look like they had very small waists.
10. _____ When Beth changed the oil in her car, she put the oil cap on too loose and it fell off.

**Practice 7B Correcting** Correct the adverb errors in Practice 7A by rewriting the incorrect sentences.

**Practice 8 Completing** Choose the correct adverb to complete the sentences in the following paragraph.

Zack and I went to Magic Mountain last weekend and had a (1) ____________ (real, really) good time. When we pulled into the parking lot, we could hear the roller coasters zooming (2) ____________ (loudly, loud) overhead, and we could smell the yummy junk food. After we got through the gates, we ran (3) ____________ (quick, quickly) to the line to ride Shockwave. The line moved along (4) ____________ (smoothly, smooth), and we were on the ride within 20 minutes. When Shockwave was over, we (5) ____________ (glad, gladly) got in line to ride it again.

**Practice 9 Writing Your Own** Write a sentence of your own for each of the following adverbs.

1. specifically ____________________________________________
2. tightly ____________________________________________
3. greatly ____________________________________________
4. sadly ____________________________________________
5. coldly ____________________________________________

## DOUBLE NEGATIVES

Another problem that involves adverbs is the **double negative**—using two negative words in one clause. Examples of negative words include *no, not, never, none, nothing, neither, nowhere, nobody, barely,* and *hardly*. A double negative creates the opposite meaning of what is intended.

**Double Negative:** She **never** had **no** time to rest. (The actual meaning of these double negatives is "She did have time to rest.")

**Correction:** She had **no** time to rest.

**Double Negative:** My brother does **not** give me **nothing.** (The actual meaning of these double negatives is "My brother does give me something.")

**Correction:** My brother does **not** give me **anything.**

Double negatives often occur with contractions.

**Double Negative:** There **aren't hardly** any apples left. (The actual meaning of these double negatives is "There are plenty of apples left.")

**Correction:** There are **hardly** any apples left.

Using two negatives is confusing and grammatically wrong. Be on the lookout for negative words, and use only one per clause.

REVIEWING DOUBLE NEGATIVES

***What is a double negative?***

______________________________

***List five negative words.***

______ ______ ______ ______ ______

***Why should you avoid double negatives?***

______________________________

**Practice 10A Identifying** Mark each of the following sentences either correct (C) or incorrect (X).

1. _____ He didn't never study, but he always passed the tests.
2. _____ Tabitha wasn't hardly 4 years old when her mother passed away.
3. _____ Nobody showed up for none of the practices last week.
4. _____ Hawkins doesn't really know what he wants to do.
5. _____ I wouldn't go nowhere with him.
6. _____ Pauly didn't get his mother nothing for her birthday.
7. _____ Grandpa can't barely hear anymore.
8. _____ Neither of her children never came to see her.

9. ______ This was not the best decision you could have made.

10. ______ The pilot flew the jet like there wasn't nothing to fear.

**Practice 10B Correcting** Correct the double negatives in Practice 10A by rewriting the incorrect sentences.

**Practice 11 Completing** Choose the correct negative modifiers to complete the following paragraph.

Last summer, I went to the beach and (1) ____________ (was hardly, wasn't hardly) prepared for the sunshiny weather. I didn't buy (2) ____________ (any, no) sunscreen before I left because I had a decent tan already. To my surprise, I started to burn after only three hours on the beach, and there (3) ____________ (wasn't nothing, wasn't anything) I could do about it. I thought the burning feeling wouldn't (4) ____________ (ever, never) go away. And no matter what lotions and ointments I put on, I couldn't get (5) ____________ (no, any) relief. Next time, I'll remember to bring an umbrella.

**Practice 12 Writing Your Own** Write a sentence of your own for each of the following negative adverbs.

1. never ______________________________

2. not ______________________________

3. barely ______________________________

4. nobody ______________________________

5. nowhere ______________________________

## USING *GOOD/WELL* AND *BAD/BADLY* CORRECTLY

The pairs *good/well* and *bad/badly* are so frequently misused that they deserve special attention.

*Good* is an adjective; *well* is an adverb. Use *good* with a noun (n) or after a linking verb (lv).

n
**Adjective:** Juan is a **good** boy.

lv
**Adjective:** She looks **good.**

Use *well* for someone's health or after an action verb (av).

lv
**Adverb:** He is **well** again. [health]

av
**Adverb:** The baby sleeps **well** at night.

*Bad* is an adjective; *badly* is an adverb.

Use *bad* with a noun (n) or after a linking verb (lv). Always use *bad* after *feel* if you're talking about emotions.

n
**Adjective:** He seems like a **bad** person.

lv
**Adjective:** I feel **bad** that I got a ticket.

Use *badly* with an adjective (adj) or after an action verb (av).

adj
**Adverb:** The house was **badly** burned.

av
**Adverb:** He swims **badly.**

### REVIEWING *Good/Well* AND *Bad/Badly*

***When should you use the adjective* good?**

________________________________________________

*When should you use the adverb* well?

______________________________________________

*When should you use the adjective* bad?

______________________________________________

*When should you use the adverb* badly?

______________________________________________

**Practice 13A Identifying** Label each of the following sentences either correct (C) or incorrect (X).

1. ______ I want to do good in this job so my boss will like me.
2. ______ My favorite team is playing bad this week.
3. ______ Maggie sings well and is pursuing a career in opera.
4. ______ Rachel said she felt bad about Mr. Brown's accident.
5. ______ I wanted so bad to go diving, but I couldn't.
6. ______ If you do good on the midterm, you don't have to take the final exam.
7. ______ Despite his cancer, Don had a good attitude.
8. ______ He swam badly during the meet after staying up too late the night before.
9. ______ You took the bad news very good.
10. ______ This soup tastes very well.

**Practice 13B Correcting** Correct the adverb errors in Practice 13A by rewriting the incorrect sentences.

**Practice 14 Completing** Choose the correct modifiers to complete the following paragraph.

When Scott was in high school, there was only one thing he could do really (1) ______________ (good, well). He struggled with academics, he played most sports very (2) ______________ (bad, badly), and he was never popular with the girls. But his one strength was music. From the moment he picked up his first guitar, he was always (3) ______________ (good, well) at creating songs. Fortunately, his natural talent earned him several (4) ______________ (good, well) scholarship offers from big-name universities. Unfortunately, his (5) ______________ (bad, badly) study habits in high school made college more difficult for him, but he survived.

**Practice 15 Writing Your Own** Write a sentence of your own for each of the following modifiers.

1. well ______________________________________________
2. badly ______________________________________________
3. good ______________________________________________
4. bad ______________________________________________
5. well ______________________________________________

## CHAPTER REVIEW

You might want to reread your answers to the questions in the review boxes before you do the following exercises.

**Review Practice 1 Identifying** Underline the correct word in each of the following sentences.

1. Tia and Sue Ann studied together for the midterm, but Tia took notes (more, most) thoroughly.
2. We don't have (no, any) money for rent this month.
3. His speech seemed to go on (endlessly, more endlessly, most endlessly).
4. Of all the teachers at this school, Mrs. Thompson speaks the (more clearly, most clearly).
5. Jacob drives (more fast, faster) than I do.
6. During the baseball game, I struck out (less, least) often than Jack did.
7. She plays the flute very (good, well) and is in the orchestra.
8. My senior year in high school, I was voted (less, least) likely to drop out of college.
9. He hurt his knee so (bad, badly), it required medical attention.
10. The children were (real, really) tired after spending the day at the lake.

**Review Practice 2 Completing** Fill in each blank in the following paragraph with an adverb that makes sense. Try not to use any adverb more than once.

Working as a food server can be very challenging. I take my job (1) ____________________ than the other servers, so I can (2) ______________ count on coming home with better tips. But sometimes there are customers I just can't please, no matter how (3) ______________ I want to. Also, there's the occasional problem that happens (4) ______________, like the kitchen running out of chicken, or the bartender forgetting to make the drinks for my table. Because I'm determined to do a (5) ______________ job, though, my customers like me and keep coming back for my service.

**Review Practice 3 Writing Your Own** If you could prepare anything you wanted for dinner tonight, what would you make? Write a paragraph about this meal. How would you prepare it? How would you serve it? How many courses would it consist of?

## Editing Through Collaboration

Exchange paragraphs from Review Practice 3 with another student, and do the following:

1. Underline all the adverbs.
2. Circle those that are not in the correct form.
3. Put an X above any double negatives.

Then return the paper to its writer, and use the information in this chapter to correct any adverb errors in your own paragraph. Record your errors on the Error Log in Appendix 6.

# Modifier Errors

## Checklist for Identifying and Correcting Modifier Problems

- ✔ Are modifiers as close as possible to the words they modify?
- ✔ Are any sentences confusing because the words that the modifiers refer to are missing?

**Test Yourself**

Underline the modifier problem in each sentence.

- After studying together, his grades really improved.
- Before doing the laundry, the car needed to be washed.
- To get a good job, the interview must go well.
- The professor told the class he was retiring before he dismissed them.
- I wrote a letter to the newspaper that complained about rising power bills.

(Answers are in Appendix 4.)

As you know, a modifier describes another word or group of words. Sometimes, however, a modifier is too far from the words it refers to (*misplaced modifier*), or the word it refers to is missing altogether (*dangling modifier*). As a result, the sentence is confusing.

## MISPLACED MODIFIERS

A modifier should be placed as close as possible to the word or words it modifies, but this does not always happen. A **misplaced modifier** is too far from the word or words it refers to, making the meaning of the sentence unclear. Look at these examples.

**Misplaced:** The instructor explained why plagiarism is wrong **on Friday.**

(Is plagiarism wrong only on Friday? Probably not. So the modifier *on Friday* needs to be moved closer to the word it actually modifies.)

**Correct:** The instructor explained **on Friday** why plagiarism is wrong.

**Misplaced:** In most states, it is illegal to carry liquor in a car **that has been opened.**

(It is the liquor, not the car, that must not have been opened. So the modifier *that has been opened* needs to be moved closer to the word it modifies.)

**Correct:** In most states, it is illegal to carry liquor **that has been opened** in a car.

Certain modifiers that limit meaning are often misplaced, causing problems. Look at how meaning changes by moving the limiting word *only* in the following sentences:

**Only** Aunt Emily says that Lilly was a bad cook.
(Aunt Emily says this, but no one else does.)

Aunt Emily **only** says that Lilly was a bad cook.
(Aunt Emily says this, but she doesn't really mean it.)

Aunt Emily says **only** that Lilly was a bad cook.
(Aunt Emily says this but nothing more.)

Aunt Emily says that **only** Lilly was a bad cook.
(Lilly—and no one else—was a bad cook.)

Aunt Emily says that Lilly **only** was a bad cook.
(Aunt Emily says that there were some who were good cooks and Lilly was the only bad one.)

Aunt Emily says that Lilly was **only** a bad cook.
(Lilly was a bad cook, but she wasn't bad at other things.)

Aunt Emily says that Lilly was a bad cook **only.**
(Lilly was a bad cook, but she wasn't bad at other things.)

Here is a list of common limiting words.

| | | | |
|---|---|---|---|
| *almost* | *hardly* | *merely* | *only* |
| *even* | *just* | *nearly* | *scarcely* |

### Reviewing Misplaced Modifiers

***What is a misplaced modifier?***

______________________________________________

***How can you correct a misplaced modifier?***

______________________________________________

**Practice 1A Identifying** Underline the misplaced modifiers in the following sentences.

1. Tina told Tom that to win the lottery she had a great chance.
2. The car leaked all its oil by the time I called a mechanic in the driveway.
3. Brittany went to the mall with Jim wearing her favorite hat.
4. I sold Marty my old watch after I bought a new one for $10.
5. We made a pie in the kitchen with lots of blueberries.
6. Simon just bought a car from my uncle with silver pinstripes.
7. I want my hair to grow as long as Marci's in a ponytail.
8. Turn your paper in at the end of class to your teacher.
9. Debbie went to Alicia's house to get a cookie recipe next door.
10. Did you remember to turn the light off before you went to bed in the hallway?

**Practice 1B Correcting** Correct the misplaced modifiers in Practice 1A by rewriting the incorrect sentences.

**Practice 2 Completing** Fill in each blank in the following paragraph with a modifier that makes sense. Include at least two phrases.

Several years ago, Rodger owned a (1) ____________ farm in Kentucky where he grew corn and wheat. He also had (2) ____________ orchards of apples that he (3) ____________ harvested every September. His children had (4) ____________ the farm. Shortly before Rodger died, he trained his children (5) ______________ the family business.

**Practice 3 Writing Your Own** Write a sentence of your own for each of the following modifiers.

1. before summer ______________________________
2. since the company hired him ______________________________
3. while driving to the store ______________________________
4. after she bought the car ______________________________
5. though no one was there ______________________________

## DANGLING MODIFIERS

Modifiers are "dangling" when they have nothing to refer to in a sentence. **Dangling modifiers** (starting with an *-ing* word or with *to*) often appear at the beginning of a sentence. Here is an example.

**Dangling:** **Reaching the top of the hill,** the view was beautiful.

A modifier usually modifies the words closest to it. So the phrase *Reaching the top of the hill* modifies *view*. But it's not the *view* that reaches the top of the hill. In fact, there is no logical word in the sentence that the phrase modifies. It is left dangling. You can correct a dangling modifier in one of two ways—by inserting the missing word that is being referred to or by rewriting the sentence.

**Correct:** **Reaching the top of the hill,** we saw a beautiful view.
**Correct:** **When we reached the top of the hill,** the view we saw was beautiful.

**Dangling:** **To get into the movie,** an ID must be presented.
**Correct:** **To get into the movie,** you must present an ID.
**Correct:** You must present an ID **to get into the movie.**

**Dangling:** The garage was empty **after moving the tools.**
**Correct:** **After moving the tools,** we had an empty garage.

**Correct:** The garage was empty **after we moved the tools.**

**Correct:** **After moving the tools,** we had an empty garage.

### Reviewing Dangling Modifiers

***What is a dangling modifier?***

______________________________________________

***How do you correct a dangling modifier?***

______________________________________________

**Practice 4A Identifying** Underline the dangling modifiers in the following sentences.

1. To get a good deal, time must be spent comparing prices.
2. Screaming for help, the chair fell over with the little boy in it.
3. As an only daughter with four brothers, there was never enough food in the house.
4. To get a driver's license, two tests must be passed.
5. Giving the dog a bath, the bathroom floor became flooded.
6. After taking them to court, the judge ruled in our favor.
7. While weeding my flower beds, the snails were all over.
8. To avoid writing bad checks, your account balance should be checked often.
9. Giving up my seat on the bus, the old lady said, "Thank you."
10. After confessing to his smoking habit, Amy couldn't believe Jeremy's teeth were so white.

**Practice 4B Correcting** Correct the dangling modifiers in Practice 4A by rewriting the incorrect sentences.

**Practice 5 Completing** Fill in each blank in the following paragraph with a modifier that makes sense. Include at least two phrases.

(1) ____________ professional baseball teams begin spring training. The coaches plan on (2) ____________ weight lifting and lots of running. Hundreds of (3) ____________ athletes begin training each season, but within days, many get cut from the major league teams. These men usually get placed on (4) ____________ teams. These men hope to play well throughout the season and (5) ____________ move up.

**Practice 6 Writing Your Own** Write a sentence of your own for each of the following phrases.

1. warm and bright ____________________________________________
2. shaking my hand ____________________________________________
3. to understand the opposite sex ______________________________
4. getting a chance to see the ocean ___________________________
5. to win an argument _________________________________________

## CHAPTER REVIEW

You might want to reread your answers to the questions in the review boxes before you do the following exercises.

**Review Practice 1 Identifying** Underline the modifier errors in the following sentences.

1. Turning in my essay late, my computer crashed.
2. I am flying to Atlanta on Friday and returning Monday to attend a wedding.
3. To make a perfect chocolate dessert, the oven temperature must be carefully watched.

4. I put away my clothes and then filled up the bathtub in the closet.
5. Throwing the ball across the room, the lamp fell over and broke.
6. Jennifer complained that she forgot to send out invitations in an angry voice.
7. I found a pressed flower in my Shakespeare textbook from my wedding.
8. Driving to the movie theater, teenagers kept stepping out into the street in front of us.
9. Maria has a picture of her cousins at the beach in her locker.
10. To please your parents, good grades should be earned on every report card.

**Review Practice 2 Completing** Rewrite the sentences in Review Practice 1 so that the phrases you underlined are as close as possible to the words they modify.

**Review Practice 3 Writing Your Own** Write a paragraph about your greatest accomplishment. What did you do? How hard did you work for it? What was your reward?

## Editing Through Collaboration

Exchange paragraphs from Review Practice 3 with another student, and do the following:

1. Underline any misplaced modifiers.
2. Put brackets around any dangling modifiers.

Then return the paper to its writer, and use the information in this chapter to correct any modifier problems in your own paragraph. Record your errors on the Error Log in Appendix 6.

# End Punctuation

## Checklist for Using End Punctuation

✔ Does each sentence end with a period, a question mark, or an exclamation point?
✔ Are question marks used when asking questions?
✔ Do sentences that exclaim end with exclamation points?

**Test Yourself**

Add the appropriate end punctuation to the following sentences.

- How are we going to get there
- That's amazing
- Get me a Pepsi, please
- This will not happen to me
- Can you make your own dinner tonight

(Answers are in Appendix 4.)

---

End punctuation signals the end of a sentence in three ways: The period ends a statement, the question mark signals a question, and the exclamation point marks an exclamation.

## PERIOD

**A period is used with statements, mild commands, and indirect questions.**

**Statement:** The boy rode to school on the bus**.**
**Command:** Ride the bus to school today**.**

**Indirect Question:** I forgot to tell him he had to ride the bus to school today.

It is also used with abbreviations and numbers.

**Abbreviations:** Mr. Johnson lives at 9 Kings Rd., next door to Dr. Tina Lopez.

**Numbers:** $16.95 4.5 $876.98 .066

### Reviewing Periods

***What are the three main uses of a period?***

______________________________________________

***What are two other uses of a period?***

______________________________________________

**Practice 1 Identifying** In the following sentences, circle the periods used incorrectly, and add those that are missing.

1. Walt is buying the house on the corner of Sonora Ave and Eureka St.
2. I bought a new computer monitor for $210 0.0.
3. Mr Bernard just married Ms. Walters.
4. Tara's dentist is named Dr Jones, and his office is on 4th. St.
5. Bring your child to the library on Jackson Drive. and Lovejoy Pl..
6. I wonder if I should be taking vitamins
7. The normal human body temperature is 9.8.6°.
8. Rachel's new big-screen TV cost $3.425.00.
9. Platform shoes have definitely gone out of style
10. Mrs Martin has six kids.

**Practice 2 Completing** Add periods to the following paragraph where they are needed.

Jane Seymour is a very talented actress who stars in a TV series called *Dr Quinn, Medicine Woman* Ms Seymour also has twin boys who are in grade school, and she wrote a book about her experience mothering twins. Her husband is very supportive of her acting and writing activities He helps with the children and even offered quotes for her book. The book sells for about $20 50 and is published by St Martin's Press.

**Practice 3 Writing Your Own** Write a sentence of your own for each of the following descriptions.

1. a statement about cooking
2. a statement including a dollar amount
3. a statement including an address with an abbreviated street name
4. an indirect question about a psychology midterm
5. a command to do a household chore

## QUESTION MARK

**The question mark is used after a direct question.**

**Question Mark:** Do you have homework to do?

**Question Mark:** "Can you get your homework done on time?" her mother asked.

REVIEWING QUESTION MARKS

***What is the main role of a question mark?***

______________________________________________

***Give an example of a question.***

______________________________________________

**Practice 4 Identifying** In the following sentences, circle the question marks used incorrectly, and add those that are needed.

1. Did you buy that jacket only last week.
2. I wonder when the party starts?

3. Stephanie said, "Are you wearing my watch?"
4. Tina asked Whit how he was feeling?
5. Tina asked, "Whit, how are you feeling?"
6. I wish you would try to understand?
7. This is my biggest concern: How are we going to protect the rain forests.
8. Could you imagine spending the night in jail?
9. Is your mother paying your tuition.
10. Patrick wonders if the weather will be good for surfing tomorrow.

**Practice 5 Completing** Add question marks to the following paragraph where they are needed.

> What are the three most important things to remember about writing. First, choose topics that you are interested in. Why should you write about something that bores you. Second, remember that writing is a process. Should you ever turn in your first draft. No way. Writing gets better and better the more drafts you write. Third, give yourself plenty of time for editing and revision. Don't you think it's better that you catch the errors before your instructor does. Writing will be less of a chore if you remember these things and apply them to each assignment.

**Practice 6 Writing Your Own** Write a sentence of your own for each of the following descriptions.

1. a direct question about driving
2. a direct question about your favorite sport
3. a direct question about a family member
4. a direct question about the next major holiday
5. a direct question about lunch

## EXCLAMATION POINT

**The exclamation point indicates strong feeling.** If it is used too often, it is not as effective as it could be. You shouldn't use more than one exclamation point at a time.

**Exclamation Point:** Never!
**Exclamation Point:** You don't mean it!
**Exclamation Point:** Take your hands off me or I'll scream!
**Exclamation Point:** "You scared me to death!" she said.

Reviewing Exclamation Points

***What is the main use of an exclamation point?***

_______________________________________________

***Give an example of an exclamation.***

_______________________________________________

**Practice 7 Identifying** Circle the exclamation points used incorrectly, and add those that are needed.

1. That's outrageous!
2. I can't believe it.
3. He said, "Great job, Julian!"
4. What do you mean!
5. "Don't hurt my baby," yelled the mother.
6. I don't think that could ever happen!
7. Get it together, Bryan!
8. Are you positive!
9. Can you repeat that!
10. You make me so angry.

**Practice 8 Completing** Add exclamation points to the following paragraph where they are appropriate.

Paintball is my favorite pastime, and I play every weekend. It's so much fun. Last Saturday, Steve and Jay were on one team, and Tim and I were on another. Within an hour, Tim and I cornered Jay and took him out. "Pop. Pop." But suddenly, Steve came around a tree and pointed his paintball gun right at Tim.

"Duck," I yelled.

Tim quickly hit the ground, but it was too late. "Pop. Pop."

"Yeah," Steve yelled as he hit Tim right in the chest with paintballs.

But I was even quicker. "Pop." One shot and Steve had red paint right in the middle of his stomach.

"Last remaining survivor again," I screamed in delight.

**Practice 9 Writing Your Own** Write five sentences of your own using exclamation points correctly.

## CHAPTER REVIEW

You might want to reread your answers to the questions in the review boxes before you do the following exercises.

**Review Practice 1 Identifying** For each sentence, add the correct end punctuation.

1. Do you have any tattoos
2. Stop lying to me
3. "Are you sure you can help me" Susan asked.
4. No Not yet
5. Is there a problem with this software
6. Sometimes I think I'll never graduate
7. My cousin wants to know if we're going to leave soon
8. Take the keys to my car
9. That's impossible
10. You should study tomorrow while you're off work

**Review Practice 2 Completing** Turn sentences 1–5 into questions and sentences 6–10 into exclamations.

1. The plumber came today.
2. The Jets are going to win the Super Bowl.

3. Delores made the afghan.
4. You are going to be my date.
5. The baby hasn't been fed yet.
6. Don't forget to do the dishes.
7. We have ten minutes to get on the plane.
8. Are you serious?
9. I don't want to tell you.
10. This is a great day.

**Review Practice 3 Writing Your Own** Write a paragraph about an emotional experience or event in your life. Was it exciting, happy, sad, disappointing, frustrating, or challenging? What happened? Who was involved with you? Include all three types of end punctuation—period, question mark, and exclamation point.

## Editing Through Collaboration

Exchange paragraphs from Review Practice 3 with another student, and do the following:

1. Circle any errors in end punctuation.
2. Suggest the correct punctuation above your circle.

Then return the paragraph to its writer, and use the information in this chapter to correct any end punctuation errors in your own paragraph. Record your errors on the Error Log in Appendix 6.

# Commas

## Checklist for Using Commas

- ✔ Are commas used to separate items in a series?
- ✔ Are commas used to set off introductory material?
- ✔ Is there a comma before *and, but, for, nor, or, so,* and *yet* when they are followed by an independent clause?
- ✔ Are commas used to set off interrupting material in a sentence?
- ✔ Are commas used to set off direct quotations?
- ✔ Are commas used correctly in numbers, dates, addresses, and letters?

**Test Yourself**

Add commas to the following sentences.

- We drove to the beach and we had a picnic.
- Before I eat breakfast I take a multivitamin.
- "This is my favorite restaurant" said Matt.
- E-mail though makes corresponding easy and fast.
- They were married on September 21 1996 in Las Vegas Nevada.

(Answers are in Appendix 4.)

---

The comma is the most frequently used punctuation mark, but it is also the most often misused. Commas make reading sentences easier because they separate the parts of sentences. Following the rules in this chapter will help you write clear sentences that are easy to read.

## COMMAS WITH ITEMS IN A SERIES

**Use commas to separate items in a series.** This means that you should put a comma between all items in a series.

**Series:** The house had three bedrooms, two baths, and a pool.

**Series:** She caught the fish, cleaned it, and then cooked it.

**Series:** William can have a new car if his grades improve, if he gets a job, and if he does his chores at home.

Sometimes this rule applies to a series of adjectives in front of a noun, but sometimes it does not. Look at these two examples.

**Adjectives with Commas:** The foggy, cold weather is finally over.

**Adjectives Without Commas:** The loose bottom knob fell off my TV.

Both of these examples are correct. So how do you know whether or not to use commas? You can use one of two tests. One test is to insert the word "and" between the adjectives. If the sentence makes sense, use a comma. Another test is to switch the order of the adjectives. If the sentence still reads clearly, use a comma between the two words.

**Test 1:** The **foggy and cold** weather is finally over. **OK, so use a comma**

**Test 2:** The **cold, foggy** weather is finally over. **OK, so use a comma**

**Test 1:** The **loose and bottom** knob fell off my TV. **NO comma**

**Test 2:** The **bottom loose** knob fell off my TV. **NO comma**

### Reviewing Commas with Items in a Series

*Why use commas with items in a series?*

______________________________________________

*Where do these commas go?*

______________________________________________

**Practice 1 Identifying** In the following sentences, circle the commas that are used incorrectly, and add any commas that are missing.

1. In my free time, I like to read, sew, and make jelly.
2. My girlfriend is very good at tennis volleyball and golf.
3. The best things, about gardening are the relaxation, the sense of accomplishment and the feeling of oneness with nature.
4. To play professional basketball one must practice regularly, play competitively and get a big break.
5. The sofa the ottoman and the computer desk are going to be donated to Goodwill.
6. My daughter's favorite animals at the zoo were the monkeys, the hippos and, the zebras.
7. Lydia's unchanging everyday routine consists of going to work going to class, and studying.
8. *Gladiator*, *Chocolat*, and *Traffic* were nominated for best movie, of 2000.
9. The Spurs' best players are Tim Duncan, David Robinson and Sean Elliott.
10. We are having grilled chicken, asparagus and French bread for dinner tonight.

**Practice 2 Completing** Add the missing commas to the following paragraph.

We are flying to Dallas this weekend to attend a friend's wedding. Before we leave, I need to do the laundry pay the bills and arrange for a house sitter. My husband's childhood friend is the one getting married, so he also hopes to see some of his other friends there—especially Gene Brad and Dwayne. During the past two months, we bought airline tickets arranged for a rental car and reserved a hotel room. Now all we have to do is make it to the airport on time! I'm also trying to decide whether to wear navy pink or gray, and my husband is getting his best suit altered. Though it has required lots of time energy and money, we are really looking forward to this trip.

**Practice 3 Writing Your Own** Write a sentence of your own for each of the following sets of items.

1. three things to do at the mall ________________________________
2. three sports you like to play ________________________________

3. three items on a to-do list ______________________

4. three popular magazines ______________________

5. three of your favorite snack foods ______________________

## COMMAS WITH INTRODUCTORY WORDS

**Use a comma to set off an introductory word or group of words from the rest of its sentence.** If you are unsure whether to add a comma, try reading the sentence with your reader in mind. If you want your reader to pause after the introductory word or phrase you should insert a comma.

| | |
|---|---|
| **Introductory Word:** | Really**,** the weather wasn't as bad as we thought it would be. |
| **Introductory Word:** | No**,** it didn't rain. |
| **Introductory Phrase:** | On the whole**,** this is a great town to live in. |
| **Introductory Phrase:** | To prove this to my relatives**,** I took them for a driving tour of the town. |
| **Introductory Clause:** | When the movie was over**,** everyone was silent. |
| **Introductory Clause:** | As the doors opened**,** the light poured in. |

### Reviewing Commas with Introductory Words

***Why use commas with introductory words, phrases, and clauses?***

______________________

***How can you tell if a comma is needed?***

______________________

**Practice 4 Identifying** In the following sentences, circle the commas that are used incorrectly, and add any commas that are missing.

1. Since this game started, the Lakers have played better than the Mavericks.
2. When, Kelly was in high school she was a cheerleader.

3. Honestly I never thought I'd finish.
4. Wanting to get better grades Mary studied all weekend.
5. Though he never got hired, Manuel had three interviews with that company.
6. Three years, ago we lived in Boise.
7. As the fire continued, to burn the firefighters feared it would get out of control.
8. Sure I can take you to the store.
9. After spilling the water the little boy began to cry.
10. The next time you go, to Macy's can you pick up a gift certificate for me?

**Practice 5 Completing** Add the missing commas to the following paragraph.

When Terina was 7 years old we took her to Disneyland. Since she was tall enough to ride all of the rides she really enjoyed herself. First we had to take pictures with Mickey and Minnie. Of course we couldn't miss them! Next we got in line for Space Mountain, which turned out to be her favorite ride. By the end of the day we had ridden Space Mountain five times.

**Practice 6 Writing Your Own** Write a sentence of your own for each of the following introductory words, phrases, or clauses.

1. well ______________________________
2. when we thought it was almost over ______________________________
3. yes ______________________________
4. as the mail carrier arrived ______________________________
5. wanting to win the lottery ______________________________

## COMMAS WITH INDEPENDENT CLAUSES

**Use a comma before *and, but, for, nor or, so,* and *yet* when they join two independent clauses.** Remember that an independent clause must have both a subject and a verb.

**Independent Clauses:** The boy flew to London**, and** he took a boat to France.

**Independent Clauses:** He enjoyed the flight**, but** he liked the boat ride more.

HINT: Do not use a comma when a single subject has two verbs.

s v no comma v

The **boy flew** to London and **left** for France the next day.

Adding a comma when none is needed is one of the most common errors in college writing assignments. Only if the second verb has its own subject should you add a comma.

s v comma s v

The **boy flew** to London**,** and **he left** for France the next day.

### Reviewing Commas with Coordinating Conjunctions

***Name three coordinating conjunctions.***

_______________

***When should you use a comma before a coordinating conjunction?***

_______________

***Should you use a comma before a coordinating conjunction when a single subject has two verbs?***

_______________

**Practice 7 Identifying** In the following sentences, underline the subjects once and the coordinating conjunctions twice. Then circle any commas that are used incorrectly, and add any commas that are missing.

1. My computer crashed, so I lost my whole research paper.
2. The car looks great, and drives even better.
3. Going to the mountains was a good idea, and we had a very nice time.
4. The cat will curl up on the sofa, or the rug by the fireplace.

5. My cousin wants to get married, but I think she's too young.
6. The hostages were very scared, and tired.
7. That vase looks expensive, yet it was very reasonably priced.
8. I went to the movies, and I saw *The Mummy Returns*.
9. Karate is good exercise, and a good form of self-defense.
10. When the judge sentenced him, Gabe's mother cried, and his father shook his head.

**Practice 8 Completing** Add the missing commas to the following paragraph.

For my last birthday, my grandmother gave me $100 so I wanted to spend it on clothes. I went to the mall and I found three outfits that were perfect. I couldn't decide on just one but I didn't have enough money for them all. I needed the dressy outfit more yet the casual outfit was a great bargain. Finally, I settled on one pantsuit but I'm saving money to go back and get the others. I'll go back within a month or maybe I'll just wait until after my next holiday gift.

**Practice 9 Writing Your Own** Write a sentence of your own using each of the following coordinating conjunctions to separate two independent clauses.

1. or ______________________________
2. and ______________________________
3. so ______________________________
4. but ______________________________
5. yet ______________________________

## COMMAS WITH INTERRUPTERS

**Use a comma before and after a word or phrase that interrupts the flow of a sentence.** Most words that interrupt are not necessary for understanding the main point of a sentence. Setting them off makes it easier to recognize the main point.

**Word:** I didn't hear the phone ring**, however,** because I was in the shower.

**Word:** My next-door neighbor**, Carlos,** is from Portugal.

**Phrase:** One of the most popular tourist spots in America**, according to recent surveys,** is Disneyland.

**Phrase:** My textbook**, Ancient Rome,** is on the desk.

**Phrase:** Mr. Colby**, president of the school board,** has been elected mayor.

A very common type of interrupter is a clause that begins with *who, whose, which, when,* or *where* and is not necessary for understanding the main point of the sentence:

**Clause:** The new mall**, which is downtown,** has three restaurants.

Because the information "which is downtown" is not necessary for understanding the main idea of the sentence, it is set off with commas.

**Clause:** Carol Roth**, who has a Ph.D. in history,** is my new neighbor.

The main point is that Carol Roth is my new neighbor. Since the other information isn't necessary to understanding the sentence, it can be set off with commas.

HINT: Do *not* use commas with *who, whose, which, when,* or *where* if the information is necessary for understanding the main point of the sentence.

My friend **who is a circus clown** just arrived in town.

Because the information in the *who* clause is necessary to understand which friend just arrived in town, you should not set it off with commas.

HINT: Do not use commas to set off clauses beginning with *that:*

The mall **that is downtown** has three restaurants.

### Reviewing Commas with Interrupters

***Why should you use commas to set off words and phrases in the middle of a sentence?***

___

*When should you use commas with* who, whose, which, when, *or* where?

______________________________________________

*When should you* not *use commas before these words?*

______________________________________________

**Practice 10 Identifying** Label each sentence C if commas are used correctly with the underlined words and phrases or X if they are not.

1. _____ Jacquelyn Smith, who used to be a model, has a line of clothing at Kmart.

2. _____ My girlfriend, Cheri is, almost 23 years old.

3. _____ Hank is taking his wife Karen, to Hawaii.

4. _____ The AMC theater, my favorite hangout, is located on Main Street.

5. _____ Joe's leather jacket, which he's had only four months has, a broken zipper.

6. _____ *Air Force One*, the airplane, used by the United States president, is the most secure aircraft in the world.

7. _____ The preschooler, who is taking, a nap is named Bradley.

8. _____ My insurance agent, Bill likes to go fishing.

9. _____ "Little Red Riding Hood," my favorite fairy tale, has a happy ending.

10. _____ We were late to school, as usual because we had to stop for gas.

**Practice 11 Completing** Insert commas around the interrupting words and phrases in the following paragraph.

My grandmother Sally turned 80 this year. My grandfather died last August, and we didn't want Grammy living alone. She was able to take care of herself however so we didn't want to put her in a rest home. My brother and I visited Rosewood which is a very popular retirement community and were impressed with the facilities. There are group homes of course with "around the clock" care, but there are also condominiums where residents can live alone or with roommates. The entire neighborhood is monitored by security guards which is reassuring and the medical staff is always available. Grammy's been there for three weeks now and said she has never been happier.

**Practice 12 Writing Your Own** Write a sentence of your own for each of the following phrases.

1. who is very brave ______________________
2. which costs over $100 ______________________
3. however ______________________
4. the mayor's wife ______________________
5. taking the keys ______________________

## COMMAS WITH DIRECT QUOTATIONS

**Use commas to mark direct quotations.** A direct quotation records a person's exact words. Commas set off the exact words from the rest of the sentence, making it easier to understand who said what.

**Direct Quotation:** My friends often say**,** "You are so lucky."
**Direct Quotation:** "You are so lucky**,**" my friends often say.
**Direct Quotation:** "You are so lucky**,**" says my grandmother**,** "to have good friends."

**HINT:** If a quotation ends with a question mark or an exclamation point, do not use a comma. Only one punctuation mark is needed.

**NOT** "What did he want**?,**" she asked.
**Correct:** "What did he want**?**" she asked.

REVIEWING COMMAS WITH DIRECT QUOTATIONS

***Why should you use commas with a direct quotation?***

______________________

***Should you use a comma if the quotation ends with a question mark or an exclamation point? Why or why not?***

_______________________________________________

**Practice 13 Identifying** In the following sentences, circle the commas that are used incorrectly, and add any commas that are missing.

1. Tonya noted "I want the Kings to win tonight."
2. "If you go now," he said "don't come back."
3. "Are you absolutely sure?," David asked.
4. "That cat," Christine said , "sets off my allergies."
5. Mr. Avery remarked "The paper will not be accepted late."
6. "Leave me alone!," Jackie screamed.
7. "Without question" Cameron asserted ",that is the best option we have."
8. "I absolutely refuse!" yelled the man.
9. Henry asked "Did I upset you?"
10. Jawan confessed, "It was all my fault."

**Practice 14 Completing** Add the missing commas to the following passage.

"Are you going to the game tonight?" Dirk asked Brandy.
"Of course" she replied "I wouldn't miss it."
"But the Mets will probably be slaughtered" Dirk said.
"What difference does that make?" she questioned.
Dirk answered "I just don't want to pay money to watch them lose."
"Well, I'm a real loyal fan!" Brandy emphasized as she walked away.

**Practice 15 Writing Your Own** Write five sentences of your own using commas to set off direct quotations.

## OTHER USES OF COMMAS

**Use commas in the following ways.**

**Numbers:** What is 2,502,500 divided by 10,522?

**Dates:** My great grandfather was born in December 1888 in London and died on July 23, 1972, in Denver.

**Addresses:** Ashley moved from Chicago, Illinois, to 15305 Jefferson Ave., Boston, MA 09643.

**Letters:** Dear Alisha,
Yours truly,

### Reviewing Other Uses of Commas

***Give one example of commas in each of the following situations:***

***Numbers*** ______________________________

***Dates*** ______________________________

***Addresses*** ______________________________

***Letters*** ______________________________

***Why are these commas important?***

________________________________________

**Practice 16 Identifying** In the following sentences, circle the commas that are used incorrectly, and add any commas that are missing.

1. The new Honda Accord costs more than $23000.
2. Michael Finley plays basketball with the Mavericks and lives in Dallas Texas.
3. My five-year anniversary is June 16 2001.
4. Jamie lives in Los, Altos, California with her two kids.
5. About 4,500 students registered for classes this quarter.
6. There were 25,45 fans in the stadium.
7. My mother still lives at 4,901 El Sendero Ave., San Antonio TX, 78,233.
8. He made more than 2000 goals during his hockey career.
9. Dear Chenille,
10. Yours truly Deena

**Practice 17 Completing** Add the missing commas to the following paragraph.

Norma graduated from Centenary College in Shreveport Louisiana on June 5 1999. There were more than 3000 people in the audience, including Norma's friends and family. Her parents drove all the way from Tulsa Okalahoma and they stayed in Louisiana all weekend. After the graduation ceremonies, Norma and her loved ones spent the weekend visiting the New Orleans area and other parts of Louisiana that Norma didn't get to see while attending school.

**Practice 18 Writing Your Own** Write a sentence of your own including each of the following items.

1. your date of birth ______________________________
2. the city and state where you were born ______________________
3. your full address, including the ZIP code ____________________
4. the estimated number of people who attend your school __________

   ______________________________________________
5. the amount of money you would like to make per year after college graduation ______________________________

## CHAPTER REVIEW

You might want to reread your answers to the questions in the review boxes before you do the following exercises.

**Review Practice 1 Identifying** Add the missing commas to the following sentences.

1. When I was 12 years old, my father took me to Honolulu Hawaii.
2. Seth wanted more dessert but he was on a diet.
3. Although James read that book before he couldn't remember how it ended.

4. The Prelude is of course the best Honda vehicle.
5. I proudly cheered as Nick my best friend scored a touchdown.
6. "We will begin discussing genetics next Tuesday" said the professor.
7. Azaleas carnations and roses are my favorite flowers.
8. The beautiful tall brown-haired model walked down the catwalk.
9. There are 300400 people in this county.
10. Craig and I started dating on August 7 2001.

**Review Practice 2 Completing** Add the missing commas to the following paragraph.

My cat Trixie is Siamese. I still remember when she was born; it was February 14 1997 Valentine's Day. There are more than 1000 different breeds of cats but the Siamese are the most strikingly beautiful. Trixie is a friendly cat however unlike most Siamese. When I first brought her home my friends said "She'll be a spoiled brat" but I have come to love her.

**Review Practice 3 Writing Your Own** Write a paragraph about the importance of computer knowledge. What are the benefits of computer technology? Why should we be familiar with it?

## Editing Through Collaboration

Exchange paragraphs from Review Practice 3 with another student, and do the following:

1. Circle any misplaced commas.
2. Suggest corrections for the incorrect commas.

Then return the paper to its writer, and use the information in this chapter to correct any comma errors in your own paragraph. Record your errors on the Error Log in Appendix 6.

# Apostrophes

## Checklist for Using Apostrophes

✔ Are apostrophes used correctly in contractions?
✔ Are apostrophes used correctly to show possession?

**Test Yourself**

Add an apostrophe or an apostrophe and -*s* to the following sentences.

- The flight crew was surprised by the pilots rudeness when he boarded the plane.
- Its important that the car has its engine checked every 3,000 miles.
- Whats going to happen after George is gone?
- The mens bathroom is located on the third floor.
- James house is the third one on the left.

(Answers are in Appendix 4.)

The *apostrophe* looks like a single quotation mark. Its two main purposes are to indicate where letters have been left out and to show ownership.

## MARKING CONTRACTIONS

**Use an apostrophe to show that letters have been omitted to form a contraction.** A **contraction** is the shortening—or contraction—of one or more words. Our everyday speech is filled with contractions.

I have = I've (*h* and *a* have been omitted)
you are = you're (*a* has been omitted)
let us = let's (*u* has been omitted)

Here is a list of commonly used contractions.

**Some Common Contractions**

| | | | | | |
|---|---|---|---|---|---|
| *I am* | = | I'm | *we have* | = | we've |
| *I would* | = | I'd | *we will* | = | we'll |
| *I will* | = | I'll | *they are* | = | they're |
| *you have* | = | you've | *they have* | = | they've |
| *you will* | = | you'll | *do not* | = | don't |
| *he is* | = | he's | *did not* | = | didn't |
| *she will* | = | she'll | *have not* | = | haven't |
| *it is* | = | it's | *could not* | = | couldn't |

HINT: Two words that are frequently misused are *it's* and *its*.

| | |
|---|---|
| *it's* = contraction: it is (*or* it has) | **It's** too late to go to the movie. |
| *its* = pronoun: belonging to it | **Its** eyes are really large. |

To see if you are using the correct word, say the sentence with the words *it is*. If that is what you want to say, add an apostrophe to the word.

**?** I think **its** burning.
**Test:** I think **it is** burning. **YES, add an apostrophe**

This sentence makes sense with *it is*, so you should write *it's*.

**Correct:** I think **it's** burning.
**?** The dog wagged **its** tail.
**Test:** The dog wagged **it is** tail. **NO, so no apostrophe**

This sentence does not make sense with *it is*, so you should not use the apostrophe in *its*.

**Correct:** The dog wagged **its** tail.

REVIEWING CONTRACTIONS

***What is the purpose of an apostrophe in a contraction?***

______________________________________________

***Write five contractions, and tell which letters have been omitted.***

____________________ ____________________

____________________ ____________________

____________________ ____________________

____________________ ____________________

____________________ ____________________

***What is the difference between*** **it's** ***and*** **its?**

________________________________________

**Practice 1 Identifying** In the following sentences, circle the apostrophes that are used incorrectly, and add any apostrophes that are missing.

1. Ive got to find a better job.
2. The attorney said she's working overtime on this case.
3. Theyll be glad to see you at the party.
4. Its a good thing they did'nt bring their baby to the wedding.
5. Cameron doesnt get paid until Friday.
6. People should'nt start smoking because its a hard habit to break.
7. Were going to be an hour late because of this traffic.
8. Im sure well be seeing each other again soon.
9. Weve got a lot of work to do tonight.
10. Hows my old car going to make it over the mountains?

**Practice 2 Completing** Write contractions for the following words.

1. she + would = ____________________
2. did + not = ____________________
3. will + not = ____________________

4. they + will = ________________

5. should + have = ________________

**Practice 3 Writing Your Own** Write a sentence of your own for each of the contractions you wrote in Practice 2.

## SHOWING POSSESSION

1. **For a singular word, use 's to indicate possession or ownership.** You can always replace a possessive with *of* plus the noun or pronoun.

| | |
|---|---|
| the soldier**'s** rifle | = the rifle *of the soldier* |
| someone**'s** house | = the house *of someone* |
| doctor**'s** office | = the office *of the doctor* |
| yesterday**'s** paper | = the paper of *yesterday* |

2. **For plural nouns ending in -*s*, use only an apostrophe.**

| | |
|---|---|
| the soldiers**'** rifles | = the rifles *of the soldiers* |
| the doctors**'** office | = the office *of the doctors* |
| the painters**'** studio | = the studio *of the painters* |
| the students**'** grades | = the grades *of the students* |
| the brothers**'** boat | = the boat *of the brothers* |

3. **For plural nouns that do not end in -*s*, add 's.**

| | |
|---|---|
| the men**'s** pants | = the pants *of the men* |
| the deer**'s** antlers | = the antlers *of the deer* |
| the criteria**'s** importance | = the importance *of the criteria* |

### Reviewing Possessives

***How do you mark possession or ownership for a singular word?***

________________________________________

***How do you mark possession or ownership for a plural word that ends in -s?***

________________________________________

***How do you mark possession or ownership for a plural word that doesn't end in -s?***

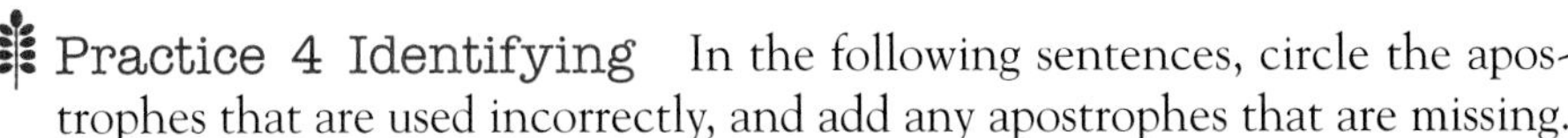

**Practice 4 Identifying** In the following sentences, circle the apostrophes that are used incorrectly, and add any apostrophes that are missing.

1. The boy's bicycle had a flat tire.
2. The disaster was Jennifers' fault.
3. Our two cat's water bowl was empty.
4. We knew the airline's food would be tasty.
5. Jacks' pet rabbit is trained to use the litter box.
6. Todays' temperature reached 83 degrees.
7. The Mets' biggest loss was against the White Sox.
8. The movies' ending was disappointing.
9. My mothers hair is brown.
10. His three uncle's briefcases are all leather.

**Practice 5 Completing** Write a possessive for each of the following phrases.

1. the feet of Charles
2. the guests of Dr. Blakeney
3. the tide of the ocean
4. the shirts of the men
5. the assignment of the students

**Practice 6 Writing Your Own** Write a sentence of your own for each of the possessives you wrote in Practice 5.

## COMMON APOSTROPHE ERRORS

Two common errors occur with apostrophes. The following guidelines will help you avoid these errors.

## No Apostrophe with Possessive Pronouns

**Do not use an apostrophe with a possessive pronoun.** Possessive pronouns are possessive without an apostrophe, so they do not need an apostrophe.

| | | **Correct** |
|---|---|---|
| **NOT** | his' | his |
| **NOT** | her's *or* hers' | hers |
| **NOT** | it's *or* its' | its |
| **NOT** | your's *or* yours' | yours |
| **NOT** | our's *or* ours' | ours |
| **NOT** | their's *or* theirs' | theirs |

## No Apostrophe to Form the Plural

**Do not use an apostrophe to form a plural word.** This error occurs most often with plural words ending in *-s*. An apostrophe indicates possession or contraction; it does *not* indicate the plural. Therefore, a plural word never takes an apostrophe unless it is possessive.

**NOT** The **clothes'** are in the dryer.
**Correct:** The **clothes** are in the dryer.

**NOT** She bought a case of **soda's** last week.
**Correct:** She bought a case of **sodas** last week.

**NOT** Get your coffee and **donut's** here.
**Correct:** Get your coffee and **donuts** here.

### Reviewing Apostrophe Errors

***List three possessive pronouns.***

________________ ________________ ________________

***Why don't possessive pronouns take apostrophes?***

________________________________________________

*What is wrong with the apostrophe in each of the following sentences?*

*The last float in the parade is ours'.* ______________________

______________________________________________

*There must be 100 floats' in the parade.* ______________________

**Practice 7 Identifying** In the following sentences, circle the apostrophes that are used incorrectly, and add any apostrophes that are missing.

1. I've been to that store five time's, and I've never seen shoes like yours.
2. My brother's are working for my fathers company.
3. Sam left his' cars window's down, and it is starting to rain.
4. The soccer player's are meeting at noon.
5. The big story in the newspaper's is yesterday's flood.
6. Emily's car is newer than our's.
7. That cookbook is their's.
8. We have to attend two wedding's in the next two week's.
9. His' short's faded in the swimming pool because there was so much chlorine.
10. Tony's leg's were sore from jumping on the trampoline.

**Practice 8 Completing** Write a possessive for each of the following phrases.

1. the house belonging to them
2. the pants she owns
3. the soda you are holding
4. the price of it
5. the feet of that man

**Practice 9 Writing Your Own** Write a sentence of your own for each of the possessives you wrote in Practice 8.

## CHAPTER REVIEW

You might want to reread your answers to the questions in the review boxes before you do the following exercises.

**Review Practice 1 Identifying** In the following sentences, circle the apostrophes that are used incorrectly, and add any apostrophes that are missing.

1. Mr. Thompson's diner serves many pasta entrée's.
2. Two plumber's came to fix the leaks.
3. I thought I picked up my purse, but it was really her's.
4. Jeff was'nt pleased with the restaurant s service.
5. The rose's in my front yard havent bloomed yet.
6. Its amazing that Tricia cut her hair as short as yours.
7. His' new house is in Highland Park.
8. Youve got to see Karens new jet ski's.
9. The schools mascot is getting a full athletic scholarship.
10. Marys parent's ordered four pizza's for her party.

**Review Practice 2 Completing** Add the missing apostrophes to the following sentences.

1. The trucks brakes went out while it was coming over the hill.
2. We havent heard from Ben since he left his fathers ranch for ours.
3. My next-door neighbors uncle is a big Hollywood actor.
4. Sarahs diet consisted of hot dogs and sodas.
5. The freeways are crowded because yesterdays fire still hasnt been contained.
6. I think its time for us to go to our house and you to go to yours.
7. Devons kids were playing dominoes.
8. Maurice cant ever beat me at backgammon.
9. Stellas going to the game with us.
10. Both cars gas tanks are empty.

**Review Practice 3 Writing Your Own** Write a paragraph about your favorite teacher. What was his or her name? What was special about this person?

## Editing Through Collaboration

Exchange paragraphs from Review Practice 3 with another student, and do the following:

1. Circle any misplaced or missing apostrophes.
2. Indicate whether they mark possession (P) or contraction (C).

Then return the paper to its writer, and use the information in this chapter to correct any apostrophe errors in your own paragraph. Record your errors on the Error Log in Appendix 6.

# Quotation Marks

## Checklist for Using Quotation Marks

- ✔ Are quotation marks used to indicate someone's exact words?
- ✔ Are all periods and commas inside quotation marks?
- ✔ Are words capitalized correctly in quotations?
- ✔ Are quotation marks used to indicate the title of a short work, such as a short story or a poem?

**Test Yourself**

Add quotation marks where needed in the following sentences.

- Can we go out to dinner tonight? she asked.
- Jeri screamed, Don't go in there!
- If you can't find my house, Tom said, call me on your cell phone.
- My favorite poem is The Red Wheelbarrow by William Carlos Williams.
- David said, I'll fix your car this weekend.

(Answers are in Appendix 4.)

---

**Quotation marks** are punctuation marks that work together in pairs. Their most common use is to indicate someone's exact words. They are also used to indicate the title of a short piece of writing, such as a short story or a poem.

## DIRECT QUOTATIONS

**Use quotation marks to indicate a direct quotation—someone's exact words.** Here are some examples. They show the three basic forms of a direct quotation.

**Direct Quotation:** "I will not lend you the money," said the banker.

Here the quoted words come first.

**Direct Quotation:** The banker said, "I will not lend you the money."

Here the quoted words come after the speaker is named.

**Direct Quotation:** "I will not," the banker said, "lend you the money."

In this example, the quoted words are interrupted, and the speaker is named in the middle. This form emphasizes the beginning words.

## INDIRECT QUOTATIONS

**If you just talk about someone's words, you do not need quotation marks.** Look at these examples of **indirect quotations.** Indirect quotations usually use the word *that*, as in *said that*. In questions, the wording is often *asked if*.

**Direct Quotation:** "I lost my job at the supermarket," said Bob.

These are Bob's exact words, so you must use quotation marks.

**Indirect Quotation:** Bob **said that** he lost his job at the supermarket.

This sentence explains what Bob said but does not use Bob's exact words. So quotation marks should not be used.

**Direct Quotation:** "The train trip took eight hours," said Kira.
**Indirect Quotation:** Kira **said that** the train trip took eight hours.

**Direct Quotation:** "Did you get the car fixed?" Mom asked.
**Indirect Quotation:** Mom **asked if** I had gotten the car fixed.

### Reviewing Quotation Marks with Quotations

***How do you show that you are repeating someone's exact words?***

______________________________________________

***What is an indirect quotation?***

______________________________________________

**Practice 1 Identifying** In the following sentences, circle the quotation marks used incorrectly, and add any quotation marks that are missing.

1. "Help me! yelled the drowning woman."
2. "If you can't take the heat," my mom used to say, stay out of the kitchen."
3. Steffan said, My goal is to "get into the Olympics."
4. Chonda said that "she enjoyed the movie last night."
5. "Go play with Sammy," said the woman to her toddler.
6. Martina asked if "I had found her jacket."
7. Martina asked, "Have you found my jacket?"
8. "I'll start this project today, Nicole promised, and with any luck be finished by tomorrow."
9. "Do you want me to drive? I asked.
10. Call me," he said, "when you get back to your house."

**Practice 2 Completing** Add the missing quotation marks to the following paragraph.

When I went into the salon, my hairdresser asked, How do you want your hair cut today? I don't really know, I replied, but I brought in a couple of pictures of haircuts I like. Those are cute, she said. Do you think my hair would look good like that? I asked. Absolutely! she exclaimed. Then she set to work with the scissors. When she was finished, I looked in the mirror in horror. That's not what I had in mind, I told her. But it looks just like the pictures, she said. How can you say that? I exclaimed. The haircuts I showed you are shoulder-length, and mine is now above my ears! Well, she said, it will always grow back.

**Practice 3 Writing Your Own** Write a sentence of your own for each of the following expressions.

1. a question asked by Claudia ______________________________
2. a statement spoken by the manager ______________________________
3. an exclamation spoken by Becky ______________________________

4. an indirect question that Jared asked ______________________________

5. a statement spoken by the electrician ______________________________

## CAPITALIZING AND USING OTHER PUNCTUATION MARKS WITH QUOTATION MARKS

Quotation marks are used around sentences or parts of sentences. Therefore, when you are quoting someone's exact sentences, begin with a capital letter and use appropriate end punctuation—a period, a question mark, or an exclamation point. You do not need to capitalize the first word of a quotation if it is only part of a sentence. Here are some examples.

> **"H**e doesn't seem very nice**,"** she said**.**
>
> **H**e said**, "T**urn off the music**."**

Capitalize the first letter of the words being quoted, and put a period at the end of the sentence if it is a statement. Separate the spoken words from the rest of the sentence with a comma.

> **H**e yelled**, "T**urn off that music**!"**
>
> **"W**hy do you want to know**?"** she asked**.**

If the quotation ends with a question mark or an exclamation point, use that punctuation instead of a comma or a period.

> **"Y**es**,"** said the bus driver**, "**this bus goes downtown**."**

In a quotation that is interrupted, capitalize the first word being quoted, but do not capitalize words in the middle of the sentence. Use a comma both before and after the interruption. End with a period if it is a statement.

> I don't think that he will ever **"**find himself**."**

You do not need to capitalize the first word of a quotation that is only part of a sentence.

**HINT:** Look at the examples again. Notice that periods and commas always go *inside* the quotation marks.

> **NOT** "Yes"**,** he said, "we're ready to leave"**.**
>
> **Correct:** "Yes**,"** he said, "we're ready to leave**."**

REVIEWING CAPITALIZATION AND PUNCTUATION WITH QUOTATION MARKS

***When you quote someone's exact words, why should you begin with a capital letter?***

______________________________________________

***Where do commas go in relation to quotation marks? Where do periods go?***

______________________________________________

 **Practice 4 Identifying** In the following sentences, circle the quotation marks and other punctuation marks that are used incorrectly, and add any missing quotation marks and punctuation.

1. "Is there a doctor in the house"? the man screamed.
2. "I can't believe", she said, "that you've never seen the ocean."
3. Margarita asked, "Are you ever going to meet me for coffee"?
4. "This is the last time" he promised, "that I come home late".
5. Garrett said, "I want to take the trolley to the restaurant on the corner".
6. "If you want to," Cheyenne suggested "we can take the elevator instead."
7. "Don't even think about it!," Janelle exclaimed.
8. Robert complained "All you do is watch television."
9. "Are we almost there yet." she asked.
10. Rose Marie said "The best thing about this house is the storage space."

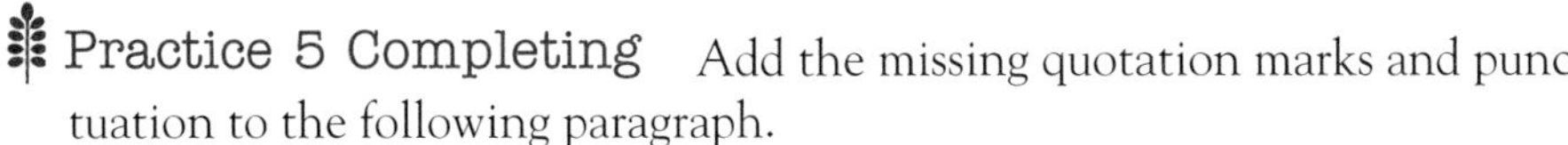

**Practice 5 Completing** Add the missing quotation marks and punctuation to the following paragraph.

I was having car problems, so I drove to the auto shop on the corner. What do you think is wrong with my car? I asked the mechanic. I can't tell you he said, until I take a look at it myself. I replied, I'll leave it with you this afternoon, and you can tell me later today what you find out. That would be great, he said. Finally, around 4:00 p.m., he called me on the phone. Your car needs a new clutch, he said. No way! I exclaimed. Sorry, mister he calmly replied, but that's all I found to be wrong with it. I explained But I just replaced the clutch four months ago. Well, he said, I hope you saved your receipt and warranty paperwork.

**Practice 6 Writing Your Own** Write a sentence of your own for each of the following direct quotations, punctuated correctly.

1. "No, I won't!" ______________________________
2. "How are we going to do that?" ______________________________
3. "This is the most important priority" ______________________________
4. "Yes" "you can come to the party" ______________________________
5. "Don't worry" "you didn't miss anything" ______________________________

## QUOTATION MARKS AROUND TITLES

Put quotation marks around the titles of short works that are parts of larger works. The titles of longer works are put in italics (or underlined).

| Quotation Marks | Italics/Underlining |
|---|---|
| "The Yellow Wallpaper" (short story) | *American Short Stories* (book) |
| "Song of Myself" (poem) | *Leaves of Grass* (book) |
| "My Girl" (song) | *The Temptations' Greatest Hits* (album) |
| "Explore New Orleans" (magazine article) | *New Orleans Monthly* (magazine) |
| "Convicts Escape" (newspaper article) | *New York Times* (newspaper) |
| "The Wedding" (episode on TV series) | *Friends* (TV series) |

### Reviewing Quotation Marks with Titles

***When do you put quotation marks around a title?***

______________________________

***When do you italicize (or underline) a title?***

______________________________________________

**Practice 7 Identifying** Put an X in front of each sentence with errors in quotation marks or italics/underlining. Add any missing quotation marks and italics or underlining.

1. _____ My favorite song by the Beatles is *Yellow Submarine.*
2. _____ When Juliet was in high school, she read Shirley Jackson's famous short story The Lottery.
3. _____ Getting through *Moby Dick* by Herman Melville took me three weeks.
4. _____ My first boyfriend recited William Blake's poem *The Garden of Love* to me on my front porch.
5. _____ The "New York Times" ran a long article called *Japan's Princess Is Pregnant* about Crown Princess Masako.
6. _____ Tomorrow night's episode of *Who Wants to Be a Millionaire* is going to be called The Couples Challenge.
7. _____ Mandy requested that the band play Britney Spears's song "Soda Pop."
8. _____ I found a great recipe in the February issue of *Good Housekeeping*.
9. _____ My girlfriend loves the TV series "Frasier," but I prefer *Third Watch.*
10. _____ We're going to the video store to rent "A Knight's Tale."

**Practice 8 Completing** Place quotation marks around the titles of short works, and underline the titles of long works in the following paragraph.

Mark got a great job with the Chicago Tribune last summer. He is now working as the editor of the entertainment section, and he writes a column called Making a Mark. In his column, he reviews celebrity events and activities, such as concerts, hit movies, and best-selling books. For one article, he interviewed several people from Survivor, the popular reality TV show. He also attended a Dixie Chicks concert and quoted lines from the song There's Your Trouble on their album Wide Open Spaces. Another article featured Nikki Giovanni, who read her poem Dream during their interview. Mark has become friends with some very interesting and well-known people, and he is now looking forward to speaking with Steven Spielberg on the set of the latest sequel to Jurassic Park.

**Practice 9 Writing Your Own** Write a sentence of your own for each of the following items. Make up a title if you can't think of one.

1. a short story ______________________________
2. a song ______________________________
3. a newspaper article ______________________________
4. a poem ______________________________
5. a magazine article ______________________________

## CHAPTER REVIEW

You might want to reread your answers to the questions in the review boxes before you do the following exercises.

**Review Practice 1 Identifying** Add the missing quotation marks and punctuation to the following sentences.

1. Patty sang Whitney Houston's You Give Good Love at the karaoke party.
2. Our next writing assignment is a critical review of Robert Browning's poem My Last Duchess.
3. You don't have to go to work today, I told Gerard.
4. Marjorie won the short story contest with a tale she wrote about her grandmother called It's a Happy Day.

5. Devonne asked Where does Jack live?
6. When Princess Diana died, the Boston Globe ran an article called Too Soon.
7. The scores came in, and our coach yelled Great job, team!
8. I can't make it to the meeting, she said but I'll call you tonight to find out what I missed.
9. What do you want to eat for breakfast? Charise asked.
10. I submitted an article to Golf Magazine called How to Swing like Tiger Woods.

**Review Practice 2 Completing** Add the missing quotation marks, commas, and underlining for italics to the following dialogue.

> Hurry up I said or we're going to be late for the Beastie Boys Concert.
>
> I'm coming John replied. Just hold your horses!
>
> The write-up in USA Today said this was going to be their biggest concert ever, I told him. I asked John if he too had read that article, but he said that he hadn't.
>
> I didn't have time to read today he explained because I was busy buying a CD of their greatest hits. Now, John said, I'm really excited about the concert tonight!

**Review Practice 3 Writing Your Own** In paragraph form, record a conversation you had this week. Who were you talking to? What did you talk about? What were your exact words?

## Editing Through Collaboration

Exchange paragraphs from Review Practice 3 with another student, and do the following:

1. Circle any incorrect or missing quotation marks.
2. Underline any faulty punctuation.
3. Put an X over any incorrect use of italics/underlining.

Then return the paper to its writer, and use the information in this chapter to correct any errors with quotation marks and italics/underlining in your own paragraph. Record your errors on the Error Log in Appendix 6.

CHAPTER 51

# Other Punctuation Marks

## Checklist for Using Semicolons, Colons, Dashes, and Parentheses

- ✔ Are semicolons used to join two closely related complete sentences?
- ✔ Are long items in a series that already contains commas separated by semicolons?
- ✔ Are colons used correctly to introduce a list?
- ✔ Are dashes used to emphasize or further explain a point?
- ✔ Are parentheses used to include additional, but not necessary, information?

**Test Yourself**

Add semicolons, colons, dashes, or parentheses to the following sentences.

- Kris left for the dance Sean decided to stay home.
- We wanted to win therefore we practiced every day.
- The computer's advertised price didn't include several important things a monitor, a printer, and speakers.
- Kyle asked the best question during the interview "Why should we vote for you?"
- Bring the jelly to a "rolling boil" a boil that cannot be stirred down.

(Answers are in Appendix 4.)

---

This chapter explains the uses of the semicolon, colon, dash, and parentheses. We'll look at these punctuation marks one by one.

## SEMICOLONS

**Semicolons** are used to separate equal parts of a sentence. They are also used to avoid confusion when listing items in a series.

1. **Use a semicolon to separate two closely related independent clauses.** An independent clause is a group of words with a subject and a verb that can stand alone as a sentence. You might use a semicolon instead of a coordinating conjunction (*and, but, for, nor, or, so, yet*) or a period. Any one of the three options would be correct.

| | Independent Independent |
|---|---|
| **Semicolon:** | Sam never drove to school**;** he always rode his bike. |
| **Conjunction:** | Sam never drove to school**, for** he always rode his bike. |
| **Period:** | Sam never drove to school**. He** always rode his bike. |

2. **Use a semicolon to join two independent clauses that are connected by such words as *however, therefore, furthermore, moreover, for example,* or *consequently.*** Put a comma after the connecting word.

| | Independent Independent |
|---|---|
| **Semicolon:** | Traveling can be expensive**; nevertheless,** it's always enjoyable. |
| **Semicolon:** | My nephew William is very smart**; furthermore,** he was offered seven scholarships. |
| **Semicolon:** | He has trouble in math**; therefore,** he hired a tutor. |

3. **Use a semicolon to separate items in a series when commas are already part of the list.**

**NOT** On the flight to New York, Maria read a popular new thriller with a surprise ending, took a long, relaxing nap, and watched an incredibly dull movie about a rock star.

**Correct:** On the flight to New York, Maria read a popular new thriller with a surprise ending; took a long, relaxing nap; and watched an incredibly dull movie about a rock star.

### Reviewing Semicolons

***How are semicolons used between two independent clauses?***

______________________________________________

***How are semicolons used with items in a series?***

______________________________________________

**Practice 1 Identifying** In the following sentences, circle the semicolons that are used incorrectly, and add any commas and semicolons that are missing.

1. The car needed new front tires the old ones were quite bald.
2. Lisa's 10-month-old son didn't take a nap today; however; he was very pleasant.
3. I must have lost my keys I can't; find them anywhere.
4. Our team is the strongest; and we are prepared to win.
5. Mr. Gravelle teaches Spanish; writes novels; books; and short stories; and reviews movies in his spare time.
6. My sister joined the army last June she committed to four years.
7. Julie left the coffee pot burning all day consequently; it cracked from the heat.
8. We have many laws against drinking and driving nonetheless, hundreds of people die every year in alcohol-related accidents.
9. During our shopping spree, we bought a bedroom set; a living room set with a sofa, chair, and end tables and a new refrigerator.
10. We could go to the movies we could also go to the theater.

**Practice 2 Completing** Add semicolons to the following paragraph.

When I was in junior high, my school had a big dance I dreaded it from the day it was announced. I didn't have a boyfriend I didn't have the right clothes, shoes, or hairstyle and I didn't have any money saved up for things like that. Even worse, I knew my parents felt I was too young to go nonetheless, I knew my friends would keep asking me if I was going. Finally, I thought of a good excuse: I told my friends my grandmother was having major surgery. My friends probably knew I was lying however, nobody said anything more to me about it.

**Practice 3 Writing Your Own** Write five sentences of your own using semicolons correctly.

## COLONS

The main use of the colon is to introduce a list or thought. Here are some examples:

**Colon:** Buy the following items for the trip: toothpaste, toothbrush, razor, soap, and makeup.

**Colon:** The fair had some new attractions: a double ferris wheel, a roller coaster, and a merry-go-round for young children.

**Colon:** The choice was simple**:** return the merchandise.

The most common error with colons is using one where it isn't needed. Do not use a colon after the words *such as* or *including*. A complete sentence must come before a colon.

**NOT** Cook only fresh vegetables, **such as:** green beans, broccoli, and spinach.

**Correct:** Cook only fresh vegetables, **such as** green beans, broccoli, and spinach.

**NOT** We went to many countries in Europe, **including:** Spain and Portugal.

**Correct:** We went to many countries in Europe, **including** Spain and Portugal.

In addition, you should not use a colon after a verb or after a preposition. Remember that a complete sentence must come before a colon.

**NOT** The movies to be reviewed **are:** *American Beauty* and *Wonder Boys*.

**Correct:** The movies to be reviewed **are** *American Beauty* and *Wonder Boys*.

**NOT** The box was full **of:** books, old dolls, and scrapbooks.

**Correct:** The box was full **of** books, old dolls, and scrapbooks.

### Reviewing Colons

***What is the main use of a colon?***

________________________________________________

***Why should you not use a colon after such words as* is *or* of?**

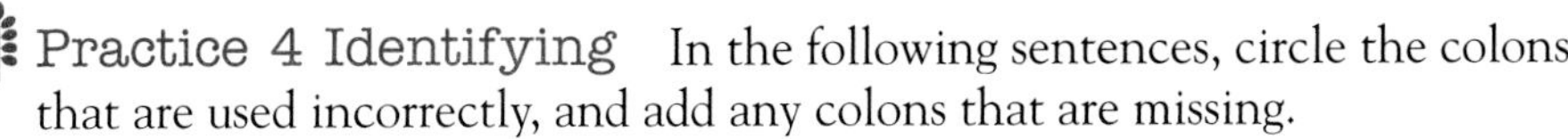

**Practice 4 Identifying** In the following sentences, circle the colons that are used incorrectly, and add any colons that are missing.

1. The best things about summer are: swimming, biking, and picnics.
2. The man asked me for the following items: my driver's license, my Social Security number, and my credit cards.
3. We accidentally left many things at home, such as: my toothbrush, our hair dryer, and the baby's bottle.
4. The conference will cover three important issues race relations, the economy, and global warming.
5. Luke bought three animals at the fair: a chinchilla, a hamster, and a boa constrictor.
6. I was most impressed by: the atmosphere, the prices, and the service.
7. The most expensive parts to repair were: the carburetor, the ignition system, and the fuel injector.
8. My favorite movies are: romances, dramas, and horror films.
9. Sharon's hair has been several colors recently: green, blue, yellow, purple, and pink.
10. That old barn was the location for many events, including: dances, dinner parties, and hoedowns.

**Practice 5 Completing** Add colons to the following paragraph.

Reading is an excellent way to spend free time. A good book can do many things take you to a faraway place, introduce you to different people, and expose you to extraordinary experiences. I especially like two kinds of books science fiction and romance novels. These genres are totally opposite, I know, but they have just what I like action, strange characters, and suspension of disbelief. When I am reading, I am in a world of my own. I escape all of my everyday problems my ungrateful job, my nagging mother, and sometimes even my homework.

**Practice 6 Writing Your Own** Write five sentences of your own using colons correctly.

## DASHES AND PARENTHESES

**Use dashes to emphasize or draw attention to a point.**

**Dash:** I know what I want to be—a doctor.

In this example, the beginning of the sentence introduces an idea, and the dash then sets off the answer.

**Dash:** Money and time—these are what I need.

In this example, the key words are set off at the beginning, and the explanation follows. Beginning this way adds some suspense to the sentence.

**Dashes:** I know what I want in a husband—a sense of humor—and I plan to get it.

The dashes divide the sentence into three distinct parts, which makes the reader pause and think about each part.

While dashes set off material that the writer wants to emphasize, **parentheses** do just the opposite: **Use parentheses to set off information that is interesting or helpful but not necessary for understanding the sentence.**

**Parentheses:** When in Rome **(as the saying goes),** do as the Romans do.

**Parentheses:** The senator's position on the proposal **(on Senate Bill 193)** has changed several times.

Parentheses are also used to give a person's life span and to number items in a sentence. They are always used in pairs. Here are some examples:

**Parentheses:** Herman Melville **(1819–1891)** wrote the classic *Moby Dick*.

**Parentheses:** My boss gave me three things to do today: **(1)** answer the mail, **(2)** file receipts, and **(3)** send out bills.

### Reviewing Dashes and Parentheses

***What is the difference between dashes and parentheses?***

______________________________

*When do you use dashes?*

______________________________________________

*When do you use parentheses?*

______________________________________________

**Practice 7 Identifying** Place dashes or parentheses around the underlined words in the following sentences.

1. One powerful tool for student research is becoming more popular than the library <u>the Internet</u>.
2. My brother <u>the police chief</u> keeps his phone number unlisted.
3. Nick <u>head of the math department</u> hires the new teachers.
4. The people I spend the most time with also take me for granted <u>my friends</u>.
5. I signaled the oncoming car <u>by flashing my lights</u>, but it still didn't turn its headlights on.
6. My old jeans were too loose, which means one thing <u>I must have lost weight</u>!
7. Norman works as a food server <u>at Denny's</u> and makes good tips.
8. Cheryl got her passport so she can <u>1</u> visit other countries, <u>2</u> go diving in all of the seven seas, and <u>3</u> meet a rich European man.
9. Jack London 1876–1916 wrote many great novels during his short life.
10. Brad Pitt's worst movie ever <u>*Fight Club*</u> was still better than the best Mike Myers movie <u>*Austin Powers*</u>.

**Practice 8 Completing** Add dashes and parentheses to the following paragraph.

In high school, I volunteered to work on the yearbook. Mrs. Brady was our instructor a round lady with bright red cheeks and a strange laugh. She immediately set us to work on several things mostly outside class, as we accumulated photos and news about the school's major events. I remember one lesson I learned in that class never procrastinate. If I failed to finish an assignment something that rarely happened, someone else would do it instead, and that person's work would be published instead of mine. I'll never forget my year with Mrs. Brady.

**Practice 9 Writing Your Own** Write three sentences of your own using dashes and two using parentheses.

## CHAPTER REVIEW

You might want to reread your answers to the questions in the review boxes before you do the following exercises.

**Review Practice 1 Identifying** Add semicolons, colons, dashes, and parentheses to the following sentences.

1. We are going to the grocery store we have nothing in the pantry to eat.
2. There are only three people I trust Krista, Kay, and Lucy.
3. He is always home however, he doesn't ever help out around the house.
4. I bought the car in my favorite color neon yellow.
5. Put the flowers on the table outside the one by the wall, and the presents can go there too.
6. My favorite book was made into a movie *Beloved.*
7. There are many things to do today pick up the dry cleaning, vacuum the carpets, and wash the dishes.
8. The chicken coop needs to be cleaned out it is full of leaves and tree branches.
9. We will pick up Jim, Jenny, and Karen go to the beach and lay out all day.
10. I got your favorite ice cream for your birthday fudge ripple.

**Review Practice 2 Completing** Add semicolons, colons, dashes, and parentheses to the following paragraph.

Today was an extremely windy day, so we decided to fly kites. We drove to Kite Hill a place where I went as a kid, and we climbed to the very top. We took out the kites and other necessary things masking tape, string, and ribbons. This way we were prepared to repair our kites, if necessary. The wind was perfect we couldn't have asked for better. There was only one thing we forgot the picnic lunch! Fortunately, Lamar remembered to pack the cooler with sodas mostly Diet Coke for something to drink when we got thirsty. After about four hours of flying kites it felt like 14, the group decided to head back home.

**Review Practice 3 Writing Your Own** Write a paragraph explaining some of your five-year goals. What do you plan to be doing in five years? What do you want to have accomplished?

## Editing Through Collaboration

Exchange paragraphs from Review Practice 3 with another student, and do the following:

1. Circle any incorrect or missing semicolons.
2. Circle any incorrect or missing colons.
3. Circle any incorrect or missing dashes.
4. Circle any incorrect or missing parentheses.

Then return the paper to its writer, and use the information in this chapter to correct any punctuation errors in your own paragraph. Record your errors on the Error Log in Appendix 6.

# Capitalization

## Checklist for Editing Capitalization

✔ Are all proper nouns capitalized?
✔ Are all words in titles capitalized correctly?
✔ Have you followed the other rules for capitalizing correctly?

**Test Yourself on Capitalization**

Correct the capitalization errors in the following sentences.

- According to uncle Bob, mother makes the best texas sheet cake.
- Antonio is a native american.
- "the shortest path," he said, "Is down baker street."
- Issa loves to go to walt disney world.
- Last year, I saw the red hot chili peppers in concert.

(Answers are in Appendix 4.)

---

Because every sentence begins with a capital letter, capitalization is the best place to start discussing the mechanics of good writing. Capital letters signal where sentences begin. They also call attention to certain kinds of words, making sentences easier to read and understand.

## CAPITALIZATION

Correct capitalization coupled with correct punctuation add up to good, clear writing. Here are some guidelines to help you capitalize correctly.

1. **Capitalize the first word of every sentence, including the first word of a quotation that forms a sentence.**

**M**y favorite city is Rome.

"**R**ome is my favorite city," he said.

**H**e said, "**M**y favorite city is Rome."

Do not capitalize the second part of a quotation that is split.

"**M**y favorite city," he said, "is Rome."

2. **Capitalize all proper nouns. Do not capitalize common nouns.**

| **Common Nouns** | **Proper Nouns** |
|---|---|
| person | Eleanor Roosevelt |
| state | Minnesota |
| building | Empire State Building |
| river | Mississippi River |
| airplane | *Air Force One* |

Here are some examples of proper nouns.

| | |
|---|---|
| **People:** | Sarah, Julia Roberts, Tiger Woods |
| **Groups:** | Australians, Apaches, Europeans, British, Latino |
| **Languages:** | Russian, Italian, French |
| **Religions, Religious Books, Holy Days:** | Catholicism, Buddhism, Koran, Bible, Yom Kippur, Kwanzaa, Easter |
| **Organizations:** | Boston Red Sox, Democratic Party, American Civil Liberties Union, Kiwanis Club, Alpha Gamma Delta |
| **Places:** | Smoky Mountains National Park, Antarctica, Louisville, Jefferson County, Madison Avenue, Highway 101, Golden Gate Bridge, John F. Kennedy International Airport |
| **Institutions, Agencies, Businesses:** | Washington High School, Baltimore Public Library, United Way, Grady Memorial Hospital, Time Warner |
| **Brand Names, Ships, Aircraft:** | Mustang, Wisk, Pepsi, U.S.S. *Alabama*, *Challenger* |

3. **Capitalize titles used with people's names or in place of their names.**

Mr. Ralph W. Gerber, Ms. Rachel Lorca, Dr. Leticia Johnson
Aunt Jane, Grandpa Bob, Cousin Mary, Sis, Nana

Do not capitalize words that identify family relationships.

| | |
|---|---|
| **NOT** | I saw my Grandfather yesterday. |
| **Correct:** | I saw my grandfather yesterday. |
| **Correct:** | I saw Grandfather yesterday. |

4. **Capitalize the titles of creative works.**

| | |
|---|---|
| **Books:** | *The Catcher in the Rye* |
| **Short Stories:** | "Sonny's Blues" |
| **Plays:** | *The Glass Menagerie* |
| **Poems:** | "My Last Duchess" |
| **Articles:** | "Two New Inns Now Open for Business" |
| **Magazines:** | *Newsweek* |
| **Songs:** | "Cheeseburger in Paradise" |
| **Albums or CDs:** | *Jimmy Buffet's Greatest Hits* |
| **Films:** | *Lady and the Tramp* |
| **TV Series:** | *The West Wing* |
| **Works of Art:** | *The Bedroom at Arles* |
| **Computer Programs:** | Apple Works |

Do not capitalize *a, an, the*, or short prepositions unless they are the first or last word in a title.

5. **Capitalize days of the week, months, holidays, and special events.**

Monday, July, Presidents' Day, Thanksgiving, Cinco de Mayo, Mardi Gras

Do not capitalize the names of seasons: *summer, fall, winter, spring.*

6. **Capitalize the names of historical events, periods, and documents:**

the French Revolution, the Jurassic Period, World War II, the Sixties, the Battle of Bunker Hill, the Magna Carta

7. **Capitalize specific course titles and the names of language courses.**

Economics 201, Philosophy 101, Spanish 200, Civilizations of the Ancient World

Do not capitalize a course or subject you are referring to in a general way unless the course is a language.

> my economics course, my **p**hilosophy course, my **S**panish course, my **h**istory course

8. **Capitalize references to regions of the country but not words that merely indicate direction.**

> If you travel **n**orth from Houston, you will end up in the **M**idwest, probably in Kansas or Nebraska.

9. **Capitalize the opening of a letter and the first word of the closing.**

> **D**ear **D**r. **H**amlin, **D**ear **S**ir,
> **B**est wishes, **S**incerely,

Notice that a comma comes after the opening and closing.

### Reviewing Capitalization

*Why is capitalization important in your writing?*

______________________________________________

______________________________________________

*What is the difference between a proper noun and a common noun?*

______________________________________________

**Practice 1 Identifying** Correct the capitalization errors in the following sentences.

1. The irs is auditing aunt Joan.
2. Debbie and Sue bought their mother a bottle of chanel's coco perfume for mother's Day.
3. In our History class, we are studying the great wall of china.
4. After lunch at the hard rock café, let's shop on Rodeo drive.
5. This Winter, emileo will visit uncle Norman, who lives somewhere in the south.

6. "That looks great," said the hairdresser, "But we need to take a little more off the top."
7. David Bowie's song "changes" is a classic from the seventies.
8. This semester, I plan on taking psychology 101 and sociology 200.
9. Charlton Heston is a vocal member of the national rifle association (NRA).
10. The letter opened with these words: "my dearest Ralph."

**Practice 2 Completing** Fill in each blank with words that complete the sentence. Be sure to capitalize words correctly. (You can make up titles if necessary.)

1. In my ____________ class, we had to read ____________.
2. Blanca bought a new truck, a ____________.
3. ____________ should be in charge of the charity drive.
4. I wish I could get tickets to see ____________ in concert.
5. We are going to ____________ for our vacation.

**Practice 3 Writing Your Own** Write five sentences of your own that cover at least five of the capitalization rules.

## CHAPTER REVIEW

You might want to reread your answers to the questions in the review boxes before you do the following exercises.

**Review Practice 1 Identifying** Correct the capitalization errors in the following sentences.

1. In April's edition of *people* magazine, LeAnn rimes talks about her love of Country music.
2. We decided to get married even though he's a member of the democratic party and I am a member of the republican party.

3. Raphael was born on October 31, 1972—he was a halloween baby.
4. Many Fathers, Sons, and Brothers fought against each other in the american civil war.
5. Joan's uncle has a beautiful statue of the buddha in his garden.
6. I watch *late night with David Letterman* for entertainment.
7. Christy can speak both english and spanish.
8. We celebrate both christmas and kwanzaa.
9. My Father used to drive me around town in his 1968 convertible ford mustang.
10. The spider said to the fly, "welcome to my home."

**Review Practice 2 Completing** Fill in each blank with words that complete the sentence. Be sure to capitalize words correctly.

1. Over the weekend, I watched my favorite movie, ______________.
2. In history, we are studying the ______________.
3. I was born on ______________.
4. Ashley wears nothing but ______________ clothes.
5. Fred and ______________ both plan to major in ______________.
6. He has an unusual accent because he's from ______________.
7. If you travel ______________ on Highway 101, you will eventually reach Santa Cruz.
8. My favorite relative, ______________, will visit soon.
9. Every summer, we go to ______________ to fish.
10. Even though she's a ______________ and I'm a ______________, we are still the best of friends.

**Review Practice 3 Writing Your Own** Write a paragraph about the most unusual person you've met or the most unusual place you've visited. What made this person or place unusual?

## Editing Through Collaboration

Exchange paragraphs from Review Practice 3 with another student, and do the following tasks:

1. Circle any capital letters that don't follow the capitalization rules.
2. Write the rule number next to the error for the writer to refer to.

Then return the paper to its writer, and use the information in this chapter to correct any capitalization errors in your own paragraph. Record your errors on the Error Log in Appendix 6.

# Abbreviations and Numbers

## Checklist for Using Abbreviations and Numbers

- ✔ Are titles before and after proper names abbreviated correctly?
- ✔ Are government agencies and other organizations abbreviated correctly?
- ✔ Are numbers *zero* through *nine* spelled out?
- ✔ Are numbers 10 and over written as figures (10, 25, 1–20, 324)?

**Test Yourself**

Correct the abbreviation and number errors in these sentences.

- He earned two million three hundred thousand dollars last year.
- My cat had 5 kittens.
- Sherril moved from England to the U.S.
- Mister Johnson always drinks hot chocolate in the mornings.
- I work for the Internal Revenue Service.

(Answers are in Appendix 4.)

## ABBREVIATIONS

Like capitalization, abbreviations and numbers are also mechanical features of writing that help us communicate what we want to say. Following the rules that govern their use will make your writing as precise as possible.

1. **Abbreviate titles before proper names.**

**Mr.** Michael Charles, **Mrs.** Marschel, **Ms.** Susan Deffaa, **Dr.** Frank Hilbig, **Rev.** Billy Graham, **Sen.** Diane Feinstein, **Sgt.** Arturo Lopez

Abbreviate religious, governmental, and military titles when used with an entire name. Do *not* abbreviate them when used only with a last name.

**NOT** We thought that **Gov.** Peterson would be reelected.

**Correct:** We thought that **Governor** Peterson would be reelected.

**Correct:** We thought **Gov.** Richard Peterson would be reelected.

*Professor* is not usually abbreviated.

2. **Abbreviate academic degrees.**

**B.S.** (Bachelor of Science)

**R.N.** (Registered Nurse)

3. **Use the following abbreviations with numbers.**

**a.m.** or **A.M.** **p.m.** or **P.M.**

4. **Abbreviate *United States* only when it is used as an adjective.**

**NOT** The **U.S.** is in North America.

**Correct:** The **United States** is in North America.

**Correct:** The **U.S.** Senate will consider this bill today.

5. **Abbreviate the names of certain government agencies, businesses, and educational institutions by using their initials without periods.**

**FBI** (Federal Bureau of Investigation)

**NBC** (National Broadcasting Corporation)

**USC** (University of Southern California)

**ACLU** (American Civil Liberties Union)

6. **Abbreviate state names when addressing mail or writing out the postal address. Otherwise, spell out the names of states.**

Maria's new address is 7124 Funston Street, San Francisco, **CA** 90555.

Maria has moved to San Francisco, **California.**

### Reviewing Abbreviations

***When you write, are you free to abbreviate any words you want?***

______________________________________________________________

**Practice 1 Identifying** Correct the underlined words in each of the following sentences.

1. Prof. Smith said that I was a wonderful writer.
2. The United States economy has many markets.
3. When I can't sleep, I watch Music Television.
4. Of all the countries my aunt has visited, the U.S. is her favorite.
5. Last night, sergeant David Montgomery devised the winning strategy.
6. The police officer clocked me driving too fast in front of the Columbia Broadcasting System.
7. I wake up at exactly 5:30 ante meridiem every morning.
8. My brother plans to earn his bachelor of science in physics.
9. Bro. Thomas visited me in the hospital.
10. Candice moved to 237 Bella Ave., Houma, Louisiana 79337.

**Practice 2 Completing** In each sentence, write either an abbreviation or the complete word, whichever is correct.

1. We were caught speeding at 10 ____________________ (p.m., post meridian).
2. Alisha will be attending ____________________ (CSU, California State University) and will get her ____________________ (B.A., bachelor of arts) degree in English.
3. Dink and Pat are visiting relatives in Houston, ____________________ (TX, Texas).

4. We moved to the __________________ (U.S., United States) when I was four years old.
5. __________________ (Sen., Senator) Matthews always has a kind word.

**Practice 3 Writing Your Own** Write a sentence of your own for each of the following abbreviations.

1. Mr. ______________________________
2. a.m. ______________________________
3. ABC ______________________________
4. A.A. ______________________________
5. U.S. ______________________________

## NUMBERS

Most writers ask the same question about using numbers: When should a number be spelled out, and when is it all right to use numerals? The following simple rules will help you.

1. **Spell out numbers from *zero* to *nine*. Use figures for numbers 10 and over.**

   I have **three** dogs.

   My mother-in-law has **19** grandchildren and **11** great-granchildren.

Do not mix spelled-out numbers and figures in a sentence if they refer to the same types of items. Use numerals for all numbers in that case.

**NOT** I have **three** dogs, **18** goldfish, and **two** canaries.

**Correct:** I have **3** dogs, **18** goldfish, and **2** canaries.

2. **For very large numbers, use a combination of figures and words.**

   The state's new budget is approximately **$32 million.**

   Computer sales for the company reached **2.1 million** units.

3. **Always spell out a number that begins a sentence.** If this becomes awkward, reword the sentence.

> **Thirty-five** people died in the crash.
>
> Approximately **260,000** people live in Mobile, Alabama.

4. **Use figures for dates, addresses, ZIP codes, telephone numbers, identification numbers, and time.**

> On August **1, 1965,** my parents moved to **215** Circle Drive, Santa Fe, NM **71730.**
>
> My new telephone number is **(555) 877-1420.**
>
> My Social Security number is **123-45-6789.**
>
> My alarm went off at **5:00** a.m.

5. **Use figures for fractions, decimals, and percentages.**

> To make the dessert, you need **1/2** cup of butter and **16** ounces of chocolate.
>
> His blood-alcohol level was **.09.**
>
> Over **5** percent of Californians are of Hispanic background.

Notice that *percent* is written out and is all one word.

6. **Use figures for exact measurements, including amounts of money. Use a dollar sign for amounts over $1.**

> The room measures **9** feet by **12** feet.
>
> She bought gas for **$2.79** a gallon today—**25 cents** more than yesterday.

7. **Use figures for the parts of a book.**

> Chapter **10** page **120** Exercise **8** questions **1** and **7**

Notice that *Chapter* and *Exercise* are capitalized.

### Reviewing Numbers

***What is the general rule for spelling out numbers as opposed to using numerals?***

____________________________________________

**Practice 4 Identifying** Correct any errors with numbers in each of the following sentences.

1. On August third, 2001, sixteen dogs escaped from the pound.
2. The park, which measures approximately two thousand square feet, will cost five thousand dollars to landscape.
3. Mr. Thompson's old telephone number was three, nine, nine, four, two, zero, nine.
4. Almost twenty-five percent of my income comes from sales.
5. The earthquake that hit at six forty-five last night measured 6.0 on the Richter scale.
6. The owners of the company expect profits of six million five hundred thousand dollars this year.
7. The fence will cost five hundred dollars to fix.
8. Before taking the exam, review questions 5 through twenty in Exercise twenty-nine.
9. Monique purchased three bags of balloons, 10 rolls of streamers, two banners, and one piñata for the party.
10. In a pinch, you can substitute one-half cup of shortening for one-half cup of butter.

**Practice 5 Completing** Fill in each blank in the following sentences with numbers in the proper form.

1. Please read Chapter __________ and answer questions __________ through __________.
2. I have __________ pencils, __________ bluebooks, and __________ note cards; I am ready for this test.
3. __________ percent of my time is spent doing homework.
4. Christmas is on __________ every year.
5. He made $__________ million last year.

**Practice 6 Write Your Own** Write a sentence demonstrating each of the following rules for numbers.

1. Spell out numbers *zero* through *nine*. Use figures for numbers 10 and over.
2. For very large numbers, use a combination of figures and words.
3. Always spell out a number that begins a sentence.
4. Use figures for dates, addresses, ZIP codes, telephone numbers, identification numbers, and time.
5. Use figures for fractions, decimals, and percentages.

## CHAPTER REVIEW

You might want to reread your answers to the questions in the review boxes before you do the following exercises.

**Review Practice 1 Identifying** Circle the abbreviation errors and underline the number errors in each of the following sentences. Some sentences contain more than one error.

1. According to Prof. Gleason, there is a process to writing.
2. At exactly 7:00 post meridiem, everyone will jump out of his or her hiding place and yell, "Surprise!"
3. The crew will need explosives to blast the twenty-nine-ton boulder.
4. Gen. Brevington's retirement banquet will be held on January twenty-nine, 2002.
5. Only 2 of the 8 children remembered their permission slips.
6. Of all the people polled, only ten percent were in favor of the new law.
7. 9 days from now, Columbia Broadcasting System is airing a special on former United States President Bill Clinton.
8. You can receive an associate of arts degree from your local community college.
9. The answers to questions four and five are in Chapter 21.
10. After winning the lottery for two million five hundred thousand dollars, Janene moved to Beverly Hills, CA.

**Review Practice 2 Completing** Correct the errors in Review Practice 1 by rewriting the sentences.

**Review Practice 3 Writing Your Own** Write a paragraph explaining the quickest route from your house to your school. Use numbers and abbreviations in your paragraph.

## Editing Through Collaboration

Exchange paragraphs from Review Practice 3 with another student, and do the following:

1. Underline all abbreviations, numbers, and figures.
2. Circle any abbreviations, numbers, or figures that are not in their correct form.

Then return the paper to its writer, and use the information in this chapter to correct any abbreviation and number errors in your own paragraph. Record your errors on the Error Log on Appendix 6.

# Varying Sentence Structure

## Checklist for Varying Sentence Patterns

- ✔ Do you add introductory material to vary your sentence patterns?
- ✔ Do you occasionally reverse the order of some subjects and verbs?
- ✔ Do you move sentence parts to add variety to your sentences?
- ✔ Do you sometimes use questions and exclamations to vary your sentence structure?

**Test Yourself**

Turn each of the following pairs of sentences into one sentence that is more interesting.

- I work too much. I am tired.
- My cat is very lazy. She sleeps more than 14 hours a day.
- He enjoys reading. He likes mysteries.
- I live in an old house. My family has lived here for generations.
- My brother loves to eat. He will eat anything.

(Answers are in Appendix 4.)

---

Reading the same sentence pattern sentence after sentence can become very monotonous for your readers. Look at the following example.

I have always loved animals. I am about to get my own dog for the first time. I think I am ready to be responsible enough to take care of it. I am excited about this new phase in my life. I got a part-time job. I can't wait to get my own dog.

This paragraph has some terrific ideas, but they are expressed in such a monotonous way that the readers might doze off. What this paragraph needs is variety in its sentence structure. Here are some ideas for keeping your readers awake and ready to hear your good thoughts.

1. Add some introductory words to your sentences so that they don't all start the same way.

> **For as long as I can remember,** I have always loved animals. **Now** I am about to get my own dog for the first time. I think I am ready to be responsible enough to take care of it. I am excited about this new phase in my life. **To pay for my new friend,** I got a part-time job. I can't wait to get my own dog.

**Practice 1 Identifying** Underline the sentence in each pair that could be turned into an introductory word, phrase, or clause.

1. Misty had a terrible stomachache. It was late last night.
2. We went to the river. We skipped over the rocks.
3. We went to McDonald's for breakfast. We saw our friends.
4. The sunsets are beautiful. It was spring.
5. He is afraid of dogs. He was bit by a dog once.
6. Our car broke down. Jenny and I decided to fly to Las Vegas.
7. We went on a trip to Texas. We visited many relatives we had never even met.
8. Hanna loves working with small children. She's a babysitter.
9. The two boys dared each other to jump into the cold pool. It was 3 a.m.
10. You are smart. You will understand this problem.

**Practice 2 Completing** Rewrite the sentences in Practice 1 by turning each sentence you underlined into an introductory word, phrase, or clause.

**Practice 3 Writing Your Own** Write five sentences of your own with introductory elements.

2. Reverse the order of some subjects and verbs. For example, instead of *I am so excited*, try *Am I ever excited*. You can also add or drop words and change punctuation to make the sentence read smoothly.

> For as long as I can remember, I have always loved animals. Now I am about to get my own dog for the first time. I think I am ready to be responsible enough to take care of it. **Am I ever excited** about this new phase in my life. To pay for my new friend, I got a part-time job. I can't wait to get my own dog.

**Practice 4 Identifying** Underline the words you could reverse in each of the following sentences.

1. I am happy to know you.
2. All the ingredients went into the pot.
3. The cat jumped out of the hat.
4. The children were happy.
5. The strange creature appeared out of nowhere.

**Practice 5 Completing** Rewrite the sentences in Practice 4 by reversing the words you underlined.

**Practice 6 Writing Your Own** Write five sentences of your own with subjects and verbs reversed.

3. Move some parts of the sentence around. Experiment to see which order works best.

> For as long as I can remember, I have always loved animals. Now I am about to get my own dog for the first time. I think I am ready to be responsible enough to take care of it. Am I ever excited about this new phase in my life. **My part-time job can help me pay for my new friend.** I can't wait to get my own dog.

**Practice 7 Identifying** Underline any parts of the following sentences that can be moved around.

1. To bake these cookies, you will need 2 cups of flour.
2. Finally, I knew the truth.

3. I was very full after lunch.
4. You will find your shoes underneath your bed.
5. If you enjoyed the film, you will probably like the book.
6. Sam does, however, like to play checkers.
7. Science in some ways cannot always answer our questions.
8. Benjamin found the job hard at first.
9. I guess she doesn't want to go.
10. My mother doesn't like pizza, unlike me.

**Practice 8 Completing** Rewrite the sentences in Practice 7, moving the words you underlined.

**Practice 9 Writing Your Own** Write two sentences of your own. Then rewrite each sentence two different ways.

4. Use a question, a command, or an exclamation occasionally.

For as long as I can remember, I have always loved animals. **Have you?** Now I am about to get my own dog for the first time. I think I am ready to be responsible enough to take care of it. **Am I ever excited about this new phase in my life!** My part-time job can help me pay for my new friend. I can't wait to get my own dog.

**Practice 10 Identifying** Identify each of the following sentences as a statement (S), a question (Q), a command (C), or an exclamation (E).

1. ______ When is the meal being served
2. ______ Did you see that object flying in the sky
3. ______ Bring me a glass of iced tea and a bowl of grapes
4. ______ First do the prewriting exercises
5. ______ How can he be so calm
6. ______ I just hate it when that happens
7. ______ That man just stole my shoes
8. ______ Take this letter to the post office for me

9. ______ What is the matter with Dan

10. ______ This apple tart tastes fantastic

**Practice 11 Completing** Complete the following sentences, making them into questions, commands, or exclamations. Then supply the correct punctuation.

1. Wow, I can't believe ______________________________
2. At the first intersection ______________________________
3. Why is ______________________________
4. Hand me ______________________________
5. Did you hear ______________________________

**Practice 12 Writing Your Own** Write two statements, two questions, two commands, and two exclamations of your own.

### Reviewing Ways to Vary Sentence Patterns

***Why is varying sentence patterns important in your writing?***

______________________________

***Name four ways to vary your sentence patterns.***

______________________________

______________________________

______________________________

______________________________

***What other kinds of sentences besides statements can you use for variety?***

__________ __________ __________

## CHAPTER REVIEW

You might want to reread your answers to the questions in the review boxes before you do the following exercises.

**Review Practice 1 Identifying** Underline the words or groups of words that have been added or moved in each revised sentence. Then use the following key to tell which rule was applied to the sentence:

1. Add introductory words.
2. Reverse the order of subject and verb.
3. Move parts of the sentence around.
4. Use a question, a command, or an exclamation occasionally.

1. Eat your peas. You aren't finished with dinner yet.

   ______ If you eat your peas, you'll be finished with dinner.

2. He did what?

   ______ What did he do?

3. I went to the store around the corner. I bought some milk and bread.

   ______ At the store around the corner, please buy some milk and bread.

4. To the park went he.

   ______ To the park he went.

5. The fireflies flew. They flew all around us.

   ______ All around us, the fireflies flew.

6. I believe that was mine.

   ______ Hey, that was mine!

7. How many times a day do you brush your teeth?

   ______ You brush your teeth how many times a day?

8. You are amazing!

   ______ Are you amazing or what?

9. Out of the darkness came a terrible noise.

 ______ Out of the darkness, a terrible noise came.

10. Carl does enjoy a good hamburger every now and then.

 ______ Every now and then, Carl does enjoy a good hamburger.

**Review Practice 2 Completing** Vary the structure of the following sentences with at least three of the four ideas you just learned.

> A good teacher should be encouraging toward students. He or she should understand when a student is having problems and spend some one-on-one time together. The teacher should then help the student identify problems and give helpful instruction to solve the problem. A good teacher never makes fun of a student.

**Review Practice 3 Writing Your Own** Write a paragraph about a good deed you have performed. What made you decide to do what you did? Try to use each of the four ways you have learned to make sentences interesting.

## Editing Through Collaboration

Exchange paragraphs from Review Practice 3 with another student, and do the following:

1. Put brackets around any sentences that sound monotonous.
2. Suggest a way to vary each of these sentences.

Then return the paper to its writer, and use the information in this chapter to vary the sentence structure in your own paragraph. Record your errors on the Error Log in Appendix 6.

# Parallelism

## Checklist for Using Parallelism

✔ Can you use parallelism to add coherence to your sentences and paragraphs?

✔ Are all items in a series grammatically balanced?

**Test Yourself**

Underline the parts in each of the following sentences that seem awkward or unbalanced.

- Tony enjoys hockey, football, and runs.
- My mom and dad give money to help the homeless and for building new homes.
- I finished high school, started college, and I am beginning a new job.
- I love the mountains because they're cool, clean, and feel refreshing.
- Listening to music, watching television, or to read a book are good ways to relax.

(Answers are in Appendix 4.)

---

When sentences are **parallel,** they are balanced. That is, words, phrases, or clauses in a series start with the same grammatical form. Parallel structures make your sentences interesting and clear. Here is a paragraph that could be greatly improved with parallel structures.

> My brother Wayne was not excited when he was called in to work at the hospital today. He had been looking forward to this day off—his first in three weeks. He was planning to work out in the morning,

swimming in the afternoon, and going to a movie in the evening. Instead he will be helping the patients, assisting the nurses, and will aid the doctors.

Words and phrases in a series should be parallel, which means they should start with the same type of word. Parallelism makes your sentence structure smoother and more interesting. Look at this sentence, for example.

**NOT** He had planned to **work out** in the morning, **swimming** in the afternoon, and **going** to a movie in the evening.

**Parallel:** He had planned to **work out** in the morning,<br>**swim** in the afternoon, and<br>**go** to the movies in the evening.

**Parallel:** He had planned on **working out** in the morning,<br>**swimming** in the afternoon, and<br>**going** to the movies in the evening.

Here is another sentence that would read better if the parts were parallel:

**NOT** Instead he **will be helping** the patients, **assisting** the nurses, and **will aid** the doctors.

**Parallel:** Instead he will be **helping** the patients,<br>**assisting** the nurses, and<br>**aiding** the doctors.

**Parallel:** Instead he will be helping **the patients,**<br>**the nurses**, and<br>**the doctors**.

Now read the paragraph with these two sentences made parallel or balanced.

My brother Wayne was not excited when he was called in to work at the hospital today. He had been looking forward to this day off—his first in three weeks. He had planned to work out in the morning, swim in the afternoon, and go to a movie in the evening. Instead he will be helping the patients, the nurses, and the doctors.

## Reviewing Parallelism

***What is parallelism?***

________________________________________

***Why should you use parallelism in your writing?***

______________________________________________

**Practice 1 Identifying** Underline the parallel structures in each of the following sentences.

1. Scott plans to hide in his cabin, do some fishing, and work on his novel.
2. The car needs new windows, tires, and paint.
3. Georgia believes that she is the most wonderful person in the world and that she deserves everyone's love and attention.
4. They camped under the stars, swam in the cool lakes, and enjoyed the fresh air.
5. Because of the pouring rain, extreme cold, and bitter wind, we decided to stay inside.
6. Cheating, cussing, and drinking alcohol will get you kicked out.
7. He raced across the field, jumped over the hedges, and fell into the pond.
8. We decided we would do nothing but relax, read, and swim this weekend.
9. My nieces are sleeping in my bed, wearing my clothes, and driving me crazy.
10. He isn't going to work today because he feels ill and because he has plenty of sick leave left.

**Practice 2 Completing** Make the underlined elements parallel in each of the following sentences.

1. He will only wear clothes that have designer labels and they are expensive.

   ______________________________________________

2. Regular exercise, drinking plenty of water, and eating lots of good food will help keep you healthy.

   ______________________________________________

3. Dierdra went to the mall to get a bite to eat, to do some shopping, and will visit friends.

_______________________________________________

4. Please do not tap pens, talk to others, or eating food during the exam.

_______________________________________________

5. On his trip, he took pictures of mountains, fed animals, and some enjoyable people.

_______________________________________________

**Practice 3 Writing Your Own** Write five sentences of your own using parallel structures in each.

## CHAPTER REVIEW

You might want to reread your answers to the questions in the review boxes before you do the following exercises.

**Review Practice 1 Identifying** Underline the parallel structures in each of the following sentences.

1. Football, basketball, and hockey are all competitive sports.
2. Because of the terrible weather, the horrible traffic, and the missed bus, we didn't make our flight.
3. When I'm in love, the sun always shines, the stars always sparkle, and the moon always glows.
4. Marilyn went to the city's annual air show because she wanted to see the jet planes and because she wanted to try the interesting foods.
5. The biting mosquitoes, barking dogs, and burning sun made me miserable.
6. Please feed, bathe, and change the baby before I get home.
7. If Harvey cleans the house, does his homework, and begs for forgiveness, he may get out of his punishment.
8. I believe that people should be treated fairly and that everyone should get a second chance.

9. He was suspended because he fought, cheated, and disrespected others.
10. Today Mother paid the bills, balanced the checkbook, and washed the car.

**Review Practice 2 Completing** Complete each of the following sentences with parallel structures.

1. I enjoy ____________, ____________, and ____________ in the summer.
2. Because of ____________ and because of ____________, Miriam didn't go to the movies.
3. You can be successful in college if you ____________, ____________, and ____________.
4. Even though Jeremy ____________, ____________, and ____________, he still can't find the problem.
5. ____________, ____________, and ____________ are essential items when hiking.
6. She cooks foods that ____________ and ____________.
7. My favorite foods are ____________, ____________, and ____________.
8. If I have to hear her ____________, ____________, and ____________ one more time, I'm going to scream.
9. The instructor has already explained ____________, ____________, and ____________.
10. If you ____________, ____________, and ____________, you just might survive boot camp.

**Review Practice 3 Writing Your Own** Write a paragraph about the best holiday you've ever had. What was the holiday? Why was it the best? Use two examples of parallelism in your paragraph.

## Editing Through Collaboration

Exchange paragraphs from Review Practice 3 with another student, and do the following:

1. Underline any items in a series.
2. Put brackets around any of these items that are not grammatically parallel.

Then return the paper to its writer, and use the information in this chapter to correct any parallelism errors in your own paragraph. Record your errors on the Error Log in Appendix 6.

# Combining Sentences

## Checklist for Combining Sentences

✔ Do you combine sentences to avoid too many short, choppy sentences in a row?

✔ Do you use different types of sentences?

**Test Yourself**

Combine each set of sentences into one sentence.

- My brother is taking tennis lessons. He takes his lessons from a professional player.
- The baby is crying. She's hungry.
- It's too hot outside. Let's go for a swim.
- We moved overseas when I was 11 years old. I learned much about different cultures.
- I like to travel. Africa has many interesting animals and plants. I want to go to Africa.

(Answers are in Appendix 4.)

Still another way to add variety to your writing is to combine short, choppy sentences into longer sentences. You can combine simple sentences to make compound or complex sentences. You can also combine compound and complex sentences.

## SIMPLE SENTENCES

A **simple sentence** consists of one independent clause. Remember that a clause has a subject and a main verb.

In the following examples, notice that a simple sentence can have more than one subject and more than one verb. (For more on compound subjects and compound verbs, see Chapter 30.)

s v
I have several very good friends.

s v v
I have good friends and enjoy being with them.

s s v
Martin and Louis are good friends.

s s v v
Martin and I do interesting things and go to interesting places.

### REVIEWING SIMPLE SENTENCES

***What does a simple sentence consist of?***

______________________________________________

***Write a simple sentence.***

______________________________________________

**Practice 1 Identifying** Underline the subjects once and the verbs twice in each of the following sentences. Then label the simple sentences SS.

1. ______ Most cats don't like the water, but most dogs do.
2. ______ Tommy and I like listening to the same types of music and watching the same types of shows.
3. ______ I feel that our luck is about to change.

4. ______ We left quickly because of the smell.

5. ______ We have pictures of the family throughout the house.

6. ______ I worked late last night because I had a deadline to meet on my project.

7. ______ The monkeys, who are a lively bunch, are jumping from tree to tree.

8. ______ The neighbors are complaining about the loud noises.

9. ______ The lawnmower is in back of the garage.

10. ______ The bills have fallen between the books.

**Practice 2 Completing** Make simple sentences out of the sentences in Practice 1 that are not simple.

**Practice 3 Writing Your Own** Write a simple sentence of your own for each of the following subjects and verbs.

1. Jessy and Miguel ________________________________

2. we're eating and drinking ________________________________

3. the playful kittens ________________________________

4. looking and listening ________________________________

5. the hot pan ________________________________

## COMPOUND SENTENCES

A **compound sentence** consists of two or more independent clauses joined by a coordinating conjunction (*and*, *but*, *for*, *nor*, *or*, *so*, or *yet*). In other words, you can create a compound sentence from two (or more) simple sentences.

**Simple:** I can swim fast.

**Simple:** I am a good long-distance swimmer.

s v s v
**Compound:** I can swim fast**, and** I am a good long-distance swimmer.

**Simple:** She has a very stressful job.
**Simple:** She works out at the gym three times a week.

s v s v
**Compound:** She has a very stressful job**, so** she works out at the gym three times a week.

**Simple:** My parents are leaving for Hawaii on Tuesday.
**Simple:** They won't be here for my birthday party.

s v v s
**Compound:** My parents are leaving for Hawaii on Tuesday**, so** they

v
won't be here for my birthday party.

**HINT:** As the examples show, a comma comes before the coordinating conjunction in a compound sentence.

### REVIEWING COMPOUND SENTENCES

***What does a compound sentence consist of?***

________________________________________

***Write a compound sentence.***

________________________________________

**Practice 4 Identifying** Underline the independent clauses in the following sentences, and circle the coordinating conjunctions.

1. I am not sick, and I feel fine.
2. You cannot bring food or drink in this building, but you can eat in the cafeteria.
3. She's been in trouble before, but she usually gets out of it.
4. We try not to gossip, for we know the damage loose lips can cause.

5. I do not like raspberries, yet I do like raspberry pie.
6. Leo shouldn't watch so much television, nor should he stay up so late at night.
7. Christy likes fast cars, so she is going to buy a sports car.
8. Myra should not eat before swimming, or she will get sick.
9. The trees and flowers are in bloom, and they look lovely.
10. The house is clean, but the yard is a mess.

**Practice 5 Completing** Combine each pair of simple sentences into a compound sentence.

1. I am leaving. I am late for an appointment.
2. Quickly, move out of the way. The angry elephant is going to charge us.
3. We usually take a month-long vacation. We are always happy to return home.
4. This food has been sitting out all day in the hot sun. It smells awful.
5. I have a lot of cousins. I haven't met them all.

**Practice 6 Writing Your Own** Write five compound sentences of your own.

## COMPLEX SENTENCES

A **complex sentence** is composed of one independent clause and at least one dependent clause. A **dependent clause** begins with either a subordinating conjunction or a relative pronoun.

**Subordinating Conjunctions**

| | | | |
|---|---|---|---|
| *after* | *because* | *since* | *until* |
| *although* | *before* | *so* | *when* |
| *as* | *even if* | *so that* | *whenever* |
| *as if* | *even though* | *than* | *where* |
| *as long as* | *how* | *that* | *wherever* |
| *as soon as* | *if* | *though* | *whether* |
| *as though* | *in order that* | *unless* | *while* |

**Relative Pronouns**

| *who* | *whom* | *whose* | *which* | *that* |
|---|---|---|---|---|

You can use subordinating conjunctions and relative pronouns to make a simple sentence (an independent clause) into a dependent clause. Then you can add the new dependent clause to an independent clause to produce a complex sentence that adds interest and variety to your writing.

How do you know which simple sentence should be independent and which should be dependent? The idea that you think is more important should be the independent clause. The less important idea will then be the dependent clause.

Following are some examples of how to combine simple sentences to make a complex sentence.

**Simple:** Myra has a large collection of movie videos.

**Simple:** Myra watches the same few films over and over.

Dep

**Complex:** **Even though** Myra has a large collection of movie

Ind

videos, she watches the same few films over and over.

This complex sentence stresses that Myra watches the same films over and over. The size of her collection is of secondary importance.

Ind

**Complex:** She has a big collection of movie videos, **though** she

Dep

watches the same few films over and over.

In this complex sentence, the size of the collection is most important, so it is the independent clause.

**Simple:** The winner of the lottery was Laura.

**Simple:** Laura is my cousin.

Ind Dep

**Complex:** The winner of the lottery was Laura, **who** is my cousin.

This complex sentence answers the question "Who won the lottery?" The information about Laura being the cousin is of secondary importance.

Ind Dep

**Complex:** My cousin is Laura**, who** won the lottery.

This complex sentence answers the question "Who is your cousin?" The information that she won the lottery is secondary.

### Reviewing Complex Sentences

***What does a complex sentence consist of?***

______________________________________________

***Write a complex sentence.***

______________________________________________

**Practice 7 Identifying** Label the underlined part of each sentence as either an independent (Ind) or a dependent (Dep) clause.

1. ______ Although I was tired, I still went to school.
2. ______ Here is the furniture that you ordered.
3. ______ Trish moved to the coast because she likes the beach.
4. ______ Though I like the water, I don't know how to swim.
5. ______ My doctor is Jack Blake, who is also my dad.
6. ______ Becky likes math, which is her major.
7. ______ You will have to buy lunch, unless you bring your own.
8. ______ If we cannot study at your house, then let's study at the library.
9. ______ Please bring me the newspaper before you leave.
10. ______ I helped him because he is my friend.

**Practice 8 Completing** Finish each sentence, and label the new clause either dependent (Dep) or independent (Ind).

1. ______ Whenever John's face turns red, ______________.

2. ______ ______________ because he forgot to call home.

3. ______ Joan's mother, who ______________, is a great cook.

4. ______ I like the blue one, ______________.

5. ______ He climbed the mountain ______________.

**Practice 9 Writing Your Own** Write five complex sentences, making sure you have one independent clause and at least one dependent clause in each.

## COMPOUND-COMPLEX SENTENCES

If you combine a compound sentence with a complex sentence, you produce a **compound-complex sentence.** That means your sentence has at least two independent clauses (to make it compound) and at least one dependent clause (to make it complex). Here are some examples.

**Simple:** My cousin likes scuba diving.
**Simple:** He is planning a trip to Hawaii.
**Simple:** He is excited about diving in Hawaii.

**Compound-Complex:** My cousin likes scuba diving (Ind)**, so** he is planning a trip to Hawaii (Ind)**, which** he is very excited about (Dep).

**Simple:** She bought a new house.
**Simple:** It has a pool and a spa.
**Simple:** The house was very expensive.

**Compound-Complex:** She bought a new house (Ind)**, which** has a pool and a spa (Dep)**, but** it was very expensive (Ind).

**Simple:** Today's weather is very bad.
**Simple:** The rain could make it difficult to drive.
**Simple:** This could delay your departure for home.

**Compound-Complex:** Today's weather is very bad (Ind)**, and** the rain could make it difficult to drive (Ind)**, which** could delay your arrival home (Dep).

HINT: Notice that we occasionally have to change words in combined sentences so that they make sense.

### REVIEWING COMPOUND-COMPLEX SENTENCES

***What does a compound-complex sentence consist of?***

________________________________________

***Write a compound-complex sentence.***

________________________________________

**Practice 10 Identifying** Underline the clauses in each of the following compound-complex sentences. Then identify each clause as either independent (Ind) or dependent (Dep).

1. Whenever I travel, I take an alarm clock, and I also arrange for a wake-up call.
2. Sandy likes Anthony because he is nice, but she also likes Mark.
3. After they fought, they decided to make up, and now they are inseparable.
4. The traffic, which is usually bad around noon, is very heavy today, so you'd better leave soon.
5. We went to the Virgin Islands because we love the sun, yet it rained the whole time.

6. My teacher is Ms. Idoux, who is also my mother's friend, and I like her very much.
7. Salsa dancing is hard, but you can do it if you practice.
8. Even though Martha doesn't like Mexican food, she should still go to the restaurant, for I know she'll have fun.
9. After we eat dinner, let's go to the mall, or else let's go to the show.
10. You shouldn't be late for class, nor should you forget your books because these actions could cause problems.

**Practice 11 Completing** Expand each sentence into a compound-complex sentence.

1. The boy likes oranges and pears. ______________________
2. The box was very heavy, but he lifted it anyway. ______________________
3. Jill says that she will never fly in a plane. ______________________
4. John will be 21 soon. ______________________
5. I am watching MTV and getting some rest. ______________________

**Practice 12 Writing Your Own** Write five compound-complex sentences of your own.

## CHAPTER REVIEW

You might want to reread your answers to the questions in the review boxes before you do the following exercises.

**Review Practice 1 Identifying** Underline the independent clauses in each sentence. Then label the sentence simple (SS), compound (C), complex (CX), or compound-complex (CCX). The following definitions might help you.

| | | |
|---|---|---|
| Simple | = | one independent clause |
| Compound | = | two or more independent clauses joined by *and*, *but*, *for*, *nor*, *or*, *so*, or *yet* |

| | | |
|---|---|---|
| Complex | = | one independent clause and at least one dependent clause |
| Compound-complex | = | at least two independent clauses and one or more dependent clauses |

1. ______ Casey and Floyd have left the building.
2. ______ Even though he is quiet, he is very friendly.
3. ______ Marcy and David are boyfriend and girlfriend, and they are going to the prom together.
4. ______ The dog and cat ate my dinner last night.
5. ______ Mrs. Glancy is my close friend, and she visits me often.
6. ______ Marc is happy because Sheila is here, and he wants to ask her on a date.
7. ______ The folders are in the desk drawer.
8. ______ The dog needs to be fed, and he needs a bath.
9. ______ The gifts, which you bought yesterday, have been wrapped, and they are ready to be delivered.
10. ______ Because her alarm didn't go off, she was late for work.

**Review Practice 2 Completing** Combine each set of sentences to make the sentence pattern indicated in parentheses. You may need to change some wording in the sentences so they make sense. The list of sentence types in Review Practice 1 may help you with this exercise.

1. George bikes in the morning. He wants to stay in shape. He goes to the gym every weekend. (compound-complex)
2. I like to play in the mud. I always get dirty. (compound)
3. You should leave now. You should be at your appointment 15 minutes early to fill out paperwork. (complex)
4. Penny brought a stray dog home. Penny loves animals. Her mother wouldn't let her keep it. (compound-complex)

5. I slammed the car door on my thumb. I broke it. (complex)
6. I love to chew gum and pop bubbles. I can't chew gum in class. (complex)
7. The little girl lost her doll. She has looked everywhere for it. She is crying. (compound-complex)
8. The sun is shining. The birds are singing. (compound)
9. The reports are missing. I need them now. (compound)
10. It is October. The leaves are turning brown and falling from the tree. (complex)

**Review Practice 3 Writing Your Own** Write a paragraph about your fondest wish. What is it, and why do you wish for it?

## Editing Through Collaboration

Exchange paragraphs from Review Practice 3 with another student, and do the following:

1. Put brackets around any sentences that you think should be combined.
2. Underline sentences that are incorrectly combined (for example, ones that have a weak connecting word or no connecting word).

Then return the paper to its writer, and use the information in this chapter to combine sentences in your own paragraph. Record your errors on the Error Log in Appendix 6.

# Standard and Nonstandard English

## Checklist for Choosing the Right Word

- ✔ Do you consistently use standard English in your paper?
- ✔ Is your paper free of nonstandard, ungrammatical words?
- ✔ Have you changed any slang to standard English?

**Test Yourself**

Label the following sentences as standard English, ungrammatical English, or slang.

- You shoulda seen Claudia's new hairstyle. ______________
- Where are my friends at? ______________
- Your new bike is really hot. ______________
- Randy was enthused about his date. ______________
- Fatboy Slim's new video rocks. ______________

(Answers are in Appendix 4.)

Choosing the right words for what you want to say is an important part of effective communication. Look, for example, at the following sentences. They all have generally the same message, expressed in different words.

I want to do good in college, being as I can get a good job.

I be studying hard in college, so I can get a good job.

I'm going to hit the books so I can rake in the bucks.

I want to go to college, graduate, and get a good job.

Which of these sentences would you probably say to a friend or to someone in your family? Which would you most likely say in a job interview? Which would be good for a college paper?

The first three sentences are nonstandard English. They might be said or written to a friend or family member, but they would not be appropriate in an academic setting or in a job situation. Only the fourth sentence would be appropriate in an academic paper or in a job interview.

## STANDARD AND NONSTANDARD ENGLISH

Most of the English language falls into one of two categories—either *standard* or *nonstandard*. **Standard English** is the language of college, business, and the media. It is used by reporters on television, by newspapers, in most magazines, and on Web sites created by schools, government, business, and organizations. Standard English is always grammatically correct and free of slang.

**Nonstandard English** does not follow all the rules of grammar and often includes slang. Nonstandard English is not necessarily wrong, but it is more appropriate in some settings (with friends and family) than others. It is not appropriate in college or business writing. To understand the difference between standard and nonstandard English, compare the following paragraphs.

**Nonstandard English**

I was stoked to find out I would be getting a $300 refund on my taxes. My first thought was to blow it on a trip, maybe somewheres like Las Vegas. But none of my friends was enthused by that. Then I thought being as I watch television alot, I would buy a new TV with a built-in VCR. My brother got hisself one last year. Then it hit me, hey, I'm gonna need some money to buy new duds for my job. Alright, I decided, I gotta buy clothes with the dough, irregardless of what I'd like to do with it.

**Standard English**

I was thrilled when I found out I would be getting a $300 refund on my taxes. My first thought was to spend it on a trip, maybe somewhere like Las Vegas. But none of my friends was enthusiastic about that. Then I thought that since I watch television a lot, I would buy a new TV with a built-in VCR. My brother got himself one last year. Then I realized that I am going to need some money to buy new clothes for my job. All right, I decided, I have to buy clothes with the money, regardless of what I'd like to do with it.

In the rest of this chapter, you will learn how to recognize and correct ungrammatical English and how to avoid slang in your writing.

### Reviewing Standard and Nonstandard English

***Where do you hear standard English in your daily life?***

______________________________

***What is nonstandard English?***

______________________________

***Give two examples of nonstandard English.***

______________ ______________

## NONSTANDARD ENGLISH

Nonstandard English is ungrammatical. It does not follow the rules of standard English. The academic and business worlds expect you to be able to recognize and avoid nonstandard English. This is not always easy because some nonstandard terms are used so often in speech that many people think they are acceptable in writing. The following list might help you choose the correct words in your own writing

ain't

**NOT** My economics professor **ain't** giving us the test today.
**Correct** My economics professor **isn't** giving us the test today.

anywheres

**NOT** Lashawn buys her clothes **anywheres** she can find them.
**Correct** Lashawn buys her clothes **anywhere** she can find them.

be

**NOT** I **be** so happy.

**Correct** I **am** so happy.

(For additional help with *be*, see Chapter 38, "Verb Tense.")

being as, being that

**NOT** Emilio will not get to go home over the weekend, **being as** he has to work.

**Correct** Emilio will not get to go home over the weekend **because** he has to work.

coulda/could of, shoulda/should of

**NOT** He **could of** earned a better grade on the test if he'd studied.

**Correct** He **could have** (or **could've**) earned a better grade on the test if he'd studied.

different than

**NOT** She is **different than** us.

**Correct** She is **different from** us.

don't

**NOT** James **don't** listen well because he daydreams too much.

**Correct** James **doesn't** listen well because he daydreams too much.

(For additional help with *do*, see Chapter 38, "Verb Tense.")

drug

**NOT** She **drug** the mattress across the room.

**Correct** She **dragged** the mattress across the room.

enthused

**NOT** Mary was **enthused** about the wedding.

**Correct** Mary was **enthusiastic** about the wedding.

everywheres

**NOT** My dog follows me **everywheres** I go.

**Correct** My dog follows me **everywhere** I go.

goes

**NOT** Then Lorie goes, "I'm leaving without you."

**Correct** Then Lorie said, "I'm leaving without you."

**Correct** Then Lorie said she was leaving without me.

has/have/had

**NOT** My friend Doug **have** three cars.

**Correct** My friend Doug **has** three cars.

(For additional help with *have*, see Chapter 38, "Verb Tense.")

hisself

**NOT** Jackson made **hisself** a cheeseburger.

**Correct** Jackson made **himself** a cheeseburger.

in regards to

**NOT** We received a letter **in regards to** your complaint.

**Correct** We received a letter **in regard to** your complaint.

irregardless

**NOT** **Irregardless** of how long you study French, you'll never speak it like a native.

**Correct** **Regardless** of how long you study French, you'll never speak it like a native.

kinda/kind of, sorta/sort of

**NOT** The rooms smells **kinda** sweet, **sorta** like vanilla.

**Correct** The room smells **rather** sweet, **much** like vanilla.

most

**NOT** **Most** everyone accepted the invitation.

**Correct** **Almost** everyone accepted the invitation.

must of

| | |
|---|---|
| **NOT** | I **must of** lost my purse at the party. |
| **Correct** | I **must have** lost my purse at the party. |

off of

| | |
|---|---|
| **NOT** | Billy jumped **off of** the back of the truck. |
| **Correct** | Billy jumped **off** the back of the truck. |

oughta

| | |
|---|---|
| **NOT** | Sometimes I think I **oughta** watch less television. |
| **Correct** | Sometimes I think I **ought to** watch less television. |

real

| | |
|---|---|
| **NOT** | My boyfriend was **real** mad when I went out with another boy. |
| **Correct** | My boyfriend was **really** mad when I went out with another boy. |

somewheres

| | |
|---|---|
| **NOT** | Your jeans are **somewheres** in that pile of clothes. |
| **Correct** | Your jeans are **somewhere** in that pile of clothes. |

suppose to

| | |
|---|---|
| **NOT** | You were **suppose to** turn that paper in yesterday. |
| **Correct** | You were **supposed to** turn that paper in yesterday. |

theirselves

| | |
|---|---|
| **NOT** | They helped **theirselves** to the food in the buffet line. |
| **Correct** | They helped **themselves** to the food in the buffet line. |

use to

| | |
|---|---|
| **NOT** | I **use to** have a truck. |
| **Correct** | I **used to** have a truck. |

ways

| | |
|---|---|
| **NOT** | Curt's car broke down a long **ways** from home. |
| **Correct** | Curt's car broke down a long **way** from home. |

where . . . at

**NOT** **Where** is the nearest bakery **at?**

**Correct** **Where** is the nearest bakery?

### Reviewing Nonstandard English

***What is one reason using nonstandard English in written work is easy to do?***

_______________________________________________

***Give four examples of nonstandard English; then correct them.***

_______________________ _______________________

_______________________ _______________________

_______________________ _______________________

_______________________ _______________________

**Practice 1A Identifying** Underline the ungrammatical words or phrases in each of the following sentences.

1. Do you know where the children are at?
2. Then John goes, "There is no way I'm going to touch that."
3. Our production of *Romeo and Juliet* is kinda like the original, but sorta modern.
4. I coulda stayed at home instead of sitting here listening to this boring lecture.
5. Justin was suppose to mail the invitations.
6. You be the person who hid my car keys.
7. Sam must of forgotten that we were supposed to have lunch today.
8. I use to walk to work, but now I have a car.
9. Marisa has to go to the dentist, irregardless of how much crying she does.
10. I ain't going to listen to you anymore.

**Practice 1B Correcting** Correct the ungrammatical words and expressions in Practice 1A by rewriting the incorrect sentences.

**Practice 2 Completing** Underline the ungrammatical word or words in each phrase, and change them to standard English.

1. Anywheres I go ____________
2. She drug it ____________
3. We are a long ways ____________
4. He made hisself ____________
5. Being that Susan ____________

**Practice 3 Writing Your Own** Write five sentences of your own using the grammatical words and phrases you chose in Practice 2.

## SLANG

Another example of nonstandard English is **slang,** popular words and expressions that come and go, much like the latest fashions. For example, in the 1950s, someone might call his or her special someone *dreamy*. In the 1960s, you might hear a boyfriend or girlfriend described as *groovy*, and in the 1990s, *sweet* was the popular slang term. Today your significant other might be *hot* or *dope*.

These expressions are slang because they are part of the spoken language that changes from generation to generation and from place to place. As you might suspect, slang communicates to a limited audience who share common interests and experiences. Some slang words, such as *cool* and *neat*, have become part of our language, but most slang is temporary. What's in today may be out tomorrow, so the best advice is to avoid slang in your writing.

REVIEWING SLANG

***What is slang?***

______________________________________________

***Give two examples of slang terms that were popular but aren't any longer.***

_______________ _______________

***Give two examples of slang terms that you and your friends use today.***

_______________ _______________

**Practice 4 Identifying** Underline the slang words and expressions in each of the following sentences.

1. *Return of the Mummy* rocks!
2. "Wassup?" I yelled to my homies.
3. This pizza is da bomb.
4. My mom tripped out when I got my tattoo.
5. She is such a babe.
6. I'm just hangin' out with my buds.
7. Stewart is zoning on the video game.
8. Let's hook up at my house later on.
9. My best friend got busted for staying out too late.
10. He's definitely weirded out.

**Practice 5 Completing** Translate the following slang expressions into standard English.

1. Talk to the hand _______________
2. hella good _______________
3. flyboy _______________
4. right back atcha _______________
5. a wanna-be _______________

**Practice 6 Writing Your Own** List five slang words or expressions, and use them in sentences of your own. Then rewrite each sentence using standard English to replace the slang expressions.

## CHAPTER REVIEW

You might want to reread your answers to the questions in the review boxes before you do the following exercises.

**Review Practice 1 Identifying** Underline the ungrammatical or slang words in the following sentences.

1. You really need to chill out.
2. He don't know what's going on.
3. I was so enthused when I won the contest.
4. He's really jammin' to the music.
5. Hey, stop buggin' me.
6. Oops, I fell off of the ski lift.
7. He's no different than you or me.
8. She's thinks she's all that.
9. You oughta take art lessons.
10. Sandra is really phat.

**Review Practice 2 Completing** Correct any nonstandard English in each of the following sentences by rewriting the sentences.

1. I be wide awake and can't sleep.
2. I think Eustice don't know what he's talking about.
3. Tony's making big money at his new job.
4. Those army boots are bad.
5. My girlfriend was real mad when I forgot Valentine's Day.
6. In regards to your question, I don't have an answer.
7. Watcha doin'?
8. Who's the real slim shady?
9. Jane have extra blankets if you're cold.
10. You are solid, man.

**Review Practice 3 Writing Your Own** Write a paragraph on how you spend your free time. Do you spend it with your friends or alone? What do you do and why?

## Editing Through Collaboration

Exchange paragraphs from Review Practice 3 with another student, and do the following:

1. Underline any ungrammatical language.
2. Circle any slang.

Then return the paper to its writer, and use the information in this chapter to correct any nonstandard or slang expressions in your own paragraph. Record your errors on the Error Log in Appendix 6.

CHAPTER 58

# Easily Confused Words

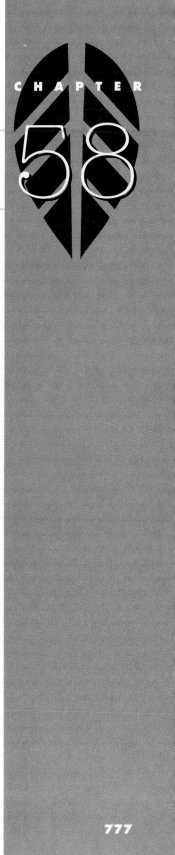

## Checklist for Easily Confused Words

- ✔ Is the correct word chosen from the easily confused words?
- ✔ Are the following words used correctly: *its/it's*, *their/there/they're*, *to/too/two*, *who's/whose*, *your/you're?*

**Test Yourself**

Choose the correct word in parentheses.

- Sally couldn't (choose, chose) a college.
- (It's, Its) time to leave for the show.
- I can't (hear, here) with all this noise.
- (Weather, Whether) you go or not, I'm still going to attend.
- (Who's, Whose) responsible for this mess?

(Answers are in Appendix 4.)

Some words are easily confused. They may look alike, sound alike, or have similar meanings. But they all play different roles in the English language. This chapter will help you choose the right words for your sentences.

## EASILY CONFUSED WORDS, PART I

**a/an:** Use *a* before words that begin with a consonant. Use *an* before words that begin with a vowel (*a*, *e*, *i*, *o*, *u*).

**a** bill, **a** cat, **a** zebra

**an** artichoke, **an** Indian, **an** occasion

**accept/except:** *Accept* means "receive." *Except* means "other than."

Mary will not **accept** the gift.

Everyone went **except** Harry.

**advice/advise:** *Advice* means "helpful information." *Advise* means "give advice or help."

My mother usually gives me very good **advice.**

My mother **advises** me when I'm trying to make an important decision.

**affect/effect:** *Affect* means "influence." *Effect* means "bring about" or "a result."

She hopes having children won't **affect** her chance at promotion.

I believe that changes in the law will **effect** positive changes in society.

The weather had a bad **effect** on his health.

**already/all ready:** *Already* means "in the past." *All ready* means "completely prepared."

I have **already** taken that class.

We had packed the car and were **all ready** to go when the accident happened.

**among/between:** Use *among* when referring to three or more people or things. Use *between* when referring to only two people or things.

The students discussed the issues **among** themselves.

I can't decide **between** the two dresses.

**bad/badly:** *Bad* means "not good." *Badly* means "not well."

That meat is **bad,** so don't eat it.

He felt **bad** about the accident.

He was hurt **badly** in the accident.

**beside/besides:** *Beside* means "next to." *Besides* means "in addition (to)."

She sat **beside** him at lunch.

**Besides** sleeping, I can think of nothing else I want to do.

**brake/break:** *Brake* means "stop" or "the parts that stop a moving vehicle." *Break* means "shatter, come apart" or "a rest between work periods."

She didn't **brake** soon enough to avoid the other car.

I watched the limb **break** off the tree.

Can we take a **break?**

**breath/breathe:** *Breath* means "air." *Breathe* means "taking in air."

Take long, slow **breaths.**

The air we have to **breathe** is unhealthy.

**choose/chose:** *Choose* means "select." *Chose* is the past tense of *choose.*

Please **choose** an answer.

He **chose** the wrong answer.

### Reviewing Words That Are Easily Confused, Part I

***Do you understand the differences in the sets of words in Part I of the list?***

______________________________________________

***Have you ever confused any of these words? If so, which ones?***

______________________________________________

**Practice 1 Identifying** Underline the correct word in each of the following sentences.

1. I can (advice, advise) you on what courses to take.
2. The little boy behaved (bad, badly) when his father left.
3. We were (already, all ready) to leave the house when she realized she didn't have her purse.
4. (Among, Between) the three of us, we should have enough money to buy lunch.

5. The cold water took my (breath, breathe) away.
6. (Beside, Besides) giving me a mother's unconditional love, my mom is also my best friend.
7. The (affect, effect) was devastating on my ego.
8. I need (a, an) rest from all this work.
9. Please (accept, except) my congratulations on your promotion.
10. Leanne (choose, chose) to volunteer at the homeless shelter.

**Practice 2 Completing** Complete the following sentences with a correct word from Part I of this list.

1. I ____________ you to be on my team last year.
2. ____________ for the humidity, we had a wonderful trip.
3. We have to keep the secret ____________ you and me.
4. Corkey was a ____________ dog; he chewed up my shoes.
5. Take my ____________ and bring a jacket.

**Practice 3 Writing Your Own** Use each pair of words correctly in a sentence of your own.

1. a/an
2. breath/breathe
3. affect/effect
4. already/all ready
5. beside/besides

## EASILY CONFUSED WORDS, PART II

**coarse/course:** *Coarse* refers to something that is rough. *Course* refers to a class.

This pavement is **coarse.**

My **course** in math is very interesting.

**desert/dessert:** *Desert* refers to dry, sandy land or means "abandon." *Dessert* refers to the last course of a meal.

It is difficult to live in the **desert.**

He **deserted** his family.

We had strawberry shortcake for **dessert.**

**HINT:** You can remember that *dessert* has two *s*'s if you think of ***s****trawberry* ***s****hortcake*.

**does/dose:** *Does* means "performs." *Dose* refers to a specific portion of medicine.

My sister **does** whatever she wants.

Children should have only a small **dose** of the medicine.

**fewer/less:** *Fewer* refers to things that can be counted. *Less* refers to things that cannot be counted.

There are **fewer** cotton fields than there used to be.

She has much **less** time now that she has a new job.

**good/well:** *Good* modifies nouns. *Well* modifies verbs, adjectives, and adverbs. *Well* also refers to a state of health.

Bill looks **good** in his new suit.

I'm afraid I didn't do **well** on the test.

Kate isn't feeling **well** today.

**hear/here:** *Hear* refers to the act of listening. *Here* means "in this place."

My father can't **hear** as well as he used to.

**Here** is the book you asked for.

**it's/its:** *It's* is the contraction for *it is* or *it has*. *Its* is a possessive pronoun.

The teacher said **it's** important to answer all the questions.

The dog chased **its** tail.

**knew/new:** *Knew* is the past tense of *know*. *New* means "recent."

I thought everyone **knew** I had a **new** boyfriend.

**know/no:** *Know* means "understand." *No* means "not any" or is the opposite of *yes*.

We all **know** that we have **no** hope of defeating the other team.

**lay/lie:** *Lay* means "set down." (Its principal parts are *lay, laid, laid.*) *Lie* means "recline." (Its principal parts are *lie, lay, lain.*)

He **lays** brick for a living.

He **laid** down the heavy sack.

She **lies** down at 2 p.m. every day for a nap.

I **lay** in the grass.

(For additional help with *lie* and *lay*, see Chapter 37, "Regular and Irregular Verbs.")

**loose/lose:** *Loose* means "free" or "unattached." *Lose* means "misplace" or "not win."

Hal's pants are too **loose.**

If I **lose** another $10, I'm going to quit gambling.

**passed/past:** *Passed* is the past tense of *pass. Past* refers to an earlier time or means "beyond."

John **passed** by his old house on the way to school.

It is interesting to study the **past.**

The dog ran **past** me and into the street.

### Reviewing Words That Are Easily Confused, Part II

***Do you understand the differences in the sets of words in Part II of the list?***

_______________________________________________

***Have you ever confused any of these words? If so, which ones?***

_______________________________________________

**Practice 4 Identifying** Underline the correct word in each of the following sentences.

1. We (passed, past) Edward on the freeway.
2. I think you have made a (good, well) choice.
3. With her second job, Marsha has (fewer, less) time to spend with her friends.
4. (It's, Its) going to be a beautiful day.
5. I cannot (loose, lose) this ring; it was given to me by my grandmother.
6. My mother used to give me a (does, dose) of castor oil when my stomach was upset.
7. The (coarse, course) material scratched the baby's skin.
8. Speak louder—I can't (here, hear) you.
9. I plan to (lay, lie) in my bed all day reading a good book.
10. I (know, no) I left my sunglasses here.

**Practice 5 Completing** Complete the following sentences with a correct word from Part II of this list.

1. The restaurant served peach cobbler for ______________.
2. How do you like my ______________ car?
3. Mike ______________ not want to go to the concert with us.
4. This business ______________ will benefit me on the job.
5. I am not feeling ______________ today.

**Practice 6 Writing Your Own** Use each pair of words correctly in a sentence of your own.

1. fewer/less ______________________________________________
2. knew/new ______________________________________________
3. hear/here ______________________________________________
4. it's/its ______________________________________________
5. lay/lie ______________________________________________

## EASILY CONFUSED WORDS, PART III

**principal/principle:** *Principal* means "main, most important," "a school official," or "a sum of money." A *principle* is a rule. (Think of *princip**le*** and ***rule***—both end in *-le.*)

My **principal** reason for moving is to be closer to my family.

Mr. Kobler is the **principal** at Westside Elementary School.

He lives by certain **principles**, including honesty and fairness.

**quiet/quite:** *Quiet* means "without noise." *Quite* means "very."

The house was **quiet.**

I am **quite** happy with my new car.

**raise/rise:** *Raise* means "increase" or "lift up." *Rise* means "get up from a sitting or reclining position."

The state is going to **raise** the tax on cigarettes.

Jane **rises** slowly from her wheelchair.

**set/sit:** *Set* means "put down." *Sit* means "take a seated position."

**Set** the vase on the table.

I don't like to **sit** at a desk for long period of time.

(For additional help with *sit* and *set*, see Chapter 37, "Regular and Irregular Verbs.")

**than/then:** *Than* is used in making comparisons. *Then* means "next."

My mother is younger **than** my father.

I took piano lessons; **then** I took guitar lessons.

**their/there/they're:** *Their* is possessive. *There* indicates location. *They're* is the contraction of *they are.*

**Their** house burned down last year.

Too many people are living **there.**

**They're** all going to London.

**threw/through:** *Threw,* is the past tense of *throw,* means "tossed." *Through* means "finished" or "passing from one point to another."

The pitcher **threw** the ball.

I am **through** with dinner.

My brother and I rode **through** the forest on our bikes.

**to/too/two:** *To* means "toward" or is used with a verb. *Too* means "also" or "very." *Two* is a number.

I went **to** the store **to** buy some bread.

I bought some artichokes, **too**, even though they were **too** expensive for my budget.

My mother has **two** sisters.

**wear/were/where:** *Wear* means "have on one's body." *Were* is the past tense of *be*. *Where* refers to a place.

Can you **wear** shorts to school?

**Where were** you yesterday?

**weather/whether:** *Weather* refers to outdoor conditions. *Whether* expresses possibility.

No one knows **whether** the **weather** will get better or worse.

**who's/whose:** *Who's* is a contraction of *who is* or *who has*. *Whose* is a possessive pronoun.

**Who's** going to decide **whose** car to take?

**your/you're:** *Your* means "belonging to you." *You're* is the contraction of *you are*.

**Your** attention to details proves **you're** a good worker.

### Reviewing Words That Are Easily Confused, Part III

***Do you understand the differences in the sets of words in Part III of this list?***

______________________________________________

***Have you ever confused any of these words? If so, which ones?***

______________________________________________

**Practice 7 Identifying** Underline the correct word in each of the following sentences.

1. Janene was (quiet, quite) pleased with your work.
2. (Your, You're) the best choice for this task.
3. Please (set, sit) here and wait for the doctor.
4. (Who's, Whose) planning on going to tonight's game?
5. Our (principal, principle) is retiring at the end of the year.
6. If the students work hard, they can (raise, rise) enough money for their trip.
7. You are going to have to move (weather, whether) you want to or not.
8. (Their, There, They're) already on the plane.
9. Brad lost his surfboard (to, too, two).
10. Cassie is better with computers (than, then) he is.

**Practice 8 Completing** Complete the following sentences with a correct word from Part III of this list.

1. After the performance, the audience ____________ flowers at the performer's feet.
2. Susan's ____________ reason for quitting her job was the pay.
3. Finish your homework, and ____________ you can watch television.
4. ____________ are you going dressed like that?
5. Why did you ____________ shorts in the winter?

**Practice 9 Writing Your Own** Use each set of words correctly in a sentence of your own.

1. raise/rise ____________________________________
2. their/there/they're ______________________________
3. your/you're ___________________________________

4. set/sit ______________________________

5. who's/whose ______________________________

## CHAPTER REVIEW

You might want to reread your answers to the questions in the review boxes before you do the following exercises.

**Review Practice 1 Identifying** Underline the correct word in each of the following sentences.

1. Your influence is having a positive (affect, effect) on people's lives.
2. (Who's, Whose) that girl with Paul?
3. Jade needs to stand (hear, here) when her name is announced.
4. (Your, You're) the one for me.
5. There are many different plants that grow in the (desert, dessert).
6. Sydney (choose, chose) the smallest puppy of the litter.
7. The picture has come (loose, lose) from its frame.
8. Please sit (beside, besides) me during the ceremony.
9. Your counselor gave you good (advice, advise), and you should take it.
10. Over (their, there, they're) is the house where I grew up.

**Review Practice 2 Completing** Complete the following sentences with a correct word from all three parts of the list.

1. We ____________ each other when we were children.
2. Contestants should send in ____________ photographs of themselves.
3. The ____________ outside was so nice that we decided to walk.
4. If you leave now, you will ____________ up our happy home.
5. The crowd was so ____________ that you could hear people breathing.

6. Quantitative analysis is the most challenging ____________ I have ever taken.
7. Jeffrey did not ____________ the phone ringing.
8. I laughed so hard that I couldn't catch my ____________.
9. Because of our uninvited houseguests, we have ____________ food in the house.
10. Faith has ____________ donated to the cause.

**Review Practice 3 Writing Your Own** Write a paragraph explaining the qualities of a good friend. What are the qualities, and why do you think they are important? Try to use some of the easily confused words from this chapter.

## Editing Through Collaboration

Exchange paragraphs from Review Practice 3 with another student, and do the following:

1. Circle any words used incorrectly.
2. Write the correct form of the word above the error.

Then return the paper to its writer, and use the information in this chapter to correct any confused words in your own paragraph. Record your errors on the Error Log in Appendix 6.

# Spelling

## Checklist for Identifying Misspelled Words

- ✔ Do you follow the basic spelling rules?
- ✔ Are all words spelled correctly?

**Test Yourself**

Correct the misspelled words in the following sentences.

- What is your new addres?
- Turn left on the third avenu.
- I was using the wrong calender when I made out the schedule.
- The dealer delt me a good hand.
- Please get all the items on the grocry list.

(Answers are in Appendix 4.)

If you think back over your education, you will realize that your teachers think spelling is important. There is a good reason they feel that way: Spelling errors send negative messages. Misspellings seem to leap out at readers, creating serious doubts about the writer's abilities in general. Because you will not always have access to spell-checkers—and because spell-checkers do not catch all spelling errors—improving your spelling skills is important.

## SPELLING HINTS

The spelling rules in this chapter will help you become a better speller. But first, here are some practical hints that will also help you improve your spelling.

1. Start a personal spelling list of your own. Use the list of commonly misspelled words on pages 794–799 as your starting point.
2. Study the lists of easily confused words in Chapter 58.
3. Avoid all nonstandard expressions (see Chapter 57).
4. Use a dictionary when you run across words you don't know.
5. Run the spell-check program if you are writing on a computer. Keep in mind, however, that spell-check cannot tell if you have incorrectly used one word in place of another (such as *to*, *too*, or *two*).

### Reviewing Hints for Becoming a Better Speller

***Name two things you can do immediately to become a better speller.***

________________________________________

***Why can't you depend on a spell-check program to find every misspelled word?***

________________________________________

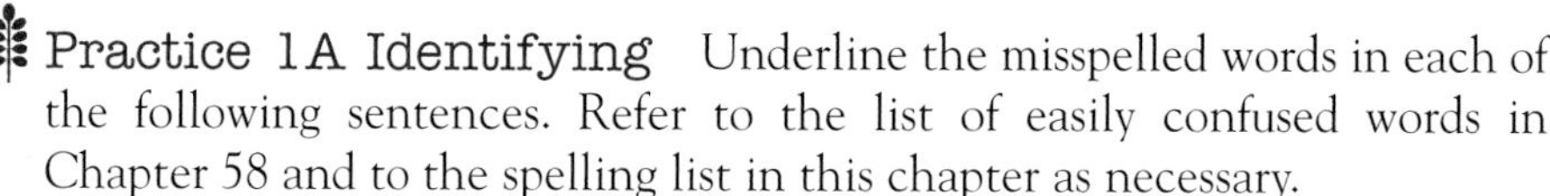

**Practice 1A Identifying** Underline the misspelled words in each of the following sentences. Refer to the list of easily confused words in Chapter 58 and to the spelling list in this chapter as necessary.

1. "We want to go to," cried the children.
2. The baloon floated away on the breeze.
3. With John's promotion came a better salry.
4. This vacation has had a relaxing affect on my attitude.
5. It was an akward situation when the bride wouldn't say, "I do."
6. Bernard is on a vegatable diet.
7. This flu makes me ake all over.
8. My grandmother willed me her beautiful jewlry.
9. Please be quite while in the library.
10. When she realized her zipper was open, she was very embarassed.

**Practice 1B Correcting** Correct the spelling errors in Practice 1A by rewriting the incorrect sentences.

**Practice 2 Completing** Fill in each blank in the following sentences with hints that help with spelling.

1. Use a ______________ to look up words you don't know.
2. You can always use the ______________ on your computer, but you should remember that it cannot catch confused words, only misspelled words.
3. Start a ______________ to help you remember words you commonly misspell.
4. Study the list of ______________ in Chapter ______________.
5. Try to avoid all ______________ English.

**Practice 3 Writing Your Own** Choose the correctly spelled word in each pair, and write a sentence using it. Refer to the spelling list on pages 794–799 if necessary.

1. concieve/conceive ______________________________
2. absence/absense ______________________________
3. vaccum/vacuum ______________________________
4. library/libary ______________________________
5. delt/dealt ______________________________

## SPELLING RULES

Four basic spelling rules can help you avoid many misspellings. It pays to spend a little time learning them now.

1. **Words that end in *-e*:** When adding a suffix beginning with a vowel (*a*, *e*, *i*, *o*, *u*), drop the final *-e*.

| | | |
|---|---|---|
| achieve + -ing | = | achieving |
| include + -ed | = | included |
| value + -able | = | valuable |

When adding a suffix beginning with a consonant, keep the final *-e*.

| | | |
|---|---|---|
| aware + -ness | = | awareness |
| improve + -ment | = | improvement |
| leisure + -ly | = | leisurely |

2. **Words with *ie* and *ei*:** Put *i* before *e* except after *c* or when sounded like *ay* as in *neighbor* and *weigh*.

| **c + *ei*** | **(no c) + *ie*** |
|---|---|
| receive | grieve |
| conceive | niece |
| deceive | friend |
| neighbor | relief |

3. **Words that end in *-y*:** When adding a suffix to a word that ends in a consonant plus -y, change the *y* to *i*.

| | | |
|---|---|---|
| happy + -er | = | happier |
| dry + -ed | = | dried |
| easy + -est | = | easiest |

4. **Words that double the final consonant:** When adding a suffix starting with a vowel to a one-syllable word, double the final consonant.

| | | |
|---|---|---|
| big + -est | = | biggest |
| quit + -er | = | quitter |
| bet + -ing | = | betting |

With words of more than one syllable, double the final consonant if (1) the final syllable is stressed and (2) the word ends in a single vowel plus a single consonant.

| | | |
|---|---|---|
| begin + -ing | = | beginning |
| transmit + -ing | = | transmitting |
| wrap + -ed | = | wrapped |

The word *travel* has more than one syllable. Should you double the final consonant? No, you should not, because the stress is on the *first* syllable (trá vel). The word ends in a vowel and a consonant, but that is not enough. Both parts of the rule must be met.

### Reviewing Four Basic Spelling Rules

*What is the rule for adding a suffix to words ending in* -e *(such as* date + -ing*)?*

______________________________________________

______________________________________________

*What is the rule for spelling* ie *and* ei *words (such as* receive, neighbor, *and* friend*)?*

______________________________________________

*When do you change* -y *to* i *before a suffix (such as* sunny + -est*)?*

______________________________________________

*When do you double the final consonant of a word before adding a suffix (such as* cut, begin, *or* travel + -ing*)?*

______________________________________________

______________________________________________

**Practice 4A Identifying** Underline the spelling errors in each of the following sentences.

1. It's not like we're commiting a crime.
2. The boundarys have been clearly marked.
3. You are so wierd.
4. Our bagage was lost somewhere in New York.
5. The facilitys are near one another.

6. I cannot decieve you; I ate the last cookie.
7. Alyssa strolled leisurly through the garden.
8. Your behavior is only aggravateing the situation.
9. If our star player doesn't get here soon, we will have to forfiet the game.
10. If he doesn't stop spending his money foolishly, he'll end up a begar.

**Practice 4B Correcting** Correct the spelling errors in Practice 4A by rewriting the incorrect sentences.

**Practice 5 Completing** Complete the following spelling rules.

1. When adding a suffix beginning with a vowel to a word that ends in *-e*, ____________.
2. With words of more than one syllable, ____________ the final consonant if (1) the final syllable is ____________ and (2) the word ends in a single ____________ plus a single ____________.
3. Put *i* before *e* except after ____________ or when sounded like ____________ as in ____________.
4. When adding a suffix starting with a ____________ to a one-syllable word, ____________ the final consonant.
5. When adding a suffix to a word the ends in a consonant plus *-y*, change the ____________ to ____________.

**Practice 6 Writing Your Own** Make a list of words you commonly misspell. Then choose five of the words, and use each correctly in a sentence.

## MOST COMMONLY MISSPELLED WORDS

Use the following list of commonly misspelled words to check your spelling when you write.

*abbreviate*
*absence*
*accelerate*
*accessible*
*accidentally*
*accommodate*
*accompany*
*accomplish*
*accumulate*
*accurate*
*ache*
*achievement*
*acknowledgment*
*acre*
*actual*
*address*
*adequate*
*advertisement*
*afraid*
*aggravate*
*aisle*
*although*
*aluminum*
*amateur*
*ambulance*
*ancient*
*anonymous*
*anxiety*
*anxious*
*appreciate*
*appropriate*
*approximate*
*architect*
*arithmetic*
*artificial*
*assassin*
*athletic*
*attach*
*audience*
*authority*
*autumn*
*auxiliary*
*avenue*
*awkward*
*baggage*
*balloon*
*banana*
*bankrupt*
*banquet*
*beautiful* ***(50)***
*beggar*
*beginning*
*behavior*
*benefited*
*bicycle*
*biscuit*
*bought*
*boundary*
*brilliant*
*brought*
*buoyant*
*bureau*
*burglar*
*business*
*cabbage*
*cafeteria*
*calendar*
*campaign*
*canoe*
*canyon*
*captain*
*career*
*carriage*
*cashier*
*catastrophe*
*caterpillar*
*ceiling*
*cemetery*
*census*
*certain*
*certificate*
*challenge*
*champion*
*character*
*chief*
*children*
*chimney*
*coffee*
*collar*
*college*
*column*
*commit*
*committee*
*communicate*
*community*
*comparison*
*competent*
*competition*
*complexion*
*conceive* ***(100)***
*concession*
*concrete*

*condemn*
*conference*
*congratulate*
*conscience*
*consensus*
*continuous*
*convenience*
*cooperate*
*corporation*
*correspond*
*cough*
*counterfeit*
*courageous*
*courteous*
*cozy*
*criticize*
*curiosity*
*curious*
*curriculum*
*cylinder*
*dairy*
*dangerous*
*dealt*
*deceive*
*decision*
*definition*
*delicious*
*descend*
*describe*
*description*
*deteriorate*
*determine*
*development*
*dictionary*
*difficulty*
*diploma*
*disappear*
*disastrous*
*discipline*
*disease*
*dissatisfied*
*divisional*
*dormitory*
*economy*
*efficiency*
*eighth*
*elaborate*
*electricity* ***(150)***
*eligible*
*embarrass*
*emphasize*
*employee*
*encourage*
*enormous*
*enough*
*enthusiastic*
*envelope*
*environment*
*equipment*
*equivalent*
*especially*
*essential*
*establish*
*exaggerate*
*excellent*
*exceptionally*
*excessive*
*exhaust*
*exhilarating*
*existence*
*explanation*
*extinct*
*extraordinary*
*familiar*
*famous*
*fascinate*
*fashion*
*fatigue*
*faucet*
*February*
*fiery*
*financial*
*foreign*
*forfeit*
*fortunate*
*forty*
*freight*
*friend*
*fundamental*
*gauge*
*genius*
*genuine*
*geography*
*gnaw*
*government*
*graduation*
*grammar*
*grief* ***(200)***
*grocery*
*gruesome*
*guarantee*
*guess*

*guidance*
*handkerchief*
*handsome*
*haphazard*
*happiness*
*harass*
*height*
*hesitate*
*hoping*
*humorous*
*hygiene*
*hymn*
*icicle*
*illustrate*
*imaginary*
*immediately*
*immortal*
*impossible*
*incidentally*
*incredible*
*independence*
*indispensable*
*individual*
*inferior*
*infinite*
*influential*
*initial*
*initiation*
*innocence*
*installation*
*intelligence*
*interfere*
*interrupt*
*invitation*
*irrelevant*
*irrigate*
*issue*
*jealous*
*jewelry*
*journalism*
*judgment*
*kindergarten*
*knife*
*knowledge*
*knuckles*
*laboratory* ***(250)***
*laborious*
*language*
*laugh*
*laundry*
*league*
*legible*
*legislature*
*leisure*
*length*
*library*
*license*
*lieutenant*
*lightning*
*likable*
*liquid*
*listen*
*literature*
*machinery*
*magazine*
*magnificent*
*majority*
*manufacture*
*marriage*
*material*
*mathematics*
*maximum*
*mayor*
*meant*
*medicine*
*message*
*mileage*
*miniature*
*minimum*
*minute*
*mirror*
*miscellaneous*
*mischievous*
*miserable*
*misspell*
*monotonous*
*mortgage*
*mysterious*
*necessary*
*neighborhood*
*niece*
*nineteen*
*ninety*
*noticeable*
*nuisance*
*obedience* ***(300)***
*obstacle*
*occasion*
*occurred*
*official*
*omission*
*omitted*

*opportunity*
*opponent*
*opposite*
*original*
*outrageous*
*pamphlet*
*paragraph*
*parallel*
*parentheses*
*partial*
*particular*
*pastime*
*patience*
*peculiar*
*permanent*
*persistent*
*personnel*
*persuade*
*physician*
*pitcher*
*pneumonia*
*politician*
*possess*
*prairie*
*precede*
*precious*
*preferred*
*prejudice*
*previous*
*privilege*
*procedure*
*proceed*
*pronounce*
*psychology*
*publicly*
*questionnaire*
*quotient*
*realize*
*receipt*
*recipe*
*recommend*
*reign*
*religious*
*representative* **(350)**
*reservoir*
*responsibility*
*restaurant*
*rhyme*
*rhythm*
*salary*
*satisfactory*
*scarcity*
*scenery*
*schedule*
*science*
*scissors*
*secretary*
*seize*
*separate*
*significant*
*similar*
*skiing*
*soldier*
*souvenir*
*sovereign*
*spaghetti*
*squirrel*
*statue*
*stomach*
*strength*
*subtle*
*succeed*
*success*
*sufficient*
*surprise*
*syllable*
*symptom*
*technique*
*temperature*
*temporary*
*terrible*
*theater*
*thief*
*thorough*
*tobacco*
*tomorrow*
*tongue*
*tournament*
*tragedy*
*truly*
*unanimous*
*undoubtedly*
*unique*
*university* **(400)**
*usable*
*usually*
*vacuum*
*valuable*
*various*
*vegetable*
*vehicle*
*vicinity*
*villain*
*visible*
*volunteer*

| | | |
|---|---|---|
| *weather* | *width* | *yearn* |
| *Wednesday* | *worst* | *yield* |
| *weigh* | *wreckage* | *zealous* |
| *weird* | *writing* | *zoology* **(425)** |
| *whose* | *yacht* | |

---

## Reviewing Commonly Misspelled Words

***Why is spelling important in your writing?***

______________________________________________

***Start a personal spelling log of your most commonly misspelled words.***

| | | | |
|---|---|---|---|
| ________ | ________ | ________ | ________ |
| ________ | ________ | ________ | ________ |
| ________ | ________ | ________ | ________ |
| ________ | ________ | ________ | ________ |

**Practice 7A Identifying** Underline any words that are misspelled in the following sentences.

1. This steak and lobster dinner is incredable.
2. You shouldn't condem others for doing what you do.
3. Valentine's Day is in Febuary.
4. How long have you been writting that novel?
5. I know you will suceed in college.
6. Tommorow Mary is moving to a foreign country.
7. We can start the party the minite Sarah gets here.
8. The house needs new cieling fans.
9. The comittee voted in favor of the proposal.
10. The theif stole Rhonda's stereo.

**Practice 7B Correcting** Correct any spelling errors that you identified in Practice 7A by rewriting the incorrect sentences.

**Practice 8 Completing** Correct the spelling errors in the following paragraph.

> I was eating a plate of spagetti when the phone rang. It was my nieghbor. He said, "The big fight is begining in 15 minutes, and my television's screen just went out." He then beged me to let him come over and watch it at my house. So I told him that was fine and that he could come on over. He neglected to tell me, however, that he wouldn't be alone. He and seven of his rowdy freinds invaded my house, ate my spagetti and drank my soda, and left a catastropy behind. I think the next time I have a party, I'll have it at his house.

**Practice 9 Writing Your Own** Write a complete sentence for each word listed here.

1. appreciate ______________________________
2. laundry ______________________________
3. marriage ______________________________
4. excellent ______________________________
5. opposite ______________________________

## CHAPTER REVIEW

You might want to reread your answers to the questions in the review boxes before you do the following exercises.

**Review Practice 1 Identifying** Underline the misspelled words in each of the following sentences.

1. I'm trying to catch the rythm of this music.
2. You ate my desert.

3. This essay shows improvment.
4. Cheryl is a genis with figures.
5. The firy-hot peppers made my eyes water.
6. Most teenagers want their independance.
7. If we stick to the scedule, we should make it home before tomorrow.
8. Breath deeply, and put your head between your legs.
9. My family lives in seperate states.
10. Dr. Murphy rides his bycicle to work every day.

**Review Practice 2 Completing** Correct the spelling errors in Review Practice 1 by rewriting the incorrect sentences.

**Review Practice 3 Writing Your Own** Write a paragraph explaining how to become a better speller. Are there any hints that may help?

## Editing Through Collaboration

Exchange paragraphs from Review Practice 3 with another student, and do the following:

1. Underline any words that are used incorrectly.
2. Circle any misspelled words.

Then return the paper to its writer, and use the information in this chapter to correct any spelling errors in your own paragraph. Record your errors on the Spelling Log in Appendix 7.

# APPENDIX 1 Critical Thinking Log

Circle the critical thinking questions that you missed after each essay you read. Have your instructor explain the pattern of errors.

| Reading | Content | Purpose and Audience | Paragraphs | Number Correct |
|---|---|---|---|---|
| **Describing** | | | | |
| Mario Suarez | 1 2 3 | 4 5 6 | 7 8 9 10 | |
| Linda Hogan | 1 2 3 | 4 5 6 | 7 8 9 10 | |
| **Narrating** | | | | |
| Lynda Barry | 1 2 3 | 4 5 6 | 7 8 9 10 | |
| Stan Higgins | 1 2 3 | 4 5 6 | 7 8 9 10 | |
| **Illustrating** | | | | |
| Miek Rose | 1 2 3 | 4 5 6 | 7 8 9 10 | |
| Chana Shoenberger | 1 2 3 | 4 5 6 | 7 8 9 10 | |
| **Analyzing a Process** | | | | |
| Roger Flax | 1 2 3 | 4 5 6 | 7 8 9 10 | |
| Geeta Dardick | 1 2 3 | 4 5 6 | 7 8 9 10 | |
| **Comparing and Contrasting** | | | | |
| Stephaine Coontz | 1 2 3 | 4 5 6 | 7 8 9 10 | |
| Patricia McLaughlin | 1 2 3 | 4 5 6 | 7 8 9 10 | |
| **Dividing and Classifying** | | | | |
| Marion Winik | 1 2 3 | 4 5 6 | 7 8 9 10 | |
| Bernice Reagon | 1 2 3 | 4 5 6 | 7 8 9 10 | |
| **Defining** | | | | |
| Lois Smith Brady | 1 2 3 | 4 5 6 | 7 8 9 10 | |
| Michael Norlen | 1 2 3 | 4 5 6 | 7 8 9 10 | |
| **Analyzing Causes and Effects** | | | | |
| Michael Alvear | 1 2 3 | 4 5 6 | 7 8 9 10 | |
| Stacey Colino | 1 2 3 | 4 5 6 | 7 8 9 10 | |
| **Arguing** | | | | |
| Thomas Lickona | 1 2 3 | 4 5 6 | 7 8 9 10 | |
| Richard Willard and David Cole | 1 2 3 | 4 5 6 | 7 8 9 10 | |

The legend on the reverse side will help you identify your strengths and weaknesses in critical thinking.

## Legend for Critical Thinking Log

| Questions | Skill |
|---|---|
| 1–2 | Literal and interpretive understanding |
| 3–6 | Critical thinking and analysis |
| 7–9 | Analyzing sentences |
| 10 | Writing paragraphs |

# APPENDIX 2A Revising
## Describing
## Peer Evaluation Form

Use the following questions to evaluate your partner's essay. Direct your comments to your partner.

**Writer:** ______________________________ **Peer:** ______________________________

### Describing

1. Is the dominant impression clearly communicated? Explain your answer.

2. Does the essay use objective and subjective descriptions when needed? Explain your answer.

3. Does the essay draw on all five senses? Explain your answer.

4. Does the essay *show* rather than *tell*? Explain your answer.

### Thesis Statement

5. Does the thesis statement contain the essay's controlling idea and appear as the last sentence of the introduction? Explain your answer.

### Basic Elements

6. Does the essay have all the basic elements? Is each one effective? Explain your answer.

### Development

7. Does each paragraph support the thesis statement? Does each paragraph contain enough specific details to develop its topic sentence? Explain your answer.

### Unity

8. Do all the essay's topic sentences relate directly to the thesis statement? Do the details in each paragraph support its topic sentence? Explain your answer.

### Organization

9. Is the essay organized logically? Is each body paragraph organized logically? Explain your answer.

### Coherence

10. Are transitions used effectively so that paragraphs move smoothly and logically from one to the next? Do the sentences move smoothly and logically from one to the next? Explain your answer.

# APPENDIX 2A Editing
# Describing
# Peer Evaluation Form

Use the following questions to help you find editing errors in your partner's essay. Mark the errors directly on your partner's paper using the editing symbols on the inside back cover.

**Writer:** ______________________________ **Peer:** ______________________________

### Sentences

1. Does each sentence have a subject and verb?

   Mark any fragments you find with ***frag.***

   Mark any run-on sentences you find with ***r-o.***

2. Do all subjects and verbs agree?

   Mark any subject-verb agreement errors you find with ***sv.***

3. Do all pronouns agree with their nouns?

   Mark any pronoun errors you find with ***pro agr.***

4. Are all modifiers as close as possible to the words they modify?

   Mark any modifier errors you find with ***ad*** (adjective or adverb problem), ***mm*** (misplaced modifier), or ***dm*** (dangling modifier).

### Punctuation and Mechanics

5. Are sentences punctuated correctly?

   Mark any punctuation errors you find with the appropriate symbol under Unit 5 of the editing symbols (inside back cover).

6. Are words capitalized properly?

   Mark any capitalization errors you find with ***lc*** (lowercase) or ***cap*** (capital).

### Word Choice and Spelling

7. Are words used correctly?

   Mark any words that are used incorrectly with ***wc*** (word choice) or ***ww*** (wrong word).

8. Are words spelled correctly?

   Mark any misspelled words you find with ***sp.***

# APPENDIX 2B Revising
# Narrating
# Peer Evaluation Form

Use the following questions to evaluate your partner's essay. Direct your comments to your partner.

**Writer:** ________________________ **Peer:** ________________________

**Narrating**

1. What is the essay's main point? If you're not sure, show the writer how he or she can make the main point clearer.

2. Does the writer use the five *W*'s and one *H* to construct the essay? Where does the essay need more information?

3. Does the writer develop the essay with vivid details? Where can more details be added?

4. Does the writer build excitement with careful pacing? Explain your answer.

**Thesis Statement**

5. Does the thesis statement contain the essay's controlling idea and appear as the last sentence of the introduction? Explain your answer.

**Basic Elements**

6. Does the essay have all the basic elements. Is each one effective? Explain your answer.

**Development**

7. Does each paragraph support the thesis statement? Does each paragraph contain enough specific details to develop its topic sentence? Explain your answer.

**Unity**

8. Do all the essay's topic sentences relate directly to the thesis statement? Do the details in each paragraph support its topic sentence? Explain your answer.

**Organization**

9. Is the essay organized logically? Is each body paragraph organized logically? Explain your answer.

**Coherence**

10. Are transitions used effectively so that paragraphs move smoothly and logically from one to the next? Do the sentences move smoothly and logically from one to the next? Explain your answer.

# APPENDIX 2B Editing
# Narrating
# Peer Evaluation Form

Use the following questions to help your partner find editing errors in his or her essay. Mark the errors directly on your partner's paper using the editing symbols on the inside back cover.

**Writer:** ______________________ **Peer:** ______________________

### Sentences

1. Does each sentence have a subject and verb?

   Mark any fragments you find with ***frag.***

   Mark any run-on sentences you find with ***r-o.***

2. Do all subjects and verbs agree?

   Mark any subject-verb agreement errors you find with ***sv.***

3. Do all pronouns agree with their nouns?

   Mark any pronoun errors you find with ***pro agr.***

4. Are all modifiers as close as possible to the words they modify?

   Mark any modifier errors you find with ***ad*** (adjective or adverb problem), ***mm*** (misplaced modifier), or ***dm*** (dangling modifier).

### Punctuation and Mechanics

5. Are sentences punctuated correctly?

   Mark any punctuation errors you find with the appropriate symbol under Unit 5 of the editing symbols (inside back cover).

6. Are words capitalized properly?

   Mark any capitalization errors you find with ***lc*** (lowercase) or ***cap*** (capital).

### Word Choice and Spelling

7. Are words used correctly?

   Mark any words that are used incorrectly with ***wc*** (word choice) or ***ww*** (wrong word).

8. Are words spelled correctly?

   Mark any misspelled words you find with ***sp.***

# APPENDIX 2C Revising Illustrating Peer Evaluation Form

Use the following questions to evaluate your partner's essay. Direct your comments to your partner.

**Writer:** ______________________________ **Peer:** ______________________________

**Illustrating**

1. What is the essay's main point? If you're not sure, show the writer how he or she can make the main point clearer.

2. Did the writer choose examples that are relevant to the main point? If not, which examples need to be changed?

3. Does the writer choose examples that the reader can identify with? If not, which examples need to be changed?

4. Does the writer use a sufficient number of examples to make his or her point? Where can more examples be added?

**Thesis Statement**

5. Does the thesis statement contain the essay's controlling idea and appear as the last sentence of the introduction? Explain your answer.

**Basic Elements**

6. Does the essay have all the basic elements? Is each one effective? Explain your answer.

**Development**

7. Does each paragraph support the thesis statement? Does each paragraph contain enough specific details to develop its topic sentence? Explain your answer.

**Unity**

8. Do all the essay's topic sentences relate directly to the thesis statement? Do the details in each paragraph support its topic sentence? Explain your answer.

**Organization**

9. Is the essay organized logically? Is each body paragraph organized logically? Explain your answer.

**Coherence**

10. Are transitions used effectively so that paragraphs move smoothly and logically from one to the next? Do the sentences move smoothly and logically from one to the next? Explain your answer.

# APPENDIX 2C Editing Illustrating Peer Evaluation Form

Use the following questions to help you find editing errors in your partner's essay. Mark the errors directly on your partner's paper using the editing symbols on the inside back cover.

**Writer:** ______________________________ **Peer:** ______________________________

### Sentences

1. Does each sentence have a subject and verb?

   Mark any fragments you find with ***frag.***

   Mark any run-on sentences you find with ***r-o.***

2. Do all subjects and verbs agree?

   Mark any subject-verb agreement errors you find with ***sv.***

3. Do all pronouns agree with their nouns?

   Mark any pronoun errors you find with ***pro agr.***

4. Are all modifiers as close as possible to the words they modify?

   Mark any modifier errors you find with ***ad*** (adjective or adverb problem), ***mm*** (misplaced modifier), or ***dm*** (dangling modifier).

### Punctuation and Mechanics

5. Are sentences punctuated correctly?

   Mark any punctuation errors you find with the appropriate symbol under Unit 5 of the editing symbols (inside back cover).

6. Are words capitalized properly?

   Mark any capitalization errors you find with ***lc*** (lowercase) or ***cap*** (capital).

### Word Choice and Spelling

7. Are words used correctly?

   Mark any words that are used incorrectly with ***wc*** (word choice) or ***ww*** (wrong word).

8. Are words spelled correctly?

   Mark any misspelled words you find with ***sp.***

# APPENDIX 2D Revising
# Analyzing a Process
# Peer Evaluation Form

Use the following questions to evaluate your partner's essay. Direct your comments to your partner.

**Writer:** ________________________ **Peer:** ________________________

### Analyzing a Process

1. Does the writer state in the thesis statement what the reader should be able to do or understand by the end of the essay? If not, what information does the thesis statement need to be clearer?

2. Does the writer know his or her audience? Explain your answer.

3. Does the remainder of the essay explain the rest of the process? If not, what seems to be missing?

4. Does the writer end the process essay by considering the process as a whole? Explain your answer.

### Thesis Statement

5. Does the thesis statement contain the essay's controlling idea and appear as the last sentence of the introduction? Explain your answer.

### Basic Elements

6. Does the essay have all the basic elements? Is each one effective? Explain your answer.

### Development

7. Does each paragraph support the thesis statement? Does each paragraph contain enough specific details to develop its topic sentence? Explain your answer.

### Unity

8. Do all the essay's topic sentences relate directly to the thesis statement? Do the details in each paragraph support its topic sentence? Explain your answer.

### Organization

9. Is the essay organized logically? Is each body paragraph organized logically? Explain your answer.

### Coherence

10. Are transitions used effectively so that paragraphs move smoothly and logically from one to the next? Do the sentences move smoothly and logically from one to the next? Explain your answer.

# APPENDIX 2D Editing
# Analyzing a Process
# Peer Evaluation Form

Use the following questions to help you find editing errors in your partner's essay. Mark the errors directly on your partner's paper using the editing symbols on the inside back cover.

**Writer:** ______________________________ **Peer:** ______________________________

### Sentences

1. Does each sentence have a subject and verb?

   Mark any fragments you find with ***frag.***

   Mark any run-on sentences you find with ***r-o.***

2. Do all subjects and verbs agree?

   Mark any subject-verb agreement errors you find with ***sv.***

3. Do all pronouns agree with their nouns?

   Mark any pronoun errors you find with ***pro agr.***

4. Are all modifiers as close as possible to the words they modify?

   Mark any modifier errors you find with ***ad*** (adjective or adverb problem), ***mm*** (misplaced modifier), or ***dm*** (dangling modifier).

### Punctuation and Mechanics

5. Are sentences punctuated correctly?

   Mark any punctuation errors you find with the appropriate symbol under Unit 5 of the editing symbols (inside back cover).

6. Are words capitalized properly?

   Mark any capitalization errors you find with ***lc*** (lowercase) or ***cap*** (capital).

### Word Choice and Spelling

7. Are words used correctly?

   Mark any words that are used incorrectly with ***wc*** (word choice) or ***ww*** (wrong word).

8. Are words spelled correctly?

   Mark any misspelled words you find with ***sp.***

# APPENDIX 2E Revising Comparing and Contrasting Peer Evaluation Form

Use the following questions to evaluate your partner's essay. Direct your comments to your partner.

**Writer:** ______________________________ **Peer:** ______________________________

### Comparing and Contrasting

1. Does the writer state the point he or she is trying to make with a comparison in the thesis statement? If not, what part of the comparison does the writer need to focus on?
2. Does the writer choose items to compare and contrast that will make his or her point most effectively? What details need to be added to make the comparison more effective?
3. Does the writer use as many specific details and examples as possible to expand the comparison? Explain your answer.
4. Is the comparison developed in a balanced way? Explain your answer.

### Thesis Statement

5. Does the thesis statement contain the essay's controlling idea and appear as the last sentence of the introduction? Explain your answer.

### Basic Elements

6. Does the essay have all the basic elements? Is each one effective? Explain your answer.

### Development

7. Does each paragraph support the thesis statement? Does each paragraph contain enough specific details to develop its topic sentence? Explain your answer.

### Unity

8. Do all the essay's topic sentences relate directly to the thesis statement? Do the details in each paragraph support its topic sentence? Explain your answer.

### Organization

9. Is the essay organized either subject by subject, point by point, or a combination of the two? Is each body paragraph organized logically? Explain your answer.

### Coherence

10. Are transitions used effectively so that paragraphs move smoothly and logically from one to the next? Do the sentences move smoothly and logically from one to the next? Explain your answer.

# APPENDIX 2E Editing Comparing and Contrasting Peer Evaluation Form

Use the following questions to help you find editing errors in your partner's essay. Mark the errors directly on your partner's paper using the editing symbols on the inside back cover.

**Writer:** ______________________ **Peer:** ______________________

## Sentences

1. Does each sentence have a subject and verb?

   Mark any fragments you find with ***frag.***

   Mark any run-on sentences you find with ***r-o.***

2. Do all subjects and verbs agree?

   Mark any subject-verb agreement errors you find with ***sv.***

3. Do all pronouns agree with their nouns?

   Mark any pronoun errors you find with ***pro agr.***

4. Are all modifiers as close as possible to the words they modify?

   Mark any modifier errors you find with ***ad*** (adjective or adverb problem), ***mm*** (misplaced modifier), or ***dm*** (dangling modifier).

## Punctuation and Mechanics

5. Are sentences punctuated correctly?

   Mark any punctuation errors you find with the appropriate symbol under Unit 5 of the editing symbols (inside back cover).

6. Are words capitalized properly?

   Mark any capitalization errors you find with ***lc*** (lowercase) or ***cap*** (capital).

## Word Choice and Spelling

7. Are words used correctly?

   Mark any words that are used incorrectly with ***wc*** (word choice) or ***ww*** (wrong word).

8. Are words spelled correctly?

   Mark any misspelled words you find with ***sp.***

# APPENDIX 2F Revising Dividing and Classifying Peer Evaluation Form

Use the following questions to evaluate your partner's essay. Direct your comments to your partner.

**Writer:** ______________________________ **Peer:** ______________________________

**Dividing and Classifying**

1. What is the overall purpose for the essay, and is it stated in the thesis statement? If not, where does the essay need clarification?

2. Did the writer divide the topic into categories that don't overlap? Explain your answer.

3. Did the writer clearly explain each category? Explain your answer.

**Thesis Statement**

4. Does the thesis statement contain the essay's controlling idea and appear as the last sentence of the introduction? Explain your answer.

**Basic Elements**

5. Does the essay have all the basic elements? Is each one effective? Explain your answer.

**Development**

6. Does each paragraph support the thesis statement? Does each paragraph contain enough specific details to develop its topic sentence? Explain your answer.

**Unity**

7. Do all the essay's topic sentences relate directly to the thesis statement? Do the details in each paragraph support its topic sentence? Explain your answer.

**Organization**

8. Are the categories organized logically in the essay? Is each body paragraph organized logically? Explain your answer.

**Coherence**

9. Are transitions used effectively so that paragraphs move smoothly and logically from one to the next? Do the sentences move smoothly and logically from one to the next? Explain your answer.

# APPENDIX 2F Editing
# Dividing and Classifying
# Peer Evaluation Form

Use the following questions to help you find editing errors in your partner's essay. Mark the errors directly on your partner's paper using the editing symbols on the inside back cover.

**Writer:** ______________________ **Peer:** ______________________

### Sentences

1. Does each sentence have a subject and verb?

   Mark any fragments you find with ***frag.***

   Mark any run-on sentences you find with ***r-o.***

2. Do all subjects and verbs agree?

   Mark any subject-verb agreement errors you find with ***sv.***

3. Do all pronouns agree with their nouns?

   Mark any pronoun errors you find with ***pro agr.***

4. Are all modifiers as close as possible to the words they modify?

   Mark any modifier errors you find with ***ad*** (adjective or adverb problem), ***mm*** (misplaced modifier), or ***dm*** (dangling modifier).

### Punctuation and Mechanics

5. Are sentences punctuated correctly?

   Mark any punctuation errors you find with the appropriate symbol under Unit 5 of the editing symbols (inside back cover).

6. Are words capitalized properly?

   Mark any capitalization errors you find with ***lc*** (lowercase) or ***cap*** (capital).

### Word Choice and Spelling

7. Are words used correctly?

   Mark any words that are used incorrectly with ***wc*** (word choice) or ***ww*** (wrong word).

8. Are words spelled correctly?

   Mark any misspelled words you find with ***sp.***

# APPENDIX 2G Revising Defining Peer Evaluation Form

Use the following questions to evaluate your partner's paragraph. Direct your comments to your partner.

**Writer:** ______________________________ **Peer:** ______________________________

### Defining

1. Did the writer choose a word or idea carefully and give readers a working definition of it in the thesis statement? Explain your answer.
2. Does the writer define his or her term or idea by synonym, category, or negation? Is this approach effective? Why or why not?
3. Does the writer use examples to expand on his or her definition of the term or idea? Where does the definition need more information?
4. Does the writer use other rhetorical strategies, such as description, comparison, or process analysis, to support the definition? Explain your answer.

### Thesis Statement

5. Does the thesis statement contain the essay's controlling idea and appear as the last sentence of the introduction? Explain your answer.

### Basic Elements

6. Does the essay have all the basic elements? Is each one effective? Explain your answer.

### Development

7. Does each paragraph support the thesis statement? Does each paragraph contain enough specific details to develop its topic sentence? Explain your answer.

### Unity

8. Do all the essay's topic sentences relate directly to the thesis statement? Do the details in each paragraph support its topic sentence? Explain your answer.

### Organization

9. Is the essay organized logically? Is each body paragraph organized logically? Explain your answer.

### Coherence

10. Are transitions used effectively so that paragraphs move smoothly and logically from one to the next? Do the sentences move smoothly and logically from one to the next? Explain your answer.

# APPENDIX 2G Editing
# Defining
# Peer Evaluation Form

Use the following questions to help you find editing errors in your partner's essay. Mark the errors directly on your partner's paper using the editing symbols on the inside back cover.

**Writer:** __________________________ **Peer:** __________________________

## Sentences

1. Does each sentence have a subject and verb?

   Mark any fragments you find with ***frag.***

   Mark any run-on sentences you find with ***r-o.***

2. Do all subjects and verbs agree?

   Mark any subject-verb agreement errors you find with ***sv.***

3. Do all pronouns agree with their nouns?

   Mark any pronoun errors you find with ***pro agr.***

4. Are all modifiers as close as possible to the words they modify?

   Mark any modifier errors you find with ***ad*** (adjective or adverb problem), ***mm*** (misplaced modifier), or ***dm*** (dangling modifier).

## Punctuation and Mechanics

5. Are sentences punctuated correctly?

   Mark any punctuation errors you find with the appropriate symbol under Unit 5 of the editing symbols (inside back cover).

6. Are words capitalized properly?

   Mark any capitalization errors you find with ***lc*** (lowercase) or ***cap*** (capital).

## Word Choice and Spelling

7. Are words used correctly?

   Mark any words that are used incorrectly with ***wc*** (word choice) or ***ww*** (wrong word).

8. Are words spelled correctly?

   Mark any misspelled words you find with ***sp.***

# APPENDIX 2H Revising Analyzing Causes and Effects Peer Evaluation Form

Use the following questions to evaluate your partner's essay. Direct your comments to your partner.

**Writer:** ______________________ **Peer:** ______________________

**Analyzing Causes and Effects**

1. Does the thesis statement make a clear statement about what is being analyzed? If not, what information does it need to be clearer?
2. Did the writer choose facts and details to support the topic sentence? What details need to be added?
3. Does the writer confuse coincidence with causes or effects? Explain your answer.
4. Does the writer include the *real* causes and effects for his or her topic? What details are unnecessary?

**Thesis Statement**

5. Does the thesis statement contain the essay's controlling idea and appear as the last sentence of the introduction? Explain your answer.

**Basic Elements**

6. Does the essay have all the basic elements? Is each one effective? Explain your answer.

**Development**

7. Does each paragraph support the thesis statement? Does each paragraph contain enough specific details to develop its topic sentence? Explain your answer.

**Unity**

8. Do all the essay's topic sentences relate directly to the thesis statement? Do the details in each paragraph support its topic sentence? Explain your answer.

**Organization**

9. Is the essay organized logically? Is the body paragraph organized logically? Explain your answer.

**Coherence**

10. Are transitions used effectively so that paragraphs move smoothly and logically from one to the next? Do the sentences move smoothly and logically from one to the next? Explain your answer.

# APPENDIX 2H Editing
# Analyzing Causes and Effects
# Peer Evaluation Form

Use the following questions to help you find editing errors in your partner's essay. Mark the errors directly on your partner's paper using the editing symbols on the inside back cover.

**Writer:** ______________________________ **Peer:** ______________________________

### Sentences

1. Does each sentence have a subject and verb?

   Mark any fragments you find with ***frag.***

   Mark any run-on sentences you find with ***r-o.***

2. Do all subjects and verbs agree?

   Mark any subject-verb agreement errors you find with ***sv.***

3. Do all pronouns agree with their nouns?

   Mark any pronoun errors you find with ***pro agr.***

4. Are all modifiers as close as possible to the words they modify?

   Mark any modifier errors you find with ***ad*** (adjective or adverb problem), ***mm*** (misplaced modifier), or ***dm*** (dangling modifier).

### Punctuation and Mechanics

5. Are sentences punctuated correctly?

   Mark any punctuation errors you find with the appropriate symbol under Unit 5 of the editing symbols (inside back cover).

6. Are words capitalized properly?

   Mark any capitalization errors you find with ***lc*** (lowercase) or ***cap*** (capital).

### Word Choice and Spelling

7. Are words used correctly?

   Mark any words that are used incorrectly with ***wc*** (word choice) or ***ww*** (wrong word).

8. Are words spelled correctly?

   Mark any misspelled words you find with ***sp.***

# APPENDIX 2I Revising
## Arguing
## Peer Evaluation Form

Use the following questions to evaluate your partner's essay. Direct your comments to your partner.

**Writer:** ______________________ **Peer:** ______________________

**Arguing**

1. Does the writer state his or her opinion on the subject matter in the thesis statement? What information is missing?
2. Who is the intended audience for this essay? Does the writer adequately persuade this audience? Why or why not?
3. Does the writer choose appropriate evidence to support the thesis statement? What evidence is needed? What evidence is unnecessary?
4. Does the writer anticipate the opposing points of view? Explain your answer.
5. Does the writer find some common ground? Explain your answer.
6. Does the writer maintain a reasonable tone? Explain your answer.

**Thesis Statement**

7. Does the thesis statement contain the essay's controlling idea and appear as the last sentence of the introduction? Explain your answer.

**Basic Elements**

8. Does the essay have all the basic elements? Is each one effective? Explain your answer.

**Development**

9. Does each paragraph support the thesis statement? Does each paragraph contain enough specific details to develop its topic sentence? Explain your answer.

**Unity**

10. Do all the essay's topic sentences relate directly to the thesis statement? Do the details in each paragraph support its topic sentence? Explain your answer.

**Organization**

11. Is the essay organized logically? Is each body paragraph organized logically? Explain your answer.

**Coherence**

12. Are transitions used effectively so that paragraphs move smoothly and logically from one to the next? Do the sentences move smoothly and logically from one to the next? Explain your answer.

# APPENDIX 2I Editing
# Arguing
# Peer Evaluation Form

Use the following questions to help you find editing errors in your partner's essay. Mark the errors directly on your partner's paper using the editing symbols on the inside back cover.

**Writer:** ______________________________ **Peer:** ______________________________

### Sentences

1. Does each sentence have a subject and verb?

   Mark any fragments you find with ***frag.***

   Mark any run-on sentences you find with ***r-o.***

2. Do all subjects and verbs agree?

   Mark any subject-verb agreement errors you find with ***sv.***

3. Do all pronouns agree with their nouns?

   Mark any pronoun errors you find with ***pro agr.***

4. Are all modifiers as close as possible to the words they modify?

   Mark any modifier errors you find with ***ad*** (adjective or adverb problem), ***mm*** (misplaced modifier), or ***dm*** (dangling modifier).

### Punctuation and Mechanics

5. Are sentences punctuated correctly?

   Mark any punctuation errors you find with the appropriate symbol under Unit 5 of the editing symbols (inside back cover).

6. Are words capitalized properly?

   Mark any capitalization errors you find with ***lc*** (lowercase) or ***cap*** (capital).

### Word Choice and Spelling

7. Are words used correctly?

   Mark any words that are used incorrectly with ***wc*** (word choice) or ***ww*** (wrong word).

8. Are words spelled correctly?

   Mark any misspelled words you find with ***sp.***

# APPENDIX 3A Revising
# Writing a Research Paper
# Peer Evaluation Form

Use the following questions to evaluate your partner's paper. Direct your comments to your partner.

**Writer:** ______________________________ **Peer:** ______________________________

### Writing a Research Paper

1. Did the writer choose a subject that is neither too broad nor too narrow to write a research paper on? Explain your answer.
2. Did the writer find sources that are relevant, reliable, and recent to support the thesis? Explain your answer.
3. Do you see any problems with plagiarism in the writer's paper? Explain your answer.
4. Check the writer's sources and documentation format—in the paper and at the end. Does the writer incorporate sources and document properly? Explain your answer.

### Thesis Statement

5. Does the thesis statement contain the essay's controlling idea and appear as the last sentence of the introduction? Explain your answer.

### Basic Elements

6. Does the essay have all the basic elements? Is each one effective? Explain your answer.

### Development

7. Does each paragraph support the thesis statement? Does each paragraph contain enough specific details that develop its topic sentence? Explain your answer.

### Unity

8. Do all the essay's topic sentences relate directly to the thesis statement? Do the details in each paragraph support its topic sentence? Explain your answer.

### Organization

9. Is the essay organized logically? Is each body paragraph organized logically? Explain your answer.

### Coherence

10. Are transitions used effectively so that paragraphs move smoothly and logically from one to the next? Do the sentences move smoothly and logically from one to the next? Explain your answer.

# APPENDIX 3B Editing
# Writing a Research Paper
# Peer Evaluation Form

Use the following questions to help you find editing errors in your partner's essay. Mark the errors directly on your partner's paper using the editing symbols on the inside back cover.

**Writer:** ______________________ **Peer:** ______________________

### Sentences

1. Does each sentence have a subject and verb?

   Mark any fragments you find with ***frag.***

   Mark any run-on sentences you find with ***r-o.***

2. Do all subjects and verbs agree?

   Mark any subject-verb agreement errors you find with ***sv.***

3. Do all pronouns agree with their nouns?

   Mark any pronoun errors you find with ***pro agr.***

4. Are all modifiers as close as possible to the words they modify?

   Mark any modifier errors you find with ***ad*** (adjective or adverb problem), ***mm*** (misplaced modifier), or ***dm*** (dangling modifier).

### Punctuation and Mechanics

5. Are sentences punctuated correctly?

   Mark any punctuation errors you find with the appropriate symbol under Unit 5 of the editing symbols (inside back cover).

6. Are words capitalized properly?

   Mark any capitalization errors you find with ***lc*** (lowercase) or ***cap*** (capital).

### Word Choice and Spelling

7. Are words used correctly?

   Mark any words that are used incorrectly with ***wc*** (word choice) or ***ww*** (wrong word).

8. Are words spelled correctly?

   Mark any misspelled words you find with ***sp.***

# APPENDIX 4 Test Yourself Answers
## Handbook

Here are the answers to the Test Yourself questions from the beginning of each chapter in the Handbook (Part V): Where are your strengths? Where are your weaknesses?

**Introduction: Parts of Speech (p. 503)**

*adj n v adv adj n adj adj n adj n*
Professional basketball is definitely this nation's best spectator sport. The talented players
*v prep conj prep n adv adv pro n adv v n prep v n*
move up and down the court so quickly that the audience never has a chance to become bored.
*int pro/v adv v pro adj n adj n conj pro adj n v pro prep v*
Boy, I'll never forget that Saturday night last February when my favorite uncle took me to see
*adj n prep n pro v adj adj n pro n conj*
the Spurs game against the Trailblazers. It was an important home game for San Antonio, so
*n v adj n v adv prep pro prep n conj pro v*
the arena was packed. The Spurs were behind throughout most of the game, but they pulled
*prep conj v prep adj n prep adj adj n int pro v adv v adv adj*
through and won with a three-pointer in the last few seconds. Wow! I have never seen so many
*n prep pro n conj v prep n prep pro n*
people on their feet and screaming at the top of their lungs.

**Introduction: Phrases (p. 522)**

**Define a phrase.**

A phrase is a group of words that function together as a unit but are missing a subject, a verb, or both.

**Give two examples of a phrase.**

the man down the street, running up the mountain, will have been married, during the night.

**Introduction: Clauses (p. 524)**

**Define a clause.**

A clause always contains a subject and a verb.

**How is a clause different from a phrase?**

A phrase is missing a subject, a verb, or both.

**Give an example of a clause.**

Independent: My family is small. Dependent: Because my family is small.

**Chapter 34: Subjects and Verbs (p. 529)**

**You** **are** my best friend.

**Hang** up your clothes. (**You**)

**They** really **wanted** to be here tonight.

**He** **made** a sandwich and **put** it in a brown paper bag.

**Susie** and **Tom** **went** to the dance.

The insurance **agent** never **called** me today.

**Chapter 35: Fragments (p. 538)**

________ I wanted to go to the gym yesterday.

___X___ Whose tie doesn't match his suit.

___X___ Giving up his seat for an elderly woman.

________ Paul asked for the most popular menu item.

___X___ While the captain was away from the cockpit.

**Chapter 36: Run-Ons (p. 552)**

The rainstorm washed out my garden, **/** I had just planted spring bulbs.

When we cleaned the house, we found the TV remote control **/** it was between the sofa cushions.

People in authority are often criticized and seldom thanked.

The kids didn't find all of the Easter eggs during the hunt, **/** when we finally found them, they were rotten.

You should ask Aubri to cut your hair **/** she's been cutting mine for four years.

### Chapter 37: Regular and Irregular Verbs (p. 561)

__X__ The pipe **has bursted**.

_____ Sim **reacted** to the scene calmly.

_____ I **bought** my car at an auction.

__X__ We **had hid** in the basement.

__X__ Sorry, I **eated** all the cookies.

### Chapter 38: Verb Tense (p. 573)

__X__ Jea always **laugh** when I tell that joke.

_____ Mark **jumped** over the hurdle and **crossed** the finish line.

__X__ I **had spoke** to the sales clerk about a discount.

__X__ Students **ain't allowed** to bring food and drink into the computer lab.

__X__ My two cats **be playing** in the sunshine.

### Chapter 39: Subject-Verb Agreement (p. 590)

__X__ Neither the **shorts** nor the **shirt** **fit** me.

_____ **Chips and dip** **is** my favorite snack.

__X__ There **were** a large **storm** last night.

__X__ Some of the **soil** along with the **fertilizer** **are** for the orchard.

__X__ **Cotton** and **silk** **are** more comfortable than wool.

### Chapter 40: More on Verbs (p. 605)

_____ George raced across the field and caught the ball.

__P__ The old record was broken by Justin.

__P__ That painting was done by a famous artist.

I In the future, we may live on Mars, and we produce our foods in greenhouses.

I First, the baker prepares the dough, and then she will cut out the cookies.

**Chapter 41: Pronoun Problems (p. 613)**

The shirt was ~~**mines'**~~ **mine** to begin with.

Tom told Valerie and ~~**I**~~ **me** the most exciting story.

James can type a lot faster than ~~**me**~~ **I**.

Those ~~**there**~~ running shoes are Kim's.

Becca and ~~**me**~~ **I** are going to the movies tonight.

**Chapter 42: Pronoun Reference and Point of View (p. 626)**

**It**[X] says to schedule **your** own appointments.

Millie and Tanya were going to go to Las Vegas, but **her**[X] car broke.

**I** created a backup plan, because **you**[X] should always be prepared for the unexpected.

**You** know **they**[X] are covering up evidence of alien beings.

Jimmy forgot the answer to questions 1 and 10, but **he** remembered **it**[X] the next day.

**Chapter 43: Pronoun Agreement (p. 634)**

**Somebody** left **his**[X] lights on in **his** car.

A judge must put aside **her**[X] bias.

**Each** of the children needs **their**[X] permission slip signed.

**None** of the fans could keep **their**[X] voices quiet.

A motorcyclist must take care of **her**[X] gear.

### Chapter 44: Adjectives (p. 642)

The kites were very **colorful**.

She has the **worstest**[X] **hair** color.

We were **more busier**[X] **this** week than **last** week.

He is the **oldest**[X] of the **two** brothers.

The **Ford** Mustang is **more better**[X] than the **Nissan** Sentra.

### Chapter 45: Adverbs (p. 655)

The pants fit me **too** **loose**[X], so I returned them to the store.

When Madeline returned from Paris, she said she had a **real**[X] good time.

We **happily** made more ice cream when our first supply ran out.

Tori was**n't**[X] **never** **so** happy as after she won the lottery.

I wanted **so** **bad**[X] to win the race, but I could**n't** catch up.

### Chapter 46: Modifier Errors (p. 671)

After studying together, **his** grades really improved.

**Before doing the laundry**, the car needed to be washed.

**To get a good job**, the interview must go well.

The professor told the class he was retiring **before he dismissed them**.

I wrote a letter to the newspaper **that complained about rising power bills**.

**Chapter 47: End Punctuation (p. 678)**

How are we going to get there**?**

That's amazing**!**

Get me a Pepsi, please**.**

This will not happen to me**.**

Can you make your own dinner tonight**?**

**Chapter 48: Commas (p. 685)**

We drove to the beach**,** and we had a picnic.

Before I eat breakfast**,** I take a multivitamin.

"This is my favorite restaurant**,**" said Matt.

E-mail**,** though**,** makes corresponding easy and fast.

They were married on September 21**,** 1996**,** in Las Vegas**,** Nevada.

**Chapter 49: Apostrophes (p. 699)**

The flight crew was surprised by the pilot**'**s rudeness when he boarded the plane.

It**'**s important that the car has its engine checked every 3,000 miles.

What**'**s going to happen after George is gone?

The men**'**s bathroom is located on the third floor.

James**'**s house is the third one on the left.

**Chapter 50: Quotation Marks (p. 708)**

"Can we go out to dinner tonight?" she asked.

Jeri screamed, "Don't go in there!"

"If you can't find my house," Tom said, "call me on your cell phone."

My favorite poem is "The Red Wheelbarrow" by William Carlos Williams.

David said, "I'll fix your car this weekend."

**Chapter 51: Other Punctuation Marks (p. 717)**

Kris left for the dance; Sean decided to stay home.

We wanted to win; therefore, we practiced every day.

The computer's advertised price didn't include several things: a monitor, a printer, and speakers.

Kyle asked the best question during the interview—"Why should we vote for you?" (or :)

Bring the jelly to a "rolling boil" (a boil that cannot be stirred down).

**Chapter 52: Capitalization (p. 726)**

According to **U**ncle Bob, **M**other makes the best **T**exas sheet cake.

Antonio is a **N**ative **A**merican.

"The shortest path," he said, "is down **B**aker **S**treet."

Issa loves to go to **W**alt **D**isney **W**orld.

Last year, I saw the **R**ed **H**ot **C**hili **P**eppers in concert.

### Chapter 53: Abbreviations and Numbers (p. 733)

He earned **$2,300,000** last year.

My cat had **five** kittens.

Sherril moved from England to the **United States.**

**Mr.** Johnson always drinks hot chocolate in the mornings.

I work for the **IRS**.

### Chapter 54: Varying Sentence Structure (p. 741)

**Answers will vary.**

### Chapter 55: Parallelism (p. 748)

Tony enjoys **hockey**, **football**, and **runs**.

My mom and dad give money **to help the homeless** and **for building new homes**.

I finished **high school**, **started college**, and **I am beginning a new job**.

I love the mountains because they're **cool**, **clean**, and **feel refreshing**.

**Listening to music**, **watching television**, or **to read a book** are good ways to relax.

### Chapter 56: Combining Sentences (p. 754)

**Answers will vary.**

### Chapter 57: Standard and Nonstandard English (p. 766)

You **shoulda** seen Claudia's new hairstyle. **(Ungrammatical)**

**Where** are my friends **at**? **(Ungrammatical)**

Your new bike is really **hot**. **(Slang)**

Randy was **enthused** about his date. **(Slang)**

Fatboy *Slim's* new video **rocks**. **(Slang)**

**Chapter 58: Easily Confused Words (p. 777)**

Sally couldn't (**choose**, chose) a college.

(**It's**, Its) time to leave for the show.

I can't (**hear**, here) with all this noise.

(Weather, **Whether**) you go or not, I'm still going to attend.

(**Who's**, Whose) responsible for this mess?

**Chapter 59: Spelling (p. 789)**

What is your new ~~**addres**~~ **address?**

Turn left on the third ~~**avenu**~~ **avenue.**

I was using the wrong ~~**calender**~~ **calendar** when I made out the schedule.

The dealer ~~**delt**~~ **dealt** me a good hand.

Please get all the items on the ~~**groery**~~ **grocery** list.

# APPENDIX 5 Editing Quotient Error Chart

Put an X in the square that corresponds to each question that you missed.

| | a | b | c | d | e | f | g |
|---|---|---|---|---|---|---|---|
| 1 | | | | | | | |
| 2 | | | | | | | |
| 3 | | | | | | | |
| 4 | | | | | | | |
| 5 | | | | | | | |
| 6 | | | | | | | |
| 7 | | | | | | | |
| 8 | | | | | | | |
| 9 | | | | | | | |
| 10 | | | | | | | |

Then record your errors in the categories below to find out where you might need help.

| | | | | | | |
|---|---|---|---|---|---|---|
| Fragments | 1b_____ | 1c_____ | 2b_____ | 2e_____ | 4d_____ | 4e_____ |
| | 5d_____ | 6d_____ | 10c_____ | | | |
| Run-ons | 1a_____ | 1d_____ | 2d_____ | 3d_____ | 5c_____ | 8b_____ |
| | 8e_____ | 9a_____ | 10b_____ | 10f_____ | | |
| Subject-verb agreement | 6e_____ | | | | | |
| Verb forms | 3a_____ | 3c_____ | 9e_____ | | | |
| Pronoun errors | 7b_____ | | | | | |
| Pronoun agreement | 3b_____ | 4a_____ | 10a_____ | | | |
| Modifiers | 5b_____ | 10e_____ | | | | |

| | |
|---|---|
| End punctuation | 6g______ |
| Commas | 4f______ 4g______ 5a______ 7e______ 7f______ 9b______ 9c______ |
| Apostrophes | 10d______ |
| Capitalization | 2a______ 2c______ 7c______ 7d______ |
| Confused words | 4b______ 4c______ 6c______ 7g______ 8a______ 9d______ |
| Spelling | 6a______ 6b______ 6f______ 7a______ 8c______ 8d______ 9f______ |

# APPENDIX 6 Error Log

List any grammar, punctuation, and mechanics errors you make in your writing on the following chart. Then, to the right of this label, record (1) the actual error from your writing, (2) the rule for correcting this error, and (3) your correction.

| | |
|---|---|
| Error | Example **I went to the new seafood restaurant and I ordered the lobster.** |
| **Comma** | Rule **Use a comma before *and, but, for, nor, or, so,* and *yet* when they join two independent clauses.** |
| | Correction **I went to the new seafood restaurant, and I ordered the lobster.** |
| Error | Example |
| | Rule |
| | Correction |
| Error | Example |
| | Rule |
| | Correction |
| Error | Example |
| | Rule |
| | Correction |
| Error | Example |
| | Rule |
| | Correction |
| Error | Example |
| | Rule |
| | Correction |
| Error | Example |
| | Rule |
| | Correction |
| Error | Example |
| | Rule |
| | Correction |

| | |
|---|---|
| Error | Example |
| | Rule |
| | Correction |
| Error | Example |
| | Rule |
| | Correction |
| Error | Example |
| | Rule |
| | Correction |
| Error | Example |
| | Rule |
| | Correction |
| Error | Example |
| | Rule |
| | Correction |
| Error | Example |
| | Rule |
| | Correction |
| Error | Example |
| | Rule |
| | Correction |
| Error | Example |
| | Rule |
| | Correction |

# APPENDIX 7 Spelling Log

On this chart, record any words you misspell, and write the correct spelling in the space next to the misspelled word. In the right column, write a note to yourself to help you remember the correct spelling. (See the first line for an example.) Refer to this chart as often as necessary to avoid misspelling the same words again.

| Misspelled Word | Correct Spelling | Definition/Notes |
|---|---|---|
| there | their | there = place; their = pronoun; they're = "they are" |
| | | |
| | | |
| | | |
| | | |
| | | |
| | | |
| | | |
| | | |
| | | |
| | | |
| | | |
| | | |
| | | |
| | | |
| | | |
| | | |
| | | |
| | | |
| | | |
| | | |
| | | |
| | | |
| | | |

# Credits

**CHAPTER 1**

"Aspiring Author Inspires Writing Even in Death," by Eric Zorn, *Chicago Tribune*, April 23, 2001. Copyright © 2001 Tribune Co. All rights reserved. Reprinted by permission.

**CHAPTER 9**

"Dust Changes America," by Margaret Bourke-White, from the May 22, 1935 issue of *The Nation*. Reprinted by permission of The Nation and The Estate of Margaret Bourke-White.

*Photo:* Jim Mone/ AP/Wide World Photos.

**CHAPTER 10**

"Girl," by Jane Maher. Reprinted by permission of the author.

*Photo:* Kim Mould/Omni-Photo Communications, Inc.

**CHAPTER 11**

"Hold the Mayonnaise," by Julia Alvarez, *The New York Times*, January 12, 1992. Reprinted by permission of The New York Times, Co.

*Photo:* White/Packert/Getty Images, Inc.

**CHAPTER 12**

"Dare To Change Your Job and Your Life in 7 Steps," by Carole Kanchier, *Psychology Today*, March 2000. Reprinted by permission of the author.

*Photo:* David Buffington/Getty Images, Inc. PhotoDisc. Inc.

**CHAPTER 13**

"Thrills & Chills" by Eric Minton, *Psychology Today* May, 1999. Reprinted by permission of the author.

*Photo:* Massimo Mastrorillo, Corbis/Stock Market.

**CHAPTER 14**

"The Sound of Music: Enough Already," from *Metropolitan Life*, by Fran Lebowitz (New York: Dutton, a division of Penguin Putnam, Inc., 1978).

*Photo:* Marc P. Anderson/Pearson Education/PH College.

**CHAPTER 15**

"Dumpster Diving" by Lars Eighner, *Utne Reader*, March 1992. Reprinted by permission of Utne Reader and the author.

*Photo:* Laimute E. Druskis/Pearson Education/PH College.

**CHAPTER 16**

"Why Do Schools Flunk Biology?" from *Newsweek*, February 19, 1996. Copyright © 1996 Newsweek, Inc. All rights reserved. Reprinted by permission.

*Photo:* Tony Freeman/PhotoEdit.

## CHAPTER 17

"Racial Profiling Is Unjust" by Bob Herbert, *The New York Times*, June 13, 1999. Copyright © 1999 the New York Times Co. Reprinted by permission.

*Photo:* Charles Gatewood/Pearson Education/PH College.

## CHAPTER 24

*Photo:* Tony Freeman/PhotoEdit.

## CHAPTER 25

"El Hoyo," by Mario Suarez, as it appeared in *Short Takes* by Elizabeth Penfield (NY: Longman, 1998).

"Dwellings" from *Dwellings: A Spiritual History of the Living World* by Linda Hogan. Copyright © 1995 by Linda Hogan. Reprinted by permission of W. W. Norton & Company, Inc.

## CHAPTER 26

"The Sanctuary of School" by Lynda Barry, *New York Times, Educational Supplement*, January 1992. Copyright © 1992 The New York Times Co. Reprinted by permission.

"Writer's Retreat," by Stan Higgins, as it appeared in *The Writer*, November 1991. Reprinted by permission of the author.

## CHAPTER 27

"I Just Wanna Be Average," from *Lives on the Boundary*, by Mike Rose. Copyright © 1989 The Free Press, a division of Simon & Schuster, Inc. Reprinted by permission.

"Getting to Know About You and Me" by Chana Schoenberger, *Newsweek*, September 20, 1993. Copyright © 1993 Newsweek, Inc. All rights reserved. Reprinted by permission.

## CHAPTER 28

"Don't Be Cruel" by Roger Flax, as it appeared in *TWA Ambassador*, March 1992. Reprinted by permission of the author.

"Access Activism" by Geeta Dardick, as it appeared in *Whole Earth Review* (Fall 1992). Reprinted by permission of the author.

## CHAPTER 29

"The American Family," by Stephanie Coontz, as it appeared in LIFE, November 1999. Copyright © 1999 Time Inc. Reprinted by permission.

Republished with permission of The Philadelphia Inquirer, from "Venus Envy," by Patricia McLaughlin, as it appeared in *Philadelphia Inquirer Magazine*, November 5, 1995. Permission conveyed through Reprint Management Services, Inc.

## CHAPTER 30

"Black Music in Our Hands," by Bernice Reagon. Reprinted by permission of the author.

From *Telling: Confessions, Concessions, & Other Flashes of Light* by Marion Winik. Copyright © 1994 by Marion Winik. Reprinted by permission Villard, a Division of Random House, Inc.

## CHAPTER 31

From *Love Lessons: Twelve Real-Life Love Stories* by Lois Smith Brady. Copyright © 1999 by Lois Smith Brady. Reprinted with the permission of Simon & Schuster, Inc.

"Healing Myself with the Power of Work," from *Newsweek*, October 25, 1999. Copyright © 1999 Newsweek, Inc. All rights reserved. Reprinted by permission.

## CHAPTER 32

"A Family Dilemma: To Scout or Not to Scout" from *Newsweek*, November 6, 2000. Copyright © 2000 Newsweek, Inc. All rights reserved. Reprinted by permission.

"Happiness is Catching: Why Emotions Are Contagious," by Stacey Colino, as it appeared in *Family Circle*, March 12, 1996. Reprinted by permission of the author.

## CHAPTER 33

"The Neglected Heart," by Thomas Lickona, from *The American Educator*, Summer 1994. Copyright © 1994 by Thomas Lickona. Reprinted with the permission of American Educator and the author.

"Anti-Loitering Laws Can Reduce Gang Violence," by Richard Willard, as it appeared in *Supreme Court Debates*, February 1999. Copyright © 1999 Congressional Digest Corp. All rights reserved. Reprinted by permission.

"Anti-Loitering Laws Are Ineffective and Biased," by David Cole, from the January 4, 1999 issue of *The Nation*. Reprinted by permission of The Nation and the author.

# Index